THE PALACE OF THE SUN

ALSO BY ROBERT W. BERGER:

Antoine Le Pautre: A French Architect of the Era of Louis XIV (CAA Monograph XVIII)

Versailles: The Château of Louis XIV (CAA Monograph XL)

In the Garden of the Sun King: Studies on the Park of Versailles Under Louis XIV

Robert W. Berger

THE PALACE OF THE SUN
The Louvre of Louis XIV

*With a Chapter on
Materials and Structure
Written in Collaboration with
Rowland J. Mainstone*

The Pennsylvania State University Press
University Park, Pennsylvania

Publication of this book has been aided by a grant from the
Millard Meiss Publication Fund of the College Art Association.

| MM |

Published with the assistance of the Getty Grant Program.

Library of Congress Cataloging-in-Publication Data

Berger, Robert W.
　　The palace of the sun: the Louvre of Louis XIV / Robert W. Berger;
with a chapter on materials and structure written in collaboration
with Rowland J. Mainstone.
　　　　　p.　　　cm.
　　Includes bibliographical references and index.
　　ISBN 0-271-00847-4
　　1. Louvre (Paris, France)　2. Classicism in architecture—France
—Paris.　3. Architecture, Modern—17th–18th centuries—France
—Paris.　4. Paris (France)—Buildings, structures, etc.　I. Title.
NA7736.P2B47　1993
725′.17′0944361—dc20　　　　　　　　　　　　　　　　　　91-42726
　　　　　　　　　　　　　　　　　　　　　　　　　　　　　　　　CIP

Copyright © 1993 The Pennsylvania State University
All rights reserved

Printed in the United States of America

Published by The Pennsylvania State University Press,
Barbara Building, Suite C, University Park, PA 16802-1003

It is the policy of The Pennsylvania State University Press to use acid-free paper for the first printing of all
clothbound books. Publications on uncoated stock satisfy the minimum requirements of American National
Standard for Information Sciences—Permanence of Paper for Printed Library Materials, ANSI Z39.48–1984.

In Memory of My Dear Sister

CONTENTS

List of Illustrations ... ix
Preface and Acknowledgments ... xvii
Abbreviations ... xix

    I   Regia Solis ... 1
   II Early Projects for the East Wing ... 9
  III The Petit Conseil (1667–1668) ... 25
  IV Three Proposals by Claude Perrault ... 47
   V Building the Louvre ... 57
  VI Materials and Structure (in collaboration with Rowland J. Mainstone) ... 65
 VII In the Eye of the Connoisseur ... 75
VIII The Attribution Question ... 83

Appendixes
A The Work of the Petit Conseil (1667–1668): A Catalogue Raisonné of the Surviving Drawings and One Medal ... 87
B The Coupled-Columns Debate ... 94
C Claude Perrault and the Piliers de Tutelle, Bordeaux ... 99
D The Palmyra-Baalbek Hypothesis ... 104
E *Colonnade, Péristyle, Galerie, Portique:* A Note on Seventeenth- and Eighteenth-Century Nomenclature ... 109

Sources I. Building the Louvre (1667–1680). Allocations and Payments from the *Comptes des bâtiments du roi* ... 111
Sources II: Documents and Writings on the Louvre (1667–1792) ... 121

Bibliography ... 219
Index ... 227
Illustrations ... 233

LIST OF ILLUSTRATIONS

1. Anonymous Flemish, *Phaethon before Apollo*. Manuscript illumination, 1470–80. London, British Library, Royal MS 17 E.IV.
2. Anonymous Venetian, *Phaethon before Apollo*. Painting, ca. 1500–1510. Vienna, Kunsthistorisches Museum.
3. Johann Wilhelm Baur, *Phaethon before Apollo*. Engraving, 1639.
4. Eustache Le Sueur, *Phaethon before Apollo*. Painting, early 1650s. Paris, Louvre.
5. Charles Le Brun, Design for the Cupola of Vaux-le-Vicomte. Drawing, late 1650s, Paris, Louvre, Cabinet des Dessins, Inv. 29638.
6. Charles Le Brun, *Supper in the House of Simon*. Painting, ca. 1653. Venice, Academy.
7. Charles Le Brun, *The Palace of the Sun or the Course of the Year (Assembly of the Gods)*. Engraving by Gérard Audran, 1681. From *Gazette des beaux-arts,* LXVI, 1965.
8. Detail of Figure 7.
9. Louvre, Pavillon du Roi and west and south façades. Engraving from Jacques Androuet Du Cerceau the Elder, *Les plus excellents bastiments de France,* Paris, 1576, I.
10. Louvre, Cour Carrée, Lescot wing.
11. Louvre, Cour Carrée, Lescot wing. Details of *Premier Étage*. Engraving from Pierre Patte, *Mémoires sur les objets les plus importans de l'architecture,* Paris, 1769.
12. Detail of Figure 10.
13. Louvre, west façade with the Pavillon de l'Horloge. Engraving from L. P. Baltard and A. P. Duval, *Paris et ses monumens . . . ,* Paris, 1803, I.
14. Louvre, Cour Carrée with the Pavillon de l'Horloge. Engraving by Israël Henriet.
15. Eustache Le Sueur, *Allegory of Magnificence*. Painting, 1654–55. Dayton Art Institute, Gift of Mr. and Mrs. Harry S. Price, Jr.
16. Louvre, Pavillon du Roi and south façade before 1660. Engraving from A. Berty and H. Legrand, *Topographie historique du vieux Paris: Région du Louvre et des Tuileries,* Paris, 1868, II.
17. Louvre, south façade, 1660–63, by Louis Le Vau. Engraving by Jean Marot.
18. Louvre, south façade, central pavilion, 1660–63, by Louis Le Vau. Engraving by Jean Marot.
19. Louis Le Vau, design for the central pavilion of the south façade of the Louvre, ca. 1660. Drawing, Paris, Louvre, Cabinet des Dessins, Recueil du Louvre, I, Inv. 26076.
20. Anonymous architect, Louvre project, shortly after 1600. Painting by Toussaint Dubreuil (restored), Château de Fontainebleau, Galerie des Cerfs.

21. Anonymous architect, design for the east façade of the Louvre, early seventeenth century. Drawing, Paris, Archives Nationales, F²¹ 3567, no. 4.
22. Jacques Lemercier, design for the east façade of the Louvre, before 1654. Engraving by Jean Marot.
23. Antoine Léonor Houdin, design for the east façade of the Louvre, 1661. Engraving by François Bignon.
24. François Le Vau, design for the east façade of the Louvre, ca. 1662–64. Drawing, Stockholm, Nationalmuseum, CC 1.
25. Detail of Figure 24.
26. Detail of Figure 24.
27. Detail of Figure 24.
28. François Le Vau, design for the central pavilion, east façade of the Louvre. Engraving by Isaac Durant.
29. François Le Vau, design for the central pavilion, east façade of the Louvre. Engraving by Claude Olry de Loriande.
30. François Le Vau, design for the end pavilion, east façade of the Louvre. Engraving by Claude Olry de Loriande.
31. François Le Vau, design for the east wing of the Louvre, section. Engraving by Claude Olry de Loriande.
32. François Le Vau, design for the east wing of the Louvre, plan. Engraving by Claude Olry de Loriande.
33. Louis Le Vau, Louvre project, plan, 1663–64. Drawing, Paris, Bibliothèque Nationale, Cabinet des Estampes, Va 440, cartes max.
34. Louis Le Vau, Louvre project, section of the east façade, 1663–64. Drawing, Paris, Archives Nationales, O¹ 1667³, no. 77.
35. Louis Le Vau, design for the east façade of the Louvre, 1663–64. Reconstructed elevation by Trevor K. Gould (from *Revue de l'art,* no. 4, 1969).
36. François Mansart, Louvre project, plan, 1664. Drawing, Paris, Bibliothèque Nationale, Cabinet des Estampes, Va 217.
37. Jean Marot, design for the east façade of the Louvre, 1664(?). Engraving by Jean Marot.
38. Pierre Cottart, design for the east façade of the Louvre. Engraving, 1665.
39. Louvre and Tuileries. Engraving by Noël Cochin.
40. Gianlorenzo Bernini, design for the east façade of the Louvre, elevation, 1665. Engraving by Jean Marot.
41. Gianlorenzo Bernini, design for the east façade of the Louvre, elevation, 1665. Drawing, Stockholm, Nationalmuseum, THC 1244.
42. Louvre, east (Colonnade) and south façades.
43. Louvre, Colonnade.
44. Louvre, Colonnade.
45. Louvre, Colonnade with moat.
46. Louvre, Colonnade. Windows of ground floor.

47. Louvre, Colonnade. Detail of ground-floor window.
48. Louvre, Colonnade. Central pavilion.
49. Louvre, Colonnade. Northern end pavilion.
50. Detail of Figure 49.
51. Louvre, Colonnade.
52. Louvre, Colonnade.
53. Louvre, Colonnade.
54. Louvre, Colonnade. Capitals.
55. Louvre, Colonnade. Balustrade.
56. Louvre, Colonnade. Details of the order. Engraving from L. P. Baltard and A. P. Duval, *Paris et ses monumens . . . ,* Paris, 1803, I. (The entasis diagram is distorted.)
57. Pantheon, Rome. Interior columnar order. Engraving from Antoine Desgodets, *Les édifices antiques de Rome . . . ,* Paris, 1682.
58. Pantheon, Rome. Pilaster order of the portico. Engraving from Antoine Desgodets, *Les édifices antiques de Rome . . . ,* Paris, 1682.
59. Studio of Louis Le Vau, elevation of the east façade with the Colonnade. Spring 1667. Drawing, Paris, Louvre, Cabinet des Dessins, Inv. 26077 (Appendix A, A1).
60. François de Poilly after Charles Le Brun, frontispiece for Jean Baptiste Colbert, Marquis de Seignelay, *Conclusiones ex universa Philosophia de Logicis* (1668), engraving (detail).
61. Charles Le Brun, preparatory drawing for Figure 60. Paris, Louvre, Cabinet des Dessins, Inv. 29423.
62. Studio of Louis Le Vau, elevation of the end pavilion of the east façade. Spring 1667. Drawing, Paris, Musée Carnavalet, Cabinet des Estampes et Dessins, Réserve, D 6944 no. 19 (série GC) (Appendix A, A2).
63. Studio of Louis Le Vau, design for a triumphal arch. Drawing, Stockholm, Nationalmuseum, CC 2218.
64. Studio of Louis Le Vau, plan of the Cour Carrée. Spring 1667. Drawing, Paris, Louvre, Cabinet des Dessins, Recueil du Louvre, I, fol. 13 (Appendix A, A3).
65. Claude Perrault (?), plan of the Cour Carrée. Spring 1667. Drawing, Stockholm, Nationalmuseum, THC 1240 (Appendix A, A4).
66. Elevation of central portion of the east façade with the Colonnade. 1667. Medal, Paris, Bibliothèque Nationale, Cabinet des Médailles et Antiques, série royale no. 679 (Appendix A, A5).
67. Claude Perrault, perspective bird's-eye view of the Louvre from the east. Early 1668. Drawing, Paris, Bibliothèque Nationale, Cabinet des Estampes, Va 217c, fol. 16 (Appendix A, A6).
68. Claude Perrault, perspective bird's-eye view of the Observatoire, Paris. Early 1667. Drawing, Paris, Bibliothèque Nationale, Cabinet des Estampes, Va 304, I, fol. 76.
69. Claude Perrault, elevation study of end (south) pavilion of the east façade with the Colonnade. 1668. Drawing, Paris, Archives Nationales, O¹ 1667³, no. 73 (Appendix A, A7).
70. Variant of Figure 69.

71. Variant of Figure 69.
72. Variant of Figure 69.
73. Studio of Louis Le Vau, François d'Orbay, draftsman. Elevation of end (north) pavilion of the east façade with the Colonnade. 1668. Drawing, Paris, Archives Nationales, O^1 1667^4, no. 84 (Appendix A, A8).
74. Anonymous draftsman, east façade with the Colonnade. 1668. Drawing, Stockholm, Nationalmuseum, CC 789 (Appendix A, A9).
75. Detail of Figure 74.
76. Anonymous draftsman, plan of the Cour Carrée. 1668. Drawing, Paris, Louvre, Cabinet des Dessins, Recueil du Louvre, I, fol. 26 (Appendix A, A10).
77. Studio of Louis Le Vau, François d'Orbay, draftsman. Studies of the rear wall and ceiling of the Colonnade. 1668. Drawing, Paris, Musée des Arts Décoratifs, Cabinet des Dessins, no. 394 (Appendix A, A11).
78. Anonymous draftsman, studies of the iron reinforcement system of the Colonnade. 1668. Drawing, Paris, Louvre, Cabinet des Dessins, Recueil du Louvre, II, fol. 74 (Appendix A, A12).
79. Louvre, Colonnade. Iron reinforcement system. Engraving from Pierre Patte, *Mémoires sur les objets les plus importans de l'architecture,* Paris, 1769.
80. Louvre, Colonnade. View of tunnel within the north entablature, with iron tie-rods.
81. Louvre, Colonnade. Iron tie-rods with *moufles.*
82. Louvre, Colonnade. Pediment of the central pavilion showing the iron reinforcement system and relieving arches. Engraving from Jacques François Blondel, *Cours d'architecture . . . ,* Paris, 1777, Atlas, III.
83. Iron "free chain," French, fifteenth century. Engraving from E. E. Viollet-le-duc, *Dictionnaire raisonné de l'architecture française du XIe au XVIe siècle,* Paris, 1875, II.
84. Iron cramps, Notre-Dame, Paris, late twelfth century. Engraving from E. E. Viollet-le-Duc, *Dictionnaire raisonné de l'architecture française du XIe au XVIe siècle,* Paris, 1875, II.
85. Michel Molart, medal of the Louvre Colonnade, 1673. Paris, Bibliothèque Nationale, Cabinet des Médailles et Antiques.
86. Sébastien Le Clerc, *Lifting of the Louvre Pediment Stones, 1674.* Engraving, 1677.
87. Machines for moving and lifting the Louvre pediment stones. Engraving from Claude Perrault, trans. and ed., *Les dix livres d'architecture de Vitruve,* 2d ed., Paris, 1684.
88. Louvre, Colonnade. Elevation and plan. Engraving by Jean Marot, 1676.
89. Louvre, Colonnade. Elevation and section (details) of the central pavilion. Drawing, 1678. Paris, Louvre, Cabinet des Dessins, RF 29934 bis.
90. Louvre, Cour Carrée. Plan of the ground floor, 1754. Engraving from Jacques François Blondel, *Architecture françoise,* Paris, 1756, IV.
91. Louvre, Cour Carrée. Plan of the first floor. Engraving from Jacques François Blondel, *Architecture françoise,* Paris, 1756, IV.
92. Studio of Louis Le Vau, François d'Orbay, draftsman. Elevation of the east façade without

the Colonnade. Spring 1667. Drawing, Paris, Archives Nationales, O^1 1667^4, no. 88 (Appendix A, B1).

93. Studio of Charles Le Brun, elevation of the east façade without the Colonnade. Spring 1667. Drawing, Louvre, Cabinet des Dessins, Inv. 27641 (Appendix A, B2).
94. Studio of Charles Le Brun, elevation of the central pavilion of the east façade. Spring 1667. Drawing, Paris, Louvre, Cabinet des Dessins, Inv. 30227 (Appendix A, B3).
95. Louvre, south façade.
96. Studio of Louis Le Vau, François d'Orbay, draftsman. Elevation and section of the south façade, with a section of the Petite Galerie. 1668. Drawing, Paris, Archives Nationales, O^1 1667^3, no. 69 (Appendix A, C1).
97. Studio of Louis Le Vau, François d'Orbay, draftsman. Partial elevation of the western façade of the Cour Carrée and the Pavillon du Roi, with section of link to the Petite Galerie. 1668. Drawing, Paris, Archives Nationales, O^1 1667^4, no. 82 (Appendix A, C2).
98. Studio of Louis Le Vau, François d'Orbay, draftsman. Elevation of the south façade. 1668. Drawing, Paris, Archives Nationales, O^1 1667^4, no. 85 (Appendix A, C3).
99. Louvre, south façade. Elevation, section, and plan (details). Drawing, 1678. Paris, Louvre, Cabinet des Dessins, RF 29935 bis.
100. Louvre, south façade. Elevation and plan. Engraving by Jean Marot, 1678.
101. Louvre, north façade (from Louis Hautecoeur, *Le Louvre et les Tuileries de Louis XIV,* Paris and Brussels, 1927).
102. Louvre, north façade. Elevation, section, and plan of the central pavilion (details). Drawing, 1678. Paris, Louvre, Cabinet des Dessins, RF 29935.
103. Louvre, north façade. Elevation and plan. Engraving by Jacques François Blondel (from Blondel, *Architecture françoise,* Paris, 1756, IV).
104. Louvre, north façade, central pavilion. Elevation and plan. Engraving. Paris, Bibliothèque Nationale, Cabinet des Estampes, Va 217e.
105. Louvre, Cour Carrée.
106. Louvre, Cour Carrée. Elevation and plan. Engraving by Jacques François Blondel (from Blondel, *Architecture françoise,* Paris, 1756, IV).
107. Studio of Louis Le Vau, François d'Orbay, draftsman. Study for the top floor of the Cour Carrée, Louvre. 1668. Drawing, Paris, Archives Nationales, O^1 1667, no. 80 (Appendix A, D1).
108. Studio of Louis Le Vau, François d'Orbay, draftsman. Study for the top floor of the Cour Carrée, Louvre. 1668. Drawing, Paris, Archives Nationales, O^1 1667, no. 81 (Appendix A, D2).
109. François d'Orbay, Project for Lescot wing, Cour Carrée, Louvre. Ca. 1675. Drawing, Paris, Musée des Arts Décoratifs, Cabinet des Dessins, no. 830.
110. François d'Orbay, Project for Lescot wing, Cour Carrée, Louvre. Ca. 1675. Drawing, Berlin, Staatliche Museen, Kunstbibliothek, Hdz 6640.

111. Anonymous draftsman, studies for the top floor of the Cour Carrée, Louvre. Ca. 1676. Drawing, Paris, Archives Nationales, O¹ 1667, no. 20.

112. Louvre, Cour Carrée. Elevation, profile, and plan of the top floor (details). 1678. Drawing, Paris, Louvre, Cabinet des Dessins, RF 29936.

113. Claude Perrault, elevation of the Cour Carrée of the Louvre with sections of the north and south wings. Ca. 1676. Drawing, Paris, Archives Nationales, O¹ 1667³, no. 71.

114. Elevation, section, and plan of the ground floor of the east wing of the Louvre (details). 1678. Drawing, Paris, Louvre, Cabinet des Dessins, RF 29934.

115. Elevation of the ground floor of the Cour Carrée (detail) and section of passageway from the vestibule of the east wing to the Cour Carrée, Louvre. 1678. Drawing, Paris, Louvre, Cabinet des Dessins, RF 29936 bis.

116. Claude Perrault, obelisk project. 1666. Drawing, Stockholm, Nationalmuseum, CC 2824.

117. Gérard Scotin after Sébastien Le Clerc, engraved frontispiece to Claude Perrault, trans. and ed., *Les dix livres d'architecture de Vitruve,* Paris, 1673.

118. Detail of Figure 117.

119. Sébastien Le Clerc, engraving from Claude Perrault, trans. and ed., *Les dix livres d'architecture de Vitruve,* Paris, 1673.

120. Claude Perrault, Arc de Triomphe du Trône, Paris. Engraving by Sébastien Le Clerc, 1679.

121. Louvre, Colonnade. Anonymous engraving.

122. Louvre, Colonnade. Engraving by Nicolas de Fer, 1705.

123. Piliers de Tutelle, Bordeaux. Engraving from Elias Vinet, *Commentarius in Ausonii,* Bordeaux, 1580.

124. Piliers de Tutelle, Bordeaux. Engraving by Pierre Le Pautre. From Claude Perrault, trans. and ed., *Les dix livres d'architecture de Vitruve,* 2d ed., Paris, 1684.

125. Piliers de Tutelle, Bordeaux. Diagram of entablature. Engraving from Pierre Patte, *Mémoires sur les objets les plus importans de l'architecture,* Paris, 1769.

126. Courtyard façade, Palmyra. Reconstruction by Robert Wood (1757). Engraving from Robert Wood, *The Ruins of Palmyra and Balbec,* London, 1827.

127. Baalbek, Engraving from Balthasar de Monconys, *Journal des voyages . . . ,* Lyon, 1665, I.

128. Plan of Baalbek. Engraving by Jean Marot from *L'architecture françoise,* Paris, [ca. 1670] ("*Le Grand Marot*").

129. Bird's-eye view of Baalbek. Engraving by Jean Marot from *L'architecture françoise,* Paris, [ca. 1670] ("*Le Grand Marot*").

130. "Temple de Balbec" (Temple of Bacchus). Plan. Engraving by Jean Marot from *L'architecture françoise,* Paris, [ca. 1670] ("*Le Grand Marot*").

131. "Temple de Balbec" (Temple of Bacchus). Elevation. Engraving by Jean Marot from *L'architecture françoise,* Paris, [ca. 1670] ("*Le Grand Marot*").

132. "Temple de Balbec" (Temple of Bacchus). Elevation and detail of order. Engraving by Jean Marot from *L'architecture françoise,* Paris, [ca. 1670] (*"Le Grand Marot"*).
133. "Temple de Balbec" (Temple of Bacchus). Elevation and section. Engraving by Jean Marot from *L'architecture françoise,* Paris, [ca. 1670] (*"Le Grand Marot"*).
134. "Temple de Balbec" (Temple of Bacchus). Section and plan. Engraving by Jean Marot from *L'architecture françoise,* Paris, [ca. 1670] (*"Le Grand Marot"*).
135. Temple of Bacchus, Baalbek, after De Monceaux. Engraving from Bernard de Montfaucon, *L'antiquité expliquée et représentée en figures,* 2d ed., Paris, 1722, II.
136. Baalbek. Aerial view (from Theodor Wiegand, *Baalbek,* Berlin and Leipzig, 1921, I).
137. Baalbek. Reconstruction by Bruno Schulz (from Theodor Wiegand, *Baalbek,* Berlin and Leipzig, 1921, I).
138. Propylon, Baalbek. Reconstruction (from Theodor Wiegand, *Baalbek,* Berlin and Leipzig, 1921, I).
139. Propylon, Baalbek. Reconstruction by Robert Wood (1757). Engraving from Robert Wood, *The Ruins of Palmyra and Balbec,* London, 1827.
140. Propylon, Baalbek, with Arab fortifications. Engraving from Robert Wood, *The Ruins of Palmyra and Balbec,* London, 1827.
141. Propylon, Baalbek, with Arab fortifications (from Theodor Wiegand, *Baalbek,* Berlin and Leipzig, 1921, I).
142. Claude Perrault, plan for the union of the Louvre and the Tuileries, 1674. Engraving, Paris, Bibliothèque Nationale, Cabinet des Estampes, Va 217.
143. Sebastiano Serlio, plan for the Louvre, 1540s. Drawing. New York, Columbia University, Avery Architectural and Fine Arts Library (from Myra Nan Rosenfeld, *Sebastiano Serlio on Domestic Architecture,* Cambridge, Mass., and London, 1978).

Photographic Credits

Alinari/Art Resource, New York: 6; Archives Nationales, Paris, 21, 34, 69–73, 92, 96, 98, 107, 108, 111, 113; Archives Photographiques/S.P.A.D.E.M., Paris, 4, 9, 17, 44; Robert W. Berger, 10, 12, 42, 43, 45, 50, 53, 55, 80, 95, 105; Bibliothèque Nationale, Paris, 8, 14, 18, 23, 28–33, 36, 38–40, 60, 66–68, 85, 86, 88, 104, 117, 120–122, 142; Boston Public Library, Courtesy of the Trustees, 11, 13, 56, 79, 125, 126, 128–134, 139, 140; British Library, London, 1; Dayton Art Institute, 15; Frances Loeb Library, Graduate School of Design, Harvard University, Cambridge, Mass., 82; Giraudon/Art Resource, New York, 52; Harvard College Library, Cambridge, Mass., 16, 83, 84, 136–138, 141; Houghton Library, Harvard University, Cambridge, Mass., 22, 37, 57, 58, 87, 90, 91, 103, 106, 118, 119, 123, 124, 127, 135; Kunsthistorisches Museum, Vienna, 2; Rowland J. Mainstone, 81; Musée Carnavalet, Paris, 62; Musée des Arts Décoratifs, Paris, 77, 109; Musées Nationaux, Paris, 5, 19, 20, 59, 61, 64, 76, 78, 89, 93, 94, 99,

102, 112, 114, 115; Nationalmuseum, Stockholm, 24–27, 41, 63, 65, 74, 75, 116; New York Public Library, Print Collection, Miriam & Ira D. Wallach Division of Art, Prints and Photographs, Astor, Lenox and Tilden Foundations, 3; Caroline Rose, Paris, 51; Staatliche Museen Preussischer Kulturbesitz, Kunstbibliothek, Berlin, 110.

PREFACE AND ACKNOWLEDGMENTS

This book is primarily concerned with the parts of the Louvre that were designed and actually built under Louis XIV from 1667 to the late 1670s: the east façade (the Colonnade), the south and north façades, and the courtyard. The many unrealized projects, French and Italian, which preceded the executed work are reviewed in Chapter II, but no attempt is made to repeat in any depth the oft-told story of Bernini's proposals and visit to Paris.

In Sources I and II, I have gathered together all documents and writings about the Sun King's Louvre from 1667 to 1792. I cannot claim that all such material is here included; some writings have surely escaped my net, although I do believe that I have included all significant ones. I have, however, omitted as unnecessary a transcription of the measurements of the Louvre (*toisés de maçonnerie;* Paris, Bibliothèque Nationale, Département des manuscrits, Mélanges Colbert, vols. 316 [1667, 1668], 317 [1669, 1670]), referring to them only in the notes.

In Chapter VII, I present critical judgments about the Sun King's Louvre, drawing upon seventeenth- and eighteenth-century texts that are given *in extenso* in Sources II. No attempt is made to examine later nineteenth- and twentieth-century attitudes, which may reflect a significant change in sensibility and would provide material for a separate study.

It was necessary to print Figures 128–134 from microfilm; every effort has been made to reproduce them as satisfactorily as possible.

In the course of research, I have been assisted in many different ways by the following people, whom I would like to thank here: Michel Barbier, Allan Braham, Jacques de Caso, Richard Chafee, Dietrich Feldmann, Georges Gachot, Neil Levine, Robin Middleton, David Van Zanten, and Rochelle Ziskin. The staff of the drawings collection in the Nationalmuseum, Stockholm, was very helpful, and I owe a debt of thanks to Professor Patrik Reuterswärd for inviting me to present some of my findings to his students at the University of Stockholm and to hold a seminar meeting in the Nationalmuseum with the original Louvre drawings before us.

Rowland Mainstone and I are particularly grateful to M. Tachat, of the office of the Architecte-en-Chef du Louvre, and to Stephen Rustow, of Pei, Cobb, Freed & Partners, for facilitating access to the "tunnel" within the entablature of the Colonnade.

Finally, I wish to express deep appreciation to my wife and daughters for their understanding and support during the long years of gestation that resulted in this book.

French units of measurement:
   1 *toise* = 1.949 m = 6 *pieds*
   1 *pied* = 32.4 cm = 12 *pouces*
   1 *pouce* = ca. 2.7 cm

ABBREVIATIONS

AB	*Art Bulletin*
AN	Archives Nationales, Paris
Blondel, 1675	François Blondel, *Cours d'architecture enseigné dans l'Académie royale d'architecture,* Paris, 1675 (Part I)
Blondel, 1683	François Blondel, *Cours d'architecture enseigné dans l'Académie royale d'architecture,* Paris, 1683 (Parts II–V)
BMon	*Bulletin monumental*
BN, Estampes	Bibliothèque Nationale, Paris, Cabinet des Estampes
BN, Manuscrits	Bibliothèque Nationale, Paris, Département des Manuscrits
BSHAF	*Bulletin de la Société de l'histoire de l'art français*
BSHP	*Bulletin de la Société de l'histoire de Paris et de l'Île-de-France*
BurlM	*Burlington Magazine*
CBR	Jules Guiffrey, ed., *Comptes des bâtiments du roi sous le règne de Louis XIV,* Paris, 1881–1901, 5 vols.
GBA	*Gazette des beaux-arts*
G-M	Jean Guiffrey and Pierre Marcel, *Inventaire général des dessins du Musée du Louvre et du Musée de Versailles: Ecole française,* Paris, 1908–13, 10 vols.
Hautecoeur, *HAC*	Louis Hautecoeur, *Histoire de l'architecture classique en France II: Le règne de Louis XIV,* Paris, 1948, 2 vols.
Hautecoeur, *Louvre et Tuileries*	Louis Hautecoeur, *Le Louvre et les Tuileries de Louis XIV,* Paris and Brussels, 1927
Herrmann, *Perrault*	Wolfgang Herrmann, *The Theory of Claude Perrault,* London, 1973

JSAH	*Journal of the Society of Architectural Historians*
JWCI	*Journal of the Warburg and Courtauld Institutes*
Laprade, *d'Orbay*	Albert Laprade, *François d'Orbay, architecte de Louis XIV,* Paris, 1960
Louvre, Dessins	Louvre, Paris, Cabinet des Dessins
MC	Minutier Central, Archives Nationales, Paris
MHF	*Monuments historiques de la France*
Perrault, *Vitruve,* 1673	Claude Perrault, trans. and ed., *Les dix livres d'architecture de Vitruve,* Paris, 1673
Perrault, *Vitruve,* 1684	Claude Perrault, trans. and ed., *Les dix livres d'architecture de Vitruve,* 2d ed., Paris, 1684
PV	Henry Lemonnier, ed., *Procès-verbaux de l'Académie royale d'architecture,* Paris, 1911–29, 10 vols.
RA	*Revue de l'art*
RAAM	*Revue de l'art ancien et moderne*
RHV	*Revue de l'histoire de Versailles et de Seine-et-Oise*
T-B	Ulrich Thieme and Felix Becker, *Allgemeines Lexikon der bildenden Künstler von der Antike bis zur Gegenwart,* Leipzig, 1907–50, 37 vols.
VU	*Vie urbaine*
ZfK	*Zeitschrift für Kunstgeschichte*

I
REGIA SOLIS

The Louvre and Ovid

In 1670, as the fabric of the Louvre Colonnade (Fig. 43) was rapidly rising, a long poem was published in Paris with the title *Le superbe dessein du Louvre* (Sources II, no. 9). Its author, Claude Olry de Loriande, was a rather obscure *ingénieur du roi* who practiced architectural engraving and literary composition.[1] Lines 98–108 of his poem are richly allusive:

> Connoist que c'est de toy [the Louvre] qu'Ovide a deu parler
> Lors qu'il nous a décrit sous de sçavantes fables
> Les beautez d'un Palais que tu rends veritables:
> Si l'éclat du Soleil n'eut ses yeux éblouïs,
> Il nous auroit prédit que c'estoit pour LOVIS,
> Que le grand Apollon, ce pere de lumieres,

---

1. He calls himself "Ingenieur du Roy" on the title page of *Le superbe dessein du Louvre*. In 1669 he had published in Paris *Le heros tres-chrestien*, dedicated to Turenne; in its *extrait du roy*, Olry is described with the same phrase.

> L'animoit à parler de ces riches matieres:
> Cela se justifie en voyant ce Soleil,
> La devise d'un Roy qui n'a point de pareil
> Et qui cherit si fort cét Astre & ses images,
> Qu'il le fait figurer sur ses plus grands ouvrages.

> (Know that it is about you [the Louvre] that Ovid must have spoken
> When he described to us by means of learned fables
> The beauties of a palace that you make real:
> If the glare of the sun had not dazzled his eyes,
> He would have foretold to us that it was for LOVIS,
> That the great Apollo, that father of light,
> Inspired him to speak of these rich materials:
> That becomes clear in seeing this sun,
> The device of a king who has no equal
> And who cherishes so strongly that star and its images,
> That he has it depicted on his greatest works.)

Olry here alludes to the description of the palace of the sun, the subject of the opening lines of book II of Ovid's *Metamorphoses,* where the tragic story of Phaethon is related:

> Regia Solis erat sublimibus alta columnis,
> clara micante auro flammasque imitante pyropo,
> cuius ebur nitidum fastigia summa tegebat,
> argenti bifores radiabant lumine valvae.
> materiam superabat opus.
>   (lines 1–5)

> (The palace of the Sun stood high on lofty columns, bright with glittering gold and bronze that shone like fire. Gleaming ivory crowned the gables above; the double folding-doors were radiant with burnished silver. And the workmanship was more beautiful than the material. [Trans. F. J. Miller, Loeb Classical Library])

The Roman poet continues (lines 5–18) with a description of the decoration of the doors and then describes Phaethon's arrival before Apollo:

> Quo simul adclivi Clymeneia limite proles [Phaethon]
> venit et intravit dubitati tecta parentis,
> protinus ad patrios sua fert vestigia vultus
> consistitque procul; neque enim propiora ferebat

> lumina: purpurea velatus veste sedebat
> in solio Phoebus claris lucente smaragdis.
> a dextra laevaque Dies et Mensis et Annus
> Saeculaque et positae spatiis aequalibus Horae
> Verque novum stabat cinctum florente corona,
> stabat nuda Aestas et spicea serta gerebat,
> stabat et Autumnus calcatis sordidus uvis
> et glacialis Hiems canos hirsuta capillos.
>
> (lines 19–30)

(Now when Clymene's son [Phaethon] had climbed the steep path which leads thither, and had come beneath the roof of his sire whose fatherhood had been questioned [in 1, 750f.], straightway he turned him to his father's face, but halted some little space away; for he could not bear the radiance at a nearer view. Clad in a purple robe, Phoebus sat on his throne gleaming with brilliant emeralds. To right and left stood Day and Month and Year and Century, and the Hours set at equal distances. Young Spring was there, wreathed with a floral crown; Summer, all unclad with garland of ripe grain; Autumn was there, stained with the trodden grape, and icy Winter with white and bristly locks.)

The Colonnade's prominent array of columns reminded Olry of Ovid's first line—"Regia Solis erat sublimibus alta columnis"—which the critic Louis Petit de Bachaumont quoted specifically some years later (1751) in a footnote to an enthusiastic appreciation of the Louvre façade (see Sources II, no. 75). This comparison of the Louvre with Ovid's sun palace could be dismissed as a whimsical thought in the minds of these two writers alone; on the other hand, Olry de Loriande was not only alive when the Louvre Colonnade was designed and built, he was also the engraver of the architectural designs (including a project for the Louvre) of François Le Vau, the younger brother of Louis Le Vau, First Architect of the King and a member of the triumvirate that designed the Colonnade in 1667–68 (see Chapter III). It is therefore quite possible that Olry had knowledge of a *concetto* underlying the Louvre that was surely known to its designers, to court intellectuals, and to the Monarch: the Louvre as Ovid's palace of the sun, suitable for Louis XIV, the Sun King.

Ovid's first line had usually been translated in French editions as "La sale á Phebus estoit assise sur haultes colonnes"[2] or "Le Palais du Soleil estoit élevé sur des Colomnes magnifiques,"[3] but the plural ablative "columnis" could just as accurately be translated as "avec colonnes," thus perfectly congruent with the visual composition of the Colonnade.

---

2. *Les XV. livres de la Metamorphose d'Ovide . . .*, Paris, 1539, fol. 20r.

3. *Les Métamorphoses d'Ovide . . .*, trans. P. du Ryer, Paris, 1655, 54.

THE PALACE OF THE SUN IN ART

If the Louvre Colonnade had indeed been designed as an illustration of Ovid's first line, were there precedents that its designers could have drawn upon? I know of no actual palaces prior to the Louvre that were devised with this *concetto* in mind. Depictions of the palace of the sun can be found, of course, in the figural arts, where the meeting of Apollo and Phaethon, as recounted by Ovid, is specifically portrayed (the moment is when Phaethon begs permission to drive the sun chariot).[4]

Many versions of *Phaethon before Apollo* omit the architecture entirely (e.g., Poussin's painting in Berlin-Dahlem, Staatliche Museen) and are therefore not relevant in this context.[5] The number of Medieval, Renaissance, and Baroque representations of Ovid's sun palace that precede the Louvre Colonnade is small. Two of the earliest attempts known to me (Figs. 1, 2) omit the columns or clumsily interpret them as piers. We have to leap ahead to the seventeenth century to find more faithful attempts to illustrate Ovid. In 1639, the German artist Johann Wilhelm Baur made an etching (Fig. 3) of *Phaethon before Apollo* that ambitiously depicts Apollo's palace as a two-story structure of freestanding Ionic and Corinthian columns.[6] In the early 1650s, the French artist Eustache Le Sueur painted a version of the theme as part of the decoration of the Hôtel Lambert in Paris (Fig. 4).[7] Although Le Sueur's sun palace is without a colonnade, it does feature paired freestanding columns.

---

4. A catalog of depictions is provided by A. Pigler, *Barockthemen*, 2d ed., Budapest, 1974, II, 217–218. Pigler's list can be supplemented with the following versions of *Phaethon before Apollo*:

(a) Italian manuscript illumination, ca. 1450 (Oxford, Bodleian Library, MS 266, fol. 49r); see F. Saxl and H. Meier, *Verzeichnis astrologischer und mythologischer illustrierter Handschriften des lateinischen Mittelalters, 3: Handschriften in englischen Bibliotheken*, London, 1953, I, 294–295.

(b) Florentine cassone, ca. 1450 (London, coll. Lord Crawford); see P. Schubring, *Cassoni*, Leipzig, 1915, II, pl. XXXI, no. 152.

(c) Flemish manuscript illumination, 1470–80 (Fig. 1); see Saxl and Meier, *Verzeichnis*, I, 213–214.

(d) Francesco Primaticcio and Nicolò dell'Abbate, fresco, Salle de Bal, Château de Fontainebleau, between 1552 and 1556/58; see D. Rondorf, *Der Ballsaal im Schloss Fontainebleau: Zur Stilgeschichte Primaticcios in Frankreich*, publ. diss., Bonn, 1967, 156f., and B. Lossky, *The National Museum of the Château de Fontainebleau*, Paris, 1971, fig. 42.

(e) Roman cassone, 1570 (London, Victoria and Albert Museum); see Schubring, *Cassoni*, I, 413, no. 865; II, pl. CLXXI, no. 865.

(f) Antonio Tempesta, *Metamorphoseon*, Amsterdam, [1606?], pl. 11 (engraving).

(g) Johann Wilhelm Baur, engraving, 1639 (see Figure 3, text, and note 6).

(h) Laurent de La Hyre, drawing, before 1656 (Munich, Staatgraphische Sammlung, Inv. 34110); see A. Schnapper, "Colonna et la 'quadratura' en France à l'époque de Louis XIV," *BSHAF*, 1966, fig. 1 (between 72 and 73).

See also E. Krause, *Die Mythen-Darstellungen in der venezianischen Ovidausgabe von 1497*, Würzburg, 1926, 15f.; M. D. Henkel, "Illustrierte Ausgaben von Ovids Metamorphosen im XV., XVI., und XVII. Jahrhundert," *Vorträge der Bibliothek Warburg, 1926–1927*, Leipzig, 1930, 58–144. The only surviving ancient depiction of this scene I know of that includes the sun palace is a relief found in a Mithraeum at Dieburg (Rhineland); in the Mithraic cult, Phaethon was sometimes identified with Mithras, bringer of the world conflagration. In the relief, the upper parts of four Corinthian columns appear, supporting a pediment with a medallion of the head of the sun god (?) in the center. See M. J. Vermaseren, *Corpus inscriptionum et monumentorum religionis mithriacae*, The Hague, 1960, II, 105–106, fig. 324.

5. Paintings in Nero's Golden House, known through modern copies, depict Apollo enthroned beneath a baldachin with Phaethon and the Seasons, but the sun palace itself is not depicted (C. Robert, *Die antiken Sarkophag-Reliefs*, Berlin, 1909, III, part 3, 406 top, 407 top).

6. The print was published in Vienna in 1641 as part of a collection of illustrations for the *Metamorphoses*.

7. It formerly decorated the Chambre des Muses. See now A. Mérot, *Eustache Le Sueur (1616–1655)*, Paris, 1987, 272–273, no. 131.

Le Brun's Sun Palace for Vaux-le-Vicomte

All of these attempts to depict Ovid's building fade in comparison with a large drawing by Charles Le Brun dating from the late 1650s (Fig. 5).[8] This is a preparatory drawing for the painting intended (but never executed) for the cupola of the large oval salon of the château of Vaux-le-Vicomte. Le Brun must have made this design between 1656 (when the building was begun) and March 1660, because its composition is described in detail in volume 5 of Madeleine de Scudéry's novel *Clélie,* printed in that month and year.[9] De Scudéry describes some of the colors of the design, thus indicating that a colored *modello* once existed; a grisaille *modello* ("un tableau camayeux") was cited by Claude Nivelon, Le Brun's biographer.[10]

Le Brun's drawing does not depict *Phaethon before Apollo* but rather an allegorical pageant in praise of the owner of Vaux, the ill-fated Superintendent of Finance, Nicolas Fouquet. We see the palace of the sun and a vast array of figures, including the Olympian gods, the Winds, and personifications of time mentioned in Ovid's verses. In the center the "star" (heraldic shield) of Fouquet is received by Jupiter, Mars, and Saturn, while the figure of Dawn flies toward it at the command of Apollo, who is seated within an arched portico. The drawing, like the entire decorative program of the château, is a glorification of Fouquet, who was identified with Apollo and Hercules.[11]

Le Brun's palace of the sun consists of a colonnade of coupled freestanding Ionic columns framing a central motif: a barrel-vaulted portico supported by ranges of paired Ionic columns. The painter had used a similar architectural setting once before, in *Supper in the House of Simon* (Fig. 6), dating from ca. 1653.[12] Here the background is filled with a colonnade of coupled Ionic columns on a high, stepped podium, as in the drawing for Vaux-le-Vicomte.[13]

In her description of Le Brun's design for the cupola of Vaux, Madeleine de Scudéry noted: "The sun is there depicted in his palace, with all the embellishments (*ornemens*) that the poets attribute to him."[14] She was alluding here to the verses of Ovid quoted above, which describe

---

8. G-M, VII, 127 (no. 5886). Guiffrey and Marcel wrongly identified the drawing as a design for the Château de Sceaux; the error was rectified by J. Cordey, *Vaux-le-Vicomte,* Paris, 1924, 58–59.

9. M. de Scudéry, *Clélie,* Paris, 1660, v, part 3, 1105f.

10. C. Nivelon, *Vie de Charles Le Brun & description détaillée de ses ouvrages,* BN, Manuscrits, MS fr. 12987, 119 (ca. 1700): "Il fit un tableau camayeux en ovale long de cinq pieds sur la largeur proportionnée pour servir de modèle du plafond du grand dome de ce lieu qui est une représentation du Palais du Soleil ou pour mieux l'expliquer une représentation de tout ce qui se passe dans le cours de l'année." This *modello* is mentioned in the inventory after death (July 17, 1699) of Suzanne Butay, Le Brun's widow (H. Jouin, *Charles Le Brun et les arts sous Louis XIV,* Paris, 1889, 561).

11. The iconographic details are in Scudéry, *Clélie,* v, part 3, 1105f. See also U. V. Chatelain, *Le surintendant Nicolas Foucquet,* Paris, 1905, 396f.; J. Cordey, "Le grand salon ovale de Vaux-le-Vicomte et sa décoration," *RAAM,* XLVI, 1924, 232–248; idem, *Vaux-le-Vicomte,* 58–59; J. Montagu, "The Early Ceiling Decorations of Charles Le Brun," *BurlM,* CV, 1963, 405–406.

12. *Charles Le Brun, 1619–1690, peintre et dessinateur,* exhib. cat., Versailles, 1963, 47 (entry by J. Thuillier).

13. A drawing by Le Brun that depicts Jupiter and the Olympian gods is closely related to the drawing for Vaux (Louvre, Dessins, Inv. 27652; illustrated in G-M, VII, 128, no. 5898). The palace of Jupiter resembles Le Brun's palace of the sun, but the columns that flank the elaborate central motif are single, not paired. The drawing is for an unknown destination and probably dates from the 1650s (see Montagu, "The Early Ceiling Decorations," 405 n. 60). On Le Brun's ceiling decorations, see also R. W. Berger, *Versailles: The Château of Louis XIV,* University Park, Pa., and London, 1985, 35f., 85 n. 58.

14. "Le Soleil y est représenté dans son Palais, avec tous les ornemens que les Poëtes luy attribuent" (Scudéry, *Clélie,* v, part 3, 1105).

Phoebus Apollo accompanied by personifications of Day, Month, Year, Century, the Hours, and the Four Seasons; all of these reappear in Le Brun's drawing, with Year symbolized by the hoary motif of a great serpent biting its tail, which unfolds along the perimeter of the design.

Although Le Brun's project for the cupola of Vaux-le-Vicomte was never executed (because of the arrest of Fouquet in 1661 and the termination of all work at Vaux), it was by no means relegated to obscurity. As we have seen, Madeleine de Scudéry published a detailed description of it in 1660. In the early 1660s, Colbert wanted it to be painted in the Salon Carré of the Louvre, a project that was vetoed by the then Superintendent of the King's Buildings, Antoine de Ratabon.[15] In 1665, Le Brun sent the drawing to Bernini, who was in Paris, and Chantelou has recorded the great Italian's reaction to it:

> The eleventh of October, having gone to the Cavaliere's, I found in his antechamber the drawing Le Brun had made to be painted in the salon of Vaux; he had sent it to show to the Cavaliere, who, having returned from Mass, stopped to look at the drawing and studied it very attentively and at length; then he said: *It is beautiful, it has abundance without confusion* [*E bello, ha abbondanza senza confusione*]. Since it [the cupola] is an oval, he said that if the palace of the sun depicted there had been of the same shape or even round, perhaps it would have better suited the location and even the sun itself.[16] There are the Four Seasons, which are represented in this drawing with the Four Elements. Because it is for the vault of a dome, the work entails great difficulties, since everything must respond to one point of view and almost must appear foreshortened, being viewed from bottom to top. I said that Raphael had avoided these sorts of compositions. The Cavaliere had the drawing turned to see it better from all sides and afterward said that M. Colbert must have it executed somewhere, as it would be a pity not to do so.[17]

---

15. Nivelon, *Vie de Charles Le Brun*, 163–164: "On peut juger que c'eut été un magnifique ouvrage si le dessein que M. Colbert avoit formé qu'il [Le Brun] peignit dans le sallon qui est entre la petite et la grande galerie le grand plafond du Palais du Soleil, on n'aura pas de peine à croire que ce lieu seroit le plus accompli et le plus superbe du monde, mais l'envie qui trouve partout entrée empêcha dans son tems l'exécution du salon. M. de Ratabon qui étoit sous intendant sacrifia aux intérêts de M. Herard [Charles Errard] ce grand ouvrage qui ne sera peut être jamais vu que dans cet ouvrage." This incident must have occurred before January 1, 1664, when Colbert replaced Ratabon as *Surintendant des bâtiments du roi*. See Montagu, "The Early Ceiling Decorations," 406, and A. Mérot, "Décors pour le Louvre de Louis XIV: La mythologie politique à la fin de la Fronde (1653–1660)," in *La monarchie absolutiste et l'histoire en France,* Paris, 1987, I, 119.

16. Bernini's comment is difficult to understand in connection with Figure 5.

17. P. Fréart de Chantelou, *Journal du voyage du Cavalier Bernin en France,* ed. L. Lalanne, Paris, 1885, 224: "Le onzième d'octobre, étant allé chez le Cavalier, j'ai trouvé dans son antichambre le dessin que Le Brun avait fait pour être peint au salon de Vaux; il l'avait envoyé pour le faire voir au Cavalier, lequel étant revenu de la messe, il s'est arrêté à regarder ce dessin et l'a considéré fort attentivement et longtemps, puis il a dit: *E bello, ha abbondanza senza confusione*. Comme c'est une ovale, il a dit que si le palais du soleil, qui y est représenté, avait été de même forme ou bien ronde, peut-être aurait-il mieux convenu au lieu et au soleil même. Ce sont les quatre saisons de l'année qui sont représentées dans ce dessin avec les quatre éléments. Comme c'est pour une voûte de dôme, l'ouvrage est de grande sujétion, tout devant répondre à un seul point et tout devant presque paraître en raccourci, étant vu de bas en haut. J'ai dit que Raphaël avait fui ces sortes de représentations. Le Cavalier a fait tourner ce dessin de tous les côtés pour le mieux voir, et après a dit qu'il fallait que M. Colbert le fît exécuter quelque part, que ce serait dommage qu'il ne le fût pas." Montagu ("The Early Ceiling Decorations," 406) implies that Bernini saw the grisaille *modello* (see above, note 10), but Chantelou specifically refers to a "dessin."

Le Brun's drawing was never translated into paint, as Bernini recommended, but it later served as the basis for a large engraving of 1681 (Fig. 7) that referred allegorically to Louis XIV (see Chapter VIII). More important, as I shall attempt to show, the drawing stimulated a series of projects for the Louvre during the 1660s, projects that eventually resulted in the great east façade (Figs. 43, 44) that is the central concern of this book.

II
EARLY PROJECTS FOR THE EAST WING

We have seen that Le Brun's drawing for Vaux (Fig. 5), dating from the 1650s, was well known in the highest French artistic circles. Le Brun himself had attained positions of great power at the time of and shortly after his Vaux cupola project. From at least 1658 on, he was referred to in documents as First Painter of the King, officially assuming that title in 1664;[1] in 1663 he was appointed Director of the Gobelins factory, where he had actually been in charge since the preceding year.[2] In addition, beginning in 1663 or 1664 Le Brun was in contact with the Petite Académie, a small committee formed by Colbert in 1663 to work out the iconography of Louis XIV.[3] Also in 1663, he was appointed Chancellor for life of the Royal Academy of Painting and Sculpture.[4]

Given these facts, it is intriguing to note that projects for the east façade of the Louvre that feature a prominent display of columns, and in some instances a trabeated colonnade of free-

---

1. *Charles Le Brun, 1619–1690, peintre et dessinateur*, exhib. cat., Versailles, 1963, liii.
2. Ibid., lviii.
3. On this group and Le Brun's involvement with it, see R. W. Berger, *In the Garden of the Sun King: Studies on the Park of Versailles under Louis XIV*, Washington, D.C., 1985, chap. 2, esp. 9. Le Brun must have been in contact with the Petite Académie by May 1663, when contracts were drawn up for the Galerie d'Apollon in the Louvre.
4. *Charles Le Brun, 1619–1690*, lvii.

standing coupled columns (as in Figure 5), begin to appear in the early 1660s, soon after Le Brun devised his idea for Vaux-le-Vicomte. To see the question of the east façade in art-historical perspective, it is necessary to review the earlier projects.

THE EARLY SEVENTEENTH CENTURY

Pierre Lescot's sixteenth-century exterior façades of the Louvre (Fig. 9) were austere and totally without the classical orders, in complete contrast to the decorative profusion and display of the orders in his court elevations (Fig. 10). Lescot's design had an authority that influenced later efforts to design an appropriate façade for the all-important eastern (entrance) wing. The earliest known suggestion, dating from shortly after 1600, is recorded in a fresco (much restored) by Toussaint Dubreuil in the Galerie des Cerfs, Château de Fontainebleau (Fig. 20).[5] Here we see an approximate continuation of Lescot's design spread across the façade; the central and end pavilions, based on Lescot's Pavillon du Roi (Fig. 9), are entirely conjectural, the product of modern restoration. The orders remain banished, and the entrance wing preserves a fortress-like quality despite the numerous windows. The architect is unknown.

During the first half of the seventeenth century, activity at the Louvre concentrated on the expansion of the western wing of the Cour Carrée (Square Court), its center marked by the new Pavillon de l'Horloge (Figs. 13, 14).[6] Nevertheless, a few projects for the east wing were created. One of these (Fig. 21), an anonymous drawing probably dating from the reign of Louis XIII,[7] relies for its effect on channeled rustication and, for the pavilions, two-story frontispieces with rusticated columns tied together by segmental pediments in a formula recalling the façade of Saint-Étienne-du-Mont (anonymous, begun 1610) or the courtside frontispiece of the *corps-de-logis* of the Luxembourg Palace (by Salomon de Brosse, begun 1615), both in Paris. The columns, small in scale and placed against piers, blend with the rustication and are not noticeable at first glance. Bolder in the use of the orders is the project by Jacques Lemercier (Fig. 22), First Architect of the King from 1639 until his death in 1654. Lemercier's design is of uncertain date; although the columns are again confined to the pavilions, they are larger in scale than in Figure 21, embracing one story and a mezzanine, and they stand out more prominently upon a rusticated *rez-de-chaussée*. Still, no one would be tempted to declaim Ovid's "Regia Solis etc." when contemplating Lemercier's façade.

---

5. On this fresco, see A. Berty and H. Legrand, *Histoire générale de Paris: Topographie historique du vieux Paris: Région du Louvre et des Tuileries,* Paris, 1868, II, 97f. (the fragments of the original fresco are illustrated in the figure between 96 and 97); L. Batiffol, "Le Louvre et les plans de Lescot," *GBA,* ser. 4, III, 1910, 282; L. Hautecoeur, "Le Louvre de Pierre Lescot," *GBA,* ser. 5, XV, 1927, 201–203.

6. For a recent summary of this activity, see J. P. Babelon, "La Cour Carrée du Louvre: Les tentatives des siècles pour maîtriser un espace urbain mal défini," *BMon,* CXLII, 1984, 43.

7. A. Erlande-Brandenburg, "Un projet d'élévation pour la façade orientale du Louvre," *BSHAF,* 1965, 115–118.

Louis Le Vau's Projects (ca. 1659–1664)

During most of the Regency period (1643–61), when Louis XIV was very young and the government of France was administered by the Italian Jules Cardinal Mazarin, there was no significant architectural work at the Louvre. The Cour Carrée, however, was in a sadly unfinished condition, a mixture of wings in Renaissance style, medieval remnants awaiting demolition, and partially built recent work. The southwest corner of the court stood complete, consisting of two blocks in Renaissance style forming a right angle, with the Pavillon du Roi at the corner (Figs. 9, 10). All of these structures, by Pierre Lescot, had been built from 1546 to the 1580s. The west wing had been extended and completed in the seventeenth century by a central unit, the Pavillon de l'Horloge, and by a repetition of Lescot's block and corner pavilion to the north, all the work of Lemercier (1624–41; Figs. 13, 14). The lower fragment of the north wing, also built under Lemercier, was standing when Louis XIII died in 1643 (Fig. 14). Within the Cour Carrée, facing the completed west wing, stood a remnant of the original medieval Louvre (Fig. 16).

Not until after the Fronde (1648–52) was artistic activity revived at the Louvre, but at first only in the form of interior decoration. Between 1653 and 1660, the apartments of the Queen Mother, Anne of Austria, of the King and Queen, and of Mazarin and his ministers were adorned with paintings, stuccoes, and woodwork, some in a new Italian Baroque style by Romanelli and Grimaldi.[8] A painting by Le Sueur of 1654–55 (Fig. 15), originally placed in the woodwork of a *cabinet* next to the *chambre du roi,* is from this period. In this *Allegory of Magnificence*,[9] the seated figure of Magnificence holds an architectural plan of a probably imaginary building at which the seated Historia gazes as she writes in her book. The idea, directly derived from Ripa, is that the effect of Magnificence is the construction of "tempi, palazzi e altre cose di maraviglia" (temples, palaces, and other marvelous things). The painting is an intimation of the royal architectural magnificence achieved under Louis XIV from the 1660s on.

Only when a secure peace with Spain was achieved in 1659 (with the Treaty of the Pyrenees) was the completion of the Cour Carrée seriously considered. Louis Le Vau, who had succeeded to the post of First Architect of the King when Lemercier died in 1654, was entrusted with finishing the south wing and with the design of a new eastern (entrance) wing.[10] The westerly part of the south wing, with the Pavillon du Roi and the outer façade of the adjoining ten-bay *logis* (Fig. 16), had been standing since the sixteenth century. From 1660 to 1663,[11] Le Vau simply duplicated

---

8. On these decorations, some of which are extant, see Hautecoeur, *Louvre et Tuileries,* 23f.; C. Aulanier, *La Petite Galerie,* Paris, 1955; and idem, *Le Pavillon du Roi,* Paris, 1958 (*Histoire du Palais et du Musée du Louvre,* vols. v and vii); D. Bodart, "Une description de 1657 des fresques de Giovanni Francesco Romanelli au Louvre," *BSHAF,* 1974, 43–50; P. Rosenberg, "Quelques dessins inédits de Romanelli préparatoires à la décoration du Louvre," ibid., 51–53; A. Mérot, "Décors pour le Louvre de Louis XIV: La mythologie politique à la fin de la Fronde (1653–1660)," in *La monarchie absolutiste et l'histoire en France,* Paris, 1987, i, 113–137.

9. On this picture, see N. Rosenberg Henderson, "Le Sueur's Allegory of Magnificence," *BurlM,* cxii, 1970, 213–217; A. Mérot, *Eustache Le Sueur (1616–1655),* Paris, 1987, 314–315, no. 182.

10. Hautecoeur, *Louvre et Tuileries,* 97f.

11. Ibid., 101f.

these units to the east, but he designed an original central pavilion (Figs. 17, 18) that broke with Lescot's austereness by introducing a colossal order of engaged Corinthian columns embracing the two lower stories. The straight entablature carried an attic richly decorated with reliefs and punctuated by vigorous *ressauts,* forming pedestals for large statues. The upper part of the pavilion repeated the top floor of the Pavillon du Roi, and Le Vau capped the whole with a four-sided dome, following Lemercier's Pavillon de l'Horloge (Figs. 13, 14). A preliminary study for Le Vau's pavilion (Fig. 19)[12] reveals strong similarities to his court façade of Vaux-le-Vicomte (1656–61); the decisive change to much taller and slenderer columns resting on a lower plinth may have been impelled by the desire to form the pavilion into an effective *point de vue* when seen from the Left Bank (it was on axis with Le Vau's Collège des Quatre Nations, begun in 1662).

Much more novel and daring was Le Vau's proposed east wing.[13] This evolved from ca. 1659 on, at first with a rectilinear central pavilion containing a passageway to the court. Then, beginning ca. 1661–62, Le Vau replaced this unit with an oval vestibule bowing outward from the plane of the façade (Fig. 33). A sectional drawing (Fig. 34) reveals a domed two-story space richly articulated with Composite columns on the ground floor, Composite pilasters above, and a narrow gallery and an open ironwork balustrade allowing viewing from the first-floor level. The cupola, densely filled with moldings and decorative compartments, surprisingly opens into a very wide oculus, open to the sky, defined by a low drum with dwarf pilasters. The vestibule is derived from the *salons à l'italienne* found in Le Vau's châteaux (Le Raincy, Meudon, Vaux-le-Vicomte),[14] here used for the passage of pedestrians and vehicles into the Cour Carrée. The open oculus was undoubtedly meant to recall the Roman Pantheon, thus summoning up associations with Roman antiquity, and the light entering from above may have been intended as a metaphor for the Sun King. The exterior elevation of Le Vau's east wing has not been preserved, but a modern reconstruction (Fig. 35) indicates the display of engaged colossal columns and the bizarre Baroque top of the central pavilion—a drum-without-dome borrowed directly by Le Vau from an ideal château design published by Antoine Le Pautre.[15]

Antoine Léonor Houdin (1661)

In 1661, soon after Le Brun devised his idea for the cupola of Vaux-le-Vicomte (Fig. 5), there appeared an engraved project for the east façade of the Louvre that rings out the columnar

12. I agree here with the suggestion of D. del Pesco that the drawing is for the central pavilion of the south façade (*Il Louvre di Bernini nella Francia di Luigi XIV,* Naples, 1984, 86, fig. 49); it had previously been identified as a study by Le Vau for the north façade, dating from 1663 [?], by M. Petzet (in E. Hubala, *Die Kunst des 17. Jahrhunderts* [*Propyläen Kunstgeschichte* 9], Berlin, 1970, 250, pl. 273a).

13. See M. Whiteley and A. Braham, "Louis Le Vau's Projects for the Louvre and the Colonnade—I," *GBA,* ser. 6 LXIV, 1964, 285–296; A. Erlande-Brandenburg, "Les fouilles du Louvre et les projets de Le Vau," *VU,* n.s., XXXI, 1964, 241–263, and XXXII, 1965, 12–22; F. Salet, "Le Vau et le Bernin au Louvre," *BMon,* CXXIII, 1965, 144–148; M. Whiteley and A. Braham, "Les soubassements de l'aile orientale du Louvre," *RA,* I, no. 4, 1969, 30–43; A. Braham and P. Smith, *François Mansart,* London, 1973, I, 262–264; R. W. Berger, "Louis Le Vau's Château du Raincy," *Architectura,* VI, no. 1, 1976, 43.

14. See Berger, "Louis Le Vau's Château du Raincy," 36–46; idem, "Louis Le Vau's Château du Raincy: An Addendum," *Architectura,* XIV, 1984, 171.

15. Berger, "Antoine Le Pautre and the Motif of the Drum-without-Dome," *JSAH,* XXV, 1966, 165–180.

theme in a sustained way (Fig. 23).[16] The author of this design was Antoine Léonor Houdin, an obscure *architecte-ingénieur* whose entire known *oeuvre* consists of visionary projects for the Louvre and the Tuileries.[17] The Louvre elevation contains almost-literal quotations of Palladio's Villa Rotonda to form the upper floors of the end pavilions. The Ionic columns of the porticoes of the "villas" are supported below by Roman Doric columns that are continued through the *premier étage* and central pavilion to suggest a trabeated colonnade. The latter clearly differentiates the *étage noble* from the rusticated *rez-de-chaussée* with its spare arch-on-pier motif. It should be noted, however, that Houdin's columns are single, not paired, and are applied against the façade wall, as indicated on the engraved plan.[18] Hence, there is no true colonnade. The design is precocious and difficult to relate to earlier French architecture. The columnar display distinguishes Houdin's design from earlier Louvre projects and, along with the podium, suggests a connection with Le Brun's design for Vaux.

François Le Vau (ca. 1662–1664)

Houdin's façade design and related projects for the Louvre and the Tuileries were not solicited by the Crown, as far as we know, but that is not true of the next design to be considered, that by François Le Vau, *architecte-ingénieur du roi* and the younger brother of the *premier architecte*. On December 4, 1664, the younger Le Vau wrote a letter to Colbert with an important passage:

> You will remember, please, that you had ordered me some time ago to work on the design of the Grande Galerie of the Louvre, on which I am at present engaged. . . . I will show you in a few days the project of my design. I will speak to you about the model of the Louvre that I have seen these past days on your order, since *about two years ago I worked on a design of the great façade which it pleased you to have me make; I will show it to you if it pleases you* [my emphasis]; and may I say to you in advance that you may find in it things that could satisfy you and that could be used without displeasing my brother [Louis Le Vau], for whom I have all the respect due him; but when it is a matter of your

---

16. Although Figure 23 is undated, the year 1661 appears on accompanying plans and bird's-eye view (BN, Estampes, Va 217).

17. His bird's-eye-view project of the Louvre and the Tuileries is published in Hautecoeur, *Louvre et Tuileries,* pl. XXIX, bottom, and in A. Chastel and J. M. Pérouse de Montclos, "L'aménagement de l'accès oriental du Louvre," *MHF,* n.s., XII, 1966, 182–184, fig. 3. See Louvre, Dessins, Recueil du Louvre, I, fols. 1, 2; BN, Estampes, Va 217. In a document of March 24, 1665 (MC, XLII, 157), Houdin is described as an "architecte et Ingenieur du Roy" living in the rue de la Lingerie in Paris. The document reveals him to have been a designer of pontoon bridges ("ponts flottans") for all the rivers of France. He was still active in 1689 and living in the rue des Deux-Écus in Paris (MC, LXX, 189 [April 2, 1689]).

18. Louvre, Dessins, Recueil du Louvre, I, fol. 1 (left). The columns in the end pavilions, however, are freestanding.

glory I feel myself obliged to show to you everything my work and industry give me in the way of wisdom in my art.[19]

In this letter François Le Vau states unambiguously that about two years earlier (end of 1662?) he had made a design for the great (east) façade of the Louvre on orders of Colbert;[20] now, in December 1664, he is ready to show the design to the minister (presumably, François continued to work on the project between 1662 and 1664). The design to which François Le Vau refers can only be the large presentation drawing in Stockholm (Figs. 24–27) that is supplemented by several engravings, all undated and four of which are by our friend Claude Olry de Loriande (see Chapter I; Figs. 28–32).[21] The engraved elevation of an end pavilion (Fig. 30) corresponds

---

19. "il vous souviendra s'il vous plait que vous m'aviez commandé il y a quelque temps de travailler au dessingt de la grande gallerie du Louvre ce que jé faict à présent . . . je vous en feray voir dans peu de jours le projet de mon dessingt. Je vous entretiendray du modelle du Louvre que j'ay vu cest jours passés par votre ordre comme *il y a environ deux ans que jé travaillay à un dessingt de la grande façade qu'il vous plust me faire faire je vous le representeray s'il vous plais* [my emphasis]; et vous puis dire par avance que vous y trouveries peut estre des choses qu'il vous pourroient satisfaire desquelles on se pourroit servir sans toutefois avec aucun dessingt de desplaire à mon frère [Louis Le Vau] lequel j'ay tout le respect que je luy doict: mais quand il s'agit de votre gloire je me sens obligé de vous faire voire tout ce que mon travaille et mon industrie me donne de lumière dans mon art" (BN, Manuscrits, Mélanges Colbert, vol. 126, fol. 145). Previously published in Laprade, *d'Orbay*, 137, and in a slightly less accurate form in A. Jal, *Dictionnaire critique de biographie et d'histoire*, 2d ed., Paris, 1872, 787.

20. In 1662 Colbert was not yet *surintendant des bâtiments du roi;* nevertheless, he had been insinuating himself into the arts before his official appointment on January 1, 1664 (see, e.g., his letter of late 1662 to Jean Chapelain proposing commemorative medals for Louis XIV; Berger, *In the Garden of the Sun King,* 7).

21. François Le Vau's Louvre project and its evident relationship to the Louvre Colonnade were first discussed by L. Hautecoeur, "L'auteur de la colonnade du Louvre," *GBA,* ser. 5, IX, 1924, 158f.; idem, *Louvre et Tuileries,* 148, 167; and Hautecoeur, *HAC,* I, 120, 275. Not many later writers on seventeenth-century French architecture have taken notice of it. Exceptions are E. Langenskiöld and C. D. Moselius, *Arkitekturritningar, planer och teckningar ur Carl Johan Cronstedts Fullerösamling,* exhib. cat., Stockholm, 1942, 2; E. Langenskiöld, "Louvren, Tuilerierna och Versailles: Slottens byggnadshistoria i belysning av ritningar i Cronstedtsamlingen på Nationalmuseum," *Nationalmusei Årsbok,* 1942–43, 117f.; R. Josephson, *Kungarnas Paris,* Stockholm, 1943, 85f.; idem, *Barocken,* 2d ed., Stockholm, 1967, 151; A. Blunt, *Art and Architecture in France, 1500 to 1700,* 2d rearranged impression, Harmondsworth, Middlesex, 1957, 279 n. 28; B. Teyssèdre, *L'art au siècle de Louis XIV,* Paris, 1967, 65, figs. 33, 66; and A. Picon, *Claude Perrault, 1613–1688, ou la curiosité d'un classique,* Paris, 1988, 163, fig. 120. Blunt questioned the early date of the design, unjustly declaring the evidence to be "uncertain." He omitted this note in the last (4th) edition of his book (1980), but the caption to the Stockholm drawing (Fig. 24) is misdated "1644(?)" on 328, fig. 270. The drawing (Fig. 24) measures 73.7 by 190.0 cm and consists of three pieces of paper glued together. The medium is pen, gray ink, and gray, blue, and pink washes. The verso is signed "Levau le jeune" and "Leveux." The watermark is a chaplet with cross (also found on Figure 65), a common mark of the later seventeenth century (see E. Heawood, *Watermarks, Mainly of the 17th and 18th Centuries,* Hilversum, 1950, pl. 37, no. 226; Heawood on 69 cites as an example Parisian paper of 1683). Langenskiöld and Moselius (*Arkitekturritningar,* 2) judged that the signature "Levau le jeune" is fairly close to Louis Le Vau's hand and therefore ascribed the drawing to both Le Vau brothers (!). This position was maintained by Langenskiöld ("Louvren, Tuilerierna och Versailles," 117–118) and adopted by Josephson in his two publications cited above. However, François's signature, although written with a flourish, is not identical to Louis Le Vau's as found on Stockholm, Nationalmuseum, CC 9, CC 6, CC 3, CC 19, CC 20, and CC 21 (Langenskiöld, "Louvren, Tuilerierna och Versailles," figs. 31–36).

The engravings bear the following inscriptions. *Central pavilion I (Fig. 28):* "Dessin du Sr. Le Vau le jeune pour le Grand Portail du Louvre suivant sa pensée." "Durant. Scul." The engraver is Isaac Durant. *Central pavilion II (Fig. 29):* "Dessein du principal pavillon et portail du Louvre du costé de la grande face, ainsi que le Sieur Le Vau le Jeune l'avoit proposé." *End pavilion (Fig. 30):* "Dessein de l'un des gros pavillon[s] du bout de la grande face de L'entrée du Louvre sur la grande place, ainsi que le Sieur le Vau le Jeune l'avoit proposé." "F. Le Vau in." "C. Olry De Loriande." *Section (Fig. 31):* "Dessein du profil du gros Pavillon de l'entrée du Louvre au droit de la gallerie chambres et peristil Suivant le dessein proposé par le Sr. Le Vau le Jeune." "F. Le Vau Inv." "C. Olry Deloriande." *Ground plan (Fig. 32):* "Dessein du plan du gros pavillon du milieu de l'entrée du Louvre avec une partie de la gallerie et peristil, ainsi que le Sieur le Vau le Jeune l'avoit proposé." "F. Le Vau In. C. Olry Deloriande Sculpsit." Note that the plan renders simultaneously the *rez-de-chaussée* and the *premier étage* with its colonnade.

almost exactly to the left (south) pavilion in the presentation drawing (Figs. 24, 26), except that the statues on the *premier étage* in the drawing have been omitted and a chimney is visible. There are two engraved versions of the central pavilion: one (Fig. 28) is based on the drawing, with some changes in the statuary (most notably in the statue of Apollo just beneath the pediment); the other central pavilion (Fig. 29) accords with the ground plan (Fig. 32) and sectional view (Fig. 31) and constitutes a radical revision of the composition. In the Stockholm drawing (Fig. 24) and in Figure 28, the *premier étage* of the central pavilion is closely unified with the flanking colonnades by means of the continuation of the pedimented windows and freestanding columns (although single, not paired in the center of the pavilion). In the revision (Fig. 29), the pavilion is more strongly contrasted with the flanking elevations because of the omission of the pedimented windows and freestanding columns. There is now a greater vertical emphasis: the recessed center is flanked by a rising sequence of piers and columns, accentuated by a prominent four-sided dome flanked by chimneys. In addition, the arch of the central portal now rises into the zone of the first floor, anticipating the Colonnade as built (Fig. 48). In all versions of the central pavilion there appears the Ludovican motto NEC PLVRIBVS IMPAR (Not Unequal to Many) and sculpture depicting Apollo and Hercules, the two major mythological *personae* of Louis XIV.[22]

The sectional view (Fig. 31) suggests that there was once a model that could open like a dollhouse for inspection. Four floors were actually projected, not three as the façade elevation seems to indicate. On the right side of the print appear the three stories with their columns of the Cour Carrée.

Returning to the presentation drawing (Figs. 24–27), we see upon careful study that Le Vau *le jeune* has depicted two alternative solutions for the articulation of the attic story—a range on the left with arched windows[23] and one on the right with rectangular windows. These differences are carried into the top floors of the end pavilions.

22. In the central pavilion of the drawing (Fig. 25), Apollo, beneath the upper pediment, drives his team of horses; Hercules appears four times below, battling (from left to right) the Nemean Lion, Cerberus, the Hydra of Lerna, and Antaeus. Hercules appears again in the end pavilions: twice in the left one (Fig. 26) (holding a pillar and fighting Cerberus again) and once in the right one (Fig. 24) (paired with Abundance). Victories appear in the main pediment, holding a crown before a shield with the French fleurs-de-lis encircled by two chaplets with a Greek cross. Apollo in his quadriga is accompanied by figures of Abundance (left) and Justice (right). Seated river gods appear next to the former; a seated Bacchus and a second Abundance (?) are next to the latter. In the engraving of the central pavilion made after the drawing (Fig. 28), a standing Apollo with the features of the King is substituted for the Apollo driving his horses; Hercules figures reappear here as well as in the alternate version (Fig. 29), where a frieze showing Apollo in his quadriga with the Muses (?) is placed beneath the pediment. (Hercules figures are omitted from the engraved end pavilion [Fig. 30], as noted in the text, above.) The motto NEC PLURIBUS IMPAR appears as early as 1658 on a medal (L. Lange, "La grotte de Thétis et le premier Versailles de Louis XIV," *Art de France*, I, 1961, 147, illus.). Concerning this motto, the King wrote: "Those who saw me managing the cares of royalty with such ease and with such confidence induced me to add the sphere of the earth, and as its motto NEC PLURIBUS IMPAR, by which they meant to flatter the ambition of a young king, in that with all my capacities, I would be just as capable of ruling still other empires as would the sun of illuminating still other worlds with its rays. I know that some obscurity has been found in these words, and I have no doubt that the same symbol might have suggested some happier ones. Others have been presented to me since, but this one having already been used in my buildings and in an infinite number of other things, I have not deemed it appropriate to change it" (*Mémoires for the Instruction of the Dauphin*, trans. and ed. P. Sonnino, New York, 1970, 104 [1662]). On the traditions linking French monarchs to Hercules, see C. Vivanti, "Henri IV, the Gallic Hercules," *JWCI*, XXX, 1967, 176–197; del Pesco, *Il Louvre di Bernini*, 140f.

23. These match the top-floor windows of Lescot's Pavillon du Roi (Fig. 9).

This major Louvre project of François Le Vau can be securely dated, as we have seen, ca. 1662–64. That it is the direct ancestor of the realized Colonnade (Fig. 44) will be discussed later. It is appropriate at this point, however, to examine the career of the younger Le Vau and attempt to understand this remarkable project in the context of his *oeuvre*.

François Le Vau: His Architectural Career

François Le Vau's date of birth has traditionally been given as 1613, one year after the birth of his brother Louis, the future First Architect, but recently it has been claimed that François was actually born ten years later, in 1623.[24] However that may be, we find him in 1643 first cited as "architecte des bâtiments du roi";[25] he probably received his formation as an architect in the same manner as his brother: by working under his father, Louis I Le Vau, described in a document of 1658 as "voyer et maistre des oeuvres des bastiments du Roy à Fontainebleau."[26] A document of 1648 describes François as "architecq Ingenieur du Roy,"[27] the latter title probably indicating that he had acquired some expertise in fortifications.[28]

François Le Vau's earliest known architectural work dates from 1651, when he renovated the Hôtel de Sully in Paris, then owned by the Maréchal de Rohan, Sully's son-in-law.[29] Three years later he became architect to Louis XIV's cousin, the Duchesse de Montpensier ("La Grande Mademoiselle") and began to remodel her Château de Saint-Fargeau in Burgundy.[30] From this time until the early 1660s, François designed substantial châteaux for highly placed clients. These buildings included the Château de Lignières (1656, for Jérôme de Nouveau, *surintendant général des postes*)[31] and the Château de Bercy (begun in or shortly after 1658 for Charles Henri de Malon, *premier président au Parlement*).[32] Lignières and Bercy are securely by

---

24. [Paris, Ministère de la Culture], *Colbert, 1619–1683*, exhib. cat., Paris, 1983, 264 (entry by N. Felkay citing the unpublished work of D. Feldmann). On François Le Vau, see mainly Hautecoeur, *HAC*, I, 114–121; Laprade, *d'Orbay*, 84–90; *Colbert, 1619–1683*, 264–265 (entry by N. Felkay, with bibliography); and R. W. Berger, "Le Vau, François," *Macmillan Encyclopedia of Architects*, ed. A. K. Placzek, New York and London, 1982, II, 695.

25. AN, Z¹ʲ 277 (April 4, 1643). See M. Dumolin, *Études de topographie parisienne*, Paris, 1931, III, 84–85.

26. Jal, *Dictionnaire critique*, 788. The document is François Le Vau's act of marriage.

27. BN, Manuscrits, Fichier Laborde, nouv. acq. franç. 12072, fol. 13726: Godfather at the baptism of the daughter of the architect Pierre Cottart (September 30, 1648).

28. See A. Blanchard, *Les ingénieurs du "Roy" de Louis XIV à Louis XVI*, Montpellier, 1979, 8, for a discussion of the word "ingénieur."

29. MC, LXXXVII, 175 (May 16, 1651).

30. The work was finished in 1657. Laprade, *d'Orbay*, 85, gives 1652 as the start of work at Saint-Fargeau. The château still stands, but it was devastated by fire in 1752 and "restored." On this building, see J. de Foville and A. Le Sourd, *Les châteaux de France*, Paris, n.d., 436; L. Hautecoeur, *La Bourgogne: L'architecture*, Paris and Brussels, 1927, I, 17–18, and II, pl. 16; Hautecoeur, *HAC*, I, 114–115.

31. Destroyed; recorded in engravings by Claude Olry de Loriande (Hautecoeur, *HAC*, I, figs. 103–106; Laprade, *d'Orbay*, pl. III.6, top). On this château, see Foville and Le Sourd, *Les châteaux de France*, 79; Hautecoeur, *HAC*, I, 115–117. According to Laprade (*d'Orbay*, 85 n. 3), the contract dates from May 9, 1654.

32. Destroyed; recorded in engravings by Claude Olry de Loriande (Hautecoeur, *HAC*, I, figs. 108–110; Laprade, *d'Orbay*, pl. III.5A). On this château, see L. Lambeau, *Bercy*, Paris, 1910; L. Deshairs, *Le château de Bercy*, Paris, [1911]; Hautecoeur, *HAC*, I, 118–120.

François: possibly by him are the Château de Saint-Sépulchre (between ca. 1654 and 1662, for Louis Hesselin, *maître d'hôtel ordinaire du roi*)[33] and the extant but derelict Château de Sucy-en-Brie (1660–61 for Nicolas Lambert, *grand maître des eaux et forêts de Normandie*).[34] Another château by the younger Le Vau, perhaps from this period and known only by a single engraving, is the curious Château de Monpipaux.[35] Other works from the 1650s include the court façade and interiors of the Hôtel de La Rivière, Place Royale (des Vosges), Paris (for the Abbé de La Rivière),[36] and modest row houses on the Île Saint-Louis,[37] the Parisian "fief" of the Le Vau clan. In connection with the house on the Place Royale, Henri Sauval (d. 1676), the contemporary historian of Paris, wrote: "The Abbé de La Rivière . . . [was] content with the young Le Vau . . . because he was esteemed at Court."[38] This statement may refer to François's employment by La Grande Mademoiselle, but it may have significance in light of the architect's involvement with the Louvre in the 1660s.

About 1662, as we have seen, Colbert ordered François Le Vau to produce a design for the east façade of the Louvre, a project the architect evidently completed by December 1664. In 1662 or 1663, however, his career took a new turn when he started to work under Colbert in the royal office of the Ponts et Chaussées (Bridges and Roads).[39] In his new capacity, François traveled during most of the year, inspecting and overseeing the building and repair of bridges and roads.[40] This activity continued until 1673.[41] In the early 1670s, he was also engaged at the

33. Destroyed. The building has traditionally been attributed to Louis Le Vau, who designed the Hôtel Hesselin in Paris (ca. 1640–44). On the Château de Saint-Sépulchre, see C. Gurlitt, *Geschichte des Barockstiles, des Rococo und des Klassicismus in Belgien, Holland, Frankreich, England*, Stuttgart, 1888, 76; Hautecoeur, *HAC*, I, 91–93, figs. 80–82 (engravings by Jean Marot); D. Feldmann, *Maison Lambert, Maison Hesselin und andere Bauten von Louis Le Vau (1612/13–1670) auf der Île Saint-Louis in Paris*, publ. diss., University of Hamburg, 1976. One of Marot's prints attributes the château to "Monsieur Le Veaux, architecte du roi," without specifying Louis or François; an inscription on a drawing in Stockholm (Nationalmuseum, THC 8108) of the chapel of the château states that the chapel is "du dessein du Sieur le Veau Architecte du Roy." Because François was usually referred to by the epithet "le jeune," these attributions would seem to refer to the elder brother. However, an attribution of the château to François on stylistic grounds has been argued by C. Tooth, "The Private Houses of Louis Le Vau," unpubl. diss., University of London, 1961, 29, following a suggestion by Blunt (*Art and Architecture in France*, 266 n. 88). The possibility of François's authorship is conceded by J. P. Babelon (*Demeures parisiennes sous Henri IV et Louis XIII*, Paris, 1965, 253); Feldmann, however, gives the building to Louis (*Maison Lambert, Maison Hesselin*, 122 n. 53).

34. See J. P. Babelon, "Le château de Sucy-en-Brie, oeuvre de François Le Vau," *BSHP*, CI/CII, 1974–75, 83–102. Babelon's attribution to François is on stylistic grounds, following Blunt, *Art and Architecture in France*, 266 n. 88. See also H. Soulange-Bodin, "Le château de Sucy-en-Brie," *BSHAF*, 1925, 32–36; Hautecoeur, *HAC*, I, 84–86.

35. Was it ever executed? The patron is unknown. Known from a print signed "F. Le Vau Invent. Cl. Olry Deloriande" (Laprade, *d'Orbay*, pl. III.5B).

36. Ibid., 85, and n. 2.

37. Nos. 6 and 8, rue Poulletier (1655f.); nos. 45–47 and 51, quai de Bourbon (1659). See Dumolin, *Études*, III, 88, 246.

38. "L'abbé de La Rivière . . . s'étant contenté du jeune le Vau . . . parce qu'on l'estimoit à la cour" (H. Sauval, *Histoire et recherches des antiquités de la ville de Paris*, Paris, 1724, III, 21). Sauval gives a scathing critique of the architecture on 21f.

39. In a contract of July 28, 1663, for the repair of bridges at l'Isle-Adam, François was referred to as an "ingénieur et architecte ordinaire des bastimens du Roy, nommé pour cet effect par arrest du Conseil d'Estat de Sa Majesté du quatorziesme juillet mil six cens soixante et trois" (F. Mazerolle, "Réfection des ponts de l'Isle-Adam [28 juillet 1663–8 janvier 1666]," *BSHP*, XXIII, 1896, 128). François had already been in touch with Colbert about these bridges in 1662 (ibid., 124).

40. See Laprade, *d'Orbay*, 86f., for details of this activity.
41. Ibid., 89; *Colbert, 1619–1683*, 264.

arsenal of Rochefort, inspecting the works and devising a plan of the town (unexecuted).[42] There are only a few additional independent designs from his later years: a project of 1667 for the south transept façade of Sainte-Croix, Orléans[43] and the transept of Saint-Louis-en-l'Île, Paris (designed in 1669).[44]

In 1668, François wrote the "Advis" (Sources II, no. 6), an important document concerning the new Louvre that is discussed in Chapter III. In the "Advis" he reveals that he has been to Rome (sec. 11b), a trip that probably took place before 1662–63, when he began his busy schedule in the office of the Ponts et Chaussées. In 1671, François was appointed a founding member of the Royal Academy of Architecture. He died in Paris in 1676.[45]

François Le Vau's Louvre design of ca. 1662–64 (Figs. 24–32) is somewhat difficult to understand when considered in the context of his architectural *oeuvre* outlined above. Only parts or details of his elevation can be related to his earlier work. These include the quoining strips, abundant sculpture (Lignières, Bercy, Sucy-en-Brie), and multiple, shallow wall planes, which appear in the attic level of the Louvre design (also found in the above-named châteaux). François used freestanding single columns in a trabeated design in the main pavilions of Bercy and Sucy-en-Brie (now walled up in the latter); these pavilions can thus be related to the central and end pavilions of the Louvre design.[46] However, the ranges of coupled freestanding columns—the colonnade motif—are unprecedented in his work and were inspired, I believe, by Le Brun's Vaux design (Fig. 5) and Houdin's proposal (Fig. 23), the latter in turn probably stimulated by the Vaux project.[47] The grandiose designs of Le Brun and Houdin opened François Le Vau's eyes to the use of the colonnade motif to give the necessary breadth between the pavilions, which exhibit his personal, complex style.

Contemporary texts provide important clues to the seminal role of the younger Le Vau's Louvre project in the evolution of the final Colonnade (Fig. 44). In the "Advis" of 1668, in the course of replying to an anonymous critic's objection to enlarging the end pavilions of the east façade, François refers to

---

42. Laprade, *d'Orbay*, 89f.; J. F. Konvitz, "Grandeur in French City Planning under Louis XIV: Rochefort and Marseille," *Journal of Urban History*, II, 1975, 11f., fig. 5; idem, *Cities & the Sea: Port City Planning in Early Modern Europe*, Baltimore and London, 1978, 105f., fig. 44.

43. The architect's drawing (destroyed in 1940) is reproduced in Laprade, *d'Orbay*, pl. III.6, bottom. See G. Chenesseau, *Sainte-Croix d'Orléans*, Paris, 1921, II, 128–131.

44. M. Rambaud, "Nouvelles recherches sur Saint-Louis-en-l'Île," *Cahiers de la rotonde*, V, 1982, 17–41.

45. Two brief theoretical statements by François Le Vau have survived; they date from the first two working sessions of the Academy and are direct responses to questions put to the academicians by the director, François Blondel (Paris, Institut de France, Archives de l'Académie des beaux-arts, carton B9: "En quoy consiste le bon goust de l'architecture" [January 7,

1672]; "Ce qui a pû obliger les antiens [sic] autheurs de faire des ordres et quelles raisons ils ont eüs" [January 14, 1672]). Hautecoeur (*HAC*, I, 96 n. 2) has suggested that François, not Louis, designed the project for the façade of Saint-Eustache, Paris, known from a print by Pierre Patte. This façade was pulled down before completion in 1754. However, Patte's print (based on a model; ibid., I, fig. 85) specifically attributes the façade to Louis Le Vau. Also attributed to François is the Carmelite church, Troyes (ibid., I, 121).

46. All of these pavilions with widely spaced columns derive ultimately from the main courtyard pavilion of Louis Le Vau's Hôtel Lambert, Paris (1641–44); the motif reappears at the Château de Saint-Sépulchre, which traditionally has been ascribed to the elder Le Vau (see above, note 33).

47. François's attic recalls Figure 21.

the models and designs, *the one I made has had the knack to please [le don de plaire] and to be approved* [my emphasis], in which the said pavilions have scarcely less width, and if I had not been constrained then, I would have made them as wide as those that they propose to make. [Sources II, no. 6 (7b)]

François's mention of being constrained is a reference to the situation before 1668, when the south wing of the Cour Carrée was still only one room deep (Figs. 64, 65); his final clause refers to the final design, reflecting the 1668 decision to double the width of that wing. François's statement agrees with his engraved pavilion project (Fig. 30), in which the width of the pavilion at the base of the *rez-de-chaussée* is about 71.6 *pieds* (almost 12 *toises*),[48] less than the width of 80 *pieds* (about 13 *toises, 2 pieds*) given in the earliest detailed drawings of the end pavilion as it approaches its final form (Figs. 69–72), and the pavilion was built to this measurement.

Most important is François Le Vau's statement that this Louvre design "has had the knack to please and to be approved." But in what sense was it approved, and by whom? I address these questions in Chapter III. Here, however, I turn to another contemporary text that shows the importance of François's project: the opening lines (1–8) of Olry de Loriande's poem of 1670 (see Chapter I and Sources II, no. 9):

> Palais le plus charmant qui soit dans l'Univers,
> Vray miracle de l'Art digne des plus beaux vers,
> Puisque du grand COLBERT la sagesse profonde
> Te destine pour estre un chef d'oeuvre du monde,
> Et que *sur les desseins de l'illustre le Vau,*
> *En cuivre j'ay gravé ton merveilleux Tableau* [my emphasis]
> Je te veux derechef dépeindre en ce volume,
> Puisque ma main sçait l'Art du fer, & de la plume.

> (O Palace, the most attractive in the universe,
> True miracle of art, worthy of the most beautiful verses,
> Since the profound wisdom of the great COLBERT
> Destines you to be a masterpiece of the world,
> And since *according to the designs of the famous Le Vau,*
> *I have engraved your marvelous picture on copper* [my emphasis];
> I want to portray you anew in this book,
> Since my hand knows the arts of engraving and writing.)

---

48. Measurements of the floor heights along the right edge of Figure 30 provide a scale; although two scales of 30 *pieds* are indicated (one for the *rez-de-chaussée,* another for the *premier étage*), they do not match. The latter scale renders the width of Figure 30 as 71.6 *pieds* at the base of the *rez-de-chaussée.*

In 1670, Olry was able to see the Louvre Colonnade well advanced in construction. Already at the end of 1668, Colbert, in a *mémoire* concerning work to be accomplished in 1669, jotted down "Élever le péristyle sur la face du devant jusqu'à la corniche" (Erect the peristyle on the entrance façade up to the cornice) (Sources II, no. 8), and payments for 1669 and 1670 (see Sources I) suggest feverish building activity. Olry evidently recognized the strong visual relationship between the façade by Le Vau *le jeune* that he had recently engraved (Figs. 29–32) and the actual Colonnade rising before him (Figs. 43, 44). This relationship was sufficiently close for him to have regarded François Le Vau's design as the basic model, only varied and slightly changed by the official architects of the Petit Conseil (see Chapter III). In line 269 of his poem, Olry writes of an "Attique en trophée avec . . . riche aspect," evidently in expectation that François's attic (Figs. 24–30) would eventually be added. Olry's "l'illustre le Vau" can only be a reference to François Le Vau, whose designs he had engraved.

THE FRENCH AND ITALIAN PROJECTS OF 1664 AND 1665

By the time the younger Le Vau wrote to Colbert about his Louvre design on December 4, 1664, many events leading inevitably to the invitation to Gianlorenzo Bernini to come to Paris to design the Louvre had already transpired. Eleven months earlier, on January 1, 1664, Colbert officially became Superintendent of the King's Buildings (replacing Antoine de Ratabon), halted Louis Le Vau's ongoing east wing of the Louvre (Figs. 33–35), invited criticism of it, and encouraged French architects to submit new designs.[49] In March, Colbert wrote his first letter to Bernini, then widely regarded as Europe's greatest living architect. Colbert thus initiated the process that resulted in Bernini's first Louvre design (sent to Paris on June 24), as well as projects by the Italians Carlo Rainaldi, Candiani (designs sent to Paris on July 15), and Pietro da Cortona (design sent to Paris in mid-September).[50] Just a few days before François Le Vau wrote his letter, Bernini in Rome had been visited (December 1) by the French ambassador and the Abbate Elpidio Benedetti, who prevailed upon him to embark on a second Louvre design to replace the first, which had been much criticized by Colbert.

Bernini's second design was sent off in February 1665 and received in Paris the next month. Although it too was censured by Colbert, the French were eager to retain Bernini's services; he was invited to France and arrived in the capital on June 2, remaining there until October 20. This chronology is an indication that, by December 1664, events had moved too far along in favor of Bernini for Colbert to have given serious attention to François Le Vau's remarkable

---

49. See Hautecoeur, *Louvre et Tuileries*, 145f.
50. For this oft-told story, see, above all, H. Brauer and R. Wittkower, *Die Zeichnungen des Gianlorenzo Bernini*, Berlin, 1931, I, 129f. and C. Gould, *Bernini in France: An Episode in Seventeenth-Century History*, Princeton, 1982.

project. The engravings of that scheme (Figs. 28–32) must have been made sometime in 1665 or 1666.[51]

Colbert's invitation to French architects at the start of 1664 to submit new Louvre designs—an open competition, in effect—produced several important projects that must have been displayed before December, when the younger Le Vau announced he was ready to submit his. The first, and most significant, was that of the physician and scientist Claude Perrault, displayed anonymously in Paris. His brother Charles has written about this design in his autobiography (ca. 1700):

> [Claude Perrault] made a design quite similar to the one that he gave afterward and that was executed [the Colonnade]. M. Colbert, to whom I showed them [the designs], was delighted by them and didn't understand how a man who wasn't an architect by profession could make such a beautiful thing. These drawings, which are two—one geometrical and the other in perspective—are in two quite plain wooden frames and are in the large closet of my *garde-meuble*. The idea of the peristyle was mine, and, having communicated it to my brother, he approved of it and put it into his drawing, but beautifying it infinitely, as he was able to do.[52]

Charles Perrault's statement that these drawings were in his personal collection ca. 1700 means they had not been included in the two folio volumes of Claude's drawings assembled by Charles in 1693 (these albums were destroyed in 1871). However, there evidently was another record of Claude's 1664 design—a façade elevation—that was in one of the albums and that J. F. Blondel described briefly in 1756:

> We find, page 87 [of the 1693 manuscript *recueil*], another project by *Perrault* for the main façade of the Louvre, and still with the aim of retaining the old pavilions. The decoration of this façade is also Corinthian, but the columns are not coupled; the center is terminated by a dome of a form and elegance worthy of the building and its author.[53]

No visual record of Perrault's "First Project" has come down to us. Its essential elements evidently were a central domed pavilion, end pavilions like the corner pavilions of the Cour Carrée (Figs. 9, 14, 16), and single Corinthian columns forming a colonnade.[54] To what degree

---

51. Despite Bernini's hegemony during 1665, Pierre Cottart issued engravings of his Louvre project during that year (Figure 38).

52. For the French text, see Sources II, no. 53[a].

53. For the French text, see Sources II, no. 84[b] (last paragraph). Blondel continues: "Enfin aux pag. 97 & 99 du même manuscrit, se voyent encore deux autres projets pour la même façade, qui méritent également l'attention des connoisseurs" (ibid.).

54. The description of Claude's 1664 project given by L. Vitet ("Le Louvre," *Revue contemporaine*, I, no. 3, 1852, 411) cannot be based on an examination of the then still-extant 1693 manuscript *recueil*, because Vitet states that the columns were coupled and does not mention the dome. His "description" is evidently a fantasy. The description of Claude's "First Project" given by A. E. Brinckmann (*Baukunst des 17. und 18. Jahrhunderts in den romanischen Ländern*, 4th ed., Berlin-Neubabelsberg, 1919, II, 232–233) conflates features specified by J. F. Blondel (*Architecture françoise*, Paris, 1756, IV, 49) as belonging to several different projects. Brinckmann's statement that half-columns decorated the central pavilion is unsubstantiated.

it actually anticipated the later-realized east façade (Figs. 43, 44) we shall perhaps never know, but Charles Perrault was not a dispassionate commentator. To the end of his days, Charles championed his brother as the real designer of the Louvre Colonnade. Charles's claim that the Colonnade idea was his does not ring true, for colonnades were "in the air" in 1664. In that year François Mansart showed Colbert a variety of ideas for the Louvre.[55] Colonnades of freestanding coupled columns appear in one of Mansart's plans (Fig. 36), with the central columns of each range also coupled in depth. There is no elevation to join to this plan, but Mansart almost certainly intended a trabeated design, judging by his surviving Louvre elevations. As in the latter, the columns would have risen from a low plinth through the *rez-de-chaussée;* Mansart did not adopt the podium idea we found in the designs of Houdin (Fig. 23) and François Le Vau (Figs. 24–31). Probably also from 1664 is an anonymous *mémoire* that proposes a Louvre façade with open colonnades providing views of the *corps-de-logis* (the west wing) at the far end of the court.[56]

Two other French Louvre projects—Jean Marot's (1664?; Fig. 37) and Pierre Cottart's (1665; Fig. 38)—although lacking colonnades, display a profusion of columns and pilasters in harmony with the trend of the 1660s to adorn the originally austere Louvre exteriors with the

---

55. On Mansart's Louvre drawings, see Braham and Smith, *François Mansart,* I, chap. xv and 255f. (app. c); II, figs. 470–474, 477, 480, 482–501, 506–508, 511–517, 522–539.

56. AN, O¹, 1669, no. 51, published in part by Hautecoeur, "L'auteur de la colonnade du Louvre," 159–160; idem, *Louvre et Tuileries,* 168. The key passage reads (spelling slightly modernized): "Je voudrois donc que la face de l'entrée du Louvre ne fut ny sy grande ny sy riche, que le Corps du bastiment que les aisles fussent fort inferieurs au pavillon du milieu, que ce pavillon fut plus grand et plus magnifique que tout le reste de l'ediffice et quil parust comme la teste de ce grand corps. Pour cela ma pensée seroit de faire deux pavillons aux deux angles de ladite face, que le reste fust une grande terrasse soustenüe de colonnes et de portiques terminée par une balustrade avec des pieds destaux sur lesquels seroient des statues de nos Roys, que le portail fust en forme d'arc de triomphe sur le frontispice duquel seroit la figure du Roy dans un char de triomphe tiré par quatre chevaux, que toute la terrasse ne fust que de la hauteur du premier ordre des colonnes affin de laisser la veue libre du grand corps de logis. Et c'est à ce corps de logis que ie voudrois que l'on employast toute l'industrie des architectes, que l'on fist un grand portique avec un dosme magnifique fort eslevé orné de figures et de choses qui montrassent que c'est le logement du maistre. Pour les aisles on les pouvoit laisser de la façon qu'elles sont aujourd'huy y augmentant seulement des terrasses ainsy quelles sont représentées au modelle affin de servir de désgagemens aux appartemens des costez" (fol. 1v). On fol. 2v we read: "Cette maniere de bastiment imiteroit ces magnifiques edifices des anciens, tels que nous les connoissons par les vestiges qui sont restez des palais des Cesars et autres grands bastimens."

The anonymous author of this proposal states that he has seen a model of the Louvre that features a "vestibule quil [the architect] dispose en forme de sallon orné de pilastres et de colomnes de marbre" (fol. 1r). This description accords with Louis Le Vau's model, which was on display in 1664 (Ch. Perrault, *Mémoires de ma vie,* ed. P. Bonnefon, Paris, 1909, 52–53 [ca. 1700]) and which contained an oval salon articulated with columns and pilasters in two stories (see text above and Figure 34). The document states (fol. 1, r and v) that the *corps-de-logis* of the model was doubled, and this detail, along with the others, corresponds precisely to Le Vau's "Project V" (1663–64) as analyzed and dated by Whiteley and Braham, "Les soubassements," 33f.

Folio 2v is inscribed "M Perrault," and M. Petzet has speculated that the document describes Perrault's lost "First Project" ("Entwürfe zur Louvre-Kolonnade," *Neue Zürcher Zeitung,* October 4, 1964 [Beilage: Literatur und Kunst, 5]; idem, "Entwürfe zur Louvre-Kolonnade," in *Stil und Überlieferung in der Kunst des Abendlandes: Akten des 21. Internationalen Kongresses für Kunstgeschichte in Bonn 1964,* Berlin, 1967, III, 159–160). However, the description of the anonymous project does not correspond to what is known of Perrault's 1664 project (see text above). "M Perrault" may here refer to Charles, first clerk to Colbert in the Bâtiments since 1664.

classical orders.⁵⁷ The Italian projects of 1664, and Bernini's of 1664 and 1665 (Figs. 40, 41), follow this trend.⁵⁸

An engraving of perhaps 1664 (Fig. 39),⁵⁹ showing a bird's-eye view of a completed and interconnected Louvre and Tuileries, bears the following suggestive verses:

> Soleil si tu ne vois dans le reste du monde
> Rien de si magnifique en ornemens divers
> C'est que de nostre Roy la grandeur sans seconde
> Est le plus bel obiect qui soit dans L'univers.
>
> Ces superbes palais qu'avec tant davantage
> Nous veut representer la vaine Antiquité
> A ce Louvre bien-tost viendront rendre l'homage
> Que tous ils luy devront, malgré leur vanité.

> (O Sun, if you do not see in the rest of the world
> Anything as magnificent in divers ornaments,
> It is because the unrivaled grandeur of our King
> Is the most beautiful object in the universe.
>
> Vain Antiquity wishes to show us
> Those proud palaces and so much more.
> They will soon render homage to this Louvre
> For everything they shall owe it, despite their vanity.)

The idea expressed in the second stanza seems to be that the new east wing of the Louvre shall surpass in beauty the older, extant parts of the Louvre and the Tuileries. The first verse is an apostrophe to the sun, the emblem of Louis XIV, which spreads its radiance over the buildings. The south façade of the Cour Carrée is depicted as completed in 1663 to the design of Louis Le Vau (cf. Figs. 17, 18). The outer façade of the east wing is averted from us, for in 1664 (the presumed date of the print) a definitive design had not yet been chosen. The engraver safely

---

57. For a recent suggestion that a drawing in Stockholm (Nationalmuseum, CC 1565) may also be a French project of 1664, see *Colbert, 1619–1683*, 287–288, no. 416 (entry by D. Feldmann), illus. on 290.

58. For the Italian projects of Carlo Rainaldi, Pietro da Cortona, and Candiani, see K. Noehles, "Die Louvre-Projekte von Pietro da Cortona und Carlo Rainaldi," *ZfK*, XXIV, 1961, 40–74, and P. Portoghesi, "Gli architetti italiani per il Louvre," in *Saggi di storia dell'architettura in onore del professor Vincenzo Fasolo* (Quaderni dello Istituto di storia dell'architettura, ser. 6–8, fascs. 31–48), Rome, 1961, 243–268.

59. The engraver Noël Cochin the Younger was in Paris throughout the 1660s, leaving for Venice ca. 1670 (T-B, VII, 140–141).

depicts a four-sided dome over its central pavilion to match the others around the courtyard. The engraving expresses the excitement and anticipation of 1664.

Before moving on to the creation and realization of the new Louvre of Louis XIV (Chapters III–VI), a feature directly linked to the solar imagery adopted for the King—the Galerie d'Apollon,[60] housed on the *premier étage* of the Petite Galerie—must be noted. Designed by Le Brun in 1663 (at the moment when Le Vau was pressing ahead with his ill-fated east wing [Figs. 33–35]) but left unfinished in 1677, it has survived and still conveys its claim as the most sumptuously decorated room in the Louvre. Its ceiling paintings and stucco sculptures proclaim the power of the sun in creating the seasons and times of day and in animating land and sea. All was easily understood as an allegory referring to the King. A major decorative scheme of Apollonian imagery was thus being created within the Louvre during the 1660s, concurrently with attempts to design a suitable façade for the sun palace of the Sun King.

60. There is no comprehensive modern study of this room. See P. de Chennevières, *Notice historique et descriptive sur la Galerie d'Apollon au Louvre,* 2d ed., Paris, 1855; Hautecoeur, *Louvre et Tuileries,* 113f., and T. Hedin, *The Sculpture of Gaspard and Balthazard Marsy,* Columbia, Mo., 1983, 34f., 114f.

III
THE PETIT CONSEIL (1667–1668)

The East Façade

By the spring of 1667, Louis XIV and Colbert had resolved to see the Louvre speedily completed according to a new design. The Bernini episode was in the past; the King and his *surintendant* were now convinced—probably for reasons of national pride—that only a native French design would suffice. Whether the King and his minister at this juncture specifically desired a design that would proclaim a new French aesthetic to contrast with the Italianate Baroque qualities of Louis Le Vau's and Bernini's rejected final projects (Figs. 35, 40, 41) is an open question. However, instead of bestowing the commission once again solely on Louis Le Vau (still *premier architecte*), a committee of three was created, consisting of Le Vau, Charles Le Brun, the First Painter, and, surprisingly, the physician, scientist, and fledgling architect and theorist Claude Perrault (Charles's older brother), then at work on his Vitruvius edition and his design for the Observatoire in Paris.[1] The idea of design-by-committee (in contrast to a competi-

---

1. On the Vitruvius edition, see Herrmann, *Perrault*, 17–19, and A. Picon, *Claude Perrault, 1613–1688, ou la curiosité d'un classique,* Paris, 1988, 115f.; it had been commissioned by the Crown in 1666 or 1667. Claude Perrault first came to the

tion) was most unusual in this period, but even while Bernini was in Paris in 1665 a rumor had circulated that a committee consisting of Le Vau, Le Brun, and François Mansart had been assembled to devise a design.[2] The rumor may have been without foundation. In any event, Mansart died in September 1666.

The primary document chronicling the deliberations of the Le Vau–Le Brun–Perrault committee (the Petit Conseil) is the "Registre ou Journal des délibérations & résolutions touchant les Bâtimens du Roi," first published by Piganiol de La Force in 1742 (see Sources II, no. 1). Probably drawn up by Charles Perrault, secretary of the committee,[3] and accepted as authentic by J. F. Blondel,[4] the "Registre" bore a marginal notation in Colbert's hand: "vu & approuvé au camp de Charleroy le 7. juin 1667."[5] The "Registre" records the activities of the Petit Conseil during April and May 1667, the first two months of its existence; the minutes of its subsequent meetings, which extended at least into 1668, are lost.

The "Registre" first records Colbert's dissatisfaction with the French and Italian Louvre projects and states his decision that there must be a committee to allow for mutual consultation. Le Vau, Le Brun, and Perrault were chosen in April and instructed to work together harmoniously so that their designs for the Louvre would be regarded as joint productions; furthermore, no member could claim sole responsibility for the designs. Colbert then ordered the architects to create an entrance façade facing the church of Saint-Germain–l'Auxerrois.

After several meetings, the Petit Conseil arrived at different ideas and produced two designs: "l'un étoit orné d'un Ordre de colonnes formant un perystile ou galerie au dessus du premier étage,[6] & l'autre étoit plus simple & plus uni sans Ordre de colonnes" (one was adorned with an order of columns forming a peristyle or gallery above the first floor [i.e., the ground floor], and the other was simpler and more unified, without an order of columns). Wooden models[7] were made after these designs, and the architects were ordered to continue to refine the two projects.

---

attention of Colbert through his obelisk designs of 1666 (see M. Petzet, "Der Obelisk des Sonnenkönigs. Ein Projekt Claude Perraults von 1666," *ZfK*, XLVII, 1984, 439–464) and possibly before that (if his brother Charles is to be believed), in 1664, through his "First Design" for the Louvre (see text). In early 1667 he had designed the Observatoire in Paris, construction of which began in June (idem, "Claude Perrault als Architekt des Pariser Observatoriums," *ZfK*, XXX, 1967, 1–54). See also Picon, *Claude Perrault*, 197f. (Observatoire), 230f. (obelisk).

2. P. Fréart de Chantelou, *Journal du voyage du Cavalier Bernin en France*, ed. L. Lalanne, Paris, 1885, 129. No work by this committee is recorded.

3. Charles Perrault in his *Mémoires* asserted that he was the secretary and that he kept a "registre" (see Sources II, no. 53[b]). Perrault at this time was *premier commis* to Colbert in the Royal Building Administration and a member and secretary of the Petite Académie (on this group, see R. W. Berger, *In the Garden of the Sun King: Studies on the Park of Versailles under Louis XIV*, Washington, D.C., 1985, chap. 2).

4. *Architecture françoise*, Paris, 1756, IV, 5 n. d(7). Blondel published only parts of the "Registre."

5. Colbert had gone to the front during the War of Devolution.

6. "Premier étage" here refers to the *rez-de-chaussée*; seventeenth-century usage is variable with respect to names of floor levels.

7. Payments from 1667 to 1674 for Louvre models are recorded in *CBR*, I, cols. 180, 181, 183–185, 188, 189, 215, 218, 219, 243, 245, 317, 320, 322, 401, 402, 405. The payment on January 9, 1668, for work on a model "du dessein de M. Le Vau" (I, col. 185) could represent a late payment for Le Vau's model of his ill-fated scheme that Colbert stopped in 1664 (Figs. 33–35). None of the models has survived, although a model of the Colonnade was reported extant as late as 1782 (*PV*, IX, 69).

On May 14, at the royal Château de Saint-Germain-en-Laye, the designs were shown to the King, who chose the colonnade scheme. The architects of the designs are not identified in the "Registre."

Another account of the Petit Conseil is contained in Leibniz's report of a 1676 conversation with his friend Claude Perrault (Sources II, no. 19). According to this source, after the departure of Mattia de' Rossi (Bernini's assistant) and the Italian masons (spring 1667), Colbert offered Claude the post of First Architect of the King (this is almost certainly a fabrication, because Perrault had no executed buildings to his credit by that date). The physician declined, proposing instead a committee under the direction of Colbert. Thus was the "Conseil d'Architecture" created, consisting of Perrault, Le Brun, Le Vau, and (be it noted) "quelques autres." After some disagreements, Le Vau abandoned his design and supported Perrault's, leaving the latter's and Le Brun's proposals. These were shown to the King, who, following Colbert's preference, chose Perrault's proposal. (In claiming sole responsibility for the Colonnade, Perrault violated the terms of the establishment of the Petit Conseil, as recorded in the "Registre" [see above]; he never made such a claim in any of his publications.)

A third version of the events was given in Charles Perrault's *Mémoires de ma vie,* written ca. 1700, long after the meetings of the Petit Conseil (Sources II, no. 53[b]). According to Perrault, it was shortly *before* the committee of three was formed in the spring of 1667 that Louis XIV was presented with two designs, one by Louis Le Vau and another by Claude Perrault. The King (again reported in residence at Saint-Germain) invited Colbert to choose first, and the minister selected Le Vau's design (drawn by his draftsman François d'Orbay), which had no colonnade. Louis then chose Perrault's, which had this feature. Only *after* this incident was the Petit Conseil established, at the suggestion of Charles Perrault.

In weighing the "Registre" against Leibniz's report and Perrault's *Mémoires,* the historian must choose the first source as the more accurate record because it is contemporary with the events themselves and because neither Claude in his conversation nor Charles in his autobiography is a detached observer; they are, rather, partisans in a campaign to extol Claude as the sole inventor of the Louvre Colonnade.

To return to the "Registre": On May 18, Colbert announced the royal decision about the Colonnade design to the officers of the Royal Building Administration and ordered large-scale drawings of the plans and elevations. Soon after, the Louvre *chantier* was to be opened for work in the Cour Carrée and on the foundations for the new façade. More models were ordered: another wooden one and a larger one in plaster or stucco. The "Registre" calls for measured drawings of each part of the design for the use of the entrepreneurs; the foundations were to be evenly built up; a drawing of a dome for the (north) façade facing the rue Saint-Honoré was to be made; an estimate was to be drawn up of sculpture remaining to be executed on parts of the Louvre already built; and Le Brun was to have general supervision of the sculpture and make drawings of the sculpture for Colbert. The "Registre" then states that the new façade shall be continued around the corner pavilions but no farther.

In late May, the architects intensified their work. They were meeting twice weekly for a total of four hours, and Le Vau provided an accurate plan of the extant eastern foundations in order to be able to lay the foundations for the Colonnade precisely.[8]

Again in late May, Le Vau was commanded to prepare two copies of the Colonnade design—one for Le Brun, one for Perrault—so each architect could create a variant design conforming "en gros" to the basic scheme. In the course of this process, the three architects were to arrive at one design based on all three drawings. (On May 28, Le Vau gave a copy of the Colonnade design to Le Brun, who in turn promised to make a copy for Perrault.) This refining process may be diagramed thus:

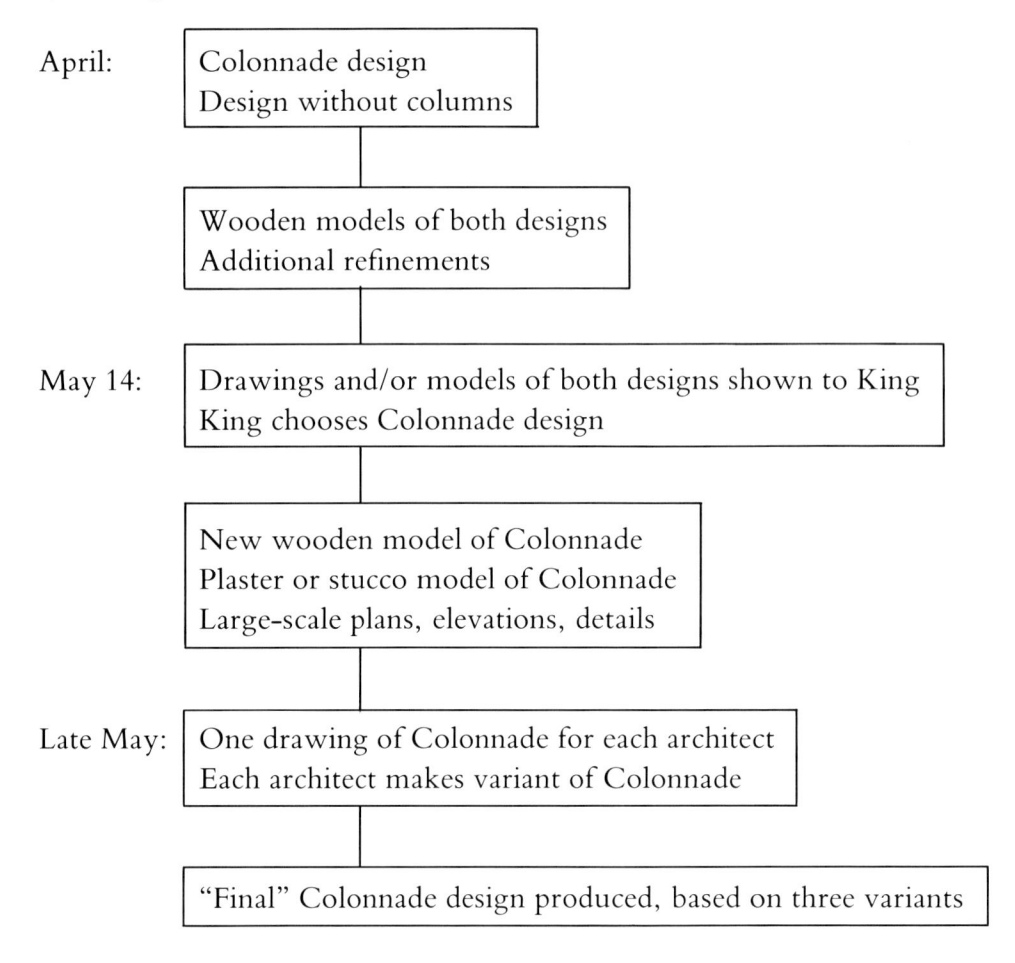

April:
- Colonnade design
- Design without columns

- Wooden models of both designs
- Additional refinements

May 14:
- Drawings and/or models of both designs shown to King
- King chooses Colonnade design

- New wooden model of Colonnade
- Plaster or stucco model of Colonnade
- Large-scale plans, elevations, details

Late May:
- One drawing of Colonnade for each architect
- Each architect makes variant of Colonnade

- "Final" Colonnade design produced, based on three variants

Having examined the first phase of the evolution of the Colonnade design as revealed by the "Registre," we turn to the rejected project for the east façade, "plus simple & plus uni sans Ordre de colonnes." Hautecoeur was the first writer to connect—correctly, I believe—three drawings in Paris with the rejected Louvre design (Figs. 92–94; Appendix A, nos. B1–B3).

---

8. The foundations for Le Vau's (early 1660s) and Bernini's (1665) aborted east façades (see A. Erlande-Brandenburg, "Les fouilles du Louvre et les projets de Le Vau," VU, n.s., XXXI, 1964, 241–263, and XXXII, 1965, 12–22; M. Whiteley and A. Braham, "Les soubassements de l'aile orientale du Louvre," RA, no. 4, 1969, 30–43).

Figures 92 and 93 are large drawings, either of which might have been shown to Louis XIV on May 14. Figure 92 is from the hand of d'Orbay, but Figure 93 is from the studio of Le Brun, as is Figure 94, a variant of the central pavilion.[9] All three drawings are closely related, the main differences being in their drums and domes, in the ranges between the pavilions, and in the decorative details. As in Figure 59 (to be discussed below), the end pavilions are narrow two-bay compositions that are variants of Lescot's Pavillon du Roi (Fig. 9); in particular, the end pavilions of Figures 59 and 92 are almost identical. The ranges between the central and end pavilions are repetitions of the ranges of the then-extant south façade (Fig. 17), with projecting *ressauts* in the centers of the ranges in Figure 93 that break the monotony. As in Figure 59, there are no visible roofs between the pavilions.

The main architectural inventiveness appears in the central pavilions, quite different from the main pavilion of Le Vau's south façade (Figs. 17, 18). These central pavilions repeat the two-step projection of the outer (western) façade of Lemercier's Pavillon de l'Horloge (Fig. 13), and this large-scale composition encloses the entrance portal with its arch rising into the *premier étage,* as in Figure 59. The most progressive features in these rejected projects are the domes—not the traditional four-sided (wooden) type initially proposed for the east façade (Fig. 66), but classical (presumably masonry) domes with stepped haunches, as in the dome of the Roman Pantheon. The portal is flanked in two of the drawings (Figs. 93, 94) by versions of the Quirinal Dioscurii,[10] and all three drawings depict statues of Apollo slaying the Niobids high up on the pavilion—allusions to a bellicose Louis XIV, wreaker of retribution.[11] The medallion-and-swag motif, which we will find in the rival colonnade project (Fig. 59), appears in Figures 92 and 94.

The repetitive fenestrated bays between the pavilions in Figure 92 recall Le Vau's south façade (Fig. 17) and suggest that Figure 92 precedes Figure 93; the projecting one-bay *ressauts* between pavilions in Figure 93 suggest that the latter is a variant on Figure 92, as do the decorative friezes of Figure 93. Figure 92 was drawn by d'Orbay, Le Vau's chief draftsman, and this corresponds to Charles Perrault's assertion that the design without colonnade was drawn by d'Orbay. That, however, does not necessarily corroborate Perrault's claim that the architect of the project without the orders was Le Vau. We shall see that the earliest extant drawing of the Colonnade (Fig. 59) is from Le Vau's office and may be from the hand of the *premier architecte* himself. We

9. The attribution of Figure 92 to d'Orbay was first proposed by Laprade (see Appendix A, no. B1) and is confirmed by a comparison with Figure 73, signed by d'Orbay. Particularly revealing (as Laprade pointed out) is a comparison of the renderings of the balusters. The attribution of Figures 93 and 94 to Le Brun, first proposed by Hautecoeur (see Appendix A, nos. B2, B3) has been accepted unanimously by later writers (some of whom assign the drawings to Le Brun's studio).

10. Roland Fréart de Chambray (*Parallèle de l'architecture antique et de la moderne,* Paris, 1650, "Epistre") had judged the horse-tamers to be the finest sculptures of antiquity, and he recommended that bronze replicas be placed at the entrance to the Louvre. For more on Fréart de Chambray, see text below.

11. The Slaying of the Niobids theme may appear here for the first time in the iconography of Louis XIV. One year later (1668), Nicolas Mignard painted the subject for the King's *appartement bas* in the Tuileries Palace (Hautecoeur, *Louvre et Tuileries,* 131, pl. XXVI(A) [preparatory drawing]; N. de Sainte Fare Garnot, *Le décor des Tuileries sous le règne de Louis XIV,* Paris, 1988, 108, no. 5). Félibien, writing about Mignard's decorations, explained that "L'histoire de Niobé montre la perte inévitable de ceux qui manqueraient au respect qu'ils doivent à la personne sacrée d'un si puissant monarque" (quoted in Hautecoeur, *Louvre et Tuileries,* 131). The theme was later proposed but was rejected for the vault of the Galerie des Glaces, Versailles, ca. 1678–79 (R. W. Berger, *Versailles: The Château of Louis XIV,* University Park, Pa., and London, 1985, 52).

cannot interpret these data to mean that Le Vau was the architect of both designs. A plausible explanation is that Le Vau's *atelier,* with d'Orbay as chief draftsman, was where the presentation drawings were actually produced; the creative architectural ideas, however—whether generated by Le Vau, Le Brun, or Perrault—could have emerged in oral discussions and rough sketches, now lost. We do know from a passage in the "Registre" for May 24 (see Sources II, no. 1) that Le Vau was ordered to have two copies made of the Colonnade design, one for Le Brun and one for Perrault, so that each could make additional refinements (see text, above). This suggests that Le Vau's office—more fully staffed for architectural work because he was the *premier architecte du roi*—was used for the making of copies and presentation drawings.

It is difficult to believe, however, that a project for the entrance façade of the Louvre bereft of the apparatus of the classical orders could have been seriously regarded in 1667 as a viable candidate, particularly when the central pavilion of Le Vau's recently completed south façade (Fig. 18) featured a colossal Corinthian order. For the entrance façade the classical orders were inevitable; they had been proposed in all of the other Louvre designs of the 1660s, French and Italian.[12] It would appear that an alternative Louvre design without the orders was presented to Louis XIV on May 14, 1667, so that the monarch could exercise his power of choice and demonstrate his *bon goût*. This is suggested by an anecdote related by Charles Perrault (Sources II, no. 53[b]):

> Although M. Colbert very much liked my brother's design [with a colonnade], he did not omit to have one made by M. Le Vau. After which he presented both to the King to choose the one which pleased him most. . . . The King looked at both very attentively, following which he asked M. Colbert which of the two he found the most beautiful and the most worthy of being executed. M. Colbert said that, if he were master, he would choose the one which had no gallery [colonnade]. . . . That drawing was the one by M. Le Vau, which astonished me very much. But no sooner had he spoken for this design than the King said: "And as for me, I choose the other one, which seems to me more beautiful and more majestic." I realized that M. Colbert had acted as a skillful courtier who wished to give all honor of choice to his master. Perhaps it was a game played between the King and him. Be that as it may, the incident took place in this way.

---

12. These include the designs of Louis Le Vau (1659–64; Figs. 33–35), Houdin (1661; Fig. 23), François Le Vau (ca. 1662–64; Figs. 24–32), François Mansart (1664; Fig. 36), Jean Marot (1664?; Fig. 37), Pierre Cottart (1665; Fig. 38), and the Italian projects of Rainaldi (1664), Pietro da Cortona (1664), Candiani (1664), and Bernini (1664–65; Figs. 40, 41). An elevation drawing in Stockholm (Nationalmuseum, CC 1565) has recently been proposed as a French Louvre project of perhaps 1664. In this anonymous drawing, pairs of coupled, engaged columns appear on the *premier étage* of the central pavilion ([Paris, Ministère de la culture], *Colbert, 1619–1683,* exhib. cat., Paris, 1983, 287–288, no. 416, illus. on 290; entry by D. Feldmann). See also the following dialogue from Charles Perrault, *Parallèle des anciens et des modernes . . . ,* Paris, 1688, I, 127–128 (dialogue between le President, a defender of the Ancients, and l'Abbé, a champion of the Moderns):

> *Le President:* Cela se peut-il dire, sans une effroyable ingratitude envers les Inventeurs de l'Architecture, si un bastiment n'avoit ny colonnes, ny pilastres, ny architraves, ny frises, ny corniches, & qu'il fust tout uni, pourroit-on dire que ce fust un beau morceau d'Architecture.
> *l'Abbé:* Non assurément.

Shortly after the King decided in favor of the Colonnade design on May 14, the Louvre *chantier* was opened. In late May and early July, quarrymen were paid for stones for the Louvre:

> May 25 [1667]: to the quarrymen of Saint-Cloud, on account of columns and blocks of stone they are providing for the Louvre building, . . . 12,500 *livres*.[13]

> [July 2, 1667]: To Renault, quarryman, on account of blocks of stone and columns of Saint-Cloud stone he is furnishing for the Louvre, . . . 200 *livres*.[14]

In late July, payments began for construction work:

> July 29, 1667–February 19, 1668: to [André Mazière(s) and Antoine Bergeron, masonry entrepreneurs of the buildings of the King], on account of masonry work they are doing at the château of the Louvre, . . . 74,000 *livres*.[15]

> October 28, 1667–January 9, 1668: to [Mazière(s) and Bergeron], on account of work they are doing at the new building of the Louvre, . . . 175,000 *livres*.[16]

On October 15, 1667, the King visited the Louvre and found the construction to be "tres-avancez."[17]

Sometime in 1667, while construction of the Colonnade was proceeding, a medal was issued (Fig. 66; Appendix A, no. A5).[18] Dated 1667 and bearing the inscription •MAIESTA-TI•AC•AETERNIT[ATI]•GALL[ICI]•IMPERII•SACRUM• (Sacred to the Majesty and Eternity of the French Empire), it was probably among the medals Colbert placed in the eastern foundations on November 19 (see Sources II, no. 4). The medal can be correlated with an elevation drawing and two ground plans (Figs. 59, 64, 65), which collectively provide a clear idea of the first Colonnade scheme of 1667, arrived at by the end of May through the refining process outlined above.

The medal features a central pavilion with a temple-front motif of four columns at *premier étage* level supporting a triangular pediment. Above this rises a drum topped by a four-sided dome. The same composition recurs in Figure 59, an unusually large drawing that may have been the presentation drawing with a colonnade, shown to the King on May 14 (it may originally have extended to the left to show the entire façade; see Appendix A, no. A1).[19] The main difference between the drawing and the medal is that the drum of the former contains two large, arched openings crowned by a second pediment. (The curve of the four-sided dome can

---

13. Sources I, no. 1.
14. Ibid., no. 2.
15. Ibid., no. 3.
16. Ibid., no. 4.
17. *Gazette de France,* October 22, 1667, 1189. See also Sources II, nos. 2, 3.
18. This medal in gold and two others were placed in the foundations of the east façade on November 19, 1667 (see Sources II, no. 4); payment to the workmen who placed the medals was made on June 18, 1668 (see Sources I, no. 7).
19. Parts of Figure 59 appear again in the background of an engraving of 1668 by François de Poilly after Le Brun (Fig. 60; see Appendix A, no. A1).

just be discerned above the right edge of the drum. This difference may represent a revision of the drum design between May [Fig. 59] and a date before November [Fig. 66].) Close examination of the medal and drawing also reveals the same treatment of the colonnades themselves: the walls behind the arrays of coupled columns have rectangular windows alternating with rectangular niches holding statues, with oval medallions with swags above. Sculpted trophies appear along the balustrades above the full entablatures that the colonnades support. The ground-floor elevation in both medal and drawing features an array of segmental-headed windows with keystone masks, with the windows more elongated in the drawing. Pier-like masses flank the central arched portal, which rises into the sculpted field of the temple front at first-floor level.

Figure 59, then, tallies in all essentials with the medal, and because it presents more than half the full extent of the façade, we can readily grasp the appearance of the entire Colonnade. Each columnar range was to consist of eight pairs of coupled Composite columns, with single columns abutting the central and end pavilions. The latter are narrow, two-bay units, with attics corresponding to the drum of the central pavilion (arched openings and pediment). The three-pavilion composition was clearly intended to match the recently completed south façade (Fig. 17), although the pavilions of the latter were one bay broader. The left (westerly) pavilion of the south façade was, of course, Lescot's Pavillon du Roi (begun 1551; Figs. 9, 17, left), which Le Vau repeated to form the right (easterly) pavilion. The ground floor of the proposed columnar east façade was an exact repetition of that of the south façade, which merely extended the design of Lescot's ground floor of the Pavillon du Roi. Into this *retardataire* framework of *rez-de-chaussée,* corner pavilions, and domed central pavilion were fitted the avant-garde motifs of the colonnades.

The colonnades surely were derived directly from François Le Vau's project of ca. 1662–64 (Figs. 24–32; discussed in Chapter II), and this suggests that when the Petit Conseil began its deliberations in the spring of 1667, François's presentation drawing (Fig. 24)—probably known to Colbert and readily available to his brother Louis Le Vau—was studied by the committee and used as a *composition de base*. The three architects must have clearly recognized the appropriateness of the colonnades for the theme of *regia solis*. However, François's wide and elaborate end pavilions were rejected in favor of pavilions closely based on the Pavillon du Roi, apparently for stylistic uniformity. The central pavilion was also redesigned, but the younger Le Vau's idea of a monumental arch rising into the level of the *premier étage* (Fig. 29) was adopted.

A drawing in the Musée Carnavalet (Fig. 62; Appendix A, no. A2) records an alternate design for the end pavilions of the east façade, with pairs of columns flanking the windows of the *premier étage,* these windows now subsumed under a shared pediment. A tall, sloping roof covers the pavilion, as in Figure 59. Braham and Whiteley, who first published the Carnavalet sheet, noted its identical correspondence in drawing style with Figure 59 and convincingly connected the style of these drawings with designs of 1665 for the Tuileries Palace, signed by Louis Le Vau.[20] We may therefore confidently attribute Figures

---

20. A. Braham and M. Whiteley, "Louis Le Vau's Projects for the Louvre and the Colonnade—II," *GBA,* ser. 6, LXIV, 1964, 348f., figs. 5, 6 (Stockholm, Nationalmuseum, CC 2272, CC 20; the latter is inscribed "arresté par Monsieur Colbert le

59 and 62 to the First Architect's office, if not to Le Vau himself; both date from spring 1667.

Two ground plans in Paris (Fig. 64; Appendix A, no. A3) and Stockholm (Fig. 65; Appendix A, no. A4) correspond perfectly to Figure 59 and the Carnavalet variant (Fig. 62).[21] Both plans delineate the Cour Carrée, with north and south wings containing single files of rooms (these wings determined the narrow, two-bay elevations of the end pavilions in Figures 59 and 62). The Paris plan indicates full paired columns flanking the windows of these pavilions, thus corresponding to the Carnavalet elevation (Fig. 62).[22] Both plans depict colonnades of eight pairs of columns, with single columns placed against the end and central pavilions, the latter with two pairs of columns around the central portal—all features that correspond to Figure 59. The Paris plan, moreover, reveals that the King's apartment was to be relocated behind the southerly range of the Colonnade, along with other ceremonial rooms.[23] The plans, which can

18ᵉ Mars 1665" and "Donné aux entrepreneurs led. jour Le Vau"). Other drawings for the Tuileries signed by Le Vau that are in Stockholm are CC 19 and CC 21, the latter dated March 26, 1665; see E. Langenskiöld, "Louvren, Tuilerierna och Versailles. Slottens byggnadshistoria i belysning av ritningar i Cronstedtsamlingen på Nationalmuseum," *Nationalmusei Årsbok*, 1942–43, 122, fig. 34; 124, fig. 36. Laprade (*d'Orbay*, 122) rejected an attribution of the Tuileries drawings to Louis Le Vau or d'Orbay, his principal draftsman.

Braham and Whiteley (349f.) have correctly attributed another Stockholm drawing (Fig. 63) to the same draftsman of Figures 59 and 62 (whom they identify as Le Vau himself) and have proposed that it is a Le Vau project of 1665 for the east façade of the Louvre. Specifically, these authors claim the drawing is for a radically new type of east range: a low screen wall with columns and a triumphal arch in the center. The authors add (352): "This building would have been remarkably close to the Colonnade of the Louvre in its decoration, for the garlanded oval medallions applied to the surface of the wall and the trophies of armour encased in two shields placed on the piers of the balustrade above, to mention only the most striking correspondences, are too close to be explicable merely as stylistic peculiarities of Le Vau's late style. They must rather indicate that both drawings [Figs. 59 and 63] are studies for the same building." (Figure 63 is also reproduced in M. Petzet, "Das Triumphbogenmonument für Ludwig XIV auf der Place du Trône," *ZfK*, XLV, 1982, 160, fig. 14, with the caption "Louis Le Vau [?], Entwurf für die Louvre-Ostfassade.")

I doubt that Figure 63 is for the east façade of the Louvre. Braham and Whiteley connect the drawing with an anonymous *mémoire* of 1664–65 (quoted in Chapter II, note 56) that proposes a low wall of columns and porticoes in place of a massive wing and criticizes Le Vau's project with a central oval salon. There is no independent evidence that Le Vau then adopted this critic's proposal, which in any event suggests an open columnar screen, not present in Figure 63. Instead, I would not rule out (as Braham and Whiteley do on 350) that the drawing depicts ideas for the royal Château de Vincennes, specifically for the outer façade of the central entrance pavilion

on the south. The exterior of Le Vau's executed pavilion (La Porte du Bois, 1658) is very severe, in harmony with the medieval architecture, but Vincennes in the seventeenth century was not in need of fortification (contrary to Braham and Whiteley, 350), and Le Vau's initial ideas could have suggested a richer, more festive design. The north, court side of the Porte du Bois was built as a classical triumphal arch, related stylistically to Figure 63. Although the executed Porte du Bois rises much higher above the screen wall than is the case in Figure 63, a preliminary drawing (Paris, Bibliothèque de la Ville de Paris; repr. in Laprade, *d'Orbay*, pl. III.3C), perhaps by d'Orbay, proposes a lower arch, with the screen wall at entablature level, as in the Stockholm drawing. However, the moat in Figure 63 is much shallower than the actual moat at Vincennes. Figure 63 cannot be connected with the competition for the Arc de Triomphe du Trône (1668–69) because of the indication of a moat, a feature never planned for the arch (see Petzet, "Das Triumphbogenmonument," 145–194).

21. In the Paris plan (Fig. 64), some of the expected window openings of the southern (left) range of the Colonnade are closed as niches.

22. The Stockholm plan (Fig. 65) depicts the *rez-de-chaussée* except for the northern range of the Colonnade itself and half of the central pavilion; the end pavilion to the north is again a plan at ground-floor level (contrary to Braham and Whiteley, "Louis Le Vau's Projects—II," 358).

23. East wing, from north to south: chapel (in the northern pavilion), stair, *salle des gardes, antichambre*, "*cabinet du cercle*" (in the central pavilion), *chambre de parade, chambre [à coucher]*, two *cabinets, grand cabinet, vestibule, salon* (in the southern pavilion); notations indicating these rooms are in the hand of Louis Le Vau (see below in this note). In Figure 65, faint pencil inscriptions indicate a stair (?) in the northern pavilion, followed by a *salle des gardes, antichambre*, and *petite antichambre*, all in the north range of the east wing.

Figure 64 bears the handwriting of Louis Le Vau (Laprade, *d'Orbay*, pl. VI.8A); the plan itself could have been drawn by Le Vau, d'Orbay, or someone else in Le Vau's office. Figure 65 was first published by Josephson as from the hand of Claude also be assigned to the spring of 1667, reveal why the "Registre" specified "Que l'Architecture, frise & corniche de la façade vers saint Germain, tourneront autour des pavillons sans continuer plus avant" (That the architecture, frieze, and cornice of the façade toward Saint-Germain [-l'Auxerrois] will turn around the pavilions without continuing farther): the south façade of Le Vau (Fig. 17) was to be preserved, and the north façade was to be completed following the design of its western half, already built earlier in the century under Lemercier (Fig. 14; see below).[24] All three façades would have been different in design, and the projected four-sided dome of the Colonnade of 1667 (Figs. 59, 66) would have harmonized with those of the other three wings.[25]

On December 7, 1667, after about six months of construction work on the Colonnade, François Le Vau wrote the following in a letter to Colbert (Sources II, no. 5):

> Monseigneur, Since my return [to Paris] I have been curious to see the buildings of the Louvre. I have seen the very high foundation of the great façade, where I have found, according to my sense, the foundations begun for the two corner pavilions and the one in the center very narrow for the proportion of the width of the said great façade and of the height the said pavilions must have,[26] and moreover the roofing, having to be made only with a spindle or finial [*espit ou amortissement*[27]], will appear instead [as something]

Perrault (R. Josephson, "Quelques dessins de Claude Perrault pour le Louvre," *GBA*, ser. 5, XVI, 1927, 182f.). The plan belongs to the Tessin collection in Stockholm, and Josephson drew attention to a letter (June 6, 1695) of Daniel Cronström to Nicodemus Tessin the Younger, wherein the former writes: "J'envoye toujours quelques feuilles du Louvre pour ne pas trop grossir les paquets. J'ay le plan du Louvre de Mr. Perrault que Monsieur son frère [Charles Perrault] m'a donné" (Sources II, no. 43). Josephson maintained that the ink plan and pencil annotations were all by Claude Perrault and must date from 1667. The question was taken up again by Braham and Whiteley ("Louis Le Vau's Projects—II," 354), who suggested that the plan was drawn up by the Petit Conseil and given to Perrault, who then added his jottings. But Braham and Whiteley did not suggest which member of the Petit Conseil (or his assistant) actually drew Figure 65. Pinprick holes suggest that the drawing either was used to make a copy or is itself a copy. Because THC 1240 is a plan, conventionally rendered in black ink, it is impossible to attribute it to a specific hand. In 1667, Le Vau had d'Orbay as his chief draftsman; Claude Perrault seems to have been working without assistance at that date. In 1671, the draftsman Louis Vigneux was paid for drawings of two buildings by Perrault—the Observatoire and the Arc de Triomphe du Trône (Fig. 120)—as well as for "quelques plans de bastimens pour le Roy" (*CBR*, I, col. 546), but his activity prior to 1671 is unknown, and hence Vigneux cannot be securely linked to the Louvre drawings of 1667–68. In 1673 he was paid for "divers plants [*sic*] des Maisons royalles" (*CBR*, I, col. 734; see also col. 671).

24. Noted by L. Hautecoeur, "L'auteur de la colonnade du Louvre" *GBA*, ser. 5, IX, 1924, 163; idem, *Louvre et Tuileries*, 170.

25. A domed northern façade is specified in the "Registre." The western wing contains the extant domed Pavillon de l'Horloge (by Lemercier, 1624–41; Fig. 14). Braham and Whiteley have proposed that the origins of the Colonnade can be traced back to notations found in the oval and square rooms in the center of the east wing in Figure 33 (one of Le Vau's drawings for his ill-fated east wing). These authors date the plan to 1663 but suggest that the small circles in chalk were added by Le Vau as early as 1665. They interpret them as freestanding columns, suggesting a triumphal arch type of entrance related to Figure 63 ("Louis Le Vau's Projects—II," 357). These notations make no architectural sense in relation to the plan (notice that the easternmost row is set back considerably from the line of the façade). What these rough notations do suggest is an interior columnar passageway, to be substituted for the oval vestibule and room behind, not an exterior colonnade.

26. Measurements (*toisés*) of the foundations of the east wing at the end of 1667 are in BN, Manuscrits, Mélanges Colbert, vol. 316, fols. 3r–5r.

27. Probably a reference to the high, narrow roofs of the end pavilions (cf. Fig. 59).

for the side pavilions of the building rather than for the main front façade. My brother asked my advice about it, and I have told him my opinion, and in order to fulfill my duty with the little experience I have, I have thought, with very humble submission and the respect that I owe you, to tell it to you also.

François's letter must have had an effect, for sometime in 1668 the width of the south wing was doubled, resulting in an east façade with widened end pavilions and a wider central pavilion, all of a new design.[28] The new scheme is revealed in a bird's-eye view drawing (Fig. 67; Appendix A, no. A6), where we find an elevation much closer to the executed one (Fig. 44), except for the *rez-de-chaussée,* which is lower, with squat, rectangular windows; there is also no moat. The wide central pavilion resembles a classical temple-front, and the attic with a four-sided dome is eliminated entirely. Four pairs of columns now articulate this pavilion instead of two pairs (as in Figs. 59 and 66), and the colonnades now consist of seven (instead of eight) pairs of coupled columns—a further step toward the final design, as is the use of the Corinthian, instead of the Composite, order. The wide end pavilions are of an entirely new design, vaguely reminiscent of François Le Vau's (cf. Figs. 26, 30), with column-pilaster pairs flanking a very wide, blank central opening (unfinished?). Gone are the attics; sloping roofs cover the end pavilions. Within the colonnades we can discern rear walls with pedimented (not rectangular) niches, with oval medallions and swags above; the windows (cf. Figs. 59, 64) have been entirely eliminated. This drawing constitutes a decisive step forward toward the final design.

To whom can we attribute this drawing? It is at once apparent that we are in the presence of a draftsman whose style we have not yet encountered. The sheet was first published by Petzet, who assigned its draftsmanship and conception to Claude Perrault. In arguing for this authorship, Petzet compared Figure 67 to a bird's-eye view drawing of Perrault's Observatoire (Fig. 68) showing an early, unexecuted project for the south façade.[29] Since Figure 68 must date from early 1667, it is surely from Perrault's hand, because Perrault had no known assistants at that time.[30] The drawings are sufficiently similar in technique, style, and viewpoint to sustain Petzet's attribution of both to Perrault. Figure 67 may indicate Perrault's decisive intervention, probably early in 1668, which revised the upper stories of the Colonnade. But the change of the central pavilion into a temple-front, the substitution of the Corinthian for the Composite order, and the entirely new end pavilions suggestive of antique triumphal arches may be the results of critiques solicited by the Crown from the foremost living architectural theorist of the moment, Roland Fréart de Chambray (1606–76). The *Comptes des bâtiments du roi* record an allocation and payment in 1668 to Fréart de Chambray:

---

28. I have found no evidence for C. Tadgell's statement that in June 1668 the Petit Conseil decided to double the south wing ("Claude Perrault, François Le Vau, and the Louvre Colonnade," *BurlM,* CXXII, 1980, 333, 334).

29. Petzet, "Claude Perrault als Architekt des Pariser Observatoriums," 4–5. The inscription ("Elevation perspective de l'observatoire") is not by Perrault (as claimed by Petzet) but by d'Orbay (cf. the latter's signed plan of the Grande Galerie of the Louvre [August 5, 1692], Louvre, Dessins, Recueil du Louvre, I, fol. 42).

30. See above, note 23.

> June 5: from [Sébastien François de La Planche, treasurer of the Royal Building Administration,] to deliver to the sieur Chambré [*sic*], as much for having come from the city of Le Mans to Paris as for having devoted himself there *during six months* [my emphasis] to the inspection and examination of all the drawings which have been made to finish the building of the Château du Louvre, taxations included, . . . 4,033 *livres, 6 sols, 8 deniers.*[31]

On July 15 the sum of 4,000 *livres* was paid to Fréart:

> July 15: to the sieur de Chambré, as much for having come from the city of Le Mans, place of his usual residence, to that of Paris, as for having devoted himself *during six months* [my emphasis] to the inspection and examination of the drawings of the Louvre, . . . 4,000 *livres*.[32]

Fréart de Chambray was a highly respected authority on architectural and artistic matters and the cousin of François Sublet de Noyers (d. 1645), who had been Superintendent of the King's Buildings from 1638 to 1643.[33] Fréart's publications include the *Parallèle de l'architecture antique et de la moderne* (Paris, 1650; dedicated to the memory of Sublet de Noyers) and the *Idée de la perfection de la peinture démonstrée par les principes de l'art* (Le Mans, 1662). In addition, he was the translator of Palladio, Leonardo da Vinci, and Euclid.[34] In 1665, he was in Paris during Bernini's visit and scrutinized the Italian's Louvre plans along with Colbert and Paul Fréart de Chantelou, his younger brother. There are many references to this in the latter's journal,[35] and Charles Perrault in his autobiography also mentions Fréart de Chambray as viewing Bernini's Louvre project in 1665.[36] This evidence shows clearly that Chambray was rated highly as an architectural authority (even by Bernini) and that his expertise extended to matters of construction.[37] Highly significant is that on August 30, 1665, Colbert personally appointed Fréart de Chambray to be supervisor of the erection of Bernini's Louvre after the Italian's expected departure later that year.[38]

The payment to Fréart de Chambray has been thought to be a belated payment for his service

---

31. "5 juin: de luy [Sébastien François de La Planche, trésorier des Bâtiments], pour dellivrer au s^r Chambré [*sic*], tant pour estre venu de la ville du Mans à Paris, que pour y avoir vaqué pendant six mois à la visitte et examen de tous les desseins qui ont esté faicts pour parachever le bastiment du chasteau du Louvre, y compris les taxations . . . 4033 [livres] 6 [sols] 8 [deniers]" (*CBR*, I, col. 234). On Fréart de Chambray, see H. Chardon, *Amateurs d'art et collectionneurs manceaux. Les frères Fréart de Chantelou,* Le Mans, 1867.

32. "15 juillet: au s^r de Chambré [*sic*], [tant] pour estre venu de la ville du Mans, lieu de son séjour ordinaire, en celle de Paris, que pour avoir vacqué pendant six mois à la visitte et examen des desseins du Louvre . . . 4000 [livres]" (*CBR*, I, col. 277).

33. On Sublet de Noyers, see Chardon, *Amateurs d'art,* and C. Michaud, "François Sublet de Noyers, Superintendant des bâtiments de France," *Revue historique,* CCXLI, 1969, 327–364.

34. *Les quatre livres d'architecture d'André Palladio,* Paris, 1650; Leonardo da Vinci, *Traité de la peinture,* Paris, 1651; Euclid, *La perspective,* Le Mans, 1663.

35. Fréart de Chantelou, *Journal.*

36. Ch. Perrault, *Mémoires de ma vie,* ed. P. Bonnefon, Paris, 1909, 68.

37. See Fréart de Chantelou, *Journal,* 140 (September 6, 1665).

38. Ibid., 126. Fréart de Chantelou later explained to Bernini the same day that his brother "n'avait pas cherché cet emploi, que son humeur était fort éloignée d'en briguer aucun, qu'il ne demandait plus que le repos et le divertissement qu'il trouvait dans son cabinet, étant d'un tempérament fort délicat et qu'il avait encore affaibli par l'étude, l'application aux mathématiques et une vie sédentaire" (ibid., 127).

during 1665 in connection with Bernini's Louvre.[39] Yet the entries in the *Comptes* refer to "tous les desseins" and "des desseins" of the Louvre without any mention of Bernini, thus according better with the situation of 1668, not 1665. Furthermore, if the payment was for six months of service that began with Fréart's appointment as supervisor on August 30, 1665, then he would have worked only until the end of February 1666, a date that does not correspond to any real construction at the Louvre or to the work on the models begun by Mattia de' Rossi in May 1666. The payment appears for the year 1668 and, in my view, fits perfectly with the timeframe of the revision of the 1667 Colonnade design previously analyzed. I submit that the payment allocated on June 5, 1668, and paid to Fréart a month and a half later, on July 15, was for transportation costs and expertise concerning the Louvre drawings from December 1667 to January 1668. Fréart de Chambray's presence in Paris in 1668 is also indicated by the anonymous critic of François Le Vau's "Advis" (see Sources II, no. 6). In a discussion about the number of floors in Louis Le Vau's south façade of 1660–63 (Fig. 17), the critic wrote:

> The apartments of the Louvre, as much [those on] the first floor as [those on] the ground floor, having the maximum height that can be given to the rooms, and the attic above also being of a suitable height, it seems to me unreasonable that they complain that this building is too low, since in order to raise it one must place either a main floor or two small ones above the King's, either of which goes against *la bienséance*—the first has been condemned already by *the leading man of our century in these sorts of knowledge* [my emphasis].[40]

It has been claimed that the savant here referred to was Bernini or Claude Perrault,[41] but I believe neither suggestion is correct. Chantelou's journal contains no record of the Italian having spoken this way; as for Perrault, in 1668 (the date of the "Advis") he had not yet achieved a reputation as an architectural theorist—that had to await the publication of his first Vitruvius edition in 1673. By 1668, in contrast, Roland Fréart de Chambray had been long esteemed as an architectural (and artistic) connoisseur, his reputation based mainly on his publications of 1650 and 1662 cited above.

Fréart de Chambray, then, had been recalled from Le Mans in December 1667 and remained in Paris until July 1668. This is precisely the period when the Petit Conseil—undoubtedly reacting to François Le Vau's criticism contained in his letter to Colbert of December 7, 1667 (see above)—was grappling with the problem of redesigning the central and end pavilions of the east façade. It may well have been during these same months that the decision was made to double the depth of the south wing and provide it with a new façade (see below). Fréart surely voiced his opinions about all these designs, although the only one recorded is contained in the

---

39. Chardon, *Amateurs d'art*, 151; F. d'Amat, "Fréart," in *Dictionnaire de biographie française*, fasc. 83, Paris, 1979, col. 1136. M. Vachon, *Le Louvre et les Tuileries*, Lyon, 1926, 138, correctly connected the payments with the Louvre plans of 1668.

40. For the French text, see Sources II, no. 6(5a).
41. Laprade, *d'Orbay*, 149 (Bernini); Tadgell, "Claude Perrault, François Le Vau and the Louvre Colonnade," 337 (Perrault).

passage from the "Advis" quoted above. In effect, Fréart may have become a member *pro tempore* of the Petit Conseil during the first half of 1668, and this conjecture is strengthened by Leibniz's report, based on information provided by Claude Perrault, that, in addition to Perrault, the council was composed of Le Brun, Le Vau, and "quelques autres" (among whom would have been the secretary, Charles Perrault).[42] The fact that, according to Chantelou, he and his brother Fréart de Chambray recommended to Colbert in June 1668 that Bernini's Louvre design be executed[43] does not invalidate the preceding arguments, although it is surprising that the classicistic Fréart would have preferred Bernini's Baroque palazzo to the Colonnade. (It can be inferred, but not proved, that the letter, dated June 15, also indicates Fréart's presence in Paris at that date.)

Finally, it might be asked: If the payment made to Fréart in 1668 was for work during that year, where is the record of payment for his services in connection with Bernini's Louvre that began on August 30, 1665? The answer, I believe, is that no payments were ever made for this because no construction work was done on Bernini's project.

Let us return to Figure 67, probably dating from early 1668. Although probably drawn by Claude Perrault, the new proposals for the central and terminal pavilions may reflect Fréart's direct intervention as an adviser and connoisseur, not as a draftsman (he did not draw, as far as we know). His *Parallèle* of 1650 was a manifesto of classicism that praised the ancient Greeks as the supreme artists, condemned contemporary architecture in France and Italy as corrupt, but praised Palladio and Scamozzi as the two greatest modern masters, probably in the (vain) hope of spurring on a neo-Palladian movement in France.[44] The transformation in Figure 67 of the frontispiece of Figures 59 and 66 into a more overt temple-front is in harmony with Fréart's taste and his pronouncement that the portico is the most magnificent element in architecture[45] (although the columns in Figure 67 are placed against or are engaged to the wall). The end pavilions in the bird's-eye view suggest the rhythms of a triumphal arch, and this form was to become more explicit in a subsequent study (see below). In this context we should note that Fréart, in the *Parallèle*, praised the Arch of Titus in Rome as the first and finest triumphal arch,[46] an arch in an a-B-a rhythm, like the new terminal pavilions. Finally, we should remark that, in his *Parallèle*, Fréart had severely criticized the Composite order as monstrous;[47] the adoption of the Corinthian order in Figure 67 instead of the Composite of the preceding elevations (Figs. 59, 62) would appear to corroborate Fréart's influence further.

---

42. See Sources II, no. 19. Charles Perrault, however, in his account of the Petit Conseil, does not mention Fréart de Chambray (Sources II, no. 53[b]).

43. On June 15, 1668, Chantelou wrote to Colbert: "L'obligation récente que mon frère et moi vous avons, nous fait, Monsieur, prendre la liberté de vous représenter que nous ne jugeons pas que rien pût servir davantage à votre gloire dans les bâtiments que de faire exécuter au Louvre le dessein du cavalier Bernin" (Fréart de Chantelou, *Journal*, 264). On June 23, Chantelou saw Colbert in person about the matter, to no avail (ibid., 264–265).

44. I have commented on Fréart de Chambray's *Parallèle* in my *Antoine Le Pautre: A French Architect of the Era of Louis XIV*, New York, 1969, 10. For his Palladio translation, see note 34, above. This was the first complete French translation of *I quattro libri*.

45. Fréart de Chambray, *Parallèle*, 58 (in a discussion of the Temple of Fortuna Virilis, Rome).

46. Ibid., 102.

47. Ibid., 97–99.

Fréart de Chambray was still associated with the Petit Conseil when it turned to the detailed articulation of these pavilions. A drawing in Paris with attached flaps (Figs. 69–72; Appendix A, no. A7) reveals in full detail the working-out process for the design of the new, wide pavilions. The podium and the high *rez-de-chaussée* with tall, segment-headed windows have been restored, complete with keystone masks (cf. Figs. 59, 62). The designers then experimented with various solutions for articulating the wide, three-bay pavilion. In one proposal (Fig. 69), the central bay was made equal in width to its neighbors, resulting in unequal narrow spacings within the pilaster pairs; this must have been quickly rejected. In all of the other variants (Figs. 70–72) the central bay was made wider. In Figs. 70 and 71 coupled pilasters were again used, but now the narrow spaces within the pairs are equal, and variants are proposed for the central opening and its decoration above. Again one suspects that the awkward wide oval and swag of Figure 71 were rapidly rejected. Figure 72 was ultimately chosen, with a wide central bay flanked by column-pilaster pairs, as in Figure 67. Now the central bay is articulated with a high rectangular opening with a semicircular arch above—essentially the final design and most reminiscent of an antique triumphal arch.

We encounter in these drawings the same crisp style of draftsmanship found in Figure 67, and Petzet would again appear to be correct in attributing the hand to Perrault (see Appendix A, no. A7). The drawings allow us to study the details of the niches within the colonnades— semicircular in plan and pedimented—which first appeared in Figure 67. These niches are more classical than the rectangular ones present in the designs of 1667 (cf. Figs. 59, 66) and are repeated in every bay. In addition, Figures 69–72 also reveal a single freestanding column terminating the series of coupled columns and adjoining the end pavilion. This represents once more a reversion to Figure 59; in Figure 67, single columns flank the main pavilion while pairs of columns abut the end ones—an eccentric, asymmetrical proposal that was regularized in the design process.

After the variant shown in Figure 72 was selected, it was drawn separately and in greater detail as the north pavilion (Fig. 73; Appendix A, no. A8). Statues appear in the niches, the oval medallions are filled with figural reliefs, and decorative flourishes are placed in the central bay of the pavilion. Whereas in Figures 69–72 an attic with a high sloping roof over the pavilion was suggested in light pencil, no such feature appears in Figure 73, where the blocking course, balustrades, and trophies of Figure 59 reappear. The drawing bears an inscription in the hand of d'Orbay, to whom the sheet was first correctly attributed by Laprade. Although similar to Perrault's drawing style as seen in Figures 69–72, d'Orbay's touch makes bolder use of the brush and washes in such details as the capitals and swags; Perrault is in most places harder, more linear (cf., e.g., the moldings around the windows of the *rez-de-chaussée* in Figures 69–72) (see also Appendix A).

The above analyses of Figures 67 and 69–72 reveal Perrault—probably under the direct influence of Fréart de Chambray—producing critically important drawings that move toward the final design, while d'Orbay appears merely as a draftsman supplying a final redaction enriched by decorative details. Another, unknown, draftsman—probably from Le Vau's studio or Le Brun's studio—was then entrusted (probably in 1668) with an elevation drawing of the entire east façade in its final form, without visible roofs and with six pairs of coupled columns in each range of the Colonnade (Figs. 74, 75; Appendix A, no. A9).[48] In this "architect's drawing," without the decorative enrichments of Figure 73, even the columns and pilasters are unfluted. The drawing is on two pieces of paper pasted together, one of which has a watermark with the Colbert coat-of-arms. It is tempting to think that the drawing was made under the auspices of the Petit Conseil as a gesture of homage to the *surintendant*. Note that this drawing, while preserving the conventional balusters at roof level (already indicated in Figure 59), changes the lower range at *premier étage* level to a balustrade of interlaced ovals; this solution with two types of balustrades was indeed executed (Fig. 58).[49]

A plan in the *Recueil du Louvre* (Fig. 76; Appendix A, no. A10) probably dates from 1668 and shows the final disposition of the Colonnade wing and the new south wing with doubled suites of rooms. Another surviving drawing from the deliberations of the Petit Conseil, probably also to be dated 1668, is concerned with the details of structure and ornament within the colonnaded ranges of the east façade (Fig. 77; Appendix A, no. A11). The top half of the drawing depicts the rear wall with its pilasters and medallion-swag motif; within the medallion appears a relief (unexecuted) of a female figure and a putto with a bow, the former holding a bell or mirror. The lower half shows the ceiling and undersides of the architraves, with details that differ from the executed work (cf. Figs. 52–54). In the drawing, one of the architraves is decorated with a motif of crossed quivers, replaced in the final work by the guilloche motif that appears on the other architraves on the sheet. But even here we find that the guilloche pattern with seven equal circles was altered to a design with five large and four small circles in alternation. Furthermore, in the built ceilings, the radiant Apollo-heads are smaller in relation to the circular wreaths, and smaller acorn leaves within triangular frames replace the more exuberant unframed fleur-de-lis motifs of the drawing. In the executed ceiling, the square frames enclosing these motifs are decorated with bead-and-reel and egg-and-tongue moldings. In addition, the jointing of the stonework, seen in section, differs from the execution (cf. Fig. 79), and the conventional, semicircular relieving arches were eventually rejected, to be replaced by an ingenious corbeled passageway; however, the iron reinforcement is not indicated. (For these structural matters, see Chapter VI). These decorative and structural differences between Figure 77 and the realized building prove that the drawing must have been produced by the Petit Conseil and that Laprade's proposal that d'Orbay was the draftsman is probably correct.

---

48. This anonymous draftsman draws the balusters at the top of the building in a peculiar shorthand form ( ) that is found in none of the other drawings and that establishes this draftsman's individuality. The drawing is surely not from the hand of Perrault, as claimed by Josephson, who first published it (see Appendix A, "Criteria of Attribution, Other Draftsmen," and Appendix A, no. A9).

49. The interlaced balustrades were replaced by iron railings in the early nineteenth century; the original ones remain in place only in the central pavilion (Fig. 55). This type of balustrade with interlaced ovals appears in some drawings by Claude Perrault (designs for a Louvre stair, Stockholm, Nationalmuseum, THC 2203, THC 2204). Perrault did not invent this type, however; it appears in some of the engravings of François Le Vau's Louvre project (ca. 1662–64; Figs. 29, 30) and also much earlier in the Petit Château, Versailles (1631–34; A. Marie, *Naissance de Versailles: Le château, les jardins*, Paris, 1968, I, pl. v, top) and over the windows of the *premier étage* of the Petit Hôtel de Sully, Paris (1634–41, perhaps by Jean Androuet Du Cerceau). See also Figures 96, 97.

THE SOUTH FAÇADE

Probably early in 1668, the decision was made to transfer the King's *appartement* to the south wing to take advantage of the southern exposure and views of the Seine and Left Bank. This occasioned the doubling of the wing and the widening of the terminal pavilions of the Colonnade. The Petit Conseil took up the task of designing the new wing and façade, which were to cover Le Vau's recent front of 1660–63 (Figs. 17, 18).

Much less documentation and far fewer drawings have come down to us concerning this phase. The earliest surviving drawing is shown in Figure 96 (Appendix A, no. C1). Here we clearly see the doubled wing in section at the extreme right, with Le Vau's four-sided dome (shown with a somewhat lower profile than in Figures 17 and 18); at the left appears the three-bay link between the southwestern pavilion (the Pavillon du Roi) of the Cour Carrée and the Petite Galerie (shown in section; the three-bay elevation at the extreme left is the north side of the Cour du Sphinx). A separate study (Fig. 97; Appendix A, no. C2) depicts the west elevations of the Pavillon du Roi and three bays of the outer façade of Lescot's wing; the connecting link to the Petite Galerie is shown in section. The draftsman of both drawings is probably d'Orbay, as first proposed by Laprade (1960).

Although these drawings already show the formula of a colossal Corinthian pilaster order on a high ground story—the eventual, realized articulation (Fig. 95)—we note that this *rez-de-chaussée* is heavily scored with horizontal channeling, producing a rusticated effect. This proposed treatment clashes with all renderings of the east façade reviewed above, where smoothly drafted masonry without channeling or rustication appears (except occasionally at corners or changes in plane). In an oblique view of the Louvre from the southeast (Fig. 42), texturally contrasting east and south ground stories would have been unacceptably discordant. Because the decision to double the depth of the south wing was made well after the basic design of the Colonnade had been created, it is difficult to understand the renderings of the ground floor in Figures 96 and 97 unless we assume there was a brief moment in 1668 when such channeled rustication was being considered for all the outer façades of the Louvre.[50]

Be that as it may, Figures 96 and 97 depict the stage in the evolution of the south façade that is contemporaneous with an important document, the "Advis de M. le Vau le jeune sur le nouveau dessin du Louvre" (Sources II, no. 6).[51] In a number of passages in the "Advis" (secs. 1–5, 7–9),

---

50. The channeled rustication may have been suggested by Bernini's Louvre Project (Figs. 40, 41) or by François Le Vau's scheme (Figs. 24–31), where the ground floors of the central and end pavilions are treated in this manner. François's drawing and engravings may have been meant to suggest two alternative ways of treating this floor—rusticated or smooth.

51. For previous analyses of this document, see Laprade, *d'Orbay*, 148f., and Picon, *Claude Perrault*, 174f. Laprade's transcription of the document contains a faulty reading on 346, no. 11, right column; the first part of the second sentence should read: "De plus, sa profondeur sera beaucoup moindre que l'espace *des entrecolonnemens* . . . ," not "*d'un entrecolonnement*." This has been corrected in Sources II, no. 6 (11a). Picon postulated (177) that the "Advis" relates to "un état intermédiaire du projet élaboré en 1668," but by "l'espace des entrecolonnemens" the writer is surely referring to the *height* of each bay, as the reading of the rest of his sentence bears out.

Laprade improbably maintained that the passages nominally by François Le Vau were really written by d'Orbay and that the criticisms are by the Perrault brothers (!); if this were so, then the latter would have been arguing in 1668 (in 6a) *against* the colossal order of the Colonnade, a design feature that had already been accepted by the King in 1667. Laprade is correct, however, in pointing out some close similarities in wording an anonymous critic and François Le Vau debate the proposal to double the depth of the south wing and create a new river façade. The critic opposes these ideas and defends Louis Le Vau's still-exposed south façade of 1660–63 (Fig. 17), which he describes as having an attic above the two lower floors. The younger Le Vau—who, surprisingly, appears in this document as a loquacious theoretician—stoutly defends the proposal and criticizes his brother's attic as inadequate functionally and symbolically in relation to its intended occupants, "les enfants de France, princes et grands seigneurs," and officers and attendants, including the King's. For these individuals there could be several floors above the royal *premier étage,* perhaps "une grande et une autre médiocre au-dessus" or only "un second étage raisonnablement haut." The critic had noted (5a) that "un grand étage" above the King's floor "has been condemned already by the leading man of our century in these sorts of knowledge" (i.e., Fréart de Chambray; see above); thus, Figures 96 and 97, which correspond to this arrangement, may well have been the very drawings seen and criticized by Fréart. They are surely of this moment (early 1668), because a number of other comments in the "Advis" correlate precisely. These include discussions of a colossal order (6a,b); a "galerie à jour" with a terrace above (seen in section in Figure 97) that will alleviate (according to François) the overlap of two bays of the Petite Galerie by the new south wing (8b);[52] and the critic's condemnation of the absence of visible roofs between the pavilions (9a).

The appearance of François Le Vau in the deliberations concerning the new Louvre of Louis XIV—in December 1667 (see above) and again early in 1668—adds to the complexity of the *dramatis personae* and suggests that Louis Le Vau may have consulted his brother throughout the process. François's reference in the "Advis" (8b) to "l'architecte" suggests that Figures 96 and 97 (and others with more stories, now lost?) are attributable to one designer rather than to the Petit Conseil—that is, to Louis Le Vau, whose "revised" design philosophy François is defending at the same time that he is criticizing Louis's first south façade of 1660–63.

If Figure 96 was indeed the First Architect's conception (a total revision of his earlier south façade, Figure 17), then it documents the moment of his much-discussed stylistic metamorphosis, which resulted in the façades of the Enveloppe at Versailles, designed in the same year, 1668.[53] Like the Enveloppe, Figure 96 features a *rez-de-chaussée* of channeled rustication, serving as a podium for the upper floors; the use of a colossal pilaster order was also proposed by Le Vau in an early project for the Enveloppe.[54] In both instances, Le Vau broke with his previous

---

between some of the critic's passages in the "Advis" and later writings by Charles and Claude (see, e.g., Chapter V, note 10). These similarities indicate that the Perraults were influenced by the anonymous critic, whoever he was. Picon is inconclusive about the identities of the writers of the "Advis," although in a note (272 n. 44) he suggests that d'Orbay collaborated with the younger Le Vau in composing the document. Laprade, followed by Picon, maintained that François Le Vau never visited Rome; hence, the passage in the "Advis" where the writer states that he had been in the Eternal City (11b) proves that the younger brother could not have written that part of the document that bears his name. However, there is no firm evidence that François Le Vau did *not* visit Rome; a plausible time for that sojourn would have been during the Fronde, 1648–51 (he is recorded in Paris on September 30, 1648, and next on May 16, 1651, when he undertook the renovation of the Hôtel de Sully; see Chapter II, notes 27 and 29).

52. Tadgell, "Claude Perrault, François Le Vau and the Louvre Colonnade," 334 n. 27, pointed out this feature.

53. On the Enveloppe and Le Vau's change of style, see Berger, *Versailles: The Château of Louis XIV,* chaps. II, III.

54. Ibid., 15–16, 23–24, figs. 13, 14.

practice at the Louvre, where the colossal order rose from the ground floor (Figs. 18, 35). The reason for this change in composition for a new south façade at the Louvre is obvious: it had to conform to the *ordonnance* of the Colonnade. But to what point had the Colonnade design evolved when Le Vau proposed Figure 96? The end pavilions of the former still must have been projected with visible roofs. Such roofs (though lower) appear in Perrault's perspective view (Fig. 67) and also in Figures 69–72, where the left edge of a very high roof on a base is faintly outlined in pencil.[55] Nevertheless, even if we disregard the question of smooth versus textured ground floor, this proposed southern elevation would have formed a dissonance with the Colonnade in its upper story: in the drawing, the latter is the same height as the *premier étage* and is articulated with round-arched windows based on those of Lescot's top floor of the old Pavillon du Roi (Fig. 9), a type of window that had never been proposed for the Colonnade, as far as we can determine from surviving drawings.[56]

The criticisms of Fréart de Chambray, the anonymous critic of the "Advis," and the palpable lack of agreement of Figures 96 and 97 with the Colonnade, forced a revision, which is preserved in Figure 98 (Appendix A, no. C3). Once again the draftsman is d'Orbay, although the same composition may have appeared on one of Perrault's sheets, since destroyed (see Appendix A, no. C3). Now the *rez-de-chaussée* is smooth and untextured to match the east façade; the *premier étage,* with its pedimented windows, is unchanged, but the royal floor is surmounted by a distinctly lower, subordinate *deuxième étage,* with the same segment-headed windows with slight breaks in the moldings at top and bottom that derive from Le Vau's earlier façade (Figs. 17, 18) and, before that, from Lescot's outer façades (Figs. 9, 13). Each bay is defined, as in the preceding design, by colossal Corinthian pilasters, but now there are ten bays instead of nine (as in Figure 96) between the central pavilion and each end pavilion—the final arrangement. The end pavilions have been totally redesigned with the medallion-swag motif to harmonize with the end pavilions of the Colonnade, but all three bays are now identical in width, with single pilasters framing the central one. The medallion-swag motif appears again in the central pavilion, which is emphasized by a *ressaut* and by engaged or full columns set against the wall; now the wider central bay with its semicircular arch subtly approaches the design of the terminal pavilions of the east front, resulting in much greater unity between the two great façades. At this stage, high roofs still rise above the corner pavilions, with a *troisième étage* with Lescot-type windows corresponding to the pavilion roof outlined in Figures 69–72. Again, visible roofs are absent between the pavilions. Le Vau's drum and dome from the campaign of 1660–63 are faintly indicated above the central pavilion, suggesting that the designers considered these superfluous vestiges. In the final revision, resulting in the built façade (Fig. 95), these were eliminated along with the roofs over the end pavilions, and pilasters were substituted for columns in the central pavilion.[57]

Although the few surviving drawings (Figs. 96–98) are all from the hand of d'Orbay and

55. The roof in Figure 97 is lower than in Figure 96.
56. Lescot's windows had been repeated in Lemercier's Pavillon de l'Horloge (1624–41).

57. Le Vau's dome was not finally dismantled until 1758 (C. Tadgell, *Ange-Jacques Gabriel,* London, 1978, 198).

hence ascribable to Louis Le Vau, our analysis indicates the close advisory role François Le Vau and Fréart de Chambray played in the evolution of the façade. The contributions of Le Brun and Perrault in this process are lost to view, but it could be hypothesized that the changes in the south façade that brought it into close harmony with the Colonnade were due to Perrault, an idea that receives some support from J. F. Blondel's 1756 description of a lost Perrault drawing that may have resembled Figure 98 (see Appendix A, no. C3). In any case, the south façade, like the Colonnade, is surely the result of the collaboration of the Petit Conseil with outside advisers.

The North Façade

The history of the north wing has been recounted by Hautecoeur[58] and can be briefly presented here. The foundations of the western half of the north wing were slowly put in place under Lemercier beginning in 1639.[59] The wing was to be one-room deep (like the west wing) and was to continue broadly the massing and exterior and courtyard elevations of the older sections of the palace.

Louis Le Vau, as First Architect, continued the wing, beginning in 1660, and in April 1661 the northwest corner pavilion (the Pavillon de Beauvais) was roofed. A print (Fig. 14) showing the completed pavilion may date from that year. It shows the incomplete north wing; its extension toward the east had been blocked by the abutting Hôtel de Rostaing, which had been ordered demolished in January 1661.[60]

Work on the north wing presumably continued during the 1660s under Le Vau. The "Registre" of the Petit Conseil for May 28 describes its condition by the spring of 1667 (Sources II, no. 1). There we learn that the unequal window spacing of the part of the wing already standing was to be copied in the corresponding part to be built (Fig. 101), for reasons of symmetry and to avoid adverse foreign opinion. The "Registre" refers at one point to the central pavilion of this wing as having a dome "à bâtir," but another section describes the domed pavilion as in existence. That it was never built is indicated by the Plan Turgot (1739), where it is completely absent.[61]

By the end of 1667, the north wing was standing for more than half its length at the height of slightly more than five *toises* (thirty *pieds*), to just above the ground-floor cornice.[62] A year later,

58. Hautecoeur, *Louvre et Tuileries*, 181–182.
59. *Le Louvre et son quartier. 800 ans d'histoire architecturale*, exhib. cat., Paris, 1982, 36.
60. The *hôtel* is shown on the survey plan of the area (1657–59) from Le Vau's office, published by Erlande-Brandenburg, "Les fouilles du Louvre," 1965, 15, fig. 17, and J. P. Babelon, "D'un fossé à l'autre. Vingt ans de recherches sur le Louvre," *RA*, no. 78, 1987, 15, fig. 22.
61. J. F. Blondel reported finding projects for this dome drawn by Perrault and accompanied by his "explications" in the (later destroyed) 1693 manuscript *recueil* (*Architecture française*, IV, 6 n. 10).
62. BN, Manuscrits, Mélanges Colbert, vol. 316, fol. 1v (*toisé du Louvre*): "Au corps de logis en retour vers les Pères de l'Oratoire, le mur de face du costé de la court contient 42 [toises] de long depuis l'angle du mur premier declaré jusques au viel tableau de la croisée de l'encien de la première corniche." The *toisé* was drawn up at the end of 1667 or the beginning of 1668. It is not clear from exactly what point the length of 42 *toises* was measured.

on December 24, 1668, the sculptors Le Hongre and Tuby were paid for sculpting the frieze and keystone masks of this façade, and Le Gendre and Massou were paid on February 15 of the next year for four more keystone masks (see Sources I, nos. 21 and 36).[63]

Because the "Registre" indicates that the central pavilion of the north wing (but not its dome) had been finished by the time the Petit Conseil met in May 1667, it follows that the pavilion is by Le Vau (Figs. 101, 103, 104). It is far simpler than his southern central pavilion (Fig. 18), eschewing the orders and relying for its effect on quoining strips dominated by a pediment. I suspect the medallion-swag motifs were added for visual unity after the design for the Colonnade had been adopted, and we can assume that this decision, like all others affecting the completion of this façade, was the result of a collaborative process within the Petit Conseil and was supplemented by the advice of François Le Vau and Fréart de Chambray.

The Courtyard

See Chapter V.

When did the Petit Conseil stop meeting? Although the above analyses indicate that the committee met in 1668, we do not know how far into that year their deliberations extended or whether they continued into 1669. The group surely had disbanded before September 12, 1669, when Claude Perrault left Paris for a trip through France.[64]

---

63. A payment to Tuby on March 22, 1668 (see Sources I, no. 19) may also be for work on the north façade (masks and frieze).

64. Cl. Perrault, *Voyage à Bordeaux* (1669), ed. P. Bonnefon, Paris, 1909. See also Appendix C.

IV
THREE PROPOSALS BY CLAUDE PERRAULT

The Colonnade as a Closed Façade

In the discussion in Chapter III concerning the evolution of the Colonnade it was noted that in the spring of 1667 the Petit Conseil first proposed that the inner wall behind the arrays of coupled columns should have an alternation of rectangular windows and rectangular statue niches (Figs. 59, 64–66).[1] In the perspective drawing of early 1668 attributed to Perrault (Fig. 67), there are no windows at all in these walls; instead, there are rows of niches of a new, more classical form, pedimented and semicircular in plan. These appear in all subsequent drawings (Figs. 69–76) and in the building as originally constructed; Figures 73, 85, and 88 show that the niches were intended to hold statues (never executed). In 1807, after the Louvre had been

---

1. In Figure 64, some of the windows in the southern (left) half of the Colonnade have been converted to niches to assure greater privacy for the King's intimate rooms.

transformed into a public museum, all the niches were replaced by the windows we see today (Figs. 43, 44, 48, 49).[2]

The Colonnade was begun in 1667, and construction proceeded rapidly (see Chapter V). A famous engraving by Le Clerc (Fig. 86)—showing the monolithic stones of the raking cornices of the central pavilion being hoisted into place by an incredible machine—reveals that the main fabric of the structure was virtually complete in 1674, when this engineering feat was accomplished. But one year earlier, in 1673, the first edition of Perrault's Vitruvius translation was published, with its well-known frontispiece again engraved by Le Clerc (Fig. 117). Here we see the figure of Abundance seated behind that of France, pointing out to her a number of architectural marvels, all connected with the name of Claude Perrault: his French order (capital and entablature in the foreground; note the fleur-de-lis on the capital); his Arc de Triomphe du Trône on the eastern outskirts of Paris, construction of which had been begun in 1670; his astronomical observatory on the Left Bank in Paris, under construction since 1667; and, in the middle distance, the new Louvre façade (Fig. 118). This engraved elevation deserves special scrutiny.

The building, adorned with a balustrade with trophies and an equestrian statue (of Louis XIV, of course) above the pediment, seems virtually complete. Construction machinery appears above the southern end pavilion. The latter does not appear in its executed form, but rather with the composition given to the end pavilions of the new south façade (Fig. 95). The main difference, however, between the frontispiece and the constructed Colonnade appears in the ground floor in the engraving. Here, beneath the ranges of coupled columns, are indicated not windows but military trophies; these reappear in the headpiece (also by Le Clerc) in the Vitruvius edition, set above the dedication to the King (Fig. 119).[3] Jacques François Blondel, the eighteenth-century architect and theoretician who had consulted the 1693 manuscript collection of Claude Perrault's drawings and commentaries (destroyed in 1871), wrote in 1756:

> The ground floor below this peristyle is pierced [in the executed building] by windows with curved tops. These openings had been made against the wishes of our architect [Claude Perrault], who had preferred, he says, military trophies [*trophées d'armes*], in the helmets of which one would have pierced small openings to light the interior of this ground floor.[4]

Blondel continues:

---

2. J. Hillairet, *Dictionnaire historique des rues de Paris,* 2d ed., Paris, 1963, II, 68. During the creation of these windows in 1807, it was discovered that "cette colonnade fut destinée d'abord à recevoir des fenêtres, et la bâtisse des niches formées de cloisons légeres a encore confirmé l'existance de ce fait" (J. G. Legrand and C. P. Landon, *Description de Paris et de ses édifices . . . ,* Paris, 1809, II, 40).

3. In Figure 119, Apollo appears next to a framed picture of the Colonnade; Minerva on the right points to another, showing Perrault's Observatoire.

4. Sources II, no. 84(b).

> We find . . . a design for the ground floor much richer than the one that was built; it was composed of large plaques, frames, projections, and quoining strips in rather good taste, concerning which he [Perrault] expressly notes that he had preferred this sort of design to the windows . . . in order to preserve for that building the aspect of a château, the name the Louvre still bore at that time.[5]

An anonymous, undated engraving (Fig. 121) shows masks instead of trophies but is surely an echo of Perrault's idea of military trophies.

Perrault's intended closed ground floor would have reinforced a feature of the design that was indeed executed: the niches in the two recessed walls behind the ranges of coupled columns, discussed above. The substitution of all niches for an alternating pattern of windows and niches in the *premier étage* as well as the proposed trophies or other features (plaques, etc.) instead of windows for the *rez-de-chaussée* are Perrault's ideas: the array of niches without windows first appears in the perspective drawing attributed to Perrault (Fig. 67), and we have Blondel's testimony about Claude's thoughts concerning the ground floor (as well as Le Clerc's engravings, executed, of course, under the supervision of Perrault).

Why was Perrault so insistent about a mainly closed façade? His reasons for this stem directly from his translation and interpretation of a passage in Vitruvius. In book v, chapter 6 (which Perrault and earlier editors numbered chapter 8), the Roman architect wrote his famous lines about the painted stage-sets of the ancient theater:

> Genera autem sunt scaenarum tria: unum quod dicitur tragicum, alterum comicum, tertium satyricum. Horum autem ornatus sunt inter se dissimili disparique ratione, quod tragicae deformantur columnis et fastigiis et signis reliquisque regalibus rebus; comicae autem aedificiorum privatorum et maenianorum habent speciem profectusque fenestris dispositos imitatione communium aedificiorum rationibus; satyricae vero ornantur arboribus, speluncis, montibus reliquisque agrestibus rebus in topeodi speciem deformati [v.6.9]. [See note 7 for two English translations.]

Here is Perrault's French translation of this passage:

> Il y a trois sortes de Scenes, sçavoir, la Tragique, la Comique, & la Satyrique. Leurs Decorations sont differentes en ce que la Scene Tragique a des colonnes, des frontons élevez, des Statues & de tels autres ornemens *qui conviennent à un Palais Royal* [my emphasis]. La Decoration de la Scene Comique represente des maisons particulieres, avec leurs Balcons & leurs croisées disposées à la manière des Bastimens communs & ordinaires. La Satyrique est ornée de bocages, de cavernes, de montagnes, & de tout ce qu'on voit representé dans les païsages des Tapisseries.[6]

---

5. Ibid.

6. Perrault, *Vitruve*, 1673, 170; 1684, 180 (v.8). Perrault does not illustrate the painted scenes.

(There are three types of scenes, namely, the Tragic, the Comic, and the Satyric. Their decorations differ in that the Tragic Scene has columns, elevated pediments, statues, and such other ornaments *which are suitable for a royal palace* [my emphasis]. The decoration of the Comic Scene shows private houses with their balconies and their windows arranged in the manner of common and ordinary buildings. The Satyric is adorned with groves, caves, mountains, and everything one sees depicted in the landscapes of tapestries.)

We see that, in Perrault's translation, a royal palace as represented in painted stage-scenery has columns, pediments, statues, and other suitable features (but no windows), whereas common and ordinary buildings depicted in such scenery have only balconies and windows. But "qui conviennent à un Palais royal" is a quite free, if not erroneous, translation of "reliquisque regalibus rebus" (literally, "and with other royal things"). Granger translated the phrase as "and other royal surroundings," and Morgan gives "and other objects suited to kings."[7] Italian sixteenth-century translations give "& altre cose (or ornamenti) regale," and Jean Martin in his 1547 French translation (the only one before Perrault's) has "& autres appareilz sentans leur Royaulté ou Seigneurie."[8] In Perrault's translation, the Tragic Scene of the ancient theater is patterned after ancient royal palaces (a type not discussed by Vitruvius), but this is an idea Vitruvius does not really state. Perrault's free translation gave him the opportunity to express his ideas about a real royal palace in a footnote appearing in the 1673 Vitruvius edition and in an expanded form in the second (1684) edition:

It is easily concluded from the comparison here made of the Tragic Scene with the Comic one that it is necessary to have something other than the greatness of elevation in making a contrast between a royal palace and a private house. [The latter] has windows on the main entrance side, whereas a palace must have only columns, statues, and

---

7. Vitruvius, *On Architecture* (Loeb Classical Library), trans. F. Granger, Cambridge, Mass., and London, 1955, I, 289: "There are three styles of scenery: one which is called tragic; a second, comic; the third, satyric. Now the subjects of these differ severally one from another. The tragic are designed with columns, pediments and statues and other royal surroundings; the comic have the appearance of private buildings and balconies and projections with windows made to imitate reality, after the fashion of ordinary buildings; the satyric settings are painted with trees, caves, mountains and other country features, designed to imitate landscape."

Vitruvius, *The Ten Books on Architecture,* trans. M. H. Morgan, New York, 1960, 150: "There are three kinds of scenes, one called the tragic, second, the comic, third, the satyric. Their decorations are different and unlike each other in scheme. Tragic scenes are delineated with columns, pediments, statues, and other objects suited to kings; comic scenes exhibit private dwellings, with balconies and views representing rows of windows, after the manner of ordinary dwellings; satyric scenes are decorated with trees, caverns, mountains, and other rustic objects delineated in landscape style."

8. *Di Lucio Vitruvio Pollione de architectura libri dece . . . ,* trans. C. Cesariano, Como, 1521, fol. LIII v; *M. L. Vitruvio Pollione de architectura . . . ,* trans. Durantino, Venice, 1524, fol. 51v; *Architettura con il suo commento et figure Vetruvio,* trans. G. B. Caporali, Perugia, 1536, fol. 120r; *I dieci libri dell'architettura di M. Vitruvio,* trans. D. Barbaro, Venice, 1556, 159; *Architecture ou art de bien bastir,* trans. J. Martin, Paris, 1547, fol. 77v. In a German edition, the passage is translated as "das Tragicum wird geziert mit Columnen, Fastigiis unnd bildern, und andern herlichen dingen" (*Vitruvius teutsch . . . ,* trans. W. Ryff, Nuremberg, 1548, fol. CLXXX v).

balustrades. [Thus far the 1673 edition;[9] the edition of 1684 continues:] And it is in this that our palaces in France differ from those of Italy, most of which have no other quality in the main façade than that of the house of a bourgeois. The design the Cavalier Bernini made for the Louvre [Figs. 40, 41] was of this sort, having nothing of grandeur except its length, width, and height. By contrast, in Paris, not only the royal palaces, like the Louvre and the Luxembourg, are in another style, which has nothing except nobility and magnificence, but even many of those of private individuals, like the Hôtel Mazarin, the Hôtel de la Vrillière, and several others.[10]

In citing the Luxembourg Palace, the Hôtel Mazarin (Chevry-Tubeuf), and the Hôtel de La Vrillière, Perrault was surely thinking of the unpierced entrance screens between the central portals and end pavilions of those buildings. (The screen of the Luxembourg Palace was pierced with arches in the early nineteenth century.)[11]

In Perrault's mind, therefore, a royal palace, whether painted or real, to be in conformity with Vitruvius and antique usage, must not have any (or perhaps only a few) windows. An additional clue to Perrault's thinking about the Louvre—in particular, about the ground floor of the east façade—is found in another footnote in his Vitruvius editions. In a passage justifying the use of the colossal order for the new Louvre façades, he states that the order "is placed upon the ground story, which serves as a pedestal and which is properly called the rampart of the château."[12] Thus, Perrault regarded the *rez-de-chaussée* as a fortification wall or rampart, a feature to be pierced with a minimum of openings even if it was only a symbolic, not a real, fortification.

The windows of the ground floor of the executed east façade (Figs. 43, 46) can be found in the earliest drawing of our series (Fig. 59); they were meant to conform to Lescot's ground-floor windows of the sixteenth-century Louvre (Fig. 9). A deviation from this canonical form is found, perhaps significantly, in the perspective drawing attributed to Perrault (Fig. 67), where the *rez-de-chaussée* is lower than that built (or found in the other drawings) and the windows are

9. "Il est aisé de conclure de la comparaison qui est icy faite de la Scene Tragique avec la Comique, qu'il doit y avoir autre chose que la grandeur de l'ex[h]aussement qui fasse la difference d'un Palais Royal d'avec une Maison particuliere qui a des fenestres sur la principale entrée, au lieu qu'un Palais ne doit avoir que des colonnes, des Statuës & des Ballustrades" (Perrault, *Vitruve,* 1673, 170 n. 2). The passage to this point was first quoted by W. D. Brönner, *Blondel-Perrault. Zur Architekturtheorie des 17. Jahrhunderts in Frankreich,* publ. diss., Bonn, 1972, 108. Brönner was the first to indicate its significance in connection with the Colonnade.

10. "Et c'est en quoy nos Palais en France sont differens de ceux d'Italie, qui la pluspart n'ont point d'autre caractere à la principale face que celuy de la maison d'un Bourgeois. Le dessein que le Cavalier Ber[n]in avoit donné pour le Louvre estoit de cette espece n'ayant rien de grand, que la longueur, la largeur & la hauteur: au contraire à Paris non seulement les Palais Royaux, comme le Louvre & Luxembourg, sont de l'autre maniere qui n'a rien que de noble & de magnifique, mais mesme beaucoup de ceux des particuliers comme l'Hostel Mazarin, l'Hostel de la Vrill[i]ere & plusieurs autres" (Perrault, *Vitruve,* 1684, 180 n. 2). In his *Ordonnance des cinq espèces de colonnes selon la méthode des anciens,* Paris, 1683, Perrault defended the use of coupled columns by claiming that they better permitted unobstructed doors and windows (see Sources II, no. 25), but he was not referring specifically to the Louvre, a "Palais Royal."

11. R. Coope, *Salomon de Brosse and the Development of the Classical Style in French Architecture from 1565 to 1630,* University Park, Pa., and London, 1972, 117, figs. 141, 150, 151.

12. Perrault, *Vitruve,* 1673, 204 n. 2: ". . . est posé sur l'étage Terrain qui luy sert comme de Piedestail, & qui est proprement le rempart du Château."

squat and without keystone masks. There is also no moat. The ungainly windows, in marked contrast to the generously large and elegant windows based on Lescot's, may indicate Perrault's first step toward his final proposed solution with no windows at all in the ground story.

The Petit Conseil accepted Perrault's idea of substituting niches for windows but rejected his final proposal for military trophies instead of windows. The tall windows based on Lescot's were built, thus lightening the appearance of the ground floor and, it is important to note, providing much light for the rooms within.

THE LION-HEAD WATERSPOUTS (1674)

In June 1674, the builders of the Colonnade were ready to hoist two stones of prodigious length to form the raking cornices of the great pediment (on these stones and the construction history, see Chapter V). On June 25, before this operation took place, Claude Perrault suddenly appeared before the Royal Academy of Architecture (see Sources II, no. 17). Although Perrault rarely attended meetings, both he and his brother Charles were regarded as full members.[13] Claude wanted that body to consent to his suggestion that the lion-head waterspouts, which had evidently been affixed to the horizontal and/or the raking cornices of the central pavilion, should be eliminated. The academicians agreed with Perrault, and this decision must have entailed last-minute adjustments by the stone-carvers before the raking cornices (if indeed they had received the spouts) were hoisted. Thus, the horizontal and raking cornices of the great pediment of the Colonnade (as well as those on the north and south façades) appear today without waterspouts; waterspouts do appear, however, on the topmost cornice moldings (simae) elsewhere (Figs. 49, 53).[14]

This episode reveals that Claude Perrault was busying himself with the smallest details of the Louvre and, in this instance, engrossed with a feature specifically discussed by Vitruvius, whose treatise Perrault had just published in a translated and annotated edition (1673). In the Roman architect's discussion of the cornice of the Ionic order (and, by extension, that of the Corinthian order, which Vitruvius says may employ an Ionic entablature [IV.1.2]), we read (III.5.15):

> On the mouldings, which are above the cornice on the sides of temples, lions' heads are to be carved, and arranged firstly so as to be set over against the tops of the several columns; the others at equal intervals so as to answer to the middle of the roof tiling. But these which will be against the columns are to be pierced for a gutter which takes the rainwater from the tiles. The intervening heads are to be solid so that the water which falls over the tiles into the gutter may not fall down through the intercolumniations

---

13. Herrmann, *Perrault*, 28–30.

14. The spouts first appear in Figures 69–72.

upon the passers by. But those which are against the columns are to seem to vomit and let fall streams of water from their mouths.[15]

The designers of Louis XIV's Louvre had placed the lion-head spouts only over columns and pilasters and not between (Figs. 49, 53) (as the above passage reveals, Vitruvius had recommended the latter usage as well, but with "solid," unpierced heads). The Roman architect, however, had not discussed the issue of waterspouts in the cornices of pediments. Evidently such spouts had been carved on the cornices of the Louvre pediment. Perrault had noticed this, pondered over it, and finally informed the Academy of his judgment. That judgment accorded with ancient practice—as illustrated, for example, by the well-known Temple of Fortuna Virilis, Rome, where the spouts appear only on the flanks of the building, not at the pedimented ends.

The Attics (1676–1679)

Chapter III notes that designs for the east façade in 1667 and early 1668 (Figs. 59, 62, 67, 69–72) included an upper story and/or high roofs over the corner pavilions; not until the detailed study in the Archives Nationales (Fig. 73) do we have a first indication of the renunciation of such ideas. Le Clerc's frontispiece for Perrault's 1673 *Vitruve* (Fig. 117) shows the flat skyline that we know in the actual structure (Figs. 42–44). In 1676, however, Jean Marot engraved an elevation of the Colonnade with attics over the end pavilions (Fig. 88), and these reappeared two years later in his print of the south façade (Fig. 100). Between these dates, on March 29, 1677, Claude Perrault appeared before the Royal Academy of Architecture with a model of the Louvre attic, "fait par M. Perrault" (Sources II, no. 20[a]). The minutes for that date read as follows:

> The Academy also saw the model of the attic of the Louvre pavilions, made by M. Perault, which it found very beautiful; it [the Academy] has only one doubt concerning how thick the attic walls must be in order to carry the carpentry of the cupola with

---

15. Vitruvius, *On Architecture* (Loeb Classical Library), I, 197. This passage was accurately translated by Perrault (*Vitruve*, 1673, 97–98), except that he translated *tegula* not as "roof tiling" (made of terra-cotta) but as "stone" (*pierre*). In a note (97–98 n. 10), Perrault defended his translation by observing that ordinary tiles "fait couler l'eau également partout," whereas only stones "font des rebords à droit et à gauche qui amassent l'eau dans leur milieu . . . ," which thereby can be channeled to the lion-head waterspouts. And in his 1673 Vitruvius edition—evidently with the construction of the Louvre in mind—he had criticized Palladio's reconstructions of ancient temples as follows: "Palladio n'a pas observé ce precepte de Vitruve [that the edges of roofing stones should be aligned with the spouts] dans ses Temples anciens qu'il couvre de grandes pierres plattes: car leurs milieux répondent entre les colonnes, & non au droit des testes de lion, par lesquelles l'eau doit s'écouler: car bien qu'il n'y ait que les testes de lion que l'on met au droit du milieu des colonnes, qui soient percées pour jetter l'eau, la Symmetrie demande que toutes les pierres qui font la couverture, se rapportent par tout d'une mesme façon aux testes de lion" (*Vitruve*, 1673, 98 n. 10). Cf., e.g., A. Palladio, *Les quatre livres d'architecture*, trans. R. Fréart de Chambray, Paris, 1650, pl. on 234 (Temple of Jupiter, Quirinal Hill, Rome).

which it will be covered, [the Academy] not knowing if the walls below are sufficiently thick to support it [the cupola], in view of the stepback which the balustrade that turns around it has to make there. Because of this matter [the Academy] has postponed resolution of the difficulties until the next meeting, when it will have seen the accurate plans, which must be sent to it.

The cupola of the model agreed with a destroyed drawing by Perrault that featured, according to J. F. Blondel (1756), "a depressed cupola [*une calotte surbaissée*] on a circular plan, surmounted by a balustrade and lantern," the whole placed upon the attic to give it more prominence (Sources II, no. 84[b]). However, the cupolas are absent from Marot's prints of 1676 and 1678 (Figs. 88, 100), but these clearly show the drums of the attics set back from the corners of the façade to accommodate the balustrades, and the three-dimensional form of these attics with their curved roofs is clearly revealed in de Fer's engraving of 1705 (Fig. 122).

After the 1677 meeting, the academicians did not take up the question of Perrault's attics for more than a year and a half. On December 5, 1678, the minutes of a further consideration were recorded (Sources II, no. 20[b]):

> Afterward, concerning what has been proposed to [the Academy] on the part of Monseigneur Colbert about the subject of the roofing of the Louvre, for which Monsieur Perault has given the design and has had the model brought to the Academy, on which the Academy has not found it apropos to dwell in order to approve it, after what it has said before about the advantage of the manner of good building by Philibert de l'Orme;[16] [the Academy] is only interested in considering the rendered drawing [*la figure du trait*], which it has very much approved concerning the given widths, observing the intervals of the curves, according to the weight requirements of the roofing. The tie-beam placed in the same model must not be considered an absolutely necessary piece, because one can do without it since that work [de l'Orme's wooden framework], which produces neither thrust nor weight, is particularly suitable for [constructions] of great height and width. Thought was given, concerning the vaults that they would like to paint [*sic*], that it would be necessary to make a double roof or arch.

This entry shows the Academy approving both the general form of the attics and their structure—apparently a direct copy of one of de l'Orme's curved wooden roofs (the cupola idea had apparently been discarded by Perrault).

One week later, on December 12, the Academy returned to Perrault's proposal (Sources II, no. 20[c]). The minutes state that Perrault brought his attic designs, which were in conformity with the models the Academy had already received. The question for the Academy was to decide on Perrault's two structural proposals: (1) to step back the attics from the edges of the

---

16. Perrault's attics used a wooden framework derived from Philibert de l'Orme's *Nouvelles inventions pour bien bastir et à petits fraiz . . .* , Paris, 1561 (possibly the design illustrated on fol. 10r and discussed on fols. 7r–10v [I, v–vii]). This book had been read in the Académie in 1677 (*PV*, I, 153f.).

building to leave room for a passage and balustrade on the roof or (2) to place the walls of the attics directly on the exterior walls. After lengthy discussion, the Academy chose the first alternative, judged to be "plus noble et plus agréable," but with the proviso that the attics be raised in height "to restore what the balustrade removes from it [the attic] by optics" (i.e., when viewed from ground level).

The next month, on January 23, 1679 (Sources II, no. 20[d]), the Academy studied the models of the Colonnade with the attics added, but the opinions of each member, requested by Colbert, were not recorded.

Marot's engraving of the south elevation (1678; Fig. 100) depicts Perrault's attic above the southwest pavilion (the Pavillon du Roi) of the Cour Carrée; as in Figure 88 of 1676, the attics are stepped back from the walls below to accommodate a passage and a balustrade. The attics in Figure 100, however, are slightly higher than those in Figure 88, thus incorporating the Academy's recommendation of December 12; Marot presumably made this engraving immediately after that date. The other alternative discussed on December 12—to place the attic walls directly over the outer ones below—appears in one of Perrault's drawings (Fig. 113).[17] In this large, finished sheet principally showing courtyard elevations (two proposals for the top floor are depicted; see Chapter V), there is no balustrade around the attics, which are of the low form seen in Marot's 1676 engraving; we may safely date the drawing ca. 1676. Perrault here proposes curious, open columnar finials (miniature temple-fronts), supporting royal globes and fleurs-de-lis. These (as well as the low balustrades atop the attics in Figure 88) were totally eliminated by 1678, if Marot's print of that year is accurate (Fig. 100).

Figures 88 and 113 depict the attics densely decorated with framed scenes, trophies, and garlands reminiscent of Perrault's proposed decorations for his triumphal arch (Figs. 117, 120). In Marot's engraving (Fig. 88) the scenes have a distinctly military flavor; in Perrault's drawing, classical or allegorical subjects are suggested. These presumably sculpted decorations are omitted in Figure 100; perhaps by that date Perrault had judged them useless, because of their distance from the spectator.[18]

Perrault's proposed attics may have been a response to criticisms that the Colonnade was too low. In 1683, François Blondel, Director of the Royal Academy of Architecture, published the second and last installment of his *Cours d'architecture,* in which he wrote:

> I forgot to say that doubling the columns extremely alters the beautiful proportions of buildings, the width of which is so greatly increased by them [the coupled columns] that they [the buildings] appear dwarfish and crushed [*nains & ecrasez*], whatever pains one

---

17. On this drawing, see Chapter V. J. F. Blondel reported in 1756 that the manuscript *recueil* of Claude's designs (destroyed in 1871) contained several drawings of the attics, one of which featured "une colonnade percée à jour, en forme de petit Temple terminé par un fronton qui lui servoit de toît" (see Sources II, no. 84[b], where Blondel briefly describes several drawings by Perrault for the attics). Another Perrault drawing noted by Blondel without the open colonnade but with a balustrade corresponds to Figure 88.

18. Charles Perrault in 1690 kept the idea of an attic alive in the engraving representing "L'Architecture," published in his *Le cabinet des beaux-arts . . . ,* Paris, 1690, between 23 and 24 (reproduced in [Paris, Ministère de la culture], *Colbert, 1619–1683,* exhib. cat., Paris, 1983, 302, no. 443).

takes to raise them either by attics or by other means. These flat styles [*manieres plattes*] that Vitruvius calls Barices or Barycephales [III.3.5] are absolutely contrary to the good taste of the ancients, who were, as Vitruvius says, *gracilioribus modulis delectati* [III.1.8], that is, who took great pleasure in slender and open styles [*manieres "suelte[s]" & degagées*]. [See Appendix B]

Blondel's *Cours* was based on his lectures delivered in the Academy. It is possible, although not provable, that he began to criticize the Colonnade along these lines in the mid-1670s and that Perrault then attempted to remedy the criticism ca. 1676, in which year Marot published the earlier of his prints (Fig. 88). In any event, the attics were never executed.[19]

19. The temporary roof that appears in some prints above the southeast pavilion of the Cour Carrée was not put up for the erection of Perrault's attic; rather, it served to facilitate the demolition of the top floor of Le Vau's corner pavilion of 1660–63 (Fig. 17; see, e.g., A. Picon, *Claude Perrault, 1613–1688, ou la curiosité d'un classique,* Paris, 1988, 170, fig. 127).

V
BUILDING THE LOUVRE

The construction of the Colonnade began during the summer of 1667; the first payment to entrepreneurs André Mazières and Antoine Bergeron is dated July 29 (Chapter III; see Sources I, no. 3). We have noted that construction activity in 1667 followed an initial design with narrow, conservative end pavilions based on Lescot's Pavillon du Roi of the preceding century (cf. Figs. 9 and 59). Probably in the first half of 1668 the entire design was revised, with notably wider terminal pavilions, one of which corresponded to the new doubled depth of the south wing, which was to receive a new façade (Figs. 76, 95). Once the Petit Conseil had finished its task of redesign, construction activity resumed at a frantic pace. The change of design necessitated amendments to the foundations,[1] but, already by the end of

---

1. The revelation of the dry moat and foundations (1964–67) allowed a careful inspection of the masonry, which clearly accords with the known construction history. The report of the chief architect is worth quoting *in extenso*:

> L'édification du soubassement de la façade de la Colonnade . . . laisse apparaitre l'élargissement en cours d'exécution, de l'avant-corps central et des deux pavillons extrêmes. Au centre, les maçonneries de fon-

dation sont appareillées assez régulièrement, correspondant à un avant-corps relativement étroit, fondations élargies après coup par un blocage moins soigné d'appareil, ne suivant pas les mêmes lits d'assises et permettant d'asseoir l'avant-corps central actuel. . . .

L'élargissement des pavillons d'angle est très net, tant dans les sous-sols de la Colonnade que sur le parement extérieur du soubassement; les bossages des

1668, Colbert could write in a *mémoire* on projected Louvre construction for 1669 (Sources II, no. 7):

> Carefully examine everything to be done at the Louvre.
> Erect the doubled wing on the river side.
> Erect the peristyle on the façade up to the cornice.
> Promptly resolve everything that concerns the peristyle, together with the attic elevation within [the courtyard], in order to be able to work without stop from the first day of March.

The erection of the new Louvre façades from 1667 on—by an army of laborers and their machines, instruments, tools, and materials—must have presented a daily spectacle indicative of the wealth and artistic ambitions of the Crown. In 1673 a medal (Fig. 85) was struck, suggesting that the east façade had been completed. Yet a special feat of engineering and construction lay ahead: placement of the two stones of the raking cornice of the central pediment. In July 1673, the scientist Christian Huygens reported that one of the stones had already reached Paris by boat. Huygens had gone to the quarry near Meudon, whence the stone had come, and reported its incredible dimensions: 52 *pieds* long, 8 *pieds* wide, and only 1½ *pieds* (18 *pouces*) thick (16.85 by 2.59 by 0.16 m), an unprecedented combination of great length and extreme thinness (Sources II, no. 14).[2] Furthermore, each stone weighed more than 80,000 French pounds, according to Claude Perrault.[3] By June 1674, both stones, apparently complete in all carved details, were lying in the Louvre *chantier* waiting to be hoisted into place. The June issue of the *Mercure galant* expressed popular amazement: "Never has a stone of such prodigious

---

chaînes d'angle sont toujours les mêmes depuis Pierre Lescot, mais les chaînes de Le Vau [of his project halted in 1664, Figures 33–35] et de la Colonnade n° 1 [Figs. 59, 64] présentent des décrochements d'une assise sur deux, tandis que les plus récents, de la Colonnade n° 2 [Figs. 74, 76], plus longs sont alignés verticalement. Au Sud, on a construit le pavillon d'angle rapidement en enjambant provisoirement les soubassements de Le Vau. Au Nord, le soubassement de Le Vau n'existant pas, on a construit définitivement. Nous devons également signaler, dans les deux angles rentrants de la Colonnade sur les pavillons d'angle, des décrochements n'existant qu'en soubassement et que les pierres des parements du soubassement de la Colonnade viennent s'appliquer, en découpe, sur les bossages pénétrants à l'intérieur du mur, laissant à penser que le parement actuel est en avant d'un parement plus ancien. Du côté Nord, sur la rue de Rivoli, en élargissant le pavillon d'angle de la Colonnade, fut amorcé sur 2 mètres environ de longueur, en soubassement seulement, le doublage de la façade Nord, comme il fut réalisé au Sud. [J. Trouvelot, "Le dégagement des fossés de la Colonnade du Louvre," *MHF,* n.s., XIII, 1967, 36/38] On the foundations, see also M. Whiteley and A. Braham, "Les soubassements de l'aile orientale du Louvre," *RA,* no. 4, 1969, 40f.

2. According to André Félibien (Sources II, no. 18[b]), the two stones came from one large piece, cut in two. A. C. d'Aviler judged stone from or near Meudon to be similar to Arcueil (the hardest stone of the Parisian region), "mais elle n'est pas si bonne pour resister aux injures du tems. [Elle] sert à faire des premieres assises, des marches & des tablettes" (*Cours d'architecture . . . ,* Paris, 1694, I, 204). It is therefore curious to find Meudon stone chosen for such an exposed location, but, as d'Aviler notes (I, 205), it could be found in pieces of extraordinary length. Félibien judged the stone to be similar to Liais. Payments for quarry excavations for these stones began as early as December 6, 1670 (see Sources I, no. 56).

3. Perrault, *Vitruve,* 1684, 339 n. 4.

length been seen since the loss of the secret that the Egyptians had discovered to melt (*fondre*) stones" (Sources II, no. 16).[4]

In Chapter IV we discussed Claude Perrault's role in having the lion-head waterspouts removed from the raking cornices and/or the horizontal cornice of the pediment, the latter member already in place. In September, the two huge stones were lifted and set in place by means of ingenious machines designed by Poncelet Cliquin, a celebrated carpenter (Fig. 87).[5] The operation was recorded in an engraving by Le Clerc (Fig. 86).[6] The feat was explicitly regarded by the French as their answer to the celebrated removal and reerection of the obelisk of Piazza San Pietro in Rome (1585–87, under Domenico Fontana), which had been illustrated by engravings published in 1590 and again in 1604.[7] French pride in this engineering feat is conveyed by an anonymous passage added to Sauval's history of Paris, where the comparison with the Vatican obelisk is made, the latter being "much easier to put in place than these two great stones." Moreover (the passage continues), "the Italians, great admirers of their [own] inventions, have spoken of this machine as something quite remarkable and without precedent" (Sources II, no. 64).

Drawings made in 1678 by the members of the Royal Academy of Architecture (see Chapter VI) lead us to other parts of the new Louvre of Louis XIV. Figure 114 is a sectional view and plan of part of the *rez-de-chaussée* of the east range, showing two bays of the Galerie Basse (left) and half of the central vestibule in its original, pre-Napoleonic condition (cf. Fig. 88, plan, right half).[8] The drawing suggests that the ground floor was still unvaulted in 1678, and this impression is reinforced by another sheet in the same series (Fig. 115, right), a section of the inner (courtside) wall, showing the evidently unvaulted vestibule to the right, the courtside columns on high pedestals to the left. Work on the Louvre was halted after 1680 (see Sources I), and these interior spaces were not vaulted until the mid-eighteenth century.

4. Cf. this passage from F. Blondel's "Discours" (December 31, 1671), published in Blondel, 1675: "Voyons ensuite ce que firent les Egyptiens? Ces Temples monolytes ou faits d'un seul morceau de marbre foüillé dans des carrieres éloignées & amené à force de bras par des machines inconcevables?"

5. Herrmann (*Perrault*, 191–192) argues convincingly that these machines were due to Cliquin and that the central machine in Figure 87 illustrates Perrault's improved mechanism, which would have obviated the need to test the cables continually. Cliquin received his first payment for the machines as early as December 6, 1672 to January 5, 1673; later payments are recorded in 1674 (Sources I, nos. 101, 126–130). On these machines and their operation, see also R. Blomfield, *A History of French Architecture from the Death of Mazarin till the Death of Louis XV, 1661–1774*, London, 1921, I, 78–79. The machine is also illustrated in an engraving of "La Mechanique," published in Ch. Perrault, *Le cabinet des beaux-arts . . .* , Paris, 1690, between 39 and 40. Perrault writes (39–40): "Nous avons vû des pierres plus grandes et plus lourdes que des rochers s'élever par les forces de son Art sur le frontispice du plus grand de tous les palais."

6. Two medals were designed in 1675 to commemorate the event. One bears the inscription NEC·PONDVS·OBSTITIT· (illus. in T. Sauvel, "Les auteurs de la colonnade du Louvre," *BMon*, CXXII, 1964, 329, fig. 5, bottom). A second, attributed to Sébastien Le Clerc, has the motto NVLLVM NON MOVEO LAPIDEM, with reference to Colbert. The drawing for this medal, contained in a manuscript volume of *devises*, is accompanied by verses, also referring to Colbert: "Par mille beaux succes ma puissance est connue, / Les plus pesans fardeaux ne sont faits que pour moy: / Sur tout quand il s'agit de la gloire du Roy / Il n'est rien que je ne remuë" (*Collections de Louis XIV, dessins, albums, manuscrits*, exhib. cat., Paris, 1977, 240, fig. 234, 241, no. 234.)

7. D. Fontana, *Della trasportatione dell'obelisco vaticano*, ed. A. Carugo, Milan, 1978 (Facsimile of the Rome 1590 and Naples 1604 eds.). Fontana's book contains numerous prints of the undertaking.

8. The Doric pilasters seen in Figure 114 still survive in the Galerie Basse (now filled with Egyptian and Assyrian antiquities). The present vestibule with decorated Roman Doric columns was created under Napoleon by Percier and Fontaine, beginning in 1807 or 1808. The reliefs of *Religion* and *Justice*, attributed to the studio of Jean Goujon, were removed from the sixteenth-century south wing and transported to this location in 1807.

The Cour Carrée, into which this last drawing (Fig. 105) brings us, has a complex history.⁹ The northward expansion of the courtyard under Lemercier (1624–41) ensured that Lescot's Renaissance design (Fig. 10) would be faithfully reproduced around the court, at least for the two lower stories, articulated by a Corinthian order surmounted by a Composite one. In Lescot's design, these lower floors, of approximately equal height, are topped by a low story, or attic, decorated with dwarf pilasters and relief sculpture. Lemercier had repeated this scheme to the north (Fig. 14).

Sometime during 1668, after the designs for the Colonnade and the new south façade had been finalized, the Petit Conseil turned to the task of completing the design of the Cour Carrée. Charles Perrault, in a note included in the 1693 manuscript *recueil* of his brother's drawings (see Sources II, no. 38[d]), revealed that some people believed Lescot's attic was sufficiently high only for a courtyard one-fourth the area of the present one; the latter, however, demanded to be surrounded by higher wings because of its much greater size. Charles indicated that he and his brother disagreed with this judgment, and particularly with those who maintained that the height of a building should be proportioned to its length. In addition, Charles, at least, believed that it was inappropriate for the King's *premier étage* to be surmounted by a story "as beautiful, as large, and with a ceiling as high as the one which he [the King] occupies and to which it is necessary to climb almost one hundred and twenty-six steps."[10] Charles Perrault, for one, believed that Lescot's attic was more appropriate for lodging the officers who had to be near the King's person than was a full *deuxième étage*.

An early indication of what the Petit Conseil thought about this matter is seen in Figure 67, where the attic is omitted entirely all around the court. If this drawing is indeed by Claude Perrault, omission of the attic is not in accord with Charles's testimony, just reviewed, that he and his brother approved of Lescot's top story. In any event, Claude's thinking was soon to change. Two drawings by d'Orbay, probably also from 1668 (Figs. 107, 108), depict a full top story without visible roofs; the paired Composite pilasters would have aligned with the columns of the *avant-corps* of the *premier étage* below. This suggestion was not adopted.

A document of 1669 or 1670 (Sources II, no. 8) reveals, in the stated opinions of seven architects and masons, that three models showing three ideas for the top floor of the courtyard had been constructed.[11] One version featured an engaged Composite order with pilasters be-

9. Hautecoeur, *Louvre et Tuileries,* 182–186; Hautecoeur, *HAC,* I, 450f.; J. P. Babelon, "La cour carrée du Louvre: Les tentatives des siècles pour maîtriser un espace urbain mal défini," *BMon,* CXLII, 1984, 43f.; A. Picon, *Claude Perrault, 1613–1688, ou la curiosité d'un classique,* Paris, 1988, 187f.

10. Charles's argument here is quite similar to one by the anonymous critic in the "Advis de M. le Vau le jeune sur le nouveau dessin du Louvre" (Sources II, no. 6[5a]); in this passage the critic, in turn, echoed the thinking of Roland Fréart de Chambray (see Chapter III). The relationship between the two passages was noted by Picon (*Claude Perrault,* 187), who, however, wrongly attributed the passage in the 1693 manuscript *recueil* to Claude.

11. Payments for these models are recorded in *CBR*:
[December 24, 1668]: A [Étienne] Le Hongre, . . . sculpteur, à compte des chapiteaux et autres ornemens qu'il fait au modèle du troisième ordre du bastiment du Louvre . . . 200 [livres]. [I, col. 245]

[May 17, 1669]: au sʳ Le Hongre, pour parfait payement de la sculpture du modelle de l'eslévation du 3ᵉ estage du dedans de la cour du Louvre . . . 325 [livres]. [I, col. 321]

[June 11, 1671]: à Estienne Le Hongre, sculpteur, pour parfait payement de 636 [livres] à quoy monte la sculpture qu'il a faite au modelle du troisième ordre du

tween the *avant-corps* and windows like those of the *premier étage*—essentially a repetition of Lescot's main floor. The top floor of this first model, therefore, was as high or almost as high as the floor below, and this rejection of Lescot's low attic for a full story was probably motivated by a desire to avoid visible, sloping roofs that would clash with the new east, south, and north façades, with their roofless skylines. A high *deuxième étage* was probably the case in the other two models as well. The second model displayed caryatids holding baskets of flowers and fruit, while the third seems to have been rather complex, with niches and figures on pedestals apparently supporting columns (see Sources II, no. 8e).

The second model, the one with caryatids, followed the design of Claude Perrault, as a note by Charles Perrault accompanying Claude's destroyed drawing attests:

> *Claude Perrault* proposed caryatids for all of this top floor. This type of decoration was heartily applauded, but, having considered that one hundred and forty figures of women aligned on the same level in poses that would be impossible to vary would create a monotonous decoration, they decided upon the French Composite order, which today is found erected above the Italic Composite order.[12]

Because the second model displayed Perrault's proposal, it is tempting to surmise that the other two embodied the ideas of Le Vau (the first model?) and Le Brun (the third model?). Unfortunately, there is scant further trace of these designs. Charles Perrault's indication of 140 caryatids in Claude's model suggests strongly that Claude ranged these figures around all four sides of the courtyard,[13] thus replacing the western attic of Lescot and Lemercier with a higher story. This probably called for the dismantling of the visible roofs of this wing, so that in Claude's proposal all sides of the court had a uniform balustraded skyline without visible roofs.

We have seen that Colbert, thinking late in 1668 about work at the Louvre for the coming year, called for prompt resolution of the question of the upper story of the courtyard. Not until 1669 or 1670, however, did he receive the opinions of the experts on the three models (Sources II, no. 8). One of those consulted, the architect Thomas Gamard, had suggested that a new, French order be invented as the solution to the problem (Sources II, no. 8[a][9]), and in 1671 Colbert took up Gamard's idea and proclaimed an open competition for a French order for the top floor of the Cour Carrée.[14] Proposals were presented in 1671 and 1672, and one of the

---

Louvre au dedans de la cour, en 1669 . . . 336 [livres]. [1, col. 495]

A payment to François Girardon must be for work on one of the models, although that is not explicitly stated [April 12, 1670]: "à Girardon, sculpteur, à compte de la sculpture qu'il fait au troisième ordre du Louvre . . . 400 [livres] (1, col. 406).

12. For the French text, see Sources II, no. 38(d). Charles is confirmed by J. F. Blondel, who wrote: "On voit dans le premier volume manuscrit de *Perrault,* page 51, une élévation où il avoit substitué aux colonnes des figures de femmes" (*Architecture françoise,* Paris, 1756, IV, 64 n. q).

13. One hundred forty caryatids distributed on four sides of the court is 35 caryatids per side. This number accords better with the solid-void distribution of the upper floor than does 46.6 per side (= 140 caryatids ÷ 3).

14. On this competition, see Sources II, no. 38(d) (Charles Perrault); Hautecoeur, *Louvre et Tuileries,* 184f.; J. M. Pérouse de Montclos, "Le sixième ordre d'architecture, ou la pratique des ordres suivant les nations," *JSAH,* XXXVI, 1977, 226f. See also Sources II, note 156.

competitors was Claude Perrault, whose design for a French order appears in the frontispiece of his 1673 Vitruvius edition (Fig. 117). In the left foreground, we see a Corinthianesque capital of ostrich feathers, from which peers the head of the Gallic cock; fleurs-de-lis run around the base of these feathers. The fragment of a cornice in the right foreground is surely part of the order, although it features no overt French symbolism.[15] Another former member of the Petit Conseil, Charles Le Brun, also came forward with a French order in 1671.[16]

The proposals of Perrault, Le Brun, and others have been studied elsewhere and need not detain us here.[17] By 1678, however, only a few bays of the *deuxième étage* on the east side of the court had been erected, but with columns, pilasters, and some decorative forms left unfinished, awaiting the sculptor's hand (Fig. 112). According to Charles Perrault, the capitals were to be of a French Composite order of Claude's design (Sources II, no. 38[c, d]), but this is difficult to understand in the light of the Corinthianesque capital in Claude's frontispiece (Fig. 117). The new *deuxième étage* was essentially a repetition of the *premier étage,* with the height of the story slightly decreased—the approximate form of the first model. Two almost-identical drawings by d'Orbay (Figs. 109, 110), probably dating from the mid-1670s,[18] depict the almost-final scheme[19] as applied (probably) to Lescot's western range, where the original high roof was to be retained. The top floor in this solution would not have been in horizontal alignment with the Pavillon de l'Horloge (cf. Fig. 14), and this may explain why, in the end, Lescot's attic was retained. In Figure 110, flaps pasted within the arches of the ground floor propose two new portals flanked by niches—another suggestion not carried out. An anonymous working drawing with detailed measurements (Fig. 111)[20] brings us closer to the definitive design, except that the detailing of the capitals is omitted and the proposed medallion-swag motif sketched in black chalk above the left niche was rejected in favor of rectilinear tablets. This last sheet probably dates from slightly later than Figures 109 and 110.

The courtyard remained unfinished from this time (1678) until the campaigns of the mid-eighteenth century (Gabriel) and early nineteenth century (Percier and Fontaine). In 1806, the decision was made to preserve the attic and visible roofs of the west wing and to finish the other

15. On Perrault's French order, see d'Aviler, *Cours d'architecture,* I, 298. D'Aviler interpreted the ring of fleurs-de-lis as a princely (open) crown. See also Pérouse de Montclos, "Le sixième ordre," 230–231.

16. On Le Brun's French order, see the bibliographical note in R. W. Berger, "Charles Le Brun and the Louvre Colonnade," *AB,* LII, 1970, 402–403, to which should be added C. Nivelon, *Vie de Charles Le Brun & description détaillée de ses ouvrages,* BN, Manuscrits, MS fr. 12987, 357 (ca. 1700); J. Langner, "Zum Entwurf der französischen Ordnung von Le Brun," *Kunstgeschichtliche Studien für Kurt Bauch zum 70. Geburtstag von seinen Schülern,* Berlin, 1967, 233–240; Pérouse de Montclos, "Le sixième ordre," 229; 230, fig. 9; and 231.

17. See above, note 14.

18. Figure 109: 26.5 by 35.0 cm, black ink, washes, framed; Laprade, *d'Orbay,* pl. VI.12, top (attrib. to d'Orbay); [Paris, Ministère de la culture], *Colbert, 1619–1683,* exhib. cat., Paris, 1983, 291, no. 427 (attrib. to d'Orbay (?) [entry by N. Felkay]). Figure 110: 28.9 by 37.6 cm, graphite, gray ink, blue wash; E. Berckenhagen, *Die französische Zeichnungen der Kunstbibliothek Berlin,* Berlin, 1970, 124–125 (attrib. to d'Orbay).

19. Niches are absent in the *avant-corps* of the top floor (cf. Figs. 109, 110).

20. Measuring 29.3 by 42.3 cm, brown ink, wash, black chalk; several inscriptions and numerous measurements.

three sides with the high *deuxième étage* worked out under Louis XIV (Fig. 105). This decision necessitated the destruction of Lescot's attic of the south wing and resulted in the nonuniform appearance of the Cour Carrée we see today.[21]

A large drawing by Perrault (Fig. 113)[22] showing his proposed attics over the corner pavilions (see Chapter IV) offers alternative designs for the *deuxième étage:* the right side repeats Lescot's pedimented windows of the floor below, the left shows arched openings based on the top floor of Lescot's Pavillon du Roi (Fig. 9), with a radiant Apollo's head above the apex of the arch and cornucopia and branches filling the spandrels. The capitals appear to be in Perrault's Corinthianesque French order. Because several bays of the right-hand proposal had been built by 1678, it seems likely that Perrault's drawing dates from ca. 1676, the date that appears on a Marot engraving (Fig. 88; see Chapter IV), which is the earliest securely dated document concerning the attics.[23] Apparently, a final decision by the King and Colbert had not yet been made at the moment of this drawing.

As the 1670s wore on, Louis XIV became increasingly engrossed in the development of Versailles. At the end of the decade, work came to a halt (see Sources I). The dry moat, which is indicated in virtually all projects and depictions, was filled in. This may have occurred in 1674, to judge from Le Clerc's engraving (Fig. 86), in order to facilitate placement of the pediment stones; by not reexcavating the moat and not building a *contrescarpe,* expenses were saved, although the *soubassement,* or podium, was now hidden.[24] However, the new Louvre of the Sun King was not entirely finished: the wings were not properly roofed, the courtyard's top floor was incomplete, and much decorative detailing was still to be carved. No matter. The Colonnade with its prodigious pediment appeared finished, a sun palace that made all Europe blink in

---

21. On the later history of the courtyard, see L. Hautecoeur, *Histoire du Louvre: Le château—le palais—le musée à nos jours, 1200–1928,* Paris, [1928], 74, 84; Tadgell, *Ange-Jacques Gabriel,* 194f.; Babelon, "La cour Carrée du Louvre," 50.

22. Measuring 90.0 by 195.0 cm, black ink, gray and black washes; somewhat damaged. Attributed to Perrault by Hautecoeur, *Louvre et Tuileries,* 184, pl. XLVI; Hautecoeur, *HAC,* I, 451, fig. 370; implausibly attributed to the studio of Louis Le Vau by Laprade, *d'Orbay,* pl. appendix C1C (attics only given to Perrault). Contrary to Laprade, the drawing has no *retombes* and must date from the mid-1670s at the earliest; hence, it cannot be ascribed to Le Vau's office (Le Vau died in 1670). The drawing is clearly by the same hand as Figures 69–72.

23. A drawing in the Nationalmuseum, Stockholm (THC 1238), depicting the eastern elevation of the courtyard was first published by R. Josephson as by Perrault ("Quelques dessins de Claude Perrault pour le Louvre," *GBA,* ser. 5, XVI, 1927, 180, 184 [wrongly described as the west elevation of the court]). In my opinion, this is an eighteenth-century project to complete the Louvre. Laprade (*d'Orbay,* pl. VI.6B) published it as an anonymous project of ca. 1666.

24. On the moat, see Whiteley and Braham, "Les soubassements," 43. The reference by J. F. Blondel to a moat visible in 1756 (*Architecture françoise,* IV, 42) is probably to fragments of a moat along the western exterior of the Cour Carrée, as indicated on the Plan Turgot (1739) and in Figure 90. The original eastern moat was uncovered and completed in the 1960s (see Fig. 45). G. Bazin has subsequently argued that Louis XIV, for aesthetic reasons, did not want a moat at the foot of the Colonnade and that the campaign of the 1960s was a mistaken venture ("L'erreur du fossé du Louvre," *Le Monde,* August 20, 1981, 2).

astonishment. It was left to other reigns—those of Louis XV and Napoleon—to restore and complete the architectural masterpiece of *le grand siècle*.[25]

25. On the mid-eighteenth-century work, see Hautecoeur, *Histoire du Louvre,* 72f.; M. Roland-Michel, "The Clearance of the Colonnade of the Louvre: A Study Arising from a Painting by De Machy," *BurlM,* cxx, September 1978, i–vi (Supplement); idem, "Soufflot urbaniste et le dégagement de la colonnade du Louvre," in *Soufflot et l'architecture des lumières,* Paris, 1980, 54–67. See also above, note 21.

VI

MATERIALS AND STRUCTURE

Written in Collaboration with Rowland J. Mainstone

The stone masonry of the new Louvre of Louis XIV was inspected in 1678 by the Royal Academy of Architecture on orders of Colbert as part of a broader survey of the building stones of Paris and its environs. The Academy submitted a report[1] and made several revealing drawings (Figs. 89, 99, 102, 112, 114, 115)[2] that bear detailed annotations of the types of stones used

---

1. The report, written by André Félibien (secretary of the Academy), bears the title *Rapport de l'Académie d'Architecture sur la provenance et la qualité des pierres employées dans les anciens édifices de Paris et des environs* (BN, Manuscrits, MS fr. 12341). The only specific comment on the new Louvre is found under the date July 18: "On a aussi observé au Batiment neuf du Louvre qu'il y a de la pierre de S. Cloud qu'on a employé au Socle attenant le Portail, tant du coté du levant, qu'à celui du Septentrion, laquelle se gate et devient farineuse" (7). The report has been published in L. de Laborde, ed., "Rapport demandé par Colbert en 1678 à l'Académie d'architecture," *Revue générale de l'architecture et des travaux publics,* x, 1852, cols. 194–242, 273–293, 321–344, and in idem, *Mémoires et dissertations,* Paris, 1852, 151–290. A version of the report was entered into the minutes of the Academy (see *PV,* I, 168–249 [July 12– September 22, 1678]; notes by Lemonnier on the report are in I, 325–335). There are some differences in wording between the two published versions. In 1699 the Academy again reviewed the variety of French stones and studied the 1678 report (*PV,* III, 66f. [June 1, 1699]).

2. The drawings were first published by G. Monnier, "Dessins inédits pour la Colonnade du Louvre," *MHF,* n.s., 1972, no. 3–4, 130–137. In the space of this short article, Monnier proposes two different dates for the drawings: 1667–68 (130) and before 1674 (135). But she herself points out (133–134) the close connections between the drawings and the report of the Academy. There can be little doubt that the drawings were made at the same time as the report and were not "modèles destinés au chantier," as described by Monnier on 130. See also [G. Monnier], *Dessins d'architecture du XVe au*

and can be supplemented by another set, probably made ca. 1755 by Pierre Patte.[3] These depictions, as well as payments recorded in the *Comptes* (Sources I), indicate that the new Louvre, like the old, was constructed of a number of esteemed limestones of the Parisian region.[4] Blocks of these stones were laid up in the traditional manner to form the bearing walls of the south and north façades as well as the courtyard elevations (Figs. 95, 101, 105). The Colonnade (Figs. 43, 44), however, was a structural *tour de force,* embodying a revolutionary system of hidden iron reinforcement.

The structural problems of the Colonnade are the result of the large dimensions of the intercolumniations and the weight of the flat ceilings covering the bays between the columns and the rear wall (Figs. 51–53). The distance of the large intercolumniation measured from the side of one column to the other is 12 *pieds,* $2\frac{1}{2}$ *pouces;* the distance between the side of a column and the surface of the corresponding pilaster on the wall behind is 12 *pieds*. If an attempt were made to span these intervals with monolithic stones, serious cracking would occur at the centers of the wide intercolumniations, aggravated by the weight of the flat ceilings resting on the architraves of each bay. For this reason, the architraves and friezes were constructed of a number of voussoirs to form flat arches (*platebandes*) (Fig. 79, top left). The voussoirs, carefully fitted together, inevitably produce outward thrusts. Thrusts generated parallel to the façade are sufficiently absorbed, of course, by the great masses of the central and end pavilions, but thrusts generated at right angles to the façade threatened to push over the freestanding columns with their entablatures in an outward direction, which would be a catastrophic event.

To solve this problem, the masonry was reinforced by embedding within it a network of iron tie rods and cramps completely hidden from view (Figs. 78, 79).[5] In this system, the tensile strength of the iron is used to resist displacements of the columns and slips of the voussoirs, leaving the masonry to act as it is best fitted to do: purely in compression.

Columns. The drums were bored through their centers to receive an iron rod about 2 to 3

XIXe siècle dans les collections du Musée du Louvre, Paris, 1972, 25–27. These drawings were perhaps among the ones referred to in the minutes of the Royal Academy of Architecture (March 15, 1756) as showing "le détail des différentes natures de pierre" (Sources II, no. 87).

3. BN, Estampes, Va 217a.

4. These included several *pierres dures* (Arcueil, Liais, Saint-Cloud, Bonbanc, and Vernon) and *pierres tendres* (Saint-Leu and Trossy). On these stones and their properties, see mainly A. C. d'Aviler, *Cours d'architecture . . . ,* Paris, 1694, I, 202–208. See also A. Félibien, *Des principes de l'architecture, de la sculpture, de la peinture, et des autres arts qui en dependent,* Paris, 1676, 65f.; *PV,* I, 186 (July 27, 1678; Liais), 200–201 (August 5, 1678; Saint-Leu), 246 (September 14, 1678; Saint-Cloud); A. Félibien, *Mémoires pour servir à l'histoire des maisons royales et bastimens de France,* ed. A. de Montaiglon, Paris, 1874 [1681], 76–81; L. Savot, *L'architecture françoise des bastimens particuliers,* ed. F. Blondel, Paris, 1685, 271f.; P. Bullet, *Architecture pratique . . . ,* new ed., Paris, 1768, 282–289 [1st ed. 1691]; N. de Blegny (A. du Pradel), *Le livre commode des adresses de Paris pour 1692,* ed.

E. Fournier, Paris, 1878, II, 111–115; J. F. Blondel, *Architecture françoise,* Paris, 1752, I, 129f. Félibien (*Des principes de l'architecture,* 65) boasted that French stones were finer than Italian stones. The marble columns reported in the *CBR* (Sources I, nos. 17, 35, 59, 65) may have been intended for interiors.

5. This discussion of the structure of the Colonnade is based on Patte (Sources II, no. 94 [1769]); the fine accuracy of his engraved analytical renderings (Fig. 79) was confirmed by the authors of this chapter in a site visit in 1990. The analysis of the central pediment is dependent on Sources II, no. 100 (Patte as continuator of Blondel, 1777). Patte's analyses form the basis for the discussions in J. B. Rondelet, *Traité théorique et pratique de l'art de bâtir* (1st ed., Paris, 1802–17; modified discussions in later editions). Two recent studies bearing on the Louvre structure are P. Saddy, "A 'Construct' of Modernity: The Reinforced Lintel," *Daidalos,* no. 8, June 15, 1983, 54–65, and R. Middleton, "Architects as Engineers: The Iron Reinforcement of Entablatures in Eighteenth-Century France," *AA Files,* no. 9, Summer 1985, 54–64.

pouces in diameter; this rod (in three segments joined together) reaches from the base of the column, through the capital, and into the entablature as high as the cornice (Fig. 79, top row, left and right). Tradition has it that between each pair of column drums there is also a flat, cross-shaped piece (Fig. 79, lower row, right, marked "A"). The vertical rod passes through the center of the column drum, and the four ends of the piece have vertical flanges; two flanges were set into the drum below, two into the drum above (Fig. 79, top row, left, showing only the downward flanges, marked "A"). This system of vertical reinforcement is connected to a horizontal system to form a network as follows:

Architraves. Above each column was placed a large stone block (*sommier*; Fig. 79, top row, left, marked "M"). The large intercolumniations are spanned by flat arches composed of voussoirs (*claveaux*) cut *à crossettes* (/ /). It is especially in these voussoirs that much thrust is created. Each voussoir is secured to its neighbor by a Z-shaped iron joggle cramp (about 15 *pouces* long; Fig. 79, top row, left, marked "L" and "K"). Then a groove was cut into the tops of the *sommiers* and voussoirs to receive horizontal iron rods (Fig. 79, top row, left, marked "B" and "C"; bottom row, center, marked "H" and "I"), each rod having an eye at each end threaded over the projecting end of one of the vertical rods on the axes of the columns. These horizontal rods thus form a chain along the entire length of the façade from one end pavilion through the central pavilion to the other end. Other flat arches span at right angles between the *sommiers* and the rear walls and have iron rods (Fig. 79, top row, left, marked "E," right, marked "b"; bottom row, center, marked "K") set in similar grooves cut in the tops of the voussoirs. These rods are likewise attached to the vertical rods on the axes of the columns by means of an eye at one end and are held at the other end by a vertical rod set against the inside face of the rear wall and passing through a second eye. Additional rods with an eye at each end (Fig. 79, top row, left, marked "D"; bottom row, center, marked "L") run in the same direction from the centers of the small intercolumniations to the inside faces of the rear walls. They are similarly anchored at these inside faces and are secured over the intercolumniations by threading the rods marked "I" (Fig. 79, bottom row, center) and "C" (Fig. 79, top row, left) through their outer eyes. But they differ from the rods previously mentioned in consisting of two approximately equal shorter lengths joined together by a special connector or *moufle* (Fig. 79, bottom row, far left; Fig. 5 and Fig. 81) with double wedge-shaped keys to permit tensioning.

Friezes. These were constructed just like the architraves, except the voussoirs were not cut *à crossettes* (Fig. 79, top row, left). Horizontal rods were again placed in grooves cut into the tops of the stones forming the friezes. Running back to the anchorages already referred to inside the rear walls, however, are two sets of rods differently aligned. One set, identical to those immediately below, runs at right angles to the Colonnade from the centers of the small intercolumniations (Fig. 79, top row, left, marked "H," right, marked "f"; lower row, left, marked "S"). The other set (Fig. 79, lower row, left, marked "R") runs back diagonally from the centers of the columns, forming X-shaped patterns above the ceilings. Each rod of both these sets consists again of two lengths joined together by *moufles* (Fig. 81).

Ceilings. The flat ceilings over each bay of the Colonnade consist of a jigsaw-puzzle pattern of stones set around a large circular central stone (top diameter 6 *pieds,* bottom diameter $5\frac{1}{2}$ *pieds;*

Fig. 79, bottom row, left and right). Between this circular stone and its neighbors, irons shaped as upside-down T's were placed (Fig. 79, bottom row, far left, marked "Fig. 4") to help distribute the weight of the central stone more evenly to the surrounding stones. The ceiling stones thrust outward in all directions onto the friezes of the bay, but the ceiling is in thickness only about one-half the height of the frieze (Fig. 79, top row, right). Patte's cross-section also reveals the large space above the ceilings (about 6 *pieds* in height) that greatly lightens the structure and provides a tunnel in which a person can walk to perform inspection and maintenance (Fig. 80). Accessible within the tunnel are the special connectors (*moufles;* Fig. 81).[6] Thus it is possible to drive in further or loosen their wedge-shaped keys, thereby tightening or slackening, as may be necessary, the rods running from above the Colonnade to the rear wall. The tunnels (still extant and accessible) are within the entablatures above the north and south ranges of the paired columns.

Cornices. The cornices are set in three conventional horizontal courses corbeled over the interior passageway (as is the masonry opposite) to enhance stability. A single flat stone over the "tunnel" in turn forms a flat terrace with balustrade (Fig. 79, top row, right).

Pediment and Entablature of the Central Pavilion (Fig. 82). This entablature is constructed in a manner similar to those of the colonnades, but it is curved slightly upward so that at its center it is about $1\frac{1}{2}$ *pouces* above the horizontal. The entablature was built this way to help support the weight of the pediment.

The simae of the raking cornices comprise two great monolithic slabs (see Chapter V). The lower courses of these cornices consist of stone blocks with vertical joints instead of joints perpendicular to the slope (the latter system was usual). The downward pressures at the corners of the pediment, and the threat of a seesaw movement of the horizontal cornice, are counteracted by large blocks at the level of the balustrade, embedded in the wall (Fig. 48).

The tympanum of the pediment contains three hidden discharging arches, the central one ogival, the flanking ones rampant. These relieve the weights over the intercolumniations and distribute them to the columns. A network of iron rods and chains brace and interconnect the raking cornices.

The brilliance of this structural system is threefold: (1) the coupling of the columns permits increased main spans without reducing the number of points of support; (2) if the reinforcement behaves as intended, thrusts generated by the masonry are absorbed by the iron that acts in tension, so that vertical loads only are imposed on the columns and walls as in genuine trabeated construction; and (3) provision is made for varying the tension in the iron rods that restrain the tendencies of the transverse flat arches and the ceilings to thrust outward against the Colonnade and overturn it. The scheme was a notable innovation in the history of building technology. In Patte's words:

---

6. The rods between the architrave and the frieze marked "T" in Figure 79 (top row, center) and "L" (bottom row, center) are placed in open troughs so their *moufles* are accessible from within the tunnel. The adjacent buried rods marked "S" and "K" are not shown as having *moufles* and probably had none.

The iron carries nothing, and its only role is precisely that of exerting [inward] pulls to counter the [outward] thrusts of the architraves, thereby stabilizing the axes of the columns, a procedure that necessarily produces the greatest resistance that can be expected from iron. [Sources II, no. 94(b), last par.]

Although the system used for the Louvre Colonnade was dramatically new, it did not spring forth into being from a technological vacuum. Various forms of iron reinforcement in masonry structures had been commonly employed in Europe since medieval times.[7] Exposed iron tie-rods were used in Early Christian and Byzantine architecture from at least the early sixth century and entered Western European architecture ca. A.D. 1000; they became quite common during the Gothic period. Hidden or partially concealed iron reinforcement (aside from cramps connecting adjacent stones, used from classical Greek times on) appears in France beginning in the twelfth century[8] and was often used in window frames during the Gothic period.[9] Because great medieval buildings had to be maintained and repaired, the "secrets" of their construction were passed on, however imperfectly, to postmedieval architects and builders. Hence, it is fascinating to note that the connecting piece (*moufle*) between the iron rods of the Colonnade (Fig. 81) is virtually identical to that used in France in the fifteenth century for "free chains" (not encased in masonry; Fig. 83), even to the detail of the double wedge-shaped keys (to permit tensioning). The cramps connecting the adjacent voussoirs at the Louvre (Fig. 79, top row, left) are similar to those used in the exterior cornice of the choir of Notre-Dame, Paris, dating from the late twelfth century (Fig. 84). Medieval builders discovered from unhappy experience that iron embedded in stone masonry was likely to rust and thereby swell, and in so doing crack the masonry or even lift whole courses of it. If iron was in direct contact with stone, there was also a risk that highly uneven bearing could lead directly to local splitting or crushing. In order to prevent these mishaps, medieval masons sometimes coated the grooves in which iron rods were placed with molten lead or mortar; even better was a type of thick mastic apparently composed of powdered sandstone, minium, litharge, and oil.[10] Charles Perrault, in a document (Sources II, no. 46) recommending the reinforcement system of the Louvre Colonnade for his brother's proposed church of Sainte-Geneviève, prescribed that the horizontal iron bars of the entablature be coated with "two or three coats of oil to protect them against rust." Perrault's recommenda-

---

7. On iron reinforcement in medieval masonry buildings, see mainly R. P. Wilcox, *Timber and Iron Reinforcement in Early Buildings* (*The Society of Antiquaries of London, Occasional Paper*, n.s., II), London, 1981, and W. Haas, "Hölzerne und eiserne Anker an mittelalterlichen Kirchenbauten," *Architectura*, XIII, 1983, 136–151, esp. 147f. See also E. E. Viollet-le-Duc, *Dictionnaire raisonné de l'architecture française du XIe au XVIe siècle*, Paris, 1875, II, 396–404 (s.v. "Chaînage"), and J. Fitchen, *The Construction of Gothic Cathedrals*, Oxford, 1961, 275–279 (appendix J, "Arch and Vault Ties in Medieval Construction").

8. Perhaps the earliest examples are in Vézelay (nave, ca. 1104–32, composite iron and wood reinforcement; see Viollet-le-Duc, *Dictionnaire*, II, 397–398, 398, fig. 1; 399, fig. 2) and Bourges Cathedral (iron chain in floor of high triforium of the chevet, 1195–1214; see R. Branner, *La cathédrale de Bourges et sa place dans l'architecture gothique*, Paris and Bourges, 1962, 82, fig. 67a; 83 and n.). At Vézelay, the exposed hooked ends of the embedded rods may have held tie-rods across the nave. As for Bourges, Branner wrote (ibid., 83): "Il est impossible de savoir si ce chaînage est rattaché aux piles par des crampons verticaux ou si sa fonction est réellement de relier les supports entre eux."

9. Viollet-le-Duc, *Dictionnaire*, II, 401; Haas, "Hölzerne und eiserne Anker," 149.

10. Viollet-le-Duc, *Dictionnaire*, II, 403.

tion indicates the procedure used at the Louvre, and this is confirmed by a payment in the *Comptes*.[11]

These instances suggest some continuity with medieval French building traditions. It is significant in this respect that in 1669 or 1670 the views of several French architects *and masons* were solicited concerning models of the Colonnade, the Arc de Triomphe du Trône (Fig. 120), and the Observatoire (the last two structures are securely by Claude Perrault) (Sources II, no. 8). Among the comments are some on the use of iron for the Louvre.

Thomas Gamard (or Jamard) condemned the iron on the grounds that it could break, adding that because the ancients never used that material their buildings were never threatened by such danger. Daniel Gittard approved of the iron, provided it was well made and well hammered, and he hoped the iron rods were composed of several flat bars beaten and joined *en liaison*. A certain Duval recommended that the rods be placed below the flat arches ("plattes bandes") for greater strength, and it could be said that this was carried out for the frieze.[12] Jean Pastel (Patel) entirely approved of the structural system but criticized the cutting of the voussoirs. Pierre Cottart agreed with Pastel's last point and did not think it was necessary to recess the flat ceilings "in order to further strengthen the cut stones" (probably meaning that the stones of the architraves could withstand the thrusts of the ceilings if they had been placed at the level of the architrave instead of the frieze; see Fig. 79, top row, right). Charles Chamois praised the Colonnade as "one of the most beautiful and daring works ever made" and recommended that the vault above the ceilings be adjusted to align with the surfaces of the pilasters of the rear wall (a suggestion given at a time when vaults with semicircular arches were still planned [as in Figure 77] instead of the eventual corbeled vaults [Fig. 79, top row, right]). He approved of the manner in which the voussoirs were to be cut and recommended that, in addition to the architrave, the frieze be built as a *platebande* and that it should be convex (this very last suggestion was not adopted).

The most extended comments were those of Pierre Thévenot, a mason whose name appears frequently from 1667 on in the royal building accounts and who later worked on Perrault's triumphal arch.[13] He also approved of the stone-cutting and structural design, noting that the

---

11. See Sources I, no. 103. D'Aviler reported in 1694 that it was the practice to coat iron embedded in stone not with oil but with a thin layer of lead, "ce qui à la verité le garantit un peu de l'humidité de la pierre, mais ne peut cependant empêcher qu'il ne jette sa roüille au dehors" (*Cours d'architecture*, I, 217). J. F. Blondel wrote in 1756 that only the iron rods of the central pavilion of the east façade were coated with lead; the others were coated with oil (Sources II, no. 84[b]). The use of iron in French domestic buildings was discussed as early as 1624 by Louis Savot (*L'architecture françoise des bastimens particuliers*, ed. F. Blondel, Paris, 1673, 296–297, 298, 301f.). Iron in combination with stone was criticized by Philibert de l'Orme (*Nouvelles inventions pour bien bastir et à petits fraiz . . .*, Paris, 1561, fols. 5v–6r) and by the Royal Academy of Architecture in 1677 (citing de l'Orme) and in 1683, with Blondel, the director, present (*PV*, I, 154 [November 29, 1677];

II, 30–31 [May 24, 1683]); for Blondel's criticism of the iron of the Colonnade, see Appendix B. There are discussions of iron in P. Bullet, *L'architecture pratique . . .*, Paris, 1691, 273, 390, and in d'Aviler, *Cours d'architecture*, I, 216–219.

12. Because, both between architrave and frieze and between frieze and cornice, the iron rods were set in the upper surface of the course below and anchored to the vertical rods passing through the column axes, it seems likely that the primary role of the rods was to prevent the column heads from being pushed aside by the thrusts generated—the role Patte ascribed to them (Sources II, no. 94[b]) and the role this manner of incorporation best fitted the rods to play.

13. His name first appears in *CBR*, I, col. 218. For his work on the arch, see M. Petzet, "Das Triumphbogenmonument für Ludwig XIV. auf der Place du Trône," *ZfK*, XLV, 1982, 179f.

end pavilions would absorb the lateral pressures, but he cautioned that the iron rods to be set perpendicularly to the façade should be without flaw (which suggests Thévenot was speaking from experience). He went on to criticize the circular stones in the centers of the ceilings (Fig. 79, bottom row, left and right); he preferred square ones on structural grounds. Then Thévenot advised that the arches above the ceilings be pointed (*en tiers point*), not semicircular (as they appear in Figure 77; cf. Chamois's comment, above); pointed arches will produce less thrust and will better load the large stones (*sommiers*) above the capitals. Although the latter are of Saint-Leu stone (a *pierre tendre*), they are more than sufficient in strength to support their loads, and the mason cited pillars left standing in the quarries of Saint-Leu-d'Esserent. Thévenot's last recommendation is the following:

> To be more assured that the *sommiers* will not break, it will be best to leave the part of the joint which overhangs [*qui porte à faux*] directly over the empty [narrow] intercolumniation.

If Patte's diagrams are to be relied on (Fig. 79, top row, left and center), the Colonnade was indeed originally built with vertical joints between the large stones over the capitals, with small overhangs over the narrow intercolumniations.[14] This was apparently Thévenot's idea, and Claude Perrault later elaborated its rationale in his second Vitruvius edition (1684), where, in replying to a point made by François Blondel about architraves resting on capitals, Perrault wrote:

> I also do not understand why one affirms that the end of an architrave that rests entirely on a column is not more secure than when it rests only on half the column, and that it does not bend more easily when it is only supported by its end than when that end passes beyond the column supporting it, because I have always believed that the end that passes beyond the column directly over the small intercolumniation has a weight that resists the bending of the opposite part, the one directly over the large intercolumniation. [Sources II, no. 26(a); see Appendix B]

Perrault's analysis applies to monolithic stone lintels but not to the flat-arch *platebandes* of the Colonnade. However, Perrault probably wrote this passage with the Louvre in mind, thus revealing a lack of clarity in his thinking about the distinctions between the two types of lintel.

14. The alteration of this arrangement to the present condition, where a single wedge-shaped stone rests on both capitals (see Fig. 54), is probably attributable to the architect Charles Percier, working in the first decade of the nineteenth century (see L. Vitet, *Le Louvre et le nouveau Louvre,* new ed., Paris, 1882, 166). Unfortunately, I have not been able to discover the documentary records of his work. In 1803 it was reported that "les fers incrustés dans les pierres, ne furent point placés assez profondément pour être à l'abri de toute humidité: ils se sont oxidés et se dissolvent toujours de plus en plus. La rouille en pénétrant dans les joints des pierres les a rongées et désunies. Une partie des plafonds de ce fameux portique est aujourd'hui menacée d'une destruction prochaine" (L. P. Baltard and A. P. Duval, *Paris et ses monumens . . . ,* Paris, 1803, I, 37). See also P.F.L. Fontaine, *Texte explicatif joint au n^{os} du Journal des monuments de Paris . . . ,* Paris, [1891], 31 (November 1809).

The above summary of the opinions contributed in 1669 or 1670 by several French architects and masons reveals the important fact that at least one feature of the structural system of the Colonnade—the *porte à faux* over the narrow intercolumniations—was the idea of a mason (Thévenot) and that the final corbeled vault over the flat ceilings (Figs. 79, top right, 80) is probably the result of critiques by Chamois and Thévenot of an earlier scheme with semicircular arches (Fig. 77). But the document of 1669–70 does not suggest that the iron reinforcement system itself was devised by minor figures, such as Chamois, Thévenot, and the others. Could it be that, after all, the revolutionary system was invented by some member of the Petit Conseil?

Of the three members, we can immediately rule out Charles Le Brun. Although he was active to a limited extent in architecture,[15] nothing about his career indicates an interest in the structural use of iron. Louis Le Vau, however, was commercially involved in the production of sheet iron coated with tin (*fer-blanc*), as well as firearms and cannon made of iron.[16] In 1665, the King established a factory at Beaumont-la-Ferrière (Nièvre) in the Nivernais region, and Le Vau was placed in charge.[17] The firearms division was sold in 1668,[18] but Le Vau still headed the *fer-blanc* manufactory at the time of his death in 1670. This connection of Le Vau with iron is intriguing, but *fer-blanc* was not used at the Louvre[19] or in other buildings. Besides, the iron employed for the Louvre was made in Normandy.[20]

In contrast to Le Brun and Le Vau, Claude Perrault had a lively interest in the use of metal in architecture. In his obelisk design of 1666 (Fig. 116), he had proposed an iron cage for spectators at the top of the monument; the iron struts were to be sheathed in gilt copper and to descend the entire length of the obelisk, linking the masonry together.[21] In the Observatoire of Paris, designed and begun in 1667, Perrault may have used a discrete amount of iron for reinforcement.[22] His scientific interest in iron—its properties when heated, beaten, and combined with

---

15. For a checklist of his architectural activity, see R. W. Berger, "Charles Le Brun and the Louvre Colonnade," *AB*, LII, 1970, 402–403. For his competition designs for a triumphal arch (1668–69), see Petzet, "Das Triumphbogenmonument," 148f.

16. See A. Laprade, "François d'Orbay (1634–1697)," *BSHAF*, 1953, 91f. and idem, *d'Orbay*, 1960, 78f.

17. *CBR*, I, col. 96 (with the specific mention of *fer-blanc*). A letter from Le Vau to Colbert (November 5, 1665, written at Beaumont-la-Ferrière) mentions muskets, cannon, and bullets (G. B. Depping, ed., *Correspondance administrative sous le règne de Louis XIV*, Paris, 1852, III, 743 n. 1). In a letter to Le Vau (October 26, 1669), Colbert complains that the *fer-blanc* is not being produced (P. Clément, ed., *Lettres, instructions et mémoires de Colbert*, Paris, 1863, II, 2, 493–494 [doc. 67]; reprinted in Laprade, *d'Orbay*, 82). Well before this, in 1650, Le Vau had invested in a metal forge at Conches (Eure) (ibid., 79).

18. Ibid., 81.

19. Iron for the Louvre (payments began in 1669 for iron delivered in 1668; see Sources I, no. 33) is regularly called "gros fer" in *CBR*. Payments for "gros fer" for the Louvre and Tuileries are recorded as early as 1664–66 (*CBR*, I, cols. 12, 68–69, 242); the use of this iron then is unknown.

20. As mentioned by Charles Perrault in his *mémoire* on a proposed church of Sainte-Geneviève (Sources II, no. 46), where Perrault speaks of "une barre de fer de Normandie."

21. "La cage est composée de vingt montants, quatre à chaque face, sans ceux des quatre coins, qui laissent 20 ouvertures d'un pied de large pour regarder. Ces montants sont couverts de grosses lames de cuivre doré de la largeur de huit pouces qui descendent tout le long de l'obélisque, en lient la maçonnerie et représentent les rayons du soleil qui partent du globe doré qui en est comme le corps" (Cl. Perrault, "Dessin d'un obélisque" [October 20, 1666], in Ch. Perrault, *Mémoires de ma vie*, and Cl. Perrault, *Voyage à Bordeaux (1669)*, ed. P. Bonnefon, Paris, 1909, 238). The publication of Perrault's essay in A. Hallays, *Les Perrault*, Paris, 1926, 258–263 is incomplete. On the obelisk monument, see M. Petzet, "Der Obelisk des Sonnenkönigs: Ein Projekt Claude Perraults von 1666," *ZfK*, XLVII, 1984, 439–464, esp. 442.

22. C. Wolf, *Histoire de l'Observatoire de Paris de sa fondation à 1793*, Paris, 1902, 13.

other metals—is revealed in one of his scientific papers published in 1680 but perhaps reflecting experiments conducted over twenty years.[23] Claude's brother Charles—who always claimed that Claude was the real designer of the Colonnade—wrote in his autobiography (ca. 1700) about a special Louvre model and stated that some of Claude's drawings illustrated the details of the intricate reinforcement:

> In order to dispel all worries that M. Colbert could have about the construction of this building, I suggested to him that it would be a good idea to make a small model of the peristyle with small cut stones of the same shape and number that the full-size work was to have. When it was finished and secured by small bars of iron, proportional in size to those to be used in the actual building,[24] M. Colbert was entirely satisfied about the firmness and solidity of the entire work, in which the iron carries nothing and only resists the thrust of the architraves with such strength that there is no weight, whatever it might be, that can break it, only making it clench more while carrying nothing. There was made, moreover, a space between the ceiling of the peristyle and the covering above, where several men can walk and work without difficulty to correct problems that could arise over the course of time. The entire work has been so well built that nothing has given way, and it is likely that the building will stand forever. The details of this construction are in the first volume of my brother's architectural designs, which are among my books. [Sources II, no. 53(b)]

Charles here refers to the two manuscript volumes of Claude's drawings that were later destroyed in 1871. Charles's familiarity with the details of the Colonnade's structure is also revealed in his *mémoire* of 1697 on Claude's unexecuted project of the 1670s for Sainte-Geneviève, Paris (Sources II, no. 46; see above).[25] Charles's technical knowledge about the Louvre can be attributed to the fact that Claude Perrault was his brother and that Charles was intimately familiar with Claude's drawings (which he inherited in 1688). On the other hand, Charles Perrault, by virtue of his key position in the Royal Building Administration under Colbert, could have acquired his special knowledge through that post alone.

Other evidence suggests that Claude Perrault (along with Le Vau and Le Brun) may indeed have devised the iron-reinforcement system in collaboration with Parisian masons and/or *serruriers*. Leibniz, who was personally acquainted with Claude Perrault in the 1670s, wrote in 1676: "M. Le Brun believed the Louvre design of M. Perrault, although beautiful, would be

---

23. Cl. Perrault, "De la pesanteur des corps, de leur ressort, et de leur dureté," in his *Oeuvres diverses de physique et de mechanique,* Leiden, 1721, I, 1–51 (1st ed.: *Essais de physique . . . ,* Paris, 1680–88, 4 vols.). Perrault discusses hardening by heat of a range of building materials (brick, marble, stone; 1721 ed., I, 24f.).

24. This is perhaps the first explicit reference to a model used in a test of this sort. The test described could have demonstrated the validity of the basic concept, but it would have given a totally misleading idea of the cross-sections of iron called for, both because it ignored the likely greater unit strength of thin model bars and, more serious—if "grosses proportionellement à celles qu'on employeroit dans l'ouvrage effectif" means the model bars were cut to the same linear scale as the rest of the model—because it ignored the fact that, whereas weights increase proportionately to the cube of linear dimensions, strengths increase proportionately only to the square of these dimensions.

25. See also Sources II, no. 37[a].

very difficult to execute. But M. Perrault found a very able entrepreneur, Preaux or Preat, I believe, who is admirably precise; the stones are well cut, everything is done with admirable beauty" (Sources II, no. 19). Leibniz was undoubtedly referring here to Pierre Bréau, described in documents (beginning in 1668) as a royal mason, and as a master mason and *entrepreneur des bastimens de sa Majesté* in a document of 1670 in which he was one of several masons who gave their opinions about the foundations of Perrault's Arc de Triomphe du Trône (Fig. 120).[26] Leibniz characterized Bréau only as a master stone-cutter, not as someone skilled in the use of structural iron; that person may have been Étienne Doyart, the master *serrurier* who appears regularly in the *Comptes* as supplying iron for the Louvre (see Sources I, nos. 33, 34, 57, 58, 83, 102, 125).[27] However that may be, Leibniz's account (the result of a personal conversation with Perrault) suggests the type of communication between architects and builders that is an integral part of the architectural process and that must have taken place in the planning and execution of the Colonnade. (On Claude Perrault's silence about iron reinforcement in his theoretical writings, see Appendix B.)

It was argued in Chapter III that François Le Vau's Louvre project of ca. 1662–64 (Figs. 24–32) was the immediate source for the Petit Conseil when it first met in 1667. The younger Le Vau had proposed wide intercolumniations of $12\frac{1}{2}$ *pieds* (Fig. 32), slightly more than those eventually executed (see above). Hence François's design, like the Colonnade, could only have been realized with a system of iron reinforcement, but such a system is not indicated in the sectional view (Fig. 31), where the entablature over the peristyle is shown with voussoirs arranged in a flat arch.[28] It may have been that, when François Le Vau's design was taken up by the Petit Conseil in 1667, the architects consulted with masons experienced in the use of iron in architectural structure and that from these discussions the system of rods and cramps was devised.

26. In 1681 he rose to the rank of *architecte des bâtiments du roi* (see Sources II, note 106).

27. Doyart appears in *CBR* from 1664 on.

28. It is doubtful that the sketchy, double lines of the entablature in Figure 31 were meant to indicate iron rods.

VII
IN THE EYE OF THE CONNOISSEUR

The Colonnade was regarded by the French in the late seventeenth and eighteenth centuries as their greatest architectural masterpiece and a monument that at least equaled, and perhaps surpassed, the finest buildings of ancient Greece and Rome. Yet despite their encomiums, French connoisseurs were not hesitant to criticize the Colonnade (and the other parts of Louis XIV's Louvre). In their writings, particularly those of the two eighteenth-century critics who wrote the longest and most detailed discussions of the Colonnade—Jacques François Blondel (Sources II, no. 84 [1756]; supplemented by nos. 96 [1771] and 97 [1772]) and Pierre Patte (Sources II, no. 94 [1769])—we can observe the manner of thinking and the criteria that inform the sophisticated architectural criticism of Old Regime France.

From its inception, the Colonnade was almost invariably praised as "superbe" and "magnifique," but aside from such vague clichés, precise comments on its aesthetic qualities can be gleaned beginning with some of the earliest writings. In 1668, while the Colonnade was still on the drawing board, François Le Vau (Sources II, no. 6[6b]) commented on the suitability of the ground floors of both the new east façade and the south façade as pedestals for the upper floors, supporting a colossal order that was effective when viewed from a distance—as, for example, from the Pont-Neuf. Claude Perrault later repeated these observations in his writings (Sources II, nos. 12[b] [1673], 25[c] [1683]; cf. Fig. 42).

Critical attention turned very early to the Louvre's Corinthian order. The mason Duval, in 1669 or 1670 (Sources II, no. 8[c]), commented that the capitals (Figs. 54, 56), although resembling those of the Roman Pantheon (Figs. 57, 58), were not so beautiful as those of the Val-de-Grâce. Desgodets in 1682 (Sources II, no. 23) observed that the Louvre capitals were proportionately tall for Corinthian capitals but said this was justified by their high placement. The tall proportions, Desgodets added, were especially effective for the pilasters of the east and south façades (Figs. 49, 95); because these pilasters have no entasis (following the usual antique practice), their high capitals obviate the otherwise low and crushed effect produced where the untapered pilaster and capital meet (Fig. 56). Perrault himself in 1683 (Sources II, no. 25[a]) noted that the capitals were taller in their proportions than those of the Pantheon, and his mention of the renowned Roman building confirms that its order had indeed served as the model.[1] Much later, in 1749, the Royal Academy of Architecture opined that the three most admired Corinthian capitals were those of antiquity ($2\frac{1}{3}$ modules; no building was specified), the Versailles chapel ($2\frac{1}{2}$ modules), and the Louvre Colonnade ($2\frac{2}{3}$ modules), with the Versailles example having the best proportions and the Louvre model recommended when columns or pilasters are coupled (Sources II, no. 72). At the next session that year (Sources II, no. 73), the Academy recorded the measurements of the Louvre order in great detail, but its efforts were refined some years later by J. F. Blondel and Patte.

More important than discussions of the Louvre's Corinthian order itself was the debate about the pairing of the Colonnade's columns that flared during the 1670s and 1680s, pitting Perrault (their apologist) against François Blondel (their critic). This controversy, discussed in detail in Appendix B, is an example of how architecture played an important role in the Quarrel of the Ancients and Moderns that developed in the later seventeenth century.[2]

Much Old Regime criticism is concerned with the classical orders, a topic that sometimes strikes a modern observer as pedantic and secondary to the larger issues of function, structure, and siting. (This view may be changing in the current vogue of Post-Modernism.) The orders, however, were not the exclusive interest of the writers. For example, in 1756 J. F. Blondel (Sources II, no. 84[b]) began his analysis with a discussion of faults of the Colonnade that violate the basic demands of *convenance, bienséance,* and *vraisemblance*.[3]

---

1. The capitals of the Louvre are 2.66 modules high; those of the Pantheon are 2.47 modules in height. In 1707, the Royal Academy of Architecture criticized the high proportions of the Louvre capitals (Sources II, no. 57).

2. On this broad topic, see A. O. Aldridge, "Ancients and Moderns in the Eighteenth Century," *Dictionary of the History of Ideas,* ed. P. P. Wiener, New York, 1968, I, 76–87 (with background material, including the French seventeenth century, and bibliography).

3. *Convenance, bienséance,* and *vraisemblance*—general aesthetic terms used for all the arts—have variable and overlapping meanings in French late-seventeenth- and eighteenth-century usage. For these terms in architectural writings, see A. Röver, *Bienséance: Zur ästhetischen Situation im Ancien Régime, dargestellt an Beispielen der Pariser Privatarchitektur,* Hildesheim and New York, 1977, esp. 77f.; W. Szambien, "Bienséance, convenance et caractère," *Les cahiers de la recherche architecturale,* no. 18, 1985, 38–43; idem, *Symétrie, goût, caractère: Théorie et terminologie de l'architecture à l'âge classique, 1550–1800,* Paris, 1986. For their general meaning and usage, particularly in literature, see R. G. Saisselin, *The Rule of Reason and the Ruses*

In using the first term, Blondel asks how the exterior design of the Colonnade communicates the building's function to a viewer. Because of its niches and few windows (see Chapter IV), the Colonnade suggests to Blondel that it could be a magnificent monument or a library, not a habitation. *Convenance* has been violated; to restore the message that the structure is something meant to be lived in, even sham windows instead of niches would have been preferable.

Bienséance, the next category, for Blondel concerns the practical, functional use of the building. He imagines a prince, whose habitation the Louvre is, displaying himself to his subjects assembled before the east façade. The prince appears in one of the peristyles, but if he wants to proceed to the other one he will have to traverse a small, mean passage within the central *avant-corps* (Fig. 90). The large central arch that rises into the *premier étage* (Fig. 48)—a motif derived from the younger Le Vau's Louvre project (Fig. 29)—only accentuates the inadequate circulation, a failure of *bienséance.*

By *vraisemblance,* Blondel means credibility, achieved by correct proportional relationship between motifs. He faults the central portal (Fig. 48), which, although subsumed within the monumental arch just discussed, is by itself too small an entrance for such a large building.

Blondel returns to some of these broader considerations at the end of his discussion. But at this point, after noting ratios between the larger subdivisions of the façade, he proceeds to a close analysis of the Corinthian order (Figs. 48, 51, 56).

The height of the order is twenty-one modules, one module more than the usual twenty given to this order. Blondel surmises that this extra touch of slenderness was meant to counteract the stocky effect of coupled columns. And because these columns appear against a solid wall, the extra module restores to them a more svelte appearance in accordance with Vitruvius's authorization of the alteration of modules (III.3.13). This gracefulness accords well with the rich display of carved ornament and is accentuated by the entasis of the shafts in their lower third, which Blondel finds elegant. Similarly, the ratio of the height of the entablature to the column height (including capital and base) slightly exceeds Vignola's canonical 1 : 4, and this is justified, in Blondel's judgment, by the great length of the façade and the few *ressauts* in its entablature (Fig. 43).

After recording additional modular relationships among the parts of the order, Blondel turns to the Corinthian capitals (Figs. 54, 56). He notes that the leaves are olive, not acanthus, and pronounces the volutes to be "très-agréable." The width at the base of the capitals of the columns is 1 module, 13 parts (1 module = 18 parts), that of the pilasters is 2 modules. The difference is caused, of course, by the fact that the columns have entasis whereas the pilasters do not. Thus, to give more elegance to the pilaster capitals, they are given extra height, matching those of the columns. (This analysis is an elaboration of Desgodet's; see above.)

In the cornice (Figs. 54, 56), dentils are omitted from the fascia between the lower ovolo (with its egg-and-tongue pattern) and the upper cyma reversa (with its acanthus enrichment),

---

of the Heart: A Philosophical Dictionary of Classical French Criticism, Critics, and Aesthetic Issues, Cleveland and London, 1970, and P. E. Knabe, *Schlüsselbegriffe des kunsttheoretischen Denkens in Frankreich von der Spätklassik bis zum Ende der Aufklärung,* Düsseldorf, 1972.

and Blondel applauds this restraint, which he finds produces an area of repose among the other, richly ornamented moldings (Blondel again makes this point in Sources II, nos. 81, 96).

The column shafts, with unornamented fluting, lead down to the bases (Fig. 56), which, according to Blondel, are patterned after Vignola's Corinthian model[4] but perhaps are too subdivided. The Louvre bases, however—with their upper and lower tori between which are two scotia moldings in turn separated by two astragals—are no more articulated than Vignola's and are in fact closer to the bases of the order of the Pantheon, particularly the portico order with its higher plinth (Figs. 57, 58). This is consonant with the use of the Pantheon order as the model for the capitals (see above) and for a detail of the cornice (see below).

Blondel then turns his attention to the crowning balustrade (Fig. 49). Here he finds the height of the balusters to be insufficient in relation to the diameter of the order, and the *tablette* (an inconspicuous molding between the base of the blocking course and the blocking course itself) to be "un peu forte" (!)—an observation of a rarefied sensibility.

Blondel continues: The horizontal molding that appears about one-third the distance below the capitals is praised for giving an "air d'élégance" in keeping with the richness of the order. But the windows are too small in relation to the other openings and the colossal order, and Blondel repeats his earlier point that windows instead of niches behind the paired columns would have better announced the domestic nature of the building.[5] He muses that the *rez-de-chaussée*, which he later judged to be "un peu élevé" (Sources II, no. 96), would be improved if it had no windows at all.

Blondel's tone becomes increasingly critical: The oval medallions (Fig. 49),[6] he believes, were intended to be filled with reliefs of "actions d'éclat," which would, however, be difficult to see from a distance. But such medallions are not suitable for a palace; they are more appropriate adorning a triumphal arch or a similar monument of glorification (a view repeated in 1772; Sources II, no. 97).[7] The end pavilions (Fig. 49) are somewhat too wide for their height, and he again states that the windows are out of scale with the central arches of the pavilions. On the other hand, Blondel praises the pairing of columns and pilasters in the terminal pavilions: the former repeat the columns of the peristyles and central pavilion, while the latter form a transition to the south front (Fig. 42). In another section (Sources II, no. 84[f]), Blondel again attacks the interruption of the colonnades by the central pavilion.

In the third volume of the *Cours d'architecture* (1772) (Sources II, no. 97), published two years

---

4. R. Fréart de Chambray, *Parallèle de l'architecture antique et de la moderne*, Paris, 1650, 75, right.

5. Blondel in 1772 again made this point (Sources II, no. 97). The niches were defended by an anonymous writer in 1756 (Sources II, no. 86).

6. The medallion-swag motif appears above the right portal in Figure 63, a drawing from Louis Le Vau's studio that may be for the Château de Vincennes and hence from the 1650s (see Chapter III). The motif appears on the façade of Perrault's project for Sainte-Geneviève, Paris (1670s; A. Picon, *Claude Perrault, 1613–1688, ou la curiosité d'un classique*, Paris, 1988, 238, fig. 205) and is suggested in one of his obelisk designs of 1666 (Fig. 116). For a variant that appears on his triumphal arch, see the following note.

7. Oval medallions topped by ribbons in irregular curvilinear patterns (instead of hanging swags) were to have appeared in profusion on Perrault's Arc de Triomphe du Trône (Fig. 120). It is interesting that the Royal Academy of Architecture in 1685 had condemned these ornaments as inappropriate for a triumphal arch and considered them more suitable for festival architecture (*PV*, II, 99).

before his death, Blondel reaffirmed that the Colonnade was one of the masterpieces of French architecture and launched into a rhapsodical passage of praise:

> This work must be regarded not only as the triumph of architecture and sculpture but again as the masterpiece of art because of the boldness of its construction. In effect, there is nothing as regular as the architectural order that presides there, nothing as interesting as the members that accompany it, no ornaments better understood than those distributed throughout its composition; finally, there is nothing as magnificent as its construction: everything there is noble, imposing. Such are the great features that characterize that edifice; such is the sentiment that connoisseurs must carry away after having examined it according to its true aspect (*point de vue*); but let us consider it now as an architect.

Honing his critical knife, Blondel then notes the disparity between the imposing east façade (Figs. 43–45) and the courtyard with its small-scale motifs (Figs. 105, 106). His criterion now seems to be that in truly correct architecture there is an overall unity of design, which he finds lacking at the Louvre, despite attempts by Louis XIV's architects (for Blondel this means exclusively Perrault) to repeat or echo in the new façades motifs found on older parts of the palace. Specifically, Blondel rightly points to the windows of the *rez-de-chaussée* (Figs. 43, 95, 101) as repetitions of Lescot's ground-floor openings (Figs. 9, 10) and to the medallion-swag motif (Fig. 53) as a variant of a motif found on the same architect's Renaissance courtyard elevation (Fig. 12). However, these gestures do not compensate for the perceived lack of unity, and the great critic again condemns the central monumental arch of the Colonnade (Fig. 48) as wrongly rising into the floor above and oppressively weighed down by a solid at a point where an opening is called for.

Blondel is not content to end his critique of the Colonnade here, for he proceeds to a radical proposal to "improve" the façade (which he had just called "le triomphe de l'Architecture") by adding, among other features, a monumental exterior stair leading to the *premier étage!* The interested reader can consult Blondel's suggestion on his own.[8] It is a testament to the critical spirit of the Enlightenment, for which even so esteemed a building as the Colonnade was not sacrosanct.[9]

Patte's critical evaluation of the Colonnade (Sources II, no. 94[d]) dates from 1769, thirteen years after Blondel's lengthy exposition in the *Architecture françoise*. Patte was the first writer to analyze the structural system at length (see Chapter VI), but he also commented on the aesthetic qualities of the design with a connoisseur's sensitivity and an architect's knowledge.

Apparently in response to criticisms that the ground floor of the Colonnade was too high, Patte begins his critique (commentary to pl. XIX) by observing that this floor at the Louvre is slightly less in proportion to the order above than is the case at the Place des Victoires, the

---

8. *Cours d'architecture . . .* , Paris, 1772, III, 69–73, pls. VII, VIII.

9. "Les oeuvres des plus grands Maîtres ne sont pas toujours à l'abri de la censure de la postérité" (ibid., III, 73).

Château de Saint-Cloud, and the Place Louis XV (de la Concorde). The column height is 21 modules, 4 parts (slightly more than Blondel reported), greater than that authorized by authorities for the Corinthian order. Like Blondel, Patte believes that this increased height succeeds perfectly, counteracting both the heavy appearance of fluted, coupled columns and the foreshortened effect produced by the considerable height at which the columns are set. Patte notes that, in addition to their normal entasis, the columns taper in their lower third (Fig. 51), a practice not found in antiquity. Patte cannot discover the justification for this in Perrault's notes to Vitruvius, but he observes (commentary to pl. xxv) that Lescot's *premier étage* in the courtyard (Fig. 11) also has columns with this lower entasis. Furthermore, the profile of the cornice above the courtyard windows at this level resembles the profile of the horizontal cornice over the niches of the east façade, and because of these correspondences Patte concludes that Perrault (whom Patte, like Blondel, believed to be the sole designer of the Colonnade) consciously sought to unify the new work with the old.

Like Blondel, Patte gives the modular measurements of the order (commentary to pl. xx) and similarly praises the tall capitals of "très bonne grace," which he finds especially effective set upon pilasters without entasis. Again in agreement with Blondel, Patte praises the decision to have the fascia of the cornice without denticules (Figs. 54, 56) in order to avoid visual confusion, and correctly cites the Pantheon (the model for the Corinthian capitals, Figures 57, 58; see above) as the antique source for this.[10]

Blondel and Patte viewed the Louvre Colonnade within the traditions of classical architecture. Indeed, the great façade is remarkably reminiscent of an ancient Roman peripteral temple set upon a high stylobate and spread out in one plane. The Corinthian order and detailing derive, as we have seen, from classical antiquity. It is therefore remarkable that in 1673 Claude Perrault thought of the coupled columns of the Colonnade as having a "Gothic" quality. As he put it (Sources II, no. 12[a]):

> The taste of our century, or at least of our nation, is different from that of the Ancients, and perhaps in that it takes a bit after the Gothic (*il tient un peu du Gothique*): because we love air, light, and openness (*l'air le jour & les dégagemens*). That has led us to invent a sixth manner of arranging these columns, which is to couple them and join them two by two, and also to put the space of two intercolumniations in one.

This statement is all the more surprising in that it associates two entirely different structural systems, one arcuated (the Gothic), the other trabeated (the Colonnade). But Perrault's perception of the latent Gothicism of the latter, with its open, airy web of broad intercolumniations and slender Corinthian columns, stands in bewildering contrast to his proposal for a closed

---

10. It should be noted that the Louvre cornice (Figs. 53, 56)—with its cyma reversa with acanthus, set above a blank fascia, in turn above an ovolo with egg-and-tongue and an astragal with bead-and-reel—is an exact inversion of the interior cornice of the Pantheon (which is typical in its placement of these enrichments of the ancient Corinthian order).

ground floor and niches instead of windows behind the paired columns (see Chapter IV). The idea of a closed façade sprang, as we have seen, from his peculiar and free translation and interpretation of Vitruvius. His perception of a Gothic quality in the peristyles must have arisen from an innate aesthetic sensibility that could look beyond the physical structure of things to grasp their optical relatedness.

Perrault's precocious willingness to take the Gothic seriously is shown by his use of the phrase "ordre gothique" in 1669[11] (perhaps its first appearance) and by an additional comment in his second Vitruvius edition of 1684 (Sources II, no. 26[a]):

> Granted that the Gothic in general and everything that composes it was not the most beautiful type of architecture, I don't think everything in Gothic is to be rejected. The light in buildings and the openness (*les dégagemens*) in question are the things in which the Goths (*les Gothiques*) differ from the Ancients: but it is not in that that Gothic is to be criticized; and the Ancients who in the beginning were greatly removed from that style approved it subsequently when they made windows in their temples, which previously received light only by the portal; and before that they had enlarged the central intercolumniations.

The Louvre Colonnade and Perrault's comments on the Gothic are the sources of the "Graeco-Gothic" strand of architectural practice and theory that developed in late seventeenth- and eighteenth-century France.[12] The adherents of that tradition, like Perrault, viewed the Colonnade as a paradoxical structure, overtly classicist, covertly Gothic. Milestones in this development in the practical sphere are Perrault's own design (unexecuted) for the reconstruction of the church of Sainte-Geneviève, Paris (1670s),[13] and Hardouin-Mansart's extant chapel at Versailles (1688/89–1710).[14] In both, freestanding columns (single, not paired) support a straight entablature (with iron reinforcement, incidentally), an innovation in ecclesiastical design in France. The adaptation of the Louvre Colonnade for these two church interiors was consonant with the perception that the Gothic was preeminently a sacred style, and this contrasted with the contemporary view that the other new Louvre elevation, the south façade, could be an ideal model for domestic elevations, as witnessed by its adoption for the Hôtel Lully (1671, by Daniel Gittard), the Place des Victoires (1685–90, by Hardouin-Mansart), and the Place Louis le Grand or Vendôme (final version begun 1699, also by Hardouin-Mansart), all in Paris. But architectural theory lagged behind practice, for it was not until 1706 that the Colonnade was explicitly recommended for church design by Cordemoy in his *Nouveau traité de toute*

---

11. Cl. Perrault, *Voyage à Bordeaux (1669)*, ed. P. Bonnefon, Paris, 1909, 155; see also R. D. Middleton, "The Abbé de Cordemoy and the Graeco-Gothic Ideal: A Prelude to Romantic Classicism," *JWCI*, xxv, 1962, 298. Perrault's admiration for the Gothic sculpture of the Chapel of Saint Hubert at Amboise also should be noted (*Voyage à Bordeaux*, 145).

12. On this important topic, see Middleton (as in note 11), 278–320; idem, "The Abbé de Cordemoy and the Graeco-Gothic Ideal: Part II," *JWCI*, xxvi, 1963, 90–123; W. Herrmann, *Laugier and Eighteenth-Century French Theory*, London, 1962, chap. v; M. Hesse, *Von der Nachgotik zur Neugotik*, Frankfurt-am-Main, 1984.

13. See M. Petzet, "Un projet des Perrault pour l'Église Sainte-Geneviève à Paris," *BMon*, cxv, 1957, 81–96.

14. There is no comprehensive modern study of the Versailles chapel; see M. Petzet, "Quelques projets inédits pour la chapelle de Versailles," *Art de France*, i, 1961, 315–319, and [G. Walton et al.], *Versailles à Stockholm*, exhib. cat., Stockholm, 1985, 81–98.

l'architecture. Cordemoy's sources and influence are beyond the scope of this chapter and have been ably discussed elsewhere.[15] But just as the Colonnade was of interest to those who, like Cordemoy, admired the Gothic, so too did the great façade stir the hearts and minds of those who looked to a return to classical antiquity and to the era of Louis XIV for the reformation of architecture. In the eyes of connoisseurs, the Colonnade was truly protean.

15. See above, notes 11 and 12, to which may be added D. Nyberg, "*La sainte Antiquité:* Focus of an Eighteenth-Century Architectural Debate," in D. Fraser et al., eds., *Essays in the History of Architecture Presented to Rudolf Wittkower,* London, 1967, 159–169.

VIII
THE ATTRIBUTION QUESTION

The authorship of the Louvre Colonnade has been debated, at times fiercely, since the late seventeenth century. Because of the great importance of this work, its attribution has become *the* crucial problem within the field of French architecture of the classical period.

The debate first erupted into public view at the beginning of 1694, when François d'Orbay (then sixty years old and still active as a *dessinateur* in the Royal Building Administration) suddenly challenged the growing consensus that Claude Perrault had designed the Louvre Colonnade, maintaining instead that it had really been designed by Louis Le Vau and himself (Sources II, no. 41). D'Orbay's claim (made verbally, not in print) was reported in the same year by Nicolas Boileau in his *Réflexions critiques sur quelques passages du rheteur Longin* (Sources II, no. 39). Although Boileau here claimed neutrality on the issue (at the same time declaring his "voeux" in favor of Perrault), he fueled the dispute in the same year with a letter to Antoine Arnauld (Sources II, no. 40) in which he categorically denied that Claude was the architect not only of the Colonnade but also of the Observatoire and the Arc de Triomphe du Trône (!). Charles Perrault, who had first claimed the Colonnade for his brother in print in 1690 (Sources II, no. 37[c]), soon responded with a vigorous defense of Claude in his *Hommes illustres* of 1696 (Sources II, no. 44) and especially in his posthumously published autobiography, written ca. 1700 (Sources II, no. 53). Modern studies of this controversy have focused on the personalities and writings just cited, to the neglect of earlier documents, to which I now turn.

The earliest known attribution of the Louvre Colonnade is contained in Claude Olry de Loriande's poem of 1670, *Le superbe dessein du Louvre* (Sources II, no. 9). In Chapter II, we noted that in his opening lines Olry ascribed the façade to François Le Vau, whose project of ca. 1662–64 (Fig. 24) Olry had recently engraved (Figs. 29–32). De Loriande apparently had correctly noted the strong relationship of the younger Le Vau's design to the rising Louvre façade and attributed it on this basis. A few years later, however, we find the Colonnade ascribed to Perrault by two well-placed writers, François Blondel and André Félibien. The former was the director of the Royal Academy of Architecture, to which François Le Vau and François d'Orbay belonged (Claude Perrault seems to have been an unofficial member);[1] the latter was secretary of the same academy and official historiographer of the King's buildings. In 1673 (and again in 1685), Blondel, in a note in his edition of Savot's book on domestic architecture (Sources II, no. 13), referred to "les plus magnifiques Ouvrages des Bastimens du Roy" as by "Monsieur Perrault Docteur en Medecine" (presumably Blondel had the Colonnade in mind, as well as Perrault's other structures). Félibien, in the preface to his *Principes* of 1676 (Sources II, no. 18[a]), was more explicit in citing Perrault not only as the translator of Vitruvius but also as the designer of the Louvre, the Arc de Triomphe du Trône, and the Observatoire. (It was also in 1676 that Claude Perrault claimed the Colonnade as his design in his conversation with Leibniz; see Chapter III and Sources II, no. 19.)

This early testimony in favor of Perrault by Blondel and Félibien—two very highly placed intellectuals within the French artistic establishment—would seem to be conclusive. There exists, however, another primary document that points in a somewhat different direction and that correlates precisely with the surviving preparatory drawings discussed in Chapter III. In 1687, the Swedish architect Nicodemus Tessin the Younger, while on a visit to Paris, was escorted around the Royal Academy of Architecture by André Félibien, who showed him a large room containing several models of the Louvre. In his diary, Tessin reported seeing models of Bernini's Louvre design and staircase. Tessin continued:

> The other complete Louvre model, inside which one could see the courtyard and the other façade facing the Tuileries, was by the late Mr de Vaux, and the largest model with the Louvre Colonnade on one side is by Mr Perault, but entirely in imitation of the one by M. de Vaux [*aber in allen nach dass von Mr de Vaux imitiert*]. [Sources II, no. 33]

---

1. See Herrmann, *Perrault*, 28f.

Tessin's *Studieresor,* from which this text is taken, and his journal of visits to the most important châteaux around Paris in 1687,[2] are commonly recognized by art historians as unusually accurate and objective. Tessin evidently saw a model of the Colonnade in its final or near-final version, which, according to the argument in Chapter III, owes its form primarily to Perrault and Fréart de Chambray. But the Swedish visitor also viewed Louis Le Vau's comprehensive model, which undoubtedly featured an east front corresponding to the presentation drawing of spring 1667 (Fig. 59), a design drawn in Le Vau's studio and directly dependent on the younger brother's seminal proposal of ca. 1662–64 (Fig. 24).[3]

In a sense, Blondel and Félibien were correct in attributing the Colonnade to Perrault but their ascriptions, like those of all later writers who championed the Perrault camp, are incomplete. The Louvre of Louis XIV—particularly its *pièce de résistance,* the Colonnade—is a profoundly collaborative work of architecture, as Hautecoeur clearly recognized long ago.[4] Early chapters of this book have attempted to more clearly define that collaboration, which not only took place among the three members of the Petit Conseil but also included the input of François Le Vau (December 1667) and Fréart de Chambray (early 1668). The first Colonnade design produced by the Petit Conseil in the spring of 1667 (Fig. 59) took as its point of departure the younger Le Vau's earlier scheme (Fig. 24), which in turn was probably indebted to Houdin's 1661 proposal (Fig. 23). What part Perrault's lost "First Design" of 1664 played in this evolution is impossible to determine. Yet all these designs could trace their lineage to Le Brun's unexecuted sun palace for the cupola of Vaux-le-Vicomte (Fig. 5).

It is paradoxical that, according to Leibniz's report of his conversation with Claude Perrault in 1676 (Sources II, no. 19), it was Le Brun who thought that the Colonnade design would be too difficult to execute. Charles Perrault in his *Mémoires* stated that Le Vau and Le Brun "always said

---

2. P. Francastel, ed., "Relation de la visite de Nicodème Tessin à Marly, Versailles, Clagny, Rueil, et Saint-Cloud en 1687," *RHV,* XXVIII, 1926, 149–167, 274–300. A French translation from the *Studieresor* of Tessin's visit to Paris in 1687 was published by R. A. Weigert, ed., "Notes de Nicodème Tessin le Jeune relative à son séjour à Paris en 1687," *BSHAF,* 1932, 220–279.

3. The importance of Tessin's passage was first noted and quoted (in French) by R. Josephson ("Quelques dessins de Claude Perrault pour le Louvre," *GBA,* ser. 5, XVI, 1927, 190, with 1681 erroneously given as the date of the visit), but I do not agree with him when he writes: "Ce renseignement souligne donc la similitude des deux projets définitifs, mais il n'indique naturellement pas *qui* de Perrault ou de Le Vau eut le premier l'idée de la création." To have written his note, Tessin must have been told by Félibien that Le Vau's model preceded Perrault's. Apparently for Félibien (who attributed the Colonnade to the latter alone; see text), the author of a work was the one who devised its final form; contributions by others to earlier phases of the design process were not relevant in the matter of attribution. Tessin's passage was also quoted by Laprade (*d'Orbay,* 302, also with the wrong date of 1681), who surmised (302 n. 5) that Perrault's model was the one that showed Perrault's proposed attic (which Laprade dates to 1678, but which was presented by Perrault to the Royal Academy of Architecture the previous year; see Chapter IV). However, the minutes of the Academy mention a model of the Louvre attic only, not a model of the entire building, of which Tessin speaks. Finally, it may be noted that Tessin's observation was recorded by T. Sauvel ("Les auteurs de la colonnade du Louvre," *BMon,* CXXII, 1964, 332–333), but without appreciation of its significance.

On the Louvre models, see Chapter III, note 7. A payment for "le model du bastiment entier" was recorded in 1664 (*CBR,* I, col. 14); later models for the east façade could probably have been fit into this one. In 1674 a payment was made for the transport of "plusieurs modelles du Louvre" to the Royal Academy of Architecture (*CBR,* I, col. 781).

4. L. Hautecoeur, "L'auteur de la colonnade du Louvre," *GBA,* ser. 5, IX, 151–168; idem, *Louvre et Tuileries,* chap. VII; Hautecoeur, *HAC,* I, 441f.

[Claude's design] was only beautiful in painting" (Sources II, no. 53[b]). We may be confident that only Le Brun objected with these words.[5] He must have realized how his own unexecuted sun palace for Vaux (Fig. 5) had stimulated architects concerned with the Louvre during the 1660s. Le Brun, whose knowledge of architectural structure was surely unequal to either Le Vau's or Perrault's, was hesitant about a design that appropriately realized in actual construction the Ovidian sun palace imagery of his own devising.

The suitability of the First Painter's Vaux project as the *Urbild* for the Louvre of *le roi-soleil* is demonstrated by the fact that it served as the basis for a later design by Le Brun, the *Palace of the Sun or the Course of the Year (Assembly of the Gods)*, engraved in 1681 by Gérard Audran (Fig. 7).[6] There are numerous changes, and most important is the fact that the engraving refers no longer to Nicolas Fouquet (the ill-fated owner of Vaux-le-Vicomte) but to Louis XIV: the sun's orb held by Saturn in the center of the composition is now filled with fleurs-de-lis, and Jupiter holds a "closed" royal French crown instead of the "open" crown of Fouquet. The palace of the sun has also been altered: the colonnade is almost totally obscured by figures and clouds, and the central motif now consists of a coffered barrel vault on piers flanked by paired Composite pilasters supporting a straight entablature. Now this new architectural design retains a certain relationship to the Louvre Colonnade: the central motif recalls the composition around the central windows of the end pavilions (Fig. 49). Furthermore, a small area of the colonnade is revealed just to the right of the central motif, behind Mercury's caduceus (see Fig. 8, detail). Here we discover a single Composite column, a feature absent in the drawing for Vaux (Fig. 5) but corresponding to the executed east façade, where single columns appear at the ends of the ranges of coupled supports, flanking the central and end pavilions (Fig. 49). Thus, in a subtle and somewhat indirect manner, but parallel to the use of classical imagery and allusion, the sun palace in the engraving of 1681 refers to the new Louvre, just as the seated Apollo refers to the King. Upon viewing Audran's print, Le Brun may well have taken pride in the power of his old design to have served as the basis for a florid, panegyrical engraving as well as for the greatest palace façade in Europe, both works proclaiming the glory of the Sun King's monarchy at its zenith.

---

5. See also Sources II, nos. 35(b), 37(b), 44 (publications by Charles Perrault [1688–96] in which he reports opposition to the Colonnade on the basis that the design could only be realized in painting).

6. Because of its many alterations and date, the engraving cannot be described as Le Brun's unexecuted project for Vaux-le-Vicomte, as it so often is. It is described in great detail in C. Nivelon, *Vie de Charles Le Brun & description détaillée de ses ouvrages*, BN, Manuscrits, MS fr. 12987, 119–126 (ca. 1700), where it is called "Le Palais du Soleil ou Le Cours de l'Année." For the Latin text that accompanies the engraving, see R. W. Berger, "Charles Le Brun and the Louvre Colonnade," *AB*, LII, 1970, 401 n. 48 (with translation).

APPENDIXES

APPENDIX A

THE WORK OF THE PETIT CONSEIL (1667–1668): A CATALOGUE RAISONNÉ OF THE SURVIVING DRAWINGS AND ONE MEDAL

Criteria of Attribution

The connoisseurship of architectural drawings made in connection with the royal projects of Louis XIV is yet to be established on a scientific basis. The presence of studio assistants complicates the attribution process. Nevertheless, some progress toward a surer connoisseurship has been made in recent decades. In the following comments, I clarify the criteria for my own attributions, most of which depend on the work of earlier writers who are cited in the catalog entries.

Louis Le Vau and His Studio (Including François d'Orbay). Le Vau, as *premier architecte* since 1654, seems to have had several assistants, chief of whom was François d'Orbay. Le Vau's personal drawing style has never been conclusively established, although his cursive writing style has been analyzed (Laprade, *d'Orbay,* 351); drawings that bear his often flamboyant signature may have been prepared by others (e.g., Stockholm, Nationalmuseum, CC 3, 6, 9, 19, 20, 21 [all for the Tuileries palace]). Braham and Whiteley have noted that in CC 20, and especially in CC 2272 (unsigned, also for the Tuileries), the same hand appears that we find in Figures 59 and 62 (A1, A2), the earliest surviving Colonnade elevations from Le Vau's *atelier*. These drawings are all in pencil, with the windows shaded with parallel lines sloping from upper right to lower left and reinforced by short strokes along the left edges. The column fluting is strengthened by darker short sloping strokes along the right edges of the columns. Balusters are abbreviated by means of superposed circular notations.

This draftsman's style is clearly different from that of d'Orbay, who entered Le Vau's *atelier* in the mid-1650s, traveled to Rome in 1660, and rejoined Le Vau in 1663, functioning as Le Vau's chief *dessinateur* until his master's death in 1670. (D'Orbay continued to make drawings for the Louvre during the 1670s; see Figures 109, 110.) D'Orbay's signed drawing of 1668 for the north end of the Colonnade (Fig. 73, A8) provides a firm basis for attributions. D'Orbay invariably worked with pen, brush, and ink, sometimes over light preliminary sketching in pencil. He is fond of chiaroscuro and abrupt light-dark contrasts, as in the rear wall of the Colonnade and the garland swags draped over the medallions. Balusters are rendered as open loops united by a jagged vertical wash of dark ink that suggests shade.

Studio of Charles Le Brun. Two drawings in the Cabinet des Dessins of the Louvre for an east façade without orders (Figs. 93, 94, B2, B3) form part of the *fonds Le Brun,* the collection of the First Painter's studio seized by the Crown upon his death in 1690. Sculptural details are more firmly indicated than in d'Orbay's elevation (Fig. 92, B1), shadows are lighter and more transparent, and the balusters are more carefully rendered, with dark accents applied to the bottoms of the central, rounded elements.

Claude Perrault. During the time the Petit Conseil met (1667–68), Perrault was working alone, without assistants. His drawing style is revealed in the designs for the Obelisk (Figure 116 and Paris, Bibliothèque Nationale) of 1666 and especially in the spring 1667 bird's-eye-view project for the Observatoire (Fig. 68). On the basis of the last drawing, Petzet convincingly attributed Figure 67 (A6) to Perrault; this key drawing (1668) is the first to reveal an important revision of the east façade (see Chapter III). Figures 67 and 68 share a marked linear style, with thin, ruled pen lines; light, transparent shading; and an awkwardness in the drawing of details (see the window surrounds in both sheets). The balusters in Figure 67 are abbreviated in a manner unlike those in the drawings previously discussed, with a lower range of squares topped by circles, a blank space, and then half-circles "hanging" from above.

In his more finished elevation (Figs. 69–72, A7), Perrault approaches d'Orbay's style (cf. Fig. 73) but keeps his shaded areas lighter and is more linear, as in the window frames of the ground floor. In general, Perrault uses less wash than d'Orbay.

Other Draftsmen. Other drawings executed for the Petit Conseil are clearly by other *dessinateurs,* who are as yet anonymous. We cannot even be sure in whose *atelier* they worked. Figure 74 (A9), for example, has Perrault's linearity, but the balusters (those tell-tale details, pointed out by Laprade; see Figure 75) are rendered by an entirely different abbreviated formula: a whimsical combination of a hanging curved hook, open to the left, attached to a "foot" of two curved strokes, with a tiny touch of light wash to suggest the convexity of the baluster. Other unidentified hands can be studied in Figures 78 (A12), 111, and 112.

(In the measurements below, height precedes width.)

A. East Façade (with Colonnade)

A1. Figure 59. Drawing. Studio of Louis Le Vau.
Elevation of east façade.
Spring 1667.
Paris, Louvre, Cabinet des Dessins, Inv. 26077.
61.0 by 117.9 cm. Three sheets with a strip added at top.
Pencil, with several notations also in pencil; portal of central pavilion marked 30 by 10 p[ieds]. In a modern frame.

On August 29, 1668, Colbert's eldest son, Jean Baptiste Colbert, Marquis de Seignelay, submitted to the Collège de Clermont in Paris an academic *thèse,* "Conclusiones ex universa Philosophia de Logicis." The frontispiece of this work was designed by Le Brun and engraved by François de Poilly (Fig. 60, detail). It shows the lower portion of Le Brun's unexecuted Louvre monument (R. Josephson, "Le monument du triomphe pour le Louvre: Un projet de Charles Le Brun retrouvé," *RAAM,* LIII, 1928, 21–34), and, in the background, a partial view of the east façade of the Louvre. The preparatory drawing by Le Brun is preserved (Fig. 61). Because the central pavilion in the drawing and engraving follow Figure 59 (note the column arrangement and the beginning of the drum above the pediment), it follows that Le Brun made his design in 1667, before the central pavilion was changed in early 1668. Figure 60 differs from Figure 59 mainly in the decorative details.

On the engraving, see H. Jouin, *Charles Le Brun et les arts sous Louis XIV,* Paris, 1889, 594–595 (where the building is wrongly identified as the Tuileries Palace). It has been published by T. Sauvel, "Les auteurs de la colonnade du Louvre," *BMon,* CXXII, 1964, 325–326, fig. 2 (detail); D. Wildenstein, "Les oeuvres de Charles Le Brun d'après les gravures de son temps," *GBA,* ser. 6, LXVI, 1965, 56, no. 294; J. Lothe, "Images et monarchie: Les thèses gravées de François de Poilly," *Nouvelles de l'estampe,* no. 29, September–October 1976, 10, fig. 5. The preparatory drawing is listed in G-M, VIII, no. 6386; see also *Collections de Louis XIV, dessins, albums, manuscrits,* Paris, 1977, 259, 260; [Paris, Musée du Louvre, Cabinet des Dessins], *Le Brun à Versailles,* Paris, 1985, 74, fig. 93, 75, no. 93.

The central part of this design appears (although quite sketchily) in an engraving by François Chauveau after Le Brun, which serves as the headpiece to Charles Perrault's *La peinture: Poëme,* Paris, 1668, 3: Apollo points to a number of framed pictures surrounding the King's portrait; the one to the right of the portrait is the Louvre, with a domed central pavilion.

Bibliography. Y. Christ, *Le Louvre et les Tuileries,* Paris, 1949, 60, fig. 64; Laprade, *d'Orbay,* pl. VI.8b (attrib. to studio of Le Brun, based on lost original by François d'Orbay); A. Braham and M. Whiteley, "Louis Le Vau's Projects for the Louvre and the Colonnade—II," *GBA*, ser. 6, LXIV, 1964, 348f., 348, fig. 1 (attrib. to Louis Le Vau, 1667); M. Petzet, "Entwürfe zur Louvre-Kolonnade," in *Stil und Überlieferung in der Kunst des Abendlandes: Akten des 21. Internationalen Kongresses für Kunstgeschichte in Bonn 1964*, Berlin, 1967, III, 160, pl. 35, fig. 2 (1667); M. Whiteley and A. Braham, "Les soubassements de l'aile orientale du Louvre," *RA*, no. 4, 1969, 40, 41, fig. 15 (attrib. to Louis Le Vau, 1667); R. W. Berger, "Charles Le Brun and the Louvre Colonnade," *AB*, LII, 1970, 400, fig. 1; E. Hubala, *Die Kunst des 17. Jahrhunderts (Propyläen Kunstgeschichte 9)*, Berlin, 1970, 251, 253, text fig. 20b (1667) (entry by M. Petzet); C. Tadgell, "Claude Perrault, François Le Vau, and the Louvre Colonnade," *BurlM*, CXXII, 1980, 330, fig. 64, 333f. (attrib. to Louis Le Vau).

A2. Figure 62. Drawing. Studio of Louis Le Vau.
Elevation of end pavilion of east façade.
Spring 1667.
Paris, Musée Carnavalet, Cabinet des Estampes et Dessins, Réserve, D6944 no. 19 (série GC).
58.0 by 29.2 cm. *Watermark:* Bunch of grapes.
Pencil. Preliminary ruled lines. Trimmed along left profile of drawing.

Bibliography. Braham and Whiteley, "Louis Le Vau's Projects—II," 349, fig. 2, 354, 358 (attrib. to Louis Le Vau, 1667); Petzet, "Entwürfe zur Louvre-Kolonnade," 161, pl. 34, fig. 1.

A3. Figure 64. Drawing. Studio of Louis Le Vau.
Plan of Cour Carrée.
Spring 1667.
Paris, Louvre, Cabinet des Dessins, Recueil du Louvre, I, fol. 13.
68.5 by 72.5 cm. Two sheets with central horizontal crease (repaired). Chaplet watermark on larger piece.
Pen, gray ink, gray wash. Pencil inscription in center of court: "premier Etage du louvre." Pen inscription (in Le Vau's hand) identifying rooms (counterclockwise beginning in right [north] wing): "Antichamb[re], Salle des Gardes, Chappelle, Salle des Gardes, Antichamb[re], Cabinet du Cercle [central room, east range], Chambre de Parade, Chamb[re] Cabinet (2), Grand Cabinet, Vestibulle, Sallon [southeast corner pavilion], Salle des Gardes, Antichamb[re], Cabinet du Cercle, Chambre (2)." In pencil in southeast corner of the Cour Carrée: two rows of freestanding columns, aligned with the engaged columns of the east side of the court.

Bibliography. L. Hautecoeur, "L'auteur de la colonnade du Louvre," *GBA*, ser. 5, IX, 1924, 162–164, illus. on 163, 164, 167, left (attrib. to Louis Le Vau, François d'Orbay, draftsman; inscriptions attrib. to d'Orbay); idem, *Louvre et Tuileries*, 169–171, pl. XXXVIII, top (attribs. as in preceding reference); R. Josephson, "Quelques dessins de Claude Perrault pour le Louvre," *GBA*, ser. 5, XVI, 1927, 183 (illus.), 183–184 (attrib. to d'Orbay); L. Hautecoeur, *Histoire du Louvre: Le château—le palais—le musée des origines à nos jours, 1200–1928*, Paris, [1928], 59, fig. 76, 60 (attrib. to d'Orbay as draftsman); E. Langenskiöld, "Louvren, Tuilerierna och Versailles: Slottens byggnadshistoria i belysning av ritningar i Cronstedtsamlingen på Nationalmuseum," *Nationalmusei Årsbok*, 1942–43, 115, fig. 29a, 116 (attrib. to Louis Le Vau and d'Orbay); Hautecoeur, *HAC*, I, 444–445, fig. 362 (attrib. to Louis Le Vau, d'Orbay, draftsman); Laprade, *d'Orbay*, 144, pl. VI.8A (attrib. to d'Orbay, inscriptions by Louis Le Vau; summer 1667); Braham and Whiteley, "Louis Le Vau's Projects—II," 354f., 356, fig. 10 (attrib. to d'Orbay, 1667); Petzet, "Entwürfe zur Louvre-Kolonnade," 160 (inscriptions by Louis Le Vau); D. del Pesco, *Il Louvre di Bernini nella Francia di Luigi XIV*, Naples, 1984, 175, 183, fig. 124 (attrib. to studio of Louis Le Vau, d'Orbay, draftsman).

A4. Figure 65. Drawing. Claude Perrault (?).
Plan of Cour Carrée.
Spring 1667.
Stockholm, Nationalmuseum, THC 1240.
65.6 by 63.0 cm. Two sheets. *Watermark:* Chaplet with cross (E. Heawood, *Watermarks, Mainly of the 17th and 18th Centuries,* Hilversum, 1950, pl. 37, no. 226, 69 [Paris, 1683]).
Black ink. Numerous measurements in ink and pencil. Pinprick holes. Rooms behind the north part of the east wing identified in pencil (from right to left): "escalier[?] [in the northern corner pavilion], Salle des gardes, antichambre, petite antichambre." Pencil studies in right lower part

of sheet: column arrangements for central pavilion. Plan in pencil in center of the court (probably a shed for the workers; cf. Louvre, Dessins, Recueil du Louvre, II, fol. 79: "Plan des Baraques de la Cour du Louvre" [18th cent.]). Inscription on verso: "Encien projet du [?]/plan de la cage [carré?] du louvre."

Provenance: Probably from Charles Perrault's collection of Claude's drawings, sent by Daniel Cronström in Paris to Nicodemus Tessin the Younger in Stockholm in 1695 (see Sources II, no. 43).

Bibliography. Josephson, "Quelques dessins de Claude Perrault," 181 (illus.), 182f. (attrib. to Perrault); Laprade, *d'Orbay,* 144, pl. VI.8C (summer 1667); Braham and Whiteley, "Louis Le Vau's Projects—II," 354f., 357, fig. 11 (attrib. to studio of Louis Le Vau); Petzet, "Entwürfe zur Louvre-Kolonnade," 160.

A5. Figure 66. Medal.
Elevation of central portion of east façade.
1667.
Paris, Bibliothèque Nationale, Cabinet des Médailles et Antiques, série royale no. 679.
Diameter: 5 cm.
Inscription: • MAIESTATI • AC • AETERNIT[ATI] • GALL[ICI] • IMPERII • SACRVM • Exergue: • MDCLXVII •

This medal in gold may have been placed in the foundation of the east façade by Colbert on November 19, 1667 (see Sources II, no. 4).

Bibliography. C. F. Menestrier, *Histoire du roy Louis le Grand par les médailles . . . ,* new ed., Paris, 1691, pl. 16, top left; A. Babeau, "Note sur les fossés du Louvre," *Mémoires de la Société nationale des antiquaires de France,* ser. 7, III, 1902, 157–158; Hautecoeur, *Louvre et Tuileries,* 170–171; Laprade, *d'Orbay,* pl. VI.8D (November 1667); Sauvel, "Les auteurs de la colonnade," 325, fig. 1, 331; Braham and Whiteley, "Louis Le Vau's Projects—II," 349, fig. 3, 354, 358 (November 1667); Berger, "Charles Le Brun and the Louvre Colonnade," 396, text fig. 3, 399.

A6. Figure 67. Drawing. Claude Perrault.
Perspective bird's-eye view from the east.
Early 1668.

Paris, Bibliothèque Nationale, Cabinet des Estampes, Va 217c, fol. 16.
37.3 by 51.9 cm.
Pen and gray wash.

Bibliography. Petzet, "Entwürfe zur Louvre-Kolonnade," 161, pl. 34, fig. 2 (attrib. to Claude Perrault, early 1668 at the latest); idem, "Claude Perrault als Architekt des Pariser Observatoriums," *ZfK,* XXX, 1967, 6, fig. 5 (attrib. to Perrault); Hubala, *Die Kunst des 17. Jahrhunderts,* 252–253, fig. 274 (attrib. to Perrault, late 1667 or early 1668) (entry by M. Petzet); del Pesco, *Il Louvre di Bernini,* 175, 184, fig. 125; A. Picon, *Claude Perrault, 1613–1688, ou la curiosité d'un classique,* Paris, 1988, 180, fig. 139.

A7. Figures 69–72. Drawing. Claude Perrault.
Elevation studies of end (south) pavilion of the east façade, with three bays of the Colonnade.
1668.
Paris, Archives Nationales, O¹ 1667³, no. 73.
99.9 by 71.8 cm. Flaps attached to show alternate designs for the elevation and plan of the pavilion.
Black ink, gray wash, pencil.

Bibliography. Laprade, *d'Orbay,* pl. App. C2, top (details) (attrib. to Claude Perrault, François d'Orbay, draftsman); Petzet, "Entwürfe zur Louvre-Kolonnade," 162, pl. 34, fig. 4 (attrib. to Perrault, 1668); W. D. Brönner, *Blondel-Perrault: Zur Architekturtheorie des 17. Jahrhunderts in Frankreich,* publ. diss., Bonn, 1972, 109, fig. 22 (attrib. to Perrault); Picon, *Claude Perrault,* 173, figs. 130–133.

A8. Figure 73. Drawing. Studio of Louis Le Vau, François d'Orbay, draftsman.
Elevation of end (north) pavilion of the east façade, with two bays of the Colonnade.
1668.
Paris, Archives Nationales, O¹ 1667⁴, no. 84.
51.8 by 76.0 cm.
Black ink, gray and black washes. *Inscriptions:* Recto, lower right, "Elevation d'un des Pavillons de la fasse du Louvre du coste de l'Eglise de Sᵗ Germain." Verso, same inscription as recto but in a different hand; crossed out, "Divers plants [sic] et elevations du Louvre."

The medallions are filled with scenes that were probably allegorical in meaning, alluding to the King. This type of scene, containing few figures, reappears in drawing A11 (see below). In Marot's engraving of 1676 (Fig. 88), such depictions are replaced by many-figured historical ones and direct representations of Louis XIV. However, the medallions were never carved under Louis XIV.

Bibliography. Hautecoeur, *Louvre et Tuileries*, 176–177, pl. XLI (attrib. to Claude Perrault); Hautecoeur, *HAC*, I, 446–447, 448, fig. 366 (attrib. to Perrault); Laprade, *d'Orbay*, 147, pls. VI.9, VI.10, bottom (detail) (drawing and recto inscription attrib. to d'Orbay); Sauvel, "Les auteurs de la colonnade," 342–343; Petzet, "Entwürfe zur Louvre-Kolonnade," 162, pl. 34, fig. 5 (drawing and recto inscription attrib. to d'Orbay, after 1670); Brönner, *Blondel-Perrault*, 109, fig. 22 (attrib. to Perrault); [Paris, Ministère de la culture], *Colbert, 1619–1683,* exhib. cat., Paris, 1983, 290, no. 424 (illus.), 291, no. 424 (attrib. to d'Orbay, 1669; crossed-out verso inscription attrib. to Charles Perrault) (entry by N. Felkay); Picon, *Claude Perrault,* 182, fig. 140 (attrib. to d'Orbay).

A9. Figures 74, 75. Drawing. Anonymous draftsman.
Elevation, east façade (final design).
1668.
Stockholm, Nationalmuseum, CC 789.
23.5 by 74.8 cm. Two sheets. *Watermarks:* Right half, Colbert's coat-of-arms (Heawood, *Watermarks,* I, pl. 108, no. 690; 80 [Paris, 1689]). Left half: cartouche (similar to ibid., I, pl. 109, no. 695; 80 [Paris, 1687]).
Pen, black ink, gray wash. Modern Swedish inscription, lower right corner.

Bibliography. R. Josephson, *L'architecte de Charles XII, Nicodème Tessin,* Paris and Brussels, 1930, pl. X (attrib. to Claude Perrault); idem, *Kungarnas Paris,* Stockholm, 1943, 86, fig. 45 (probably by Perrault).

A10. Figure 76. Drawing.
Plan of Cour Carrée (final design).
1668.
Paris, Louvre, Cabinet des Dessins, Recueil du Louvre, I, fol. 26.

85.0 by 87.0 cm. Four sheets, no watermarks.
Pen, black ink. Numerous measurements.

Previously unpublished.

A11. Figure 77. Drawing. Studio of Louis Le Vau, François d'Orbay, draftsman.
Studies of the rear wall and ceiling of the Colonnade.
1668.
Paris, Musée des Arts Décoratifs, Cabinet des Dessins, no. 394.
39.7 by 26.9 cm.
Pen, black ink, gray wash. *Watermark:* bunches of grapes(?).

Bibliography. Laprade, *d'Orbay,* pl. VI.10, top (attrib. to d'Orbay, 1669); Sauvel, "Les auteurs de la colonnade," 342–343; *Colbert, 1619–1683,* 291, no. 426, 293, no. 426 (illus.) (attrib. to d'Orbay[?]) (entry by N. Felkay).

A12. Figure 78. Drawing. Anonymous draftsman.
Studies of iron reinforcement system of the Colonnade.
1668.
Paris, Louvre, Cabinet des Dessins, Recueil du Louvre, II, fol. 74.
39.0 by 55.6 cm. *Watermark:* Bunch of grapes.
Gray and brown ink; some pencil markings. Numerous measurements.

Previously unpublished.

The semicircular arch indicated in pencil in the upper right corner accords with A11 (Fig. 77), thus revealing the initial, unrealized design for the space above the ceilings of the Colonnade, a space that was eventually built with a corbeled vault (Figs. 79, upper right, 80). The iron reinforcement depicted in the drawing essentially agrees with the executed system as recorded by Patte (Fig. 79, upper left), except that the Z-cramps between the voussoirs and the cross-shaped cramps between the column drums are not indicated. The *porte-à-faux* between the paired columns is also not shown (see Chapter VI and Appendix B).

Folio 75 in the same *recueil* appears to be an eighteenth-century copy of A12. Probably also of eighteenth-century date are folios 71, 72, and 73, which show the iron system in the central pavilion. Folio 75 bears an inscription in pencil on the verso: "4 desseins pretes a *M*. moreau par M. Soufflot le 2 1761 (?)." (The reference is probably to the architect Pierre Louis Moreau-Desproux; Soufflot would have had access to the drawings in the course of his restoration of the Louvre under Gabriel from 1756 on.) These four drawings, along with others now also in the Cabinet des Dessins (Figs. 89, 99, 102, 112, 114, 115; see Chapter VI), may be the drawings Claude Guillot-Aubry presented to the Académie royale d'architecture in 1756 (see Sources II, no. 87). The drawings in the Cabinet des Dessins came to the Louvre in 1951 from the collection of the Duke of Wellington, but they could have left the Academy's collection at the time of the French Revolution. See G. Monnier, "Dessins inédits pour la colonnade du Louvre," *MHF*, n.s., 1972, nos. 3/4, 130–137.

B. *East Façade (without Colonnade)*

B1. Figure 92. Drawing. Studio of Louis Le Vau, François d'Orbay, draftsman.
Elevation.
Spring 1667.
Paris, Archives Nationales, O¹ 1667⁴, no. 88.
48.0 by 105.2 cm.
Black and gray ink, wash, pencil.
Standing (probably allegorical) female figures flank the portal. Statues at the level of the drum depict Apollo in a quadriga slaying the Niobids.

Bibliography. Hautecoeur, *Louvre et Tuileries,* 167 (attrib. to Le Brun); Hautecoeur, *HAC,* I, 444 (attrib. to Le Brun); Laprade, *d'Orbay,* 144, pl. VI.7, top (detail) (attrib. to d'Orbay, beginning of 1667); Braham and Whiteley, "Louis Le Vau's Projects—II," 348 (attrib. to Le Brun); Petzet, "Entwürfe zur Louvre-Kolonnade," 160, pl. 35, fig. 1 (attrib. to Louis Le Vau, d'Orbay, draftsman); Berger, "Charles Le Brun and the Louvre Colonnade," 400, fig. 5 (attrib. to Le Brun); Hubala, *Die Kunst des 17. Jahrhunderts,* 251, 252, text fig. 20a (detail) (attrib. to d'Orbay, 1667; entry by M. Petzet); idem, "Das Triumphbogenmonument für Ludwig XIV. auf der Place du Trône," *ZfK,* XLV, 1982, 161 (studio of Louis Le Vau).

B2 Figure 93. Drawing. Studio of Charles Le Brun.
Elevation.
Spring 1667.
Paris, Louvre, Cabinet des Dessins, Inv. 27641.
42.0 by 146.2 cm. Three sheets.
Brown ink, gray wash, black chalk. In a modern frame.
Inscription above central portal: "LVDOVICVS XIIII GAL[LIAE] REX."

Provenance: From Le Brun's studio, seized by the Crown in 1690 for the royal collections.

The Dioscurii flank the portal with flying figures of Fame above its arch, holding festoons attached to a radiant sun- (or Apollo-) head on a shield. Statues at the base of the dome depict Apollo slaying the Niobids.

Bibliography. Hautecoeur, *Louvre et Tuileries,* 167, pl. XXXVII (detail) (attrib. to Le Brun); Hautecoeur, *HAC,* I, 444, fig. 361 (detail) (attrib. to Le Brun); Laprade, *d'Orbay,* 144, pl. VI.7, bottom (wrongly given as AN, O¹ 1667) (attrib. to studio of Le Brun); Braham and Whiteley, "Louis Le Vau's Projects—II," 348 (attrib. to Le Brun); Berger, "Charles Le Brun and the Louvre Colonnade," 400, fig. 6 (attrib. to Le Brun); Hubala, *Die Kunst des 17. Jahrhunderts,* 251 (attrib. to Le Brun) (entry by M. Petzet); *Collections de Louis XIV,* 258–260, no. 258 (attrib. to Le Brun); Petzet, "Das Triumphbogenmonument," 161 (attrib. to studio of Le Brun); del Pesco, *Il Louvre di Bernini,* 151, 175, 180, fig. 121 (attrib. to Le Brun); J. C. Daufresne, *Louvre & Tuileries: Architectures de papier,* Liège, 1987, 67, fig. 85 (attrib. to Le Brun).

B3. Figure 94. Drawing. Studio of Charles Le Brun.
Elevation of central pavilion.
Spring 1667.
Paris, Louvre, Cabinet des Dessins, Inv. 30227 (G-M 8430).
45.0 by 33.0 cm. Laid down.
Brown ink, gray wash, black chalk, pencil.
Inscription above central portal: "LVDOVICVS XIIII GAL[LIAE] REX."

Provenance: From Le Brun's studio, seized by the Crown in 1690 for the royal collections.

The Dioscurii flank the portal, with reliefs of Athena(?) and Hercules in the oval medallions above. Statues at the level of the drum depict Apollo in a quadriga slaying the Niobids.

Bibliography. Hautecoeur, *Louvre et Tuileries,* 167 (attrib. to Le Brun); Hautecoeur, *HAC,* I, 444 (attrib. to Le Brun); Braham and Whiteley, "Louis Le Vau's Projects—II," 348 (attrib. to Le Brun); Berger, "Charles Le Brun and the Louvre Colonnade," 400, fig. 4 (attrib. to Le Brun); Hubala, *Die Kunst des 17. Jahrhunderts,* 251, fig. 273b (attrib. to Le Brun, 1667) (entry by M. Petzet); del Pesco, *Il Louvre di Bernini,* 172, fig. 120.

C. *South Façade*

C1. Figure 96. Drawing. Studio of Louis Le Vau, François d'Orbay, draftsman.
Elevation and sections.
1668.
Paris, Archives Nationales, O¹ 1667³, no. 69.
43.3 by 142.0 cm.
Black ink, gray and blue washes.

Bibliography. Hautecoeur, *Louvre et Tuileries,* pl. XLII (detail); Laprade, *d'Orbay,* pl. VI.6c, c' (attrib. to d'Orbay, ca. 1666); W. Graf Kalnein, review of idem, *ZfK,* XXV, 1962, 187, 189, fig. 1 (detail) (attrib. to d'Orbay, ca. 1666); Tadgell, "Claude Perrault, François Le Vau and the Louvre Colonnade," 327, 330, fig. 65, 334.

C2. Figure 97. Drawing. Studio of Louis Le Vau, François d'Orbay, draftsman.
Western elevations of southwest pavilion of the Cour Carrée and part of the western façade; section of link to the Petite Galerie.
1668.
Paris, Archives Nationales, O¹ 1667⁴, no. 82.
43.8 by 28.5 cm.
Black ink, gray and blue washes. Pen inscription, upper left: "Soixante toises (?)."

Previously unpublished.

C3. Figure 98. Drawing. Studio of Louis Le Vau, François d'Orbay, draftsman.
Elevation.
1668.
Paris, Archives Nationales, O¹ 1667⁴, no. 85.
43.0 (scant) by 123.0 cm.

Black ink, gray, black, blue washes, pencil. In damaged condition.

Previously unpublished.

This drawing, although from the hand of d'Orbay, may correspond to a destroyed drawing for the south façade attributed by J. F. Blondel to Perrault (Sources II, no. 84[c]): "On voit le dessein à colonnes proposé par *Perrault* pour l'avant-corps du milieu, page 55 de son manuscrit; il paroît aussi qu'il avoit projeté d'élever au-dessus de cet avant-corps, un Attique couronné d'un dôme dans le genre de celui qu'on y remarque aujourd'hui, reste du vieux Louvre, & dont le mur de face qui le soutient, doit servir de mur de réfend [the reference is to Le Vau's pavilion of 1660–63, Figs. 17, 18]: il paroît encore qu'il avoit eu envie de rendre les combles apparens, & de pratiquer un Attique sur les pavillons des extrêmités de cette façade."

D. *Courtyard*

D1. Figure 107. Drawing. Studio of Louis Le Vau, François d'Orbay, draftsman.
Study for top floor.
1668.
Paris, Archives Nationales, O¹ 1667, no. 80.
17.0 by 29.5 cm.
Brown ink and wash, black chalk.

Bibliography. Laprade, *d'Orbay,* pl. VI.11, bottom (detail); Picon, *Claude Perrault,* 190, fig. 149.

D2. Figure 108. Drawing. Studio of Louis Le Vau, François d'Orbay, draftsman.
Study for top floor.
1668.
Paris, Archives Nationales, O¹ 1667, no. 81.
29.2 by 44.2 cm.
Brown ink and wash.

Bibliography. Laprade, *d'Orbay,* pl. VI.11, top (detail); Picon, *Claude Perrault,* 190, fig. 150.

(For other courtyard drawings not produced by the Petit Conseil and dating from the 1670s, see Chapter V and Figures 109–113.)

APPENDIX B

THE COUPLED-COLUMNS DEBATE[1]

Vitruvius, in book III, chapter 3 (1–6) of *De architectura*, discusses the various types of intercolumniations of the columns of temples. The different spacings have specific names: pycnostyle ($1\frac{1}{2}$ diameters); systyle (2 diameters); diastyle (3 diameters); araeostyle (more than 3 diameters). The best intercolumniation, according to Vitruvius, is a fifth type, the eustyle—$2\frac{1}{4}$ diameters, with 3 diameters between the two central columns of a row. Vitruvius attributed the eustyle system to the Greek architect Hermogenes,[2] who also invented (again according to Vitruvius) the pseudodipteral octastyle temple plan. In Perrault's translation we read:

> Hermogene est celuy qui a trouvé toutes ces proportions & qui le premier a inventé l'Octostyle & la maniere du Pseudodiptere, lorsqu'il a trouvé à propos d'oster du Diptere le rang des Colonnes du milieu qui sont au nombre de trente-quatre, afin qu'il y eut moins d'ouvrage & de dépense. Ce qu'il y a de beau en cette invention, est qu'il a trouvé le moyen d'augmenter l'espace qui est fait pour se promener au tour du Temple, sans diminuer le nombre des Colonnes qui font l'aspect de dehors, en ordonnant si bien tout son ouvrage qu'il n'a rien ôsté au Diptere de ce qu'il a de recommandable, & à quoy on puisse avoir regret; mais seulement ce qui y estoit de superflu. Car on a inventé ces Ailes de colonnes ainsi arrangées au tour des Temples, pour leur donner plus de majesté par l'aspreté des entrecolonnemens. Cét élargissement a encore cette utilité, qu'il peut mettre à couvert de la pluye un grand nombre de personnes. Cette disposition & cette ordonnance des Pseudodipteres font connoistre avec quelle subtilité d'esprit Hermogene conduisoit ses ouvrages, qui meritent d'estre considerez comme la source où la posterité a puisé les meilleurs preceptes de l'Architecture.[3]

The phrase "par l'aspreté des entrecolonnemens"[4] in the latter part of this passage prompted Perrault to write a long and important footnote of commentary in his 1673 Vitruvius edition. After remarking on the fondness of the ancients for close columnar groupings, resulting in closed visual effects, Perrault continued:

> Le goust de nostre siecle, ou du moins de nostre nation, est different de celuy des Anciens, & peut-estre qu'en cela il tient un peu du Gothique: car nous aimons l'air le jour & les dégagemens. Cela nous a fait inventer une sixiéme maniere de disposer ces Colonnes, qui est de les joindre deux à deux, & de mettre aussi l'espace de deux entrecolonnemens en un.[5]

Other French writers before Perrault had written favorably, even enthusiastically, of Gothic churches,[6] but Perrault seems to have been the first to claim Gothic style as an expression of a national taste for open, perforated structure. He uses a diagram (see Sources II, no. 12[a]) to demonstrate how the coupled columns of the Louvre Colonnade were derived from a systyle range of columns, leaving a wide span between each group. This, according to Perrault, "imitates" Hermogenes's eustyle, with its wider central intercolumniation. Perrault proceeds to assert that the new ranges of coupled columns of the Colonnade—which he calls "Pseudosystyle"—accomplish what Hermogenes's pseudodipteral plan produced: a more open composition. Perrault then notes that "plusieurs" disapprove of the "pseudosystyle" as not authorized by the ancients. To this Perrault argues that just as the ancients themselves improved upon past accomplishments by not slavishly following precedent, so too the moderns should be entitled to add to the past. The "pseudosystyle" combines all the advantages found separately in the Vitruvian systems: "aspreté" and "serrement" of the columns (favored by the ancients); "dégagement," the quality sought by the moderns; and structural solidity. This last is achieved by not making the architraves of monolithic stones and by not resting the end of the architrave on only half of the top of the capital, as was the practice of the ancients. In modern construction, Perrault continues, the architraves shall be made of several stones, with one resting entirely on top of the capital. Also, "les Poutres estant doublées de mesme que les colonnes, elles ont beaucoup de force pour soûtenir les Planchers."[7]

This method, Perrault asserts, has been put into practice "avec beaucoup de magnificence" in the Louvre Colonnade. He continues:

> Les Colonnes qui ont trois piez & demy de diametre sont jointes deux à deux, & ont leurs Entrecolonnemens de douze piez, estant distantes d'autant de leurs Pilastres qui sont au mur. Cela a esté fait ainsi pour garder la symmetrie en donnant un espace égal à tous les Entrecolonnemens dans le reste de l'Edifice [the south façade, Figure 95], qui n'a que des Pillastres un à un, mais qui n'ont pû estre plus proches que de douze piez, à cause de la largeur des Croisées, qui sont ornées de Chambranles, de Consoles & de Frontons qui demandoient cette distance entre les Pillastres; & ces grandes distances dans les Portiques n'auroient pas esté supportables si les Colonnes n'avoient esté doublées.[8]

In 1674, one year after publication of Perrault's Vitruvius edition, the topic of coupled columns was discussed at a meeting of the Royal Academy of Architecture (April 30). The members of the Academy were reading Palladio's treatise, where there is a brief description and several plates of Santa Costanza in Rome.[9] Palladio had noted that its interior columns are coupled radially to support the dome. The Academy merely commented that the ancients used paired columns for "dégagement" and "solidité" when required.[10] The topic arose again on May 7, when the members reached book IV, chapter XXV in Palladio, where there is a description of a small prostyle Roman temple near Trevi with two coupled pier-and-column sets.[11] The Academy this time noted (wrongly) the presence of coupled columns.[12] Neither on April 30 nor on May 7 did it take a position on the question of coupled supports.

Seven years later, in 1681, the French architect and theoretician Augustin Charles d'Aviler noted that the issue of paired columns was at the moment a very controversial one. In his discourse on an ideal mid-century château design by Antoine Le Pautre that displays coupled columns, he tended to condemn their usage:

> Pour ce qui est de l'Acouplement des Colonnes, il n'y a presque d'autre exemple dans l'Antique que les Temples de Scisi[13] & de Trevi que rapporte Palladio, qui ne sont pas de grande consideration; mais, les Modernes en ont tellement introduit l'usage, mesme dans les plus beaux ouvrages de nostre temps, que si cela paroist tolerable, l'accoustumance y aura plus de part que la raison; & il y a tant de choses à dire, soit pour établir ou pour détruire cette disposition d'Ordonnance, qu'il en faut laisser agiter la question aux Maistres de l'Art qui s'accorderont difficilement sur ce sujet, & particulierement ceux dont la capacité est fondée sur la connoissance de l'Antiquité.
>
> Le premier ordre de ce Palais [Le Pautre's ideal design] est dorique, & qui paroist estre distribué selon la regle qui en est inviolable [concerning the placement of metopes and triglyphs?], & qui en fait la plus grande beauté, excepté lorsque les Colonnes sont accouplées, parce que l'on tombe dans l'un des deux inconveniens, ou du Portail de l'Eglise de saint Gervais, ou de celuy des Peres Minimes, qui avec ces deffauts ne laissent pas d'estre les chefs-d'oeuvres de deux des plus grands Architectes de nostre siecle.[14]

This passage is important because d'Aviler cites two distinguished French precedents for coupled columns: Salomon de Brosse's façade of Saint-Gervais (begun 1616) and François Mansart's façade of the Église des Minimes (1657–65), both in Paris.[15] However, the columns of these façades were placed right next to the wall, not producing a colonnade, as at the Louvre. And at the Minimes, the "paired" columns were spaced more than one column diameter apart, thus weakening the coupled effect.

Two years later, in 1683, François Blondel, director of the Royal Academy of Architecture, replied at length to Perrault. In his 1673 edition of Savot's book on domestic architecture, Blondel implied that the Louvre Colonnade was by Perrault and was among the most magnificent buildings of Louis XIV (Sources II, no. 13). Nevertheless, in three chapters of his *Cours d'architecture,* Blondel mounted a sharp attack against paired columns.[16]

Blondel first notes that coupled columns (or pilasters) were rarely found in ancient architecture. They started to appear, however, and with some frequency, during the Italian Renaissance. Blondel views them as vestiges of the clustered colonnettes of Gothic compound piers: coupling constitutes the compromise sought by Renaissance architects between the Antique (single supports) and the Gothic (numerous supports). French architects of the sixteenth and seventeenth centuries, he continues, then indulged in a craze for coupled columns and pilasters, so that there are few modern French buildings without them. The coupling of supports, Blondel concedes,

est pardonnable à ceux qui n'ont point vu d'autres Exemples: Mais il y a sujet de s'estonner que tant de beaux Genies qui professent l'Architecture aient fait voyage à Rome & ailleurs, sans s'etre depris de ces pratiques; & que la preoccupation des usages de Paris, dont ils n'ont trouvé que trop d'exemples dans les ouvrages modernes d'Italie [!], les ait empesché de gouter ces proportions admirables qui se rencontrent dans les Colonnes des edifices anciens entre leurs hauteurs, leurs grosseurs & leurs Entrecolonnes; dont les distances sont si judicieusement compassées, qu'ils ne sçauroient jamais plaire comme ils font, si elles estoient disposées dans d'autres mesures. Je m'estonne, dis-je, qu'ils n'ayent pas veu la difference qu'il y a entre ces restes qui ont l'approbation universelle, & ces bâtimens demi Gothiques ou les Anciens ont couplé des Colonnes ou des Pilastres.[17]

Blondel then moves to the question of whether the ancients used coupled supports at the corners of edifices for additional strength. This may have been the case in a few undistinguished ancient buildings (and in works by Palladio and Scamozzi). The practice, however, is not found in any ancient examples of high quality; the corners of cellas merely received single columns or pilasters. And where Vitruvius writes of widening the end column, he recommends this for optical, not structural, reasons (III.3.11). Blondel states that there are no ancient examples of porticoes with coupled columns at the corners or in the center. He notes, furthermore, that the radially disposed coupled columns inside Santa Costanza in Rome (Blondel's "Temple de Bacchus") function to support the arches and vaults and cannot be taken as a model (cf. the meeting of April 30, 1674, of the Royal Academy of Architecture, summarized above). Finally, coupled end pilasters, Blondel maintains, can be used only if the wall behind them is broad.

Blondel then takes up purely structural considerations. He rejects Perrault's claim that an architrave is better supported at its ends by coupled columns instead of single ones. That is because the weakness or strength of the architrave depends on its length between the supports and not on whether the latter are single or paired. The weight of an architrave is better distributed over four equally spaced columns than over two pairs of coupled ones.

After summarizing Perrault's Vitruvius note (discussed above), Blondel first attacks Perrault's logic in claiming that his derivation of the pseudosystyle from the systyle arrangement is analogous to Hermogenes's derivation of the pseudodipteral from the dipteral plan. According to Blondel, the analogous logical process would be to remove every other column of a systyle plan, not to move every other column closer to the others, à la Perrault (see diagram, Sources II, no. 12[a]). After some remarks on how the idea of progress in architecture has led to abuses (Gothic and German styles), Blondel returns to the pseudosystyle arrangement. Rather than combining all the advantages of the different systems of columnar spacing (as claimed by Perrault), the pseudosystyle actually combines a number of disadvantages: some columns are closer together than in the pycnostyle, others are farther apart than in the araeostyle arrangement.

Blondel continues the offensive: Perrault is wrong to claim that the pseudosystyle system is stronger, because the architrave rests on the entire surface of the capital, not just on half of it. The point of weakness of an architrave is its midpoint; a failure there results in damage only to the part of the abacus closest to the point of collapse. Thus, the architrave is not less supported if it only rests on half of the column; the outermost columns in a coupled column arrangement support little. These arguments, Blondel adds, are the same for wood construction. The director then at last comments on the actual embodiment of the pseudosystyle composition, the Louvre Colonnade (Figs. 43, 44):

> C'est, comme je crois, pour ne pas tomber dans les inconveniens que j'ay rapportez cy-devant, que les Architectes avoient évité jusques icy de faire des Peristyles isolez à Colonnes couplées, car tous ceux que nous voyons sont faits avec des Pilastres ou des Colonnes engagées, afin que les architraves fussent en partie soutenus dans le mur. Il n'y en a qu'un seul au monde, au moins que je sçache, & qui est pourtant tres-considérable. Il s'est fait depuis peu dans Paris, & c'est où l'on dit que l'on a heureusement suivi l'exemple d'Hermogene. Il est pourtant vray que l'on n'y a pas eu toute la confiance que l'on devoit avoir à sa solidité, aprés avoir si bien assuré qu'elle n'y estoit point diminuée: Car le fer n'y a point esté épargné pour aider à soutenir & à arrester les architraves dans leur grande portée.[18]

Blondel ends this section by pointing out the costliness of the pseudosystyle arrangement, because extra columns are always needed, and supplies a diagram to prove his point (Sources II, no. 24[b], p. 153, right col.).

Then, in a final chapter on coupled columns, he writes about the difficulties of using paired Roman Doric columns (citing De Brosse's façade of Saint-Gervais) and concludes his entire critique with a damning afterthought:

> J'oubliois à dire que l'usage de doubler les Colonnes altere extremement les belles proportions des edifices, dont elles augmentent tellement la largeur, qu'ils en paroissent nains & ecrasez, quelque soin que l'on prenne de les elever ou par des attiques[19] ou autrement. Ces manieres plattes que Vitruve appelle Barices ou Barycephales[20] estant absolument contraires au bon goust des Anciens, qui estoient, comme dit Vitruve, *gracilioribus modulis delectati,* c'est à dire qui prenoient grand plaisir aux manieres *svelte[s]* & degagées;[21] Mais je n'en ay que trop dit sur ce sujet.[22]

These chapters from Blondel's *Cours* were published in 1683. In the same year, Claude Perrault published his *Ordonnance des cinq espèces de colonnes selon la méthode des anciens*. The section on coupled columns[23] is a repetition of points Perrault put forward in the footnote in his 1673 Vitruvius edition, previously summarized. In 1684, however, Perrault issued the second edition of his *Vitruve* and responded at length to Blondel's critique of the preceding year.[24]

Perrault first vigorously defends the right to advance the art of building through innovation, even if that means departing from ancient practice. It would be much worse to close the door on fine inventions than to allow whatever is bizarre or capricious; the latter, once permitted, will eventually die through disuse. The inventions of the ancients were once new; if they had never been permitted, there would have been no progress in the arts and sciences. And Perrault reminds his readers that the ancients themselves never claimed to have reached perfection.

As for Blondel's point that Perrault's analogy of Hermogenes' pseudodipteral plan with the modern pseudosystyle is a false one, Perrault replies that he was not claiming that the moderns "imitated" Hermogenes, but only attempting to show that

> Hermogene a pris une license, il n'est point necessaire pour l'imiter de prendre la mesme license, mais qu'il suffit d'en prendre une pareille, & à plus forte raison une moindre, comme on a fait, puisque déplacer simplement une Colonne [i.e., the pseudosystyle arrangement] est quelque chose de moins que de l'oster absolument [i.e., the pseudodipteral system].[25]

Perrault then moves on to the more specific and technical points raised by Blondel. First, while it is true that the distance between the coupled columns is less than in the pycnostyle (the latter = $1\frac{1}{2}$ diameters), this does not detract from the "dégagement" because such openness is not necessary at every point. Then, Blondel's claim that the large intercolumniation of the pseudosystyle renders the architrave too weak is untenable, according to Perrault, because the distance is no greater than that found in the diastyle (3 diameters). (Here, however, Perrault slightly alters the measurement: the large intercolumniation of the Colonnade is 3.4 diameters, which technically places it in the araeostyle category, where, according to Vitruvius, wood and not stone must be used as lintels [III.3.5].) Perrault adds that criticism of the coupled columns arises simply from the term "pseudosystyle," to which some object; "pseudopycnostyle" could just as well have been used, but Perrault chose the former because it is easier (*plus douce*) to pronounce. It merely indicates a column arrangement different from all others previously used.

Perrault proceeds to the question of whether the end of an architrave should rest entirely or partially on top of a column. He reaffirms the preferability of the first alternative on structural grounds: its end will be above the small intercolumniation between the paired columns, and the weight of this end of the architrave—a *porte-à-faux* overhanging the narrow span—will resist the bending of the architrave above the center of the large intercolumniation. (This is true for a monolithic lintel but not for the flat arches of the Louvre Colonnade, which both Blondel and Perrault probably had in mind when discussing this question.)[26]

Perrault then passes to the question of the Gothic:

> Mais le plus grand reproche que l'on croit faire à nostre Pseudosystyle est de dire qu'il tient du Gothique. J'estois demeuré d'accord du fait dans ma notte; mais supposé que le Gothique en general, & à considerer tout ce qui le compose ne fust pas le plus beau genre d'Architecture, je ne pensois pas que tout ce qui est dans le Gothique fut à rejetter. Le jour dans les Edifices & les dégagemens dont il s'agit, sont des choses en quoy les Gothiques different des Anciens: mais ce n'est pas en cela que le Gothique est à reprendre; & les Anciens qui dans les commencemens

s'éloignoient beaucoup de cette maniere, l'ont approuvée dans la suite lorsqu'ils ont fait des fenestres à leurs Temples, qui auparavant ne prenoient du jour que par la porte; & avant cela ils avoient élargi les entrecolonnemens du milieu, ainsi qu'il a esté dit.[27]

Finally, Perrault urges modern architects to adopt the coupled arrangement and renounce ideas of fixed, true proportions, comparable to musical sounds.[28] Since their appearance, paired supports have been liked by "tout le monde," including numerous modern architects, Italian and French. And there is reason to believe that the ancients also would have appreciated them if they had been counseled to use them.

Yet to Blondel's point that the masonry structure of the Colonnade holds together only because of a lavish use of iron (see Chapter VI), Perrault is silent. Perrault is also mute regarding his adversary's comment about the costliness of paired-column construction and makes no reply to Blondel's final remark about the necessarily spoiled proportions of buildings with coupled columns.

Perrault's muteness about these matters perhaps placed Blondel ahead in debating points, but Claude's silence about the iron reinforcement calls for special examination. Whether or not he was the inventor of this revolutionary system (see Chapter VI), he certainly was familiar with all its details, as was his brother Charles, Colbert's first assistant in the *Bâtiments*. But Charles Perrault revealed his intimate knowledge of the iron reinforcement only in manuscripts: in a *mémoire* of 1697 accompanying Claude's unexecuted project for the church of Sainte-Geneviève in Paris (Sources II, no. 46) and in his *Mémoires de ma vie*, composed ca. 1700 for his family. In this autobiography, Charles stated that Claude's drawings of the details of the iron system were in his possession (Sources II, no. 53[b], last par.). These drawings, along with many others by Claude, tragically perished by fire in 1871.

Claude Perrault, then, kept silent about the iron and discussed the Louvre Colonnade as if it were a purely masonry structure. In his commentary on a passage in Vitruvius where iron cramps for walls are mentioned (II.8.4), Claude makes no mention of the Louvre. His brother Charles wrote about the iron only in manuscripts not intended for publication. These facts suggest that, for the Perrault brothers, the moment for discussing iron reinforcement in architecture *in print* had not yet arrived. Perhaps the Perraults retained vestiges of traditional notions about the need for self-sufficiency in masonry construction.

Blondel died in 1686, Claude Perrault in 1688. In the latter year, Charles Perrault published the first volume of his *Parallèle des anciens et des modernes*. In this dialogue, the Abbé who speaks for the Moderns [the Perraults] comments on the Greek temple of Ephesus, the huge architraves of which (more than 15 *pieds*) were miraculously put in place by the goddess Diana, after the architect had prayed to her (and had fallen asleep):[29]

Si cet Architecte avoit sçu la coupe des pierres, il n'auroit pas esté embarassé, il auroit fait son architrave de plusieurs pieces taillées selon le trait qu'il leur faut donner, & elle auroit esté beaucoup plus solide. . . . L'impossibilité de faire de larges entrecolonnemens, parce qu'ils [the ancients] ne faisoient l'architrave que d'une seule piece, les a aussi empesché d'accoupler les colonnes & d'élargir par ce moyen les intervales, maniere d'arranger des colonnes qui donne beaucoup de grace & beaucoup de force à un édifice. [Sources II, no. 35(a)]

The coupled-columns debate effectively ended in the seventeenth century with the *Parallèle*.

Notes

1. Other recent discussions of this debate are in A. Hernandez, *Grundzüge einer Ideengeschichte der französischen Architekturtheorie von 1560–1800*, publ. diss., University of Basel, 1972, 63–65, and G. Germann, *Einführung in die Geschichte der Architekturtheorie*, Darmstadt, 1980, 184f. The relevant texts by Claude Perrault and François Blondel are published in their entirety in Sources II, nos. 12 and 24–26.

2. On Hermogenes (active ca. 220–190 B.C.), see J. J. Coulton, "Hermogenes," *Macmillan Encyclopedia of Architects*, ed. A. K. Placzek, New York and London, 1982, II, 359–361.

3. Perrault, *Vitruve*, 1673, 76–77; ibid., 1684, 78–79 (book III, chap. 2, in these editions).

4. Perrault's "aspreté" is his translation of Vitruvius's "asperitatem" (from "asperitas" = roughness, unevenness), translated as "high relief" in modern English translations. Perrault explained the phrase "aspreté des entrecolonnemens" thus: "Cette façon de parler est assez significative pour representer l'inégalité de superficie qu'un grand nombre de Colonnes donne aux costez d'un Temple lorsqu'on le regarde par les Angles. L'effet de cet aspect est de faire paroistre les Colonnes serrées l'une contre l'autre, & cette maniere plaisoit grandement aux Anciens" (Perrault, *Vitruve*, 1684, 78–79 n. 16). Blondel understood "aspreté" to mean "serrement" (Blondel, 1683, 235 [part III, book I, chap. XI]).

5. Perrault, *Vitruve*, 1673, 76 n. 3; ibid., 1684, 79 n. 16.

6. See P. Frankl, *The Gothic: Literary Sources and Interpretations through Eight Centuries*, Princeton, 1960, 336f.; R. D. Middleton, "The Abbé de Cordemoy and the Graeco-Gothic Ideal: A Prelude

to Romantic Classicism," *JWCI,* xxv, 1962, 290f. Claude Perrault and his Vitruvius note quoted above in the text are discussed by Middleton on 299. He points out (298) that in his diary of 1669 for his trip to Bordeaux, Perrault used the then highly unusual phrase "l'ordre Gothique." Middleton adds (298–299): "The term indicates a readiness, scarcely conscious perhaps, to accept Gothic as a recognizable and valid counterpart to the classical style."

7. Perrault, *Vitruve,* 1673, 76 n. 3; ibid., 1684, 79 n. 16.

8. Ibid., 1673, 76–77 n. 3; ibid., 1684, 79 n. 16.

9. A. Palladio, *Les quatre livres d'architecture . . . ,* trans. R. Fréart de Chambray, Paris, 1650, 279–280 (IV, xxi). Palladio refers to the building as the Church of Saint Agnes and reports that some think it was originally a temple of Bacchus.

10. *PV,* I, 70–71.

11. Palladio, *Les quatre livres,* 292. This was the Temple of Clitumnus, now the church of San Salvatore.

12. *PV,* I, 72.

13. Palladio, *Les quatre livres,* 297, figs. on 298–300 (IV, xxvi), where, however, the columns are not coupled.

14. [A. C. d'Aviler], *Les oeuvres d'architecture d'Anthoine Le Pautre,* Paris, [1681], 2–3. The date of this publication is given in *Le journal des sçavans,* April 14, 1681, 87. Le Pautre's ideal château is illustrated in R. W. Berger, *Antoine Le Pautre: A French Architect of the Era of Louis XIV,* New York, 1969, figs. 16–20 (First Design).

15. On the façade of Saint-Gervais, see R. Coope, *Salomon de Brosse and the Development of the Classical Style in French Architecture from 1565 to 1630,* University Park, Pa., and London, 1972, 135f., 266–267, pl. 17b. On the Minimes, see A. Braham and P. Smith, *François Mansart,* London, 1973, I, 111f., 247f.; II, pl. 436.

16. Blondel, 1683, 228–240 (part III, book I, chaps. x–xii).

17. Ibid., 230.

18. Ibid., 237. In another place in the *Cours d'architecture,* Blondel wrote that iron reinforcement corrodes stone in time and is not meant for the "longue durée" (ibid., 434 [part IV, book VI, chap. XIV]).

19. A reference to Perrault's proposed attics for the east and south façades (Figs. 88 and 100; see Chapter IV).

20. Vitruvius's text reads: "In araeostylis autem nec lapideis nec marmoreis epistyliis uti datur, sed inponendae de materia trabes perpetuae. Et ipsarum aedium species sunt varicae [*baryce* in some mss.], barycephalae, humiles, latae" (III.3.5). This is translated by F. Granger (Loeb Library ed., I, 173) as: "In araeostyle buildings it is not given to use stone or marble architraves, but continuous wooden beams are to be employed. And the designs of the buildings themselves are straddling, top-heavy, low, broad." Perrault's translation (*Vitruve,* 1673, 74; ibid., 1684, 76) reads: "Mais aux Araeostyles on ne peut pas mettre des Architraves de pierre ny de marbre comme on en met autre part, & on est contraint de coucher des poutres tout du long: cette maniere rend encore les faces des Edifices *écartées, pesantes,* basses & larges." Perrault's note on Vitruvius's terms is in *Vitruve,* 1673, 74 n. 1, and ibid., 1684, 76 n. 9.

21. Vitruvius's text reads: "Subtilitateque iudiciorum progressi et gracilioribus modulis delectati septem crassitudinis diametros in altitudinem columnae doricae, ionicae novem constituerunt" (III.1.8). This is translated by F. Granger (Loeb Library ed., I, 207) as: "Advancing in the subtlety of their judgments and preferring slighter modules, they [the Greeks] fixed seven measures of the diameter for the height of the Doric column, nine for the Ionic." Perrault's translation (*Vitruve,* 1673, 102; ibid., 1684, 106) reads: "Les Architects qui succederent à ces premiers, & qui se rendirent de plus en plus subtils & habiles, approuvant grandement la delicatesse des petits modules, donnerent à la hauteur de la colonne Dorique sept de ses diametres, & huit & demy [!] à l'Ionique." Perrault's willful change of Vitruvius's Ionic proportions should be noted.

22. Blondel, 1683, 240 (part III, book I, chap. XII).

23. Cl. Perrault, *Ordonnance des cinq espèces de colonnes selon la méthode des anciens,* Paris, 1683, 115–116 (from chapter VIII: "De quelques autres abus introduits dans l'architecture moderne").

24. Perrault, *Vitruve,* 1684, 79–80 n. 16.

25. Ibid., 79 n. 16.

26. If Patte is to be trusted (cf. Fig. 79), the Louvre Colonnade was originally constructed with a *porte-à-faux* over the small intercolumniation (of small extent, to judge from Fig. 54). On the resetting of the entablature stones, see Chapter VI, note 14.

27. Perrault, *Vitruve,* 1684, 80 n. 16.

28. On this aspect of Perrault's thought, see Herrmann, *Perrault,* chap. II.

29. The story about the Greek architect (named Chersiphron) and Diana is related in Pliny the Elder's *Natural History,* XXXVI, 95–97. Pliny does not report that the architect had prayed to Diana.

APPENDIX C

CLAUDE PERRAULT AND THE PILIERS DE TUTELLE, BORDEAUX

In September 1669, Claude Perrault left Paris for a trip through France in the company of his elder brother Jean and some friends. Perrault kept a diary, published in 1909 by Bonnefon.[1] Why did Perrault take this trip? Bonnefon posed and answered this question thus:

> Quelle était la raison de cette longue excursion? L'architecte, qui avait entrepris et mené à bien la

colonnade du Louvre et l'Observatoire, voulait-il se délasser en parcourant la France et en promenant ses yeux, au hasard des chemins, sur des objets nouveaux et changeants? Ou bien ce désir de s'instruire, ce besoin de tout connaître qui l'animaient, poussaient-ils Claude Perrault à faire, au travers des provinces françaises, une tournée qui serait aussi agréable qu'utile? Toutes ces raisons, sans doute, servirent à décider Claude Perrault, sans que nous puissons dire laquelle l'emporta.[2]

Perrault's travels took him to notable monuments of French architecture, and his diary is filled with detailed architectural notes on the châteaux of Chambord, Blois, Amboise, the town and château of Richelieu, the château of Bonnivet, then the towns and buildings of Poitiers, Lusignan, Saint-Maixent, Niort, Fontenay-le-Comte, Luçon, and La Rochelle. Later the group passed through Rochefort and villages along the river Garonne, reaching Bordeaux on September 29 by boat. Upon arrival at Bordeaux, Jean Perrault was already ill, and his worsening condition forced the others to remain in that city for more than a month. Jean died on October 30, and after his burial Claude Perrault left Bordeaux on November 6 to return to Paris. The diary breaks off suddenly on that day's entry; his companions continued their travels toward Toulouse.

If we consider the voyage to Bordeaux in the context of Claude's activities in 1669, we will find that he was at a busy point in his career and that, rather than being a vacation trip, the journey had a specific goal and purpose.

In September 1669, Claude Perrault was in the midst of work on his Vitruvius edition. He had begun this ca. 1667,[3] and the manuscript was granted a *privilège du roi* on April 4, 1672. Additions were made that year,[4] and the magnificent volume was published in 1673. In September 1669, in addition to this labor, Perrault saw construction continuing on the Louvre and the Observatoire[5] and on the early phase of his full-scale mockup of the Arc de Triomphe du Trône (first payments in July and August 1669).[6] His work at the Académie royale des sciences in 1669 included his memoir on blood coagulation (August 10, 1669)[7] and publication of a book on animal dissection, published anonymously.[8]

Perrault was therefore in the thick of his work in 1669. I believe his decision to embark on the voyage to Bordeaux was sparked by curiosity to see with his own eyes an ancient Roman monument that had features in common with the Louvre Colonnade—the Piliers de Tutelle in Bordeaux (Fig. 124).[9] Dating from ca. A.D. 200, this hypaethral structure may have been a temple dedicated to the protective divinity of Burdigala (the Roman name of the city), or it may have been a secondary forum. It consisted of a high podium supporting twenty-four Corinthian columns in a rectangular arrangement, eight columns on each long side, six on each short side. A broad staircase at one of the short ends led up to the platform, open to the sky. The columns held up an architrave, with *ressauts* over the columns; this in turn supported arches on piers, with high-relief caryatid figures set against the piers and sculpted vases in the spandrels. An unbroken architrave terminated the elevation.

On his first full day in Bordeaux (September 30), Perrault began his sightseeing after attending Mass. He visited the Palais des Plaideurs, the Hôtel de Ville, the Bourse, and several other monuments, including the Cathedral of Saint-André.[10] Then he reached the Piliers de Tutelle, the first antique structure he examined in the city:

Après dîner nous fûmes voir un édifice fort antique, qu'on appelle les piliers de Tutèle. Il est au milieu de la ville; on y entre par un cabaret à qui cet édifice sert de jardin. Il y a un stylobate continu haut environ de onze pieds, compris sa base et sa corniche. Ce stylobate en soutient un second pareil, sur lequel des colonnes disposées selon le genre pycnostyle sont posées. Ces colonnes, qui ont quatre pieds et demi de diamètre, sont composées de plusieurs tambours de deux pieds de hauteur, d'une belle et bonne pierre. Les jointures des tambours sont si serrées qu'on ne peut y introduire la pointe d'un couteau. Ces colonnes étoient au nombre de 24, mais il y en a 7 qui manquent. Elias Vinet, qui a commenté Ausone, il y a cent ans, dit que de son temps il n'y en manquait que six, et il paroît par la figure qu'il a mise dans son livre [Fig. 123] que celle qui est marquée A[11] est tombée depuis ce temps-là. Celles qui sont marquées B et C[12] sont endommagées de coups de canon, ayant été battues au dernier siège de Bordeaux du château Trompette qui est l'opposite. Ceux de Bordeaux avoient mis une batterie au milieu de ces colonnes qui servoient de gabions. Ces colonnes sont d'ordre corinthien; les feuillages des chapiteaux sont à feuilles d'acanthe assez mal taillées; toutes les volutes sont rompues. Les canelures sous l'astragale sont évasées contre l'ordinaire, comme il est ici marqué.[13] Par le bas, au-dessus de la base, elles sont comme on a accoutumé de les faire.

Il y a quelques-unes de ces colonnes qui ne sont point achevées par le bas et qui ont été construites selon cette manière des anciens dans laquelle on ne tailloit que les joints des pierres et on réservoit à tailler les parements après les avoir posées. Ces colonnes ne soutiennent point d'autres ornements que l'architrave, ayant au lieu de frise des arcades dont les impostes sont soutenues par des figures de demi-relief, en forme de cariatides, et sur les impostes au droit des figures il y a des vases qui ne sortent aussi qu'à moitié du mur. Au-dessus des arcades et des vases il y a encore un architrave et on ne sauroit dire s'il y avoit quelque chose au-dessus.

Les stylobates dont il a été parlé ne sont que par dehors; car par dedans les bases des colonnes posent sur le plancher, qui est, à ce qu'on peut juger, le ciel d'une carrière dont on a tiré des pierres, car ce plancher est par dessous tout plat, et non vouté, mais soutenu par un mur bâti de petites pierres qui n'ont pas plus de cinq pouces en carré. Cet édifice a dans oeuvre treize toises de long et neuf de large. Il est bien difficile de juger ce qu'il étoit, car il ne peut passer ni pour temple ni pour basilique, et il n'y a point d'apparence qu'il ait été couvert que de charpenterie, n'ayant point d'arcs-boutants qui pussent soutenir la poussée d'une voute de neuf toises de large.[14]

Perrault's description is the longest of any entered in his journal, and he drew sketches of the plan, elevation, and column fluting of the Piliers. His entry reveals that he knew the print published by Vinet (Fig. 123), and Perrault's comparison of it with the monument suggests that he had Vinet's Ausonius edition in hand and probably took it with him from Paris.

The reasons for Perrault's interest in the Piliers de Tutelle are obvious. Here was an authentic building from Roman antiquity that featured a spectacular array of huge, freestanding columns set upon a monumental podium—features at once reminiscent of the Louvre Colonnade (Fig. 43).

In his 1673 Vitruvius edition, Perrault made brief references to the Bordeaux structure.[15] In 1677, however, the wondrous building was destroyed by order of Louis XIV because it stood in the way of an enlargement of a fortress.[16] In the second (1684) Vitruvius edition,

Perrault added a long and enthusiastic description of the Piliers accompanied by a full-page engraving (Fig. 124):

Il y a un exemple de cette suppression d'ornemens [the omission of frieze and cornice in an entablature] au superbe Edifice des Tuteles à Bordeaux que l'on tient avoir esté basti peu de temps après Auguste: car les colonnes ne soutiennent qu'un Architrave sur lequel au lieu du second ordre de colonnes, il y a des Cariatides.

J'ay cru qu'il ne seroit pas hors de propos de mettre icy une planche que j'ay fait graver de ce celebre edifice, qui a esté abatu depuis peu pour bâtir à sa place les fortifications des dehors de la Citadelle; parce que les figures que nous en avons qui sont celle de Ducerceau,[17] & celle qu'Elias Vinetus a mises dans son Commentaire sur Ausone [Fig. 123], ne sont point exactes. Quoyque les particularitez de la construction & de la Figure de ce bastiment qui fournissent des exemples singuliers pour l'explication de plusieurs endroits du texte de Vitruve, soient les principales raisons qui m'ont porté à mettre icy cette Planche, que j'ay dessinée sur le lieu quatre ans avant la demolition de cet edifice; il m'a semblé aussi que je ne devois pas laisser passer cette occasion de conserver & de laisser à la posterité l'idée de ce superbe monument, qui estoit un des plus magnifiques & des plus entiers qui fussent restez en France, de tous ceux que les Romains y ont autrefois basti.

On ne sçait point certainement ny quand ny par qui cet edifice a esté construit: il y a seulement quelques conjectures qui peuvent faire croire qu'il est du temps de l'Empereur Claudius, & la principale est fondée sur ce qu'en foüillant il y a environ soixante & dix ans, on a trouvé trois Statuës antiques, qu'on croit estre de l'Empereur Claudius, de Drusus son pere & de Messaline sa femme: car on a trouvé avec ces S[t]atuës des fragmens de marbre gravez d'inscriptions qui font voir assez clairement que deux de ces statuës estoient l'une de Drusus & l'autre de l'Empereur Claudius. L'inscription pour la statue de Drusus est DRVSO CAESARI PATRI GERMANICI CAESARIS ET CLAVDII AVGVSTI NEPOTVM DIVI AVGVSTI PRAEFECTO VRBIS AVGVSTALI. Celle de la statuë de Claudius est TIBERIO CLAVDIO DRVSI FILIO CAESARI AVGVSTO PONTEFICI MAXIMO CONSVLI SECVNDUM PATRI PATRIAE CAIVS JVLIVS. Ce qui fait croire que la troisieme statuë qui n'a point de teste est de

Messaline [est] que ce C. Julius surnommé Vindex qui avoit fait eriger ces statuës & construire les anciens edifices de Bordeaux, gouverna les Gaules au commencement de l'Empire de Claudius, auquel temps Messaline avoit toute la puissance & tout le gouvernement entre les mains; car il y a apparence que Vindex ayant fait bastir quelque bel edifice comme les Romains faisoient ordinairement dans leurs Provinces, soit de Temples, soit de Bains, soit de Theatres, il fit mettre les statuës de ces Princes avec celle de Messaline. Ces trois statuës avec les inscriptions sont dans la cour de l'Hostel de Ville de Bordeaux.

Cet edifice estoit au penchant d'une colline, sur laquelle est située la partie de la Ville de Bordeaux qui descend vers la Garonne où est le Port. Il estoit basti de grandes pierres aussi dures & aussi blanches qu'est nostre Liais. Sa figure estoit un quarré oblong de quinze toises de long sur onze de large, & sur vingt-deux piez de haut, sur lequel vingt-quatre colonnes estoient posées; huit aux grandes faces & six aux petites. Ce quarré qui estoit comme une base ou stylobate continu estoit presque tout solide de maçonnerie, revêtu en dehors de grandes pierres taillées, & rempli par dedans de moilons jettez à l'avanture dans du mortier; n'y ayant de vuide que pour une cave qui estoit au bas, dont la voute ou plancher n'avoit pas plus de neuf piez de haut. Ce plancher estoit tout droit & tout plat, & n'estoit point soutenu par le couppe des pierres, mais par l'épaisseur du massif qui avoit plus de douze piez, estant selon la maniere dont les anciens faisoient leurs planchers qui avoient ordinairement sans compter les poutres & les solives plus de deux piez d'épaisseur, ainsi que Vitruve l'enseigne au premier chapitre du septiéme livre. Ce plancher par dessous estoit fait comme le ciel d'une carriere, & il paroissoit que les murs d'alentour ayant esté bastis, on avoit laissé la terre en dedans à la hauteur que devoit estre le plancher; & que sur cette terre on avoit jetté le mortier & les pierres, dont on avoit rempli le reste jusqu'en haut, & que le massif estant sec, on avait osté la terre de dessous. Cette sorte de plancher de mesme que les autres que Vitruve décrit pourroient estre appellez des planchers fusils, estant faites d'une matiere coulante que l'on jette comme en moule.

Ce stylobate continu estoit double, y en ayant un posé sur un autre; & il y a lieu de croire que celuy de dessous estoit pour gagner la hauteur de la pente de la colline, & que le second commençoit au droit du rez de chaussée de l'entrée: de maniere qu'on montoit sur l'aire où les colonnes estoient placées par un perron de vingt & une marches.

Les colonnes avoient quatre piez & demy de diametre, & n'estoient distantes l'une de l'autre que de sept piez, ce qui faisoit que leur disposition approchoit du genre Pycnostyle. Elles estoient cannelées & composées de plusieurs assises ou tambours de deux piez de hauteur: ces tambours de mesme que tout le reste des pierres taillées estoient posez sans mortier & sans plomb; en sorte que les joints estoient presque imperceptibles. La pluspart des bases n'estoient que commencées à tailler. Les cannelures sous l'astragale du haut de la colonne n'estoient point en maniere de niche, comme elles sont ordinairement, mais elles avoient une figure toute contraire, ainsi que l'on peut remarquer dans la planche où tout cet edifice est fidelement représenté en l'état qu'il estoit quand on l'a abattu à la reserve des coins des tailloirs avec les volutes, & de quelques unes des feüilles des chapiteaux qui estoient rompuës. Les chapiteaux estoient selon la proportion que Vitruve enseigne, n'ayant pas plus de hauteur que le diametre du bas de la colonne: ils estoient aussi selon Vitruve taillez à feüilles d'Acanthe. L'Architrave estoit composé d'un sommier posé sur chaque colonne & d'un claveau au milieu appuyé sur deux sommiers; Cet Architrave faisoit un ressaut d'environ six pouces au droit de chaque colonne pour soutenir des caryatides en bas-relief de dix piez de hauteur, adossées contre les piez droits des arcades qui estoient au dessus de l'Architrave à la place de la Frise. Les Caryatides avoient la teste sous les impostes des arcades & au droit de chaque caryatide au dessus de l'imposte, il y avoit un vase dont le pié estoit en pointe à la maniere des Urnes où les anciens mettoient les cendres des morts.

Ces Arcades soutenoient un autre Architrave pareil au premier, au dessus duquel il n'y avoit rien. Le dedans de mesme que le dehors estoit garny de caryatides qui estoient au nombre de quarante-quatre; parce qu'il ne pouvoit y en avoir en dedans au droit des colonnes des angles.

De vingt-quatre colonnes de cet edifice, il n'en restoit que dix-sept, & il paroist par la figure d'Helias Vinetus [Fig. 123] que de son temps il y a environ six-vingt ans, il y en avoit encore dix-huit. Deux des colonnes de la face qui regardoit sur le port au droit de la Citadelle, estoient fort endommagées de coups de canon qui avoient emporté en quelques endroits, jusqu'au quart d'un tambour sans les avoir pu abattre: ce qui fait connoistre combien le pouvoir que le temps a de ruïner insensiblement les choses, à plus de force pour les détruire que n'en ont les autres forces, qui pour le même effet agissent avec violence.[18]

In an anonymous article in the *Mercure galant* of 1696, the Louvre Colonnade was called an "imitation" of the Piliers de Tutelle:

> Ces colonnes [of the Piliers] estoient construites de grandes pierres, ce qui marquoit l'antiquité & la noblesse de l'édifice; car c'estoit là la maniere d'Architecture du temps d'Auguste. . . .
>
> Il y a aujourd'huy une Imitation royale de cette superbe structure des Empereurs Romains. Le Fronton qui est sur la porte de la principale entrée du Louvre, est couvert de deux grandes pierres, qui ont chacune cinquante-deux pieds de long sur huit de large. Elles pesent aussi chacune plus de quatre vingt milliers, & ont esté tirées de la Carriere qui est sur la montagne de Meudon.[19]

The comparison is between the very large stones of both structures, but could a more general comparison and similarity have been present in the writer's mind?

The architrave carried by the columns at Bordeaux was not monolithic (even though the columns were closely spaced), but was composed of voussoirs. According to Patte, this was a unique feature among ancient buildings.[20] As Patte's engraving clearly shows (Fig. 125), one voussoir (G) was inserted over each intercolumniation between the *sommiers* (F). Now Perrault noted this feature in both his sketch[21] and engraving (Fig. 124) and described it in the long note in his 1684 Vitruvius edition quoted above: "L'Architrave estoit composé d'un sommier posé sur chaque colonne & d'un claveau au milieu appuyé sur deux sommiers." The relationship to the entablature of the Louvre Colonnade (Fig. 79) is evident, although the latter is far more complex, being composed of two rows of nine voussoirs over each large intercolumniation. The stereotomy of the Louvre façade must have been worked out in 1667–68, before Perrault visited Bordeaux. Although the voussoirs at Bordeaux are suggested in Vinet's print (Fig. 123; possibly known by the Petit Conseil during those years),[22] it is unlikely that the Piliers served as a model for either the stereotomy of the Colonnade's entablature or its overall composition. If the Petit Conseil had consciously drawn upon the Piliers de Tutelle as a source, its members surely would have visited it, but there is no evidence for such a site visit before Perrault's in 1669.

Notes

1. Cl. Perrault, *Voyage à Bordeaux (1669)*, ed. P. Bonnefon, Paris, 1909.
2. P. Bonnefon, "Claude Perrault architecte et voyageur (premier article)," *GBA*, ser. 3, XXVI, 1901, 218.
3. Herrmann, *Perrault*, 18.
4. Ibid., 19 n. 53.
5. M. Petzet, "Claude Perrault als Architekt des Pariser Observatoriums," *ZfK*, XXX, 1967, 1–54.
6. M. Petzet, "Das Triumphbogenmonument für Ludwig XIV. auf der Place du Trône," *ZfK*, XLV, 1982, 165–166.
7. Herrmann, *Perrault*, 219.
8. *Description anatomique d'un caméléon, d'un castor, d'un dromedaire, d'un ours et d'une gazelle*, Paris, 1669.
9. On this monument, see R. Céleste, "Les Piliers de Tutelle," *Revue philomathique de Bordeaux et du Sud-Ouest*, IX, 1906, 1–22; R. Etienne, "Bordeaux," *Enciclopedia dell'arte antica, classica e orientale*, Rome, 1959, II, 138–139. Its relationship to a Roman structure called "Las Incantadas," formerly in Salonica, is discussed by L. Guerrini, " 'Las Incantadas' di Salonico," *Archaeologia classica*, XIII, 1961, 40–70. See also M. Lyttleton, *Baroque Architecture in Classical Antiquity*, London, 1974, 281–282.
10. Cl. Perrault, *Voyage à Bordeaux*, 178–182.
11. Marked on Perrault's sketch plan, reproduced in ibid., 183.
12. Marked on Perrault's sketch plan, reproduced in ibid.
13. Sketch reproduced in ibid., 185.
14. Ibid., 183–185.
15. Perrault, *Vitruve*, 1673, 88 n. 3, 102 n. 3, 275 n. 3. The Piliers de Tutelle were mentioned in a meeting of the Académie royale d'architecture in 1673: "Sur le 10ᵉ chapitre [book I], il [Palladio] dit que les anciens, dans les grands ouvrages, n'avoient accoutumé de tailler que les joints et les lits des pierres, laissans les testes et paremens bruts, pour estre taillez sur le tas, ainsy qu'il se voit encore aux Tutelles [sic] de Bordeaux" (*PV*, I, 26 [March 21]).
16. Céleste, "Les Piliers," 15.
17. J. A. Du Cerceau the Elder's print is reproduced in H. de Geymüller, *Les Du Cerceau*, Paris and London, 1887, 105, fig. 80. It was first published in 1560 (302–303). Du Cerceau's drawing for this print (BN, Estampes) is illustrated in C. Jullian, *Histoire de Bordeaux depuis les origines jusqu'en 1895*, Bordeaux, 1895, pl. I (facing 30). For another drawing of the Piliers (Washington, D.C., National Gallery of Art) attributed to Du Cerceau, see [Brown University, Department of Art], *The Origins of the Italian Veduta*, exhib. cat., Providence, 1978, 30, no. 8, fig. 8.
18. Perrault, *Vitruve*, 1684, 217–218 n. 8. Other references to the Piliers are on 92 n. 30, 108 n. 13, 298 n. 3.
19. See Sources II, no. 45.
20. P. Patte, *Mémoires sur les objets les plus importans de l'architecture*, Paris, 1769, 262.

21. Cl. Perrault, *Voyage à Bordeaux*, 184; Herrmann, *Perrault*, fig. 22.

22. The voussoirs are not indicated by Du Cerceau (see above, note 17).

APPENDIX D

THE PALMYRA-BAALBEK HYPOTHESIS

During the mid-eighteenth century, some connoisseurs suggested that the Louvre Colonnade had been consciously modeled after the stupendous Roman architectural remains at Palmyra and Baalbek. The Englishman Robert Wood had published engravings of these monuments, both in their actual ruined state and in conjectural restorations, in his *Ruins of Palmyra* (London, 1753) and *Ruins of Balbec* (London, 1757). But the suggestion of a link between the Colonnade and Palmyra or Baalbek was immediately dismissed by the French architect and theoretician Jacques François Blondel and by Robert Wood himself. Blondel wrote in 1754 as follows (published in 1756):

> L'année derniere le Recueil des *ruines de Palmyre* fut mis au jour par M. *Robert Wood,* célèbre Anglois, qui s'étant transporté sur les lieux en 1751 avec MM. *Bouverie & Dawkins,* parcourut ces antiquités; cet Amateur n'ayant épargné ni peines ni soins, ni les moyens nécessaires à une si grande entreprise, nous a donné dans ce recueil les desseins & la description de divers monumens, dont quelques fragmens assez considérables sont encore sur pied. A peine ce Recueil parut-il à Paris, que quelques Architectes, toujours jaloux de la gloire que *Claude Perrault* s'est si justement acquise, ont prétendu que la façade du péristile ... avoit été faite sur le modele des ruines de Palmyre; la plûpart de ces monumens, disent-ils, & principalement le Temple du Soleil, étant d'Ordre Corinthien élevé à quelques endroits sur un soubassement, & dont les entrecolonnemens sont ornés de niches couronnées de frontons. A cela, nous répondrons que les estampes qu'on nous a données de ces ruines, ont été achevées, pour la plûpart, par conjectures, à dessein de donner, dit *l'Editeur,* une idée plus complette des divers monumens répandus dans cette collection; d'où l'on pourroit conclure qu'au contraire ce seroit l'exemple du Louvre, dans son état actuel, qui auroit donné l'idée de ces supplémens.[1]

Blondel here refers to Palmyra's Temple of Bel (called the Temple of the Sun in the eighteenth century), the entrances to its courtyard, and the colonnaded streets, recorded in Wood's engravings.[2] Wood's reconstruction of the inner façade of the courtyard entrance (Fig. 126) certainly recalls the Louvre Colonnade (Fig. 44), but, as Wood noted,[3] the pediment is entirely conjectural.[4] Also reminiscent of the Parisian façade is the Propylon of the sanctuary at Baalbek in Wood's reconstruction (Fig. 139). Like Blondel, however, Wood denied any influence of this structure or anything else at Baalbek and Palmyra upon the French design:

> Several artists have observed a similitude between some European buildings and some parts of the ruins of Palmyra and Balbec; from which they have, perhaps too hastily, concluded that the former were copied from the latter. The portico of the Louvre at Paris has been compared in this light with some parts of the ruins of Palmyra, as also with the portico described in this plate [Fig. 139]: but we cannot discover any foundation for inferences so injurious to the memory of the architect who built that noble structure, which is as justly admired as it is unaccountably neglected.[5]

Wood's reconstructions of the 1750s were, of course, unavailable to the designers of the Louvre Colonnade and are irrelevant as possible source material. The ruins of Palmyra were not known until the visit of William Halifax in 1691. The site of Baalbek, however, was known in some detail by the 1660s in France. Could the Colonnade have been based on earlier written and/or visual descriptions of the Baalbek Propylon or other structures at that site?

French knowledge of Baalbek in the seventeenth century has been reviewed by Blunt,[6] who rightly drew attention to Balthasar de Monconys's visit in 1647; Balthasar's account was published in 1665.[7] De Monconys recognized that the architecture was Roman and was most enthusiastic about its quality:

> Dans tous ces bastiments tant dehors que dedans, c'est la plus belle architecture qui reste auiourd' huy des Romains, & peut-estre la meilleure qu'ils ayent fait; le temple [of Bacchus] est le plus entier qu'on puisse trouver, où l'on voit bien distinctement de la façon qu'ils les faisoient dedans & dehors, par tout également une belle architecture, comme au Chasteau [the hexagonal forecourt and great court] qui est tout ordres divers, frises, & colomnes.[8]

De Monconys described the structures of Baalbek in some detail and spent almost an entire day drawing them.[9] He returned to France in 1649 and made a second voyage (this time to England, the Low Countries, Germany, and Italy) in 1663–64. When his *Journal des voyages* was published in 1665, only one plate of crude engravings illustrated the ruins of Baalbek (Fig. 127).[10] Was any use made of the drawings that he spent almost a whole day making? These are lost, but Blunt proposed that they were known to Jean Marot, who used them as the basis for his suite of seventeen engravings of Baalbek, published in the *Grand Marot* (*L'architecture françoise,* Paris, n.d.), the first detailed visual publication of the site (Figs. 128–134).[11] It is believed that Marot made his engravings in the 1660s; the *Grand Marot* was published ca. 1670. Although De Monconys was a resident of Lyon, he was in Paris by May 1663, whence he departed for his second journey;[12] contact with Marot could have been made shortly before then.

Before Blunt's proposal, Marot was believed to have relied upon drawings made at the site by a certain De Monceaux (or Des Monceaux), who had been sent on an official mission to the Levant by Louis XIV to seek out manuscripts and medals for the royal collections.[13] De Monceaux left France in 1667, reached Baalbek in 1668, and returned in 1669. The original manuscript diary of his visit is lost, but an *abrégé* published in the eighteenth century[14] tells us: "L'Auteur fait une description de ces Ruïnes, dans laquelle il seroit fort ennuyeux de le suivre, pour n'entendre parler que de frises, volutes, &c. n'ayant pas vû une Inscription, ny même un bas-relief, ou Statuë qui puisse nous instruire."[15] De Monceaux's written account was accompanied by drawings (lost), and these could have been utilized by Marot in 1669 or 1670 for the engravings published in the *Grand Marot.* At least one of De Monceaux's drawings—that of a capital from Argos—was known to Claude Perrault, who illustrated it in his Vitruvius editions of 1673 and 1684;[16] Perrault's brother Charles, in his capacity as Colbert's assistant in the Royal Building Administration, had addressed a *mémoire* to De Monceaux before his departure for the Levant[17] and so was well aware of this official expedition. (De Monceaux's drawings may have reached Claude via Charles; I shall return to these drawings shortly.)

A third French voyager to Baalbek during these years—Laurent d'Arvieux—should be mentioned.[18] This aristocratic merchant, diplomat, and adventurer initially sojourned in the Near East from 1653 to 1665 (he returned to Paris on January 1, 1667).[19] He was at Baalbek in 1660, which he described in his memoirs (begun in 1673 but not published until 1735).[20] D'Arvieux correctly judged the ruins to be Roman and described the main monuments in some detail, but he did not allude to making any drawings of them.

In arguing that Marot's prints were based on De Monconys's descriptions and drawings, Blunt correctly noted that both De Monconys and Marot indicated that the Temple of Bacchus (De Monconys's "Temple," Marot's "Temple de Balbec" [Figs. 130–134]) had fourteen columns along its long sides.[21] But Blunt's next claim—that *two* hexagonal courts, one at each end of the main court (as in Figures 128 and 129; cf. Fig. 136), were described by De Monconys—is incorrect. The French traveler clearly indicated an initial structure (the Propylon) followed by one hexagonal court, which in turn is followed by a great court preceding "le principal corps de logis basti sur des colomnes dont il reste neuf" (i.e., the Temple of Jupiter).[22] Furthermore, another detail in Marot does not accord with De Monconys's text: the engraver indicated (Figs. 131, 133) that the tops of the exterior cella walls of the Temple of Bacchus were adorned with busts set in rectangular frames, but De Monconys wrote that busts of deities appeared set into the *ceiling* covering the peripteron—which was the actual arrangement.[23] These divergences between De Monconys and Marot strongly suggest that the former was not the latter's source. And because d'Arvieux does not seem to have executed drawings, the traditional theory—that Marot utilized De Monceaux's renderings in 1669 or 1670—still appears to be the most plausible, and this is supported by the fact that Marot designed a *hôtel* for De Monceaux in Paris.[24]

The extent to which Marot accurately rendered De Monceaux's drawings is another matter. In 1719 Bernard de Montfaucon published an engraving of a temple rendered in a perspective sectional view (Fig. 135). The inscription beneath the image reads "M^r des Monceaux," and De Montfaucon explained its circumstances as follows:

> Le dessein du beau temple qui suit est tiré des memoires de feu M. des Monceaux, frere de Madame la comtesse de Bonneval, qui nous a communiqué fort obligeamment tout ce que nous avons voulu tirer des memoires de son frere. Je ne sai[s] s'il y eut jamais de voiageur plus curieux & plus habile que lui: il faisoit dessiner tout. Nous avons tiré de ses memoires bien des choses qu'on trouvera dans le cours de cet ouvrage: il marquoit sur tous ses desseins les dimensions, & les noms des choses qu'ils representoient, & de même les lieux où il les avoit trouvées. Mais il est arrivé malheureusement que la feuille où étoit le dessein de ce temple aiant été rognée, l'écriture a sauté avec la rognure; nous avons cherché inutilement dans la relation manuscrite de son voiage. Plusieurs cahiers en ont été égarez; c'étoit peutêtre dans ceux-là que la description de ce temple se trouvoit.[25]

De Montfaucon's text preceding the above passage concerns Baalbek,[26] and he republished several of Marot's engravings from the Baalbek suite. He concluded his commentary on Figure 135 this way:

> Comme il y a dans ce temple quelques choses qui paroissent avoir rapport au temple de Balbec [the Temple of Bacchus], on avoit douté d'abord si ce n'étoit pas le même dessiné moins fidelement par un de ceux qui l'ont tiré; mais les differences sont si essentielles qu'il n'y a aucun moien de le croire.[27]

De Montfaucon believed, therefore, that Marot's sectional rendering of the Bacchus temple (Fig. 134) was correct and that De Monceaux's building could not be from Baalbek. In reality, however, De Monceaux had made a highly accurate portrayal of the Temple of Bacchus, as confirmed by modern archaeological surveys,[28] with the reasonable (but erroneous) proposal of a barrel vault over the cella. It was Marot who inexplicably added two rows of freestanding columns within the cella (Fig. 130), thus converting the interior space into the traditional nave and side aisles of a Christian basilican church. And Marot covered each of these spatial units with its own barrel vault. The spurious rows of columns appear also in a plan and section in Marot's suite (Fig. 134), but in a lateral view of the temple (Fig. 133) the interior view omits the freestanding columns and accords with the print published by De Montfaucon (Fig. 135). Marot may have judged that a barrel vault as large as De Monceaux's could not have been adequately braced by the structures over the exterior peripteron.

In any case, De Monceaux's return from the Levant in 1669 and the publication of the *Grand Marot* soon afterward postdate the design of the Louvre Colonnade in 1667–68. Knowledge of Baalbek could have been available to the Petit Conseil only from De Monconys's *Journal* (published in 1665) and drawings or from conversations with d'Arvieux (in Paris from January 1667 until August 1671).[29] We shall recall that eighteenth-century critics compared the Propylon preceding the hexagonal court at Baalbek (depicted in a reconstruction by Wood in 1757, Figure 139) to the Colonnade (Fig. 44), suggesting that the former inspired the latter. De Monconys described the Propylon briefly:

> Son entrée est à l'Orient, sa figure est assez mal aisée à descrire; à la face qui est longue & double il y a de chaque costé une Tour quarrée. Ces Tours n'ont chacune qu'une chambre, mais merveilleusement ornée de niches, frises, colomnes, & portes, toutes taillées en sculptures.[30]

And De Monconys published a schematic engraving of this entrance, depicted as a solid, unarticulated wall between end towers with attached columns (Fig. 127)—hardly an image that could have inspired the Louvre Colonnade.[31]

D'Arvieux (whose *Mémoires,* begun in 1673, were not published until 1735) also described the Propylon:

> La face principale de ce Château est à l'Orient. Toutes les murailles sont doubles & fort épaisses, flanquées de grosses tours quarrées, cantonnées chacune de deux Tours rondes plus petites. Les portes de toutes ces Tours sont ornées de colonnes & d'autres membres d'architecture.[32]

As in De Monconys's description and engraving (Fig. 127), columns are indicated only on the towers.

The possibility that Baalbek may have had an influence upon the Louvre Colonnade—a question under discussion, as we have seen, in the mid-eighteenth century—was revived in 1922 by Hans Rose,[33] who claimed that the east façade of the Louvre (attributed entirely by Rose to Perrault) was a "reconstruction" of an ancient Corinthian temple adapted to a palace façade. Rose drew attention to d'Arvieux's visit to Baalbek in 1660 and speculated that it must have stimulated further expeditions and the making of drawings, the basis for Marot's prints. And Rose illustrated Marot's side view of the Temple of Bacchus (Fig. 131) as "das Urbild der Perrault-Kolonnade."[34]

A comparison, however, of Marot's engraving with the executed Colonnade reveals no real similarities. To buttress his extraordinary claim, Rose drew attention to certain details. First, he stated that the Corinthian order of the Louvre (Fig. 56) was copied directly from Marot's rendering of the Bacchus temple's peripteral order (Fig. 132), except that the eagles linked by swags in the cornice of the latter (between a lower fascia with dentils and an upper fascia) were omitted in the former, where are found an orthodox ovolo (with egg-and-tongue), a lower fascia without dentils, and a row of modilions below the upper fascia.[35] To these differences in the detailing of the cornice, however, must be added a disparity between the bases of the columns (not discussed or illustrated by Rose; cf. Figs. 56, 132): whereas the bases in Paris and Baalbek have two scotias between two torus moldings, the upper scotia at Baalbek is set well back; in Paris, the scotias are nearly equal.

Second, Rose suggested a comparison between ornamental details, such as the vault coffers and the entrance portal.[36] Marot shows, however, rows of small, square coffers filled with rosettes,[37] quite unlike the large panels covering the peristyles of the Colonnade, with their radiant Apollo heads (Fig. 52). And, contrary to Rose, there is no similarity whatsoever between the entrance portal to the cella at Baalbek and the central Louvre portal (Fig. 48).[38]

Third, Rose drew attention to the pedestals projecting through the sloped roof of the Bacchus temple in Marot's engravings (Figs. 131–133) and saw these as the sources for the balustrade of the Colonnade (Fig. 48).[39] But such pedestals (which frequently adorned ancient Roman roofs) were known to sixteenth-century architects and can be found in their antique reconstructions and actual buildings.[40] By the 1660s, such pedestals were widely diffused throughout European architecture.

Finally, we may note that in 1927 Hautecoeur suggested that the use of niches instead of windows on the walls behind the ranges of columns of the east Louvre façade (Figs. 74, 75) was a conscious attempt by Perrault to imitate the blank walls of ancient temples, and he specifically cited one of Marot's engravings of the "Temple de Balbec" (Fig. 131).[41] However, Marot's high-placed rectangular recesses with busts bear no resemblance to the niches of the Colonnade, in either their preliminary or final forms (Figs. 59, 74). (For the niches, see Chapter IV.)

The above analyses confirm the eighteenth-century judgments of Blondel and Wood that the Louvre Colonnade was not based on the monuments of Palmyra and Baalbek in any way. Yet there remain several tantalizing but (I believe) coincidental relationships between these buildings. First, both ancient sites were connected with the sun: Baalbek was the Roman Colonia Julia Augusta Felix Heliopolitana,[42] and, as previously noted, the Palmyrene Temple of Bel was thought in the eighteenth century to have been dedicated to the sun. Second, the architect of the Baalbek Propylon (Fig. 138; built during the reign of Philip the Arab, A.D. 244–249) designed attics over the end pavilions flanking his colonnade. We do know that from 1677 to 1679 Claude Perrault proposed attics over the end pavilions of the east and south Louvre façades (see Chapter IV and Figures 88, 100, 113, and 122). Third, in both the Louvre Colonnade and the Temple of Bacchus at Baalbek, iron was used to secure the masonry structure (see Chapter VI).[43] At Baalbek, iron was placed only within the columns, not in the entablature (as in the Louvre); iron rods about one foot in length connected the drums of the columns.[44] Finally, we may note that in 1674 Perrault proposed a comprehensive design linking the Louvre and the Tuileries, in which a central, monumental octagonal court is featured (Fig. 142).[45] Because Marot published his engravings of Baalbek ca. 1670, Perrault could have appropriated the polygonal court idea (octagonal in Perrault, hexagonal in Marot) from the latter's plan and views (Figs. 128, 129). And yet it is also possible that Perrault was inspired by Serlio's plan for the Louvre (1540s), unpublished but probably in France in the later seventeenth century (Fig. 143).[46] Here we find a large, central octagonal court, as in Perrault. Proof that Perrault at least had knowledge of Serlio's involvement with the Louvre is provided by Perrault himself in the prefaces to his Vitruvius editions

(1673, 1684) and to his *Abrégé des dix livres d'architecture de Vitruve* (Paris, 1674):

> Lorsque Sebastien Serlio, l'un des plus grands Architectes de son temps, vint d'Italie en France où il composa les excellens Livres d'Architecture que nous avons de luy; nos Architectes profiterent si bien de ses instructions, que le Roy ayant commandé de travailler au dessein du Louvre, qu'il entreprit de faire bâtir avec toute la beauté & la magnificence possible, le dessein d'un François fût préféré à celuy que Serlio avoit fait.

Serlio's plan is closer to Perrault's than Marot's because of the shape and placement of the Italian architect's octagonal court; in Marot's Baalbek engravings, the hexagonal courts are outside the periphery of the great court.

Notes

1. J. F. Blondel, *Architecture françoise*, Paris, 1756, IV, 40 n. a. The same judgment is found in an anonymous review of Wood's *Ruins of Palmyra* in *Année littéraire* (ed. Fréron), March 1754, I (quoted in D. Wiebenson, *Sources of Greek Revival Architecture*, London, 1969, 94): "Pour donner à ces desseins généraux plus d'agrément, on a ajouté dans plusieurs Planches des frontons, qu'on suppose avoir été élevés lors de la perfection de ces édifices, aussi-bien que d'autres parties entières, que les fragmens qui restent annoncent y avoir été. Ces additions ont déja fait croire & dire à plusieurs personnes que le Peristyle du Louvre, bâti par *Claude Perrault,* avoit été fait sur le modèle de ces ruines; & l'on se fonde encore sur ce que l'ordre de ce Temple est Corinthien, & que les niches & les croisées, couronnées de petits frontons, on[t] beaucoup de ressemblance avec le Peristyle. Mais ne pourroit-on pas dire, au contraire, que ce sont les beautés du Peristyle dans son état actuel, qui ont donné l'idée de completter dans ce Recueil ces fameuses ruines? Quoi qu'il en soit, cette imitation prétendu de la part de *Perrault,* quand elle seroit réelle, ne pourroit que lui faire honneur. Plût à Dieu que nos Artistes méritassent des reproches de cette espèce! Nous n'aurions pas tant d'édifices d'une ordonnance si négligée, & d'une décoration, pour la plûpart, si triviale."

2. I have used the following edition: R. Wood, *The Ruins of Palmyra and Balbec,* London, 1827, part I, pls. I, IV, XIV, XVI–XXI, XXVI, XXXI, XXXV, XLIII. For modern archaeological studies and reconstructions of Palmyra, see T. Wiegand, ed., *Palmyra: Ergebnisse der Expeditionen von 1902 und 1917,* Berlin, 1932, 2 vols.

3. Wood, *The Ruins of Palmyra and Balbec,* part I, 44 (note to pl. XIV).

4. For a modern reconstruction of the outer and inner façades (both pedimented), see Wiegand, ed., *Palmyra,* Tafelband, pl. 101.

5. Wood, *The Ruins of Palmyra and Balbec,* part II, 72. For modern archaeological studies and reconstructions of the sanctuary at Baalbek, see T. Wiegand, ed., *Baalbek,* Berlin and Leipzig, 1921–23, 2 vols. Modern archaeology crowns the colonnade of the Propylon with a huge triangular pediment invaded by the arched architrave over the central intercolumniation (Figs. 137, 138). The pediment is absent in Wood's reconstruction (Fig. 139) and would undoubtedly have convinced many more eighteenth-century connoisseurs of a link with the Louvre Colonnade.

6. A. Blunt, review of M. Lyttelton, *Baroque Architecture in Classical Antiquity,* London, 1974, in *BurlM,* CXVIII, 1976, 320–324.

7. B. de Monconys, *Journal des voyages . . . ,* Lyon, 1665, I, 346–355.

8. Ibid., 350.

9. Ibid.

10. Figure 127 shows, in highly schematic fashion, the Propylon, the entrance to the south tunnel, and, in the background, the Temple of Bacchus; below are a column, entablature, niche, and pediment from the latter building.

11. Blunt's review of Lyttelton (see note 6 above), 323. Marot's group of seventeen engravings, although lacking a title page, are numbered consecutively.

12. De Monconys, *Journal des voyages . . . ,* II, 1. De Monconys died in 1665.

13. On De Monceaux, see H. Omont, *Missions archéologiques françaises en Orient aux XVIIe et XVIIIe siècles,* Paris, 1902, I, 27f.

14. C. de Bruyn, *Voyages de Corneille Le Bruyn . . . ,* The Hague, 1725, V. (I used the edition of 1732, V, 383f.; Baalbek is described on 416–418.) See also P. Perdrizet, "Les dossiers de P. J. Mariette sur Ba'albek et Palmyre," *Revue des études anciennes,* III, 1901, 228–229.

15. De Bruyn, *Voyages,* V, 417.

16. Perrault, *Vitruve,* 1673, 126 n. 1: "Il se voit encore dans les ruines d'Argos quelques restes de cet ordre Attique. Les chapiteaux qui sont aux colonnes de la figure de la porte Attique [127, pl. XXXI], ont esté dessinez sur le lieu, & m'ont esté communiquez par M. de Monceaux." The note is repeated in ibid., 1684, 134 n. 29 (133, pl. XXXI). Additional references to De Monceaux appear in Perrault's Vitruvius editions, where he is cited for having supplied information about the Parthenon and the Temple of Theseus (the Hephestaion) in Athens (ibid., 1673, 81 n. 4, 118 n. 2; ibid., 1684, 85 n. 7, 125 n. 7).

17. Charles Perrault's *mémoire* is referred to in a letter (December 30, 1667) to De Monceaux from Pierre de Carcavy, keeper of the Bibliothèque du Roi (Omont, *Missions,* I, 30). De Monceaux was accompanied from 1667 to 1669 by a certain Laisné, who journeyed independently to the East in 1670–71; Laisné's manuscript account of his trip was sent to Charles Perrault (ibid., 47 and n. 2).

18. See W. H. Lewis, *Levantine Adventurer: The Travels and Missions of the Chevalier d'Arvieux, 1653–1697,* London, 1962.

19. Ibid., 130.

20. Ibid., 153. For the description of Baalbek, see L. Arvieux, *Mémoires . . . ,* ed. J. B. Labat, Paris, 1735, II, 436f.

21. De Monconys, *Journal des Voyages . . . ,* I, 349. Modern archaeology has established that the Temple of Bacchus had fifteen columns on its long sides.

22. Ibid., 348: "Le bastiment qui est au milieu dans le dedans est fait en hexagone, ouvert au fond en forme de Theatre; au bout il y a une grande cour, laquelle aussi bien que la precedente hexagonale est toute entouré d'appartements ou chambres de diverses figures ornées toutes d'une tres-belle Architecture: au fond de la grande cour vis à vis du milieu de la face devoit estre le principal corps de logis basti sur des colomnes dont il reste neuf."

23. Ibid., 349: "Dans le plat-fond de cette galerie qui va tout autour du Temple, sont quantité de busts de demy relief de Deesses ou Dieux antiques."

24. Marot published two engravings of a "Maison a bâtir" for "Monsieur de Monceaux Grand audiencier de France" in his *Grand Marot* (see Hautecoeur, *HAC*, I, 143–144). A clue to the date of the *Grand Marot* is provided by one of its prints, which depicts the mausoleum for the funeral of the former Queen of England, Henrietta Maria, at Saint-Denis, November 20, 1669.

25. I used the following edition: B. de Montfaucon, *L'antiquité expliquée et représentée en figures,* 2d ed., Paris, 1722, II, 118–119.

26. Ibid., 117–118.

27. Ibid., 119.

28. First recognized by Wiegand, ed., *Baalbek*, I, 2–3.

29. Lewis, *Levantine Adventurer*, 142.

30. De Monconys, *Journal des voyages . . .* , I, 348. For views of the recent (early 1920s) state of the Propylon, see Wiegand, ed., *Baalbek*, I, pls. 44a, 121.

31. Marot failed to depict the Propylon—which is another indication that his reconstructions were not based on De Monconys. The latter's engraving of the Propylon (Fig. 127) is not a reconstruction, but it does show its approximate condition, built over by the Arabs (cf. Figs. 140, 141).

32. D'Arvieux, *Mémoires . . .* , II, 438.

33. H. Rose, *Spätbarock*, Munich, 1922, 114f.

34. Ibid., 114.

35. In the interior order of the Baalbek temple (Marot, Baalbek suite, no. 8), the cornice has orthodox modilions and is closer to the French cornice (Fig. 56). But Marot shows an unusual frieze with outward, lower flare, and a base with only one scotia between torus moldings—all quite different from the Louvre.

36. Rose, *Spätbarock*, 115.

37. Marot, Baalbek suite, no. 8.

38. Ibid., no. 6. Rose (*Spätbarock,* 115) indicates a comparison with the Baalbek portal as reconstructed in Wood, *The Ruins of Palmyra and Balbec,* part II, pl. XXXII, but this is unrelated to the Louvre. It is possible that by "Kasettendecke" Rose meant the hexagonal coffers with sculpted busts set into the flat ceilings over the peripteron, but these were not illustrated by Marot and are unlike the Louvre panels with Apollo heads (Fig. 48).

39. Rose, *Spätbarock*, 115.

40. E.g., Palladio's drawing of the Temples of Saturn and Venus Genetrix, Rome (London, RIBA), illus. in C. Semenzato, *The Rotonda of Andrea Palladio*, University Park, Pa., and London, 1968, 12, pl. II; Palladio's own Villa Rotonda near Vicenza.

41. Hautecoeur, *Louvre et Tuileries*, 175 n. 4.

42. Wood's 1757 publication is titled *The Ruins of Balbec, otherwise Heliopolis in Coelosyria.*

43. Noted by Rose, *Spätbarock*, 115.

44. See P. Patte, *Mémoires sur les objets les plus importans de l'architecture,* Paris, 1769, 264.

45. Perrault's description of this project is in Blondel, *Architecture françoise*, IV, 9–11. The inscription on Figure 142 states that the plan was "proposé . . . en l'année 1674." Perrault may have sent the scheme directly to Colbert; no mention is made of it in *PV.* Perrault's octagonal court was to be surrounded by ceremonial apartments for winter and summer; this may indicate Perrault's knowledge of De Monconys's *Journal,* where the rooms around the hexagonal and large courts at Baalbek are described as "toute entourée d'appartements ou chambres de diverses figures" (I, 348). Leibniz also reported on Claude's scheme in 1676 (see "Le Louvre: Plans d'achèvement. Pyramide triomphale de Perrault. Fragment inédit de Leibniz," *Journal de l'instruction publique et des cultes*, XXVI, 1857, 238–239). An alternate project by Perrault within the hexagonal court is published in Blondel, *Architecture françoise*, IV, 14–15, pl. II (no. 443).

46. M. N. Rosenfeld, *Sebastiano Serlio on Domestic Architecture*, Cambridge, Mass., and London, 1978, 27. A variant of Figure 143 is in the Munich manuscript of Serlio's book VI (Munich, Bayerische Staatsbibliothek, Codex Icon 189; see ibid., 63).

APPENDIX E

Colonnade, Péristyle, Galerie, Portique: A Note on Seventeenth- and Eighteenth-Century Nomenclature

François Le Vau made a distinction in 1668 between *péristyle* and *galerie,* the former placed around "temples, avant portiques, théâtres et places publiques et autres lieux semblables," the latter used for the decoration of palaces.[1] Claude Perrault consistently referred to the east façade of the Louvre as having "deux Portiques"[2] and sanctioned the term *péristyle* only for columns within the walls of a structure, not for those on an exterior.[3] But during the later seventeenth and eighteenth centuries, others tended to use the terms interchangeably when referring to the east façade, with *péristyle* more frequent during the seventeenth century and *colonnade* more usual in the eighteenth. The "Registre" of 1667 speaks of "un perystile ou galerie" with reference to the Louvre Colonnade.[4] François Blondel wrote in 1675 of "des differentes especes de Peristyles ou Colonnates"[5] and titled one of his chapters in the *Cours d'architecture* "Des Peristyles ou Colonnates."[6] Blondel wrote:

> Les Anciens n'ont rien trouvé de plus grand ny de plus superbe pour orner leurs magnifiques Bâtimens que les Colonnes; Aussi les ont-ils quasi toûjours environnez de files de Colonnes, ou de Pilastres, qu'ils ont appellées des Portiques & des Peristyles, à qui nos Modernes ont donné le nom de Colonnates.[7]

André Félibien followed Perrault's definition of *péristyle*;[8] he defined *galerie* in its sense as a long gallery ("lieu propre pour se promener") and *portique* as "un lieu long & couvert, soit par une voute, soit par un plancher soutenu par des Colonnes."[9] Charles Perrault summarized the issue in his autobiography (ca. 1700):

> M. Colbert dit que, s'il en étoit le maître, il choisiroit celui [of the Louvre designs] qui n'avoit point de galerie (on ne donnoit pas encore [in 1667] le nom de péristile à ces rangs de colonnes qui, posés le long d'un bâtiment, forment une espèce de galerie couverte qui communique à toutes les pièces des appartemens).[10]

Notes

1. Sources II, no. 6 (11b).
2. Ibid., nos. 12 (a,b) (1673), 26 (b,c) (1684).
3. "Mais ce qui fait l'essence des Peristyles, est que ces Portiques qui les composent, ayent les colonnes en dedans & les murs en dehors, & non pas les colonnes en dehors, & les murs en dedans, comme aux Temples & aux Portiques de derriere les Theatres. . . . Cette disposition des Colonnes & du Mur, empesche les Peripteres & les Monopteres d'estre Peristyles. Parce que les Monopteres n'ont point de Mur, & que celuy des Perypteres est en dedans" (Perrault, *Vitruve*, 1673, 70 n. 1; ibid., 1684, 72 n. 36).
4. Sources II, no. 1.
5. Blondel, 1675, preface (unpaginated).
6. Blondel, 1683, 177 (part III, book I, chap. 1).
7. Ibid.
8. *Des principes de l'architecture, de la sculpture, de la peinture, et des autres arts qui en dependent*, Paris, 1676, II, 701–702.
9. Ibid., 605, 706. Also in 1676, the members of the Académie royale d'architecture used the terms "peristiles, galleries ou loges" interchangeably (*PV*, I, 120 [June 22]).
10. Sources II, no. 53[b]. On these terminologies, see also B. Jestaz, "Le Trianon de Marbre ou Louis XIV architecte," *GBA*, ser. 6, LXXIV, 1969, 272–273, 285 n. 27.

SOURCES I

BUILDING THE LOUVRE (1667–1680): ALLOCATIONS AND PAYMENTS FROM THE *COMPTES DES BÂTIMENTS DU ROI*

Note: The *Comptes* record yearly allocations from the royal treasury for the royal buildings, but in most cases a combined sum is given. For this reason, only allocations specifically earmarked for the Louvre are cited below.

1667

Masonry

[1.] May 25: aux carreyers de Saint-Cloud, à compte des colonnes et quartiers de pierre qu'ils fournissent pour le bastiment du Louvre . . . 12500 [livres] (I, col. 179)

[2.] July 2: A Renault, carreyer, à compte des quartiers et colonnes de pierre de Saint-Cloud qu'il fournit pour le Louvre . . . 200 [livres] (I, col. 189)

[3.] July 29, 1667–February 19, 1668: à eux [André Mazières et Antoine Bergeron, entrepreneurs de maçonnerie des bastimens du Roy], à compte des ouvrages de maçonnerie qu'ils font au chasteau du Louvre [3 payments] . . . 74000 [livres] (I, col. 179)

[4.] October 28, 1667–January 9, 1668: à eux [Mazières et Bergeron], à compte des ouvrages qu'ils font au bastiment neuf du Louvre [5 payments] . . . 175000 [livres] (ibid.)

Sculpture

[5.] December 31: au s^r Millet, à compte des ouvrages de sculpture qu'il fait au bastiment neuf du Louvre . . . 200 [livres] (I, col. 183)

Worker Compensation

[6.] December 31: à plusieurs pauvres maneuvres qui ont esté blessez en travaillant à l'attelier du bastiment neuf du Louvre . . . 150 [livres] (I, col. 189)

1668

Foundation Medals

[7.] June 18: aux ouvriers du Louvre, pour grattification, à cause du jour qu'ont esté posées les medailles du Roy dans les fondations du Louvre . . . 220 [livres] (ibid.)

Masonry

[8.] January 3: à André Mazières et Antoine Bergeron, entrepreneurs des bastimens du Louvre, par advance des matéreaux qu'ils voiturent et des ouvrages qu'ils feront pendant la présente année . . . 20000 [livres] (I, cols. 239–240)

[9.] January 9–June 18: au nommé Roze, à compte de la pierre de liais qu'il fournit et voiture pour le Louvre [2 payments] . . . 2500 [livres] (I, col. 179)

[10.] March 7, 1668–January 15, 1669: à eux [Mazières et Bergeron], à compte de leurs ouvrages au chasteau du Louvre [11 payments] . . . 477000 [livres] (I, col. 240)

[11.] June 18: à Mouton, autre carreyer, à compte des colonnes et quartiers de pierre de Saint-Cloud qu'il fournit pour le Louvre . . . 3000 [livres] (I, col. 179)

[12.] July 5–October 6: à Anne Billon, à compte des pierres de liais qu'il fouille à Senlis pour le Louvre [2 payments] . . . 600 [livres] (I, col. 278)

[13.] August 16–December 17: à Anne Billon, carreyer, à compte des pierres de liais qu'il fouille ez environs de Senlis, pour le Louvre [3 payments] . . . 2100 [livres] (I, col. 249)

[14.] August 16–December 6: à Arnoul Rose, carreyer, à compte des pierres de Vernon qu'il tire pour le Louvre [3 payments] . . . 3300 [livres] (ibid.)

[15.] December 3: à Jean Blondel et Mathieu Charité, voituriers, à compte des pierres de Vernon qu'ils voiturent pour le Louvre . . . 1000 [livres] (I, col. 241)

Columns, Pilasters, Capitals

[16.] February 15–October 6: à Philippes [*sic*] Caffier et Mathieu Lespagnandelle, sculpteurs, pour leur parfait payement des chapiteaux de pierre qu'ils ont faits à l'avant-corps de l'entrée du Louvre, du costé de la court [5 payments] . . . 3740 [livres] (I, col. 243)

[17.] July 20: aud. Le Greu, à compte de trente-six colonnes de marbre qu'il doit fournir au Louvre . . . 2000 [livres] (I, col. 244)

[18.] July 28: à Louis Milet, pour un chapiteau de pierre de Saint-Cloud qu'il fait à l'avant-corps de l'entrée du Louvre . . . 200 [livres] (ibid.)

Sculpture

[19.] March 22: A Tuby, à compte des masques et frize qu'il a faits et continue de faire au Louvre . . . 600 [livres] (I, col. 243)

[20.] April 28: à Coysevaux, pour un morceau de frise qu'il a fait au Louvre, et autres ouvrages de sculpture pendant l'année 1667 . . . 135 [livres] (I, col. 244)

[21.] December 24: Aud. Le Hongre[1] et à Jean Baptiste Tuby, sculpteurs, pour leur parfait payement de 1440 [livres] à quoy montent les ouvrages qu'ils ont faits de la frize et masques dans les clefs des fenestres du Louvre du costé de la rue Saint-Honoré . . . 340 [livres] (I, col. 245)

Worker Compensation

[22.] April 25: à Simonne Guillemin, veufve de Gervais Oudin, par gratiffication, en considération de ce que son mary a esté tué travaillant aux atteliers du Louvre . . . 100 [livres] (I, col. 249)

[23.] June 29: à Estienne Gresset et Jean Potel, tous deux maneuvres, qui ont esté blessez en travaillant aux atteliers du Louvre, par gratiffication . . . 160 [livres] (ibid.)

[24.] September 3–November 29: à divers maneuvres qui ont esté blessez travaillans aux atteliers du Louvre, par gratiffication [4 payments] . . . 645 [livres] (ibid.)

[25.] September 30: à la veuve Perignon, Limousin, idem . . . 100 [livres] (ibid.)

[26.] November 4: A Simon Brion, maneuvre, par gratiffication, à cause de la blessure qu'il a eue en travaillant au Louvre . . . 60 [livres] (ibid.)

1669

Masonry

[27.] January 25, 1669–January 1, 1670: à André Mazières et Antoine Bergeron, entrepreneurs du Louvre, à compte des ouvrages de maçonnerie qu'ils font aud. lieu [10 payments] . . . 600500 [livres] (I, col. 317)

[28.] February 1–August 1: à Anne Billon, pour son parfait payement des pierres de liais qu'il a fournies pour les bazes des colonnes et pillastres de la façade du Louvre [4 payments] . . . 3925 [livres] (ibid.)

[29.] February 6: A Arnoul Roze, pour son parfait payement et remboursement de 9476 [livres] 10 [sols] 8 [deniers] à quoy monte la fouille qu'il a faite de la pierre de Vernon pour le Louvre . . . 1376 [livres] 10 [sols] 6 [deniers] (I, col. 326)

[30.] February 25–November 2: à Arnoul Roze, pour parfait payement de la despense qu'il a faite à fouiller des pierres à Vernon pour les bastimens du Louvre depuis le

31 décembre 1668 jusqu'au 20 juin 1669 [3 payments] . . . 5003 [livres] 15 [sols] (I, cols. 317–318)

[31.] October 15: à eux [André Mazières et Antoine Bergeron], à compte des avances de l'année prochaine et pour payer partie des pierres de Trossy qu'ils font venir pour les chapiteaux du péristile du Louvre . . . 3000 [livres] (I, col. 317)

[32.] December 20: à eux [Mazières et Bergeron] et pour avance desd. bastimens du Louvre de l'année prochaine 1670 . . . 10000 [livres] (ibid.)

Iron

[33.] January 28–March 19: à Estienne Doyart, serrurier, à compte des ouvrages et fournitures de gros fer qu'il a faits pour le service de S.M. en 1668 [3 payments] . . . 6000 [livres] (I, col. 319)

[34.] May 11, 1669–January 1, 1670: à luy [Estienne Doyart], à compte de ses ouvrages de serrurerie et fournitures de gros fer pour le Louvre et les Thuilleries [5 payments] . . . 19000 [livres] (ibid.)

Columns

[35.] February 6–September 2: à Jean Le Gruë, marbrier, à compte des 36 colonnes de marbre qu'il fait pour le Louvre [4 payments] . . . 14500 [livres] (I, col. 320)

Sculpture

[36.] February 15: aud. Le Gendre et Massou, sculpteurs, pour leur payement de quatre masques qu'ils ont faits à la façade du Louvre, vers la rue Saint-Honoré . . . 122 [livres] (I, col. 319)

Payments to Workers

[37.] March 25: aux ouvriers travaillans au Louvre, maçons, tailleurs de pierre et autres ouvriers, pour la gratiffication que S.M. leur a faite lorsqu'elle a esté veoir ses bastimens . . . 500 [livres] (I, col. 387)

[38.] May 30: aux ouvriers travaillans aux bastimens du Louvre, par gratification et pour le May de l'Ascension de la présente année . . . 600 [livres] (ibid.)

[39.] August 16: à Denis Champion et Laurens Baron, tailleurs de pierres, tant pour eux que pour les ouvriers qui travaillent au Louvre, par gratification que S.M. leur a faite lorsqu'elle a visité ses bastimens du Louvre . . . 550 [livres] (I, col. 388)

Worker Compensation

[40.] January 19: aux religieux de la Charité, par aumosnes et en considération des malades et blessez au bastiment du Louvre qu'ilz ont traitez en 1668 . . . 300 [livres] (I, col. 283)

[41.] February 24: à la veuve de Julien Gallois, manoeuvre, qui a esté tué en travaillant pour le Louvre, 80 [livres], et à Pierre Guillaume, autre manoeuvre, qui a esté blessé, 25 [livres] . . . 105 [livres] (I, col. 387)

[42.] March 22: à Jean Meusnier, manoeuvre, qui est tombé et s'est blessé en travaillant au bastiment du Louvre . . . 60 [livres] (ibid.)

[43.] June 2: à divers ouvriers qui ont esté blessez et tués au Louvre, 195 [livres]; sçavoir: à Jean Airault, tailleur de pierre, blessé, 30 [livres]; à la veuve du nommé Jean Branche, manoeuvre, blessé à la jambe, 20 [livres]; à la veuve de Simon Boudin, tué, idem, 60 [livres]; et 85 [livres] au nommé Deslauriers, carreyer, qui a eu la jambe rompue dans la carrière de Vernon en tirant des pierres pour le Louvre . . . 195 [livres] (ibid.)

[44]. June 23: à la veuve du nommé Louis Coquart, chartier, par gratiffication, et en considération de ce qu'il a esté tué en voiturant des pierres pour le Louvre, 60 [livres]; au nommé Chaveton, Limosin, blessé, idem, 30 [livres] . . . 90 [livres] (ibid.)

[45.] August 3: à Jean Le Tendre, Suisse, 30 [livres]; à François Julien, manoeuvre, 20 [livres], par gratiffication, en considération de ce qu'ils ont esté blessez en travaillant au bastiment du Louvre . . . 50 [livres] (I, cols. 387–388)

[46.] September 22: à plusieurs ouvriers blessez travaillans aux bastimens du Louvre, sçavoir: à la veuve Oustry, dont le mary est mort, 100 [livres]; à Durant, Dumont, Demy et Simon, 60 [livres]; et à Estienne Chaumeton, 25 [livres], cy . . . 185 [livres] (I, col. 388)

[47.] October 15: à plusieurs autres, tant mortz que blessez travaillans auxd. bastimens . . . 155 [livres] (ibid.)

[48.] November 7: . . . à Guillaume Legoux, blessé au Louvre, 20 [livres] (I, col. 387)

[49.] December 3: à Jean Briant, manoeuvre, blessé au Louvre, 20 [livres]; . . . et aux héritiers de Didier Thevenin, tué en travaillant au Louvre . . . 140 [livres] (ibid.)

[50.] December 31: à Calvas, manoeuvre, blessé au Louvre, 20 [livres]; . . . à Noizet, chartier, blessé en menant des matériaux au Louvre, 50 [livres] . . . 150 [livres] (ibid.)

Expropriation

[51.] January 23: à luy [Sieur Scaron de Vaures], pour le prix dud. hostel [Petit Hôtel de Vendôme] qui se rencontre dans le dessein du bastiment du Louvre . . . 126000 [livres] (I, col. 214)

[52.] January 23: au s^r Selincart, advocat en Parlement, pour le prix d'une maison qui se rencontre dans le dessin du bastiment du Louvre . . . 16000 [livres] (I, col. 221)

[53.] October 4: à Me François Le Fouin, notaire au Chastelet, pour ses peines, salaires et vacations d'avoir, pendant lad. année, passé plusieurs contracts d'acquisitions de maisons qui se rencontrent dans le dessein du Louvre et autres héritages au proffit de S.M. . . . 500 [livres] (I, col. 223)

1670

Masonry

[54.] January 24, 1670–January 4, 1671: à Mazière et Bergeron, à compte et en avance des ouvrages qu'ils feront pendant la présente année, et en considération de ce qu'ils doivent payer aux carriers de Saint-Leu pour les grandes pierres de mesure qu'ils fouillent pour la façade principalle du Louvre [9 payments] . . . 550000 [livres] (I, col. 401)

[55.] October 9: à luy [Sieur Liégeard], pour quarante-six blocs de marbre rouge, blanc et noir, de Dinan, qu'il a livrez au guichet du Louvre . . . 2108 [livres] 7 [sols] (I, col. 454)

[56.] December 6, 1670–January 4, 1671: à Simon et La Chapelle, à compte des terres qu'ils fouillent pour découvrir une carrière à Meudon pour tirer des grandes pierres pour le Louvre [2 payments] . . . 4000 [livres] (I, cols. 410–411)

Iron

[57.] February 4, 1670–January 15, 1671: à Estienne Doyart, serrurier, à compte et pour avance de ses ouvrages de serrurerie et fourniture de gros fer pour le chasteau du Louvre [7 payments] . . . 56700 [livres] (I, col. 403)

[58.] April 25: à luy [Doyart], pour parfait payement de 33294 [livres] 2 [sols] 9 [deniers] à quoy monte la fourniture de gros fer et de menus ouvrages qu'il a faits au Louvre et autres endroits pendant l'année 1669 . . . 1294 [livres] 2 [sols] 9 [deniers] (ibid.)

Columns, Pilasters, Capitals

[59.] February 6–October 9: à Le Gruë, marbrier, à compte des trente-six colonnes de marbre de Dinan qu'il fait venir pour le Louvre [4 payments] . . . 14400 [livres] (I, col. 404)

[60.] March 1–December 16: à eux [Philippe Caffieri et Mathieu Lespagnandel, sculpteurs], pour leur parfait payement de dix chapiteaux de colonnes, deux doubles pilastres et trois pilastres simples qu'ils ont faits pour le portail et peristile du Louvre [4 payments] . . . 7166 [livres] 13 [sols] 4 [deniers] (ibid.)

[61.] March 1–December 16: à Paris, sculpteur, pour son parfait payement de quatre chapiteaux de colonnes, un pillastre et deux quarts qu'il a faits pour le portail et peristille du Louvre [4 payments] . . . 2276 [livres] 13 [sols] 4 [deniers] (I, col. 405)

[62.] March 1–December 16: à Legrand et Poissant, pour leur parfait payement de dix chapiteaux de colonnes, deux chapiteaux d'encoigneure et quatre chapiteaux pillastres simples qu'ils ont faits pour le portail et peristille du Louvre [3 payments] . . . 6233 [livres] 6 [sols] 8 [deniers] (ibid.)

[63.] March 1–December 16: à Francisque Temporiti, sculpteur, pour parfait payement de dix chapiteaux de colonnes, deux doubles chapiteaux pillastres, quatre simples et deux quarts[2] qu'il a faits pour le portail et peristille du Louvre [4 payments] . . . 6503 [livres] 19 [sols] 8 [deniers] (ibid.)

[64.] April 12–December 16: à Le Hongre,[3] sculpteur, pour parfait payement de quatre chapiteaux de colonnes, trois pillastres et deux quarts qu'il a faits pour le portail et peristille du Louvre [3 payments] . . . 2910 [livres] (I, cols. 405–406)

[65.] April 21: à Jean Le Grue, marbrier, à compte des trente-six colonnes de marbre blanc et rouge qu'il fait venir pour le Louvre . . . 10000 [livres] (I, col. 454)

[66.] June 1–December 16: à Couet, sculpteur, pour parfait payement de deux chapiteaux de colonnes et deux pillastres qu'il taille pour la façade du chasteau du Louvre [3 payments] . . . 1166 [livres] 13 [sols] 4 [deniers] (I, col. 407)

[67.] July 16: A luy [Nicholas Poissant, sculpteur], à compte des chapiteaux qu'il faict à la façade du Louvre . . . 600 [livres] (I, col. 405)

Scaffolding

[68.] January 11–November 9: à Cliquin et Charpentier, charpentiers, à compte et pour avance des échaffaux qu'ils font pour la façade du Louvre [6 payments] . . . 26500 [livres] (I, col. 401)

Worker Payments

[69.] April 11: à [Antoine Le Ménestrel, trésorier général des Bastimens du Roy, pour son remboursement de ce qu'il a avancé] aux ouvriers qui travaillent aux bastimens de S.M. suivant notre ordre, sçavoir: aux ouvriers du Louvre, 800 [livres] (I, col. 471)

[70.] May 15: à [Le Ménestrel, pour son remboursement de ce qu'il a avancé aux ouvriers qui travaillent aux bastimens de S.M. suivant notre ordre,] sçavoir: aux tailleurs de pierre du Louvre, des Thuilleries et de l'Observatoire, 300 [livres] (ibid.)

[71.] December 22: aud. s^r Le Ménestrel, pour remboursement de pareille somme qu'il a payée aux ouvriers du Louvre, de l'Arc de triomphe, compagnons sculpteurs et marbriers des manufactures dont le Roy a esté voir les ouvrages, par gratiffication . . . 1100 [livres] (I, col. 455)

Worker Compensation

[72.] January 24: aux nommez Briault, Barbillon et Langrand, manoeuvres blessez en travaillant tant au Louvre qu'à la Sainte-Chapelle et à Saint-Germain, par gratification, chacun 40 [livres] . . . 120 [livres] (ibid.)

[73.] March 27: aux nommez Jean Belleville, maçon, qui a eu les doigts coupez d'une pierre en travaillant au Louvre, par gratification, 30 [livres]; à La Taille 20 [livres], et 15 [livres] à Jean Gordier, manoeuvres blessez aud. lieu . . . 65 [livres] (ibid.)

[74.] April 7: aux veuves des nommez Jacques Hurault, apareilleur, et René Jumeau, manoeuvre, tuez en travaillant au Louvre, sçavoir: 100 [livres] à lad. veuve Hurault et 75 [livres] à lad. veuve René Jumeau . . . 175 [livres] (ibid.)

[75.] June 3: à [Le Ménestrel, pour son remboursement de ce qu'il a avancé] pour plusieurs ouvriers qui se sont tuez et blessez travaillant tant au bastiment du Louvre qu'aux appartemens des Thuilleries . . . 310 [livres] (I, col. 471)

[76.] August 14–December 22: au s^r Le Menestrel, pour remboursement de pareille somme qu'il a payée aux veuves dont les maris ont esté tuez et aux ouvriers blessez travaillans pour le Roy aux bastimens du Louvre, Saint-Germain, Versailles et la carrière de Meudon [2 payments] . . . 1439 [livres] (I, col. 455)

[77.] October 19: à Bongars, chirurgien, en considération du soin qu'il a pris de penser [*sic*] les ouvriers du Louvre depuis l'année 1662 jusqu'à ce jour . . . 600 [livres] (I, col. 480)

1671

Masonry

[78.] February 13–October 3: à eux [Mazières et Bergeron], à compte des ouvrages de maçonnerie qu'ils font au Louvre [7 payments] . . . 506500 [livres] (I, col. 492)

[79.] February 21: à Dambroiseville, Vigneron, les Nasses et les Le Noir, propriétaires des carrières de Trossy et Saint-Leu, en considération du soin qu'ils ont pris à faire débiter et tirer de leurs carrières les grandes pierres de mesure qui ont esté employées à la façade du Louvre l'année dernière [1670] . . . 300 [livres] (I, col. 498)

[80.] March 12–August 9: à Michel Rigaleau, dit La Chapelle, et Simon du Costé, à compte des terres qu'ils fouillent dans la carrière de Meudon, pour tirer de grandes pierres pour le Louvre [3 payments] . . . 1400 [livres] (I, col. 546)

[81.] July 17: à Vincent Francoeur et Simon du Costé, carreyers, à compte de la fouille qu'ils font à Meudon pour tirer de grandes pierres pour le Louvre . . . 100 [livres] (I, col. 497)

[82.] October 3: à Simon du Costé et Michel Rigalleau, à compte de la fouille qu'ils font à la carrière de Meudon pour tirer des pierres pour le Louvre . . . 150 [livres] (ibid.)

Iron

[83.] March 3–December 2: à Estienne Doyart, serrurier, à compte des ouvrages de serrurerie et fournitures de gros fer qu'il a faits et continue de faire tant au chasteau du Louvre qu'au palais des Thuilleries et autres lieux [6 payments] . . . 18800 [livres] (I, col. 493)

Worker Payments

[84.] May 11: Aux tailleurs de pierre du Louvre, des Thuilleries et de l'Observatoire, par gratification pour le May de l'Ascension . . . 600 [livres] (I, col. 567)

Worker Compensation

[85.] March 1: à la veuve de Jean Petit, eschaffaudeur, par gratification, en considération que son mary a esté tué en tombant d'un eschaffaut des bastimens du Louvre . . . 60 [livres] (ibid.)

[86.] April 21: aux cy-après nommées, sçavoir: 120 [livres] à la mère de Pierre Morin et à la veuve de Brie, manoeuvres, qui ont esté tuez travaillant au Louvre, et 90 [livres] à la veuve de Laury, charpentier, aussy tué aud. lieu . . . 210 [livres] (ibid.)

[87.] June 18: aux héritiers de Claude et Jullien René, tous deux tuez en travaillant au Louvre . . . 60 [livres] (ibid.)

[88.] September 5: à la veuve Seglas, en considération de ce que Joachim et Marin Seglas, ses enfans, ont esté tuez travaillant au Louvre . . . 60 [livres] (I, col. 568)

[89.] September 5: A Jean Jourdain, couvreur, en considération d'une chute qu'il fit travaillant au Louvre . . . 60 [livres] (ibid.)

[90.] September 25: aux cy-après nommez, sçavoir: à la veuve François Julienne, manoeuvre, tué en travaillant au Louvre, 45 [livres]; . . . et à Marchand, père de Paul Marchand, goujat, tué au Louvre, 30 [livres] (I, col. 567)

[91.] October 18: aux héritiers de François Jubé, goujat, tué au Louvre . . . 30 [livres] (I, col. 568)

[92.] November 9: à la veuve de Jean des Hayes, charpentier, tué en remuant des poutres arrivées pour le Louvre . . . 50 [livres] (ibid.)

1672

Masonry

[93.] February 25–November 9: à André Mazières et Antoine Bergeron, entrepreneurs des bastimens, à compte de leurs ouvrages de maçonnerie au Louvre [8 payments] . . . 44300 [livres] (I, col. 595)

[94.] June 10: à Estienne Friolet, poseur, en considération des soins qu'il a apporté pour poser les pierres du péristile du Louvre sans les avoir écorné . . . 300 [livres] (I, col. 651)

Pediment Stones

[95.] April 2: à Berger et Boubert, pour avoir gardé pendant trois mois le magazin pour les deux grandes pierres du fronton du Louvre . . . 152 [livres] (I, col. 655)

[96.] September 29, 1672–April 19, 1673: à Mouton et Potery pour parfait payement de 1773 [livres] 16 [sols] pour les décombres des deux grandes pierres pour la cimais du fronton du Louvre [3 payments] . . . 1773 [livres] 16 [sols] (I, col. 595)

[97.] September 29: à eux [Mouton et Potery], à compte idem . . . 282 [livres] (ibid.)

[98.] October 13: à de Baure et consors pour la taille desd. pierres . . . 126 [livres] (ibid.)

[99.] October 28: à Joseph, charpentier, par gratification et pour les soins qu'il a pris d'avoir monté les grandes pierres du péristile du Louvre sans les avoir écorné . . . 300 [livres] (I, col. 651)

[100.] December 6: aux charpentiers qui ont travaillé à la descente des deux grandes pierres de Meudon . . . 220 [livres] 19 [sols] 6 [deniers] (I, col. 596)

[101.] December 6, 1672–January 5, 1673: à Cliquin, à compte de la machine qu'il fait pour enlever lesd. deux grandes pierres [2 payments] . . . 2200 [livres] (ibid.)

Iron

[102.] March 25: à Estienne Doyart, serrurier, à compte du gros fer qu'il fournit pour le Louvre . . . 2000 [livres] (ibid.)

[103.] April 1: à La Baronnière, peintre, pour avoir peint en huille des barres de fer pour le Louvre . . . 129 [livres] 1 [sol] (I, col. 597)

Sculpture

[104.] A Jacques Houzeau, faisant ordinairement les modelles et ornemens de sculpture, tant au Louvre qu'ailleurs, pour ses gages, la somme de 400 [livres], dont il ne sera payé que de la moitié, cy . . . 200 [livres] (I, col. 658)

Worker Payments

[105.] May 27: aux ouvriers du Louvre et des Thuilleries, pour leur May de l'Ascension . . . 350 [livres] (I, col. 672)

Worker Compensation

[106.] August 6: A la veuve Hebert, en considération de ce que son mary a esté tué en travaillant au Louvre . . . 80 [livres] (I, col. 651)

1673

Pediment Stones

[107.] [Allocation:] Pour transporter, tailler et poser les deux grandes pierres du fronton du Louvre . . . 25000 [livres] (I, col. 677)

[108.] January 5–March 9: à la veufve Fleury, pour parfait payement des cordages qu'elle fournit pour le payement des deux pierres [employées au fronton du Louvre] [2 payments] . . . 1684 [livres] 8 [sols] (I, col. 599)

[109.] April 19: A La Roche, préposé aux décombres des deux grandes pierres du fronton du Louvre, pour ses gages de janvier et febvrier derniers . . . 150 [livres] (I, col. 655)

[110.] May 20: à Michel Rigalleau, dit La Chapelle, pour parfait payement de 6346 [livres] 11 [sols] 6 [deniers] à quoy monte la décombrement des terres pour les deux grandes pierres de Meudon . . . 696 [livres] 11 [sols] 6 [deniers] (I, col. 685)

[111.] June 5–September 26: à Cliquin, charpentier, à compte des ouvrages qu'il fait pour enlever les deux grandes pierres de Meudon pour servir de cimaise au fronton du Louvre [3 payments] . . . 3500 [livres] (I, col. 683)

[112.] June 18: aux ouvriers qui travaillent à remuer les deux grandes pierres de Meudon, par gratification . . . 110 [livres] (I, col. 715)

[113.] June 29–August 8: à la veuve Fleury, cordière, pour les cordes qu'elle a fournies pour le transport desd. deux pierres [2 payments] . . . 750 [livres] 13 [sols] (I, col. 685)

[114.] July 18–November 18: aux ouvriers qui travaillent aud. décombrement [3 payments] . . . 4235 [livres] 17 [sols] 6 [deniers] (ibid.)

[115.] September 1: à Grou, voiturier, qui a fourny un batteau pour led. transport . . . 535 [livres] 8 [sols] 4 [deniers] (ibid.)

[116.] October 26: à luy [Grou], pour un autre batteau qu'il a fourny . . . 306 [livres] (ibid.)

[117.] October 26: à ceux qui ont travaillé à remuer et voiturer lesd. pierres . . . 2976 [livres] 11 [sols] (ibid.)

[118.] October 26: A Mouton, pour le décombrement desd. deux pierres . . . 498 [livres] 10 [sols] (ibid.)

[119.] October 26, 1673–February 12, 1674: à La Roche, préposé à la conduitte des deux grandes pierres de Meudon pour le fronton du Louvre, pour six mois de ses appointemens [2 payments] . . . 450 [livres] (I, col. 716)

Capitals

[120.] June 16–November 18: à Caffier et Lespagnandel, sculpteurs, pour trois chapiteaux qu'ils ont faits à la façade du grand portail du Louvre [2 payments] . . . 1300 [livres] (I, col. 684)

Compensation

[121.] June 29: à Courtois, vigneron, pour le dédommager du dégat qu'il a souffert par la descente de la grande pierre de Meudon pour le fronton du Louvre . . . 225 [livres] (I, col. 710)

[122.] November 2: à Du Corroy, en considération de ce qu'il a esté blessé travaillant à remuer une desd. pierres . . . 75 [livres] (I, col. 716)

1674

Allocations

[123.] Pour tailler et poser les deux grandes pierres du fronton, en couvrir le derrière de grandes marches, et achever la balustrade . . . 25000 [livres]
  Pour faire la sculpture de toute la corniche de la façade . . . 12000 [livres]
  Pour oster le grand eschafaud qui est devant lad. façade . . . 3000 [livres] (I, col. 739)

Masonry

[124.] May 19–December 23: à Mazière et Bergeron, entrepreneurs de la maçonnerie, à compte de leurs ouvrages [4 payments] . . . 13200 [livres] (I, col. 741)

Iron

[125.] September 17: à [Doyart], à compte du gros fer qu'il fournit [for the Louvre and Tuileries] . . . 600 [livres] (I, col. 743)

Pediment Stones

[126.] March 22–August 17: à Mouton, carreyer, à compte des pierres qu'il tire à [*sic*] Meudon pour le fronton du Louvre [3 payments] . . . 2200 [livres] (I, col. 741)

[127.] June 8–July 20: à Cliquin, à compte des machines et échafauds qu'il fait pour monter les deux grandes pierres de fronton [2 payments] . . . 4300 [livres] (ibid.)

[128.] June 22, 1674–February 5, 1675: à Rigault, pour les charpentiers qui travaillent à remuer les deux grandes pierres du fronton [4 payments] . . . 6279 [livres] 9 [sols] (ibid.)

[129.] August 17: à divers charpentiers, à compte des échafauds pour lesd. pierres . . . 1500 [livres] (ibid.)

[130.] September 15: à Pierre Modène et Simon La Grande, pour divers ouvriers qui ont aydé à enlever lesd. pierres du fronton . . . 286 [livres] (I, cols. 741–742)

Sculpture

[131.] A Jacques Houzeau, . . . sculpteur, faisant ordinairement les models et ornemens, tant au Louvre qu'ailleurs, pour ses gages la somme de 400 [livres], dont il sera payé seulement de . . . 150 [livres] (I, col. 789)

[132.] May 19–October 4: à Caffiers, Lespagnandel et consors, pour parfait payement de 12321 [livres] pour les ouvrages de sculpture de la façade du Louvre [3 payments] . . . 12321 [livres] (I, col. 743)

[133.] September 17: à Le Hongre,[4] pour les chapiteaux et pilastres qu'il a faits . . . 833 [livres] 6 [sols] 8 [deniers] (ibid.)

Worker Compensation

[134.] September 28: à Le Roux, compagnon charpentier, blessé travaillant à la façade du Louvre, pour le faire médicamenter . . . 100 [livres] (I, col. 744)

[135.] October 30: A Nicolle Copin, mère de feu Louis Morel, qui a esté tué posant les deux grandes pierres du Louvre . . . 100 [livres] (I, col. 804)

1675

Allocations

[136.] Pour la sculpture de la façade du Louvre, bas-reliefs, et autres ornemens, y compris le ravallement des colonnes . . . 16600 [livres]
  Pour un petit escallier et autres dépenses à faire aud. devant du Louvre . . . 3000 [livres] (I, col. 812)

Masonry

[137.] April 12–August 6: à Mazières et Bergeron, entrepreneurs de la maçonnerie, à compte de leurs ouvrages [2 payments] . . . 3000 [livres] (I, col. 815)

Sculpture

[138.] April 12, 1675–January 14, 1676: à Caffiers et Lespagnandel, sculpteurs, à compte de leurs ouvrages à la façade du Louvre [6 payments] . . . 14200 [livres] (ibid.)

Worker Compensation

[139.] January 10: à Fournier, compagnon menuisier, qui est tombé travaillant pour le Roy au Louvre . . . 40 [livres] (I, col. 804)

Measurement

[140.] September 29: A Goujon, greffier, à compte des thoisez du Louvre et de Versailles . . . 600 [livres] (I, col. 877)

1676

Masonry

[141.] March 16–December 13: à Mazieres et Bergeron, à compte des ouvrages de maçonnerie qu'ils font au Louvre [6 payments] . . . 5500 [livres] (I, col. 885)

Capitals

[142.] May 9: à Couet, pour les chapiteaux qu'il a restaurés à la façade du Louvre . . . 157 [livres] (I, col. 887)

Sculpture

[143.] [Allocation:] Pour continuer les ornemens de sculpture de la façade du chasteau du Louvre . . . 16000 [livres] (I, col. 882)

[144.] February 26–November 13: à Caffiers, Lespagnandel et consors, à compte des ouvrages de sculpture qu'ils font à la façade du Louvre [5 payments] . . . 7220 [livres] (I, col. 887)

Scaffolding

[145.] April 8: à Cottard et Jombert, qui ont échaffaudé le péristille du Louvre, pour leurs salaires et vaccations . . . 307 [livres] 13 [sols] 6 [deniers] (I, col. 888)

1677

Allocation

[146.] Pour l'élévation des deux pavillons . . . 30000 [livres] (I, col. 937)

Masonry

[147.] March 16–December 12: à Bergeron et Mazières, à compte des ouvrages de maçonnerie qu'ils font au Louvre [3 payments] . . . 5400 [livres] (I, cols. 943–944)

[148.] May 8–December 5: au nommé Rose, carrier, pour parfait payement tant pour les pierres de liais qu'il a fournis que pour les guillochis des deux peristiles et pavillons de la façade du Louvre et autres ouvrages [4 payments] . . . 5600 [livres] (I, cols. 944–945)

Sculpture

[149.] [Allocation:] Pour continuer la sculpture de la façade du Louvre . . . 20000 [livres] (I, col. 937)

[150.] March 16–May 17: à Caffiers et Lespagnandel, sculpteurs, à compte de leurs ouvrages à la façade du Louvre [2 payments] . . . 3500 [livres] (I, col. 945)

1678

Masonry

[151.] February 20: aux entrepreneurs de la maçonnerie du Louvre, à compte des ouvrages qu'ils font . . . 500 [livres] (I, col. 1021)

[152.] March 13, 1678–January 1, 1679: à Rose, carrier, à compte des pierres de liais qu'il fournit pour le bastiment du Louvre [3 payments] . . . 4800 [livres] (ibid.)

Sculpture

[153.] [Allocation:] Pour la sculpture de la façade du Louvre . . . 20000 [livres] (I, col. 1016)

[154.] March 11: A Lespagnandel et consors, parfait payement de 25067 [livres] 16 [sols] 8 [deniers] pour ouvrages de sculpture qu'ils ont faits au peristile de la grande façade du Louvre . . . 867 [livres] 16 [sols] 8 [deniers] (I, col. 1023)

Roofing

[155.] March 6: à Charuel, couvreur, à compte des ouvrages et réparations de couvertures du Louvre et des Thuilleries . . . 1200 [livres] (I, col. 1021)

[156.] November 24: à Yvon et Charuel, à compte, idem . . . 400 [livres] (ibid.)

1679

Allocation

[157.] Pour la continuation des bastimens du Louvre . . . 300000 [livres] (I, col. 1116)

Masonry

[158.] May 7: à La Roze, carrier, parfait payement de 7541 [livres] 5 [sols] pour les pierres de liais des Chartreux qu'il a livrez pour le Louvre en 1677 . . . 741 [livres] 5 [sols] (I, col. 1229)

Pilasters, Capitals

[159.] April 16–August 27: à la veuve Francisque, sculpteur [Francesco Temporiti], à compte des chapiteaux et pilastres que led. Francisque a fait au Louvre [2 payments] . . . 600 [livres] (I, col. 1123)

Pediment Stones

[160.] May 28: à Cliquin, charpentier, par gratiffication, en considération de ses soings et industrie pour le transport et élévation de deux grandes pierres du fronton du Louvre et autres ouvrages . . . 2000 [livres] (I, col. 1213)

1680

Allocation

[161.] Pour la continuation du bastiment du Louvre . . . 300000 [livres] (I, col. 1235)

Notes

1. In his life of Étienne Le Hongre, Guillet de Saint-Georges wrote: "Il [Le Hongre] a fait encore au Louvre une partie des chapiteaux de l'ordre corinthien qui sont au portail, du côté de l'église de Saint-Germain [l'Auxerrois], avec une partie des ovales et des appuis du peristyle; même à la façade du Louvre qui regarde l'ancien hôtel de Grammont [the north façade] une partie des chapiteaux et une partie de la frise, des masques et des autres ornements qu'on y voit" (L. Dussieux et al., eds., *Mémoires inédits sur la vie et les ouvrages des membres de l'Académie royale de peinture et de sculpture,* Paris, 1854, I, 368).

2. "Deux quarts de chapiteaux, par conséquent pour des pilastres d'angle" (*CBR*, I, col. 405; note by J. Guiffrey).

3. See above, note 1.

4. See above, note 1.

SOURCES II

DOCUMENTS AND WRITINGS ON THE LOUVRE (1667–1792)

Index

1. "Registre ou Journal des délibérations & résolutions touchant les Bâtimens du Roi" (April and May 1667)
2. Letter of Carlo Vigarani to Cardinal Rinaldo d'Este, August 5, 1667
3. Letter of Carlo Vigarani to the Duchess of Modena, August 26, 1667
4. *La Gazette d'Amsterdam,* November 19, 1667
5. Letter of François Le Vau to Jean Baptiste Colbert, December 7, 1667
6. "Advis de M. le Vau le jeune sur le nouveau dessin du Louvre" (1668)
7. Jean Baptiste Colbert, "Mémoire sur ce qui est à faire pour les bâtiments en l'année 1669" (1668)
8. "Extrait et sommaire des avis des Architectes sur les modeles du Louvre, De L'arc de triomphe et de l'observatoire" (1669–70)
9. Claude Olry de Loriande, *Le superbe dessein du Louvre. Dedié a Monsiegnevr Colbert* (Paris, 1670)
10. Nicolas Catherinot, *Distiques sur le Louvre au Roy* (Bourges, 1672)
11. *Essays à la louange du roy* (Paris, 1672)
12. Claude Perrault, ed. and trans., *Les dix livres d'architecture de Vitruve* (Paris, 1673)
13. Louis Savot, *L'architecture françoise des bastimens particuliers,* ed. François Blondel (Paris, 1673)
14. Letter of Christian Huygens to Lodewijk Huygens, July 28, 1673
15. Paul Tallement, "Panégyrique du roi prononcé le 25 août 1673"
16. *Le Mercure galant,* June 1674
17. *Procès-verbaux de l'Académie royale d'architecture,* June 25, 1674
18. André Félibien, *Des principes de l'architecture, de la sculpture, de la peinture, et des autres arts qui en dependent* (Paris, 1676)
19. [Gottfried Wilhelm, Baron von Leibniz], "Le Louvre: Plans d'achèvement, Pyramide Triomphale de Perrault" (January 22, 1676)
20. *Procès-verbaux de l'Académie royale d'architecture,* March 29, 1677; December 5, 1678; December 12, 1678; January 23, 1679
21. Letter of Philips Doublet to Christian Huygens, March 9, 1679
22. *Le Mercure galant,* December 1681
23. Antoine Desgodets, *Les édifices antiques de Rome dessinés et mesurés très exactement* (Paris, 1682)
24. François Blondel, *Cours d'architecture enseigné dans l'Académie royale d'architecture* (Paris, 1683)
25. Claude Perrault, *Ordonnance des cinq espèces de colonnes selon la méthode des anciens* (Paris, 1683)
26. Claude Perrault, ed. and trans., *Les dix livres d'architecture de Vitruve,* 2d ed. (Paris, 1684)
27. Germain Brice, *Description nouvelle de ce qu'il y a de plus remarquable dans la ville de Paris* (Paris, 1684)
28. C. Le Maire, *Paris ancien et nouveau* (Paris, 1685)

29. Allain Manesson-Mallet, *Description de l'univers . . .* (Frankfurt-am-Main, 1686)
30. Claude Charles Guyonnet de Vertron, *Le nouveau Panthéon . . .* (Paris, 1686)
31. *Le Mercure galant,* November 1686
32. Germain Brice, *Description nouvelle de ce qu'il y a de plus remarquable dans la ville de Paris,* 2d ed. (Paris, 1687)
33. Nicodemus Tessin the Younger, *Nicodemus Tessin D. Y.:s Studieresor . . .* , ed. Osvald Sirén, (Stockholm, 1914)
34. Bernard de Fontenelle, "Eloge de Perrault" (1688)
35. Charles Perrault, *Parallèle des anciens et des modernes en ce qui regarde les arts et les sciences* (Paris, 1688)
36. "Eloge de Mons. Perrault" (February 28, 1689)
37. Charles Perrault, *Le cabinet des beaux-arts . . .* (Paris, 1690)
38. Manuscript collection (destroyed) of drawings by Claude Perrault, with commentaries by Claude and Charles Perrault (compiled 1693)
39. Nicolas Boileau, *Réflexions critiques sur quelques passages du rheteur Longin* (Paris, 1694)
40. Letter of Nicolas Boileau to Antoine Arnauld, June 1694
41. Letter of Daniel Cronström to Nicodemus Tessin the Younger, January 28, 1694
42. Letter of Daniel Cronström to Nicodemus Tessin the Younger, May 20, 1695
43. Letter to Daniel Cronström to Nicodemus Tessin the Younger, June 6, 1695
44. Charles Perrault, *Les hommes illustres qui ont paru en France pendant ce siècle* (Paris, 1696)
45. *Le Mercure galant,* November 1696
46. Charles Perrault, "Dessin d'un Portail pour l'Église de Sainte-Geneviève a Paris MDCXCVII fait et donné par M. Perrault de l'Academie Françoise" (1697)
47. *Procès-verbaux de l'Académie royale d'architecture* (July 8, 1697)
48. Germain Brice, *Description nouvelle de la ville de Paris . . .* 3d ed. (Paris, 1698)
49. Martin Lister, *Voyage de Lister à Paris en MDCXCVIII* (1698)
50. *Le Journal des sçavans,* April 7, 1698
51. Cassan, "La nymphe de Chanceaux, ou L'arrivée de la Seine au château de Marly" (May 1699)
52. Florent Le Comte, *Cabinet des singularitez d'architecture, peinture, sculpture, et gravure . . .* (Paris, 1699)
53. Charles Perrault, *Mémoires de ma vie* (ca. 1700)
54. Claude François Ménestrier, *Histoire du règne de Louis le Grand par les médailles . . .* new ed. (Paris, 1700)
55. Obituary of Charles Perrault, *Mercure de France,* May 1703
56. Letter of Göran Josuae Adelcrantz to Nicodemus Tessin the Younger, December 19, 1704
57. *Procès-verbaux de l'Académie royale d'architecture* (August 22, 1707)
58. Germain Brice, *Description nouvelle de la ville de Paris . . .* 6th ed. (Paris, 1713)
59. Jean Louis de Cordemoy, *Nouveau traité de toute l'architecture . . .* 2d ed. (Paris, 1714)
60. Georges Louis Le Rouge, *Les curiositez de Paris, de Versailles, de Marly, de Vincennes, de S. Cloud, et des environs* (Paris, 1716)
61. "Eloge de M.r Claude Perrault" (1721)
62. Louis Moreri, *Le grand dictionnaire historique . . .* , new ed. (Amsterdam and The Hague, 1722)
63. Jean Aymar Piganiol de La Force, *Nouvelle description de la France,* 2d ed. (Paris, 1722)
64. Henri Sauval, *Histoire et recherches des antiquités de la ville de Paris* (Paris, 1724)
65. Claude Marin Saugrain, *Dictionnaire universel de la France . . .* (Paris, 1726)
66. Pierre Nativelle, *Nouveau traité d'architecture . . .* (Paris, 1729)
67. Pierre Alexis Delamair, *La pure verité* (1737)
68. Jean Aymar Piganiol de La Force, *Description de Paris . . .* (Paris, 1742)
69. Annibale Antonini, *Memorial de Paris, et de ses environs, à l'usage des voyageurs,* new ed. (Paris, 1744)
70. [Saint-Yves], *Observations sur les arts . . .* (Leiden, 1748)
71. [La Font de Saint-Yenne], *Remerciment des habitans de la ville de Paris à Sa Majesté, au sujet de l'achevement du Louvre* (Paris, 1749)
72. *Procès-verbaux de l'Académie royale d'architecture* (July 7, 1749)
73. *Procès-verbaux de l'Académie royale d'architecture* (July 14, 1749)
74. Claude François Lambert, *Histoire littéraire du règne de Louis XIV* (Paris, 1751)
75. Louis Petit de Bachaumont, *Essai sur la peinture, la sculpture, et l'architecture* ([Paris], 1751)
76. François Marie Arouet de Voltaire, *Le siècle de Louis XIV* (Berlin, 1751)
77. Jacques François Blondel, *Architecture françoise* (Paris, 1752)
78. [Antoine Nicolas Dezallier d'Argenville], *Voyage pittoresque de Paris . . .* , 2d ed. (Paris, 1752)
79. La Font de Saint-Yenne, *L'ombre du grand Colbert, le Louvre, & la ville de Paris, dialogue . . .* , new ed. (Paris, 1752)

80. Marc Antoine Laugier, *Essai sur l'architecture* (Paris, 1753)
81. [Jacques François Blondel], "Denticule" (article) in *Encyclopédie ou dictionnaire raisonné des sciences, des arts et des métiers . . .* (Paris, 1754)
82. *Mercure de France,* April 1755
83. "Lettre de M. . . . à M. le Comte de Ch. sur le Louvre," *Mercure de France* (June 1755)
84. Jacques François Blondel, *Architecture françoise* (Paris, 1756)
85. [La Font de Saint-Yenne], *Le génie du Louvre aux Champs Élisées. Dialogue entre le Louvre, la ville de Paris, l'ombre de Colbert, & Perrault* ([Paris], 1756)
86. "Lettre pour servir de réponse à une critique du Louvre imprimée dans le Mercure d'Avril 1755" (1756)
87. *Procès-verbaux de l'Académie royale d'architecture* (March 15, 1756)
88. Pierre Patte, ed., *Mémoires de Charles Perrault . . .* (Avignon, 1759)
89. Julien David Leroy, *Histoire de la disposition et des formes différentes que les chrétiens ont données à leurs temples . . .* (Paris, 1764)
90. Pierre Patte, *Monumens érigés en France à la gloire de Louis XV . . .* (Paris, 1765)
91. Marc Antoine Laugier, *Observations sur l'architecture* (The Hague, 1765)
92. D.J., "Louvre," in *Encyclopédie . . .* (Neufchâtel, 1765)
93. [Francesco Milizia], *Le vite de' piu celebri architetti . . .* (Rome, 1768)
94. Pierre Patte, *Mémoires sur les objets les plus importans de l'architecture* (Paris, 1769)
95. *Procès-verbaux de l'Académie royale d'architecture* (June 17, 1771)
96. Jacques François Blondel, *Cours d'architecture . . .* (Paris, 1771)
97. Ibid. (Paris, 1772)
98. Ibid. (Paris, 1773)
99. Marquis de Condorcet, "Éloge de Perrault" (1773)
100. Jacques François Blondel [Pierre Patte, continuator], *Cours d'architecture . . .* (Paris, 1777)
101. [Pierre Joseph Antoine], *Série de colonnes* (Dijon, 1782)
102. Luc Vincent Thiéry, *Almanach du voyageur à Paris . . . année 1784* (Paris, [1783])
103. Antoine Nicolas Dezallier d'Argenville, *Vies des fameux architectes depuis la renaissance des arts, avec la description de leurs ouvrages* (Paris, 1787)
104. Francesco Algarotti, "Pensieri diversi sopra materie filosofiche e filologiche" (1792)

Documents and Writings

1. *April and May 1667.* "Registre ou Journal des délibérations & résolutions touchant les Bâtimens du Roi." First published in J. A. Piganiol de La Force, *Description de Paris . . .* , Paris, 1742, II, 627–637. The editor of Piganiol's guide, La Font de Saint-Yenne, apparently had seen the original (lost) manuscript, for he wrote: "C'est un acte authentique à la marge duquel on lit cette apostille de la main de M. *Colbert, vu & approuvé au camp de Charleroy le 7. Juin 1667*" (ibid., II, 627).

Monseigneur le Surintendant [Colbert] ayant considéré qu'aucun des Architectes tant de France que d'Italie, n'avoit entierement réussi dans les desseins du Louvre qu'ils ont donnés, & ayant estimé que cet ouvrage demandoit le génie, la science & l'application de plusieurs personnes qui joignant ensemble leurs differens talens, se secoureroient l'un l'autre & s'aideroient mutuellement, & pour cet effet ayant jetté les yeux sur Messieurs le Vau, le Brun & Perrault, il les manda & fit venir chez lui le   Avril 1667. & après leur avoir expliqué son intention, & fait entendre qu'il désiroit qu'ils travaillassent unanimement & conjointement à tous les desseins qu'ils y auroit à faire pour l'achevement du Palais du Louvre, en sorte que ces desseins seroient regardés comme l'ouvrage d'eux trois également, & que pour conserver l'union & bonne intelligence, aucun ne pourroit s'en dire l'auteur particulierement au préjudice des autres. Il leur ordonna de travailler incessament en commun à former un plan & une élévation de la façade de l'entrée vers saint Germain [-l'Auxerrois].

Suivant cet ordre, lesdits sieurs le Vau, le Brun & Perrault se sont assemblées plusieurs fois pour conferer ensemble, & s'étant trouvés de différens avis, au lieu d'un seul dessein pour la façade, ils en firent deux, dont l'un étoit orné d'un Ordre de colonnes formant un perystile ou galerie au-dessus du premier étage, & l'autre étoit plus simple & plus uni sans Ordre de colonnes. Monseigneur ayant vû ces desseins, & ayant souhaité d'en voir aussi les modeles en bois, cela fut exécuté en appliquant ces deux façades sur le modele qui est chez M. le Vau; ensuite de quoi il leur dit de travailler encore tous trois sur chacun de ces desseins jusqu'à ce qu'ils en fussent satisfaits, & de les tenir prêts pour les faire voir au Roi quand il les manderoit, ce qu'ils firent incessament.

Le 13. May l'ordre vint de porter ces desseins à saint Germain, où n'ayant pû être montrés à Sa Majesté le même jour, ils lui furent présentés le lendemain par Monseigneur le Surintendant qui expliqua à Sa Majesté tous les avantages de l'un & de l'autre de ces desseins.

Ensuite de quoi Sa Majesté se détermina, & choisit celui qui est orné d'un Ordre de colonnes formant un perystile. Sa Majesté vit aussi quelques autres desseins de Plans & d'élévations du reste du livre qu'elle remit à résoudre pour une autre fois.

Le 18. du même mois, Monseigneur ayant mandé les Officiers des bâtimens dans son anticabinet où se trouverent Messieurs Varin, le Nostre, le Menestrel & Petit,[1] Messieurs le Vau, le Brun & Perrault, il dit que suivant l'intention de Sa Majesté, le dessein de la façade du Louvre où il y a un perystile lequel il fit voir à toute la compagnie, seroit exécuté, & que pour cet effet les Plans & les élévations en seroient faits en grand pour lui être envoyés & présentés au Roi & ensuite signés & arrêtés par mondit Seigneur.

Que le lundi ensuivant on ouvriroit les attelliers du Louvre pour travailler à tout le carré qui sera élevé jusqu'au dessus de la premiere corniche, comme aussi à fouiller les fondations de la façade vers saint Germain, qui sera continuée & poursuivie incessament.

Qu'il sera fait un modele en Bois de cette façade pour être montée sur celui qui est chez M. le Vau, pour mieux voir encore son union avec le reste.

Qu'outre ce modele en bois, il en sera fait un plus grand de cette façade, en plâtre ou stuc, réduit de la toise au pied.

Qu'il sera fait des desseins mesurés de chaque partie d'Architecture, qui ne pourront être exécutés par les Entrepreneurs qu'ils n'ayent été signés de Monseigneur.

Que les fondations seront conduites de niveau, & s'éleveront également & par assises.

Qu'il sera fait un dessein au net du dôme vers la rue S. Honoré, & sera envoyé à Monseigneur pour être présenté au Roi, & ensuite arrêté de mondit Seigneur.

Que la sculpture qui reste à faire au Louvre sur ce qui est bâti, & à laquelle les Entrepreneurs sont obligés, sera estimée, pour le prix en être déduit ausdits Entrepreneurs sur ce qui peut leur être dû de ces ouvrages.

Que M. le Brun aura l'oeil sur la s[c]ulpture du Louvre, & en fera les desseins qui seront pareillement envoyés à Monseigneur pour être signés de lui.

Que l'Architecture, frise & corniche de la façade vers saint Germain, tourneront autour des pavillons sans continuer plus avant.

Que l'on ouvrira la terrasse de M. Regnard,[2] & sera fait un ouvrage de maçonnerie dans le fossé, suivant le dessein qui en sera fait & arrêté par Monseigneur.

Le 24. May, Messieurs le Vau, le Brun & Perrault s'étant assemblés au logis de Monseigneur, résolurent, suivant l'intention de Monseigneur, de s'assembler tous les mercredis & samedis, depuis six heures du soir jusqu'à huit, pour conferer & travailler ensemble à ce qui regarde les bâtimens.

Que Samedi prochain, M. le Vau apportera un Plan au juste de ce qui est bâti sur le devant du Louvre, pour regler l'endroit où se doit faire la fouille pour le mur qui doit porter le perystile.

Qu'il fera faire deux copies du dessein de la façade approuvée par le Roi, un pour M. le Brun, l'autre pour M. Perrault, afin que chacun d'eux fasse un dessein conforme en gros à celui-là, suivant les mesures & proportions qui lui sembleront les plus belles, pour de ces trois desseins en être fait un seul, en choisissant ce qui sera jugé le meilleur de tous les trois.

Le 28. Mai, M. le Vau donna une copie du dessein à M. le Brun qui promit d'en faire faire une copie pour M. Perrault, afin de travailler à faire chacun leur dessein, comme il est dit ci-dessus.

S'agissant de regler l'intervalle des croisées du corps de logis vers les Peres de l'Oratoire, entre le dôme & le pavillon qui sont à bâtir, & la question étant de sçavoir si on les espacera également entre elles, ou si on les espacera de la même façon qu'elles le sont dans la partie semblable qui est bâtie, où elles sont à distances inégales. Il a été trouvé à propos de les espacer de la même façon qu'elles le sont dans la partie semblable qui est bâtie, où elles sont à distances inégales. Cette raison de simetrie d'un côté à l'autre, étant plus forte que celle de l'égalité des tremeaux, & d'autant plus que cette difference qui se feroit d'un côté à l'autre, seroit non-seulement blâmée en voyant le bâtiment, mais aussi en voyant le plan qui sera vû dans tous les pays étrangers.

Le plan de cette face de bâtiment faisant voir que le dôme du milieu est plus large en la partie du dehors vers la rue S. Honoré, qu'il ne l'est en la partie du côté de la cour, & les fondations en étant faites de la sorte, on a examiné si cette difference n'étoit point une chose à réformer, & on a remis à mercredi prochain à prendre une résolution là-dessus.

2. *August 5, 1667.* From a letter of Carlo Vigarani to Cardinal Rinaldo d'Este (G. Rouchès, ed., *Inventaire des lettres et papiers manuscrits de Gaspare, Carlo et Lodovico Vigarani . . .*, Paris, 1913, 139, no. 267 [paraphrase by Rouchès]):

On travaille activement au Louvre, où il y a beaucoup d'ouvriers.

3. *August 26, 1667.* From a letter of Carlo Vigarani to the Duchess of Modena (S. Fraschetti, *Il Bernini*, Milan, 1900, 358 n. 3):

La gran Corte del Louvre è già tutta cinta attorno di fabrica à l'altezza quasi del primo piano fuori la facciata, che va un poco più lentamente per il tempo che ha bisognato perdere in disfare il primo fondamento, e il secondo anche del Caval^r Bernino.

4. *November 19, 1667. La Gazette d'Amsterdam,* no. 48, December 1, 1667. It is curious that the ceremony at the Louvre recorded here is not reported in the *Gazette de France,* even though the latter journal attests to the presence of the King in Paris on November 19. One of the medals may have been a gold version of Figure 66.

Ce fut Mons. Colbert au nom du Roy qui posa Samedi passé [November 19] la premiere Pierre du fondement du Grand Portail du Louvre, où il mit aussi 3 grandes Medailles d'or merveilleusement bien travaillés à Vincennes par un Graveur, à qui l'on a donné 100 Louïs d'or pour les faire. (Fol. 2r)

5. *December 7, 1667.* From a letter (from Paris) of François Le Vau to Jean Baptiste Colbert (BN, Manuscrits, Mélanges Colbert, vol. 146, fol. 377; published in A. Laprade, *François d'Orbay, architecte de Louis XIV,* Paris, 1960, 146):

Monseigneur, Depuis mon retour [to Paris] j'ay eu la curiosité de voir les Bastiments du Louvre. J'ay veu la fondation de la grande face fort élevée, où j'ay trouvé, selon mon sens, les fondations commencées pour les deux pavillons des encognures et celui du milieu fort estroits pour la proportion de la largeur de ladite grande face et de la hauteur que lesdits pavillons doivent avoir, et de plus la couverture ne devant estre faite qu'avec un espit ou amortissement, parestrons plutôt pour des pavillons du flanc du Bastiment que de la face principale du devant. Mon frère m'en a demandé mon avis et luy ai dit mon sentiment et pour m'acquitter de mon devoir dans le peu d'expérience que j'en ay, j'ay cru, avec la très humble soumission et le respect que je vous dois, vous le dire aussy.

6. *1668.* "Advis de M. le Vau le jeune sur le nouveau dessin du Louvre" (AN, O¹ 1669¹). Published in Laprade, *François d'Orbay,* 340–347. I have retained Laprade's modernized orthography and regularized grammar and have corrected many errors of transcription and omission; my changes, also modernized and regularized, appear within brackets.

This undated document consists of two parts, each in a different hand: twelve arguments (a) concerning the new Louvre designs written by an anonymous critic; and twelve replies (b) written by François Le Vau. For a discussion of this document, see Chapter III.

1a. [Anon. critic]: Pour bien juger du nouveau dessin que l'on propose pour le Louvre, qui est de doubler les corps de logis qui regardent la rivière, il faut comparer et mettre en balance ce qu'il a d'avantageux avec ses inconvénients.

1b. [Fr. Le Vau]: Advis du sieur le Vau le jeune sur le nouveau dessin du Louvre.

Pour bien répondre sur ce nouveau dessin que l'on propose, et sur les objections et inconvénients que l'on y apporte, il me semble qu'il faut premièrement poser en fait en quoi consiste la véritable architecture pour y fonder le principe de notre raisonnement, et nous conduire au jugement solide de tous lesdits objections et inconvénients qu'on y trouve.

C'est pourquoi revenant à notre sujet, l'Architecture consiste entre plusieurs belles parties à trois principales qui lui sont essentielles, le Solide, la Distribution et la Décoration; comme en premier lieu, la question que nous [avons] à résoudre [ms.: soudre] sur la proposition de ce nouveau dessin embrasse entièrement toute la distribution, il est bon de savoir en quoi elle consiste, qui est en l'utile et commode dispensation des choses qui sont nécessaires pour l'usage des appartements d'un édifice selon son genre, et à quoi et pour qui elle doit être faite et appliquée; ainsi considérant donc que cette distribution doit être faite et appliquée pour le logement du plus grand et magnifique monarque du monde et dans son palais qui ne doit [point] avoir son semblable, il faut donc la considérer aussi pour être faite la plus grande et magnifique qu'il se pourra et sans défaut; et partant y observer tous les avantages qui s'y rencontrent, et [y trouver tout ce qu'il y peut convenir] qui sont à mon avis trois choses très essentielles et nécessaires.

2a. [Anon. critic]: De tous les avantages qu'il a, le plus considérable est la commodité [des logements] de service du Roi et de la Reine, qui devant être situé sur l'aspect de la rivière comme étant le plus beau et le plus sain parcequ'il est tourné au midi, qui est le plus convenable qu'il faut choisir pour la saison dans laquelle leurs Majestés ont accoutumé de demeurer au Louvre. Il n'y a point de doute que cette commodité est une raison qui doit l'emporter sur toutes les autres, en cas qu'il n'y ait point d'autre moyen de rencontrer cette commodité, ce qui n'a pas encore ce me semble, été examiné pour conclure si tôt à des changements si étrangers [et] qui doivent avoir des conséquences si importantes.

2b. [Fr. Le Vau]: [Sçavoir.]

Les logements et appartements de leurs Majestés situés à la meillure et plus belle exposition qui est du côté de la rivière comme on est déjà convenu.

Les logements et appartements de la Maison Royale pour les enfants de France, princes et grands seigneurs pour quand il plaira au Roi de les y loger.

Les logements des officiers de leurs Majestés et ceux de leur Maison Royale et de leurs suites.

3a. [Anon. critic]: Car il faut considérer que les appartements dont il s'agit n'étant que pour l'usage ordinaire, et non pour la parade, la largeur des pièces qui est de 28 pieds 3 pouces, [et] de $29\frac{1}{2}$ en quelque[s] endroit[s], est plus suffisante pour les [salles], antichambres et chambre de la Reine, et que l'appartement du Roi ayant la salle des gardes, son antichambre, sa chambre de parade et ses grands cabinets assez spacieux hors [des] corps de logis dont il s'agit, il ne reste que sa chambre de service, son petit cabinet et les lieux nécessaires pour les officiers de sa garderobe, que l'on pourra peut-être trouver assez commodes si on s'applique à étudier la distribution de toutes ces pièces.

3b. [Fr. Le Vau]: Donc s'il est vrai que ces trois sortes de logements soient nécessaires et qu'ils conviennent à l'utile et commode dispensation de notre distribution et à l'usage des logements de leurs Majestés et de leurs suites, il sera vrai aussi que l'on ne se peut pas dispenser de les y faire; et pour cet effet, il faut donc de nécessité, doubler le corps de logis pour les y trouver, ce qu'on ne pourrait faire dans les[dits] corps de logis simples. Car de ne faire que les appartements de l'usage ordinaire de leurs Majestés sans y accompagner celui du beau et de la bienséance, ni ceux des enfants de France, princes et grands seigneurs, ce serait manquer à la suite de la décoration due à la magnificence des appartements de leurs dites Majestés, et par conséquent, faire un défaut notable et essentiel à notre distribution, et aux règles et principes de la véritable architecture que de ne lui pas donner l'utile et la commode dispensation de toutes les choses qui y conviennent; et partant il ne doit avoir nulle conséquence contraire à la conclusion du corps de logis double, puisque dans icelui il se pourra trouver tout l'accomplissement de notre distribution, avec tout ce qui peut convenir pour la perfection d'un si superbe palais.

4a. [Anon. critic]: Les autres avantages de ce doublement de bâtiment qui sont ceux qui regardent la beauté et la bienséance sont nécessairement attachés à des inconvénients qui pourront être trouvés assez considérables pour faire douter si en cet état ils valent le temps et la dépense qu'il faudra pour exécuter ce dessin; ces avantages sont l'exhaussement que l'on donnera et que plusieurs estiment manquer au bâtiment du Louvre, la grandeur de l'ordre et l'élargissement des pavillons sur la face de la principale entrée.

4b. [Fr. Le Vau]: A l'égard des avantages du doublement de ce bâtiment, il me semble qu'ils ne peuvent être attachés à aucuns inconvénients considérables par les raisons que j'ai dites ci-devant et que je dirai ci-après.

Et comme à mon avis, il ne s'agit pas seulement d'en bien discourir selon l'emportement de notre opinion qui nous porte quelquefois à vouloir détruire quelque chose à telle fin que de raison, mais fonder son avis sur les bons principes de l'architecture, et pour ce savoir en quoi elle consiste. C'est pourquoi je dirai pour le fondement de mon raisonnement, que l'Architecture est une science qui consiste en des principes qui ont des preuves certaines, dans leurs fins proposées, lesquelles on suppose avec raison et qu'on démontre par la pratique; partant, les fins proposées de notre architecture en cette occasion sont ces trois sortes de logements dits ci-dessus, que l'on suppose avec raison, puisqu'ils sont utiles et nécessaires à l'usage de leurs Majestés, et qu'ils conviennent à l'accomplissement de la distribution d'un si magnifique palais que l'on doit faire sans défaut. Et la preuve certaine se démontrera par la pratique que l'on aura de les y faire, et par la commodité et l'usage qu'en recevront ceux qui les occuperont; par conséquent je n'y trouve aucun[s] inconvénient[s] attaché[s].

5a. [Anon. critic]: A l'égard du premier, les appartements du Louvre, tant le noble que le terrain ayant le plus grand exhaussement dont [ses] pièces sont capables, et l'attique qui est dessus étant aussi d'une hauteur convenable, c'est ce me semble sans raison que l'on se plaint que ce bâtiment est trop bas, puisque pour le lever, il faut mettre ou un grand étage ou deux petits sur celui du Roi, ce qui l'un ou l'autre est contre la bienséance—le premier a déjà été condamné par le premier homme de notre siècle, dans ces sortes de connaissances,[3] et remarqué comme un défaut au Louvre dans le dôme qui regarde sur la rivière parce que l'on ne peut monter à ces grands et magnifiques appartements qui sont égaux à ceux du Roi que par des escaliers fort étroits et qui ont 132 marches[4]—l'autre manière qui est de mettre deux petits étages sur le grand est une chose qui n'est séante qu'à une maison de communauté. Car enfin, le hauteur des bâtiments ne doit point être proportionnée à leur étendue, mais à leur usage, et si un temple qui est fait pour les assemblées d'un très grand nombre de peuple doit être haut [à] proportion de sa grandeur, il n'est pas de même d'un lieu qui, étant fait pour se loger, est composé de plusieurs habitations mises les unes sur les autres dont l'entassement peut devenir excessif s'il n'a point d'usage qui y oblige nécessairement.

5b. [Fr. Le Vau]: Donc s'il est vrai comme j'ai prouvé ci-devant par les raisons que j'ai alléguées, qu'on soit obligé de faire ces trois sortes de logements, pour les appartements de leurs Majestés, ceux de la Maison Royale, des enfants de France, princes et grands seigneurs, et pour ceux de leur suite et officiers, l'on sera ausi obligé d'y faire les trois étages ou au moins une grande et une autre médiocre au-dessus pour trouver lesdits appartements de la grandeur convenable à ceux qui les doivent occuper et proportionnés à leurs qualités.

Car en l'étage du rez-de-chaussée il n'y peut avoir que les vestibules, galeries, passages et salles et autres commodités publiques qui en occuperont la plus grande partie, et l'autre sera occupée pour les logements des petits officiers, et pour les offices.

Le premier étage au-dessus, qui est le noble, sera entièrement occupé, pour les logements de leurs Majestés.

Donc il ne sera point contre la bienséance de faire un second étage raisonnablement haut pour y faire [les] logements et appartements des enfants de France, et grands seigneurs comme j'ai dit ci-dessus, lesquels ne seraient pas proportionnés à leurs grandeurs ni à leurs qualités dans l'étage en attique. Ainsi, il me semble qu'on a raison de le trouver trop bas et l'élever pour lesdits logements, puisqu'ils ne peuvent être faits ni mieux placés ailleurs dans leurs convenables situations. C'est ce qui ne peut être à mon avis condamné avec justice, ni même les logements du troisième étage pour les logements de leurs suites, en y faisant toutefois les escaliers et entrées plus grandes et commodes que ceux qui sont mal faits, présentement aux pavillons du Louvre qui regarde la rivière qui est un mauvais exemple de laquelle on se peut facilement corriger.[5]

Enfin par toutes ces raisons l'on ne doit pas condamner, ce me semble, la hauteur de ce bâtiment par la raison que l'on en donne, disant que la hauteur des bâtiments ne doit point être proportionné à leurs étendues, mais à leur usage, puisque la même raison dont on se sert pour la blâmer et la détruire, doit servir pour la louer et l'autoriser; car la nécessité qu'il y a d'y faire ces trois sortes de logements et par conséquent ces trois étages, lui donnera sa hauteur proportionnée à son usage, puisque son usage doit avoir la hauteur desdits étages, qui feront la hauteur de ce bâtiment.

Mais je dis plus, qu'étant proportionnée à son usage, elle le sera encore à son étendue, à quoi il faut moins manquer qu'à leur usage, autrement ce serait faire une faute notable contre la décoration des faces d'un si superbe bâtiment que de ne leur donner les justes proportions de leur hauteur, qu'ils doivent avoir aussi bien en leurs étendues comme en leur usage, et de cette façon l'une et l'autre proportions s'y trouveront par le réhaussement de ce bâtiment.

J'avoue bien qu'on pourrait dire à la rigueur contre ces trois étages qu'il pourrait peut-être avoir plusieurs appartements inutiles, mais ce qui serait blâmable dans les maisons particulières est louable dans celles des grands princes, lesquelles doivent être toujours distinguées par la magnificence de leurs grandeurs, à des choses où nuls ne peuvent arriver.

6a. [Anon. critic]: Pour ce qui est de la grandeur de l'ordre, elle peut encore devenir plus vicieuse que cet entassement d'appartements les uns sur les autres. Et c'est une faute qui ne peut être soufferte dans la régularité du reste de l'architecture du Louvre, qui est exempte des défauts et des abus que les modernes ont introduits dans l'architecture, n'y ayant rien de si peu raisonnable et de si indigne d'un illustre bâtiment que de vouloir paraître plus grand qu'il n'est en effet, et qu'il ne lui appartient, les grands ordres devant être réservés pour les édifices qui sont de [manière?] à avoir de grands exhaussements comme sont les temples, les basiliques, les vestibules et les salons des édifices simples, au lieu que ceux qui sont faits pour être habités et qui sont composés comme de plusieurs maisons les unes sur les autres, doivent avoir chacun son ordre, n'étant pas raisonnable que le plancher du second étage soit soutenu par des colonnes et que les poutres du premier soient fichées dans le milieu de ces colonnes qui soutiennent le second qui est comme accablé ou menacé de la ruine d'une grande et démesurée corniche, qui n'a aucune proportion avec ses [fenêtres] et qui fait sur elles l'effet que ferait un grand chapeau sur la tête d'un enfant.

6b. [Fr. Le Vau] A l'égard de la grandeur de l'ordre, et de l'indignité que l'on suppose à ce bâtiment de vouloir paraître plus grand qu'il n'est en effet, cela ne se peut à mon avis si bien discuter par le discours qui ne finirait point pour peu que l'on voulut raisonner sur toutes choses, comme par les dessins et modèles qui sont de fait sur lesquels l'on pourra mieux connaître la vérité, des défauts, et de la beauté desdites faces et pour en venir à cette connaissance, il faut considérer que cette question embrasse en cette occasion toute la décoration, qui est l'une des parties la plus essentielle de l'architecture. C'est pourquoi il est bon ce me semble, de savoir en quoi elle consiste pour appuyer le principe de notre raisonnement sur l'opinion que l'on a, des grands ordres qui ne doivent être appliquées qu'aux temples, basiliques et autres ouvrages simples.

Pour cet effet, je dirai donc que la décoration est celle qui est composée du beau nombre de toutes choses par l'ordre de toutes ces parties égales et inégales, avec raison et comparaison les unes aux autres par l'union de toutes ces belles proportions, distinguées par tous les membres de la belle et véritable Architecture et sculpture bien mises et placées chacune en son lieu avec relation du tout aux parties et des parties au tout, afin que le tout ensemble fasse voir ce bel aspect dit Eurythmie, qui est quand toute la symétrie est si bien gardée et concertée dans toutes ses proportions, que par son harmonie, les yeux qui la voient se délectent librement avec plaisir sans rien trouver qui la choque, comme sont les oreilles quand elles entendent l'harmonie d'une belle musique bien concertée où rien ne manque.

Partant pour arriver à la parfaite décoration desdites faces du Louvre selon la véritable Architecture, il ne s'agit que d'y trouver ce bel aspect, qui fasse le même effet pour la délectation de la vue que fait le son aux oreilles pour la délectation de l'ouïe, puisque l'architecture dans sa décoration aussi bien que la musique n'est qu'une harmonie, l'une pour contenter et délecter la vue, et l'autre l'ouïe.

Donc, comme on se sert de toutes les différentes voix et parties qu'il y a dans la musique haut et bas diézées,[6] gros et clairons, pour en composer toutes les sortes de pièces et concerts que l'on veut faire entendre convenables à son sujet, l'on se peut de même servir de toutes les différentes ordres, grandes, petites ou médiocres, membres et mesures qu'il y a dans l'architecture, pour en composer toutes les sortes d'édifices de ladite architecture pourvu qu'ils soient aussi convenables au sujet de son édifice.

Ce qui se reconnaîtra quand lesdites ordres seront proportionnées à toute l'oeuvre avec relation du tout aux parties et des parties au tout, avec raison et comparaison les unes aux autres, qui fasse voir comme j'ai dit ci-devant ce bel aspect dit Eurythmie, qui délecte la vue sans la choquer.

Cela étant fait et trouvé, avec toutes les observations que j'ai alléguées ci-dessus pour la décoration, donnera la grandeur et hauteur de l'ordre, de laquelle on ne puisse en bien juger avec raison que par la vue de ce bel aspect; donc, si ladite ordre se trouve grande et haute par la proportion qui convient à ce bel aspect, c'est une preuve évidente qu'il ne la faut pas petite, pour le sujet de la décoration desdites faces, et par conséquent elles sont donc d'une matière à recevoir aussi bien que les temples, basiliques, et autres édifices simples, les grandes ordres qui lui sont aussi convenables selon son genre—ce que l'on n'aura pas de peine à croire si l'on considère que lesdites faces se verront plus de loin que de près par la distance qu'il y a du travers de la rivière et jusque sur le Pont Neuf et par conséquent la grande ordre aura plus de majesté qu'une petite, joint qu'elle sera plus proportionnée à l'étage du dessous qui lui servira comme de piédestal que si elle était plus petite.

Partant lesdites grandes ordres ne sont pas seulement réservées pour lesdits temples, basiliques et autres édifices simples, mais encore pour toutes sortes d'édifices auxquels elles conviennent quand toutes les observations de ladite décoration y sont bien observées et fassent voir par la modération de tous ces membres, l'union et la vérité de notre décoration, ce que plusieurs cherchent mais peu la trouvent, car il ne suffit pas seulement d'en bien discourir selon notre imagination, il faut encore avoir la pratique et les yeux ajustés à connaître les belles choses pour après les avoir trouvées les donner à l'entendement pour en juger et en faire le choix, ce qui ne se peut mieux faire ni justifier que par les dessins tant faits qu'à faire.

7a. [Anon. critic]: L'élargissement des pavillons sur la principale face, bien qu'ils aient cela de mal qu'ils feront paraître la place du devant du Louvre trop large à proportion de sa longuer, pouvait être assez à propos si on le faisait plus modérément ou seulement jusque à égaler la largeur qu'ils ont sur la rivière, ce qui n'irait qu'à quinze pieds au plus, au lieu de six toises que l'on leur donne, de sorte qu'il me semble que ce doublement de logis n'a de soi ni assez de beauté ni d'utilité assez nécessaire pour faire négliger ces inconvénients qu'il attire nécessairement. J'en compte cinq, outre ceux qui ont déjà été allégués pour faire voir le peu de nécessité qu'il y a à élever le Louvre, à lui donner un grand ordre et à élargir les pavillons comme on se propose.

7b. [Fr. Le Vau]: Quant à la difficulté que l'on trouve de l'élargissement des pavillons sur la grande place de l'entrée, cela ne peut à mon avis, faire paraître ladite grande place de devant plus ou moins large à proportion de sa longueur pour les élargir un peu plus ou un peu moins, —et quand même lesdits pavillons seraient proportionnés à la place, en ne les faisant que de la même largeur que ceux du côté de la rivière, ce qui ne peut être, mais quand cela serait vrai, il y a deux fortes raisons contre cette pensée.

La première est fondée sur notre décoration, laquelle

je crois avoir assez bien expliquée ci-devant, qui est d'observer qu'en tous genres et natures d'édifices, il y a ce qui doit précéder et ce qui doit succéder, aussi bien dans notre architecture, qui est une génération artificielle comme dans la génération naturelle, où se trouve dans l'une et l'autre le pair et l'impair, l'égal et l'inégal, car si le tout était égal le tout ne serait pas, et c'est cette diversité avec relation les unes aux autres qui compose ce bel ordre de notre architecture, comme ce bel ordre [lacking in ms.] du monde, et qui nous fera voir par toutes ses parties l'union et la vérité de notre décoration, et par conséquent de notre question.

Et pour cet effet, il faut demeurer d'accord que le corps de tout un édifice comme celui du Louvre, et par conséquent la principale face qui lui est essentielle, doit succéder à tout ce qui y peut convenir par comparaison et relation, comme la grandeur de la place de devant qui ne lui est qu'accessoire, et par conséquent elle lui doit donc succéder. Partant, il ne faut donc pas à mon avis, régler ni assujettir la décoration du bâtiment qui doit précéder comme chef de toute l'oeuvre à la place qui lui doit succéder. Il y a plus de raison ce me semble de régler ladite place [au] bâtiment puisqu'il lui doit précéder.

L'autre raison est qu'il ne faut pas considérer présentement ladite place pour être faite dans sa perfection, et quand même sa longueur ne paraîtrait pas être entièrement proportionnée à sa largeur, l'on pourra bien ne la pas considérer comme une chose achevée, mais qui se peut accroître et augmenter avec le temps quand on voudra; mais quant à la face et aux pavillons, ils se doivent considérer comme une oeuvre achevée dans leurs perfections où l'on ne doit plus toucher et par conséquent il les faut donc faire avec toutes les proportions et symétrie qui leur convient pour la belle décoration de cette grande face qui ne peut être accomplie sans l'élargissement desdits pavillons à la largeur que l'on [propose] de les faire. La preuve s'en verra sur les modèles et dessins, celui que j'ai fait a eu le don de plaire et d'être approuvé, sur lequel lesdits pavillons n'ont guère moins de largeur, et si je n'eusse été contraint alors, je les aurais faits aussi larges que ceux que l'on propose de faire—j'omets que l'on peut faire en sorte par la manière de la décoration que l'on leur donnera de les faire paraître un peu moins large qu'ils ne seront en effet.

A l'égard de la beauté et de l'utilité nécessaires pour le doublement et l'élargissement du corps de logis, il y est tout entier par les raisons que je crois avoir assez bien expliquées ci-devant par la nécessité qu'il y a de faire dans un si magnifique palais comme celui du Louvre sans défaut, l'utile et la commode distribution de tous les appartements tant de leurs Majestés que ceux de leur maison et de leur suite. Reste à examiner s'il est vrai que cela puisse attirer des inconvénients auxquels on ne puisse remédier.

8a. [Anon. critic]: Le premier inconvénient est que l'avance de ce bâtiment étouffera deux fenêtres de la galerie des peintures[7] et que ce bel édifice qui fait une partie considérable de l'aspect du Louvre sera offusqué d'une manière qui fera visiblement connaître que l'on a ajouté après coup ces bâtiments qui s'avancent si mal à propos, pour cacher une partie de cette galerie, laquelle partie a correspondance à une autre qui est en une, n'y ayant rien qui fasse plus de tort à la majesté d'un grand édifice que ce qui fait connaître que l'on y a ajouté quelque chose comme des pièces recousues, cela faisant voir le peu de capacité de l'architecte qui l'a ordonné et qui n'a pas prévu avant que de commencer son ouvrage les choses qui étaient nécessaires pour son accomplissement—car bien qu'il soit impossible de prévoir tout dès le commencement, il faut néanmoins faire en sorte que l'on ne s'aperçoive pas que l'on a été contraint de faire quelque chose que l'on n'avait pas prévu. Cette grande avance fera encore cet autre effet mauvais que rétrécissant considérablement de près de la moitié le petit jardin[8] qui n'est déjà que trop étroit, elle fera encore que son milieu ne correspondra plus avec la porte et avec le vestibule du magnifique appartement qui est sous la galerie.[9]

8b. [Fr. Le Vau]: Il est bien facile de remédier à cet inconvénient de cette avance par la galerie à jour que l'on a déjà proposé de faire au rez-de-chaussée du jardin avec une terrasse dessus.[10] Par cette invention, l'industrie et la capacité de l'architecte sera louable d'avoir si bien accordé le vieux avec le nouveau. Quant au petit jardin, il n'est pas assez considérable, ni la porte avec le vestibule de l'appartement sous la galerie pour empêcher par ce petit défaut qui n'a point de suite, un si beau et magnifique dessin qui a des suites très considérables.

9a. [Anon. critic]: Les bâtiments qui sont entre les dômes et les pavillons étant élevés en sorte que l'on ne verra plus de toits par dehors, représenteront une terrasse sur laquelle les combles des dômes et des pavillons tomberont de fort mauvaise grâce, étant, en bonne architecture, comme nécessaire que l'on puisse entrer d'une terrasse dans ce qui se lève sur son pavé et non pas que l'on aille donner des pieds contre les toits sous lesquels il faudrait pouvoir passer. Car on ne peut pas, pour remédier à ces inconvénients, ôter les toits et couvrir les dômes et les pavillons aussi en plateforme, à cause du mauvais effet que cela produirait dans la cour que l'on verrait entourée de bâtiments dont les uns seraient avec des toits forts amples, les autres n'y ayant [point], ce qui aurait la forme d'un lieu ruiné par le tonnerre ou par le canon.[11]

9b. [Fr. Le Vau]: Les dômes et pavillons ne pourront pas tomber avec plus mauvaise grâce à mon avis sur les murs de faces que l'on élèvera qu'il font à présent; puisqu'ils tomberont toujours avec la même symétrie et à la même hauteur, et la terrasse qui paraîtra par la hauteur desdits murs ne pourra pas non plus apporter de défaut pour l'entrée d'icelles dans les pavillons; car en bonne architecture, pour peu que l'on s'y connaisse, l'on comprendra bien que ce n'est pas une véritable terrasse; mais bien comme il est vrai des combles en terrasse, qui ne doivent avoir entrée ni sortie que pour la commodité [de] les entretenir, et non pas pour la décoration ni pour s'y promener, ce qui ne se fait jamais sur une couverture. Ainsi, il importe fort peu de la manière que l'on pourra entrer ou sortir des combles desdits pavillons et dômes sur lesdits combles en terrasse; ce n'est pas comme si l'on faisait des véritables terrasses au premier ou second étage pour la décoration et pour l'utilité de la promenade. A la vérité, il y aurait un grand défaut à l'entrée desdits dômes et pavillons s'ils tombaient si proches desdites terrasses, mais par la raison que j'ai dit, n'étant que des combles en terrasses qui entrent dans d'autres combles en pavillons plus élevés, pour marquer lesdits pavillons. Je n'y trouve nul inconvénient, et cela se rapporte à ce que j'ai dit ci-devant, parlant de la décoration, que l'ordre ne se faisait que par l'inégalité des parties qui ont comparaison et relation au tout. Ainsi ces inégalités des combles ont relation les unes aux autres, puisqu'elles montrent ceux qu'il faut qui précèdent comme les pavillons, et ceux qui doivent succéder, comme les corps de logis qui sont entre eux.

10a. [Anon. critic]: Ces toits qui seront en appentis et qui recevront douze toises de pluie ou de neige demanderont un [chéneau] sur la cour, d'une grandeur qui aura fort mauvaise grâce, et dont l'écoulement, qui passe à présent au travers des galetas et l'attique pour s'aller décharger vers la rivière, passera justement au milieu des grands appartements du second étage, et le mieux qu'il puisse arriver aux eaux sera d'aller sortir entre deux fenêtres par une gouttière qui sera au milieu d'un pilastre.

10b. [Fr. Le Vau]: Ce n'est pas un défaut d'augmenter les combles, quand il [en] est nécessaire pourvu qu'ils ne choquent point la vue, comme celui en appentis que l'on fera pour le doublement du corps de logis, lequel ne se verra point; ainsi il ne fera point un mauvais effet. Quant à l'écoulement [de ses] eaux, il est bien difficile [de] croire que les [chéneaux] qui sont faits du côté de la cour soient si justes qu'ils ne peuvent recevoir encore les eaux desdits combles en appentis, mais quand cela serait vrai, il est bien facile d'y remédier par un autre [chéneau] que l'on peut faire au bas dudit comble en appentis, qui pourra conduire les eaux aux endroits propres à l'écoulement desdites eaux sans qu'elles passent dans aucun[s] appartement[s] ni en des lieux qui puissent [faire] un mauvais effet, ou par tels autres moyens que l'intelligence de l'architecte s'avisera, ce qui n'est pas une difficulté sans remède, ainsi cela n'est pas considérable au respect du grand dessin que l'on veut faire.

11a. [Anon. critic]: Le péristyle, qui est, en effet, un des plus beaux ornements du Louvre, n'aura plus de proportion si on le [lève] comme on prétend; car il sera aréostyle, par [la] grandeur de son entrecolonnement, laquelle en [cédera?] les trois diamètres,[12] ce qui ne s'exécute que dans les bâtiments chétifs d'ordre toscan, où les architraves sont de bois, parce que ceux de pierre auraient une trop grande portée. De plus, sa profondeur sera beaucoup moindre que l'espace [des] entrecolonnement[s] qui est tout le contraire de ce qui doit être, par la raison que la grande hauteur d'un péristyle qui n'a pas de profondeur proportionnée à la pluie fait qu'il ne donne point de couvert, pour peu qu'elle tombe obliquement. C'est pourquoi les anciens faisaient [les] grands péristyles diptères[13] ou pseudodiptères,[14] c'est-à-dire à deux rangs de colonnes, ou qui avaient en profondeur deux fois la largeur de l'entrecolonnement.

11b. [Fr. Le Vau]: Le péristyle est, en effet, un des plus beaux ornements de l'architecture quand il est mis et appliqué aux endroits qui lui sont propres et convenables, comme autour des temples, avant portiques, théâtres et places publiques et autres lieux semblables pour lesquels ils sont réservés, qui ne sont élevés que fort peu du terrain où l'on peut facilement monter et se promener pour la commodité publique, comme [j'ai] vu et remarqué à Rome, dans quelques vieux vestiges qui restent encore, et dans le traité qu'en a fait Vitruve, de son temps, où toutes ces sortes d'édifices étaient encore alors en nature; mais il ne se justifie point dans le dit traité ni en ce qui peut se voir encore en Italie, que l'on ait jamais fait le dit péristyle à un premier étage élevé comme celui du Louvre pour orner et décorer la face d'un grand et magnifique palais, ni à d'autres édifices semblables autant élevés.

Partant, il ne faut donc pas considérer, à mon avis, ce bel ornement du Louvre comme celui d'un véritable péristyle ni même aréostyle avec toutes ses proportions et circonstances, comme s'il était appliqué et joint à un autre édifice qui lui fut propre et convenable comme j'ai dit ci-devant, mais bien pour une galerie qui sert pour la décoration d'un palais où il y a toutes autres sujétions à garder et observer que celui d'un temple et autres édifices pour lesquels l'on fait lesdits péristyles, lesquels n'ont besoin de jours ni [de] lumière[s] que celle[s] de leurs entre colonnes, selon la hauteur qu'on leur donne, au sujet de quoi on leur a fixé certaines proportions convenables à leur sujet et à la décoration de leurs édifices.

Mais, en ceci il n'en est pas de même pour la décoration d'un tel palais où il y a tous les jours et lumières à observer pour les appartements qui doivent précéder et régler leurs décorations; c'est pourquoi l'on ne saurait faire lesdits péristyles dans toutes leurs circonstances et proportions; partant, on les a convertis en galeries.

Car, comme galerie et non [de] péristyle, [l]'on peut prendre telles licenses qui y seront convenables, sans toutefois déroger aux règles de la véritable architecture, pour la hauteur et entre colonnes des ordres que l'on y doit faire à cause des observations desdits jours et lumières [qu'il faut trouver pour éclairer tous les appartements] qu'il convient de faire à ce dit bâtiment, lesquelles étant bien proportionnées entre elles, et tout à l'oeuvre, avec relation des parties les unes aux autres, comme j'ai dit ci-devant, se trouveront dans leurs justes proportions, selon [leurs] genre[s] d'édifices pour lesquels ils sont faits et attachés, comme lesdits péristyles se trouvent aussi parfaitement [bien] proportionnés selon la décoration de leurs genres d'édifices pour lesquels ils sont faits et attachés.

12a. [Anon. critic]: Enfin, quand il n'y aurait rien à redire d'ailleurs à ce grand et haut ordre, il fera ce mauvais effet qu'étant sur une place qui est moins grande que la cour qu'il enferme au dedans il fera paraître en entrant les ordres des bâtiments qui environnent la cour chétifs et mal proportionnés.

Bien que la plupart de ces raisons ayent [déjà] été alléguées contre ce nouveau dessin, à l'abord qu'il a été présenté, j'ai cru qu'il était à propos de les mettre par écrit, afin de les éplucher à loisir et j'estime qu'il serait expédient qu'elles fussent insérées dans le registre,[15] avec les réponses qui les auraient détruites, en cas que l'exécution de ce dessin soit résolue, afin que si après cela, quelqu'un voulait objecter ces mêmes raisons, il [paraît] que ce n'est pas que l'on en ait ignoré, mais seulement que l'on n'y a pas eu d'égard parce que l'on en a préféré d'autres qui ont été trouvées [au] plus fortes, [et] plus considérables.

12b. [Fr. Le Vau]: Je ne vois pas selon mon sens que la hauteur du grand ordre de la grande face extérieure [puisse] faire trouver celle de la cour chétif puisqu'elle ne se voit pas toute d'une même vue; la vue de l'une fera perdre l'idée de l'autre, joint qu'elles seront proportionnées chacune selon leur application, et quand même elles paraîtraient plus petites, ce n'est pas un défaut de voir la décoration des faces renfermée dans une cour plus petite et délicate que [celle] du dehors qui doivent être toujours plus [grande] et [majestueux], d'autant qu'on les voit de loin; et joint qu'il n'est pas raisonnable de s'assujettir à la grandeur et manière d'architecture desdites faces et colonnes de la cour qui se trouvent faites, pour les modèles de celles que l'on fera au dehors tout à neuf. Car il n'est pas raisonnable, s'il était vrai que lesdites colonnes et les faces de la cour se trouvassent déjà trop chétifs, d'en faire de même à ceux de dehors et suivre pour cet effet un mauvais exemple, plutôt que de leur donner ses proportions qui conviennent à la belle décoration desdites faces. Il y a ce me semble à considérer qu'un superbe palais comme celui du Louvre ne s'achève pas souvent sous un même règne ni quelquefois en un même siècle; partant, si par la diversité des temps, l'on augmente et que l'on se perfectionne, ce n'est pas un défaut en l'architecture de le faire paraître. Au contraire, je trouve que c'est ce qui fait distinguer les temps séparés dans lesquels on édifie, que de voir, par la diversité des bons goûts et la belle manière de bâtir [mieux] en un temps qu'en l'autre; par là on reconnaît l'excellence des beaux esprits qui s'y appliquent et la grandeur et la puissance du prince qui règne et sous lequel on édifie.

7. *1668.* Jean Baptiste Colbert, "Mémoire sur ce qui est à faire pour les bâtiments en l'année 1669" (extract). Published in P. Clément, ed., *Lettres, instructions et mémoires de Colbert,* Paris, 1868, v, 277, doc. 33:

Examiner soigneusement tout ce qui est à faire au Louvre.
Élever le corps du logis double du costé de la rivière.
Élever le péristyle sur la face du devant jusqu'à la corniche.
Résoudre promptement tout ce qui concerne le péristyle, ensemble l'élévation de l'attique du dedans, pour pouvoir travailler incessamment dès le premier jour de mars.

8. *1669/1670.* "Extrait et sommaire des avis des Architectes sur les modeles du Louvre, De Larc de triomphe et de l'observatoire" (AN, O¹ 1669, no. 404). Undated and previously unpublished. The date of this document is indicated by the fact that two of the experts (Chamois and Thévenot) refer to a finished part of Perrault's Arc de Triomphe du Trône on the side of Picpus (a district near the Place du Trône, now the Place de la Nation). This must be a reference to the full-scale model of the arch, begun in mid-1669 and finished by April 1670 (see M. Petzet, "Das Triumphbogenmonument für Ludwig XIV. auf der Place du Trône," *ZfK*, XLV, 1982, 165–166). I reproduce the opinions of the seven experts only on the Louvre (the Colonnade and the top story of the courtyard).

a. [Thomas Gamard]:[16]
Louvre

Ier art. La facade de lentrée du louvre est bastie avec tout lart imaginable pour la solidité et pour la propreté.

2 Il presume que le dessein en est beau puisque Monseigneur [Colbert] la aprouvé.

3 La voute ou plat fonds de ce qu'il appelle peristyle luy semble un ouvrage bien hardi parce que sa solidité depend du fer qui se peut rompre.

4 Que les anciens en ont usé autrement et ne se sont point exposez a ce hazard.

5 Qu'il le condamne absolument.

6 Qu'on devoit prendre garde a tailler les feuilles des chapiteaux en sorte quelles fussent renforcées aux endroits ou la veue ne peut porter.

Troisie[me] ordre

7 Il desaprouve ces colonnes du troisieme ordre du dedans du louvre ou il ne voudroit que des pillastres ou des cariatides,

8 Ou du moins cet ordre de colonnes devroit estre moins haut et moins grand qu'il n'est, et qu'il devroit estre d'une autre espece que celuy de dessous.

9 Il voudroit qu'on inventast un ordre nouveau qui pust estre appelé francois.

b. [Daniel Gittard]:[17]
Peristyle

Aprouve la disposition et la coupe des architraves et plat fonds pourveu que le fer soit bien faconné et bien corroyé, souhaitteroit que les barres fussent composées de plusieurs barres plattes battues et jointes en liaison. . . .

Troisie[me] ordre

Le modelle du troisieme estage qui est fait a cariatides luy semble mieux convenir a un dernier ordre que ceux ou il y a des colonnes, il n'y a rien qui le choque que les fleurs et les fruits qui sont dans les paniers qu'il juge n'estre pas capables de soutenir [les] architraves.

c. [Duval]:[18]

Les tirans de fer devroient estre au dessous des plattes bandes a fin davoir plus de force.

Les chapiteaux nont point la beauté de ceux du val de grace quoy qu'ils ayent quelque raport avec ceux de la rotonde.[19]

Le dedans du Louvre

Le modelle ou on a mis des cariatides ne merite pas qu'on si arreste et ces femmes avec leurs paniers sur leurs testes ne scauroient convenir qu'à l'entrée d'un marché.

Dans les autres modelles la repetition des colonnes est importune de même que celle des niches, celuy qui est a la droite est le plus suportable parce qu'il est moins haut que l'autre mais deux ordres composites l'un sur l'autre sont contre l'usage, il faudroit que les colonnes fussent isolées que les figures fussent plus grandes qu'il y eut moins de scul[p]ture, que les fenestres fussent differentes de celles de dessous, et pour bien faire il ne faudroit prendre pas un des trois models mais hausser seulement quelque peu l'ancien attique.

d. [Jean Pastel (Patel)]:[20]
Le Peristile

Les precautions qu'on apporte par le moien du fer pour soutenir les plattes bandes et par se moien et la charge qui est au dessus des colonnes rendront cette structure ferme et asseurée.

La coupe des claveaux en leurs testes devroit estre aplomb pour la beauté et la propreté.

Dedans du Louvre

Le modelle ou sont les Cariatides est moins convenable au reste du bastiment que les deux autres.

e. [Pierre Cottart]:[21]
Le Peristile

Les joints par le dehors seroient mieux destre aplomb au lieu destre en couppe. Il ne faudroit point denfoncement au plat fond a fin de fortiffier davantage les coupes des pierres et le reste est bien aisé pour executer.

Le dedans du Louvre

Le premier modele a colonnes est trop haut celuy a cariatides ne convient point au reste de louvrage le troisieme a le plus du bon goust et lantique et de la belle maniere a la reserve que les piedestaux pour les figures sont trop gros et quil ne faut point de consoles pour la corniche qui est au dessus des fenestres mais qu'il faut que le chambranle fasse crossette au haut a fin d'acourcir la corniche qui aproche trop pres des colonnes, et qu'il ny faut point de frontons a fin quelles soient differentes de celles de dessous pour diversiffier encore il faut que la frise soit ronde. Les modillons sont trop gros et la corniche a trop de saillie. Il faut oster les niches et en leur place mettre des figures sur des piédestaux saillans entre les deux qui soutiennent les colonnes.

f. [Charles Chamois]:[22]
Le Peristile

C'est un des plus beaux et plus hardis ouvrages qui se soient jamais fait, on ne scauroit rien adjouster a sa solidité si ce n'est qu'il faudroit estressir la voute qui sera au dessus en la faisant porter aplomb du devant des pillastres.

A lesgard de la coupe des pierres il ne se peut rien faire de mieux. Il faudroit pourtant que la frise fut une platte bande apart de celle de larchitrave et quelle fut bombée de demy poulce et demi.

Le dedans du louvre

Le modelle qui est a gauche convient fort bien pour les avant corps mais il voudroit entre les avant corps au lieu des pillastres mettre les caryatides pourveu q[u]ils nayent point de paniers car ces trois ordres l'un sur l'autre tout autour du louvre ne feroient pas un bon effet pour l'ordre qui est a la droite au lieu des deux figures qui cachent les colonnes il n'en faudroit qu'une entre les colonnes sur un pié destat simple.

g. [Pierre Thévenot]:[23]
Le Peristyle

On ne peut rien adjouster pour la coupe des pierres et pour la solidité de l'ouvrage par ce que la poussée est puissamment retenue par la fermeté des deux pavillons qui ont chacun plus de 13 toises, et que les fers qui doivent affermir et retenir la [blank] des plattes bandes qui poussent au vuide ne scauroient manquer pourveu qu'ils soient sans paille et qu'il [sic] ce qui est aisé de connoistre en les soudant.

Les plat fonds quarrez seront meilleurs que ceux dont la coupe est en rond parceque celle cy pousse au vuide et celle qui est en quarré et droitte ne pousse que contre les plattes bandes de traverses et en ce faisant les affermit.

Il seroit a propos que les voutes qui sont au dessus du plat fond fussent en tiers point et non en plein ceintre a fin davoir moins de poussée et de charger davantage la sommiere ce qui est d'une grande importance pour les affermir sur les colonnes car il ne faut rien craindre des chapiteaux qui quoy que de St Leu sont plus que suffisant pour soustenir le fais qu'il doivent porter ce qui se prouve par les pilliers qui sont laissez dans les carrieres dou ces pierres ont esté tirées qui soustiennent [blank] du ciel et la terre qui couvre les carrieres.

Pour estre plus asseuré que les sommiers ne casseront point il sera bon de laisser la partie du joint qui porte a faux au droit de l'entrecolonement vuide. . . .

Le dedans du Louvre

Le modelle qui a esté fait le premier est le plus convenable pourvueu qu'on diminue quelque chose de sa hauteur.

9. *1670.* Claude Olry de Loriande, *Le superbe dessein du Louvre. Dedié a Monseignevr Colbert,* Paris, 1670.

In magnis voluisse sat est. [Epigraph]
AV ROY.
SONNET.

Lovis dont le merite attire nos regars,
Et jette des rayons de gloire & de lumiere,
Tes armes brilleront parmi les champs de Mars
Autant que le Soleil brille dans sa cariere.

Marche vaillant Monarque, il n'est point de hazars
Qui puisse faire obstacle à ton ardeur guerriere,
La valeur qui t'égalle au plus grands des Cesars,
Plûtôt que de bon-heur manquera de matiere.

L'ennemy qui t'atend commence à consulter,
En quel lieu favorable il pourra se poster,
Mais en vain sa prudence assiste son courage.

En te voyant paroître, ô Roy victorieux,
Il combatra toûjours avec desadvantage,
Tu luy mettras par tout le Soleil dans les yeux.

A
MONSEIGNEVR
COLBERT.
SONNET.

Qve tes soins grand Ministre enfantent de miracles,
Que l'empire François sous ton regne a d'honneurs;
Les plus doctes esprits, les plus sçavans Autheurs,
Pour embellir l'Estat consultent tes oracles.

Par toy de l'impossible on force les obstacles,
Tes faits charment les yeux & gagnent tous les coeurs,
Et les François qui sont par toy de tout vainqueurs,
Lassez de triompher admirent tes spectacles.

Le Louvre est le plus beau qui soit dans l'Vnivers,
Et si je l'ay choisi pour l'objet de mes vers,
C'est que ma Muse sçait que ton grand coeur l'aprouve.

Par toy ce grand Palais comme l'état reluit,
Ce que Rome a perdu, la France le retrouve,
Puisqu'en toy grand COLBERT un Mecene revit.

LE
SVPERBE DESSEIN
DV LOVVRE.

Palais le plus charmant qui soit dans l'Univers, 1
Vray miracle de l'Art digne des plus beaux vers,
Puisque du grand COLBERT la sagesse profonde
Te destine pour estre un chef d'oeuvre du monde,
Et que sur les desseins de l'illustre le Vau, 5
En cuivre j'ay gravé ton merveilleux Tableau;
Je te veux derechef dépeindre en ce volume,
Puisque ma main sçait l'Art du fer, & de la plume;
Mais d'un stile si fort que ce foible papier,
Avec toy durera cent fois plus que l'acier. 10
Le marbre le plus dur, le Jaspe, le Porphire,
Les plus fins Diamans, où l'Art seul peut écrire,
Le bronze le plus fier & les autres metaux
Qui relevent l'éclat des plus riches travaux
Ne sont pas à mon gré d'une trempe assez forte, 15
Pour graver ta beauté qui charme & qui transporte.
Je choisis donc cét Art qui sçait éterniser
Lors qu'il est dans les mains de qui peut tout ozer,
La mienne l'entreprend imitant ce grand hôme;
Qui par sa docte plume immortaliza Rome; 20
Et quoy que ta noblesse & ton riche dessein
Meritent en ce siecle une plus docte main,
Suivant l'Esprit du Dieu qui regne sur mon ame,
Je te donne l'encens de ma plus noble flame.
Je dis donc que c'est toy magnifique Château, 25
Que la nature & l'Art à l'envy rendent beau,
Que l'on a destiné pour loger un Monarque
Dont le nom est exempt des fureurs de la Parque.
C'est l'Auguste LOUIS le seul rival de Mars,
Et l'ame d'Alexandre, & le coeur des Cesars, 30
Prés de toy beau Palais les plus fameuses villes,
Cedent sans resistance à l'éclat dont tu brilles:
Leurs Temples merveilleux, leurs fameux monumens,
Et leurs arcs triomphaux & tous leurs ornemens,
Ne sont que des travaux qui rougissent de honte 35
Lors que de ta beauté je fais le moindre conte,
Beauté qui durera jusqu'au delà des temps,
Malgré la decadance & l'injure des ans.
L'on est si rebattu du Chasteau du grand Caire,[24]
Que j'avois presque fait le dessein de m'en taire, 40
Mais parce qu'on luy donne un mile de longueur,
Vn grand exhaussement sur un quart de largeur,
Et que l'on crie icy que ce n'est rien que marbres
Parce qu'il croit chez luy, comme chez nous les arbres;
Abbatons son orgueil & montrons luy que l'art 45
Passe son riche Trône & tout son or blaffard,
La Mecque ne peut pas resister d'avantage,

Car sa honte est écrite en ton divin ouvrage,
Et malgré le Tombeau de son faux Mahomet,[25]
Et de l'heureux destin qu'en vain il luy promet, 50
Il faut que ses beautez qu'elle croit sans pareilles
Le cedent à l'éclat de tes moindres merveilles
Mais peut-estre on croira que nous serōs vaincus,
Lors qu'on nous fera voir le Temple de Bacchus,
Temple qui sur la foy des plus doctes personnes 55
Faisoit regner un rang de douze cens colomnes;
Colomnes qui montroient une grande fierté,
Sous l'ordre de Dorus qui l'avoit inventé;[26]
Mais si le grand Dorus, cét illustre Monarque
Donna de son sçavoir par cét ordre une marque, 60
Le nostre n'a pas moins de gloire ni d'honneur,
Puisqu'on ne borne point ton immense grādeur,
Je ne passeray point pour un esprit prophane,
Quand je t'exalteray sur celuy de Diane,
Ce Temple[27] si fameux te cede le laurier, 65
Et ta seule beauté le peut faire oublier,
Encor que nous soyons éloignez de la Chine,
Qui sçait l'art de bâtir sans marteaux ni machine,
Je ne puis oublier son Gôle Mandarin,
Son Palais de rubis & son Migra japin,[28] 70
Choses qui passeront pour une vaine fable
Auprés de ta beauté solide & veritable,
Quand aussi je devrois avoir pour ennemis
Les travaux d'Arthemise[29] & le fameux Memphis,[30]
La superbe Babel & ses grandes murailles, 75
Dont tous les vieux serpens déchirent les entrailles,[31]
Le Labyrinthe Grec avec cette maison
Que la nature a fait sans art & sans Masson,[32]
La fameuse Sion,[33] les Colomnes d'Hercules,[34]
Le Colosse[35] & le Phare[36] & tes plus grands emules; 80
Cét Autel que les Grecs d'un esprit prevenu
Dresserent à ce Dieu qu'ils nommoient Inconnu,[37]
L'excés de ta beauté, l'ardeur qui me consome,
M'empesche d'oublier que tu surpasses Rome,
Le Vatican son Temple & tout son Colonat,[38] 85
Et ses antiquitez dont on fait tant d'estat;
Les Palais de Florence & Gennes sa compagne,
Le grand Escurial[39] ce chef-d'oeuvre d'Espagne;
Cette sainte Sophie, où Constantin,[40] dit-on,
S'écria, j'ay vaincu le grand Roy Salomon, 90
Salomon dont le Temple eut tant de renommée,
Qui fut fait d'une main dans les arts consommée,
Que nous voyons revivre en ta seule beauté,
Dont rien n'égalera jamais la majesté.
Laissant cette victoire ou prophane ou sacrée, 95
Ma Muse qu'à toy seul le Ciel a consacrée,
Esprise de ce feu qui nous fait deviner,

Connoist que c'est de toy qu'Ovide a deu parler
Lors qu'il nous a décrit sous de sçavantes fables
Les beautez d'un Palais que tu rends veritables:⁴¹ 100
Si l'éclat du Soleil n'eut ses yeux éblouïs,
Il nous auroit prédit que c'estoit pour LOVIS,
Que le grand Apollon, ce pere de lumieres,
L'animoit à parler de ces riches matieres:
Cela se justifie en voyant ce Soleil, 105
La devise d'un Roy qui n'a point de pareil
Et qui cherit si fort cét Astre & ses images,
Qu'il le fait figurer sur ses plus grands ouvrages.
Armide ainsi qu'Ovide eut tres-certainement
De ta construction quelque pressentiment, 110
Et lors que sur Regnault elle essaya ses charmes,
Elle avoit un Soleil pour devise & pour armes.
Elle mena l'objet de ses contentemens,
Dans un vaste Palais semé de diamans:
Puis luy dit qu'en Europe on verroit des spectacles 115
Qui passeroient la Foy des plus puissans miracles.
Elle predit aussi qu'vn Heros glorieux
Feroit faire vn Palais plus grãd que ceux des Dieux.⁴²
Que l'Vnivers chargé de richesses immenses
Ne Brilleroient pas tant que ses magnificences: 120
Quel seroit ce Heros si ce n'estoit Louïs
Qui remplit l'Vnivers de ses faits inouïs,
Venons au veritable, & méprisons la feinte,
N'est-il pas bien dépeint dans l'Escriture Sainte,
Et ce qu'elle a predit des illustres Citez 125
N'est-il pas pour Paris dont il fait les beautez.
Les Anges destinez pour veiller sur les Villes
Serviront à ce lieu de gardes tres-subtilles,
Celuy de cét Empire a sur tout un grand soin,
Qu'il enchante les yeux & de prés & de loin: 130
Cõmençons par le Quay qu'on propose de faire,
Pour embellir Paris, & la rendre plus fiere,
Ce grand Quay regnera du Cours à l'Arcenal,
Pour maintenir la Seine en son lict de cristal.⁴³
Louis ce demi-dieu de la Terre & de l'Onde 135
Qui fait que cét Empire en merveilles abonde
L'ayant fait netoyer de trains & de bateaux
Y prendra quelquefois le frais dans ses vaisseaux.
Quel honneur que la Seine emporte sur l'Hidaspe,⁴⁴
Sans doute ses rampars seront un jour de Iaspe, 140
La voyãt de ces murs qui sont plus droits qu'un fil:
Ie diray qu'elle passe & l'Euphrate & le Nil:
Ce n'est point luy donner une gloire frivole
D'y joindre le Iourdain & l'Inde & le Pactolle:
Elle de qui le nom dit fleuve de santé 145
Du Tibre abaissera l'orgueilleuse fierté,
L'Hébre & le Maragnan, le Gange & la Tamise

A ce fleuve si sain verront leur eau soûmise:
Quelle main peut dépeindre ou graver l'appareil
Dans lequel ce Grand Roy, ce vainqueur sans pareil 150
Descendra tout brillant de gloire & de lumiere
Sur les charmantes eaux d'une telle riviere:
Et quel ravissement aura toute sa Cour
De voir de ce grand Pont qu'on bastit nuit & jour,⁴⁵
Au travers du cristal d'une pompe ou machine 155
Qui tirera son eau d'une source argentine,
La riche inspection de l'Isle du Palais
Ce College & son Temple à peine encor parfaits.⁴⁶
Cette Sainte Chappelle avec sa grande fléche
A qui jamais le temps ne devroit faire bresche 160
Les arcades du vaste & renommé Pont-neuf
Et leurs fronts décorez de massacre de boeuf,⁴⁷
Tous ces grands Chevaliers dont on ceindra la place
De l'Auguste Henry qui d'un Mars a la grace.⁴⁸
Le cirque & cét aspect du nouveau S. Germain 165
Pour lequel on a fait un si fameux dessein,
Dont le compartiment est si docte & si juste
Qu'il changera ce temple en un lieu tout auguste.⁴⁹
Tous les Ponts déchargez du fardeau des maisons
Qui courent grands dangers dans les froides saisons 170
Ces riches monumens qu'on destine en leur place
Pour croistre de Paris l'ornement & la grace.⁵⁰
Mille autres beaux objets que l'oeil découvrira
De moment en moment que l'on advancera:
L'auguste Mausolée, où l'Art s'ose promettre 175
De produire un miracle à l'endroit qu'on doit mettre.⁵¹
Nostre Roy que Bernin ce Sculpteur si fameux
Fait dessus son Cheval d'un air victorieux,
Luy dont la main a fait Daphné changée en arbre
Fait l'Homme & le Cheval d'un seul morceau de
    marbre:⁵² 180
L'on ne peut pas douter qu'un tres-riche ornement
N'accompagne un chef d'oeuvre où tout est si charmant.
Car il faut que tout cede, & fasse place nette
Lors qu'il s'agit de faire une oeuvre si parfaite.
Celle de ce Chasteau doit estre un grand carre 185
Fort vaste & fort superbe & tres-bien mesuré,
C'est dans ce bel endroit qu'il faudra que l'oeil s'ouvre,
Si l'on veut bien goûter le beau dehors du Louvre,
Pour preparer les yeux à tant d'enchantemens,
Qui se presenteront en des lieux si charmans: 190
Dans le coeur de ce lieu l'on verra des Fontaines⁵³
Qui passeront l'éclat des Cascades Romaines,
Depuis les premiers rangs tous de marbres pavez
Nous verrons trois bassins l'un sur l'autre élevez;
Mais bassins enrichis du Roy de chaque fleuve, 195
Qui d'un deluge d'eau leur profondeur abreuve,

Les fleuves debordez auront dessous leurs bras
Des vases d'un cristal que l'on ne connoist pas:
Leurs rapides boüillons tombant sur des coquilles
Iront au reservoir des plus nobles familles: 200
La Naumachie éteinte en ces lieux revivra,
Avecque des succés dont on s'étonnera:
Ces grands Rostres chargez de leur ancre & cordages
En sont à nôtre égard d'assez grands témoignages.
Sur le sommet chenu de l'orgueilleux rocher, 205
Qui contient ce jet d'eau si commode & si cher,
Nos grands Ingenieurs dont les forces mouvantes
Des plus fameux travaux surpassent les attentes,
Plus feconds mille fois que les Siecles passez
Qu'on croyoit vainement nous avoir surpassez, 210
Promettent d'y placer un superbe Obelisque
Qui de tomber jamais ne doit courir de risque:
Il me semble le voir sur quatre grands griffons,
Autant d'Aigles armez avec d'affreux Lions:
Sa fléche dont la pointe ira jusques aux nuës 215
Dans le Ciel portera du Roy les armes nuës.
Afin de l'emporter sur l'orgueil des Romains
Que la pierre d'Egypte avoit rendus si vains,
Pour orner de tous points cette charmante place,
Et luy donner les traits d'une derniere grace, 220
Sur de riches Autels, sur de grands pieds destaux
Où de tous nos grands Rois seront peints les travaux,
L'on doit placer aussi de grandes piramides
Que le Roy fait venir des montagnes Arides:
Les Colomnes d'Hercule & celle de Trajan 225
Avecque l'Antonine & le Môle Adrien
N'ont jamais égalé ces masses gigantesques
Où Nature a passé la matiere Arabesques:
Nature de qui l'oeil & les vives couleurs
Mieux que la Serpentine auront l'émail des fleurs 230
Ayant de cette place envisagé ce Louvre
Où l'Art n'a rien de beau que son front ne découvre:
Advançant sur le bord de ses larges fossés
Vn grand perron se montre à trois rangs exaucez,
Qui ceint d'un grand balustre enrichy de figures 235
Montre du grand Loüis les hautes advantures:
Sur le marbre orgueilleux de ce balustre à jour
Ses chiffres sont gravez en riches lacs d'amour.
L'on y voit ce portail dont la haute structure
Fait voir ce que jamais eut de beau la nature. 240
Sur ce fameux portail où l'Art s'est surpassé
Sera nostre grand Roy dans vn Char exaucé,
Avec Louis le Iuste & le grand Henry quatre,
Qui tous trois ont sçeu l'art de vaincre & de combattre.
Monseigneur le Dauphin cét heroïque enfant 245
Qui de tout l'Vnivers se verra triomphant
D'un oeil tout martial regardera son Pere

Qu'on ayme par sur tout, & qu'un chacun revere.
Non content d'un spectacle où tout est si charmant
Pour cōble de grandeur, de pōpe & d'ornement: 250
L'on nous assure aussi que nôtre grande Reine
Que toutes les vertus tiennent pour Souveraine
Y doit accompagner son invincible Epoux
D'un maintien agreable, engageant & tres-doux:
Ce char riche & pompeux sera suivy des heures 255
Qui feindront de sortir de ces grandes demeures.
A l'aspect surprenant d'un si fameux portail
Qui montre ce que peut la vertu du travail:
Vn peristile est veu chargé de cent colonnes,
Sous leur entablement qui vaut mille Couronnes, 260
Peristile elevé d'une extreme hauteur
Sur des loges qui vont tout autour en rondeur,
Qui montre noblement ce que peut la science
Et l'art le plus subtil joint a l'experience,
Leur fuste me surprend, leurs bazes chapiteaux 265
L'emportent sur l'antique & n'ont point leurs égaux:
L'architrave & la frise avecque la corniche
Sōt encore à mes yeux d'un air cēt fois plus riche.
Leur Attique en trophée avec leur riche aspect
Aux plus doctes de l'Art imprime du respect, 270
Et le tout qui n'est point coupé par un grand dome
Vaut au gré des Sçavans le plus riche Royaume:
Mes voeux sont satisfais de voir ce lieu sans prix
Le charme & le desir des illustres esprits:
D'un Art si consommé, d'une adresse si grande 275
L'on travaille à ces murs que ma muze apprehende
D'abaisser la matiere en loüant les Autheurs
Qui s'éternisent tous par ces doctes labeurs.
Enfin n'y voyant rien que de riche & de tendre,
Et mesme des grādeurs que je ne puis comprendre, 280
Ie m'écrie, ô Chasteau! miracle de beautez!
En ta faveur les Arts se sont ressuscitez,
Dépeigne qui voudra ta visible armonie
Et l'auguste beauté de ta grace infinie
Pour moy je tiens qu'il faut un rayon du Soleil 285
Pour dépeindre un Palais comme toy sans pareil:
Si l'on est si charmé de ta grande façade
Et qu'en entrant chez toy l'on y jette une oeillade.
Je soûtiens qu'à l'éclat de ton august Cour
Les meilleurs yeux seront ébloüis en plein jour, 290
Les graces, les vertus, les Nymphes, les Deesses,
Les victoires du Roy, ses combats, ses proüesses,
Les Sages de la France & les bustes des Rois,
Tous ceux qu'ils ont rangé sous leurs augustes loix
Feront une ceinture historique & sçavante 295
De cette Monarchie invincible & puissante.
Mais ce n'est rien encor que ces grands bastimens
Cette belle ceinture & ces enchantemens,

Vn escalier à jour⁵⁴ d'un Art émerveillable
Et d'un exaucement aussi considerable 300
Abbaissant sa fierté vous offrira le dos,
Pour vous mener aux lieux destinez aux Heros
C'est à l'appartement qu'on nomme de parade,⁵⁵
Lieu d'empire & d'honneur, de faveur & de grade,
Si riche que luy seul épuiseroit vingt Rois 305
Fussent-ils des Cresus, & plus riches cent fois
Si superbe qu'on peut dire sans flatteries
Qu'un Monde ne vaut pas toutes ses pierreries,
Ses plafonds enchantez semez de diamans
Exaucez & plus clairs que quatre Firmamens, 310
Ses meubles precieux, sa charmante peinture
Qui tout ensemble imite & passe la nature
Ces parquets figurez, ces chassis de christal,
Et ces lustres taillez d'un ordre sans égal
Ces phares lumineux que l'on nomme torcheres 315
Et qui servent la nuict d'Astres pleins de lumieres:
Ces chambranles d'acier & ses portes d'argens
Cisellez par la main des plus intelligens,
Ces vases, gueridons, cassolettes & tables,
Où l'ambre gris répand des odeurs delectables: 320
Cét Air artificiel qui combat les saizons
Et qui donne le froid & le chaud par raisons,
L'incroyable succés de nos forces mouvantes
Qui charme & prive l'oeil de beautez surprenantes
Dont l'Art industrieux par des ressorts fait voir 325
D'incroyables efforts d'un merveilleux sçavoir:
Cét aspect enchanteur qui trompe & multiplie
Ta celebre demeure en tous poincts accomplie
Cause que je dédaigne, & qu'on ne pense pas
Au superbe Palais du grand Vatavoualpas⁵⁶ 330
Que je méprise aussi le Trône de la Chine,
Les Tresors de Cresus,⁵⁷ ceux de la Cochinchine:⁵⁸
Le fameux Tabernacle érigé dans Mosco,⁵⁹
Et la grotte du Camfre & son charmant Echo:⁶⁰
La perle Pennamas celle de Cleopatre⁶¹ 335
Et mille autres bijoux que la terre idolatre
Le cabinet d'Osman,⁶² son Sceptre & son Turban
Qui valent, ce dit-on, l'Empire du Persan,
Mesme des autres Rois toutes les pierreries
Qui prés de toy ne sont que pures réveries: 340
Aux deux vastes costez de ce lieu sans égal
Sont les lieux de concert, de festins & regal.⁶³
En celuy des festins, Bachus & Ganimede
Avecque des ressorts viendront soudain à l'aide,
De tous ceux que la soif ou la faim pressera, 345
Mais qui le gout & l'oeil en tout satisfera.
Au grand coeur de Musique, Orphée & Calliope
Exaucez dans vn Ciel dessus le Mont Rodope⁶⁴
Sembleront rappeller en concert d'élicat

La Reine Piereide & ses soeurs au combat:⁶⁵ 350
Mais par des tons si doux, si remplis d'armonie
Qu'Appollõ quoy que dieu de l'art de symphonie
Y verra des François plus forts que Marsias
Qui defendront leur peau de la main & des bras:
Ie croy que j'ay raison puisque rien ne resiste 355
A ce siecle entendu, sçavant, subtil artiste
Mesme où les instrumens ont je ne sçay quels sons
Qui triomphe des airs, des vers, & des chansons.
Ma main qui ne décrit que des beautez divines
Laisse à part Magazins, Offices & Cuisines: 360
Seur que dãs ces beaux lieux l'Orfevre intelligent
Y mettra d'un Perou la valeur en argent.
Je passe viste aussi sur les Salles des Gardes,
Qui sont des Arsenaux, de riches Hallebardes.
Ie diray toutesfois que dans ces lieux de Mars 365
Tous les Gardes du Corps du rival des Cesars,
Ont le coeur d'un Alcide en voyant ce Monarque
Que leur gloire interesse à sauver de la Parque,
Revenu de l'extaze & des ravissemens,
Où l'on tombe en voyant des objets si charmans, 370
Commançons à parler de ce Palais de marbre,
Où l'on doit s'attacher comme au plus fort de l'arbre.
Où l'on doit prodiguer & sans feintes & sans fard
Ce que peut le sçavoir la richesse avec l'Art.
Ce chef-d'oeuvre enchanté se presente à la veuë 375
Avec une fierté qu'on n'a point encor veuë,
Prés de luy le Palais du grand Abalipas,⁶⁶
Le Pagode,⁶⁷ & cent lieux dont on fait plus de cas,
Verront à son aspect leur majesté ternie,
Et cederont la Palme à sa grace infinie. 380
Ie change donc de style, & pour vous delasser
Sous le Temple d'Amour je vay vous le tracer,
Cette diversité rien que le nom ne change
Et c'est pour abreger que je fais ce mélange.
La repetition de tant d'appartemens 385
N'estant rien qu'un surcroist de riches ornemens
D'invention nouvelle artiste & surprenante,
Que l'oeil du spectateur trouvera tres-charmante.
Voyez ce que l'Amour dit de nôtre grand Roy,
Qui comme le Soleil n'a rien d'égal a soy. 390
Mesme à quel poinct ce dieu respecte nôtre Reine,
Luy dressant des Autels comme à sa Souveraine.
Dans ce Temple sacré du grãd Dieu de l'Amour
Louis ainsi que luy doit faire son sejour.
Auprés des doux brillans de cette solitude 395
Les feux du Firmament sont d'un éclat trop rude.
Ces globes de cristal, cét azur precieux
Qu'on nomme le partage & l'empire des Dieux
N'enchante pas si bien les esprits ni les ames
Que fait la majesté de ces lieux pleins de flames: 400

A l'aspect d'un sejour si beau, si glorieux,
Le Soleil n'a plus rien qui ravisse les yeux.
L'Vnivers tout chargé de richesses immenses
Ne brilleroit pas tant que ces magnificences.
A l'empire éclatant de ce marbre orgueilleux 405
Ie méprise la Terre & son faste pompeux:
C'est dans ce Temple auguste où les plus saints Oracles
En faveur des Amans font d'illustres miracles.
Par un charme secret mon ame en ce moment
Iure par tous les Dieux d'aimer incessamment. 410
Mon coeur tout penetré de ces saintes amorces,
Pour redoubler ses voeux sent de nouvelles forces.
Le presage assuré d'un triomphe amoureux
Est le celebre prix qu'on destine à mes voeux.
Sur de riches autels tout parsemez de roses, 415
L'Amour dessus son Trône accorde toutes choses:
Venus qui des Amans est le plus doux espoir
Dās sa plus haute pompe en ces lieux se fait voir,
Sa clemence est toujours favorable & propice
Aux Amans dont le coeur aime sans artifice. 420
On apprend l'art de plaire en ce brillant sejour,
A l'objet pour lequel on conçoit de l'amour.
Mais quel enchantement se presente à ma veuë,
La Deesse y paroist, mes yeux l'ont apperceuë:
Son bel oeil de ce temple éblouït la clarté, 425
Et son lustre auprés d'elle est plein d'obscurité:
Son geste est si divin, sa démarche si grave,
Qu'en la voyant, un Dieu deviendroit son esclave.
Son air est sans égal, & ce charme inocent
Est le seul que le Ciel a rendu tout-puissant. 430
Auprés de cette auguste & charmante Amazone
Louis avec l'Amour est assis sur son Trône.
Ce Dieu qui s'est logé dans les yeux de ce Roy
Nous montre par ces vers qu'à tout il fait la loy.
Que rien n'est cōparable à l'excedsde ses charmes 435
Et qu'il sçait triompher sans le secours des armes.
Enfin par un destin illustre & glorieux
Ie me vois tout-puissant sur les Rois & les Dieux.
C'est moy seul qui peux tout sur les plus invincibles,
Et qui flechis les coeurs tout à fait inflexibles. 440
Ie tiens dessous mes loix tout ce grand Univers,
Et mon pouvoir s'étend jusque dans les Enfers:
Je fais sentir mes feux aux fleurs ainsi qu'aux arbres,
Et sçay l'art d'animer les bronzes & les marbres.
Ie ne vois rien qui soit sous les loix du Destin, 445
Qui ne sente l'effet de mon pouvoir divin;
Les plus grandes beautez qui sont dans ses idées
De mes sacrez attraits se verront possedées.
Bref il ne fait rien voir de precieux au jour
Qu'il ne l'assujettisse au pouvoir de l'Amour; 450
Et l'art de faire aimer, & celuy d'estre aimable
Font qu'entre tous les Dieux je suis incomparable.
Ie voy pareillement la Reine qui jouit
De la mesme faveur & du mesme credit.
Ie la trouve à mes yeux si charmante & si belle, 455
Que moy qui fais aimer, je meurs d'amour pour elle.
Ce Mars tout redoutable, & furieux qu'il est
Tremble sous les regards de son oeil qui me plaist.
Mesme ce qui naistra de ce Monarque & d'elle
Domptera comme moy le coeur le plus rebelle. 460
Ie n'aurois jamais fait & serois ennuyeux
Si je voulois au vray vous dépeindre ces lieux,
Le moindre appartement n'eut jamais son semblable,
Et le tout bien dépeint paroîtroit incroyable.
Quiconque entreprendra d'en vanter les tresors 465
Sans doute il y fera d'inutiles efforts.
Passons de ce Palais aux grandes Galeries,[68]
Dont la vaste longueur va jusqu'aux Thuilleries:
Celle dont je vous offre à present le tableau
Regne superbement dessus le bord de l'eau: 470
Admirez en entrant dans cette Gallerie
Qui sert de logemens aux dieux de l'industrie
Les villes que Louis y fait representer
Sur de riches tableaux qu'on ne peut trop vanter.
Si vôtre oeil n'est charmé des Forests de Pilastres, 475
Desquels l'or & l'azur est plus pur que les astres,
Voyez les ornemens de ces riches lambris,
Ces plans dont les desseins enchantent les esprits:
Admirez en leurs noms contenus en ces listes,
La grandeur de l'esprit de nos Topographistes, 480
Henoc, Ierusalem, Athenes, Illion,
Thebes, Carthage, Rome, Ispan, Lacedemon,
Memphis, Constantinople, Aden & Babylone,
Le grād Pecquin, Ninive, Emsar, Laor, Lisbone,
Mosco, Goa, Quincé, Persepolis, Smarcan, 485
Narsingue, Calicut, Brame, Calaminlian,
Trebisonde, Maroc, Venise, Alexandrie,
Madrid, Londre, Stokolm, Amsterdam, Cracovie,
Paris, Vienne, Presbourg, Copenhague, Nancy,
Naples, Gennes, Florence, & Basle & Bude aussi. 490
Enfin ces beaux Tableaux qu'avec raison j'exalte
Finiront par Turin, Cologne, Prague & Malte.
Encor que ces lambris soient plus que suffisans
Pour enchanter les yeux des spectateurs sçavans,
Par un art tout celeste & tout astronomique, 495
Et bien plus excellent que le Topographique.
Leurs plafonds qui du Ciel font voir les raretez
En des compartimens justes & concertez,
Fait croire aux spectateurs qu'un celeste genie
En est venu tracer en ces lieux l'harmonie. 500
Ceux que ce beau sejour tient pour ses habitans
Sont les Dieux du sçavoir & les charmes du temps.

Si les Arts ont rendu quelque main signalée,
Sans doute on la verra regner dans cette allée:
La plume, le compas, le pinceau, le burin, 505
Le ciseau, ciselet, la lime, éguille & main,
Font voir entierement dans cette Gallerie
Tout ce que la science & l'art ont d'industrie.
La Deesse Minerve en ces celebres lieux
Estalle ses Tresors aux yeux des curieux. 510
Si bien que si quelqu'un veut avoir des miracles,
Il faut qu'il ait recours à ces sçavans Oracles:
Car sans se fatiguer de voyages divers
On trouvera chez eux le beau de l'Vnivers.
Vous ferez en faisant chez ces sçavans la ronde 515
En moins de quatre jours tout le grand tour du Monde,
Ou du moins le profit qu'un esprit curieux
Feroit toute sa vie errant en divers lieux:
Car la celebre Athene & toutes les deux Romes[69]
Reprennent leur vigueur en l'Art de ces grands
    hommes; 520
Et sans doute on verra que leur divin sçavoir
Enfante des beautez qu'elles n'ont point fait voir.
Admirez en passant le Theatre de Flore,[70]
Où la Cour a paru plus belle que l'Aurore,
Où l'Artiste Jessé[71] signala son esprit, 525
Par la grande Machine où sa main reüssit.
La Scene estoit si belle & si bien décorée
Que de tous les sçavans elle fut admirée.
Aprés avoir loüé ces immenses grandeurs
Voyez ce qu'on a fait pour les Ambassadeurs: 530
Jugez au mesme instant de la grande surprise,
Dont ces sages Herauts auront leur ame éprise,
Comme aprés avoir veu tous les Appartemens
Du Louvre, qui sont tous autant d'enchantemens.
Il[s] verront derechef en cette auguste Salle[72] 535
Louis avec sa Cour qui n'eut jamais d'égale.
Si je voulois encor dépeindre ce Palais,
Tous ses appartemens & ses charmans attrais
Ce seroit accabler de l'éclat de sa gloire
Des plus grands curieux l'esprit & la memoire. 540
On y voit vestibule, antichambre & sallon,[73]
Qui surpassent tous ceux dont j'ay fait mention.
Mesme on y voit aussi la salle des Antiques,[74]
Et des siecles passez les plus belles Reliques.
Les portraits d'Alexandre & des premiers Cesars, 545
Le buste d'Aristote avec celuy de Mars,
Cette Divinité qui rendit des Oracles
Y regne fierement & cent autres miracles.
C'est icy qu'épuisé je conjure Appollon
De rafraichir ma veine aux eaux de son vallon: 550
Car avant que j'arrive à ce fameux Theatre,[75]
Qui fait voir des beautez que le monde idolâtre,

Ie pourrois demeurer en un si beau chemin
Si ce Dieu refusoit son secours à ma main,
A travers l'antichambre où nôtre Roy s'habille 555
Et les appartemens de toute sa famille.[76]
Allons à l'escalier que le docte Hauzau[77]
A rendu si charmant, si superbe & si beau,
Chacun de ses balustres est un petit mystere,
Ce Globe & cette Lire ont le bel art de plaire, 560
Ces pattes de lions, ces serpens, ces lauriers,
Predisent de Louis les miracles guerriers.
De prudence & de force on les void les symboles,
Et font à mon defaut l'office des paroles.
La Chapelle[78] où l'on doit surpasser ce qu'on fait 565
D'ordinaire en tel lieu pour le rendre parfait,
N'estant pas un chemin où le vulgaire passe:
Sortez dedans la court, & venez voir la grace
De ce fameux Theatre ou Salle des Ballets,[79]
Où du grand Jupiter vous verrez le Palais. 570
Si jamais le Theatre a paru magnifique,
Voyez sa belle face, où tout est Deïfique,
Son merveilleux parterre & son riche plafond
Qui de l'Art le plus riche épuiseroit le fond:
Son riche Amphiteatre & ses charmantes loges 575
Dont ma plume ne peut bien faire les éloges:
Voyez & revoyez du fond de ces beaux lieux
Les Machines que l'Art represente à vos yeux:
Si Nature jamais parût industrieuse,
C'est par ces grãds ressorts qu'elle est miraculeuse 580
Voyez avec Louis au Ciel de Iupiter
Ces Vers que sous son nom je veux luy presenter:
Ouy je suis Iupiter, & ce glorieux tiltre
Des Heros & des Dieux me fait le seul arbitre:
Le Destin a sousmis l'Univers à mes loix, 585
Et le Ciel dans mes mains met le Sceptre des Rois.
Quand quelque temeraire a merité le foudre
De mes sanglans carreaux je le reduits en poudre,
Et qui de mes faveurs devient méconnoissant
Ressent tout aussi-tôt que je suis tout-puissant. 590
Enfin je vais finir par la grande surprise,
Dont ces objets mouvans rendront vostre ame éprise,
Voir marcher un Theatre[80] orné d'un grand Palais,
Enfler l'onde des Mers, & sans aucuns delais,
Des vents les plus mutins arrester les tempêtes, 595
Vous môtrer des Forests & les cieux sur leurs testes,
Faire voller les gens ainsi que des oiseaux,
Et fendre l'Ocean avecque des vaisseaux,
Descendre en un clin d'oeil du Ciel dessus la Terre,
Calmer les Elemens qui se faisoient la guerre, 600
Consacrer les Heros, couronner les Amans,
C'est le comble à mon gré des divertissemens.
Vn jour vous passerez par l'autre Gallerie[81]

Qui du Louvre fera la juste Symetrie.
Sitost que vous lirez entrant dans le jardin, 605
Ce Sonnet qu'à propos je vous mets dans la main,
Ie vous entretiendray de la Sainte Chapelle,[82]
Où nôtre Roy pretend que chaque chose excelle.

DEESSE l'ornement des sejours enchantez:
Flore qui mets ton Trône aux grandes Thuileries 610
Seconde les ardeurs de mes douces furies,
Qui vont pour te loüer jusqu'aux extremitez.

Voyant que dans ces lieux tous les Arts concertez
Ont fait comme un Autel, où sans idolâtrie
Les divines vertus de LOVIS *sont cheries,* 615
Ie m'écrie en voyant tant de rares beautez.

Charmante inspection, ravissantes allées
O fruicts, ô rares fleurs en beautez signalées,
Lieu sacré, lieu plaisant, magnifique jardin

Tu me fais voir Vertume au dernier poinct aimable 620
Estallant ses tresors & son pouvoir divin
Pour rendre ton aspect en tout incomparable.

Ie vous en dirois plus, mais les choses prolixes
Fatiguent les esprits, & les veut par trop fixes,
Ie m'acquiteray donc de ce que j'ay promis 625
Touchant la Gallerie & ses riches lambris.[83]
Rentrez au Pavillon de la grande Ecurie[84]
Et vous irez tout droit dans cette Gallerie.
Vn jour vous y verrez peint sur chaque tableau
Tout ce que la Nature eut iamais de plus beau, 630
Ce qu'on y dépeindra doit estre emerveillable,
Riche, grand, curieux, & sur tout admirable.
Et vous fera connoistre en fixant vos regards
Que la Frãce est l'empire où regnẽt les beaux arts.
FIN.

10. *1672.* Nicolas Catherinot, *Distiques sur le Louvre au Roy,* Bourges, 1672, 5–14 (selections). (Colophon: "Augusta Biturigum, exeunte 1671.")

[1.] *Domûs & Domini proportio.*
Haec est magna quidem, sed major debuit esse;
Ter magni ut posset Principis esse domus.

[2.] *Lutetia Luparae Appendix.*
Urbs magna est, est magna domus: dic Civis & Hospes
Qui legis. Appendix utra sit alterius.

[3.] *Unica non egent nomine.*
Antiquae Luparae tollatur inutile nomen,
Una est in mundo Regia vera domus.

[4.] *Lupara tota nova.*
Non minor incipere est, quam coepta absolvere virtus.

A fundamentis quanta sed exstruere?

[5.] *Opera Belli & Pacis.*
Ludo vices, Ludovicus ait, benè tẽpora cedunt;
Mars fervet, vinco; Pax redit, aedifico.

[6.] *Rex & Lupara.*
Omnibus ut populis potior Rex unicus, una
Sic potior tectis omnibus est Lupara.

[7.] *Imprecatio in Avaros laudis.*
Qui Luparã videt & Luparã nõ laudat; Erynnis
Huic linguam exscindat, confodiatque oculos.

[8.] *Bellitudo & magnitudo.*
Bella & magna potest haec Principis aula videri:
Bella quidẽ dom[us] est, magna tamẽ domus est.

[9.] *Dialogismus.*
Sequana siste undã & Luparã tranquilla videto.
Vidi, sed propero visa, referre volens.

[10.] *Lupara cur adeo superba.*
Viventis fiat cum Principis aula sepulcrum,
Pulcra domus Regi nulla sat esse potest.

[11.] *Roma & Lutetia.*
Tanta est sub nostro Lupara atque Lutetia Rege
Quanta sub augusto Caesare Roma fuit.

[12.] *Domus Regiae.*
Principis h[a]ec nostri dom[us] est quota, nobilis aula?
Praecipua est, sed non unica tanta Domus.

[13.] *Luparae Metamorphosis.*
Cur veterem Luparem evertit Rex? Saxea tantũ
Quae fuit, hanc statuit linquere marmoream.

[14.] *Consequentia ex Lupara.*
Qui Luparam cernit, dicat sincerior hospes:
O quantum est Gallis gentibus ingenium!

[15.] *Lupara verum Capitolium.*
A capite appellant Capitolia, quàm benè nomẽ
Convenit hoc Luparae, quae caput Imperij est.

[16.] *Votum Auctoris.*
Cum video Luparam, subit admiratio tanta;
Invigilans oculus totus ut esse velim.

[17.] *Hispanus ex Amico invidus.*
Infelix Luparam conspexit nuper Iberus;
Adventarat amans, invidus hinc abijt.

[18.] *Rex audiendus, Lupara videnda.*
Regem audi, si vis ut sit feliciter auri;
Ut sit faustè oculo, conspicias Luparam.

[19.] *Taxila, Scorialum & Lupara.*[85]
Taxila jactetur Persae, jactetur Iberi
Scorialum: Luparae cedit utrumque meae.

[20.] *Silentium & Garrulitas.*
Antiqui sileat septem miracula mundi,
Pro cunctis Luparam garrula fama canat.

[21.] *Permissio laudandi sub conditione.*

Septem orbis, quantum cupies, miracula lauda;
Dum Luparam laudans omnibus anteferas.

[22.] *Triplex Ars Regis.*
Bellificare scio, scio pacificate, canit Rex;
Idem addit verax, aedificare scio.

[23.] *Luparae Hospitium.*
Invictus Princeps coelum unum cogitat, ergo
Ad tempus tantum est haec domus hospitium.

[24.] *Luparae Situs.*
Aedificor prope magnā Urbē, prope nobile flumē.
Quis magis hoc possit commodus esse situs?

[25.] *Lupra supra Zodiacum.*
Est soli duodena domus super aethera, Regis
In terris superatior domus una domos.

[26.] *Luparae amplitudo.*
Conveniant orbis Reges, comitatus & adsit.
Sufficiet plusquam haec omnibus una domus.

[27.] *Luparae innumerae.*
Non una est domus atque invicti Principis aula;
Corda quot in Regno, tecta tot esse puta.

[28.] *Regis actuositas.*
Heic iacet, inscribes huic nunquam Principis aulae;
Cum semper vigilet, cur sitet, instet, agat.

[29.] *Oculorum usus unicus.*
Luscus sim aut coecus reliquo Polyphemus in orbe;
Argus at in Lupara dum novus esse queam.

[30.] *Expostulatio.*
Cum Rex semper agat, cum nesciat ille quietem
Cur illi (precor) est aedificata domus?

[31.] *Conservatio.*
A ventis nulli parcatur & ignibus Urbi,
Dum Luparae turbo parcat uterque meae.

[32.] *Luparae eversio.*
Diruite hos muros, haec tecta evertire Galli;
Nullis arctantur Regia corda locis

[33.] *Lutetiae transnominatio.*
In Luparam debes mutare Lutetia nomen,
A magna res est parte vocanda sui.

[34.] *Vetus & nova Lupara.*
Dices, si veterem huic nostrae contenderis aulam
Principis aula fuit, nostra sed aula Dei est.

[35.] *Res locata major loco.*
Esse locum Luparam, & Regem concedo locatū,
Rex maior tamen est & minor ille locus.

[36.] *Caput mundi & capitis oculus.*
Si caput est magni populosa Lutetia mundi,
Tanti huius capitis haec domus est oculus.

[37.] *Aedes duplici sensu.*
Aedem non Aedes hanc verè dixeris aulam,
Cum tam sit nostri Principis aula pia.

[38.] *Luparae situs.*
Nec valles humiles, nec celsos eligo montes;
Heic volui condi, dum mihi plana placent.

[39.] *Capitolium & Lupara.*
Garrula Roma sui Capitoli iactitet arcem,
Dum Luperam servat Gallia muta suam.

[40.] *Ad Sequanam.*
Ad mare volvis aquas & multos alluis agros.
An quid par Luparae Sequana fortè vides?

[41.] *Lupara inchoata & absoluta.*
Incipe, dimidium est; Reges dixêre priores;
Sed Rex perficiens, meta coronat, ait.

[42.] *Rex architectus.*
Ipse dedit Ludovix formam atque synopsim,
O quantum est nostri Principis ingenium!

[43.] *Rex non conatur, sed efficit.*
Has tantas Aedes ausi sunt condere multi,
Sed potuit Princeps unicus efficere.

[44.] *Lupara tota Gallicana.*
Gallica nostra situ domus est, dominoq[ue] potente,
Nil Berninus habet, quod petat esse suum.

[45.] *Lupara est domus sacra.*
Cum sancte tanta semper vivatur in aula,
Non est tam famae quam pietatis opus.

[46.] *Lingua impar Luparae.*
Cum Luparae vidi numerosa Palatia nostrae,
Quam cupii linguam tunc habuiste Dei.

[47.] *Ludovicus I. non LXV.*
Gallorum Imperii nuda est Praefatio tantum,
Quotquot ad hunc Reges praeteriêre meum.

[48.] *Orbis, Urbis & Domus Collatio.*
Par Urbi Dom[us] est, Orbi Urbs, Quid ma[net(?)] ut
Urbsque Domusque tamē te (Lodoice) minor.

[49.] *Lupara, domus amphibia.*
Electus Luparae locus est feliciter iste,
Ruri habitat noster Rex & in Urbe simul.

[50.] *Prosodia Luparae.*
Dicite Luparam, Luparam, qui dicitis omnes
Non tantae vox est corripienda domus.

[51.] *Lupara Luparae ornamentum.*
In Lupara fac ut videatur nulla supellex,
Parietibus nudis est decorata satis.

[52.] *Lupara Domus & Arx.*
Et bello & paci Lupara opportuna videatur:
In bello Arx fortis, pace venusta domus.

[53.] *Luparae dos triplex.*
Ista Domus cū si bene cōmoda, fortis, amoenas
In toto frustra quaerimus Orbe parem.

[54.] *Ad Hospitem vel Advenam.*

Vidisti Luparam, satis est vidisse; superstes
Effossis poteris vivere luminibus.

[55.] *Lupara peractio.*
Constructis noster sic Princeps addidit, omne
A fundamentis ut ferè construeret.

[56.] *Lupara Coelum terrenum.*
Ni coleret Princeps pietatem, dicere posset;
Iuppiter in Coelo est, in Lupara Ludovix.

[57.] *Aedifica, noxa praesto est.*
Aedificatores ferè semper poenitet; unum
Regia qui tecta haec condidit, excipias.

[58.] *Lupara biornata.*
Pulcra quidem est extus, sed longè est pulcrior intra;
Praecipuè Princeps, si suus adsit Herus.

[59.] *Concentus vocum de Lupara.*
De Lupara vox est diversa, huc pertinet omnis:
In toto non est par Domus orbe tibi.

[60.] *Roma Gallicana.*
Pulcra videre cupis, ne finibus urbis abito;
Quod tibi promittit Roma, dabit Lupara.

[61.] *Lutetia & Lupara discrimen.*
A quovis poterit fortasse Lutetia condi,
Non Luparam quivis aedificare potest.

[62.] *Lupara quasi Colossus.*
Quantum inter statuam est discriminis atque Colossum,
Tantum inter Luparam totque domos reliquas.

[63.] *Regis opera.*
Belli quaeris opus, tot captas aspicis Urbes;
Pacis quaeris opus, Regia tecta vide.

[64.] *Erga & Parerga Regis.*
Haec Domus est summum Lodoïci Principis Ergon;
Caetera quae cernis recta, parerga putes.

[65.] *Pulcritudo & venustas simul.*
Ut pulcram Luparam, sic dixeris esse venustam
Sive extendatur, seu brevietur opus.

[66.] *Lupara opus coeleste.*
Dices, cum Luparae sublimia culmina cernes,
A summo sunt haec culmina missa polo.

[67.] *Argumentum.*
Magna quidem Domus est, Dominus sed maior, & inde
Quid sequitur? Non est digna domus domino.

[68.] *Luparae & Lutetiae magnitudo.*
Lutetiam & Luparam videas, Respublica dices
Tota illic, verum est heic caput Imperij.

[69.] *Lupara urbana & rustica.*
Alternis quidam modò rure, modò Urbe fruuntur;
Rure frui Rex heic & simul Urbe solet.

[70.] *Insignia Regia & Colbertina.*
Soles & colubros[86] cur tot Domus exhibet una?
Ut malus hinc timeat, speret ut inde bonus.

[71.] *Luparae foecunditas.*
Non dom[us] est sterilis, non est sine pignore tectū;
Tot Vates cum tot carmina parturiant.

[72.] *Encomia Luparae.*
Mille modis quondā laudata est vacca Myronis;[87]
De Lupara cur non audeat omnis idem?

11. *1672.* [Anonymous], *Essays à la louange du roy*, Paris, 1672 (selections).

SUR LE DESSEIN DU LOUVRE
achevé par le Roy.
SONNET.

Louis qui sur ses voeux regle les destinées;
Parmy tous ses Travaux & ses Projets divers,
Acheve ce Palais qui depuis tant d'années,
Par son vaste dessein estonnoit l'univers.

France n'espere plus que d'heureuses Journées,
La Gloire qui conduit ce Prince que tu sers,
Tient icy la Fortune, & l'Envie enchaisnées;
Et le temps ne peut rien sur de si nobles fers.

Ne crois pas que l'honneur de finir cet ouvrage,
Soit de l'amour du Ciel un foible témoignage,
Du coeur de ce Heros il connoit la Grandeur

De ses plus tendres soins sans cesse il le seconde,
A preparer luy-méme un thrône à sa Valeur;
Pour y donner un jour des Lois à tout le monde.   (18)

INSCRIPTION
sur le mesme Sujet.

Hoc opus exegit LodoiX ne plura moreris
Quaerere, laus omnis tItVlo comprenditur uno.

TRADUCTION

Louis acheva cét ouvrage,
N'en demandez pas davantage,
Tout ce qu'on peut penser de grand
Ce nom Auguste le comprend.   (19)

SUR LE MESME SUJET.

Quod nec multa dies, ordo nec longus avorum,
Hoc potuit LodoiX, populi dIVûmque voluptas:
Terrarum sedem hic dominam, decernere fatis
Sic juvat aeternam, tanto Duce & auspice tanto.

TRADUCTION

Ce qu'apres tant d'années,
N'avoient peu faire encore tant d'illustres Ayeux,
Louis l'a fait luy-seul au gré des destinées,

Louis l'amour du peuple, & le plaisir des Dieux.
C'est ainsi que du Ciel, la sagesse profonde,
  En faveur du plus grand des Rois,
Establit en ces lieux, sous d'eternelles loix,
Pour le bien des mortels, la maistresse du monde.   (20)

POUR LE MESME LOUVRE
  au dessous de la Figure du Roy.[88]

Tecta superba vides; Authorem pronus adora:
Terrarum imperio facies haud dignior usquam:
Ingentes animos sineret superaddere marmor,
O quantum hic populos inter certamen amoris!

TRADUCTION
Passant qui que tu sois qui vois ce grand Ouvrage;
Admirant son Auteur, adore son Image:
  Si les destins ont arresté
Que ce vaste univers d'un seul soit le partage,
  Cet air de Majesté,
  Qu'on voit sur son Visage,
T'apprend que c'est à Luy qu'ils donnent leur suffrage.
Si le marbre pouvoit exprimer la grandeur,
  De son Genie & de son Coeur,
Et toutes ces Vertus qu'en Luy le Ciel assemble,
Combien de Nations verroit-on chaque jour,
Offrant icy leurs voeux, se disputer ensemble,
  De respect & d'amour.   (21)

12. *1673.* Claude Perrault, ed. and trans., *Les dix livres d'architecture de Vitruve*, Paris, 1673 (*privilège du roi*: April 4, 1672).

  a. Le goust de nostre siecle, ou du moins de nostre nation, est different de celuy des Anciens, & peut-estre qu'en cela il tient un peu du Gothique: car nous aimons l'air le jour & les dégagemens. Cela nous a fait inventer une sixiéme maniere de disposer ces Colonnes, qui est de les accoupler & de les joindre deux à deux, & de mettre aussi l'espace de deux entrecolonnemens en un; par exemple la Colonne B du Systyle[89] A B C D, estant jointe à la Colonne A, on augmente l'entrecolonnement B C, pour faire l'entrecolonnement E F.

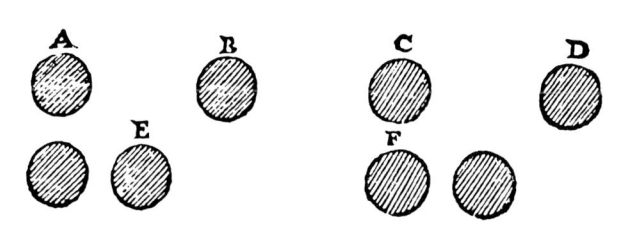

  Cela a esté fait à l'imitation d'Hermogene,[90] qui dans l'Eustyle[91] élargit l'entrecolonnement du milieu, qui rendoit l'entrée des Temples trop étroite; & pour dégager aussi le Diptere[92] qui estoit étouffé par la confusion de deux rangs de Colonnes fort serrées, fit le Pseudodiptere, mettant en une les deux Ailes que ces deux rangs de Colonnes formoient avec le mur tout à l'entour des Temples.[93] Mais ce qu'il fit en ostant un rang de Colonnes dans chaque Aile, nous le faisons dans chaque rang en ostant une Colonne du milieu de deux autres Colonnes où elle estoit, pour la ranger contre une de ses voisines. Cette maniere pourroit estre appellée *Pseudosystyle,* par analogie au *Pseudodiptere* d'Hermogene, ou *Areosystyle* à cause que de ses Colonnes les unes sont élargies comme en l'Araeostyle,[94] les autres sont serrées comme dans le Systyle. Plusieurs desapprouvent cette maniere, comme n'estant point autorisée par les Anciens. Mais s'il est permis d'ajouster quelque chose aux inventions des Anciens à l'example des Anciens mesmes, qui, comme Hermogene, n'ont point esté blâmez pour avoir changé quelque chose en l'Architecture, & pour n'avoir pas exactement suivy tous les exemples de ceux qui les avoient precedez; on peut dire que cette nouvelle maniere n'est point à rejetter, puisqu'elle a seule tous les avantages que les autres n'ont que separément: car outre la beauté de l'aspreté & du serrement de Colonnes que les Anciens aimoient tant, elle a le dégagement que les Modernes recherchent, sans que la solidité y manque: Car les Architraves que les Anciens ne faisoient que d'une pierre qui portoit d'une Colonne à l'autre, n'étoient pas si bien affermis, ne posant que sur la moitié de la Colonne, que lorsqu'ils portent sur toute la Colonne; & les Poutres estant doublées de mesme que les Colonnes, elles ont beaucoup de force pour soustenir les Planchers.

  Cette maniere a esté pratiquée avec beaucoup de magnificence aux deux grands Portiques qui sont à la face du Louvre, où les Colonnes qui ont plus de trois piez & demy de Diametre sont jointes deux à deux, & ont leurs entrecolonnemens de douze[95] piez, estant distantes d'autant de leurs Pilastres qui sont au mur. Cela a esté fait ainsi pour garder la symmetrie en donnant un espace égal à tous les entrecolonnemens dans le reste de l'Edifice,[96] qui n'a que des Pillastres un à un, mais qui n'ont pû estre plus proches que de douze[97] piez, à cause de la largeur des Croisées, qui sont ornées de Chambranles, de Consoles & de Frontons qui demandoient cette distance entre les Pillastres; & ces grandes distances dans les Portiques n'auroient pas esté supportables si les Colonnes n'avoient esté doublées. (76–77 n. 3; for the continuation of this note in Perrault's 1684 Vitruvius edition, see below, no. 26[a].)

b. La hauteur & la grandeur de l'ordre, qui en general fait la beauté & la majesté d'un grand Edifice, doit estre reputée vicieuse, si elle n'a quelque usage par tout, comme elle en a toujours naturellement dans les Temples, les Theatres, les Portiques, les Peristyles, les grands Escalliers, les Sallons, les Vestibules & les Chapelles des Palais, qui sont des parties dont l'usage demande ou du moins souffre un aussi grand exhaussement que l'on veut. Cette regle neanmoins est negligée par les Architectes modernes, qui pour donner de grands ordres à des bastimens qui de leur nature ne souffrent pas un grand exhaussement, comme sont ceux qui sont pour l'habitation, qui ne passent point 28 ou 30 piez; se sont avisez d'enfermer deux & trois étages dans un mesme ordre; ce qui à mon sens a quelque chose de chetif & de pauvre, comme representant quelque grand Palais demi ruiné & abandonné, dans lequel des particuliers se seroient voulus loger; & qui trouvant que de grands appartemens & beaucoup exhaussez ne leur sont pas commodes, ou qui voulant menager la place y auroient fait faire des entre-solles. Ce n'est pas que cela ne puisse estre permis quelquefois dans les grands Palais; mais il faut que l'Architecte ait l'addresse de trouver un pretexte à ce grand ordre, & qu'il paroisse qu'il y a esté obligé par la symmetrie qui demande qu'un grand ordre qui est necessaire à quelque partie considerable de l'Edifice, soit continué & regne tout au tour.

Cela a été pratiqué avec beaucoup de jugement en plusieurs Edifices, mais principalement dans le Palais du Louvre, lequel estant basty sur le bord d'un grand Fleuve, qui donne un espace & un éloignement fort vaste à son aspect, avoit besoin pour ne paroistre pas chetif, d'avoir un grand ordre. Celuy que l'on luy a donné qui comprend deux étages, & qui est posé sur l'étage Terrain qui luy sert comme Piedestail, & qui est proprement le rempart du Chateau, est ainsi exhaussé à cause de deux grands & magnifiques Portiques qui regnent le long de la principale face à l'entrée du Palais, & qui estant comme pour servir de Vestibule à tous les apartemens de l'étage noble, demandoit cette grandeur & cette hauteur extraordinaire que l'on a donnée à son ordre, qu'il a fallu poursuivre & faire regner ensuite tout au tour du reste de l'Edifice: ce qui authorise ou du moins excuse l'incongruité que l'on auroit pû objecter à l'Architecte, s'il avoit fait sans necessité une chose qui de soy est sans raison, sçavoir de ne donner pas à chaque étage qui est proprement un bastiment separé, son ordre propre & separé; & de faire servir une mesme colonne à porter deux planchers, supposant qu'elle en soûtient un par maniere de dire sur sa teste, & un autre comme pendu à sa ceinture. Car la longueur de l'aspec ne peut estre toute seule une raison suffisante d'élever un bastiment, qui de sa nature doit estre bas; non plus que la grandeur d'un Theatre n'oblige point à faire ses degrez & ses ballustrades & appuis avec plus de hauteur; comme Vitruve remarque au chapitre septiéme du cinquiéme livre.[98] (204 n. 2)

13. *1673.* Louis Savot, *L'architecture françoise des bastimens particuliers,* ed. François Blondel, Paris, 1673.

[Savot]: Il n'y a personne d'aucune profession, qui puisse estre plûtost capable de l'intelligence de l'Architecture que le Medecin. (3)

[Blondel]: Cecy ne s'est jamais si bien connu qu'à present, que les plus magnifiques Ouvrages des Bastimens du Roy, se font sur les desseins de Monsieur Perrault Docteur en Medecine. (3 n. a)

(Blondel repeats his note in his 1685 edition of Savot.)

14. *July 28, 1673.* From a letter (from Paris) of Christian Huygens to Lodewijk Huygens (*Oeuvres complètes de Christiaan Huygens,* The Hague, 1897, VII, 349, no. 1966):

Je fus il y a 4 ou 5 jours a la quarriere pres de Meudon d'ou l'on avoit tiré et desià embarquè sur la riviere une pierre 52 pieds de long, 8 de large et seulement $1\frac{1}{2}$ d'epais. C'est l'une des 2 qui couvriront le frontispice du Louvre, et on est maintenant apres a la tirer du bateau qui l'a amesnée. Veu le peu de force qu'ont les pierres d'icy autour, je n'avois pas creu qu'on en seroit venu a bout; et je n'admire pas peu l'industrie du charpentier[99] qui conduit cette affaire, qu'il a si bien commencée, que je ne doute nullement qu'il n'acheve de poser les pierres ou elles doivent estre, sans aucun inconvenient. Je vous donne a deviner et au frere de Moggershill[100] comment et par quelles machines tout cela se fait.

15. *August 25, 1673.* Paul Tallemant, "Panégyrique du roi prononcé le 25 août 1673" (extract). Quoted in N. Ferrier-Cavérivière, *L'image de Louis XIV dans la littérature française de 1660 à 1715,* Paris, 1981, 62:

Quelle surprise pour lui [a Frenchman absent from France for some time and just returned] de voir le palais superbe des Rois presque achevé, cette façade du Louvre, l'attente de tout le monde depuis si longtemps, ornée d'un nombre infini de superbes colonnes.

16. *June 1674.* Le Mercure galant, June 1674, 41–42: Pendant que l'on travaille à l'embelissement de la Ville, on ne s'applique pas moins à faire quelque chose de magnifique pour le Portail du Louvre; & les deux Pierres, chacune de cinquante-deux pieds de long qui sont venuës des Carrieres de Séve en font foy; elles ont esté l'admiration de tout Paris, & il a fallu quantité de machines pour les faire venir jusques au Louvre. On n'a point veu de Pierre de longueur si prodigieuse, depuis que l'on [avait] perdu le secret que les Egyptiens avoient trouvé de fondre les Pierres.

17. *June 25, 1674.* Minutes of the Académie royale d'architecture (H. Lemonnier, ed., *Procès-verbaux de l'Académie royale d'architecture,* Paris, 1911, I, 78):
Sur la proposition faite aussy par Monsieur Perault si, dans le fronton du Louvre, on ne devoit pas suprimer les mufles de lion qui servent de gargouille dans la corniche, la compagnie l'a fort aprouvé et a jugé qu'il n'y en devoit point avoir.

18. *1676.* André Félibien, *Des principes de l'architecture, de la sculpture, de la peinture, et des autres arts qui en dependent,* Paris, 1676:
 a. M. Perrault . . . a traduit Vitruve, & donné les desseins du Louvre, de l'Arc de Triomphe [du Trône], & de l'Observatoire, par lesquels on peut assez juger quelle est sa connoissance dans l'Architecture & dans les autres Arts. (Preface, unpaginated)
 b. Les deux grandes Pierres dont l'on couvrit l'année derniere [*in the margin:* Septembre 1674] le Fronton du Louvre, ont esté tirées au dessous de Meudon, & dans la Carriere ne faisoient qu'une seule Pierre que l'on a coupée en deux, qui ont chacune cinquante-deux pieds de long, sur huit pieds de large, & dix-huit pouces d'épaisseur mise en oeuvre. Ces Pierres sont tres dures, & approchent de la nature du Liais. (68)

19. *January 22, 1676.* [Gottfried Wilhelm, Baron von Leibniz], "Le Louvre. Plans d'achèvement. Pyramide Triomphale de Perrault," *Journal de l'instruction publique et des cultes,* XXVI, 1857, 235f.:
Mons. Perrault, le medecin de l'Academie royale des sciences, auteur du Vitruve françois, m'a conté aujourd'hui (22 janvier) quantité de choses remarquables touchant le bastiment du Louvre. Mons. Colbert, ayant pris la surintendance des bastimens pour achever le Louvre, fit faire des desseins par les habiles architectes de France. Mons. de Veau, premier architecte du roy, en donna un comme pour servir de base; les autres le controlerent, firent des remarques là dessus et donnèrent leur dessein. Mons. Colbert en tira de luy meme l'essence, ayant écrit 4 feuilles d'ecriture menue de sa main pour en faire rapport au roy. Mons. Perrault, frère du medecin, qui est a present le controlleur general des bastimens et jardins de France (il y en a 4 qui servent par quartier), et qui exerce sous Mons. Colbert l'intendance des bastimens etait en ce temps connu de Mons. Colbert et prestait la plume a une Academie des belles lettres [the Petite Académie] dont Mons. Colbert était le protecteur et de la quelle estaient Monsieu[r] Chapelain scavantissime pour le grec et qui a traduit Xenophon, Mons. Charpentier et quelques autres.[101] Mons. Perrault y faisant fonction de secretaire, où l'on travaille a des medailles, devises et autres choses pour la gloire du roy, il dit a son frere le medecin pourquoy il ne faisait pas aussi quelque dessein luy qui avoit travaille longtemps a l'architecture; il s'en defendit, mais a la fin il en fit un; il desseigna d'une maniere douce et agreable bien qu'en ce temps les architectes ne desseignait pas si bien et n'achevait pas, n'y finissait pas, se contentant de leurs traits et de donner les ombres par leur marche de lavis. Mons. Perrault le controlleur ayant montré ce dessein a Mons. Colbert, il luy plut fort et Mons. le Brun qui avait méprisé tous les autres s'arresta fort a celuy-ci. Mons. Colbert demandant de qui il estoit, luy dit qu'il estoit de son frère dont Mons. Colbert demanda qu'il le vint trouver, luy montra tous les autres desseins et les lui donna avec les ecrits et avec le sien qu'il en avait tiré pour luy en dire son sentiment. Mons. Perrault fit un petit traité où il establit des maximes et une espece de systeme;[102] il remarqua les defauts de tous les desseins, et fit voir qu'il y avoit remedié avant que de voir les autres desseins. Mons. Colbert en fut fort satisfait. Et on estoit sur le point de s'y arrester. Mais il arriva une chose qui pensa renverser tout. Car Mons. Colbert considerant les fautes que tant d'architectes francais avaient fait, et qu'un médecin leur avait fait la barbe, se mit en teste qu'il fallut que sous ces gens fussent des ignorants et qu'il fallait consulter aussi des architectes étrangers. [There follows an account of Bernini's Louvre project.]
 . . . Ces Italiens estant partis, Mons. Colbert dit nous voila seuls. Comment ferons nous. On offrit a Mons. Perrault le medecin la charge de premier architecte du roy, car on n'estoit point satisfait de Mons. de Veau. Il refusa et il dit qu'il n'estoit pas architecte de profession et quil ne vouloit pas non plus abandonner toute autre chose pour l'amour de l'architecture. Il proposa qu'on establit un conseil d'architecture pour cet effet, sous la direction de Mons. Colbert dont il seroit. Cela fut fait,

Mons. Perrault Mons. le Brun et M. Veau et quelques autres en estoient. Ils ne pouvoient s'accorder sur le dessein.

Enfin Mons. de Veau abandonna le sien et consentit a celuy de Mons. Perrault de sorte qu'il n'y avait que deux qui restaient a comparer, celuy de Mons. Perrault et celuy de Mons. le Brun. On les fit desseigner tous deux par un même peintre d'une meme grandeur. Chacun donna ses raisons par escrit. Le roy (suivant le sentiment de Mons. Colbert) prefera celuy de Mons. Perrault.[103] Ayant fait examiner tous deux en plein conseil, en présence de Monsieur, frere du roy,[104] mons. le prince[105] et les conseillers d'Estat. Et c'est ce dessein sur le quel on travaille a present. Il y a le devant du Louvre; il [Claude Perrault] pensait le quarré [the Cour Carrée] dont le commencement du costé de la riviere sera l'appartement de service de la reine; sur le devant meme l'appartement de ceremonie de la reine; plus bas du costé de la rivière sera l'appartement de service du roy de sorte que l'appartement de service du roy et de la reine sont tournés vers le midi, car le roy demeure principalement a Paris l'hyver et par consequent le midy est le plus agreable en hyver. . . .

Mons. le Brun croyoit que le dessein du Louvre de M. Perrault quoique beau seroit d'une execution très difficile. Mais Mons. Perrault a trouvé un très habile entrepreneur ce me semble Preaux ou Preat[106] qui est admirablement exact, les pierres sont bien taillées, tout est avec une beauté admirable. Et le roy le voyant dit en présence de plusieurs: "si Versailles pouvoit estre basti comme cela." On remarqua que le roy estoit en quelque facon jaloux de la beauté du Louvre, car il regarde le Louvre comme le bastiment des rois de France, mais Versailles comme le sien.

20. *1677–1679.* Minutes of the Académie royale d'architecture.

a. *March 29, 1677* (Lemonnier, ed., *Procès-verbaux*, I, 137):

La compagnie a veu aussy le modèle de l'attique des pavillons du Louvre, fait par M. Perault, qu'elle a trouvé fort beau; elle a seulement un scrupule sur les espaisseurs que les murs que cet attique doit avoir, pour porter la charpente de la coupole dont il doit estre couvert, ne sçachant pas si les murs de dessoubz sont assez espais pour le soutenir, veu la retraite que la balustrade qui tourne à l'entour oblige d'y faire; c'est pour ce sujet qu'elle a remis à la prochaine assemblée à résoudre les difficultés après avoir veu les plans justes qui luy doivent estre communiquez.

b. *December 5, 1678* (ibid., I, 252–253):

Ensuite, sur ce qui lui [to the Académie] a été proposé de la part de Monseigneur Colbert sur le sujet de la couverture du Louvre, dont Monsieur Perault a donné le dessein et fait apporter le modelle à l'Académie, sur lequel la compagnie n'a pas trouvé à propos de s'estendre pour l'aprouver, après ce qu'elle a dit cy devant à l'avantage de la manière de bien bastir par Philbert de Lorme;[107] elle s'est seulement attachée à considérer la figure du trait, qu'elle a fort approuvé sur les largeurs données, observant les intervalles des courbes, selon la nécessité du poids de la couverture. Le tirant qui est posé dans le mesme modelle ne doit pas y estre considéré comme une pièce absolument nécessaire, parce que l'on peut s'en passer, parce que cet ouvrage,[108] qui ne pousse ny pèse, est particulièrement propre pour ceux de grande hauteur et de grande largeur. On a fait réflexion, dans les voûtes qu'on voudroit peindre [*sic*], il faudroit faire une double couverture ou cintre.

c. *December 12, 1678* (ibid., I, 253–255):

M. Perault a aporté, par l'ordre de Monseigneur Colbert, les desseins de l'attique et des pavillons du Louvre, conformes aux modelles qui ont desjà esté mis à l'Académie, affin de se déterminer sur le choix de l'une des deux manières qu'il propose, dont la première est de les faire en retraite sur l'espoisseur du gros mur, laissant de la place en dehors pour un passage et une balustrade, ou la 2ᵉ, de continuer l'attique sur l'alignement extérieur du mur. Sur quoy, la compagnie, après s'estre long-temps arestée sur les discutions des avantages et inconvéniens de l'une et de l'autre, s'est enfin déterminée au choix de la première manière, qu'elle a estimée plus noble et plus agréable, pourveu que l'on augmente l'exaussement de l'attique, autant qu'il est nécessaire pour réparer ce que la balustrade lui oste par l'optique, si tant est que l'on soit résolu de se servir de l'une ou de l'autre.

d. *January 23, 1679* (ibid., I, 260):

L'on a examiné les modelles du devant du Louvre, pour l'élévation des pavillons de la façade, sur ce que Monseigneur Colbert a demandé que chacun de ceux de la compagnie en donne son avis en particulier.

21. *March 9, 1679.* From a letter (from The Hague) of Philips Doublet to Christian Huygens (*Oeuvres complètes de Christiaan Huygens*, VII, 154, no. 2163):

Le projet du Louvre du Sr. Perrault[109] est effectivement tres vaste, et [torn] pourroit courir quelque risque [torn (d'estre)] arresté ainssy, a moins que ces

Messr. ayent encore autant d'ascendant sur L'esprit de Monsr. Colbert, c'est a dire du Roy, comme lors qu'on a arresté la facade du Louvre, et le grand arc de Triomphe [du Trône] qui sont de leur façon. Mais il ny a pas tousiours a faire sur le aulae culmine lubrico. et je ne scay s'ils ne sont pas supplantez depuis par quelque autre en cette matiere architectonique.

22. *December 1681. Le Mercure galant,* December 1681, 255–256:

Le Roy [after a visit to the Cabinet des Tableaux in the Louvre] ayant l'imagination toute remplie de ce que la Peinture a de plus beau, alla voir un morceau d'architecture qui si l'on en excepte la Gallerie du Louvre,[110] est le plus grand qui se trouve au monde, c'est la Façade de ce magnifique Bastiment. Il l'examina long temps, mais ce qu'il en dit ne fut entendu que de Mr Colbert, qui estoit aupres de Luy.

23. *1682.* Antoine Desgodets, *Les édifices antiques de Rome dessinés et mesurés très exactement,* Paris, 1682, 147, and pl. on 149:

La proportion du chapiteau [of the Frontispiece of Nero, Rome] est extraordinaire en ce quil est beaucoup plus haut qu'il n'a de coustume d'estre. On a donné une pareille proportion aux chapiteaux des grands portiques du devant du Louvre qui font un fort bel effet: car quoique les colonnes de ces portiques qui n'ont que trois pieds sept pouces de diametre ne soient pas si grandes que celles du Frontispice de Neron; leur position qui est à trente-trois pieds sur le rez de chaussée, supplée en quelque façon à l'énorme grandeur qui leur manque: mais sur tout cette hauteur du chapiteau reüssit fort bien dans les pillastres, qui n'ayant point de diminution par en haut comme les colonnes, font toujours paroistre leurs chapiteaux bas & écrasez. Et on a eu beaucoup d'égard à cette raison parce qu'une des principales faces du Louvre qui est celle du costé de la riviere n'est ornée que de pillastres.

24. *1683.* François Blondel, *Cours d'architecture enseigné dans l'Académie royale d'architecture,* Paris, 1683.

a. *Des Colonnes couplées.*

Pour ce qui est des Colonnes & des Pilastres que Scamozzi à mis si prés l'un de l'autre, & que l'on appelle ordinairement des Colonnes ou des Pilastres couplez ou doublez; Il est à remarquer qu'au pardessus de celles qui sont à la façade de ce Temple de Trevi,[111] celles du dedans du Temple de Bacchus aupres de Rome[112] & celles qui sont à un Arc de Triomphe que l'on voit à Pole en Dalmatie;[113] il seroit malaisé d'en trouver beaucoup d'autres dans les bâtimens Antiques. Je sçai bien que l'on en voit à Rome en une maison batie par Bramante que l'on dit avoir été construite sur le dessein des anciennes maisons des Romains;[114] Mais ces desseins-là nous sont inconnus, & je ne sçai ce qui à pu porter les Architectes du dernier siecle (que nous devons neantmoins honorer comme les Restaurateurs de l'Architecture) à introduire dans la pluspart de leurs Ouvrages cette maniere de coupler les Colonnes & les Pilastres, qui a esté si peu pratiquée dans les Edifices des Anciens, au moins dans ceux que l'on peut appeller veritablement de bon goust par l'aveu même de ces Architectes.

[*In the margin:* Il y a peu d'exemples de Colonnes ou Pilastres couplez dans l'Antique.

Ce sont les Architectes modernes qui les ont introduites.]

Bramante s'est servi de Pilastres couplez en plusieurs endroits du Vatican: Mi[c]hel Ange Bonarote en a mis au dedans & au dehors de la Tribune qui soûtient la Coupole de Saint Pierre: Sangallo en a rempli les desseins qu'il avoit faits pour Saint Pierre, aussi bien que Labaco qui estoit son éleve;[115] Et quasi tous les autres Architectes de ce Temps-là, qui ont esté suivis par une infinité de Modernes.

[*In the margin:* Bramante, Mi[c]hel Ange Bonarote, Sangallo.]

L'Architecture ne faisant alors que de renaistre, ces Grands Hommes n'ont peut-estre pas osé se deprendre tout à coup des pratiques auxquelles on étoit accoustumé depuis long-temps. Ils voioient dans les bâtimens Gothiques des groupes de Colonnes entassées prés à prés autour des Pilastres, afin que dans leur hauteur extravagante elles pussent avoir assez de force ensemble pour se soûtenir; l'on estoit tellement accoustumé à ne pas mettre de grands fardeaux sur des Colonnes solitaires & principalement aux coins des edifices, que ce n'est pas merveille que ces premiers Architectes ayent pris cet usage de coupler les Colonnes comme une espece de milieu entre les belles pratiques des Anciens & les Gothiques dont la pluspart des Ouvriers se servoient encore alors.

[*In the margin:* Ce qu'ils ont fait pour s'accomoder au goust de leur temps qui étoit encore Gothique.]

C'est à peu prés dans le même temps qu'à la faveur du Cardinal d'Armagnac,[116] plusieurs de nos Architectes François passerent en Italie pour se perfectionner dans leur Art par l'estude des plus beaux restes de l'Antiquité. Il est vray que ce peu d'exemples de Colonnes couplées qu'ils y trouverent leur plût à un poinct, qu'ils firent capital de les imiter quasi dans tous leurs Ouvrages. Du Cerceau n'eut pas plutost veu cet Arc de Triomphe qui est à Pole en Dalmatie où il y a des Colonnes couplées, qu'il fut charmé de cette singularité; il ne fut touché de la beauté d'aucun des autres; Et quoy qu'il nous ait donné des desseins de la plus part des Arcs anciens, il s'est uniquement proposé celuy de Pole pour modele de tous ceux de son invention sur tous les Ordres dont il a rempli son Livre, les faisant quasi tous avec des Pilastres ou des Colonnes couplées; Ce qu'il a encore pratiqué ailleurs.[117]

[*In the margin:* Les premiers Architectes François passez en Italie ont été admirateurs de ce peu d'exemples Antiques ou il y a des Colonnes couplées.

Du Cerceau a rempli tous ses desseins de l'idée qu'il avoit prise des Colonnes couplées de l'Arc de Pole.]

Philibert de l'Orme dans ses desseins du Louvre & particulierement à ceux de cette partie de la grande Galerie la plus proche du Pont Neuf que l'on appelle la Galerie bruslée, a par tout mis des Pilastres couplez.[118] Serlio en a remplis ses desseins.[119] Et tous ceux qui sont venus dans la suite ont pris à tasche de les imiter en ce poinct. Jean Goujon luy même, quoy qu'il eust l'exemple de son maistre l'Abbé de Clagny[120] qui n'a rien fait de semblable au vieux Louvre, n'a pas pu s'empescher de coupler ses Pilastres à la fontaine des Innocens.[121]

[*In the margin:* Philibert de l'Orme. Serlio. Jean Goujon qui n'a pas suivi l'exemple de l'Abbé de Clagny son Maist[r]e.]

Je ne dis rien de ceux qui ont travaillé sous Henry quatriéme, comme de Metezeau qui a fait le Château Neuf de Saint Germain en Laye, & qui a peut-estre donné les desseins de cette autre moitié de la grande Galerie du Louvre qui est vers les Tuileries,[122] ou de Monsieur de Brosse qui a fait le Palais d'Orleans, que l'on appelloit cy devant le Luxembourg, & le portail de Saint Gervais.[123] Car il faudroit parler de tous les Architectes bons & mauvais qui se sont meslez de bâtir à Paris depuis plus de cent ans, puisqu'il n'y en a qu'un ou deux qui ne soient pas servis de Colonnes ou de Pilastres couplez. Jamais usage n'a esté reçeu avec tant de docilité de tout le monde que celuy-là; l'on s'en est fait un goust si general que l'on ne croit pas parmy les Ouvriers qu'un bâtiment puisse avoir aucune autorité si les Colonnes ou les Pilastres ne sont couplez.

[*In the margin:* Metezeau. De Brosse. Un bâtiment dans l'opinion des Ouvriers de Paris n'a point de grace s'il n'a des Colonnes ou des Pilastres couplés.]

Ce qui est pardonnable à ceux qui n'ont point vu d'autres Exemples: Mais il y a sujet de s'estonner que tant de beaux Genies qui professent l'Architecture aient fait voyage à Rome & ailleurs, sans s'etre depris de ces pratiques; & que la preoccupation des usages de Paris, dont ils n'ont trouvé que trop d'exemples dans les ouvrages modernes d'Italie, les ait empesché de gouter ces proportions admirables qui se rencontrent dans les Colonnes des edifices anciens entre leurs hauteurs, leurs grosseurs & leurs Entre-colonnes; dont les distances sont si judicieusement compassées, qu'ils ne sçauroient jamais plaire comme ils font, si elles estoient disposées dans d'autres mesures. Je m'estonne, dis-je, qu'ils n'ayent pas veu la difference qu'il y a entre ces restes qui ont l'approbation universelle, & ces bâtimens demi Gothiques ou les Anciens ont couplé des Colonnes ou des Pilastres.

[*In the margin:* Les belles proportions que nos Architectes ont vües dans les Ouvrages Antiques en Italie, n'ont pû les deprendre de la preoccupation des usages de Paris pour les Colonnes couplées.]

Les plus modestes de nos Architectes ne les ont couplez que pour fortifier les encognures de leurs edifices; En quoy ils sont aucunement excusables ayant, outre cette raison de la force qu'ils pretendent par ce moyen ajoûter à cette partie du bâtiment qui en a le plus de besoin, celle de l'exemple de l'Antique. Car c'est sur ce fondement que les Architectes de l'Arc de Pole[124] & du Temple de Trevi[125] ont couplé leurs Colonnes ou leurs Pilastres angulaires.

[*In the margin:* Les plus modestes, ne les ont couplées que pour fortifier les encognures.

A l'exemple de l'Arc de Pole & du Temple de Trevi.]

Palladio qui d'ailleurs imite avec beaucoup de soin les belles pratiques des Anciens, s'est aussi servi de Pilastres couplez dans les angles de quelques bâtimens dont il a donné les desseins: Scamozzi a fait la même chose; Mais ni l'un ny l'autre n'en ont jamais couplé ailleurs qu'aux encognures.[126]

[*In the margin:* Palladio & Scamozzi en ont fait de même, mais jamais hors des encognûres.]

Ainsi j'ay dit que cet usage étoit excusable en quelque maniere, ne voyant pas qu'il fust absolument à suivre; ces exemples de l'Antique n'ont pas comme je pense assez d'autorité pour leur donner cours. L'arc de Pole ne passe point pour estre sans deffauts, & le Temple de Trevi a des ornemens qui font voir qu'il a esté bâti dans les temps ou l'Architecture étoit des-ja fort déchüe.[127]

[*In the margin:* Les exemples de l'Antique qui ont des Colonnes couplées n'ont pas assez d'autorité pour leur donner cours.]

Pour ce qui est de la force que l'on pretend adjoûter par ce moyen dans les encognures, il me semble que les Anciens qui sçavoient si bien bâtir, n'ont pas crû qu'il fust necessaire de coupler les Colonnes pour les fortifier; au moins voyons nous qu'aux bouts des murs de leurs Temples, qu'ils appellent les murs de la Celle, ils se sont toûjours contentez ou d'une Colonne ou d'un Pilastre repondant aux Colonnes du Portique & faisant front aux faces du dedans de l'avant-nef & de l'aile. Il ne faut que voir le Portique du Pantheon, ce qui s'est fait au Temple de la Fortune Virile, à celuy de la Concorde, à celuy d'Antonin & de Faustine,[128] & à tous les autres. Et quand Vitruve enseigne qu'il faut augmenter les Colonnes angulaires d'un Portique de la cinquantiéme partie de leur diametre,[129] il ne dit pas que ce soit pour les fortifier, mais bien pour les faire paroistre égales à celles du milieu, pretendant leur rendre, par cette augmentation, la partie de leur grosseur que le grand air qui les environne nous peut derober à la veüe.

[*In the margin:* Les Anciens n'ont pas crû que les Colonnes couplées fussent necessaires pour fortifier les encognures.]

Nous n'avons donc aucun exemple ou les Anciens ayent jamais couplé les Colonnes de leurs Portiques dans les angles, & bien moins encore dans la file de celles du milieu. Les Colonnes qui sont au dedans du Temple de Bacchus auprés de Rome,[130] quoy que l'Architecture n'en soit pas fort estimée, ne sont pourtant point couplées dans la file du Peristyle, mais bien au dedans & sur l'étendue de chacun des flancs des lunettes dont elles portent les Arcs.

[*In the margin:* Il ny a point d'exemple Antique ou les Colonnes soit couplées dans la file.

Les Colonnes du dedans du Temple de Bacchus ne sont point couplées dans la file du Peristyle: mais seulement sur les flancs des lunettes dont elles portent les Arcs.]

Car c'est un Temple rond qui a dans le milieu une tribune couverte de sa coupole, & un berceau tournant en forme d'aile au tour de ce milieu. Ces deux parties du Temple sont separées l'une de l'autre par un Periptere diptere ou distique, c'est à dire par deux files de Colonnes portant des Arcs qui forment les Lunettes lesquelles aboutissent de part & d'autre dans les deux voutes; Les retombées de ces Lunettes ont beaucoup de longueur sur leur flanc, & comme elles sont appuyées sur l'entablement du Peristyle double du milieu qui luy sert d'imposte ou de coussinet, l'Architecte a esté obligé de le faire soûtenir par deux Colonnes: Ainsi estant posées de deux en deux sur le flanc, elles forment ce periptere distique de deux files de Peristyles ronds, élognez seulement l'un de l'autre de la grandeur du diametre de la Colonne. Cet entablement est coupé par les bouts sur les deux Colonnes, & les voussoirs des lunettes qui portent dessus comme sur une imposte ont quatre testes dont les deux qui sont sur la longueur de l'entablement font les naissances des lunettes; & des deux autres, l'une rachete le rond de la tribune du milieu, & l'autre rachete le berceau tournant de l'aile. Ainsi l'on ne peut tirer aucune consequence raisonnable de cet exemple pour autoriser les Colonnes couplées dans les Peristyles, puisque celles-cy ne le sont point dans leur file, ou au contraire elles sont éloignées l'une de l'autre de la largeur de l'Arc qui forme les Lunettes, mais elles le sont seulement dans la distance qui est entre les deux files.

Pour ce qui est des Pilastres que l'on engage en partie dans les murs, s'ils ne sont, ainsi que quelques uns croient, que les extremitez des murs, je ne vois point quelle raison l'on peut avoir de les coupler sur les coins? à moins que l'on ne veuille faire entendre que les murs auxquels ils repondent sont aussi couplez prés à prés au dedans de l'edifice. Car il faut tomber d'accord que les Pilastres angulaires doivent toûjours repondre au milieu de l'epaisseur du mur de l'aile; Ainsi lorsque la largeur du Pilastre est égale à cette epaisseur, il fait front & sur le coin & sur les deux faces du mur: Mais si la largeur est moindre, il laisse des alettes à droite & à gauche, & ne faisant front que d'un costé, il faut encore un Pilastre à même distance dans l'autre pour faire front à l'autre face, & le coin de retour est occupé par les deux alettes lesquelles representent la largeur de la pile qui termine les deux murs. Où l'on voit qu'en l'un & en l'autre de ces deux cas un Pilastre couplé prés de celuy de l'encognure ne peut aucunement servir à la fortifier.

[*In the margin:* Il n'y a point de raison de coupler les Pilastres, s'ils ne sont que les bouts des murs.

Le Pilastre angulaire doit repondre au milieu de l'epaisseur du mur de l'aisle.]

S'il arrive que la Pile qui repond au mur de l'aile ait beaucoup d'épaisseur & que le Pilastre qui y doit être adossé ait si peu de largeur qu'il y paroisse trop petit entre deux aletes; il seroit en ce cas pardonnable de remplir cette épaisseur par deux Pilastres l'un prés de l'aut[r]e, à l'exemple du Temple de Trevi[131] dont l'Architecte à couplé une Colonne avec un Pilastre dans les Portiques des ailes, pour les faire repondre à l'épaisseur du mur de l'avant-nef.

[*In the margin:* Il y a une Colonne couplée avec un Pilastre dans le portique des ailes du Temple de Trevi pour repondre à l'ép[ai]sseur du mur.] (II, 228–232 [part III, book I, chap. x])

b. *Suitte de la Doctrine des Colonnes couplées.*

Au reste quoy que cet usage ait été introduit purement par le hazard, ceux qui s'en servent ont neantmoins cherché des raisons pour l'autoriser; ils disent donc qu'un architrave est mieux soûtenu par deux Colonnes que par une;[132] Ce qui nest pas veritable en tout sens & qui merite d'estre soigneusement examiné.

[*In the margin:* Il n'est pas toûjours vrai qu'un architrave soit mieux soutenu de deux Colonnes que d'une.]

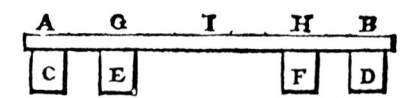

Soit donc par exemple une longueur d'architrave A B, soûtenue en ses extremitez par les deux Colonnes ou pilastres C & D: Il est premierement constant que si entre ces deux extremes vous mettez deux autres Colonnes comme E & F qui diminuent la portée de l'architrave A B & le reduisent à un Entre-Colonne plus étroit comme G H; cet architrave en ce cas sera mieux soûtenu par les quatre Colonnes que par les deux seulement, & qu'il ne se rompra pas si tost dans son milieu I. Mais supposé que le même architrave soit soutenu aux deux points G & H par les Colonnes E & F, si nous venons à y en joindre d'autres en dehors comme C & D en A & B; je ne vois pas que l'architrave en soit en ce cas beaucoup mieux soutenu par quatre que par deux Colonnes, la portée dans l'Entre-colonne G H étant toujours la même. Et les deux Colonnes ajoûtées ne servent à rien, ou si l'on veut qu'elles servent à quelque chose, c'est tout au plus à soûtenir la moitié de la partie de l'architrave comme G A ou H B, qui est en dehors de l'Entre-Colonne: Ce qui n'est point considerable. Car en un mot la force ou la foiblesse de l'architrave depend entierement de la longueur par laquelle il n'est point soutenu, c'est à dire de la la[r]geur de l'Entre-colonne. Et il luy est indifferent que ses Entre-colonnes soient faits par des Colonnes ou doubles ou simples.

[*In the margin:* Cas où un architrave n'est pas mieux soutenu de quatre Colonnes que de deux.

La foiblesse de l'architrave depend de la largeur de l'entre-colonne.]

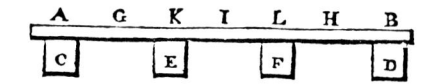

Maintenant si nous voulons nous servir des quatre Colonnes pour soutenir l'architrave A B, il est aisé de comprendre qu'il est bien plus naturel de les disposer en distances égales laissant les deux C & D aux deux extremes A & B, & mettant les deux autres E & F au points K & L, plustost qu'aux poincts G & H. Car par ce moyen le poids de tout l'architrave sera bien plus également distribué sur ses appuis, & la portée de l'architrave K L, entre les Colonnes E & F, étant moindre que la longueur G H, il s'en soûtiendra beaucoup mieux.

[*In the margin:* Quatre Colonnes ne soutiennent jamais mieux un architrave que lorsqu'elles sont en distances egales.]

Ce qui fait que l'on se trompe si facilement dans cette maniere de raisonner, c'est que l'on voit qu'une piece de bois comme une solive par exemple A B, est portée plus facilement par quatre hommes aux poincts A C H B, que par deux seulement en quelque endroits qu'ils se mettent. Mais il faut ici prendre garde qu'il y a bien de la difference entre des hommes, qui se haussent & qui se baissent pour chercher l'égalité de leurs charges, & des Colonnes qui sont toûjours dans une méme rigidité. Car ceux qui portent des fardeaux s'accommodent entre-eux de maniere qu'ils en soûtiennent chacun une égale portion; Ainsi dans le cas present si les deux hommes qui portent en C, & en H se trouvent trop chargés de la grande portée de la solive qui est entre eux, ils ont le soin de se soulager en se baissant afin qu'une partie de leur charge passe sur ceux qui sont en A & en B, lesquels autrement ne porteroient rien du tout. C'est pour le même sujet que lorsqu'ils s'entendent bien, ils placent les plus petits d'entr'eux en C & en H, & les plus grands en A & en B; ils ne se mettent même jamais en C & en H, qu'ils n'y soient obligez par quelque raison; Car quand ils sont en liberté de se placer ou ils veulent, vous voyez qu'ils s'en vont naturellement se disposer aux endroits où ils souffrent le moins, c'est à dire aux poincts A K L B, & où les distances sont égales.

[*In the margin:* Il y a bien de la difference entre des hommes qui se haussent & baissent pour chercher l'égalité de leurs charges & des Colonnes qui sont toûjours dans une même rigidité.

Les hommes qui portent un fardeau vont naturellement chercher les endroits où ils souffrent le moins, quand ils ont la liberté de le faire.]

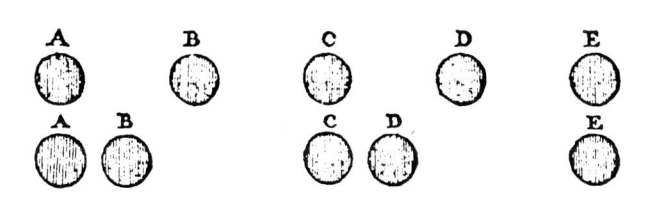

Voicy encore une raison que Mr Peraut rapporte dans ses doctes Commentaires sur Vitruve en faveur des Colonnes couplées des Peristyles, laquelle a beaucoup de subtilité. Il dit qu'outre les cinq especes d'Entrecolonnes qui sont rapportées par Vitruve, on en a inventé une sixième pour satisfaire au goust de nostre Nation qui ayme le jour & les degagemens, quoy qu'en cela il tienne peut-estre un peu du Gothique & qu'il soit fort different du goust des Anciens qui ont toûjours estimé les Entre-colonnes serrez. Cette sixième maniere met donc les Colonnes deux à deux, & l'espace de deux Entre-colonnes ordinaires en un, comme au Systyle A B C D E; elle ôte la Colonne B pour la joindre auprés de la Colonne A, & la Colonne D pour la placer auprés de la Colonne C; & ainsi des deux Entre-colonnes elle n'en fait qu'un seul B C. Ce qu'elle fait, dit-il, à l'imitation d'Hermogene qui au rapport de Vitruve, a ôté le rang des Colonnes interieures du Diptere pour en faire le Pseudodiptere. Car icy l'on oste une Colonne du milieu des deux autres dans chaque rang pour la joindre à une de ses voisines. Ce que l'on peut appeler Pseudosystyle ou Araeosystyle.

[*In the margin:* Raisons pour les Colonnes couplées.

Les Colonnes couplées font une sixième espece d'Entre-colonnes Inventées pour satisfaire au goust de nostre Nation qui ayme le jour & les degagemens.

Qui met les Colonnes deux à deux & l'espace de deux Entre-colonnes en un.

A l'imitation du Pseudodiptere d'Hermogene.

On peut l'appeler Pseudosystyle.]

Qu'il est vray que cecy n'est point authorisé des Anciens, mais qu'il ne nous doit pas estre moins permis d'ajoûter à leurs inventions, qu'il à esté permis à Hermogene de changer celles des Architectes qui l'avoient precedé. D'autant plus que cette espece d'Entre-colonnes à seule tous les avantages que les autres n'ont que separement; Car outre la beauté du serrement ou de l'apreté des Colonnes que les Anciens ont tant estimée, elle a le dégagement que les Modernes recherchent, sans rien oster de la solidité: Car les architraves qui dans les autres especes d'Entrecolonnes ne portent que sur la moitié d'une Colonne portent ici sur la Colonne entiere, outre que les planchers en sont plus forts si les poutres sont doublées comme les Colonnes.

[*In the margin:* Dont on a eu autant de droit d'introduire l'usage qu'Hermogene en a eu pour son Pseudodiptere.

Cette espece a seule les avantages que les autres n'ont que separement, c'est à dire le serrement des Colonnes estimé des Anciens, & le degagement cherché par les modernes: sans rien oster de la solidité.]

Voila à peu prés ce que l'on voit dans sa notte sur le deuxième Chapitre du troisième Livre de Vitruve, en faveur de cette pratique.[133] Sur quoy me servant de la liberté Academique que nous avons de disputer sur les choses douteuses, je dis premierement que cet exemple d'Hermogene serviroit infiniment à autoriser cet usage, si cet Architecte s'estoit contenté de changer de place le rang interieur des Colonnes du Diptere & de l'approcher auprés de l'exterieur, sans l'oster entierement, comme il a fait; Car on pourroit, à son imitation, raisonnablement faire changer de place aux Colonnes du milieu dans chaque rang d'un Systyle & la raprocher chacune auprés de sa voisine. Mais comme Hermogene, pour faire le Pseudodiptere, ôte absolument le rang interieur du Diptere sans rien ajoûter à celuy de dehors: il semble que pour faire un Pseudosystyle à son exemple, il faudroit ôter absolument une Colonne entre deux autres du Systyle sans les ajoûter à celles qui restent; Car par ce moyen les Colonnes y demeureroient solitaires comme le rang exterieur dans le Pseudodiptere, & tout le changement du Pseudosystyle se feroit aux Entrecolonnes, comme il ne se fait au Pseudodiptere qu'en la distance qu'il y a entre le rang exterieur & le mur de la Celle. Ou l'on voit qu'en toutes manieres il n'y a point de rapport entre l'exemple d'Hermogene & l'usage de coupler les Colonnes.

[*In the margin:* Reponse à ces raisons.

Comme Hermogene à osté le rang interieur du Diptere pour faire le Pseudodiptere. Il faudroit pour le bien imiter, que l'on ôtast une Colonne entre deux autres du Systyle pour en faire un Pseudosystyle.]

Je n'ay rien à dire sur cette amour que l'on attribue à nostre Nation pour le jour & les degagemens, puisqu'on avoüe en même temps qu'il tient encore du Gothique, & qu'il est en cela fo[r]t different du goust des Anciens; & sur ce qu'on dit qu'il nous doit étre aussibien permis d'ajouter aux inventions des Anciens, comme il a esté permis à Hermogene d'ajoûter aux pratiques de ceux qui l'avoient precedé; je repons qu'il n'y a rien de plus vray; C'est sans doute aux Hermogenes de produire hardiment leurs pensées nouvelles dans tous les siecles, ils sont en droit de corriger les deffauts des autres, & leurs inventions doivent passer pour regles infaillibles à la posterité.

[*In the margin:* Les Hermogenes peuvent hardiment produire leurs pensées nouvelles en tout temps.]

Il est pourtant tres veritable que c'est ce même raisonnement qui a ouvert la porte de tout temps au dereglement qui se trouve dans l'Architecture & dans les autres Arts. Nous n'avons presque point d'Ouvriers qui n'ayent assez bonne opinion d'eux mêmes & qui ne croient avoir autant de capacité qu'Hermogene; Les Architectes Goths n'ont rempli leurs edifices de tant d'impertinences, que parce qu'ils ont cru qu'il leur étoit permis d'ajoûter aux inventions des Grecs & des Romains; Et ces cartouches ridicules, ces grotesques bi[z]earres, & ces ornemens extravagans qui plaisent encore tant aux Architectes Allemans, joints au grand mepris qu'ils ont pour les mesures legitimes des parties de l'Architecture, ne viennent que de ce qu'ils sont persuadez qu'ils ont autant de droit de produire des nouveautez & d'ajoûter aux pratiques des Anciens, que les Anciens ont eü de produire les leurs & d'ajoûter à celles qui avoient esté produites par les Architectes qui les avoient devancés. Ce qui me feroit prononcer hardiment qu'il faut de necessité s'assujetir à certaines regles & arreter le caprice, si l'on veut retablir la belle Architecture; Si ce raisonnement n'avoit pas esté traité plus au long dans un autre lieu.

[*In the margin:* Mais comme il y a peu d'Ouvriers qui ne s'estime autant qu'Hermogene, Il ne faut pas s'estonner si l'on voit de si beaux fruits de cette licence. Il faut de necessité s'assujetir à certaines regles & arreter le caprice si l'on veut retablir la belle Architecture.]

Je reviens au Pseudosystyle qui a, comme on dit, luy seul tous les avantages que les autres especes d'Entre-colonnes n'ont que separement; Car il a le serrement, ou comme dit Vitruve, l'apreté des Entre-colonnes[134] que les Anciens ont tant estimée, & les degagements quoy que Gothiques, que les Modernes recherchent. A quoy j'adjoute seulement qu'il a aussi luy seul tous les desavantages que les especes, qui sont rebutées par Vitruve,[135] n'ont que separement; Car il a non seulement les incommoditez des Colonnes serrées qui font que Vitruve condamne les Pycnostyles & méme les Systyles, mais il les a d'autant plus grandes que les Colonnes dans le Pseudosystyle sont infiniment plus serrées qu'au Pycnostyle. Et il a encore les deffauts des Colonnes trop élognées qui font blamer l'Araeostyle à Vitruve.

[*In the margin:* Les Colonnes couples outre le serrement des Entrecolonnes prisé par les Anciens & les degagemens, quoy que Gotiques, recherchez par les Modernes; ont aussi seules les des-avantages des autres especes rebutées par Vitruve.]

Au reste je ne comprens pas bien la force de la raison que l'on apporte pour persuader que la solidité dans les grands intervalles du Pseudosystyle n'est pas diminuée parce, dit-on, que dans les autres especes, les architraves ne portent que sur la moitié d'une Colonne, au lieu que dans celle-cy ils portent sur la Colonne entiere. Car j'avois jusqu'icy cru qu'un architrave de quelque matiere qu'il pust estre, devoit plier & s'abaisser tant soit peu avant que de rompre à l'endroit où il se trouvoit plus chargé; c'est à dire sur le milieu du vuide de l'Entre-colonne. Comme si nous supposons que l'architrave d'une seule piece A C B, soutenu sur quatre Colonnes D E F G, ait trop de charge; il m'a toûjours semblé qu'ayant a se rompre, ce devoit être vers le milieu C, supposé la matiere par tout égale, & qu'il devoit s'affaisser en cet endroit, quoy que cela se fist imperceptiblement, avant que d'eclater. Or pour peu qu'il s'abaisse dans le milieu, il est constant qu'il s'eleve par les deux bouts A & B; à moins qu'il ne soit arresté par la trop grande charge; auquel cas il commencera des les points H & I, à s'affaisser c'est à dire sur les coins des Colonnes interieures, lesquels en toutes manieres auront tout le poids de l'architrave à soutenir, & les Colonnes extremes D & E ne porteront rien, ou tout au plus elles ne seront chargées que de la moitié des parties de l'architrave A H & I B. Et je m'estois d'autant plus confirmé dans ce sentiment que dans les Ouvrages antiques la plus part des chapiteaux sont éclatez à l'endroit des costez interieurs de leur abaque. Ce qui m'a toujours fait croire qu'un architrave n'estoit pas moins soutenu portant sur le milieu seulement d'une Colonne que lorsqu'il portoit sur toute sa largeur.

[*In the margin:* Il est faux de dire que la solidité n'y est pas diminuée.

Un architrave de quelque matiere qu'il soit plie avant que de rompre sur le milieu de l'Entre-colonne où il est le plus chargé.

La pluspart des chapiteaux antiques sont rompus au droit des costez interieurs de leur abaque.]

L'on peut dire sur le même sujet que dans les Peristyles à Colonnes doublées les bouts des architraves portent à faux, ce qui est desagreable & contre les regles de la bonne Architecture; Car les deux architraves A B & B C qui portent chacun sur deux Colonnes D E & F G, ont leur joint B dans le milieu de l'entrecolonne E F, où il porte sur le vuide & n'est soutenu de rien. Ce qui n'arrive point aux entrecolonnes ordinaires, où les joints B & C des trois architraves A B, B C, C D, portent sur le milieu des Colonnes F & G.

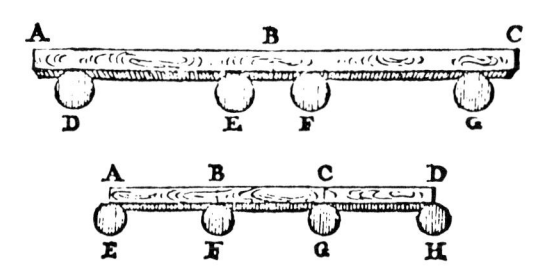

[*In the margin:* Aux Perystyles à Colon[n]es couplées les bouts des architraves portent à faux.]

Je ne crois pas au reste qu'il soit fort necessaire de répondre à ce que l'on ajoute que les planchers sont plus forts si les poutres sont doublées, comme les Colonnes, apres ce que j'ay dit des architraves, puisque tout le raisonnement que j'ay fait sur leur force se peut appliquer à celle des planchers, dont la solidité depend de la longueur des solives, c'est à dire de la largeur des travées qui sont entre deux poutres, comme celle des architraves depend de la largeur des entrecolonnes; Et comme il est indifferent aux architraves que les entrecolonnes soient terminées par des Colonnes couplées, de même il importe peu pour la solidité des solives que les travées ou les intervalles entre les poutres soient terminez par des poutres doublées.

[*In the margin:* La solidité des planchers depend de la longueur des solives, c'est à dire de la portée des travées.]

C'est, comme je crois, pour ne pas tomber dans les inconveniens que j'ay rapportez cy-devant, que les Architectes avoient évité jusques icy de faire des Peristyles isolez à Colonnes couplées, car tous ceux que nous voyons sont faits avec des Pilastres ou des Colonnes engagées, afin que les architraves fussent en partie soutenus dans le mur. Il n'y en a qu'un seul au monde, au moins que je sçache, & qui est pourtant tres-considerable. Il s'est fait depuis peu dans Paris, & c'est où l'on dit que l'on a heureusement suivi l'exemple d'Hermogene. Il est pourtant vray que l'on n'y a pas eu toute la confiance que l'on devoit avoir à sa solidité, aprés avoir si bien assuré qu'elle n'y estoit point diminuée: Car le fer n'y a point esté épargné pour aider à soutenir & à arrester les architraves dans leur grande portée.

[*In the margin:* L'on n'avoit point vu jusqu'icy des Peristyles isolez à Colonne[s] couplées.

Le fer n'a point esté épargné au Peristyle du Louvre.]

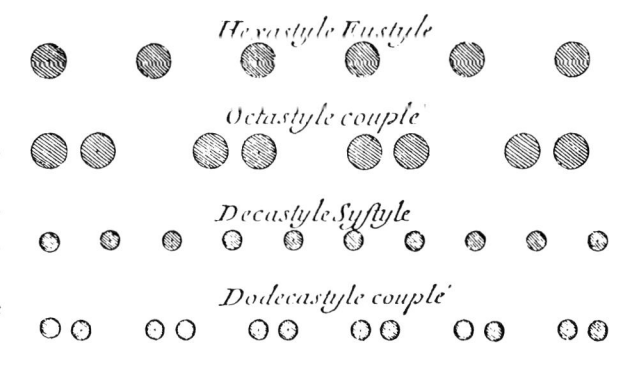

Mais pour retourner à nôtre sujet, encore que je n'estime pas que l'augmentation de la depense doive arrester un Architecte lorsqu'il s'agit de faire mieux, il me semble néanmoins qu'il y doit faire consideration quand on peut egalement bien faire. Et sur ce propos je diray que c'est augmenter notablement & assez inutilement la depense que de doubler les Colonnes, par le moyen desquelles on ne sçauroit par exemple occuper à moins de huit Colonnes la largeur d'une façade Hexastyle de Vitruve, ny un Decastyle à moins de douze Colonnes, & ainsi du reste.

[*In the margin:* L'on ne peut occuper une façade Hexastyle de Vitruve à moins de huit Colonnes couplées, ny un Decastyle à moins de douze.] (II, 232–237 [part III, book I, chap. XI])

c. J'oubliois à dire que l'usage de doubler les Colonnes altere extremement les belles proportions des edifices, dont elles augmentent tellement la largeur, qu'ils en paroissent nains & ecrasez, quelque soin que l'on prenne de les elever ou par des attiques[136] ou autrement. Ces manieres plattes que Vitruve appelle Barices ou Barycephales[137] estant absolument contraires au bon goust des Anciens, qui estoient, comme dit Vitruve, *gracilioribus modulis delectati,*[138] c'est à dire qui prenoient grand plaisir aux manieres *suelte* & degagées; Mais je n'en ay que trop dit sur ce sujet. (II, 240 [part III, book I, chap. XII])

d. Nous pouvons icy remarquer en passant sur le sujet des Peristyles Isolez que dans les exemples de l'Antique que nous avons, il ne paroist pas qu'ils ayent posé des Colonnes Isolées dans des seconds étages,[139] à moins qu'il n'y en eust d'autres aussi Isolées dans les premiers; Ceux même que l'on voit dans les bâtimens Modernes sont tres rares.

[*In the margin:* Lon ne voit point de Colonnes Antiques Isolées dans des seconds étages s'il n'y en a d'Isolées dans le premier.] (II, 253 [part III, book II, chap. V])

e. *Des Plattes-bandes.*

Les Plattes-bandes que l'on fait servir pour linteaux aux Portes & aux Fenestres, & pour architraves aux Colonnes isolées, (qui se soutiennent d'elles-mêmes parce qu'elles sont faites de claveaux ou voussoirs, c'est à dire de quartiers de pierre de taille coupez par joints tendans à un même centre,) peuvent aussi estre rapportez aux Arcades, quoiqu'elles soient de niveau & sans rondeur. Toute leur force consiste en la couppe de leurs claveaux, & le plus souvent on prend pour centre des lignes de leurs joints de teste, le sommet d'un triangle équilateral renversé, dont la base est la largeur de l'ouverture sur qui la Platte-bande est assise. Le nombre des claveaux doit estre impair comme celuy des voussoirs des Arcs, afin qu'il y en ait un dans le milieu qui serve de clef. Il est aussi necessaire quand ils ont un peu de portée de les soulager par des Arcs de decharge bâtis au dessus, qui rejettent en dehors la plus grande partie du poids du massif, & l'appuyent sur le fort des piedroits. L'on y met même souvent des barres de fer pour les fortifier, mais cette precaution n'est pas pour les rendre de longue durée, car le fer ronge la pierre & la fait rompre avec le temps. Nous n'avons point d'exemples de Plattes-bandes dans les Ouvrages antiques, quoiqu'il soit à presumer qu'elles fussent aussibien en usage parmy les Anciens que parmy nous. Ce qui nous peut faire conoître que cette maniere de bâtir a de soy par trop de foiblesse pour pouvoir subsister pendant plusieurs Siecles. (III, 434 [part IV, book VI, chap. XIV])

25. *1683.* Claude Perrault, *Ordonnance des cinq espèces de colonnes selon la méthode des anciens,* Paris, 1683.

a. L'imitation de la Nature, ny la raison, ny le bon sens ne sont donc point le fondement de ces beautez, qu'on croit voir dans la proportion, dans la disposition, & dans l'arrangement des parties d'une colonne; & il n'est pas possible de trouver d'autre cause de l'agrément, qu'on y trouve, que l'accoûtumance. De maniere que ceux qui les premiers ont inventé ces proportions, n'ayant gueres eu d'autre regle que leur fantaisie, à mesure que cette fantaisie a changé, on a introduit de nouvelles proportions qui ont aussi plû à leur tour. Ainsi la proportion du Chapiteau Corinthien, qui a esté trouvée belle par les Grecs, n'a pas esté approuvée chez les Romains, les premiers luy ayant donné la hauteur seulement du diametre de la colonne, & les derniers y ayant adjousté une sixiéme partie. Je sçay bien que l'on peut dire, que quand les Romains ont augmenté la hauteur de ce Chapiteau, ils l'ont fait avec raison, parce que cette hauteur donne lieu à rendre le contour des caulicoles & des volutes plus agreable; ce qui ne se pouvoit faire, le chapiteau estant court & large. Et c'est par cette raison que l'on a fait les chapiteaux des grandes colonnes, qui sont à la face du Louvre, encore plus hauts que ceux du Pantheon, à l'exemple de Michel-Ange, qui dans le Capitole les a encore faits plus hauts qu'ils ne sont au Louvre.[140] Mais cela ne fait rien voir autre chose sinon que le goust des Architectes qui ont approuvé ou approuvent encore la proportion que les Grecs donnoient à leurs chapiteaux Corinthiens, doit estre fondé sur quelque autre principe que sur celuy d'une beauté positive, convaicante, & aimable par elle-mesme, qui soit dans la chose comme telle, c'est-à-dire comme ayant cette proportion; & qu'il est difficile de trouver une autre raison de ce goust, que la Prevention & l'accoûtumance. A la verité, cette prevention, ainsi qu'il a esté dit, est fondée sur une infinité de beautez convaicantes, positives & raisonnables, lesquelles se rencontrant dans un ouvrage avec cette proportion, ont pû rendre l'ouvrage si beau, sans que la proportion ait rien contribué à cette beauté, que l'amour raisonnable que l'on a pour l'ouvrage entier, a fait aussi aimer separement toutes les parties qui le composent. (x–xi)

b. From Chapter VIII: De quelques autres abus introduits dans l'Architecture moderne.

Le troisiéme abus est l'accouplement des Colonnes que quelques-uns ne peuvent approuver parce qu'il n'a presque point d'exemples dans l'Antique. Mais la verité est, que s'il est permis d'adjouster quelque chose aux inventions des anciens, cette invention merite d'estre reçûë dans l'Architecture comme ayant une beauté & une commodité considerable. Pour ce qui est de la beauté elle est tout à fait selon le goust des Anciens, qui aimoient sur tout les genres d'édifices où les Colonnes estoient serrées, & ils n'y trouvoient rien à redire que l'incommodité que causoit ce serrement de la maniere qu'ils le faisoient: car cette incommodité les obligea d'élargir les entrecolonnemens du milieu, & fut aussi cause qu'Hermogene inventa le Pseudodiptere, pour élargir les ailes ou galeries aux Portiques des Temples appellez Dipteres, parce que les ailes y estoient doubles ayant deux rangs de Colonnes, lesquelles avec le mur du Temple, formoient deux galeries par le dehors. Or ce sçavant Architecte l'un des premiers inventeurs de l'Architecture ancienne, s'avisa d'oster le rang de Colonnes qui estoient au milieu, & de deux galeries étroites, il en fit une qui avoit la largeur des deux ensemble, & de plus celle d'une Colonne. A l'exemple d'Hermogene, les Modernes ont introduit cette nouvelle maniere de placer les Colonnes, & ont trouvé le moyen en les accouplant de donner plus de dégagement aux Portiques & plus de grace aux Ordres: car mettant les Colonnes deux à deux, on peut tenir les entrecolonnemens assez larges, pour faire que les portes & les fenestres qui donnent sur les Portiques, ne soient pas offusquées[141] comme elles estoient chez les Anciens, où ces ouvertures avoient plus de largeur que les entrecolonnemens; car alors dans les manieres les plus ordinaires de disposer les Colonnes, il estoit necessaire pour avoir un entrecolonnement de huit piés, que les Colonnes eussent quatre à cinq piés de diametre; au lieu qu'accouplant les Colonnes, c'est assez qu'elles ayent deux ou deux piés & demy de diametre: & par ce moyen les entrecolonnemens larges n'ont point mauvaise grace comme ils auroient, si les Colonnes estoient une à une, qui paroistroient en cet état trop foibles & incapables de soûtenir la longueur que l'Ent[a]blement a d'une Colonne à l'autre au droit de l'entrecolonnement.

Cette maniere de placer les Colonnes peut estre considerée comme un sixiéme genre ajousté aux cinq qui estoient en usage parmy les Anciens. . . . Or on peut dire que ce sixiéme adjousté, est composé des deux genres extrémes: sçavoir du Pycnostyle où les Colonnes sont beaucoup serrées, & de l'Araeostyle, où elles sont beaucoup écartées; & que cette disposition de Colonnes qui ne peut passer pour abusive que parce que les Anciens ne l'ont point pratiquée, peut estre mise au nombre de plusieurs autres choses de mesme nature que l'usage a autorisées. (115–116)

c. From Chapter VIII: De quelques autres abus introduits dans l'Architecture moderne.

Le sixiéme abus est de faire un grand Ordre, comprenant plusieurs étages, au lieu de donner un Ordre à chaque étage, ainsi que faisoient les Anciens: & il y a apparence que cette licence est fondée sur l'imitation des Cours des Anciens appellées *Cava aedium*, & principalement de celles qu'ils nommoient Corinthiennes,[142] où l'Entablement des bastimens qui les entouroient estoient soûtenuës par des Colonnes qui alloient depuis le bas jusqu'au haut, & comprenoient plusieurs étages; la difference qui estoit entre ces Cours Corinthiennes & nos bastimens à grand Ordre, estant seulement en ce que les Colonnes aux Cours Corinthiennes estoient quelque peu éloignées du mur, pour soûtenir la Saillie de l'Entablement qui servoit comme d'auvent, & que nos Colonnes sont à demy engagées dans le mur, & que mesme le plus souvent au lieu de Colonnes nous ne mettons que des Pillastres. Or, l'abus est dans l'affectation d'un grand Ordre, qui ne convient pas à toutes sortes d'Edifices; parce que de mesme qu'un grand Ordre fait la majesté des Temples, des Theatres, des Portiques, des Peristyles, des Salons, des Vestibules, des Chapelles & des autres bastimens qui souffrent, ou mesme qui demandent un grand exhaussement; on peut dire que cette maniere d'enfermer plusieurs étages dans un grand Ordre, a tout au contraire quelque chose de chetif & de pauvre, comme representant un grand Palais demy ruiné & abandonné, dans lequel des particuliers se seroient voulu loger, & qui trouvant que de grands appartemens & beaucoup exhaussez ne leur sont pas commodes, ou qui voulant menager la place, y auroient fait faire des entresoles.

Ce n'est pas que cela ne puisse estre permis quelquefois dans les grands Palais, mais il faut que l'Architecte ait l'adresse de trouver un pretexte à ce grand Ordre, & qu'il paroisse qu'il y a esté obligé par la symmetrie qui demande qu'un grand Ordre qui est necessaire à quelque partie considerable de l'Edifice, soit continué & regne dans le reste du bastiment. Cela a esté pratiqué avec beaucoup de jugement en plusieurs Edifices, mais principalement dans le Palais du Louvre, lequel estant basti sur le bord d'un grand fleuve, qui donne une espace & un éloignement fort vaste à son aspect, avoit besoin pour ne paroistre pas chetif d'avoir un grand Ordre. Celuy qu'on luy a donné qui comprend deux étages, & qui est posé sur l'étage d'embas qui luy sert comme de Piedestail, & qui est proprement le rempart du Chasteau, est ainsi exhaussé à cause de deux grands & magnifiques Portiques, qui regnent le long de la principale face à l'entrée du Palais, & qui estant comme pour servir de Vestibule à tous les appartemens du premier étage, demandoit cette grandeur & cette hauteur extraordinaire que l'on a donné à son Ordre, qu'il a falu poursuivre & faire regner ensuite tout au tour du reste de l'Edifice: Car cela autorise ou du moins excuse l'incongruité que l'on auroit pû objecter à l'Architecte, s'il avoit fait sans necessité une chose qui d'elle mesme est sans raison: sçavoir, de ne donner pas à chaque étage qui est proprement un bastiment separé, son Ordre propre & separé, & de faire servir une mesme Colonne à porter deux planchers, supposant qu'elle en soûtient un par maniere de dire sur sa teste, & un autre comme pendu à sa ceinture. Car la longueur de l'aspect ne peut estre toute seule une raison suffisante d'élever un bastiment qui de sa nature doit estre bas, non plus que la grandeur d'un Theatre n'oblige point à faire ses degrez, ses sieges, ses ballustrades, & appuis avec plus de hauteur, comme Vitruve l'a remarqué.[143] (118–119)

26. *1684.* Claude Perrault, ed. and trans., *Les dix livres d'architecture de Vitruve,* 2d ed., Paris, 1684.

a. [For the preceding paragraphs of this note, first published in the 1673 Vitruvius edition, see above, no. 12(a).]

Monsieur Blondel dans ses doctes Leçons d'Architecture, desquelles il a composé un Cours, employe trois chapitres entiers, qui sont le 10 le 11 & le 12, du premier Livre de sa troisiéme Partie,[144] pour faire voir que l'usage universel reçû aujourd'huy de doubler les Colonnes, est une licence qui ne doit point estre soufferte: & comme personne que je sçache n'avoit cherché les raisons qui peuvent establir cette nouvelle pratique, il s'estend principalement sur la refutation de celles que je viens de rapporter. La chose me semble assez importante pour meriter d'estre examinée, & je croy qu'on ne trouvera pas hors de propos que j'ajoute à cette notte ce que j'ay à répondre à la refutation qui en a esté faite.

La principale objection sur laquelle on appuye le plus, est fondée sur un prejugé & sur la fausse supposition qu'il n'est pas permis de se départir des usages des Anciens; que tout ce qui n'imite pas leurs manieres doit passer pour bizarre & pour capricieux, & que si cette Loy n'est inviolablement gardée, on ouvre la porte à une licence qui met le déreglement dans tous les Arts. Mais comme cette raison prouve trop, elle ne doit rien prouver: car il y a beaucoup plus d'inconvient à fermer la porte aux belles inventions, qu'à l'ouvrir à celles qui estant ridicules se doivent détruire d'elles-mesmes. Si cette Loy avoit eu lieu, l'Architecture ne seroit jamais parvenuë au point où l'ont mises les inventions des Anciens, qui ont esté nouvelles en leur temps; & il ne faudroit point chercher de nouveaux moyens pour acquerir les connoissances qui nous manquent, & que nous acquerons tous les jours dans l'Agriculture, dans la Navigation, dans la Medecine, & dans les autres Arts, à la perfection desquels les Anciens ont travaillé, & à laquelle ils n'ont jamais pretendu d'estre parvenus: du moins il ne se trouve point qu'aucun d'eux ait jamais prononcé d'Anatheme contre ceux qui voudroient oster ou ajouter quelque chose aux regles que l'on se figure nous avoir esté prescrites par ces grands Personnages qui dans toutes les apparences auroient esté aussi surpris s'ils avoient prevû la maniere dont la posterité les a honorez, que Jupiter & Saturne l'auroient pû estre si lorsqu'ils vivoient dans Crete, & dans l'Italie, on leur eust predit qu'on devoit un jour élever des Autels. C'est dans cet esprit d'adoration pour tout ce qui vient des Anciens, qu'on dit que les Inventeurs de la nouvelle maniere de placer les Colonnes, n'estant point des Hermogenes, ils n'ont point eu droit de l'entreprendre; comme si ce n'estoit pas estre Hermogene que d'inventer quelque chose de bon dans l'Architecture, & que ce fust une chose si difficile que d'estre Hermogene en ce sens, puis qu'Hermogene, tout Hermogene qu'il est, a inventé des choses qui n'ont point esté approuvées dans la suite; ainsi qu'il paroist par les changemens introduits depuis luy, nonobstant l'autorité qu'on veut attribuer à son nom, & qui n'est deuë qu'au merite, & à l'excellence des inventions.

C'est pourquoy sans examiner les autres objections qui ne sont faites au sujet d'Hermogene, comme de dire qu'il n'est pas vray qu'on ait imité Hermogene, puis qu'il a osté absolument une Colonne dans le Pseudodiptere, laquelle n'est que simplement deplacée dans le Pseudosystyle, & ne vouloir pas comprendre que s'agissant seulement de faire voir qu'Hermogene a pris une licence, il n'est point necessaire pour l'imiter de prendre la mesme licence, mais qu'il suffit d'en prendre une pareille, & à plus forte raison une moindre, comme on a fait, puisque déplacer simplement une Colonne est quelque chose de moins que de l'oster absolument; je me reduis à examiner les autres objections faites contre ce que j'ay avancé pour prouver que ce n'est point sans raison, & par caprice que cette nouveauté a esté introduite.

On dit qu'il n'est point vray que le Pseudosystyle ait le dégagement que je pretens, puisque les Colonnes couplées rendent leur entrecolonnement encore plus estroit que le plus étroit des Anciens qui est le Pycnostyle, comme s'il estoit necessaire que le dégagement fut par tout, & si l'on pouvoit dire que l'élargissement que les derniers des Anciens ont introduit dans l'entrecolonnement du milieu, n'est pas un dégagement pour l'entrée des Temples, parce que l'élargissement n'est pas à tous les entrecolonnemens. On dit encore avec aussi peu de raison que le grand entrecolonnement du Pseudosystyle fait un écartement qui rend l'Architrave trop foible: car cet entrecolonnement n'est pas plus grand que celuy du Diastyle qui est de trois Diametres, puisque le Systyle dont le Pseudosystyle est composé donnant un Diametre des quatre qu'il faut pour deux de ses entrecolonnemens au petit entrecolonnement du Pseudosystyle, il n'en reste que trois pour le grand entrecolonnement. Et l'on peut dire encore que cette objection n'est pas de bonne foy, n'estant fondée que sur le nom de Pseudosystyle, que l'on sçait ne rien faire à la chose, puisque l'on voit aisément que celuy de Pseudopycnostyle auroit pû estre mis en sa place, & alors son grand entrecolonnement n'auroit esté que de deux Diametres: car le nom de Pseudosystyle ou faux Systyle n'a esté choisi que parce que sa prononciation est plus douce, ne s'agissant que de signifier un genre different de ceux des Anciens, désigné par le mot de *faux,* de mesme que Hermogene avoit designé par le mot de faux Diptere une espece de Temple differente de toutes celles qui estoient en usage avant luy.

Je ne comprens pas aussi pourquoy l'on veut que le bout d'un Architrave qui pose sur une Colonne entiere, n'y soit pas mieux affermy que quand il ne pose que sur la moitié de la Colonne; & qu'il ne plie pas plus facilement quand il n'est sousten qu'il n'est sousten par son extremité, que quand cette extremité passe au delà de la Colonne qui le soustient; parce que j'ay toûjours crû que ce bout qui passe par delà la Colonne au droit du petit entrecolonnement a une pesanteur qui resiste au pliement de la partie opposée qui est celle qui est au droit du grand entrecolonnement.

Mais le plus grand reproche que l'on croit faire à nostre Pseudosystyle est de dire qu'il tient du Gothique. J'estois demeuré d'accord du fait dans ma notte; mais supposé que le Gothique en general, & à considerer tout ce qui le compose ne fust pas le plus beau genre d'Architecture, je ne pensois pas que tout ce qui est dans le Gothique fut à rejetter. Le jour dans les Edifices & les dégagemens dont il s'agit, sont des choses en quoy les Gothiques different des Anciens: mais ce n'est pas en cela que le Gothique est à reprendre; & les Anciens qui dans les commencemens s'éloignoient beaucoup de cette maniere, l'ont approuvée dans la suite lorsqu'ils ont fait des fenestres à leurs Temples, qui auparavant ne prenoient du jour que par la porte; & avant cela ils avoient élargi les entrecolonnemens du milieu, ainsi qu'il a esté dit.

Ce qui me reste à ajouster est qu'il faut que les Architectes reçoivent comme bonne cette nouvelle maniere de placer les Colonnes, ou qu'ils renoncent au principe qu'ils tiennent pour le plus infaillible dans l'Architecture, sçavoir que les veritables proportions sont des choses qui se font appro[u]ver & aimer naturellement comme les accords de la Musique le font; & que ce qui se fait ainsi aimer & approuver doit avoir la veritable beauté.[145] Car il est constant que depuis que l'on a vû des Colonnes couplées tout le monde les a aimées; & que les Modernes, comme Bramante, Michel-Ange, Sangallo, Labaco, Serlio, Palladio, Scamozzi, de l'Orme, Jean Goujon, du Cerceau, Meteseau, de Brosse, le Merchier [*sic*], Mansard, & tous les grands Architectes les ont aimées; & qu'il est croyable que les Anciens en auroient fait autant, s'ils se fussent avisez de les mettre en usage. (79–80 n. 16)

b. Ces pierres [of the pediment of the Colonnade] qui pesoient chacune plus de quatre-vingt milliers n'estoient pas tant difficiles à élever à cause de leur pesanteur, que par la raison de leur figure qui les rendoit faciles à estre rompuës si elles n'avoient pas esté soutenuës également: car ayant cinquante deux piez de long sur huit de large, elles n'avoient tout au plus que dix-huit pouces d'épaisseur.

Pour empescher que cette fracture ne leur arrivast soit dans leur transport de la carriere qui est sur la montagne de Meudon à deux lieuës de Paris; soit dans leur élévation & leur posement qui estoit à prés de vingt toises du rez de chaussée; les precautions que l'on a apportées ont esté, que l'on a fait un assemblage de charpenterie.[146] (339 n. 4)

27. *1684.* Germain Brice, *Description nouvelle de ce qu'il y a de plus remarquable dans la ville de Paris,* Paris, 1684, I, 14–15:

La Cour qui se trouve au milieu de ce bâtiment [the Louvre], est grande & parfaitement quarrée, le Roy en a fait élever trois aisles qui ne sont pas encore achevées, l'ouvrage est à trois rangs de colonnes Corinthiennes & composites, & le comble du bâtiment est en terrasse, ce qui paroît d'une beauté & d'une magnificence surprenante; la grande Porte est du côté de saint Germain l'Auxerrois, elle est au milieu d'une longue Façade revêtüe de colonnes Corinthiennes, deux à deux d'une tres-belle grandeur, qui estant hors d'oeuvre, forment un grand portique de chaque côté de la Porte, sur laquelle est le Fronton composé seulement de deux pierres d'une seule piece, qui ont chacune cinquante pieds de longueur; une grande Terrasse regne sur cette face, de laquelle on peut découvrir tout Paris.

28. *1685.* C. Le Maire, *Paris ancien et nouveau,* Paris, 1685, III, 188–190:

Loüis le Grand a fait venir de tous les endroits de l'Europe les meilleurs Ouvriers, & les plus fameux Architectes, pour donner au Louvre sa derniere perfection, & le rendre le plus beau & le plus magnifique Edifice de l'Univers. La Cour qui se trouve au milieu est grande & parfaitement quarrée, le Roy en a fait élever trois Aisles, qui ne sont pas encore achevées; l'Ouvrage est à trois rangs de Colonnes Corinthiennes & Composites, & ce qui luy donne une beauté & une magnificence surprenante, c'est que le Comble du Bastiment est en Terrasse. La grande Porte est du costé de S. Germain Lauxerrois, au milieu d'une longue Façade soûtenuë de Colomnes Corinthiennes hors d'oeuvre, au dessus est le Fronton composé seulement de deux Pierres d'une merveilleuse grandeur, elles ont chacune cinquante pieds de longueur. L'on doit poser vis-à-vis cette Porte la Statuë du Roy, avec des Vers au bas.[147] . . . C'est aussi à l'occasion des nouveaux Bastimens du Louvre que Monsieur de Fourcroy celebre Avocat a composé ce Distique.

Vrbi par domus est, Vrbs Orbi, neutra Trophaeis
  Et belli & pacis par, LODOÏCE, *tuis.*

29. *1686.* Allain Manesson Mallet, *Description de l'univers . . . ,* Frankfurt-am-Main, 1686, V, 109:

Entre les deux Pavillons qui regardent l'Orient, on voit regner une face embellie de 40 Colonnes d'ordre Corinthien, & isolées ou détachées du corps de l'Ouvrage: Elles portent une grande Terrasse, qui doit estre enrichie d'une superbe Balustrade, & chargée en plusieurs endroits de Trophées d'Armes. Le grand Portail du Château est pratiqué dans le milieu de cette face; & l'on admire à son Fronton, deux pierres qui ont chacune 52. pieds de long, qui luy servent de couverture.

30. *1686.* Claude Charles Guyonnet de Vertron, *Le nouveau Pantheon . . . ,* Paris, 1686, 52:
Victorem, LODOIX, totus te praedicat Orbis,
  Gallia te Justum, Regia Magnificum.

Tout l'univers, GRAND ROY, parle de ta vaillance;
Tu fais que ta Justice éclate en tes Sujets;
Mais qui veut être instruit de ta magnificence,
N'a qu'à considerer ce superbe Palais.

31. *November 1686. Le Mercure galant,* November 1686, part 2, 44 [From an account of the visit of the Siamese ambassadors to the Observatoire, Paris]:

Mr Perrault qui a fait le Dessein de la Façade du Louvre, a esté l'Architecte de ce Bastiment [the Observatoire].

32. *1687.* Germain Brice, *Description nouvelle de ce qu'il y a de plus remarquable dans la ville de Paris,* 2d ed., Paris, 1687, I, 15–17:

La Cour qui se trouve au milieu de ce bâtiment, est grande & parfaitement quarrée, dont le Roy a fait élever trois côtés qui ne sont pas encore achevés. L'Ouvrage est à trois étages de colonnes, le premier est Corinthien, le second & le troisiéme sont composites. Mais ce qui donne une apparence magnifique à tout ce bâtiment, est qu'au lieu de toict on a fait regner sur les combles une bâlustrade, soûtenuë d'espace en espace, par des piés-d'estaux, qui fait un effet admirable.

La grande porte est du côté de Saint Germain l'Auxerrois; elle est composée d'un premier étage uni, & d'un second orné de colonnes Corinthiennes, disposées de telle sorte, qu'elles forment un avant-corps dans le milieu, & deux Pavillons aux extremités. Il y a trois ouvertures qui sont separées l'une de l'autre, par des soubassemens propres à mettre des statuës, & tout cét avant-corps est terminé par un fronton duquel la cymaise n'est composée que de deux pierres tirées des Carrieres de Meudon, qui ont chacune plus de cinquante piés de longueur. Le reste de la façade est un peristile formé par des colonnes Corinthiennes couplées, dont le corridor est enrichi de Sculptures & les entre-colonnemens de niches couronnés de frontons. Une balustrade regne sur ce coridor, dont les piés-d'estaux, doivent estre chargés de trophées d'armes; & ce qui est assez agreable, est que de ce lieu on découvre une partie de la Ville, & que l'on s'y peut promener tres-commodement. Tout cét ouvrage & ce qui paroist du côté de la riviere, bâti sur la même ordonnance, est du dessein de PERRAULT, excellent Architecte qui a mis de tres-belles choses en lumiere: comme la traduction de Vitruve, dont on a fait une seconde édition, il n'y a pas long tems, l'ordonnance des cinq especes colonnes, selon la methode des Anciens & un traité de phisique en trois volumes in 12.[148] DORBAY, aussi tres-habile Architecte a eû quelque part au dessein de ce portique; & on peut dire à la gloire de celuy des deux qui y a le plus contribué, que de ces bas siécles, on n'a point élevé un morceau d'Architecture, où il paroisse plus de grandeur & plus de magnificence que dans cét édifice.

33. *1687.* Nicodemus Tessin the Younger, *Nicodemus Tessin D. Y.:s Studieresor . . .* , Osvald Sirén, ed., Stockholm, 1914, 92–93:

Beij Mr Felibien, Secretaïre du Roy dans l'Accademie Royalle d'Architecture . . . habe ich unterschiedliche schöne dinge gesehen, wie unter andern in einem grossen zimber[149] unterschiedliche Modellen vom Louvre, worunter dass von Cav. Bernini von ungefehr 7 qv. hoch sonderlich schön wahr, imgleichen sein Modell von einer treppen. Dass andere gantze modell vom Louvre, dar man inwendig kunte den hoff sehen, undt die andere Facciate nach der Thuilleries, wahr von Mr de Vaux, der todt ist, undt dass gröste model von der einen seiten von Louvre mit der Colonnade ist von Mr Perault, aber in allen nach dass von Mr de Vaux imitiert.

34. *1688.* Bernard de Fontenelle, "Eloge de Perrault," in *Oeuvres de Fontenelle . . .* , Paris, 1792, VII, 539. (An almost identical obituary appears in Henri Basnage, "Eloge de Mr. Perrault,"*Histoire des ouvrages des savans,* Amsterdam, 1721, IV, 310–314 [November 1688].)

Colbert ayant pris des dessins pour la façade du devant du Louvre de tous les plus fameux architectes de France et d'Italie, le dessin que Perrault donna fut préféré à tous les autres, et il a été entièrement exécuté tel qu'on le voit aujourd'hui sur les profils et sur les mesures qu'il en a donnés.

35. *1688.* Charles Perrault, *Parallèle des anciens et des modernes en ce qui regarde les arts et les sciences,* Paris, 1688:
 a. Le President.

L'architrave qui portoit sur les colonnes de la porte du Temple d'Ephese, avoit pourtant plus de quinze pieds. Il est vray que l'Architecte effrayé par la grandeur & par la pesanteur de cette pierre, desesperoit de pouvoir l'élever, & Pline[150] ajoûte que s'estant endormi aprés avoir fait sa priere à Diane, il trouva à son reveil l'architrave posée en place: Ce qui fait voir qu'on regardoit comme une chose miraculeuse l'adresse qu'il avoit euë de l'élever & de la poser.

L'Abbé.

Si cet Architecte avoit sçu la coupe des pierres, il n'auroit pas esté embarassé, il auroit fait son architrave de plusieurs pieces taillées selon le trait qu'il leur faut donner, & elle auroit esté beaucoup plus solide. Mais qu'auroit fait cet Architecte de Diane s'il avoit eu à élever deux pierres comme celles du fronton du Louvre de cinquante-quatre pieds de long chacune, sur huit pieds de largeur, & de quinze pouces d'épaisseur seulement, ce qui les rendoit tres-aisées à se casser, ny luy ny sa Deesse n'en seroient jamais venus à bout. L'impossibilité de faire de larges entrecolonnemens, parce qu'ils ne faisoient l'architrave que d'une seule piece, les a aussi empesché d'accoupler les colonnes & d'élargir par ce moyen les intervales, maniere d'arranger des colonnes qui donne beaucoup de grace & beaucoup de force à un édifice. (I, 169–171)

 b. [L'Abbé].

Je soûtiens que dans la seule face du devant du Louvre, il y a plus de beauté d'architecture qu'en pas un des édifices des Anciens. Quand on presenta le dessein de cette façade, il plut extremement. Ces Portiques majestueux dont les colonnes portent des architraves de douze pieds de long, & des plafonds quarrez d'une pareille largeur, surprirent les yeux les plus accoûtumez aux belles choses, mais on crut que l'execution en étoit impossible, & que ce Dessein estoit plus propre pour estre peint dans un tableau, parce que c'estoit encore seulement en peinture qu'on en avoit vû de semblables, que pour servir de modele au frontispice d'un palais veritable. Cependant il a esté executé entierement, & il se maintient sans qu'une seule pierre de ce large plafond tout plat & suspendu en l'air se soit dementie le moins du monde. Toute cette façade a esté d'ailleurs construite avec une propreté & une magnificence sans égales. Ce sont toutes pierres d'une grandeur demesurée, dont les joints sont presque imperceptibles, & tout le derriere des portiques a esté appareillé avec un tel soin, qu'on ne voit aucun joint montant dans toute l'étenduë de cette façade; On a eu la precaution de les faire rencontrer contre les costez des pilastres & contre les bandeaux des niches qui les cachent par leur saillie, en sorte que chaque assise semble estre toute d'une piece d'un bout à l'autre de chaque Portique; beauté de construction qui ne se trouvera point dans aucun bastiment ny des Anciens ny des Modernes. (I, 175–176)

36. *February 28, 1689.* "Eloge de Mons. Perrault," *Journal des sçavans,* February 28, 1689, 68:

La grande connoissance qu'il [Claude Perrault] avoit de l'Architecture, a paru par l'excellence de ses desseins qui ont été préférés à ceux des plus habiles maîtres de France & d'Italie, & éxécutés de la maniére que l'on les voit à la façade du Louvre, à l'Observatoire, & au modéle de l'Arc de Triomphe [du Trône].

37. *1690.* Charles Perrault, *Le cabinet des beaux-arts* . . . , Paris, 1690.

a. La coupe des pierres, invention moderne, a donné aux voutes surbaissées, et aux architraves qui se font presentement de plusieurs pieces . . . une solidité que toute l'Antiquité n'a point connuë. (24–25)

b. Où voit on rien de comparable à la beauté du devant du Louvre, et à la hardiesse de ses portiques, dont les platfonds tout plats et suspendus en douze pieds de profondeur, n'ont rien qui leur ressemble dans quelque édifice que ce soit, si ce n'est en peinture, où l'on ne se met pas en peine de la solidité. (25–26)

c. Perrault . . . a donné les desseins de la façade principale du Louvre, de l'Observatoire, de l'Arc de triomphe [du Trône], de la Chapelle de S[c]eaux etc. (26)

38. *1693.* Ms. collection (2 vols., folio) of drawings by Claude Perrault, compiled in 1693 by Charles Perrault, with commentaries by both brothers. Destroyed in 1871. Quotations from the manuscript text in Jacques François Blondel, *Architecture françoise,* Paris, 1756, iv.

a. [Charles Perrault]:

Ce Monarque [Louis XIV], ayant résolu de faire continuer le bâtiment du Louvre, & d'y ajouter une façade digne de ce qui étoit déja fait, & s'il se pouvoit, proportionnée à la splendeur de son régne, fit venir de Rome le *Cavalier Bernin,* célébre Architecte, pour y travailler. Cependant le dessein de *Perrault,* aussi Parisien, mérita la préférence, & a été exécuté avec un succès qui égale ce que les Grecs & les Romains ont fait élever de plus grand & de plus somptueux en édifices. (6–7)

b. [Charles Perrault]:

Monsieur *Colbert,* suivant les intentions de Sa Majesté, s'étant proposé d'achever ce grand Bâtiment, & de commencer par la face principale de l'entrée, ne voulut rien négliger pour le porter à sa derniere perfection; & quoiqu'il eut une très-bonne opinion de la capacité de *Claude Perrault* en fait d'Architecture, cependant comme celui-ci n'étoit pas Architecte de profession, & qu'il avoit beaucoup d'ennemis, ce Ministre crut que le plus sûr moyen de se disculper de toutes les fautes qui pourroient survenir dans la composition d'un Edifice de cette importance, étoit de préferer un Architecte dont le nom seul arrêtât la critique des plus hardis, & donnât de la réputation à l'ouvrage. Pour cet effet, il fit venir de Rome le Cavalier Bernin. . . . Il fut décidé qu'on abandonneroit son [Bernini's] dessein, lequel étoit directement opposé à la condition essentielle de ne rien abattre, sur laquelle on avoit fait venir cet Architecte en France, & il fut résolu qu'on suivroit le plan de *Claude Perrault;* ce qui a été exécuté très-heureusement, & offre à la postérité un des plus beaux édifices qui soit dans le reste du monde. (8)

c. [Charles Perrault]:

Les bâtimens qui environnent la grande cour quarrée du Louvre ont quatre-vingt-dix toises de face hors oeuvre, de chaque côté, sur dix, douze, & quatorze toises de profondeur.

La face principale du côté de Saint Germain l'Auxerrois est composée d'un grand avant-corps au milieu, de deux aîles, & de deux pavillons aux extrémités. . . . Le soubassement a trente pieds de haut; au dessus de ces aîles sont les deux péristiles, ayant chacun 14 colonnes; ces colonnes sont Corinthiennes & isolées. . . .[151]

Les plafonds de ces péristiles sont construits de pierres toutes plates entre les architraves, qui comme des poutres de pierre passent des colonnes aux pilastres; ouvrage dont la hardiesse n'a pas d'exemple, ni dans l'Architecture ancienne, ni dans la moderne.[152]

Le dessus de ces portiques est couvert de grandes pierres en terrasses. Pour aller d'une terrasse à l'autre, on passe sur le fronton de l'avant-corps du milieu, couvert de marches, la cimaise supérieure de la corniche de ce fronton est d'une seule pierre de chaque côté, dont chacune a cinquante-deux pieds de long, huit de large, & 18 pouces d'épaisseur: au haut de l'avant-corps du milieu, il y a un grand réservoir où les eaux du Ciel s'amassent & se déchargent quand le réservoir est plein, dans un espéce de puits pratiqué dans l'épaisseur du mur, par le moyen d'un gros tuyau de plomb affermi par des barres de fer qui forment comme un escalier[153] pour visiter & réparer le tuyau quand il en est besoin. Les eaux amassées dans ce réservoir sont pour servir en cas d'incendie. Par le moyen de ce puits on n'a plus besoin de goutieres ni de descentes qui ruinent & qui défigurent les bâtimens.

Les trois autres faces extérieures de ce bâtiment qui environnent la grande cour, ont aussi chacune deux pavillons aux encoignures, & un avant-corps au milieu. Celle qui regarde la riviere est de même ordonnance que la précédente, à la réserve qu'il n'y a que des pilastres, & que ces pilastres ne sont pas accouplés, afin que les trumeaux ne soient pas trop grands. Les deux autres sont simples, & ont seulement la même corniche de l'entablement, & les mêmes ornemens aux chambranles des croisées.

Le dedans de la cour est plus enrichi d'ornemens; car chaque étage a son Ordre, celui d'en bas est Corinthien, le second Composite Italien, & le troisiéme doit être Composite François.[154] (11–12)

d. [Charles Perrault]:

La pensée de faire un troisieme Ordre au Louvre [in the Cour Carrée], avoit pour fondement une raison que M. [Claude] Perrault n'a jamais bien goûtée. On prétendoit que les façades du dedans du Louvre étoient assez élevées avec l'Attique [of Lescot; Fig. 10], lorsque la cour du Louvre ne devoit avoir que le quart de sa superficie actuelle; au lieu que cette cour ayant été agrandie, il falloit donner plus de hauteur aux corps de logis qui l'environnent; mais . . . il n'est point vrai que la hauteur d'un Bâtiment doive être proportionnée avec son étendue; car il faudroit par cette raison que la galerie du Louvre sur la riviere, fût deux ou trois fois plus élevée que les tours Nôtre-Dame. D'ailleurs il n'est point convenable qu'au-dessus du logement du Prince qui doit être tout de plain-pied, & dans un même étage, il y en ait un autre aussi beau, aussi grand, & d'un plancher aussi élevé que celui qu'il occupe, & où il faille monter près de cent vingt-six dégrés. Il est certain qu'un Attique, tel que celui qu'on voit exécuté, est plus convenable pour y loger les Officiers qui doivent être proche la personne du Prince, que ce grand étage formé par le troisieme Ordre qui paroît trop beau pour ces especes de logemens. Cependant, malgré cette consideration qui n'est point du tout indifférente, le *Cavalier Bernin* ayant été aussi d'avis qu'il falloit donner au Bâtiment de la cour du Louvre plus d'exhaussement qu'il n'en a, non-seulement parce qu'il étoit bien-aise de trouver à redire à tout ce qu'il voyoit à Paris, mais encore parce qu'en Italie, où l'on aime l'ombre, on aime aussi les Bâtimens fort élevés, la chose fut résolue ainsi.

Néanmoins comme plusieurs personnes n'approuvoient pas qu'on fît un nouvel Ordre François, *Claude Perrault* proposa des cariatydes[155] dans tout ce troisieme étage. Ce genre de décoration fut fort applaudi; mais ayant considéré néanmoins que cent quarante figures de femmes rangées sur la même ligne, & dont il seroit impossible de varier les attitudes, feroient une décoration monotone, on décida l'Ordre composé François, qui se trouve élevé aujourd'hui sur l'Ordre composé Italique. . . .

On prévit néanmoins tant de difficultés pour l'invention de ce nouvel Ordre, qu'on proposa un prix de 3000 liv. à celui des Architectes qui le composeroit plus heureusement. Il en fut fait un grand nombre de desseins & de modeles, tant en France qu'en Italie; la plus grande partie fut trouvée extravagante,[156] & quelques-uns reçurent assez d'approbation; mais celui de *Claude Perrault* fut préféré. (63–64)

39. *1694.* Nicolas Boileau, *Réflexions critiques sur quelques passages du rheteur Longin,* Paris, 1694. Edition used: Nicolas Boileau, *Oeuvres complètes,* ed. A. Adam and F. Escal, Paris, 1966, 495 (réflexion I):

Je ne nierai pas cependant qu'il [Claude Perrault] ne fust Homme de tres-grand merite, et fort sçavant sur tout dans les matieres de Physique. Messieurs de l'Academie des Sciences neanmoins ne conviennent pas tous de l'excellence de sa traduction de Vitruve, ni de toutes les choses avantageuses que Monsieur son frere rapporte de lui. Je puis même nommer un des plus celebres de l'Academie d'Architecture [d'Orbay], qui s'offre de luy faire voir, quand il voudra, papiers sur table que c'est le dessein du fameux Monsieur le Vau, qu'on a suivi dans la façade du Louvre;[157] et qu'il n'est point vray que ni ce grand Ouvrage d'Architecture, ni l'Observatoire, ni l'Arc de Triomphe [du Trône], soient des ouvrages d'un Medecin de la Faculté. C'est une querelle que je leur laisse démêler entre eux; et où je déclare que je ne prens aucun interest; mes voeux mesme, si j'en fais quelques-uns, estant pour le Medecin.

40. *June 1694.* From a letter of Nicolas Boileau to Antoine Arnauld (N. Boileau, *Oeuvres complètes,* 793–794):

A la premiere édition qui paroistra de mon livre, il y aura dans la Preface un article exprés en faveur de ce Médecin [Claude Perrault], qui seurement n'a pas faict la façade du Louvre, ni l'Observatoire, ni l'Arc de Triomphe [du Trône], comme on le prouvera dans peu démonstrativement; mais qui au fond estoit un homme de beaucoup de mérite, grand phisicien, et, ce que j'estime encore plus que tout cela, qui avoit l'honneur d'estre vostre ami.[158]

41. *January 28, 1694.* From a letter of Daniel Cronström to Nicodemus Tessin the Younger (R. A. Weigert and C. Hernmarck, eds., *Les relations artistiques entre la*

France et la Suède 1693–1718: Nicodème Tessin le jeune et Daniel Cronström, correspondance (extraits), Stockholm, 1964, 44–45):

A propos de Mansard et d'architectes vous ne serez peut estre pas fasché de scavoir, quil fist elevé un grand orage contre la mémoire de feu Mr. Perrault, en ce qu'un certain Dorbais qui dessignoit soubs Mr. le Veaux s'est avisé tout d'un coup de disputer le dessein de la façade du Louvre a feu Mr. Perrault et de l'attribuer a Mr. le Veaux et a luy mesme. Il prètend faire un escrit sur cela;[159] Mr. [Charles] Perrault d'aujourdhuy, qui a des preuves plus que convaicantes du contraire, ne dit mot exprès afin qu'il s'enferra, en suitte de quoy il prétend repondre; et, ç'est ce qui donnera occasion à un ouvrage curieux et savant qu'il veut faire, dans lequel toute l'histoire du Louvre et du Cavallier Bernin sera déduite avec exactitude.[160]

42. *May 20, 1695.* From a letter of Daniel Cronström to Nicodemus Tessin the Younger (Weigert and Hernmarck, eds., *Les relations artistiques,* 78):

Je vous envoiroy une chose bien plus rare et peut estre plus belle [than engravings of Bernini's Louvre project], c'est le dessein de feu Mr. Perrault du mesme Louvre ou son contre-projet proprement à celluy du Cavallier. Il est selon moy d'une beauté singuliere. Je feroy plus. Je vous envoiroy la critique raisonnée de Messrs Perrault et de toute la petite Académie Royalle d'architecture de ce temps la,[161] sur le dessein du Cavallier, si Mr. Perrault la peut retrouver. Il m'a promis l'un et l'autre par un effort d'amitié estant choses que personne n'a absolument.

43. *June 6, 1695.* From a letter of Daniel Cronström to Nicodemus Tessin the Younger (Weigert and Hernmarck, eds., *Les relations artistiques,* 81):

J'envoye toujours quelques feuilles du Louvre pour ne pas trop grossir les paquets. J'ay le plan du Louvre de Mr. Perrault que Monsieur son frère m'a donné.

44. *1696.* Charles Perrault, *Les hommes illustres qui ont paru en France pendant ce siècle,* Paris, 1696, I, 67 (from the life of Claude Perrault):

Monsieur Colbert ayant demandé des desseins pour la façade du devant du Louvre à tous les plus celebres Architectes de France & d'Italie, & ayant fait venir à Paris le Chevalier Bernin, afin que ce grand homme executât luy-même son dessein; celuy de Monsieur Perrault fut preferé à tous les autres, & ensuite executé en la maniere que nous le voyons. Aussi peut-on dire que dans la seule façade du devant du Louvre, il y a autant de beauté d'Architecture que dans aucun des édifices des Anciens.

Quand on presenta le dessein de cette façade, il plut extremement; ce Peristile, ces Portiques majestueux dont les colonnes portent des architraves de douze pieds de long & des plafonds carrez d'une pareille largeur, surprirent les yeux les plus accoûtumez aux belles choses, mais on crut que l'execution en estoit impossible, & que ce dessein estoit plus propre pour estre peint dans un tableau, parce que c'estoit encore seulement en peinture qu'on en avoit vû de semblables, que pour servir de modele au frontispice d'un Palais veritable. Il a neanmoins esté executé entierement sans qu'une seule pierre de ce large plafond tout plat & suspendu en l'air se soit démentie.[162]

45. *November 1696. Le Mercure galant,* November 1696, 46–47:

Ces colomnes [of the Piliers de Tutèle, Bordeaux] estoient construites de grandes pierres, ce qui marquoit l'antiquité & la noblesse de l'édifice; car c'estoit là la maniere d'Architecture du temps d'Auguste. Aussi le celebre Mr Spon passant à Bordeaux, fit remarquer qu'on devoit faire grand estat d'une ancienne porte de la Ville, qu'on nommoit *la Porte Basse,* parce que les grandes pierres désignoient une structure du siecle des premiers Cesars.[163]

Il y a aujourd'huy une Imitation royale de cette superbe structure des Empereurs Romains. Le Fronton qui est sur la porte de la principale entrée du Louvre, est couvert de deux grandes pierres, qui ont chacune cinquante-deux pieds de long sur huit de large. Elles pesent aussi chacune plus de quatre vingt milliers, & ont esté tirées de la Carriere qui est sur la montagne de Meudon.

46. *1697.* Charles Perrault, "Dessin d'un Portail pour l'Église de Sainte-Genevieve a Paris MDCXCVII fait et donné par M. Perrault de l'Academie Françoise. *Mémoire touchant un portail pour l'Église de Sainte-Genevieve à Paris*" (Paris, Bibliothèque Sainte-Geneviève, réserve W 376). Published by Michael Petzet, "Un projet des Perrault pour l'Église Sainte-Geneviève à Paris," *Bulletin monumental,* CXV, 1957, 94–96 (extract):

Si le peristile du Louvre n'estoit point basti et d'une maniere plus solide qu'aucun bastiment qu'il y ayt au monde il faudroit essuyer encore toutes les mauvaises difficultes que l'on fit à mon frere et a moy sur l'impossibilité imaginaire qu'on trouvoit a bastir des plafonds qui n'ont pour soustien que des colonnes, on nous diroit encore que cela est beau en peinture mais impossible dans la verité. Nous n'avons plus ces reproches a craindre; des plafonds de 12 pieds qui subsistent au Louvre sont des garents suffisans pour des plafonds de 8 pieds que nous proposons [in the design for the Église Sainte-Geneviève]. Mais parcequ'on pourroit encore differer longtemps a le bastir e qu'il reste peu d'ouvriers de ce temps la qui en ayent une entiere connaissance je croy estre obligé de faire icy mention de ce qui doit s'observer dans la construction de ces Peristiles. Il faut percer les tambours qui composent les fusts des colonnes dans les deux tiers du hault de la colonne, les enfiler dans une barre de fer de Normandie de deux pouces ou deux pouces et demie en carré. Il faut que cette barre de fer excede le chapiteau d'un pied ou d'un pied et demi ou environ, qu'une autre barre de fer de mesme calibre percée par un bout embrasse cette barre et de l'autre bout traverse le mur vis à vis de part en part et soit retenue dans l'eglise par une ancre de fer ou descendante ou traversante le long du mur. Il faut encore une autre barre traversante de mesme grosseur que la precedente qui aille de la colonne en diagonale au travers du mur ainsi qu'on le peut voir dans cette figure. [absent]

Avant que de mettre les barres de fer il [faut] construire un ceintre bien solide sur lequel on pose toutes les pierres de la premiere assise avec la couppe que l'on leur donne ordinairement et creuser dans ces pierres comme des auges de quatre a cinq pouces de largeur et de profondeur en sortes [sic] que les pierres de l'assise de dessus ne touchent point aux dites pierres. La raison est que ces barres ne portant rien et ne travaillant qu'a retenir la poussée des pierres il est impossible qu'elles rompent jamais. Le peristile du Louvre en est un bel exemple. Il sera bon avant que de les couvrir de la seconde assise de les peindre de deux ou trois couches a l'huile pour les defendre de la rouille.

47. *July 8, 1697.* Minutes of the Académie royale d'architecture (H. Lemonnier, ed., *Procès-verbaux de l'Académie royale d'architecture,* Paris, 1913, III, 13):

M. Blondel, dans le 11ᵉ chapitre du premier livre, troisième partie de son cours d'architecture, raporte les principales raisons qui peuvent servir selon luy à combattre l'usage des colonnes couplées et ne dit que très peu de chose de ce qui peut quelques fois authoriser cet usage.[164] A ce sujet, M. Des Godets[165] a présenté un dessein de deux dispositions différentes de colonnes, dont les unes sont simples et à égale distance les unes des autres, et les autres sont accouplées comme au péristile du Louvre; sur quoy la Compagnie, après avoir examiné cette matière, a jugé que, dans des édifices où il n'y auroit pas plus de sujétions que dans les ouvrages qui nous restent des anciens aux portiques de leurs temples et autres semblables, il seroit fort mal à propos de coupler les colonnes.

Mais dans les édifices qui sont présentement usités et où l'on est obligé de mettre de grands intervalles entre des colonnes isolées, il est souvent impossible de ne pas employer des colonnes couplées pour une solidité plus grande et plus apparente,[166] et au contraire la Compagnie blasme l'abus que l'on fait de ces accouplemens de colonnes dans des lieux où il n'y a aucune nécessité.

48. *1698.* Germain Brice, *Description nouvelle de la ville de Paris . . . ,* 3d ed., Paris, 1698, I, 24–27:

LE PERISTYLE DU LOUVRE

La grande Façade du Louvre est à l'Orient, du côté de S. Germain l'Auxerrois. Elle est composée d'un premier étage simple, pareil à celui des autres Façades de l'ancien bâtiment & d'un grand ordre au dessus de Colonnes Corinthiennes couplées, & de Pilastres de même. Cette Façade, qui est de quatre-vingt-sept toises & demie de longueur, est divisée par trois avant-corps, à sçavoir, deux aux extremitez, & un autre au milieu, où la grande Porte & la principale entrée se trouve de ce côté-là par un Vestibule sans Colonnes, pour en soûtenir la voute, qui n'est pas encore achevée. Cet avant-corps du milieu est orné de huit Colonnes couplées & terminé par un grand Fronton, dont la cimaise est de deux seules pierres d'une grandeur prodigieuse, qui n'ont point de pareilles dans tous les ouvrages modernes, puisqu'elles ont chacune cinquante-quatre pieds de long, sur huit pieds de largeur, & quatorze pouces d'épaisseur seulement. Elles ont été tirées des Carrieres de Meudon. On auroit peut-être eü bien de la peine à les poser entieres, sans le secours du nommé PONCE CLIQUIN habile Charpentier, qui en vint heureusement à bout par le moïen d'une machine fort ingenieuse qu'il fit exprés,[167] comme il avoit fait d'un grand Cheval de bronze qu'il avoit amené de Nancy quelques années auparavant. La machine dont il s'est servi pour la conduite de ces deux prodigieuses pierres a paru si ingenieuse & si singuliere aux Sçavans, que pour en conserver la memoire, l'on en a fait graver une Estampe que l'on trouve dans le *Vitruve* de PERRAULT[168] . . . à l'exemple de celle du Chevalier Fontana pour l'obelisque du Vatican, que l'on éleva à Rome sous le Pontificat de Sixte V. qui étoit cependant bien moins difficile à poser que ces deux pierres, lesquelles sont beaucoup plus élevées & plus faciles à casser, ayant moins d'épaisseur & moins de massif que cet obelisque.[169]

Entre ces trois avant-corps il y a, comme on a déja dit, deux Peristyles de Colonnes Corinthiennes, couplées pour une plus grande solidité; lesquels se communiquent par un petit Coridor, pratiqué fort ingenieusement dans l'épaisseur du gros mur, au dessus de la porte quarrée du milieu. Ces belles Colonnes Corinthiennes qui sont cannelées ont trois pieds sept pouces de diametre, lesquelles forment deux grands Peristyles de douze pieds de largeur, sur vingt-sept toises de longueur chacun, dont les Plafons sont d'une beauté surprenante, non seulement par la hardiesse des Architraves de douze pieds d'étenduë qui les soûtiennent, mais encore par les sculptures excellentes que l'on y a disposées, & par la propreté avec laquelle tout cet ouvrage a été executé. Les pierres sont jointes avec tant de soin, qu'elles semblent ne faire qu'un même corps, & l'on a caché les joints montans si à propos dans les coins des pilastres & des cha[m]branles des niches, que les assises paroissent n'être que d'une seule piéce dans toutes les faces de l'Edifice. La même ordonnance d'architecture est observée à la Façade du corps de logis double du côté de la riviere, par des pilastres seulement, & il doit regner par tout une grande Balustrade, soûtenuë de pieds-destaux, qui se voit déja commencée sur la Façade de devant, ce qui embellit infiniment tout ce grand ouvrage, qui n'a pas son pareil pour la magnificence & pour la somptuosité dans tous les bâtimens élevez depuis ces derniers siécles. Les sculptures des chapitaux & quelque autres ornemens sont executez d'une maniere merveilleuse.

Ces travaux ont été commencez en 1667. & conduits en l'état où ils sont en 1670. par les soins & sur les desseins de LOUIS LE VAU Parisien, premier Architecte du Roy, qui a eu la direction des Bâtimens Royaux depuis l'année 1653. jusqu'en l'année 1670. qu'il est mort. FRANÇOIS DORBAY qui étoit sous lui ne contribua pas peu à la perfection de ce bel ouvrage; & c'est à ces deux excellens Architectes à qui l'on doit attribuer toute la gloire du dessein de ce superbe Edifice, malgré tout ce que l'on a publié au contraire jusques icy.

49. *1698.* Martin Lister, *Voyage de Lister à Paris en MDCXCVIII,* Paris, 1873, 51–52:

C'est dommage que le roi ait tant d'aversion pour le Louvre. S'il étoit fini, ce que l'on feroit aisément dans deux ou trois ans, ce seroit peut-être le palais le plus magnifique qu'il y eût sur la surface de la terre; & aussi jusque-là Paris n'atteindra pas l'apogée de sa beauté.

Il y a au fronton de la colonnade deux pierres que l'on fait remarquer aux étrangers, & qui, se joignant à la pointe, la couvrent comme feroient deux ardoises. Elles sont énormes, car elles ont cinquante-quatre pieds de long chacune, huit de large & seulement quatorze pouces d'épaisseur. C'est un chef-d'oeuvre de l'art, égal à tout ce que les anciens ont pu faire en ce genre, d'être parvenu à élever à cette hauteur deux pierres si grandes & si fragiles. Elles sortent des carrières de Meudon, la maison de plaisance de Monseigneur le Dauphin.

50. *April 7, 1698.* *Le Journal des sçavans,* April 7, 1698, 137–138:

La façade est de quatre-vingt-sept toises & demie de longueur. L'avant-corps du milieu est orné de huit colomnes couplées, & terminé par un grand fronton, dont la cimaise est de deux pierres qui ont chacune cinquante-quatre pieds de long, sur huit de large, & quatorze pouces d'épaisseur. On auroit eu beaucoup de peine à les poser entières, sans le secours de Ponce Cliquin, Charpentier, qui en vint à bout par le moyen d'une Machine qui a paru si ingénieuse, que pour en conserver la mémoire, on en a gravé une Estampe qui se trouve dans le Vitruve de M. Perrault,[170] de l'Académie des Sciences.

51. *May 1699.* Cassan, "La nymphe de Chanceaux, ou L'arrivée de la Seine au château de Marly," *Le Mercure galant,* May 1699, 136–137:

Le Louvre, à sa [the Seine's] main droite, est un si bel objet,
Qu'elle a regret d'en voir suspendre le projet,
Sur tout de ce Fronton d'ordonnance correcte,
Chef-d'oeuvre merveilleux de Perrault l'Architecte.

Si de le voir finir ce n'est pas la saison,
C'est à d'autres qu'à nous d'en sçavoir la raison.

52. *1699.* Florent Le Comte, *Cabinet des singularitez d'architecture, peinture, sculpture et gravure,* Paris, 1699, I, "Sommaire historique d'architecture et des architectes . . ." [unpaginated]:

a. Les travaux du Louvre ayant été commencés en 1667. la porte de l'entrée du Louvre fut faite sous sa [Louis Le Vau's] conduite, & il eut la direction des Bâtimens du Roy dés l'année [16]53. jusqu'en [16]70. que les ouvrages du Louvre furent conduits à l'état où ils sont.

b. Son [Claude Perrault's] dessein de la façade principale du LOUVRE, est une marque autentique & glorieuse, qu'il sçavoit allier ensemble toute le noblesse & la beauté requise pour un si superbe édifice.

53. *Ca. 1700.* Charles Perrault, *Mémoires de ma vie*, P. Bonnefon, ed., Paris, 1909.

a. Votre oncle [Claude Perrault] fit un dessein à peu près semblable à celui qu'il donna depuis et qui a été exécuté. M. Colbert, à qui je les montrai, en fut charmé, et ne comprenoit pas qu'un homme qui n'étoit pas architecte de profession eût pu faire une si belle chose. Ce dessein qui est double, l'un géométral et l'autre en perspective, sont dans deux enchassures de bois tout simple et sont dans la grande armoire de mon garde-meuble. La pensée du peristile est de moi, et l'ayant communiquée à mon frère, il l'approuva et la mit dans son dessein, mais en l'embellissant infiniment, comme il en était capable.

Dessein de M. Perrault, le médecin, exposé à la critique comme les autres.—Ce dessein fut exposé dans la salle comme les autres; ce fut un plaisir de voir les jugemens qu'on fit de ce dessein; il fut trouvé très-beau et très-magnifique, mais on ne sçavoit à qui l'attribuer. Les plus versés dans ces matières ne connoissoient personne, hors quelque étranger qu'ils nommoient, qui pût dessiner si proprement ni si correctement. M. Colbert, quoique très-content du dessein de votre oncle, ne crut pas devoir en demeurer là; il ne voulut rien omettre dans une affaire de cette conséquence, il résolut de prendre l'avis des plus excellens architectes d'Italie, et de les inviter, comme il avoit fait ceux de France, à faire des desseins. (53–54)

b. *M. Colbert présente au Roi deux desseins pour la façade du Louvre, l'un de M. Le Vau, l'autre de M. Perrault, le médecin.*—Quoique M. Colbert goûtât fort le dessein de mon frère, il ne laissa pas d'en faire faire un à M. Le Vau. Après quoi il les présenta tous deux au Roi pour choisir celui qui lui agréeroit le plus. J'étois présent lorsque ces deux desseins furent présentés. C'étoit dans le petit cabinet du Roi, à Saint Germain; il n'y avoit que Sa Majesté, son capitaine des gardes, M. Colbert et moi. Le Roi les regarda tous deux fort attentivement, ensuite de quoi il demanda à M. Colbert lequel des deux il trouvoit le plus beau et le plus digne d'être exécuté. M. Colbert dit que, s'il en étoit le maître, il choisiroit celui qui n'avoit point de galerie (on ne donnoit pas encore le nom de péristile à ces rangs de colonnes qui, posés le long d'un bâtiment, forment une espèce de galerie couverte qui communique à toutes les pièces des appartemens). Ce dessein étoit celui de M. Le Vau, ce qui m'étonna fort. Mais il ne se fut pas plutôt déclaré pour ce dessein que le Roi dit: "Et moi je choisis l'autre, qui me semble plus beau et plus majestueux." Je vis que M. Colbert avoit agi en habile courtisan, qui vouloit donner tout l'honneur du choix à son maître. Peut-être étoit-ce un jeu joué entre le Roi et lui. Quoi qu'il en soit, la chose se passa de cette manière.

Le Roi choisit le dessein de M. Perrault, le médecin.—Quelque connoissance qu'eût M. Colbert de la capacité de mon frère dans l'architecture, je m'aperçus qu'il hésitoit à faire exécuter son dessein, et qu'il lui sembloit étrange de préférer les pensées d'un médecin, en fait d'architecture, aux desseins du plus célèbre des architectes. L'envie des maîtres du métier, à Paris, ne manqua pas de s'élever contre cette résolution et à faire de méchantes plaisanteries, en disant que l'architecture devoit être bien malade, puisqu'on la mettoit entre les mains des médecins.

Établissement d'un conseil des bâtimens.—Je donnai un mémoire à M. Colbert où je lui proposai de faire un conseil des bâtimens, composé de M. Le Vau, premier architecte, qui avoit près de trente années d'expérience, de M. Le Brun, qui possédoit tous les beaux arts et qui n'ignoroit pas les principes de l'architecture, et de mon frère, qui avoit fait le dessein et qui assurément avoit beaucoup de génie et de capacité; qu'il étoit impossible que voulant bien être à la tête de ce conseil, toutes choses ne réussissent au-delà même de ses espérances. J'eus l'honneur d'être le secrétaire de ce conseil, et je tins un registre où j'écrivois toutes les résolutions que l'on y prenoit. Il s'assembloit deux fois la semaine. Ce registre que j'ai rendu avec tous les autres papiers des bâtimens, est plein de choses très-curieuses et qui seroient très-utiles à ceux qui aiment l'architecture:[171] car mon frère, étant presque toujours contredit par M. Le Vau et par M. Le Brun, étoit obligé de faire à tous momens des dissertations, ou plutôt des leçons d'architecture, qu'il rapportoit par écrit dans l'assemblée suivante. J'en ai les originaux que je garde avec plaisir. Il est vrai que M. Le Vau et M. Le Brun ne pouvoient approuver le dessein de mon frère, disant toujours qu'il n'étoit beau qu'en peinture, et qu'assurément on s'en trouveroit mal dans l'exécution, à cause de la trop grande profondeur du péristile, qui étoit de douze pieds, et que les architraves, qui poussoient au vuide, jetteroient tout à bas; mais on y a si bien pourvu que rien au monde n'est plus solide. Il n'y a rien de si hardi ni de si beau dans tous les ouvrages de l'antiquité.

Ce conseil des bâtiments et la retenue que nous avions, mon frère et moi, de publier qu'il étoit l'auteur du dessein que l'on exécutoit, donna la hardiesse au sieur Dorbay, élève de M. Le Vau, de dire que son maître en étoit l'auteur;[172] calomnie terrible, car c'étoit lui qui avoit mis au net celui de M. Le Vau qui fut présenté au Roi, et auquel celui de mon frère fut préféré.

Il ne tint pas à moi ni à mon frère que M. Le Vau n'eût l'honneur d'avoir inventé le dessein qui a été exécuté. Je proposai plus de dix fois au sieur Dorbay de faire un péristile à la façade principale du Louvre, je lui en dessinai le plan et l'élévation; mais jamais il n'y voulut mordre ni en parler à son maître, car, et je le dis en vérité, mon frère et moi avions un tel amour pour la paix et pour la concorde, qu'il n'y avoit rien que nous n'eussions fait pour maintenir l'ordre naturel, qui veut que ce soit le premier architecte des bâtiments du roi qui donne les desseins de ce qui se bâtit pour le prince, particulièrement dans une rencontre de cette nature.

On fait un modèle en petit de la façade du Louvre avec le même nombre de pierres qu'en devoit avoir le bâtiment.—Pour lever toutes les inquiétudes que M. Colbert pouvoit avoir sur la construction de cet édifice, je lui proposai de trouver bon qu'on fît un petit modèle du péristile avec de petites pierres de taille de même figure et en même nombre que l'ouvrage en grand se devoit faire. Quand il fut achevé et retenu par de petites barres de fer, grosses proportionnellement à celles qu'on employeroit dans l'ouvrage effectif, M. Colbert demeura tellement convaincu de la fermeté et de la solidité de tout l'ouvrage, où le fer ne porte rien et ne fait que retenir la poussée des architraves, en quoi il a une si grande force qu'il n'y a point de pesanteur, quelle qu'elle puisse être, qui puisse la rompre, ne faisant que river et ne portant rien. Il fut encore pratiqué un vuide entre le plafond du péristile et la couverture de dessus, où plusieurs hommes peuvent aller et travailler sans peine à remédier aux inconvéniens qui pourroient survenir dans la suite des temps. Le tout a été si bien construit que rien ne s'est démenti et il y a apparence que la durée de cet édifice ne finira jamais. Le détail de cette construction est dans le premier volume des desseins d'architecture de mon frère qui est parmi mes livres.[173] (85–89)

54. *1700.* Claude François Ménestrier, *Histoire du règne de Louis le Grand par les médailles . . . ,* new ed., Paris, 1700, 60:

Monsieur Perrault traduisit le Vitruve, & donna les desseins du Louvre, de l'Arc de Triomphe [du Trône], & de l'Observatoire.

55. *May 1703.* Obituary of Charles Perrault, *Mercure de France,* May 1703, 235:

Il [Claude Perrault] estoit aussi tres habile mathematicien, & tres excellent Architecte, la Façade du Louvre, l'Arc de Triomphe [du Trône], l'Observatoire & la Chapelle de Sceaux, sont de son dessein, & il a traduit Vitruve où il a joint des notes sçavantes.

56. *December 19, 1704.* From a letter (from Paris) of Göran Josuae Adelcrantz to Nicodemus Tessin the Younger (Stockholm, Riksarkivet, Tessinsaml., II, E 5711 [in Swedish]; French translation by R. Josephson, "Quelques dessins de Claude Perrault pour le Louvre," *GBA,* ser. 5, XVI, 1927, 189):

D'ailleurs, vous devez vous rappeler, Monsieur le Maréchal de la Cour, que le péristyle avec sa façade n'est pas de Perrault comme on l'a d'abord supposé, mais a été exécuté par d'Orbay d'après les dessins et le commencement d'exécution de Le Vau.

57. *August 22, 1707.* Minutes of the Académie royale d'architecture (H. Lemonnier, ed., *Procès-verbaux de l'Académie royale d'architecture,* Paris, 1913, III, 279):

M. Desgodets[174] a présenté à la Compagnie le dessein avec les mesures des deux premiers ordres du dedans de la cour du Louvre et les mesures et proportions du grand ordre du péristile de la face extérieure du costé de Saint Germain l'Auxerrois, pour faire voir le raport des chapiteaux des pilastres avec ceux des colonnes dans ces différens ordres.

La Compagnie a trouvé que ces proportions, particulièrement celles des colonnes et des pilastres du péristile, conviennent à ce que l'on a dit dans l'assemblée précédente pour les pilastres,[175] car pour les colonnes, les chapiteaux dans le péristile, estant de mesme hauteur que ceux des pilastres, sont beaucoup plus haut que la mesure ordinaire. Et l'on auroit pu, en assemblant ainsy des colonnes et des pilastres, prendre pour leurs chapiteaux le milieu entre la proportion ordinaire et celle qui est augmentée par raport au pilastre, comme on a dit cy devant, et par ce moyen on éviteroit l'excès qui se trouve à la hauteur des chapiteaux des colonnes du péristile.

58. *1713.* Germain Brice, *Description nouvelle de la ville de Paris* . . . , 6th ed., Paris, 1713, I, 24:

The Louvre Colonnade is described as "à la maniere des Grecs" for the first time by Brice, and this formula appears in later editions of his guide.

59. *1714.* Jean Louis de Cordemoy, *Nouveau traité de toute l'architecture* . . . , 2d ed., Paris, 1714, 139 ("Extrait d'une lettre de l'auteur au R. P. de Tournemine jesuite pour servir de réponse aux Remarques de M. Frezier[176] Ingénieur Ordinaire du Roy, insérées dans le Journal de Trevoux du mois de Septembre 1709"):

L'excellent Portique de Louvre, dont les Architraves ont au moins quatorze piéds de portée ou de longueur. Quand M. Perrault en fit voir le dessein au Roy, la plûpart des *Connoisseurs* crûrent que c'étoit plûtôt une décoration de Théâtre, qu'une chose qui pût être vrayment executée. Elle l'a été neanmoins d'une maniére aussi solide que belle. Et je suis persuadé qu'en suivant *le trait de coupe* de cet habile Architecte, on donneroit aux Architraves 16. 18. & 20. piéds de longueur, sans rien risquer.

60. *1716.* Georges Louis Le Rouge, *Les curiositez de Paris, de Versailles, de Marly, de Vincennes, de S. Cloud, et des environs*, Paris, 1716, 32:

Il [Louis XIV] se servit pour l'execution de ce grand dessein [the Louvre Colonnade] de Louis Le Vau & de François Dorbay, fameux Architectes.

61. *1721.* Anonymous, "Eloge de Mr. Claude Perrault" in idem, *Oeuvres diverses de physique et de mechanique*, Leiden, 1721, I, [9]:

Dans la seule façade du devant du *Louvre* il y a autant de beauté d'Architecture que dans aucun des édifices des Anciens.

Quand on présenta le dessein de cette façade, il plût extrêmément; ce peristyle, ces portiques majestueux, dont les colonnes portent des architraves de douze pieds de long & des plafonds carrez d'une pareille largeur, surprirent les yeux les plus accoutumez aux belles choses, mais on crud [sic] que l'execution en étoit impossible, & que ce dessein étoit plus propre pour être peint dans un tableau, parce que c'étoit encore seulement en peinture qu'on en avoit vû de semblables, que pour servir de modele au frontispice d'un Palais véritable. Il a néanmoins été executé entierement sans qu'une seule pierre de ce large plafond tout plat & suspendu en l'air se soit dementie.

62. *1722.* Louis Moreri, *Le grand dictionnaire historique* . . . , new ed., Amsterdam and The Hague, 1722, I, 212:

Il [the Louvre Colonnade] étoit du Sieur Perrau[l]t de l'Académie des Sciences, Auteur de la nouvelle Traduction de Vitruve, & il fut exécuté entierement.

63. *1722.* Jean Aymar Piganiol de La Force, *Nouvelle description de la France*, 2d ed., Paris, 1722, II, i, 205–206:

La grande façade, & les bâtimens neufs ont été commencés en 1665. [sic] par ordre de Louis le Grand. Cette façade a quatre vingt-sept toises & demie de long; & consiste en trois corps avancez, deux aux extremitez, & le troisiéme au milieu, & en deux peristyles. La principale entrée est dans le corps du milieu qui est orné de huit colonnes couplées, & terminé par un fronton dont la cimaise est de deux pierres qui ont chacune cinquante-quatre pieds de long, sur huit de large, quoiqu'elles n'ayent que dix-huit pouces d'épaisseur. Les deux perystiles sont entre ces trois avant-corps, & ont chacun vingt sept toises de long sur douze pieds de large. Leurs colonnes sont corinthiennes, canelées & couplées. Sur le comble, au lieu de toit, regne une terrasse ornée d'une balustrade sur les pilastres de laquelle on doit mettre des trophées. Ce superbe bâtiment fut commencé en 1667. & conduit en l'état où on le voit, en 1670. On croit communement qu'il est du dessein de Perrau[l]t, Medecin de la Faculté de Paris, & grand Architecte, à qui nous sommes redevables d'une sçavante traduction de Vitruve: cependant depuis quelque tems, on lui dispute cette gloire, & on assure sans en apporter de preuve convaicante, qu'il est du dessein de Louis le Vau, premier Architecte du Roi, mais dans cette incertitude les apparences sont pour le Traducteur de Vitruve.

64. *1724.* Henri Sauval, *Histoire et recherches des antiquités de la ville de Paris*, Paris, 1724, II, 61–62:[177]

LE PERISTYLE OU LA GRANDE FAÇADE du Louvre.

La grande façade du Louvre est à l'Orient, du côté de St Germain de l'Auxerrois. Les premiers fondemens en furent jettés le dix-sept Octobre 1665. sur les desseins du Cavalier Bernin, que l'on fit venir d'Italie avec bien de la depense: ce fameux Architecte n'a pas fait tout ce que l'on attendoit de lui, on en peut juger par les modeles qui subsistent: le Roi fut obligé d'avoir recours aux Architectes François, qui executerent peu de tems après ce magnifique édifice qui se voit à present.

Cette façade est composée d'un premier étage simple, pareil à celui des autres façades de l'ancien bâtiment, & d'un grand ordre au-dessus de colonnes Corinthiennes couplées avec des pilastres de même. Elle est de quatre-vingt-sept toises & demie de longueur, divisée par trois corps avancés, & par deux Peristyles; à savoir, deux corps avancés aux extremités, & un autre au milieu, où la grande porte & la principale entrée se trouve de ce côté-là par un vestibule sans colonnes, pour en soutenir la voute qui n'est pas encore achevée.

Le corps avancé du milieu est orné de huit colonnes couplées, & terminées par un grand f[r]onton, dont la cimaise est de deux pierres d'une grandeur prodigieuse, & dont on n'a point de pareille dans tous les ouvrages modernes; en effet elles ont chacune cinquante-quatre pieds de long sur huit pieds de large, & dix-huit pouces d'épaisseur seulement. Elles ont été tirées des carrieres de Meudon, où elles ne faisoient qu'un seul bloc que l'on a coupé en deux. Ces deux grandes pieces ne furent posées que dans le mois de Septembre de 1674. On auroit peut-être eu bien de l'embarras à les placer entieres, sans le secours de l'habile Charpentier Ponce Cliquin, qui par le moyen d'une machine fort ingenieuse, vint heureusement à bout de les monter où elles sont posées. Cette machine étoit dans le goût, & semblable à une autre qu'il avoit dressée pour élever le cheval de bronze, amené de Nanci quelque tems auparavant.

La machine dont il s'est servi pour la conduite de ces prodigieuses pierres, a paru si ingenieuse, & si singuliere aux Savans, que pour en conserver la memoire, l'on en a fait graver une estampe, que l'on trouve dans la derniere édition de Vitruve de Perrault,[178] dont on a parlé à l'exemple de celle du Chevalier Fontana, pour l'obelisque du Vatican,[179] élevé dans la place de St Pierre de Rome, sous le Pontificat de Sixte V. bien plus facile à poser que ces deux grandes pierres, lesquelles sont beaucoup plus exhaussées, & plus aisées à casser, parce qu'elles ont moins de solide, que cet obelisque. Cependant les Italiens grands admirateurs de leurs inventions, ont parlé de cette machine, comme d'une chose tout-à-fait merveilleuse & sans exemple.

Entre ces trois corps avancés, il y a deux peristyles de colonnes Corinthiennes, couplées pour une plus grande solidité, lesquelles se communiquent par un petit coridor pratiqué fort ingenieusement dans l'épaisseur du gros mur, au-dessus de la porte quarrée du milieu. Ces belles colonnes Corinthiennes, qui sont cannelées, ont trois pieds sept pouces de diametre, lesquelles forment deux grands peristyles, ou portiques de douze pieds de largeur, sur vingt-sept toises de longueur chacun, dont les plafonds sont d'une beauté surprenante. On doit admirer la hardiesse des architraves de douze pieds d'étendue, qui les soutiennent, de même que les sculptures excellentes que l'on y a disposées, & la propreté avec laquelle tout cet ouvrage a été executé; les pierres sont jointes avec tant de soin, qu'elles semblent ne faire qu'un même corps, & l'on a caché les joints montans si à propos dans les coins des pilastres & des chambranles des niches, que les assises paroissent d'une seule piece dans toutes la face de l'édifice. La même ordonnance d'Architecture est observée à l'exterieur du corps de logis double, du côté de la riviere, par les pilastres seulement; & il doit regner par tout, au lieu de combles, une balustrade appuyée sur des pieds d'estaux que l'on voit déja commencer sur la façade de devant: ce qui embellit infiniment tout ce grand ouvrage, qui n'a pas son pareil pour la magnificence & pour la somptuosité dans les bâtimens élevés depuis les anciens Grecs & Romains.

Les sculptures des chapiteaux & quelques autres ornemens sont recherchés d'une maniere sans pareille; & quoiqu'on eut en France des ouvriers plus habiles qu'en aucun endroit du monde, pour les exécuter comme on les souhaitoit, le Roi fit venir d'Italie d'autres Sculpteurs, auquel on donna un bon prix par jour pour les animer à bien faire.[180]

Ces grands travaux ont été commencés en 1667. & conduits dans l'état où l'on les voit à present en 1670. par les soins & sur les desseins de Louis le Vau, né à Paris, premier Architecte du Roi, lequel a eu la direction des bâtimens Royaux depuis l'année 1653. jusqu'en 1670, qu'il est mort.

François d'Orbai son éleve ne contribua pas peu à la perfection de ce bel ouvrage, & c'est à ces deux excellens Architectes à qui on doit attribuer toute la gloire du dessein, & de l'exécution de ce superbe édifice; malgré tout ce que l'on a publié de contraire; lequel causera sans doute de l'admiration aux siecles à venir, & leur donnera une haute idée de celui qui aura produit des ouvrages d'une si rare & si grande perfection.

65. *1726.* Claude Marin Saugrain, *Dictionnaire universel de la France . . . ,* Paris, 1726, II, col. 1038:

Le Roy se servit de Louis le Vau, premier Architecte, depuis 1667. jusqu'en 1670. & ensuite de François d'Orbai son Eleve; ces deux Architectes conduisirent l'édifice en l'estat où il est. Charles Pérault de l'Academie Françoise, prétend dans l'éloge qu'il a fait de son frere Claude,[181] que le dessein de la nouvelle façade exterieure est de lui; mais quoi qu'il en soit, on n'en connoît point d'autres auteurs que Louis le Vau & d'Orbai qui l'ont conduit; & on leur attribue toute la gloire d'un monument si parfait.

66. *1729.* Pierre Nativelle, *Nouveau traité d'architecture . . . ,* Paris, 1729, text for pl. 41:

[Le] plus régulier Edifice qu'il y ait au monde, . . . [est le] peristile de la façade de la principale entrée du Louvre, qui a été executé sur les desseins de Loüis Le Veaux né à Paris, premier Architecte du Roy, & qui (comme le dit le Sieur Germain Brisse [sic] Auteur de la Description de la Ville de Paris)[182] eut la direction des Bâtimens Royaux depuis l'année 1653.[183] jusqu'en 1670. qu'il est mort. François Dorbay aussi Parisien, son Eleve, & reçû en même-temps comme son Maître premier Architecte du Roy,[184] ne contribua pas peu à la perfection de ce bel Ouvrage; il continua à en avoir la conduite jusqu'à ce qu'il fut parvenu à l'état où il est resté sans avoir été achevé. On peut assurer que c'est à ces deux Illustres que la gloire en est dûë, malgré ce qu'a publié au contraire Claude Perault, plus Medecin que bon Architecte, qui néanmoins a eu la hardiesse de l'inserer dans sa Traduction de Vitruve;[185] ainsi que de l'Observatoire, dont certainement François Dorbay est l'Auteur.[186]

67. *1737.* Pierre Alexis Delamair, *La pure verité.* Manuscript, Paris, Bibliothèque de l'Arsenal, MS 3054.

a. [Claude Perrault] . . . a solidement fait connoitre la veritable beauté des colomnes couplées [in his Vitruvius edition]; Dont l'appreté favorable de l'approchement des colomnes contrastée par l'ouverture des grands entrecolonnemens qui les accompagnent toûjours, fait un merveilleux effet au coup d'oeil (comme on le voit dans la sage magnificence de la façade du Louvre). (143)

b. Je suis seur au moins que mon applaudissement par rapport à son [Louis Le Vau's] excellente façade du Louvre (mal à propos attribuée par quelques uns au Cavalier Bernin et plagiairé d'un autre côté, par le traducteur Perrault) est fondé sur tout ce qu'il y a de plus beau en composition d'Architecture non seulement en France ni même en Italie mais en Europe et peut être dans tout le monde. D'où même s'est formé ce juste dicton passé en proverbe dans les Dictionnaires: *Le Louvre est un Edifice merveilleux.* Ce qui doit faire gemir de ce que depuis si longtemps on laisse un aussi beau morceau non seulement imparfait mais d'ailleurs comme enfouy [sic] et caché aux yeux des hommes par tous les mauvais batimens qui l'entourent. (217–218)

68. *1742.* Jean Aymar Piganiol de La Force, *Description de Paris . . . ,* Paris, 1742. (Quotations are from the 1765 edition: *Description historique de la ville de Paris et de ses environs,* new ed., Paris, 1765).

a. C'est Louis le Grand qui a fait élever la plus grande partie des bâtimens de la Cour. Lorsque ce grand Prince eut résolu de faire travailler à ce bâtiment, il fit ce que font ordinairement les Rois & les Grands; il fit chercher bien loin ce qu'il avoit auprès de lui. On fit venir d'Italie avec beaucoup de faste & de dépense, le cavalier *Jean-Laurent Bernin,* le plus fameux Architecte qu'il y eut alors dans cette partie de l'Europe; mais après qu'on eut examiné ses desseins & ses modeles, on leur préféra ceux de *Claude Perrault,* Médecin de la Faculté de Paris, & un des plus riches génies pour l'architecture qu'il y ait jamais eu. (II, 246–247)

b. Ce superbe bâtiment fut donc commencé en 1665. [sic] & conduit en l'état où on le voit en 1670. Quoiqu'il ne soit point achevé, il ne laisse pas de donner une magnifique idée de ce qu'il doit être. Les quatre faces intérieures offrent à la vûe huit pavillons & huit corps de logis, qui enferme une grande cour de soixante & trois toises en quarré. Ils sont décorés de trois ordres de colonnes, dont le premier est corinthien, & les deux autres sont composites.

La grande façade est du côté de S. Germain l'Auxerrois, & a quatre-vingt-sept toises & demie de longueur. Elle consiste en trois avant-corps, & en deux peristyles. La principale porte est dans l'avant-corps du milieu qui est décoré de huit colonnes couplées, & terminé par un fronton, dont la cimaise est de deux pierres qui ont chacune cinquante-quatre pieds de longueur sur huit de largeur, quoiquelles n'ayent que dix-huit pouces d'épaisseur. Elles ont été tirés des carrieres de Meudon, où elle ne faisoient qu'un seul bloc qui fut scie en deux. On peut voir dans la derniere édition de Vitruve par *Perrault,*[187] la machine dont on se servit pour les guinder au lieu où elles sont posées: elle est de l'invention d'un charpentier, nommé *Ponce Cliquin.*

Les deux peristyles sont entre ces trois avant-corps, & ont chacun vingt-sept toises de longueur sur douze pieds de largeur. Leurs colonnes sont Corinthiennes & couplées. Sur le comble au lieu du toît, regne une terrasse ornée de balustrade, dont les piédestaux doivent porter des trophées, & des vases alternativement.

Charles Perrault dans ses Hommes Illustres,[188] dit que lorsque *Claude Perrault* son frere présenta le dessein de cette façade, *ce peristyle, ces portiques majestueux dont les colonnes portent des architraves de douze pieds de long, & des plafonds quarrés d'une pareille largeur, surprirent les yeux les plus accoutumés aux belles choses, mais qu'on crût que l'exécution en étoit impossible, & que ce dessein étoit plus propre pour être peint dans un tableau, parce que c'étoit seulement en peinture qu'on en avoit vû de semblables, que pour servir de modele au frontispice d'un Palais véritable. Il a néanmoins été exécuté entierement, sans qu'une seule pierre de ce large plafond tout plat & suspendus en l'air, se soit démentie.*

Une tradition unanime avoit toujours donné à Claude Perrault le dessein de cette superbe façade, jusqu'en 1694. que la jalousie & l'envie s'éleverent pour la contredire. Cette année-là M. Despreaux donna une nouvelle édition de ses ouvrages, & dit dans la premier de ses réflexions sur le Traité du Sublime *de Longin*,[189] que d'Orbay un des plus célèbres de l'Académie Royale d'Architecture, s'offroit de faire voir papier sur table, que le dessein qu'on a suivi pour la facade du Louvre, étoit celui de M. le Vau, mort en 1670. premier Architecte du Roi, & qu'il n'étoit pas vrai que ce grand ouvrage d'architecture, ni l'Observatoire, ni l'Arc de Triomphe [du Trône], eussent été élevés sur les desseins d'un médecin de la Faculté de Paris. Dès que ces deux hommes avoient résolu d'ôter à Claude Perrault la gloire d'avoir imaginé le dessein de la façade du Louvre, ils eurent raison de n'en pas faire à plusieurs fois, & de lui ôter celle des desseins de l'Observatoire, & de l'Arc de Triomphe; car ces trois ouvrages ont certainement été produits par le même génie, & par le génie le plus riche, en fait d'architecture. D'Orbay auroit bien dû nous dire où sont les bâtimens construits par le Vau, où l'on trouve la moindre ressemblance de leur architecture avec celle-ci. Aussi ni lui, ni Despreaux n'en imposerent-ils qu'à un petit nombre de personnes. En 1697. Charles Perrault publia les portraits & les éloges des Hommes Illustres qui ont paru en France pendant le dix-septieme siecle.[190] Dans ce Livre il donna à son frere les plus grands éloges, c'est-à-dire, ceux qui lui étoient dûs, pour avoir inventé les desseins de ces trois chefs-d'oeuvres d'Architecture, sans daigner seulement dire un seul mot de l'injustice que d'Orbay & Despreaux lui faisoient en voulant lui ravir la gloire de ces trois édifices. Il y auroit eû bien de l'impudence à Charles Perrault d'attribuer à son frere des ouvrages que le Roi Louis XIV. & Monsieur Colbert . . . , qui étoit pour lors Surintendant des bâtimens, auroient scû par eux-mêmes être de le Vau. D'ailleurs pourquoi d'Orbay a-t-il attendu la mort de Claude Perrault pour mettre *papier sur table?* C'étoit de son vivant qu'il faloit le dire, & prouver qu'il jouissoit d'une gloire qui appartenoit à un autre. Quant à Despreaux, ce Poëte si admirable, & si admiré, étoit si aigri contre les Perraults, que quand il parloit d'eux, il n'étoit plus maître de ces expressions, ni d'accord avec lui-même. Tantôt Claude Perrault de méchant Médecin, étoit devenu bon Architecte, & tantôt il étoit ignorant Médecin, mais non pas habile Architecte, &c. On peut appliquer à tant d'aigreur & à tant d'injustice l'aveu public que fit M. Despreaux, après sa réconciliation avec Charles Perrault, que le dépit de se voir critiquer, lui avoit fait dire des choses qu'il seroit mieux de n'avoir pas dites.[191] (II, 248–252)

c. [Piganiol de La Force's analysis of the "Registre ou Journal des délibérations & résolutions touchant les Bâtimens du Roi" (April and May 1667); see above, no. 1]:

Les réflexions qui résultent de ce Journal, sont:

1°. M. Colbert nous apprend d'abord qu'aucun des Architectes, tant de France que d'Italie, n'avoit entierement réussi dans les desseins du Louvre qu'ils avoient donnés. Il n'y a point à douter un moment que parmi les Architectes de France, à la tête desquels étoit le Vau, en qualité de premier Architecte du Roi, il n'eut aussi donné son dessein. Or s'il avoit été capable de produire le dessein de la façade du Louvre, pourquoi ne l'auroit-il pas fait paroître alors, & auroit-il attendu qu'on l'eût associé avec le Brun & Perrault qui n'étoient point Architectes de profession?

2°. Louis XIV. qui étoit le meilleur maître qu'il y eut au monde, comme il étoit le plus grand, ne voulut point deshonorer son premier Architecte, & l'associa à le Brun & à Perrault. Le Vau étoit le plus habile Architecte qu'il y eût à Paris, mais je m'explique: c'étoit un de ces Architectes *de tradition,* comme ils sont presque tous. Il avoit parfaitement profité de ce qu'on lui avoit enseigné, & de ce qu'il avoit vû pratiquer, mais nulle imagination, nulle invention au-delà. Le Brun étoit un grand Peintre, & ne se mêloit d'architecture qu'autant qu'elle entroit quelquefois dans la composition de ses tableaux, mais il avoit le génie si beau & si grand qu'il s'étendoit à tous les arts, & qu'il se connoissoit à tous. C'étoit une espece de surabitre que le Roi avoit nommé pour départager les deux autres. Perrault étoit né Architecte, & avoit fortifié ce talent naturel par l'étude qu'il avoit faite de *Vitruve*, dont il a donné au Public une traduction excellente.

3°. On voit par ce Journal que malgré l'ordre que le Roi avoit fait donner à ces trois Messieurs de travailler unanimement & conjointement à tous les desseins qu'il y auroit à faire pour l'achevement du Palais du Louvre, en sorte que ces desseins seroient regardés comme l'ouvrage des trois également, & qu'aucun ne pourroit s'en dire l'auteur particulierement au préjudice des autres; malgré cet ordre si respectable, il n'y eut pas moyen d'y assujettir ces trois personnes de génie & de caractere si differens. Au lieu d'un seul dessein pour la façade, ils en firent deux, dont l'un étoit orné d'un ordre de colonnes formant un péristile ou galerie au-dessus du premier étage; & l'autre étoit plus simple & plus uni sans ordre de colonnes. Or fut-ce le sieur *le Vau* & le sieur *Perrault* qui donnerent le dessein à colonnes formant un péristile? En ce cas-là ce seroit l'ouvrage de tous les deux également, & le dessein simple & uni seroit du sieur *le Brun.* Tout cela ne paroît pas vraisemblable. Ou bien seroient-ce *le Vau* & *le Brun* qui seroient les auteurs du dessein à colonnes? & en ce cas-là *Perrault* seroit l'auteur du dessein uni, tort que personne ne lui a jamais fait; ou enfin c'est *Perrault* qui est l'auteur du dessein à colonnes, & qui a été approuvé par *le Brun,* & pour lors le dessein uni restera à *le Vau,* sans que personne lui en dispute la gloire.

Voilà ce qui résulte du mérite de *Perrault,* de l'opinion presque générale, & du sentiment de ceux qui ont connu le génie des trois artistes dont il est ici question.

69. *1744.* Annibale Antonini, *Memorial de Paris, et de ses environs, à l'usage des voyageurs,* new ed., Paris, 1744, 59:

Le nouveau Louvre a été entrepris du Regne & par les ordres de Louis XIV. en trois années seulement, depuis 1667. jusqu'en 1670. sur les desseins & sous la conduite de *Louis le Vau,* natif de Paris; & après sa mort, sous les soins de *François d'Orbai,* son éleve.

Quelques-uns attribuent les desseins du Louvre à *Perrault,* le Traducteur de Vitruve.

70. *1748.* [Saint-Yves], *Observations sur les arts . . . ,* Leiden, 1748, 150:

La façade du Vieux Louvre, le plus admirable de ceux qui éxistent aujourd'hui sur la terre, le seul édifice construit sous le regne de Louis XIV. qui donneroit à la posterité une haute idée du regne de ce Prince, est aussi le seul [in Paris] qui pourroit inspirer de grandes pensées à un Architecte.

71. *1749.* [La Font de Saint-Yenne], *Remerciment des habitans de la ville de Paris à Sa Majesté, au sujet de l'achevement du Louvre,* Paris, 1749, 1–9:

SIRE [Louis XV],

Les voeux de Vos Sujets sont enfin éxaucés. Vous avez décidé du sort de l'Edifice de Vôtre Royaume le plus important à Vôtre gloire & à la sienne, & Vos ordres sont donnés pour achever le Louvre. Il n'appartient qu'aux grands Rois d'étonner la postérité par des Monumens qui immortalisent leur Regne, & le Louvre seul pouvoit remplir cet auguste projet.

C'étoit depuis long tems un sujet de douleur bien sensible aux vrais François & aux Citoyens zélés pour leur Patrie, d'avoir dans le sein de leur Capitale un Palais d'une aussi rare beauté, & de le voir non seulement imparfait, & livré par son abandon à une ruine prochaine, mais encore enseveli dans le deshonneur, & fermé aux regards même de Votre peuple, & à l'admiration des Etrangers. Nous avions d'autant plus lieu de gémir sur son déplorable état, que ce superbe Péristile est l'ouvrage d'un François, & peut-être le plus honorable à la France. Eh! qu'est-ce qui fait la gloire d'une Nation? Qu'est-ce qui met le sceau éternel à sa véritable grandeur, sinon ses chefs-d'oeuvre dans les Lettres & dans les Arts? Si Paris n'eût eu qu'un exemplaire des ouvrages divins de Corneille, de Racine, & de Moliere; & qu'un ordre bizare mais absolu, l'eût enfermé dans un cabinet inaccessible, de quelles ténèbres cette barbarie eût obscurci le génie François, supérieur par ses immortelles productions aux modeles même les plus parfaits de l'Antiquité? A quel état humiliant de médiocrité, cet attentat eût fixé sa réputation qui remplit aujourd'hui les deux Hémisphéres, & que nos meilleurs écrits présens & à venir n'eussent peut-être jamais élevée au même point de grandeur! Comment aurions-nous pû, sans la publicité de ces glorieux titres, convaincre tous les peuples sçavans de l'Europe de notre primauté Littéraire, & surtout dans le double Poëme Théatral? Il en est de même, SIRE, de l'ouvrage admirable de Perrault, & de la sublime ordonnance de ces majestueux Portiques, rivaux de ceux d'Athènes & de Rome par leurs sçavantes proportions, & leur magnifique étendue, qui forment la superbe façade de votre Palais. Elevés au milieu de nous, & interdits à nos regards, on eut été réduit à les admirer dans des descriptions, ou dans des gravures. Mais quelle froide admiration! Quel parallele en Architecture de la vûe des dessins, avec celle du corps de l'édifice! N'est-ce pas celui de l'ombre avec la réalité? L'aspect seul de la grandeur de toutes ses parties, de la justesse de leurs proportions, & de l'harmonie qui en résulte, porte à l'ame cette impression de majesté qui la ravit, & que rien ne sçauroit égaler ni suppléer.

Combien d'Etrangers dans l'impuissance de venir à Paris, ont estimé impracticable l'élévation de ce merveilleux Palais sur les dessins gravés qui leur en sont parvenus! Plusieurs Architectes concurrens de Perrault, jaloux de l'excellence & du succès de son dessin présenté à Louis XIV., & ne pouvant désavouer la sublimité de son ordonnance qui força l'envie même à l'approbation, se vengerent en soutenant son exécution impossible. Quel projet chimérique, dirent-ils, de vouloir élever une Architecture solide sur de telles proportions? A-t-on l'exemple de quelqu'édifice où les architraves & les platfonds, ayent une portée de cette étendue dans les entrecolonnes? A peine l'entablement & l'attique seront construits, que l'on verra par leur charge affaisser ces platte-bandes hardies, & la ruine de l'édifice est certaine. Génies vulgaires! Censeurs aveugles! qui ignoroient les ressources de ce grand Architecte dans la science de la Géométrie & de la Méchanique, & sur-tout dans celle du Trait, & de la Coupe des pierres; science qui tient du prodige, & dont l'oeil admire d'autant plus les merveilles, qu'il les voit avec effroi. Ce fut par elles que Perrault triompha sans peine des impossibilités qu'on lui opposoit.

Colbert, fortement persuadé que sans l'étude des hommes & de leur valeur, le Monarque est sans force, & le Ministre sans réputation, non seulement connoissoit les grands talens, mais il les mesuroit au point de calculer les différences de leur étendue. Sûr de celle de Perrault, il méprise les menaces de ses envieux, quoiqu'importantes en apparence, & adopte son plan avec une hardiesse tranquille. On travaille à l'exécution, l'ouvrage s'éleve, & leurs cris continuent. Qu'est-il arrivé? Le tems a démontré leur ignorance, & éternisé l'habileté de l'Architecte. Depuis soixante & dix-neuf ans ce miracle de l'art, cette Colonnade subsiste avec autant de fermeté & d'immobilité dans toutes ses parties, qu'aux premiers jours de sa construction.

72. *July 7, 1749.* Minutes of the Académie royale d'architecture (H. Lemonnier, ed., *Procès-verbaux de l'Académie royale d'architecture,* Paris, 1920, VI, 123–124):

L'Académie étant assemblée, on a comparé les proportions des plus beaux chapiteaux corinthiens, savoir celles des chapiteaux antiques avec celles des chapiteaux de la chapelle de Versailles et celles des chapiteaux de la colonnade du Louvre, les chapiteaux antiques ayant deux modules et un tiers de hauteur, les chapiteaux de la chapelle de Versailles ayant deux modules et demie, les chapiteaux de la colonnade du Louvre ayant deux modules deux tiers, et tous ces chapiteaux étant généralement estimés des connoisseurs comme les plus beaux models que l'on puisse suivre en architecture, l'Académie est d'avis que deux modules et demi sont la plus belle proportion moyenne qu'on puisse donner au chapiteau corinthien, et que la hauteur de ce chapiteau peut être porté jusqu'à deux modules deux tiers, principalement lorsqu'on a des pilastres ou des colonnes couplées comme à la colonnade du Louvre, et que le même chapiteau peut sans inconvénient n'avoir que deux modules et un tiers de hauteur comme dans l'antique lorsqu'on a que des colonnes non accouplées sans pilastres.

73. *July 14, 1749.* Minutes of the Académie royale d'architecture (Lemonnier, ed., *Procès-verbaux,* VI, 124–125):

L'Académie étant assemblée, on a examiné plus particulièrement les proportions du chapiteau de l'ordre corinthien du péristyle du Louvre d'après les mesures que différens Académiciens ont rapporté à la Compagnie.

Le diamètre du bas du fust de la colonne a été donné de 3 pieds 7 pouces. Le diamètre au tiers de la hauteur de la colonne a été trouvé de 3 pieds 8 pouces 8 lignes. Le diamètre du haut du fust de la colonne a été donné de 3 pieds 1 pouce. La hauteur du chapiteau entier, y compris son tailloir, a été donnée de 4 pieds 8 pouces. Suivant ces mesures, le chapiteau se trouve avoir 2 modules 10 parties 38/43, c'est-à-dire 2 modules 10 parties et environ 3/4.

La hauteur totale de la colonne y compris la base et le chapiteau est de 37 pieds 11 pouces. La hauteur de la base est de 2 pieds. La hauteur de l'entablement est de 9 pieds 6 pouces, sçavoir: architrave, 2 pieds 9 pouces; frise, 3 pieds; corniche, 3 pieds 9 pouces.

Enfin, la colonne est posée sur un socle de 3 pieds de haut.

74. *1751.* Claude François Lambert, *Histoire littéraire du règne de Louis XIV,* Paris, 1751.

a. [From the biography of Claude Perrault]:

Les superbes & magnifiques ouvrages qui ont été bâtis sur ses desseins seront des monumens éternels de sa capacité; l'on ne peut en effet disconvenir que la seule façade du Louvre ne suffise pour immortaliser la gloire de ce grand homme. (III, 100)

b. [From the biography of Claude Perrault]:

Toute la difficulté étoit de sçavoir si l'exécution en étoit possible; ce Peristille, ces Portiques majestueux dont les colonnes portent des Architraves de douze pieds de long & des platfonds quarrés d'une pareille largeur, paroissoient être autant de morceaux plus propres à faire l'ornement d'un tableau qu'à servir de modelle pour le frontispice d'un Palais véritable; ce dessein si hardi a été cependant parfaitement exécuté, sans qu'une seule pierre de ce large platfond, tout plat & suspendu pour ainsi dire en l'air, se soit démentie. (III, 100–101)

c. [From the biography of Claude Perrault]:

Ces trois ouvrages [Louvre Colonnade, Observatoire, Arc de Triomphe du Trône] dont la beauté égale tout ce que l'Architecture ancienne a pû imaginer de plus riche & de plus somptueux, assurent à leur auteur une gloire qui ne finira jamais. (III, 101).

d. [From the biography of Louis Le Vau]:

Ce fut aussi sur ses desseins . . . que la superbe porte de l'entrée du Louvre fut bâtie. (III, 137)

75. *1751.* Louis Petit de Bachaumont, *Essai sur la peinture, la sculpture, et l'architecture,* [Paris], 1751, 81–82:

Où peut-on trouver plus de noblesse, plus d'élégance, plus de magnificence, que dans la superbe Colonnade qui décore cette façade? Tous les ornemens de Sculpture qui y sont répandus avec autant de sagesse que de richesse, ne sont pas tous mis; mais on peut aisément juger par ceux qui le sont à peu près, de ce que seroit devenu le reste, si l'on eût mis la dernière main à cet Ouvrage. Quel heureux effort de génie, d'avoir réduit cette grande Décoration à un seul Ordre. [*Footnote: Regia solis erat sublimibus alta columnis. Ovide, Metam. L. 2 V. 1.*][192] Que cela lui donne de majesté! Quelle idée n'offre-t'elle pas du Palais qu'elle annonce; de celui pour qui on l'a bâti; et de celui qui l'a imaginée!

76. *1751.* François Marie Arouet de Voltaire, *Le siècle de Louis XIV,* Berlin, 1751. I have used the London edition of 1752, II, 309:

Mais quand [Bernini] arriva à Paris avec tant d'appareil, comme le seul homme digne de travailler pour Louis XIV. il fut bien surpris de voir le dessein de la façade du Louvre, du côté de Saint-Germain-l'Auxerrois, qui devint bientôt après dans l'éxécution un des plus Augustes monumens d'architecture, qui soient au monde. Claude Perrault avait donné ce dessein, éxécuté par Louis le [V]au & d'[O]rbay. Il [Perrault] inventa les machines, avec lesquelles on transporta des pierres de cinquante deux pieds de long, qui forment le frontispice de ce majéstueux édifice. On va chercher quelquefois bien loin ce qu'on a chez soi. Aucun palais de Rome n'a une entrée comparable à celle du Louvre, dont on est redevable à ce Perrault, que Boileau osa vouloir rendre ridicule.[193]

77. *1752.* Jacques François Blondel, *Architecture françoise,* Paris, 1752, II.

a. En effet les monumens que nous avons de lui [Claude Perrault], tels que le péristyle du Louvre, bâti en 1665 [*sic*], l'Observatoire dont nous parlons élevé en 1667, & l'Arc de Triomphe du Thrône, érigé en 1670, sont autant de chef-d'oeuvres qui serviront de regles à la postérité la plus reculée. (57 n. a)

b. A propos de cet ouvrage [Perrault's Vitruvius edition], je remarquerai qu'il paroît étonnant que Claude Perrault, à qui la plupart de ses contemporains donnent la composition de cet édifice [the Observatoire], ne fasse lui-même aucune mention qu'il en ait été l'auteur, en en donnant les desseins dans Vitruve, Livre premier, chap. 2. pag. 10. C'est sans doute cet excès de modestie qui a déterminé ses ennemis à lui disputer l'invention de ce monument, aussi bien que celle du peristyle du Louvre & [l'Arc de Triomphe] du Thrône, & à lui refuser jusqu'au titre d'Architecte, voyant que cet auteur n'avoit pas pris cette qualité dans l'Epitre dedicatoire adressée à Louis XIV, qui est à la tête de sa traduction de Vitruve, imprimée en 1673.[194] (60)

78. *1752.* [Antoine Nicolas Dezallier d'Argenville], *Voyage pittoresque de Paris . . . ,* 2d ed., Paris, 1752, 35–36:

LA NOUVELLE FAÇADE qui est du côté de S. Germain l'Auxerrois, est un morceau d'Architecture généralement admiré. Au-dessus d'un raiz de chaussée fort élévé est construite une Galerie couverte & séparée en deux. Le comble est soutenu de vingt-huit colonnes Corinthiennes, isolées, accouplées & cannelées, qui avec autant de pilastres placés sur le mur intérieur de la galerie, supportent des architraves de douze pieds de long. Cette superbe façade est donc distribuée en deux péristiles & en trois avant-corps. Celui du milieu est décoré de huit colonnes Corinthiennes accouplées, & terminé par un fronton dont la cymaise n'est que de deux pierres, d'une grandeur surprenante. Les deux autres sont ornés de six pilastres & de deux colonnes du même ordre & dans la même disposition. Sur le comble règne au lieu de toit, une terrasse bordée d'une balustrade dont les piédestaux doivent porter des trophées entre-mêlés de vases. La gloire de ce chef-d'oeuvre est dûe, suivant toutes les apparences, à *le Vau,* quelques personnes cependant se croient autorisées à la donner à *Claude Perrault.*

79. *1752.* La Font de Saint-Yenne, *L'ombre du grand Colbert, le Louvre, & la ville de Paris, dialogue . . . ,* new ed., Paris, 1752. First published at The Hague in 1749. The selection published here contains the author's final version and some interesting footnotes not found in the first edition.

L'OMBRE [Colbert].

La dignité de votre [the Louvre's] édifice & sa magnificence étoient aussi l'objet de mes désirs & de mes soins les plus appliqués. Eh comment aurois-je pû être attaché à mon Roi avec autant de tendresse, & ne pas épuiser tout ce que j'avois de capacité pour rendre son Palais supérieur à tous les Palais des autres Monarques! Voici les moyens que j'employai.

Pendant le tems que je faisois travailler à Versailles & au grand ouvrage de la jonction des mers,[195] les embellissemens de ma Patrie m'occupoient toujours. Je ne perdois point de vûe mon dessein de relever l'honneur de la capitale & de la venger de l'oubli & de la négligence de mes prédécesseurs pour sa décoration & ses alignemens. Mais l'édifice qui exigeoit toute l'étendue, toute l'application de mes lumieres & la plus grande célérité dans sa perfection, étoit le Palais du Souverain. Les Magistrats, le peuple, tous les citoyens, & même les étrangers soupiroient après l'achevement du Louvre. Je n'avois rien à ajouter à la face de ce Château de côté des jardins. Celui dont je venois de l'embellir si heureusement, étoit le plus grand ornement & le plus parfait que l'on y pût souhaiter. Il formoit à ce palais un aspect enchanteur, & les vûes en étoient terminées assez agréablement par les allées de l'Etoile [the Champs Elysées] fort avancée dans la campagne. Il ne me restoit plus qu'à finir le nouveau Louvre & son frontispice du côté de l'Eglise de Saint Germain l'Auxerrois, qui est celui de son entrée, & qui doit annoncer de loin le Palais du Maître de la nation. Le Roi désiroit avec la plus grande ardeur de le voir achevé, & me dit qu'il ne vouloit rien épargner pour rendre sa façade supérieure en tout à celle des Tuileries. Il m'ordonna d'y employer la magnificence la plus somptueuse dont l'architecture puisse décorer, & distinguer un édifice de cette importance. Quelque habiles que fussent nos Architectes François, je ne me bornai point à leurs idées. Le Cavalier Bernin avoit alors avec la réputation du plus grand Sculpteur, celle de premier Architecte de l'Europe par l'élévation de son génie, & le sublime qu'il répandoit dans toutes ses compositions. J'en parlai à Sa Majesté. Elle me chargea de l'engager à venir en France, & de l'attirer de Rome où il étoit alors, par des bienfaits abondans & les récompenses les plus flatteuses. Pour le presser davantage, elle lui assura une pension de 6000 livres pendant sa vie, & une gratification de 50 mille écus. Elle lui envoya en même tems son Portrait chargé de diamans. Outre les frais de son voyage qui devoient lui être payés, on lui promit encore cent francs par jour pendant sa demeure à Paris. Le Cavalier Bernin ne tarda pas de s'y rendre. Mais ses dessins pour le Frontispice du Louvre n'ayant pas rempli l'idée que l'on avoit de sa haute capacité, ni satisfait le goût de Louis XIV., ils ne furent point suivis. La fortune qui épioit toutes les occasions de servir un si grand Prince, & qui lui formoit dans ses propres Etats des hommes supérieurs à ceux des autres Nations, lui fit rencontrer dans sa Capitale ce qu'elle avoit inutilement cherché dans les pays étrangers. J'avois des espions à Paris, dans tout le Royaume, & même chez l'Etranger pour découvrir le mérite caché. L'on me parla avec de grands éloges de Claude Perrault. Il étoit né avec une étendue d'esprit capable de toutes les sciences. Il s'étoit fait un grand nom dans la Médecine & dans la Physique par des Mémoires excellens, donnés au public sur l'Histoire naturelle & sur celle des animaux. Il lut dans nos assemblées de l'Académie des Dissertations sur l'Architecture qui me parurent si sçavantes & si profondes, que j'engageai S. M. à l'obliger de travailler à la traduction de Vitruve pour l'avantage public, & surtout de l'Académie d'Architecture. Ce grand ouvrage ne l'effraya point; & pour réussir parfaitement, il s'arracha entièrement à l'étude de la Médecine & aux expériences de Physique, & abandonna les connoissances étendues qu'il avoit de la structure du corps des animaux pour se livrer à celle des bâtimens. Il abjura le culte qu'il rendoit à Hippocrate, ce célébre Philosophe, en qui il disoit que tout le bon sens de la Gréce étoit renfermé, pour porter tous ses hommages à un sçavant également illustre en son genre, & qu'il estimoit aussi nécessaire pour former les bons Architectes, que les Aphorismes Grecs pour faire d'habiles médecins. Sa traduction fut enrichie de notes excellentes par l'étendue de son érudition, & sur-tout de celle dans la partie des Mathématiques qui regarde la Mécanique & les forces mouvantes, si nécessaire à tout Architecte. A peine cette traduction parut, qu'elle eut un cours prodigieux en France & chez les étrangers. Le Vitruve François n'honorera pas moins le siécle de Louis XIV. que le Latin a illustré celui d'Auguste. C'est à l'attention que j'eus de le détourner par cette traduction, de ses autres études, que j'attribue l'entiere métamorphose du bon Physicien en excellent Architecte. Quelque foibles que fussent mes connoissances dans ce bel Art, les entretiens fréquens que j'avois eus avec ce sçavant homme, m'en avoient donné les plus hautes idées. Je lui confiai mes regrets de n'en avoir pas fait une étude particuliere dans ma jeunesse, & surtout de celui du Dessin pour pouvoir lui tracer mes pensés. Vous êtes dans une grande erreur, me dit-il, il est fort heureux pour un Ministre & encore plus pour un Souverain de se trouver dans l'impuissance de perdre un tems qui leur est si précieux, à crayonner des idées qui ne sçauroient être utiles par l'ignorance des grands principes de cet Art & le défaut de pratique. Ces foibles connoissances leur sont même nuisibles, en ce que leurs productions étant applaudies par des flateurs, quelque médiocres qu'elles soient, elles sont souvent préférées pour l'exécution aux excellentes. D'ailleurs ces sortes d'amusemens étant toujours bornés à de petits objets, ils achevent de rétrécir leur goût, & leur génie au lieu de l'agrandir. Il y a long-tems que l'on a représenté un Prince qui fait bâtir, & celui à qui il confie le soin de ses bâtimens, par l'emblême d'un homme sans mains, mais avec de bons yeux & d'excellentes oreilles;[196] pour exprimer que ni le Roi, ni le Ministre ne doivent point travailler eux-mêmes aux Dessins de leurs bâtimens, qu'ils n'ont besoin que de bons yeux pour juger de ceux qu'on leur présente, & d'excellentes oreilles pour écouter les conseils des personnes capables de leur en donner. Voilà ceux qu'ils doivent chercher avec une ardeur continuelle, & suivre ensuite leurs avis, quand ils auront eu le bonheur de les trouver. Il ne s'agit pas, me disoit-il encore, pour un Sur-intendant des bâtimens d'un Roi tel que celui d'aujourd'hui, d'élever des pierres; mais de porter ses édifices publics au plus haut dégré de perfection où l'Architecture puisse arriver. La raison en est sensible. C'est que leurs beautés existent éternellement, & que leurs défauts sont irréparables. Mais où trouver d'excellens Architectes? Combien d'hommes en usurpent le nom qui sont à peine de bons ouvriers? S'il suffisoit pour le mériter d'avoir vû l'Italie, & d'y avoir mesuré exactement ses beaux édifices anciens & modernes, de connoître les proportions des cinq Colonnes & les parties de leurs Ordres, d'en avoir élevé plusieurs l'un sur l'autre, que d'Architectes il y auroit dans le monde! Mais ce n'est point là ce qui constitue le grand Architecte, c'est le génie seul, ainsi que dans tous les autres arts. C'est de l'avoir assez élevé pour pénétrer les principes & les sources de ses vraies beautés, approfondir les raisons primitives de leurs proportions, de leurs divisions, & des ornemens assignés à chaque Ordre; sentir par la force & l'activité d'un génie vigoureux, & par une longue expérience, tous les effets d'un grand ensemble avant de le mettre en oeuvre, voir s'il doit résulter de la distribution de ses masses, cette harmonie, & cet accord qui ramene tout à l'unité. C'est enfin sçavoir prendre des licences à propos, sans paroître choquer les régles, ni s'éloigner des sages proportions, pour y jetter cette élégance & cet agrément qui charme & qui ravit; pendant que la froide correction & l'observation la plus scrupuleuse de ces mêmes régles, glace le spectateur & ne l'émeut d'aucun plaisir.

Ce furent ces difficultés de former de grands Architectes, ajouta Perrault, qui me porterent, avant de faire travailler à ces importans Edifices qui doivent servir de modéles à la postérité, à vous engager de solliciter S. M. d'envoyer des personnes habiles en cet Art dans l'Egypte, la Gréce, la Syrie, la Perse & par-tout où subsistent encore des vestiges & les ruines respectables de cette premiere Architecture presque aussi ancienne que le monde.[197] Quelle grandeur! quelle vaste étendue dans ce qui nous reste du Palais des rois de Perse à Persépolis![198] Les plus superbes demeures de nos Rois Européens, sont-elles comparables à l'immensité & à la magnificence d'une seule des piéces de ce Palais?[199] L'on ne pouvoit donc rien conseiller à Louis XIV. de plus digne de sa grandeur, & de plus utile aux Arts pour les porter à leur perfection la plus sublime, que d'envoyer dans tout l'Orient recueillir les précieux débris de ces merveilles du monde pour former parmi nous d'excellens Architectes, & élever nos idées à la majesté de celles des anciens. . . .

LE LOUVRE.
Le plaisir que j'ai de vous entendre, ô mon pere! ne me fait point oublier la suite du récit de vos travaux en ma faveur, que j'ose vous prier de continuer.

L'OMBRE.
J'y reviens. Dès que le Cavalier Bernin fut arrivé à Paris, Perrault chercha avec avidité les occasions de s'entretenir avec lui; mais ses discours ne satisfirent point l'opinion extraordinaire qu'il en avoit. Dans tous ses dessins, dont il lui fit part, il admira la beauté de son génie & la vaste étendue de son imagination digne d'une réputation si célèbre; mais ses plus belles compositions en architecture n'étoient presque jamais assujetties à des proportions exactes, & conformes à celles que Perrault s'étoit formées sur les plus beaux Monumens Grecs & Romains. A l'égard de son goût pour la décoration des Mausolées, des Pompes funébres, des Fontaines publiques, & des Ouvrages d'importance & d'une grande étendue, aucun génie de son siécle n'a égalé, & peut-être aucun n'égalera la hauteur & la magnificence de ses pensées. Perrault me fit sentir en bon juge, mais sans jalousie, les écarts, les licences & le mépris des grandes régles au travers des beautés qui brillioent dans ses dessins pour le frontispice du Louvre. Peut-être l'Italie accoutumée depuis un siécle à la licence des Sçavans de sa nation dans les Arts comme dans les Lettres, eût admiré son projet. Peut-être aussi eût-il été adopté par le nôtre sous un regne moins éclairé; mais les yeux du Roi ne furent point éblouis par de si magnifiques séductions. Après beaucoup d'accueil à l'Auteur, il me déclara en son absence qu'il n'étoit point satisfait. Quelques mois après, Perrault eut l'honneur de lui présenter un dessin pour cette façade; S. M. fut quelque tems à l'examiner, puis elle s'écria avec satisfac-

tion que c'étoit ce qu'Elle désiroit. Elle fut frappée & satisfaite de la grandeur & de la riche simplicité de cette majestueuse ordonnance, & m'ordonna d'y faire travailler sur le champ, & de prodiguer à son auteur toutes les facilités & les fonds nécessaires pour sa parfaite exécution. Et c'est où doivent toujours tendre les Souverains, dans les Ouvrage d'importance auxquels ils se determinent. L'économie de la dépense en ces occasions est une foiblesse d'esprit nécessairement suivie de la honte & de l'inutilité des regrets. La préférence que donna Louis XIV. au dessin sage & simple de Perrault, sur les beautés séduisantes, mais défectueuses de celui du Bernin, prouvoit dans ce Prince un grand discernement, & le goût du vrai beau, extrêmement rare chez tous les hommes, & sur-tout chez les Grands. Tout le monde est convenu, & même les Etrangers, que le dessin du Péristile du Louvre est un chef-d'oeuvre de grandeur de génie, & en même tems de bons sens & de raison.[200] C'est sur cette raison, me disoit souvent ce grand Architecte, sur ce concours & ce rapport général d'approbations, qu'ont été établies les régles & les belles proportions consacrées dans l'architecture à chaque Ordre. Elles ne doivent cependant jamais être si respectées qu'elles ne puissent souffrir quelque exception par la différente position des objets assujettis aux différens aspects de l'oeil qui les observe. La science même de l'Optique, si nécessaire à l'Architecte, ne sçauroit donner des régles certaines à cet égard, & ce n'est que la justesse de son génie & l'art de prevoir les effets de ses parties, suivant la diversité de leurs emplacemens, qui peuvent autoriser & faire réussir ces sortes de licences.[201]

. . . .

Je fis élever les trois faces de ce Palais sur un plan quarré, & j'en reservai toute la magnificence pour le côté de son entrée. Je n'épargnai aucune dépense pour egaler la perfection de l'exécution à celle du dessin. Les sieurs le Vau premier architecte du Roi, & le fameux le Brun, ce génie universel, toujours grand, toujours riche, & qui embrassoit tous les Arts, furent associés à Perrault pour la plus grande perfection de tout l'ouvrage, & d'Orbay habile Architecte fut chargé particulierement du soin de l'exécution. Je choisis parmi nos Sculpteurs les plus excellens pour les chapiteaux des colonnes Corinthiennes; c'est le travail le plus difficile en ce genre, & d'où dépend presque toute la grace & l'élégance de cet Ordre. C'est sur les dessins du Sr. le Brun & sous ses yeux qu'ils furent exécutés dans cette perfection qui les fait regarder par les connoisseurs François & étrangers comme des modéles de perfection en leur genre, soit par leurs belles proportions, soit par la légéreté de leurs feuilles, & les graces avec lesquels elles sont traitées. Je destinai aux autres la sculpture des ornemens des platfonds, des architraves, & de ceux de la Gallerie, les festons qui accompagnent les médaillons, les vases & les trophées sur la balustrade du comble, le timpan du grand fronton, les statues des niches, &c. Enfin j'eus la satisfaction d'entendre des cris d'applaudissemens universels à mesure que les beautés de ce Palais s'élevoient. Je laissai les murs de face portés jusqu'aux combles, & la grande façade élevée jusqu'à la balustrade, & presque entierement finie. Quel plaisir je vais goûter d'en voir en ce moment l'entiere perfection, & le majestueux spectacle![202] (116–133, 138–145, 150–152)

80. *1753.* Marc Antoine Laugier, *Essai sur l'architecture*, Paris, 1753, 3:

Un bel édifice parle éloquemment pour son Architecte. M. Perrault dans ses écrits n'est tout au plus qu'un Sçavant: la colonnade du Louvre le décide grand Homme.

81. *1754.* [Jacques François Blondel], "Denticule" (article), *Encyclopédie ou dictionnaire raisonné des sciences, des arts et des métiers . . .* , Paris, 1754, IV, 847:

L'on peut dire en général, que cette espece d'ornement [denticules] peut être employé ou supprimé dans l'Architecture, selon l'élégance de l'ordre, la richesse de la décoration, & l'importance du bâtiment; par exemple, lorsque toutes les moulures d'une corniche sont taillées d'ornemens, il est bon de les omettre, ainsi que Perrault l'a pratiqué à son péristyle, malgré l'exemple de l'intérieur du Louvre [the courtyard] qu'il avoit sous les yeux. Cette suppression emporte un repos dans les différentes moulures d'une corniche, qui produit un bon effet.

82. *April 1755.* Mercure de France, April 1755, 167–175. This anonymous, strong attack on the Louvre of Louis XIV was published at a time when the Colonnade was being completed, restored, and enthusiastically praised. Counterattacks on this article were published two months later and in 1756 (see nos. 83 and 86, below).

Si les hommes n'étoient pas aussi portés qu'ils le sont à se livrer dans leurs opinions à des excés toujours condamnables, s'ils n'autorisoient pas par des exemples trop souvent répétés, à douter de l'équité de leurs motifs, on ne pourroit leur contester le droit honorable d'étendre leurs discussions & leur critique sur les objets les plus respectables en tous genres: mais lorsqu'on voit (pour me restreindre aux matieres de goût) qu'à peine a-t-on osé substituer à l'adoration d'Homere quelques recherches sur de légers défauts, dont il est certain qu'il n'a pas dû être exempt, qu'aussi-tôt on brise ses autels, on arrache sa couronne, on méprise & on raille ses adorateurs, ne doit-on pas être porté à souhaiter, qu'à l'exemple de Mahomet, on impose un silence profond & mystérieux sur les Divinités des sciences, des arts & du goût? Mais où se trouvera le Législateur dont la mission sera assez généralement reconnue, pour établir cette loi de prévoyance que l'esprit imposeroit à l'esprit? d'ailleurs, oser montrer de nos jours une pareille méfiance, ne seroit-ce pas refuser à notre siécle ce titre respectable de philosophe dont il se pare, & dont il espere que la postérité fera son titre distinctif? Puisqu'il en arbore l'étendart, il doit être louable & permis aujourd'hui ou jamais de hazarder quelques réflexions qui ont pour objet un de ces chefs-d'oeuvres des arts faits pour être adorés aveuglément dans un siécle d'enthousiasme & de préjugés; mais faits pour être discutés dans un siécle sage, éclairé, enfin dans un siécle philosophe comme le nôtre.

Il s'agit ici de la colonade & des projets du rétablissement du Louvre.

Il est nécessaire d'établir premierement les raisons pour lesquelles, sous le regne de Louis XIV, les Architectes employés à cet ouvrage ont pris pour le finir une route différente de celle qu'avoient tenue ceux qui l'avoient commencé.

En général, il est avantageux aux progrès des connoissances humaines, que les esprits & les talens d'un siécle profitent & s'enrichissent de ce que l'esprit & le talent avoient amassé déja de thrésors & de richesses; mais le profit seroit incontestablement plus considérable & plus rapide, si les grands ouvrages & les vastes projets conduits & exécutés par la même main, qui en a tracé les esquisses, nous offroient plus souvent les idées accomplies de ceux qui les ont conçus. Il arrive malheureusement que ces auteurs ont des jours plus bornés que leur entreprise, & qu'après eux on s'écarte toujours de leurs vûes, ou bien que l'on abandonne leurs plans.

Il ne falloit pour finir l'édifice dont il est question, qu'ordonner aux Architectes de suivre ce qui étoit commencé, nous aurions sous les yeux le plus superbe palais de l'Europe. Louis XIV attribuant aux artistes les principes & les grands motifs qui le faisoient agir, fit venir des pays étrangers des hommes de réputation: tous ceux qui étoient en France furent chargés de travailler; mais l'amour propre injuste leur persuada qu'il n'y avoit aucune gloire à prétendre, s'ils suivoient des idées qu'ils n'auroient point créées.

On fit donc différens projets qui occasionnerent, comme aujourd'hui, des contestations sans nombre parmi les artistes, & des libelles sans fin de la part des critiques. Il fut résolu qu'on éleveroit la colonade pour former l'entrée du Louvre, & que l'on doubleroit l'aîle sur la riviere, pour loger le Roi plus commodément dans cette partie.

Réfléchissons sur le résultat de tant de discussions, d'observations, de critiques, & d'avis différens.

Quel est-il? une façade de palais sans croisées, dont l'usage n'a pu se faire deviner depuis qu'elle est bâtie, dont les inconvéniens sont sans nombre, & dont la beauté déplacée a cependant un droit trop juste sur notre admiration pour qu'on puisse être soupçonné de le lui refuser. L'Architecte, emporté par le desir de concevoir & d'enfanter une production neuve & grande, a-t-il donc regardé comme peu intéressant l'usage qu'on feroit de ses travaux? quelle est la destination de la magnifique colonade qu'il a placée au premier étage de cette façade? L'a-t-il faite pour placer du monde à l'arrivée, ou à la sortie du Roi? L'a-t-il ornée pour le Roi lui-même dans les occasions où l'on auroit donné des fêtes dans la place sur laquelle elle devoit dominer? Dans l'un ou dans l'autre cas, n'eût-il pas été encore à desirer que la colonade se trouvât placée dans le milieu, comme l'endroit le plus convenable & le plus décent? La supposez-vous propre à faciliter la communication d'un côté du palais à l'autre? Alors pourquoi cette interruption ménagée pour faire une mauvaise arcade, dans laquelle se voit une petite porte? C'est ainsi que les idées de grandeur & cet enthousiasme qui semblent pour nous un état violent, ne sont pas à l'abri d'un mêlange de grandes & de petites productions. J'ajoûterai encore, c'est ainsi que la perfection absolue exige que l'imagination prenne toujours l'ordre d'une sage & utile convenance, qui est la base des sciences, des arts & du goût.

Passons maintenant à l'examen de la façade, qui placée du côté de la riviere, est celle que l'Architecte a eu intention de destiner à l'appartement du Roi. A en juger par l'entrée dont nous venons de parler, & par les progrès que doit offrir la magnificence d'un palais, quelle devroit être la riche décoration de cette aîle qu'un grand Monarque avoit choisie pour son séjour? Cependant, oubliant cette convenance si juste, ou bien épuisé par l'effort qu'il vient de faire, l'Architecte ne présente à notre curiosité qu'un bâtiment froid, décoré d'architecture en bas relief, autrement dit de pilastres sans colonnes, & sans aucun avant-corps qui interrompe par des repos & par des masses l'ennuyeuse monotonie qui y regne.

Des Architectes qui n'étant pas gênés, ont été capables de commettre des fautes aussi avérées, ne nous autorisent-ils pas à examiner avec moins de scrupule ce qui a pu les engager à décorer la Cour d'un troisieme ordre, par préférence à l'attique de l'ancien projet.²⁰³

Je m'imagine que deux raisons sont les principales causes de ce changement: le desir d'innover, & les difficultés qu'ils ont rencontrées en voulant exécuter l'attique, après avoir fait les façades extérieures.

Jugeons à présent de la validité de ces deux motifs: le premier si général & si souvent ennemi du bien, n'a pas besoin d'une longue discussion. Les innovations particulieres telles que celles-ci, ne faisant jamais partie d'un plan général, ont presque toujours l'air déplacé.

Cependant il étoit nécessaire de montrer sa capacité: suivre ce qui étoit commencé, c'étoit, ou paroître plagiaire, ou montrer un génie peu capable de ressource & d'invention: d'ailleurs, par rapport au dehors, qui ne peut entrer en comparaison avec le dedans, il falloit se résoudre à supprimer les dômes, les pavillons, les combles. Si l'on exécute ces retranchemens, & si l'on place ce seul attique, ne paroîtra-t-il pas qu'on a cherché à appauvrir un édifice que le projet d'un grand Roi est d'enrichir & d'orner? Pourquoi, diront-ils, cédant à toute la solidité de ces raisons, ne formons-nous pas un troisieme ordre qui, par sa nouveauté, fera briller nos talens, & par sa richesse sera conforme au dessein de celui qui nous emploie?

L'invention n'est pas une déesse docile; elle refuse souvent ses faveurs à ceux qui les desirent. On eut beau proposer des prix à celui qui ajoûteroit un nouvel ordre à ceux que le caprice a si souvent défigurés, & que le bon goût a toujours rétablis; il ne se trouva pas de Callimachus,²⁰⁴ & l'on se vit contraint de se servir d'une de ces productions, dont la nouveauté fait le seul mérite, & qu'on se garderoit bien d'adopter aujourd'hui.

Mais en supposant même que cet ordre fût digne d'être joint à ceux que le discernement de tant de siecles nous a transmis, seroit-il bien placé, & rendroit-il l'effet qu'on s'est proposé?

J'ose répondre que non. On a eu dessein sans doute, en supprimant les pavillons, les dômes & les combles, qui ne peuvent subsister relativement au dehors, de trouver quelque chose qui réparât cette perte.

Mais en établissant ce troisieme ordre dans toute l'étendue de l'edifice, tout le bâtiment se trouvera alors couronné à la même hauteur & de niveau; au lieu qu'en conservant l'attique dans les aîles, en admettant le troisieme ordre dans les pavillons des milieux, en décorant le dessus de l'attique dans les quatre pavillons des angles, cette cour intérieure présentera une décoration, dont le jeu détruira cette uniformité dont l'architecture doit autant se garantir que les autres productions des arts.

Il seroit aisé de développer ces réflexions & de prouver que ce projet est celui qui convient mieux à l'entiere perfection, si desirée d'un des plus beaux monumens de la nation. Un nombre infini d'inconvéniens dans les partis différens qu'on peut prendre, me fourniroit une matiere qui deviendroit insensiblement trop abondante. Je souhaite seulement qu'on se représente l'effet que produira l'ordre françois exécuté dans les petits avant-corps du milieu des aîles, où s'en trouve à présent le modele en masse. Qui pourra supporter l'excessive hauteur de ces avant-corps, comparée à leur largeur, puisqu'ils sont déja trop hauts, en y employant même l'attique.

Au reste, je ne prétens pas justifier absolument l'attique des défauts qu'on peut lui imputer; surchargé d'ornemens, décoré de figures & de trophées d'une proportion trop forte, il ne peut soutenir ses droits avec avantage que contre un adversaire dont la cause est infiniment moins favorable que la sienne.

De plus, tout changement dans cet ouvrage consacré par la vénération publique, paroîtra toujours un crime à ceux qui veulent jouir du plaisir de blâmer, sans prendre la juste peine d'approfondir & de s'éclairer. Mais si la critique fondée concourt à l'avantage des arts qu'elle éclaire, & à la réputation durable des artistes qu'elle applaudit, ces murmures passagers que rien n'autorise, ne doivent jamais suspendre des résolutions que la raison & le goût d'accord ont approuvées.

83. *June 1755.* "Lettre de M.... à M. le Comte de Ch. sur le Louvre," *Mercure de France,* June 1755, II, 144–155. This reply to no. 82 is accompanied by notes "d'un Artiste aussi éclairé qu'impartial," according to the anonymous author:

Je veux vous faire part, Monsieur, d'une critique du péristile du Louvre que je viens de voir dans le Mercure d'Avril. Je connois la chaleur de votre intérêt pour ce célebre monument, & je crois vous donner une preuve singuliere de mon amitié, en vous exposant les prétendus défauts qu'attaque ce censeur anonyme.

Il m'a paru un homme de l'art, mais on découvre aisément à travers les éloges qu'il donne à ce beau monument, que son admiration est plus contrainte que sincere. Il demande d'abord *qu'on lui permette quelques réflexions hazardées sur un de ces chefs-d'oeuvres des arts faits pour être adorés aveuglément dans un siécle d'enthousiasme & de préjugés* (reconnoît-on à ces traits le siécle de Louis XIV?)²⁰⁵ *mais faits pour être discutés dans un siécle sage, éclairé, enfin dans un siécle philosophe comme le nôtre.* Ce siécle, tout philosophe qu'il est, pourra-t-il nous indiquer quelques-uns de ses chefs-d'oeuvres qui ayent surpassé ou même approché de ceux du siécle dernier dans tous les genres?

Une nouvelle preuve du peu d'équité, & j'ose dire du peu de goût de ce nouveau censeur, c'est qu'au lieu de faire élever cette admirable façade, il eût souhaité de faire achever le Louvre sur les mêmes desseins de l'ancien; & *nous aurions,* dit-il, *sous les yeux le plus superbe palais de l'Europe.* L'on ne sçauroit marquer un mépris plus injurieux pour l'architecture de Perrault qu'en lui préférant un édifice où l'on ne trouve ni composition, ni proportions, ni régles. Trois frontons enclavés les uns dans les autres, des Caryatides placées à un second étage, des ornemens à la vérité d'un bon dessein & d'une belle exécution, mais presque tous déplacés, superflus & prodigués sans choix.[206]

Sur quel fondement attribuer ensuite à l'injustice de l'amour propre des Architectes de Louis XIV, le refus de suivre cet ancien plan qu'il estime si fort, pour y substituer par vanité leurs propres idées? Ne se présentoit-il pas un motif plus naturel & plus équitable? celui de mettre à profit dans une occasion si heureuse & si rare les progrès de l'esprit humain, celui des connoissances & des talens, la science des vraies proportions, l'estime & la préférence de ce beau simple à l'abondance & à la profusion des ornemens, ressource ordinaire de l'ignorance & du défaut de goût?

Que résulte-t-il du sentiment de notre Aristarque?[207] *une façade de palais sans croisées, dont on n'a pu deviner jusqu'à présent l'usage & la destination, & dont les inconvéniens sont sans nombre, & les beautés déplacées?* Il se donne bien de garde de nous détailler aucune de ces beautés, ni d'en louer les perfections. Il commence par chercher des défauts à cette façade, pour affoiblir l'impression d'admiration dont elle frappe tous les regards, en s'efforçant de rendre cette admiration injuste & presque ridicule; mais il n'est pas aisé de combattre avec succès une approbation universelle, & soutenue pendant le cours de près d'un siécle.

Il dit que l'on n'a pû deviner jusqu'à présent la destination de cette façade; mais n'auroit-il pas dû s'en informer avant de la condamner? Je crois pouvoir l'en instruire après avoir répondu à un reproche qu'il fait à M. Perrault, & que ce grand architecte n'a point mérité.

Il l'accuse de n'avoir interrompu la communication de ce péristile que pour faire une mauvaise arcade & une petite porte. Quelle apparence qu'une porte aussi simple ait été chez un aussi grand compositeur l'objet de cette interruption! le bon sens peut-il adopter une idée si singuliere? Ces deux péristiles ont chacun deux portes à leurs deux extrêmités, qui leur sont suffisantes. Etoit-il sensé que l'architecte supprimât ou gâtât ce beau pavillon du milieu pour donner plus d'étendue à deux péristiles qui ont chacun plus de trente-cinq toises: d'ailleurs quelle raison a-t-il d'appeller une mauvaise arcade une porte dont les proportions sont excellentes, & à laquelle on ne pouvoit donner qu'une forme ceintrée sans la rendre défectueuse? Est-il mieux fondé de blâmer la petite porte placée dans un renfoncement de douze pieds de profondeur, & sans laquelle il eût été impossible de fermer le Louvre? Eût-on pû mettre des venteaux à une ouverture de quarante-deux pieds de hauteur? Il étoit donc indispensable d'en menager avec art une plus petite, que l'on pût ouvrir & fermer.[208] Je reviens à l'usage & à la destination de cette façade, qui est pour notre critique un problème, & dont je lui ai promis la solution.

Il est très-certain, & je l'ai sçu par Mrs Desgot & Boffrand[209] qui avoient connu M. Perrault dans leur jeunesse, que lorsque Louis XIV déclara qu'il vouloit le frontispice de son Louvre enrichi de tout ce que l'architecture avoit acquis de perfection sous son regne, & de tout ce qu'elle pouvoit produire de plus régulier en même-tems, & de plus conforme aux belles proportions & à la majestueuse simplicité de l'architecture antique, il n'eut aucune intention d'habiter jamais ce Palais, mais seulement d'élever à son entrée un édifice dont la magnificence égalât & la grandeur de ses idées, & la dignité d'une maison que la nation regardoit comme celle de son Roi, par les honneurs qu'il avoit attachés à ses entrées. Il vouloit encore qu'elle pût servir aux siécles à venir de monument & de témoin évident & incontestable des merveilles de son regne dans tous les genres, mais sur-tout dans celui de la perfection des beaux Arts. Il y eut encore un autre motif qui détermina à employer dans cette façade tout ce que l'architecture avoit de plus majestueux & de plus frappant. Le dessein de M. Colbert étoit d'ouvrir une large & belle rue vis-à-vis le Louvre, que auroit été continuée jusques à l'arc de triomphe du fauxbourg S. Antoine,[210] & qui auroit servi d'avenue au plus vaste palais par son enceinte qu'il y eût eu en Europe, puisqu'il étoit décidé qu'on éleveroit du côté de la rue S. Honoré une galerie parallele à l'ancienne qui est sur la riviere, & qu'il n'y auroit aucun bâtiment entre le Louvre & le palais des Tuileries. Quelle décoration n'exigeoit pas l'objet d'un point de vûe d'une si prodigieuse étendue![211]

Louis XIV, en qui l'excellence d'un goût naturel égaloit son amour pour le grand en tout, ne fut point satisfait de plusieurs desseins qui lui furent présentés, où les croisées n'avoient point été oubliées, & sur-tout dans celui du Cavalier Bernin:[212] mais Perrault sçut saisir en habile homme l'avantage unique de la destination de cet édifice, & composer cet admirable frontispice, où il n'étoit asservi ni à la structure des palais ordinaires ni à leurs façades percées à jour; c'est ce qui lui fit concevoir & enfanter ce sublime dessein, qui fut dans le même instant présenté, admiré & agréé par Louis XIV.

Voilà ce qui a échappé aux connoissances de l'auteur de la critique, & qui détruit tous ses efforts pour dégrader ce bel édifice. L'ignorance à la vérité de ce que je viens de lui exposer, peut excuser & même autoriser les erreurs qu'on trouve dans la suite de l'examen de cette façade au sujet de sa destination. Telle est l'impossibilité où l'on eût été d'y placer des spectateurs dans le milieu, à l'occasion des fêtes qui auroient été données dans l'espace en face de ce Château.[213] Il n'est cependant pas vraisemblable qu'il n'ait jamais ouï parler du superbe carrousel donné par Louis XIV dans la cour du palais des Tuileries qui en a gardé le nom, & que cette cour étant beaucoup plus spacieuse que celle du Louvre, elle eût par conséquent toujours été choisie pour des fêtes. Notre Censeur auroit encore pû deviner la destination de ce palais par une réflexion bien simple: c'est que le palais le plus superbe ne sçauroit être digne d'un Roi, s'il n'a sous ses yeux & à sa bienséance les agrémens & la promenade d'un magnifique jardin. Ces réflexions eussent peut-être moderé la vivacité de sa critique, & l'eussent obligé de donner à Perrault les éloges qu'il mérite, quoique l'on apperçoive dans ses remarques une conspiration déclarée contre notre admiration. Ce Censeur peu équitable n'ayant pû se faire illusion sur la foiblesse des coups qu'il a portés à cette façade admirable, qui se bornent à son inutilité apparente & à l'interruption des deux péristiles, a cherché des défauts dans l'architecture de la façade de ce palais du côté de la riviere, mais avec aussi peu de succès. Il prétend que c'est dans cette partie du Louvre que Perrault avoit eu intention de placer l'appartement du Roi: dans cette supposition il s'éleve vivement contre la simplicité indécente de sa décoration extérieure; il la blâme d'être sans avant-corps qui interrompent par des repos & des masses l'ennuyeuse monotonie qui y regne. Cette premiere critique tombe d'elle-même, puisque l'on voit dans cette façade trois avant-corps, l'un dans le milieu qui devoit être couronné d'un grand fronton orné de sculptures, tel qu'il est gravé dans les plans du Louvre, d'après le dessein original de Perrault, & qui sont entre les mains de tout le monde;[214] les deux autres sont placés aux pavillons des deux extrémités.[215] En second lieu, ce bâtiment dont la simplicité l'offense si fort & le rend froid à ses yeux, ne l'auroit point été si les pilastres qui en décorent la face étoient cannelés comme ils le doivent être, les chapiteaux corinthiens sculptés & les trois corps décorés de médaillons couronés de masques & de guirlandes, & de tous les ornemens dont ils devoient être enrichis.[216] Lorsqu'il desire dans ce palais un progrès de magnificence supérieure, ou au moins égale à celle de la façade de l'entrée, il auroit voulu sans doute le même péristile, mais percé par des croisées, ce qui eût été impossible. Ces croisées placées dans un renfoncement de dix-sept pieds, auroient-elles éclairé suffisamment les appartemens, & n'y auroient-elles pas plutôt jetté le sombre & la tristesse d'un faux jour plus insupportable que l'entiere obscurité? Un autre inconvénient que l'on n'auroit jamais pû sauver dans la continuation du péristile, c'étoit de ne pouvoir rendre les appartemens de cette partie doubles, & par conséquent habitables par Sa Majesté dans des jours de fêtes.

Je passe sous silence ce qu'il dit de l'intérieur de la cour: il convient avec raison de l'embarras presque invincible où furent alors les Architectes, ou de continuer l'attique, ou en le supprimant, de raccorder la nouvelle architecture avec l'ancienne. Les plus habiles de nos jours ont tenté d'imaginer pour cet accord un meilleur dessein que celui qu'on a exécuté en partie,[217] & ils ont tous avoué que leurs efforts ont été sans succès.

L'Auteur finit sa critique par une assertion dont on pourra lui disputer la vérité; c'est que tout changement dans un ouvrage consacré à la vénération publique, paroîtra toujours un crime. Je puis lui répondre que s'il eût proposé quelque chose de nouveau & d'un meilleur accord que ce que l'on a exécuté dans les façades intérieures, le public sensé & éclairé en eût été très-reconnoissant, & auroit pensé comme lui, *qu'une critique fondée concourt à l'avantage des arts qu'elle éclaire, & que les murmures ne doivent jamais empêcher de publier ce que le goût, d'accord avec la raison, [a] approuvé.*[218]

84. 1756. Jacques François Blondel, *Architecture françoise*, Paris, 1756, IV.

a. Il n'y a point de doute que ce dessein [the drawing of the east façade of the Louvre with a colonnade, presented to Louis XIV in 1667], choisi par Sa Majesté, ne fût celui de *Perrault,* non seulement par la preuve des desseins originaux, dont nous avons parlé précédemment, qui existent dans les deux volumes qui appartiennent au Roi[219] . . . ; mais encore parce que l'on ne reconnoît point dans cette production le goût de *Le Veau* . . . ; au lieu qu'il paroît certain que celui qui a imaginé l'arc de triomphe [du Trône] est l'auteur du péristile. . . . Au reste, il se pourroit bien que *Le Brun,* sur-arbitre dans cette occasion, & reconnu pour un génie grand & élevé, ait fortifié *Perrault* dans son projet; mais pour recevoir des avis, on n'en est pas moins le créateur d'un ouvrage, & cette docilité, en la supposant telle que nous la disons, seroit seule capable de faire honneur à

Perrault, n'y ayant que les demi-sçavans qui ne consultent personne, & qui épris de leur ignorance, n'applaudissent qu'à leurs productions. (6 n. 9)

b. [East façade]:

Nous voici arrivés à la partie la plus intéressante de ce vaste Palais, & nous touchons au moment où notre sentiment sera sans doute combattu par ceux qui, plains d'estime & de vénération pour la beauté & l'élégance de l'Architecture qui régne dans cette façade, ont trop négligé peut-être d'examiner cet Edifice relativement à la convenance. Quoiqu'il en soit, nous croyons devoir suivre l'ordre avec lequel nous avons consideré les bâtimens décrits dans les volumes précédens de cet Ouvrage. Comme ce n'est point un esprit de critique qui nous anime, & que nous n'avons d'autre objet que d'examiner nos Edifices avec une attention égale à notre impartialité, nous devons considerer du même oeil les chef-d'oeuvres de nos grands Maîtres, d'autant plus qu'on imite plus ordinairement leurs défauts que l'on n'en saisit les beautés & que sous prétexte qu'ils se sont quelquefois affranchis de la gêne des régles, on se permet les licences les plus déreglées. En effet, plus ces hommes célébres ont eu de talens supérieurs, & plus les libertés qu'ils ont prises sont d'un exemple dangereux. Mais si d'un côté ils ont pû se tromper dans quelques parties de leurs compositions, de l'autre nous pouvons nous abuser dans nos observations. Dans cette crainte, nous ne prétendons pas qu'elles ayent force de loi; nous les proposons plûtôt comme des doutes que comme des décisions, & nous ne hazardons même plusieurs de ces remarques que parce qu'il nous a paru qu'on en avoit déja approuvé quelques-unes.

Nous avons eu tant d'occasions d'ailleurs de faire l'éloge de *Claude Perrault,* que si nous paroissons quelquefois contraires à son sentiment, on ne pourra du moins nous accuser d'esprit de parti; toujours attentifs, autant qu'il nous est possible, à louer le beau par-tout où il se rencontre, nous relevons les inadvertances, moins pour censurer l'ouvrage, que pour faire sentir la difficulté qu'il y a d'éviter les licences dans la décoration d'un édifice d'une grande importance, & nous concevons même qu'il nous sera aussi difficile d'aprécier l'excellence des beautés réelles de cette belle façade, que de constater les défauts de convenance dont elle n'est pas entierement exempte. Ces derniers, à la vérité, sont peu de chose, si on les compare à la sublimité de l'ordonnance; aussi les expressions nous manqueront-elles plus d'une fois, lorsqu'il s'agira d'applaudir à ce chef-d'oeuvre, qui a si justement mérité les éloges & réuni les suffrages des connoisseurs les plus éclairés; au lieu que les remarques qu'on seroit obligé de faire sur les parties négligées d'un édifice quelconque, partent assez ordinairement de source. Néanmoins nous remarquerons que comme la convenance doit présider à toutes les productions d'un Architecte, & que c'est de ces principes que doit résulter le succès de l'ouvrage entier, nous commencerons nos observations par les défauts de convenance, de bienséance, & de vraisemblance, que nous serons forcés de condamner dans ce frontispice, & nous finirons cette description, en inspirant une admiration qu'on ne peut porter trop loin à l'égard de l'élégance de son architecture, du choix de ses ornemens, & du rapport heureux qui se rencontre entre certaines parties, & l'ensemble de ce vaste Edifice.

Par le défaut de convenance, nous entendons que l'ordonnance de l'architecture de cette façade annonce plûtôt celle d'un monument élevé seulement pour la magnificence, que la décoration d'un bâtiment destiné à l'habitation. Or comme le genre de cet édifice doit annoncer ces deux objets, ne convenoit-il pas qu'on remarquât des ouvertures dans les dehors, qui eussent indiqué la destination des dedans? Mais, dira-t-on, l'aîle de ce bâtiment qui est adossée à ce péristile étant simple, les piéces intérieures tirent leur jour du côté de la cour. A la bonne heure; mais il falloit au moins feindre des croisées à la place des niches, telles qu'on les a percées réellement du côté de la riviere . . . , & que l'on en a pratiquées dans les petits entre-colonnemens des trois avant-corps de cette façade; autrement cette superbe décoration semble revêtir le mur de face d'un édifice public, tel que pourroit être, par exemple, une Bibliotheque que l'on voudroit éclairer à l'Italienne, ou bien le mur d'un aqueduc, dont encore la plus grande partie se perce à jour, autant pour oeconomiser la matiere, que pour ne pas masquer entierement le coup d'oeil des environs.

A l'égard du défaut de bienséance, nous observerons que l'appareil de ce superbe péristile supposant ici une communication extérieure d'une extrémité du bâtiment à l'autre, pour le passage du Prince, lorsqu'il auroit voulu se faire voir au peuple, il devoit être sans interruption; ce qui ne se peut dans la distribution de ce péristile, par l'étranglement du passage [in the central pavilion] . . . & dont on sent visiblement la discontinuation, par l'archivolte en plein ceintre, qui se remarque au dessus de la porte comprise dans le soubassement. Nous relevons ce défaut de bienséance, qui est d'autant plus condamnable qu'il eût été essentiel que, par la communication libre que nous exigeons, on eût évité le solide qui se trouve placé dans le grand entre-colonnement du milieu, dût-on y avoir affecté une porte croisée feinte, qui auroit paru donner entrée à un grand sallon ou vestibule supérieur que ce grand avant-corps semble annoncer, & qui auroit beaucoup mieux réussi que tout l'appareil de la sculpture qu'on s'étoit proposé d'y mettre. On a cependant exprimé ici cette sculpture, pour donner une idée générale de ce que ces parties devoient produire relativement au tout.

Enfin le défaut de vraisemblance consiste en ce qu'il n'est pas naturel qu'une aussi petite ouverture que la porte [in the central pavilion] . . . donne entrée à un édifice d'une ordonnance aussi colossale & aussi imposante; ensorte qu'il semble que cette décoration ait été faite, moins pour indiquer l'entrée du Palais du Louvre, que dans le dessein d'ériger un ouvrage d'Architecture qui, par son appareil, sa régularité & sa richesse, annonçât la capacité & l'étendue du génie de l'Architecte. Il est vrai que *Claude Perrault,* pour sauver la réalité de cette petite porte, a cherché à pallier ce défaut; mais il est tombé dans un autre excès, en nichant celle-ci dans une grande arcade; car cette derniere, comme nous venons de le remarquer, non seulement semble interrompre le niveau des galeries, mais nuit absolument à l'ordonnance du grand entre-colonnement. . . .

Revenons présentement aux richesses répandues dans la décoration de ce frontispice, passons en revûe les beautés générales & particulieres de son ordonnance, & examinons avec soin la répartition de ses ornemens; enfin arrêtons-nous à considérer l'assemblage de tant de perfections, qui offre avec un si grand éclat ce beau tout qui illustre également & le siecle de Louis XIV, & les talens de *Claude Perrault.*

Le rapport de la hauteur de cette façade à sa largeur, est comme 4 est à 25, non compris l'élévation du fossé, qui . . . n'a point été exécuté. La largeur de l'avant-corps du milieu est à la longueur totale, comme 3 est à 19. La largeur des pavillons des extrémités est à la longueur totale, comme 1 est à 7. Enfin le soubassement a de hauteur les neuf 17mes de tout l'Ordre supérieur, y compris le socle qui soutient les colonnes, l'entablement qui les couronne, & la balustrade qui est au dessus. Nous remarquerons que la hauteur de ce soubassement est un peu moins considérable que celle qu'on lui donne ordinairement; sçavoir, les deux tiers de la hauteur de l'Ordre supérieur, . . . ainsi qu'on l'a observé aux Places de Vendôme & des Victoires, malgré l'exemple du Château de Versailles, où le soubassement, pris dans l'avant-corps du milieu, est égal à toute la hauteur des colonnes Ioniques; hauteur excessive, qui ne contribue pas peu à rendre mesquin l'Ordre de dessus. . . .

La hauteur de l'Ordre Corinthien est de vingt-un modules, au lieu de vingt qu'on lui donne ordinairement; la raison de ce module de plus, donné par *Perrault,* vient, sans doute, de ce qu'ayant accouplé cet Ordre, il a présumé que les colonnes, distribuées ainsi, paroissent plus fortes de diametre que celles qui sont totalement isolées, & qu'ayant pour fond le mur du péristile, il étoit nécessaire, à l'imitation des Anciens, & relativement à ce que *Vitruve* nous enseigne, de rendre le fust de ces colonnes plus svelte.[220] Cette élégance produit ici un d'autant meilleur effet, que son ordonnance est fort riche, toutes les moulures de son entablement étant taillées d'ornemens, &c. Ces colonnes ont de diametre, au dessus des bases, trois pieds 7 pouces un tiers. Je dis au dessus des bases; car nous observerons que vers le tiers inférieur, le fust est renflé de deux parties de module: *flexion* peu sensible, à la vérité, mais très-agréable, qui contribue à rendre ces colonnes bien fuselées, & d'une courbe tout-à-fait élégante & gracieuse. Ces colonnes, y compris les bases & les chapiteaux, ont 37 pieds 11 pouces. Entre deux colonnes accouplées, on a observé un demi-diametre; les plus petits entre-colonnemens des arrieres corps, ont 12 pieds 11 pouces; les moyens entre-colonnemens des pavillons, 17 pieds un quart; & enfin le grand entre-colonnement de l'avant-corps du milieu, 24 pieds 3 quarts. Ordonnance, disposition, & construction inconnues avant *Perrault;* ce qui fit douter à plusieurs de l'exécution de son projet; mais cet habile Maître, aussi sçavant Mathématicien qu'Architecte expérimenté, & aussi célèbre Théoricien que consommé dans l'expérience, ne se rebuta pas des contradictions qu'il essuya, non seulement de la part des Artistes de son tems, mais encore des ennemis que son mérite supérieur dans plus d'un genre lui avoit attiré. Enfin il sçut en homme éclairé, bien moins qu'en Courtisan, persuader M. *Colbert,* par des démonstrations évidentes, & des modeles convaincans, & n'opposa à ses ennemis qu'une prompte exécution, qui dans la suite fit taire ses Adversaires, sans néanmoins en diminuer le nombre; c'est ainsi qu'il justifia les lumieres & l'équité du Ministre qui s'étoit rendu à des talens si supérieurs.

L'entablement a de hauteur 5 mod[ules], 5 parties 7 minutes,[221] qui égalent le quart de la colonne, plus deux parties & 10 minutes de parties.[222] Il paroît que c'est *Vignole* que notre Auteur a le plus suivi dans ses proportions, & s'il a donné à son entablement quelque partie de plus que le quart, il faut considérer que cette augmentation étoit nécessaire, à cause de la grande longueur de cette façade, & du peu de ressaut de son entablement; que pour cette raison il s'est crû autorisé à s'écarter des régles les plus universellement approuvées en France, quoique susceptibles, pour la plûpart, de variations, selon les différens systêmes des Auteurs. En effet *Vignole,* comme nous venons de le remarquer, ne lui donne que le quart, *Palladio* le cinquiéme, *Scamozzi,* entre le quart & le cinquiéme,[223] &c. proportions diverses dont l'application dépend de l'étendue du Bâtiment, de son importance, de son ordonnance solide ou legere, ou enfin du mouvement affecté dans ses plans & dans ses élévations. . . .

La hauteur de l'architrave est égale à celle de la frise, & elles ont chacune un mod[ule] 10 parties 3 minutes. La corniche a de hauteur 2 mod[ules] 3 parties une minute; cette derniere est ornée de modillons, dont les intervalles sont enrichis de cassettes & de rosaces. Toutes les moulures sont aussi taillées d'ornemens, à l'exception du larmier denticulaire que *Perrault* a laissé lisse, afin de donner du repos entre les principales moulures: on ne sçauroit trop applaudir cette prudence, & elle doit être imitée dans toutes les occasions où l'on fera parade de la plus grande richesse. Les plate-bandes ou soffites des architraves, sont aussi ornées d'entrelas d'un très-bon goût, aussi bien que les plafonds quarrés de chaque entre-colonnement, dans lesquels sont placées des têtes de soleils, enfermées dans des cadres circulaires, & entourées de bordures ornées de moulures taillées d'ornemens. Tout ce plafond, exécuté actuellement,[224] est d'une beauté au dessus de toute expression. . . .

Le chapiteau de cet Ordre a deux mod[ules] 11 part[ies] 8 min[utes] de hauteur, sur un mod[ule] 13 part[ies] de largeur, la même que celle du fust supérieur de la colonne, & est composé de feuilles d'olivier d'une assez belle exécution, & dont les tigettes & les caulicoles sont d'un galbe très-agréable. Ce chapiteau paroît un peu svelte dans son élévation; mais ceux des pilastres étant de 2 mod[ules] de largeur, il étoit nécessaire, pour éviter trop de disparité entre l'un & l'autre, d'augmenter ceux des colonnes, pour donner une sorte d'élégance aux chapiteaux des pilastres.

Le fust des colonnes est entouré de 24 canelures, séparées par des listeaux seulement. Peut-être la richesse répandue dans toute l'ordonnance de cette façade, auroit-elle exigé que le fust de ces colonnes fût plus orné; néanmoins malgré la célébre exemple des colonnes Ioniques des Tuileries, dont nous parlerons ci-après,[225] il est assez raisonnable de ne pas trop affamer en apparence le tronc des colonnes, ni de les trop surcharger d'ornemens, tels que des joncs, des canaux, des rudentures, &c. Quoiqu'il paroisse essentiel de conserver une analogie intime dans toutes les parties qui constituent un Ordre d'Architecture, il est certain qu'il faut dans tous les cas, éviter la prodigalité des ornemens, principalement dans la décoration extérieure, où la retenue fait toujours bien, & où la fermeté, la grandeur de l'édifice, & la qualité de la matiere, doivent servir de régles fondamentales.

Les bases sont profilées selon *Vignole,*[226] & auroient pû sans doute être moins subdivisées, les cannelures du fust de la colonne l'étant fort peu; . . .

La balustrade qui couronne cet édifice a environ les deux tiers de la hauteur de l'entablement, étant de 6 pieds 9 pouces 5 lig[nes], & l'entablement, de 9 pieds & demi. Le socle de cette balustrade qui soutient les balustres, a la moitié de toute la hauteur de la balustrade, & la tablette, environ le tiers de la hauteur du balustre; ce dernier ayant 2 pieds 6 pouces 8 lig[nes] & la tablette 9 pouces 6 lig[nes]. Nous observerons que la hauteur du balustre paroît petite, comparée avec le diametre de l'Ordre, & la tablette un peu forte, suivant les exemples modernes les plus célébres que nous avons rapportés dans notre *Introduction.*[227] Ce changement de proportion provient sans doute, ainsi qu'il a déja été remarqué plus haut à propos de l'entablement, de ce que la longueur de cette façade, sa grande hauteur & son ordonnance colossale, ont obligé *Perrault* de chercher de nouvelles divisions pour les parties, qui répondissent aux dimensions générales de tout l'Edifice; considération pour laquelle nous avons crû qu'il étoit préférable de donner les mesures exactes de cet ouvrage, telles que nous les avons trouvées sur les lieux. . . .

Le grand avant-corps du milieu de cette façade est couronné d'un fronton qui en occupe toute la largeur. Ce fronton a de base 92 pieds sur 19 de hauteur: proportion d'environ le cinquiéme de sa largeur. Les cymaises supérieures de ce fronton sont chacune d'une seule pierre, de la longueur de 51 pieds sur 6 de largeur, & 18 pou[ces] d'épaisseur, pesant environ 80 milliers. . . .[228] Il est inconcevable comment un poids aussi considérable, non compris celui de l'entablement, peut être soutenu en l'air par le seul architrave, que nous avons dit avoir 24 pieds trois quarts d'une colonne à l'autre, ces dernieres surtout étant isolées du mur d'un demi-diametre. La maniere ingénieuse avec laquelle *Perrault* a concilié la partie de la construction avec l'ordonnance, est seule capable d'immortaliser la mémoire de ce célébre Artiste, principalement lorsque l'on considere par quelle ressource il a sçu retenir la poussée de ce fronton sur la colonne angulaire B de cet avant-corps. [The letters cited by Blondel are lacking in his engraved elevation of the Colonnade (pl. 7, no. 448).] Cette charge immense, & cette poussée, est entretenue, à la vérité, d'un côté par la proximité du mur C, & de l'autre par le mur E, qui est lié par une voûte avec le précédent; mais il étoit question d'imaginer ces différens moyens, ce qui annonce certainement une grande supériorité. Nous ne pouvons dissimuler cependant que la raison de cette solidité a produit le retrécissement F, que nous avons déja remarqué nuire à la communication intérieure des deux péristiles situés aux deux côtés de cet avant-corps; mais *Perrault,* en grand Maître, a crû devoir sacrifier la commodité à la beauté de l'ordonnance, & à cette solidité immuable qui rend cet édifice, digne de la splendeur d'un si beau siecle, & capable d'entrer en comparaison avec ce que la Grece & l'Italie nous ont offert de plus somptueux & de plus régulier. Nous remarquerons aussi que cette platebande de 24 pieds trois quarts est retenue par des barres de fer horizontales de 4 pouces de gros, portées & clavetées avec les aissieux perpendiculaires placés à chaque axe des colonnes. Ces barres de fer sont enveloppées de plomb de deux lignes d'épaisseur, & liernées par des entretoises de fer plat, qui entretiennent intérieurement cet architrave, dont la coupe & l'appareil est construit avec un art admirable, & dont les voussoirs forment autant de lancis dans le massif du mur C, retenus chacun avec des ancres & des tirans de fer; ensorte que depuis l'édification de ce monument, il a résisté à la rigueur des saisons, aux injures de l'air, & aux dégradations inévitables à tout bâtiment dont l'entretien est négligé.

Dans les petits entre-colonnemens de cet avant-corps, sont des croisées couronnées d'un fronton triangulaire. Ces ouvertures, quoique de six pieds de largeur, paroissent petites, eu égard aux autres percés de ce frontispice, & à son ordonnance colossale. Au dessus de ces croisées, sont placés des médaillons de forme elliptique de six pieds de diametre sur sept pieds 10 pouces, renfermant des bas-reliefs, & couronnés de mufles de lion, & de guirlandes ou bouquets de laurier & de chêne. Ces médaillons ont si bien réussi à *Perrault,* qu'il n'hésita pas de les employer dans la décoration de son arc de triomphe [du trône; Fig. 120].[229] . . . Ils [the medallions] sont séparés de la croisée de dessous par un plinthe horizontal, qui régne dans toute la longueur de la façade. Ce plinthe a 2 pi[eds] 8 pou[ces] & demi de hauteur, & est composé d'un gorgerin, orné de canaux; dans la plate-bande supérieure de ce plinthe, est une table ravalée qui lui donne un air d'élégance relatif à la richesse de l'Ordre. Ce membre d'Architecture est élevé environ au tiers supérieur de la hauteur de la colonne, & sert d'imposte aux grandes arcades placées dans les pavillons. . . . On voit dans [une] estampe de *Le Clerc,* au dessus du sommet du fronton, une figure équestre terrassant les ennemis de la France, ainsi que des Renommées assises sur les acroteres [see Marot's print, Figure 88]. On n'a point exprimé ici ces ouvrages de sculpture, non seulement parce que les Renommées dont nous parlons y paroissent chetives, mais aussi parce qu'il n'est pas vraisemblable de placer une figure équestre sur le sommet d'un édifice, & principalement sur l'extrémité supérieure d'un fronton triangulaire.

Les Armes de S.M. mises au dessus de l'archivolte de l'arcade du soubassement, la légende, les Renommées, & tous les ornemens de cet entre-colonnement ne sont gueres placés avec plus de succès.[230] En général ils ont trop peu de relief, & s'accorderoient mal avec la fermeté qu'on remarque dans l'architecture de ce Monument, quoique d'une ordonnace Corinthienne. . . . les parties doivent paroître engendrées par les masses: or certainement ce principe incontestable ne se rencontre point ici. . . .

A chaque côté de cet avant-corps, se voient les deux colonnades formant le péristile: elles sont composées chacune de sept entre-colonnemens de 12 pi[eds] 11 pou[ces] d'intervalle, & les colonnes en sont accouplées. Nous avons déja parlé de la beauté des ornemens de son plafond. . . . Nous rapporterons ici qu'au dessus de ce péristile on a pratiqué une voûte en plein ceintre [built as a corbeled vault; see Chapter VI and Figure 80], continue, pour décharger les colonnes du poids des plafonds, aussi bien que pour rémédier à ce dernier, en cas que quelques-unes de ses parties vinssent à se dégrader. Ces plafonds, portés sur des architraves en plate-bandes, sont construits de maniere que la clef circulaire placée dans chaque entre-colonnement, & où l'on a sculpté une tête de Soleil . . . est d'une seule pierre de 5 pieds 9 pouces de diametre, qui tient en équilibre toutes les parties de ce plafond, retenu d'ailleurs par des barres de fer de trois pouces de gros, corroyées & couvertes de plusieurs couches de peinture à huile, pour éviter la rouille. Ces barres de fer horizontales sont retenues sur le devant dans chaque extrémité par d'autres verticales qui enfilent la colonne jusqu'à la base: les premieres, qui traversent le péristile & le mur qui lui sert de fond, sont liées chacune par une ancre; ces barres de fer traversantes ne touchent à aucune pierre, ne portent rien, & ne font que tirer contre la poussée du plafond. Indépendamment de ces ancres & tirans, toujours à couvert dans la hauteur de la voûte dont nous venons de parler, il en est d'autres posées diagonalement des colonnes aux pilastres, & de ceux-ci aux colonnes, ces dernieres sont clavetées dans les précédentes; ensorte que par cet artifice ingénieux, la construction de ce plafond a acquis une solidité immuable confirmée par une assez longue expérience. On peut voir avec facilité ce genre de construction sur les lieux: de détail, pour un homme du métier, est peut-être aussi intéressant que l'ordonnance de ce superbe Edifice est satisfaisante pour les connoisseurs en Architecture.[231]

Dans chaque entre-colonnement de ce péristile, on a pratiqué des niches, accompagnées de chambranles, & couronnées de frontons, semblables aux croisées des petits entre-colonnemens de l'avant-corps du milieu.[232] Ne pourroit-on pas desirer ici, à la place de ces niches, des portes qui parussent donner entrée dans les appartemens placés derriere ce péristile? Ces portes n'auroient-elles pas donné un air d'habitation à cet édifice, qui ne s'annonce pas assez dans cette façade, destinée à présenter au spectateur le frontispice d'un Palais consacré à la demeure ordinaire d'une Tête couronnée? . . .

Au dessus de ces niches, se voyent des médaillons de même forme & grandeur que ceux dont nous avons parlé plus haut. Ne seroit-il pas aussi à craindre que les bas-reliefs que doivent contenir ces médaillons, ne soient d'un trop petit volume pour être apperçus d'en bas?[233] Ne pourroit-on pas demander encore si ces sortes de bas-reliefs, destinés à désigner des actions d'éclat, sont bien du ressort de la décoration d'un bâtiment de l'espece de celui dont nous parlons? Ne semble-t-il pas au contraire qu'il seroit plus convenable de les reserver pour celle d'un Edifice consacré à la gloire du Prince, tel qu'un Arc de triomphe, ou tout autre ouvrage de ce genre, parce qu'alors un tel monument, érigé par l'amour du Peuple, semble exiger que l'on désigne d'une maniere symbolique, les principales actions qui ont donné occasion aux Citoyens de le faire élever.

Le soubassement au dessous de ce péristile est percé de croisées bombées. Ces ouvertures ont été faites contre le sentiment de notre Architect [Claude Perrault], qui auroit préféré, dit-il, des trophées d'armes, dans les casques desquels on auroit percé de petites ouvertures pour éclairer l'intérieur de ce soubassement.[234] Quoiqu'en dise *Perrault,* cette suppression auroit encore donné un air moins habitable à ce Palais, & il auroit été à craindre que ces trophées, de la maniere dont il les avoit conçus, n'eussent été postiches, n'étant amenés par aucune table, ni corps saillant ou rentrant. D'un autre côté la grandeur des croisées de ce soubassement contribue à rendre les autres ouvertures de cette façade trop peu considérables; c'est pourquoi on auroit peut-être dû préférer de laisser ce soubassement lisse & uni, sur-tout ayant affecté si peu de percés dans toute l'étendue de ce bâtiment.

Les pavillons des extrémités de cette façade, dont la largeur est un peu considérable pour la hauteur, sont de la même décoration que ce que nous venons de remarquer précédemment, à l'exception néanmoins que les parties angulaires de ces pavillons sont revêtues de pilastres au lieu de colonnes. Plusieurs condamnent ces pilastres, parce qu'ils prétendent que cette architecture n'a pas assez d'analogie avec les colonnades, ni avec l'avant-corps du milieu. Cependant il faut considerer, non seulement que cette ordonnance présente quelque chose de plus ferme, & donne une apparence de solidité aux extrémités de cette façade, mais aussi que ces pilastres étoient essentiels en faveur de l'élévation du côté de la riviere, dont toute la décoration est en pilastres. *Perrault* néanmoins, à dessein de rappeller dans ces pavillons les Ordres de colonnes distribuées dans les péristiles & dans l'avant-corps, a pris soin de pratiquer dans leur milieu d'autres colonnes qui portent une plate-bande continue, & qui, en donnant du mouvement au plan de cette ordonnance, composent une architecture qui répond à la solidité que produit l'usage des pilastres dans la décoration. Entre ces colonnes, sont pratiquées de grandes arcades qui répondent assez bien à la grandeur de l'Ordre. . . . Les croisées placées à côté de ces arcades sont dans le même cas que celles que nous avons ci-devant trouvé trop petites, & forment ici une disparité d'ouverture qui nuit absolument à l'ordonnance colossale de ce frontispice.

On voit dans les planches du Louvre gravées anciennement par *Le Clerc,* des amortissemens qui devoient couronner les pavillons des extrémités de cette façade.[235] Ces amortissemens sont composés d'Attiques, ornés de tables contenant des bas-reliefs séparés par des trophées, & terminés par un fronton circulaire, dans le tympan duquel sont des bas-reliefs, & un oeil de boeuf pour éclairer l'intérieur de cet Attique. On remarque dans le Recueil manuscrit de *Perrault,* page 19,[236] un supplément qu'il avoit proposé pour exhausser cet amortissement; il consiste en une calotte surbaissée sur un plan circulaire, & surmonté d'une balustrade & d'un lanternon.

Nous remarquerons que ce fronton, qui a une grande base & qui est posé sur un Attique, composit une architecture lourde & pesante, qui ne répondoit pas à l'ordonnace générale de ce bâtiment. D'ailleurs, cet amortissement dominoit en hauteur sur l'avant-corps du milieu, ce qui ôtoit à cette façade la forme pryamidale que l'on remarque ici. On voit encore dans le Recueil manuscrit de *Perrault,* pag. 17 & 31, deux autres amortissemens projettés pour terminer ces pavillons. Dans l'un, au dessus des frontons circulaires, & à la place des calottes surbaissées, on avoit élevé une colonnade percée à jour, en forme de petit Temple terminé par un fronton qui lui servoit de toît; dans l'autre, on avoit seulement placé une balustrade à la place de la colonnade.

Toutes les différentes compositions dont nous venons de parler étoient assez ingénieuses, néanmoins aucune n'a eu lieu: nous ne les rapportons même ici que pour prouver combien notre Auteur avoit cherché par différens moyens à concilier les anciens bâtimens du Louvre avec ses nouveaux desseins, & que ce ne fut enfin que par des méditations profondes & des démonstrations convaicantes, qu'il parvint à prouver qu'il falloit nécessairement démolir dans l'intérieur de ce Palais tout ce qui pouvoit contribuer à rendre les dehors desagréables & peu conformes aux principes de la bonne architecture. Quelque raison même qu'on pût lui opposer, il persista à prouver que ces amortissemens, qui pourroient bien faire séparément, ne s'accorderoient jamais avec les masses totales, toujours préférables aux beautés de détail.

On trouve dans la page 91 de ce même manuscrit, un projet qui prouve la sujétion dans laquelle *Perrault* s'étoit trouvé pendant long-tems de conserver les anciens pavillons du Louvre tels qu'ils étoient: cette considération, dit-il, l'avoit même déterminé à les enrichir; mais on remarque dans son dessein, que pour que ces pavillons ne l'emportassent pas en prééminence sur le reste du bâtiment, il avoit élevé au dessus & derrière l'avant-corps du milieu, une espece de dôme, qui devoit servir de couronnement à une nouvelle chapelle qu'il avoit proposée, & dont on voit le plan & la situation marquée M. . . . A cette même page 91 du manuscrit de *Perrault,* on voit aussi qu'il avoit orné de figures les piédestaux de la balustrade qui couronne tout cet édifice; on y trouve encore des projets de niches pour les entre-colonnemens des colonnades, & un dessein de soubassement beaucoup plus riche que celui qui se voit exécuté; il étoit composé de grandes tables, de cadres, d'avant-corps, & de chaînes de refend d'assez bon goût, à propos desquels il rapporte expressément qu'il avoit préféré ce genre de dessein aux croisées . . . , afin de conserver à cet Edifice l'aspect d'un Château, nom que le Louvre portoit encore de son tems.[237]

On trouve, page 87, un autre projet de *Perrault* pour la principale façade du Louvre, & toujours à dessein de conserver les anciens pavillons. La décoration de cette façade est aussi Corinthienne, mais les colonnes n'en sont pas accouplées; le milieu est terminé par un dôme d'une forme & d'une élégance dignes du bâtiment & de son Auteur. Enfin aux pag. 97 & 99 du même manuscrit, se voyent encore deux autres projets pour la même façade, qui méritent également l'attention des connoisseurs. . . . (40–49)

c. [South façade]:

Cette façade a été aussi élevée sur les desseins de *Claude Perrault;* elle est toute décorée de pilastres de même hauteur & de même diametre que les colonnes du péristile . . . : au lieu de médaillons, on a placé, dans les arriere-corps, des croisées de proportion Attique; & au-dessous, dans toute l'étendue du Bâtiment, on a ménagé des ouvertures de même forme & grandeur que celles qui sont pratiquées dans l'avant-corps & dans les pavillons de la façade du côté de S. Germain l'Auxerrois. Cet Ordre Colossal est aussi élevé sur un soubassement percé de croisées bombées. Ce dernier est soutenu sur un mur de revêtissement qui devoit former l'un des paremens du fossé dont on avoit projeté d'entourer cet Edifice, mais qui n'as pas eu lieu pour les raisons que nous en avons rapportées précédemment.[238]

Les croisées Attiques paroissent un peu larges pour leur hauteur. On peut remarquer encore que leur forme trop bombée ne présente pas une Architecture assez grave; d'ailleurs la disparité de leur ouverture avec les médaillons des avant-corps, nuit à l'ensemble général, & paroît annoncer par les dehors, des pieces intérieurs inégalement propres à l'habitation; car, selon l'esprit de la convenance de cet Edifice, ces croisées Attiques ne doivent présenter que des ouvertures destinées à éclairer la partie supérieure des grandes pieces du dedans de ce Palais, lesquelles, par leur grand diametre, ont besoin d'une certaine élévation susceptible d'une lumiere proportionnée à leur hauteur. Or, cette idée, qui doit se présenter à tout spectateur intelligent, se trouve ici détruite; la plus grande partie de ces ouvertures ne se remarquent que dans les arriere-corps, tandis qu'au contraire les plus belles pieces doivent être placées de préférence dans le milieu du Bâtiment. C'est par cette considération qu'il falloit affecter ces mêmes ouvertures au moins dans l'avant-corps du milieu, dont les entre-pilastres, d'ailleurs inégaux, ainsi que les percés, qui s'y trouvent dissemblables de hauteur & de largeur, annoncent une décoration peu conforme aux regles de l'Art, lesquelles exigent que toutes les ouvertures d'un même corps soient d'une égale dimension.

Nous remarquerons aussi que dans l'extérieur d'un Bâtiment, les plinthes horizontaux & continus doivent annoncer les différens planchers qui divisent intérieurement la hauteur de l'Edifice; que pour cela il est nécessaire de les supprimer absolument dans la décoration d'une façade où l'on fait présider un Ordre Colossal, qui donne toujours à connoître par les dehors, l'immensité des dedans. Au reste cette division nuit en général à l'ordonnance de l'Ordre; c'est ce qu'on a pris soin d'éviter dans les façades des places de *Vendôme* &

des *Victoires,* quoique l'on soit prévenu, par leur aspect, que les dedans sont divisés dans leur hauteur par des planchers d'une élévation proportionnée à des appartemens particuliers; idée toute naturelle, qu'on ne peut certainement prendre d'un Edifice du genre de celui du Louvre.[239]

Toute cette façade est exécutée telle qu'elle se voit . . . , à l'exception de la balustrade supérieure, du fronton de l'avant-corps du milieu, & de tous les ornemens qui, au lieu d'être sculptés, sont restés en pierre d'attente, exceptés les deux chapiteaux Corinthiens qui forment la partie anguleuse de cette façade du côté de S. *Germain l'Auxerrois.* Les consoles des croisées du premier étage, & les modillons de la corniche de l'entablement ne sont même que galbés; les pilastres sont aussi sans canelures;[240] enfin nous observons que la plus grande partie de cette façade est masquée par les arbres à haute tige du jardin qui est au pied de cet édifice [the Jardin de l'Infante], & par le Garde-meuble, qui seront sans doute détruits l'un & l'autre, si l'on parvient, comme il y a tout lieu de l'espérer, à finir ce monument si digne du siécle qui l'a vu naître. A l'égard des proportions générales de cette façade, nous remarquerons que les pavillons de ses extrêmités, quoique beaucoup plus étroits que ceux du péristile, ont trop d'égalité avec l'avant-corps du milieu, celui-ci n'ayant qu'un diametre de plus de largeur; en sorte que ces trois parties principales qui n'ont guere que les deux cinquiemes des arrieres-corps, paroissent trop petites, eu egard à l'étendue du Bâtiment. Cette réfléxion sans doute avoit engagé *Perrault* à proposer de faire usage des colonnes seulement dans l'avant-corps, pour lui donner plus de relief, en empêchant cette monotonie qui se remarque ici, & pour que cette saillie eût pu lui procurer par l'optique une forme pyramidale; étant tout décoré de pilastres, il manque de mouvement; objet très-intéressant dans une élévation d'une si grande longueur, & où l'on a fait présider l'élégance Corinthienne; d'ailleurs cet Edifice étant apperçu de fort loin, exigeoit nécessairement des corps qui marquassent sensiblement, & qui fussent capables de se manifester du point de distance considérable d'où l'on peut appercevoir; étant décoré d'un Ordre Colossal, il feroit un très-bon effet, si les parties qui le divisent eussent eu quelque relief de plus dans les ressauts qui le composent.

On voit le dessein à colonnes proposé par *Perrault* pour l'avant-corps du milieu, page 55 de son manuscrit; il paroît aussi qu'il avoit projetté d'élever au-dessus de cet avant-corps, un Attique couronné d'un dôme dans le genre de celui qu'on y remarque aujourd'hui, reste du vieux Louvre, & dont le mur de face qui le soutient, doit servir de mur de réfend: il paroît encore qu'il avoit eu envie de rendre les combles apparens, & de pratiquer un Attique sur les pavillons des extrêmités de cette façade. Sans doute avoit-il conçu ce dernier projet dans l'intention de conserver les anciens pavillons; mais dans les deux desseins qu'il a donnés pour leur restauration, on remarque dans l'Attique de l'un des croisées à plein ceintre au nombre de cinq, dont on ne peut que blâmer la forme & la multiplicité; dans l'autre il avoit proposé des *yeux de boeuf* de forme circulaire au nombre de trois. Ces trois percés répondoient à plomb des trois arcades qu'il avoit placées au-dessous dans les entre-pilastres, à dessein de procurer plus de jour dans l'intérieur de cette partie anguleuse du Bâtiment, où il vouloit, dit-il, pratiquer de grands sallons. Ces arcades symétrisoient avec celles de l'avant-corps; mais leurs grandes ouvertures, la petitesse de leurs piédroits, la pésanteur de leurs claveaux, tous membres qui n'avoient aucune proportion avec le diametre de l'Ordre Colossal, ont sans doute été cause qu'il n'a pas suivi ce projet. . . .

Ce qui nous prouveroit que cet avant-corps avoit été projetté pour recevoir des colonnes, ainsi que le dit *Charles Perrault,*[241] c'est la saillie de l'avant-corps du soubassement. . . . Sans doute ces colonnes n'ont été refusées à *Perrault,* que lorsque ce soubassement a été élevé; en sorte qu'il s'est déterminé à placer après-coup sur cette saillie une balustrade, pour procurer au premier étage une terrasse à découvert, beaucoup mieux soutenue par ce mur de soubassement qui monte de fond, que par des consoles ou des encorbellemens, lesquels . . . ont toujours quelque chose de postiche, & présentent une décoration peu régulière, malgré les exemples fréquens que nous en ont laissé dans tous les tems nos Architectes, dans plusieurs Edifices même d'une assez grande importance. (54–56)

d. [North façade].

La nouvelle façade du péristile du Louvre, a donné occasion à la restauration & augmentation de celle dont nous allons parler, en sorte qu'il n'y a que le pavillon A & l'arriere-corps B qui soient restés de l'ancien Bâtiment [Fig. 103].

La diversité & l'irrégularité des rues qui communiquent de ce Palais à la rue S. Honoré, masquent la disparité qu'on apperçoit dans les pavillons de cette façade; celui C ayant dû être nécessairement de la même ordonnance que le péristile, & celui A conforme à l'ancienne décoration du côté des Thuileries [Fig. 103].

. . . A l'égard du pavillon A, l'on s'est contenté de suivre les mêmes dimensions, formes & grandeurs des croisées du pavillon C, sans y employer d'Ordre d'Architecture, dans le dessein que ce Bâtiment vu sur l'angle par la place du Louvre, parût plus uniforme & plus régulier.

Une balustrade qui couronne ce Bâtiment, annonce qu'il devoit être couvert en plate-forme, ou du moins que les combles n'en devoient pas être apparens, seul moyen, ce me semble, de distinguer d'une maniere convenable la différence des Palais des Rois, d'avec les Bâtimens destinés à la demeure des particuliers.

L'avant-corps du milieu de cette façade présente une assez belle ordonnance [Fig. 103]. On y a supprimé néanmoins les Ordres d'Architecture, avec d'autant plus de raison que cette richesse auroit été trop considérable par rapport à la simplicité des arriere-corps. Cette considération auroit dû porter à supprimer aussi la plus grande partie des ornemens[242] qui se remarquent dans cette planche [Fig. 103], leur élégance s'accordant mal avec la grandeur colossale de l'Architecture, avec la fermeté des corps quarrés qui la composent, avec les bossages qu'on a affectés dans les extrêmités de cet avant-corps, & avec le pourtour de la porte de cet Edifice. Nous répéterons aussi que la diversité des formes & la différente proportion des ouvertures des croisées nuisent à l'effet & à l'ensemble général: cette disparité est absolument condamnable, & ne présente jamais une décoration réguliere.

Les croisées des arriere-corps qui accompagnent ce frontispice sont trop sveltes au rez-de-chaussée, & leur sommet est formé d'une portion de cercle trop ressentie; celles du premier étage sont au contraire d'une proportion un peu courte, & les frontons qui les couronnent ne laissent pas assez d'intervalle entre chacun de leur retour; d'ailleurs ces corniches font rarement un bon effet; car, sans parler ici de l'origine des frontons qui semble exiger qu'on n'en place jamais ailleurs que sur les extrêmités supérieures des Edifices, il faut convenir que les angles obtus & les angles aigus ne s'allient jamais bien avec une Architecture rectiligne, dont la beauté principale consiste dans le parallelisme des lignes qui la composent, & dans les angles droits qui déterminent ses retours, principalement lorsqu'on a voulu donner à son ordonnance générale une expression ferme & solide.

Les croisées des arriere-corps B [Fig. 103] sont les mêmes que celles dont nous venons de parler, & different seulement par les trumeaux immenses qui les séparent. Certainement dans toute autre circonstance, nous condamnerions la trop grande largeur de ces trumeaux, mais nous avons déja dit que cette façade dans sa plus grande partie n'avoit été que restaurée, & que les rues & la multiplicité des Bâtimens particuliers qui sont élevés de ce côté du Louvre, rendoient cette décoration assez indifférente. Nous ajouterons cependant qu'on auroit dû supprimer l'espece de corniche horizontale, qui semble lier sans nécessité les frontons qui couronnent ces mêmes croisées. Nous venons, il est vrai, de recommander la parallélisme dans l'Architecture; mais on n'en est pas moins obligé d'éviter tout ce qui y porte de la confusion & qui la devise sans vraisemblance; rien n'est arbitraire dans l'ordonnance d'un bâtiment; les plus petits membres doivent y paroître nécessaires & amenés par quelque cause apparente qui ne laisse aucune équivoque; sans quoi tout devient licence dans la décoration; d'où naît le désordre qu'on ne remarque que trop souvent dans nos Bâtimens, sans en excepter ceux de la premiere importance.

Au reste tous les profils de cette façade sont d'une grande beauté & d'une exécution admirable, aussi-bien que la plus grande partie des croisées considérées séparément.... La plûpart de celles du premier étage different néanmoins en quelque chose de celles du péristile; mais celles du rez-de-chaussée sont absolument les mêmes. Enfin nous remarquerons, quoiqu'il paroisse dans cette planche [Fig. 103] que l'entablement Corinthien soit continué horizontalement, qu'il est dans l'exécution d'environ quatre pieds plus bas dans toute la longueur de l'arriere-corps B & du pavillon A, pour s'accorder avec celui de la façade du côté de la place du Louvre, inégalité à laquelle on auroit remédié sans doute en ragréant cette derniere façade.... (61–62)

e. [Courtyard]:

Cette planche [Fig. 106] nous offre une façade de l'intérieur de la cour du Louvre, avec trois Ordres d'Architecture élevés les uns au-dessus des autres. La suivante [pl. 18, no. 459] nous donnera une autre face où l'on a préféré un Attique au troisieme Ordre; de maniere qu'il est aisé de concevoir que la décoration des quatre façades de ce Palais est dissemblable dans leurs dimensions & dans la maniere dont elles sont terminées. Cette disparité n'a pas peu contribué peut-être à l'irrésolution où l'on a été jusqu'à présent de prendre un parti pour l'entiere perfection de cet Edifice.[243] D'un côté le troisieme Ordre rencontre des difficultés pour le concilier avec la hauteur des avant-corps déja exécutés; de l'autre, la continuité de l'Attique semble exiger des combles tels qu'on les voit dans [pl. 18, no. 459], & dont la hauteur trop considérable, semble affaisser ce petit étage supérieur.... Examinons à présent les motifs qui engagerent *Perrault* à préférer le troisieme Ordre qu'on a exécuté dans cette façade. (62–63) [Blondel next quotes

Charles Perrault's comments on the courtyard elevations, contained in the destroyed 1693 manuscript; see Sources II, no. 38(d).]

f. [Plan of *premier étage;* Fig. 91]:

L'objet le plus important qui se remarque dans cette planche, & qui soit élevé sur les desseins de *Claude Perrault,* est le péristile . . . ; nous remarquerons néanmoins que cette Architecte n'ayant donné que 12 pieds d'entrecolonnement dans la façade, & ayant voulu faire les plafonds réguliers, ce péristile devient étroit pour sa longueur. Cette circonstance a sans doute déterminé *Perrault* à l'interrompre dans le milieu de l'avant-corps; mais nous conviendrons qu'on ne sçauroit applaudir à cette discontinuité: le passage *b* [bottom of Fig. 91, facing the "L" in "L'Auxerrois"], non seulement ayant à peine quatre pieds, mais le coude qu'il fait [est] désagréable & peu commode. . . . (33)

g. [Plan of *premier étage,* south façade, Fig. 91]:

Ces distributions étoient destinées pour les appartemens de Leurs Majestés, de préférence à toutes autres, à cause de leur exposition au midi; exposition convenable, dit [Claude] *Perrault,* pour un bâtiment élevé dans une Capitale. Cette observation est judicieuse, sans doute, mais nous remarquerons qu'il est nécessaire que dans un Palais de l'importance de celui dont nous parlons, il y ait un appartement qui soit au levant; autrement ils ne pourroient être habités que l'hyver. D'ailleurs cet appartement, applaudi par [Claude] *Perrault,* seroit trop exposé à la poussiere des Quais, & au bruit continuel des voitures qui y passent; défaut qui ne sçauroit gueres être compensé, que par la superbe vûe & la variété des aspects dont jouissent de ce côté ces appartemens. Nous remarquerons encore que ces derniers manquoient absolument de commodité; que la forme des piéces, leur grandeur, & leur proportion étoient trop uniformes, la plûpart sans symmétrie, & assez mal éclairés; ensorte que la dépense immense que l'on a faite pour doubler ce corps de logis, bien loin de produire des dedans commodes, n'a contribué qu'à procurer des façades extérieures d'une architecture plus réguliere; encore faut-il convenir que l'ancienne façade du Louvre, du côté de la riviere, élevée sur les desseins de *Le Veau* [Fig. 17], étoit d'une ordonnance très-estimable. (34)

85. *1756.* [La Font de Saint-Yenne], *Le génie du Louvre aux Champs Élisées. Dialogue entre le Louvre, la ville de Paris, l'ombre de Colbert, & Perrault,* [Paris], 1756.

a. [Le Louvre]: Les admirables portiques de mon Frontispice, seront éternellement le modéle des plus belles proportions, & la voix la plus éloquente qui publiera à la postérité, l'excellence & la supériorité du génie François. (12)

b. [Le Louvre]: La justesse admirable des proportions [of the Colonnade] servira de modéle & de frein aux licenses de notre siécle dans ce bel art. (36)

c. [L'ombre de Colbert]: The design of the Colonnade is attributed to Perrault, "le Vitruve françois." (41)

d. PERRAULT.

Dites-moi si quatre-vingts années d'abandon total & de défaut de couverture, n'ont point apporté de dommage à mon Péristile?

LE LOUVRE.

Aucun, à l'exception d'une très-petite partie d'une des corniches rampantes du fronton, de la largeur d'environ deux pieds, qui s'étoit détachée il y a quelques années, & avoit fait en tombant une brêche de la même largeur à la corniche de la base. Mais elle vient d'être parfaitement rétablie, & avec les plus grandes précautions.

PERRAULT.

Quoi! les plattes-bandes des architraves, dont la grande portée paroissoit si hardie & si téméraire à tous les Architectes, qu'ils en avoient assuré la ruine avant l'élevation de l'édifice jusqu'au comble, ne se sont point affaissées depuis un si grand nombre d'années?

LE LOUVRE.

L'oeil ne sçauroit appercevoir aucun dérangement sensible ni dans les claveaux des plattes-bandes, ni dans les plat-fonds des galleries.

PERRAULT.

J'ai encore une grande impatience d'apprendre si les chapiteaux des colonnes de ces portiques, dont j'avois pris soin de modeler les belles formes sur celles de l'antique le plus parfait, & de faire tailler les feuilles avec un extrême précision par les plus savans sculpteurs d'architecture de l'Italie, n'auroient pas éprouvé quelques accidens?[244]

LE LOUVRE.

Non, mon pere, on admire encore la légereté & le travail de leurs feuilles, la grace de leur proportion & de leur contour, & ils serviront éternellement de modéle à cet ordre divin, aussi-bien que leurs colonnes, sans que peut-être on puisse égaler la précision & la perfection de leur exécution. (48–50)

e. PERRAULT.

Vous m'avez fait un grand plaisir de m'assurer que les chapiteaux de mes colonnes ont encore leur premiere beauté. Leurs saillies étant les plus délicates & les plus exposées de toutes les parties de l'architecture, on ne sçauroit répondre de leur entiere conservation pendant un si grand nombre d'années, quelques précautions que l'on prenne. A l'égard des colonnes, des entablemens, & de tout le reste de ce grand édifice, je ne suis point étonné de leur intégrité par le souvenir des attentions inexprimables que j'avois donné à la solidité des fondations. Elles ont plus de vingt pieds de profondeur; & la grandeur des assises, ma séverité dans le choix des blocs, & leur liaison inséparable à l'aide de la même machine que j'avois imaginé, & dont je m'étois servi pour les fondemens de l'Arc de Triomphe [du Trône], doivent rendre cet ouvrage éternel. J'ai employé la même méchanique dans la construction du corps de maçonnerie élevé sur les fondations dans les fossés, & je ne doute pas qu'il ne soit encore dans son premier état.[245]

LE LOUVRE.

Ces fossés furent comblés dès que l'on arrêta les travaux, ainsi je ne puis rien vous assurer à cet égard, mais ils seront certainement rétablis dès que ma façade sera découverte.[246] (56–58)

f. [Perrault]: The niches of the Colonnade were intended for statues of "les grands hommes d'Etat."[247] (58–59)

86. *1756.* "Lettre pour servir de réponse à une critique du Louvre imprimée dans le Mercure d'Avril 1755" in [La Font de Saint-Yenne], *Le génie du Louvre aux Champs Élisées*. The author of the letter is anonymous; see no. 82, above.

a. J'ai appris de Messieurs Desgot & Boffrand,[248] qui avoient connu M. Perrault dans leur jeunesse, que lorsque Louis XIV. prit la résolution de faire achever le Louvre, il déclara souhaiter que sa façade fût composée de tout ce que ses architectes pourroient imaginer de plus magnifique, & en même-tems de plus régulier & de plus parfait. Que son intention n'étant point d'habiter ce Palais, il vouloit que la décoration de son entrée fut assez frappante, pour annoncer à tous les étrangers la majesté d'une maison qui devoit être regardée comme sa demeure, & respectée par les honneurs qu'il avoit attachés à ses entrées accordées aux Princes du sang & aux Grands de sa Cour, comme une faveur distinguée. Qu'il prétendoit que cet édifice surpassât en beauté & en perfection tous ceux de ses maisons royales, & qu'il servît aux siecles à venir de monument authentique, & de preuve incontestable du dégré d'élévation & de correction, où avoient été portés les Arts sous son regne. (133–135)

b. [Louis XIV] préféra à tous ces plans celui de Perrault, qui avoit saisi en grand génie l'avantage si rare, & peut-être unique dans tous les Palais de l'Europe, d'en construire la façade sans être asservi à la percer à jour par des croisées, ce qui donnoit à son dessin la plus heureuse singularité, & relevoit merveilleusement toute son architecture. (137)

c. Il [the critic of 1755] attaque la façade qui regarde la riviere. . . . Il s'imagine que c'étoit dans cette partie du Louvre où devoit être l'appartement du Roi, & que l'Architecte auroit du rendre la plus magnifique. Dans cette supposition il s'éleve fortement contre la simplicité indécente de sa décoration extérieure. Il en blâme l'ordonnance sans avant-corps qui interrompent par des sa[i]llies & par des masses l'ennuyeuse monotonie qui y regne. Mais on voit ici un exemple sensible des égaremens où nous jettent la passion & les préjugés. Le dessein où il est de décrier ce beau Palais, & d'exténuer notre admiration à son égard, l'empêche de voir les trois avant-corps de cette façade, l'un dans le milieu qui devoit être couronné d'un grand fronton triangulaire orné de sculptures dans son timpan, tel qu'il est gravé dans les plans du Louvre, & dans le dessin original de Perrault;[249] les deux autres sont placés aux deux extrémités. D'ailleurs ce bâtiment, dont la simplicité l'offense si fort & le rend froid à ses yeux, ne lui eut point paru tel, si les pilastres étoient cannelés, comme ils doivent l'être, les chapiteaux corinthiens décorés de leurs feuilles, & les trois corps enrichis de médaillons, ornés de masques, de guirlandes & de tous les ornemens dont ils devoient être embellis. Lorsqu'il désire dans cette façade une supériorité de magnificence, ou au moins égale à celle du frontispice, en suivant le même dessin, elle eut été inhabitable par les inconvéniens des défauts de lumiere, ou du moins des faux jours. Il falloit indispensablement y ouvrir des croisées à la place des niches du Péristile, & alors les jours qu'auroient reçus les piéces de ses appartemens n'eussent-ils pas été d'une tristesse insupportable & pire qu'une entiere obscurité? J'avoue cependant que dans l'ordonnance de cette façade, telle qu'on la voit aujourd'hui, il eut été beaucoup mieux d'élever des colonnes isolées aux trois pavillons à la place des pilastres, & de leur donner plus de saillie, comme à le façade de la grande gallerie de Versailles; alors la décoration extérieure de cet édifice eut été plus riche & plus variée sans qu'il en fût résulté aucun inconvénient pour l'interieur. (140–143)

87. *March 15, 1756.* Minutes of the Académie royale d'architecture (H. Lemonnier, ed., *Procès-verbaux de l'Académie royale d'architecture,* Paris, 1920, VI, 256–257):

L'Académie étant assemblée, M. Aubry[250] a présenté un carton rempli de nombre de desseins contenant tous les détails de la construction du péristile du Louvre et du pavillon du milieu, où sont tous les plans, profils, coupes et élévations, avec le détail des différentes natures de pierre; comme aussi tous les détails de tous les ancres, tirants de fer, mandrins des colonnes, leurs emboîtures. Cet ouvrage est extrêmement curieux, toutes les mesures y étant cottées, qui en donnent une intelligence qui fait toujours plaisir à voir par MM. de l'Académie; d'autant que tous ces détails sont d'une très grande utilité pour des édifices de cette conséquence.[251]

88. *1759.* Pierre Patte, ed., *Mémoires de Charles Perrault . . .* , Avignon, 1759, 123–125 n. 1 (by Patte):

On trouve dans la bibliotheque du Roi une gravure du dessein que M. le Vau présenta en concurrence avec celui de M. Claude Perrault: il est d'une composition très-differente, & surtout n'a point de péristile.[252] Ceux qui d'après les ennemis de la réputation de M. Perrault, ont repeté que le péristile du Louvre, l'observatoire, l'arc de triomphe [du trône], sont composés par M. le Vau, ont fait voir qu'ils se connoissoient bien peu au génie & aux talens des artistes, puisqu'ils ne s'appercevoient pas de l'énorme différence qu'il y a entre le goût de ces deux architectes par la comparaison de leurs ouvrages. Si quelqu'un venoit nous dire qu'un tableau du Bourdon est de Rubens, qu'une figure du Puget est de Coisevox, qu'une simphonie de Campra est de Lulli, il ne trouveroit assurément aucune créance, parce que chaque auteur a une maniere caracteristique qui est telle que les ouvrages de l'un ne peuvent être attribués à l'autre, sans blesser le jugement de ceux qui ont du goût & des connoissances dans les arts. De même aussi dans l'architecture, la maniere de M. de Brosses n'est point celle de M. Mansard, de M. le Mercier, ni de M. François Blondel, &c. Si la composition du péristile du Louvre, de l'Observatoire & de l'Arc de triomphe [du Trône] est de M. le Vau, il faut aussi que tous les ouvrages connus pour être véritablement de lui, tels que le château de Vaux-le-Vicomte, les deux grands corps de bâtimens de Vincennes qui sont du côté du parc, les hôtels de Lionne & du président Lambert à Paris, enfin le collège des quatre Nations, soient composés dans le même esprit, dans le même caractere d'architecture que les trois premiers: mais c'est tout le contraire; il seroit même difficile de trouver deux manieres de traiter l'architecture plus opposées. Autant M. le Vau est lourd dans ses proportions générales, & mesquin dans ses profils, autant M. Perrault est élégant, noble, pur dans les détails comme dans l'ordonnance de ses édifices. Ce dernier s'étoit frayé une route dans l'architecture qu'il ne tenoit que de son genie, & que M. le Vau ne connut jamais.

89. *1764.* Julien David Leroy, *Histoire de la disposition et des formes differentes que les chrétiens ont données à leurs temples . . .* , Paris, 1764, 59–60:

Mais pour mieux nous former une idée des différens effets que produisent les peristyles, & de leur supériorité sur les décorations qui ne sont composées que de pilastres, profitons de l'avantage que nous a donné M. le Marquis de Marigny,[253] de voir dans tous les aspects, le plus beau morceau d'Architecture de l'Europe; parcourons des yeux toute l'étendue du peristyle du Louvre, en marchant le long des maisons qui lui font face; éloignons-nous-en pour en saisir ensemble, approchons-nous-en assez près pour découvrir la richesse de son plafond, de ses niches, de ses medaillons: saisissons le moment où le soleil y produit encore les effets les plus piquans, en faisant briller quelques parties du plus grand éclat, tandis que d'autres couvertes d'ombres les font resortir. Combien la magnificence du fond de ce peristyle, combinée de mille façons différentes, avec le contour agréable des colonnes qui sont devant, & avec la maniere dont il est éclairé, ne nous offriront-t-ils pas des tableaux enchanteurs. La riche variété de ce spectacle, se fera encore mieux sentir, en lui opposant celui qu'on peut se procurer sur le bord de la riviere. Qu'on s'efforce de même de découvrir de nouveaux aspects, dans la décoration de pilastres qu'on y voit, & dont les intér-[v]ales sont divisés à peu près comme ceux du peristyle, on n'y observe sans cesse que cette espece de décoration froide & monotone, que la lumiere vive du soleil qui anime toute la nature, ne change même presque pas.

Non-seulement le spectateur n'épuisera pas en quelques heures les tableaux que le peristyle du Louvre pourra lui offrir, mais même les différens momens de la journée lui en fourniront de nouveaux. Chaque nouvelle situation du soleil, y fera répondre les ombres des colonnes à différentes parties du fond, comme chaque hauteur différente de cet astre, les fera élever ou abbaiser plus ou moins sur le fond de ce peristyle.

90. *1765.* Pierre Patte, *Monumens érigés en France à la gloire de Louis XV . . .* , Paris, 1765, 197:

La colonnade du Louvre, cet admirable morceau d'architecture, dans lequel il semble que l'ancienne Rome nous ait transmis les traces pompeuses de son génie & de sa grandeur.

91. *1765.* Marc Antoine Laugier, *Observations sur l'architecture,* The Hague, 1765.

a. Sur les façades exterieures des bâtimens, l'essentiel est de rendre l'ordonnance aussi mâle qu'il est possible, sans s'écarter d'aucune des autres loix; & ce n'est pas une petite étude. On ne voit sur la plûpart des façades que petits ordres & petites parties. Aussi elles font presque toutes très-peu d'effet. Nous n'avons eu jusqu'à présent que la grande façade du Louvre qu'on pût citer comme une façade majestueuse. (39)

b. J'ai déjà dit plus haut, qu'il n'y a que les très-grands édifices où l'on puisse employer avec quelque succès plusieurs étages d'Architecture. Il faut pour cela qu'un bâtiment ait une hauteur démesurée. Au Louvre on a fait la faute de décorer les façades qui donnent sur la cour, de trois étages d'Architecture. Qu'en résulte-t-il? Les colonnes du rès-de-chaussée sont d'un diamétre médiocre. Celles du premier étage sont des bâtons, & celles du second deviennent des fuseaux. Les trois entablemens vont en s'amoindrissant, & le plus haut est d'une petitesse choquante. C'est un amas de petites parties imperceptibles la plûpart, & par conséquent sans noblesse. C'est un travail immense de sculpture & un ouvrage de petit goût. Le contraste des façades du dehors avec celles du dedans, offre un passage trop rapide du grand au petit. Quand on arrive à la grande porte du Louvre, vis-à-vis saint Germain l'Auxerrois, on croit voir un Palais de l'ancienne Rome. Quand on est entré dans la cour, on retrouve presque l'état des choses telles qu'elles furent 12 siécles après Vitruve. (87–88)

c. Les ordres grecs ont été inventés pour des pays dont les usages étoient différents des nôtres. Les Grecs n'avoient point de carrosses & il ne leur falloit point de porte cochere. On ne sçauroit croire combien l'usage des carrosses oppose de difficultés aux péristiles. On ne veut point mettre pied à terre dans la rue. On veut entrer en carrosse dans la cour. Il faut pour cela une porte très-large & d'une solidité à l'abri des ébranlemens. Absolument il est possible d'accoupler les colonnes d'un péristile, & de les rendre inébranlables. Mais les bases de ces colonnes ne peuvent être plantées à cru sur le pavé. Il faut les élever sur un socle continu, ou mieux encore sur des marches formant un perron en avant & de toute la longueur du péristile. Et voilà ce que les carrosses ne permettent pas; parce qu'ils ne peuvent entrer que dans une cour dont le pavé est au niveau de celui de la rue. On est donc obligé de couper & de creuser le pavé du péristile à l'endroit de la porte cochere; ce qui est très-désagréable.

Pour éviter cet inconvénient, on a pris le parti au Louvre de faire de tout le rès-de-chaussée une espéce de soubassement, & d'élever la colonnade au premier étage. Mais ce soubassement fait un très-mauvais effet; parce qu'il n'en a point la forme & qu'il est beaucoup trop haut. On y a percé des fenêtres, qui annoncent toute autre chose qu'un soubassement. Il faudroit supprimer ces fenêtres & leur substituer entre la base & la corniche des tables en relief ou en ravallement, telles qu'on les dessine sur le dé des piédestaux.[254] Il est vrai qu'il en résulteroit dans l'intérieur un petit corridor très-noir. Mais cet inconvénient seroit peu de chose en comparaison de ce qui existe. Avant qu'on eût culbuté les masures qui offusquoient cette belle façade du Louvre, le rès-de-chaussée n'étoit point apperçu. On ne voyoit un peu sensiblement que la partie d'en-haut, qui est d'une beauté sublime. Depuis qu'on a tout mis à découvert, la difformité du faux soubassement a frappé tout le monde, & l'effet de l'ensemble est devenu moindre.

Quoique ce faux soubassement soit d'une excessive hauteur, il auroit été impossible d'ouvrir dans le milieu une porte tant soit peu majestueuse, si on n'avoit pas pris le parti d'élever au-dessus un grand ceintre, qui empiéte sur le premier étage, & qui intercepte la communication des deux péristiles. C'est sans contredit une faute énorme; & elle est d'autant plus fâcheuse qu'on ne sçauroit y remédier. Commise par le plus grand de nos Architectes [Claude Perrault], elle prouve combien il est difficile de concilier dans les dehors de nos bâtimens l'Architecture gréque avec nos usages. (92–94)

92. *1765.* D.J., "Louvre" (article), *Encyclopédie, ou dictionnaire raisonné des sciences, des arts et des métiers . . . ,* Neufchâtel, 1765, ix, 706–707:

Louis XIV. fit exécuter la superbe façade du [L]ouvre qui est à l'orient du côté de saint Germain l'Auxerrois. Elle est composée d'un premier étage, pareil à celui des autres façades de l'ancien [L]ouvre; & elle a au-dessus un grand ordre de colonnes corinthiennes, couplées avec des pilastres de même. Cette façade, longue d'environ 88 toises, se partage en trois avant-corps, un au milieu, & deux aux extrémités.

L'avant-corps du milieu est ornée de huit colonnes couplées, & est terminé par un grand fronton, dont la cimaise est de deux seules pierres, qui ont chacune cinquante-deux piés de longueur, huit de largeur & quatorze pouces d'épaisseur.

Claude Perrault donna le dessein de cette façade, qui est devenue par l'exécution, un des plus augustes monumens qui soient au monde. Il inventa même les machines, avec lesquelles on transporta les deux pierres. . . .[255]

Le côté de saint Germain l'Auxerrois libre & dégagé, offriroit à tous les regards cette colonade si belle, ouvrage unique, que les citoyens admiroient, & que les étrangers viendroient voir.

93. *1768.* [Francesco Milizia], *Le vite de' piu celebri architetti* . . . , Rome, 1768, 374 (from a life of Claude Perrault):

Fece un disegno per la facciata del Louvre, che fu prescelto sopra tanti altri, e parve sì bello, che credevasi che per la sua gran bellezza non potesse eseguirsi. Fu posto in esecuzione, ed è quella superba facciata dalla parte di S. Germain [-l'Auxerrois] . . . che è il più bel pezzo d'Architettura che siavi tra quanti Palazzi Reali son in Europa. Sopra un'assai bello imbasamento s'erge un appartamento con finestre lisce ed alquanto centrate. Sopra questo piano è la famosa Colonnata lunga 525. piedi, di colonne Corintie appajate, e scanalate, di 3. piedi e 7. pollici di diametro sostenendo arditi architravi lunghi 12. piedi. Questa Colonnata ha tre avancorpi, due all'estremità ed uno nel mezzo. In questo è un frontone che abbraccia 8. colonne accoppiate, e son rimarchevoli i due pezzi inclinati che forman esso frontone, poichè sono ciascuno di 54. piedi di lunghezza. Questo edificio è coronato da una balustrata.

94. *1769.* Pierre Patte, *Mémoires sur les objets les plus importans de l'architecture,* Paris, 1769.

Patte had previously published a brief description of the structural system of the Colonnade in his *Études d'architecture* of 1755, but a full analysis had to await the appearance of the *Mémoires,* fourteen years later.

   a.   Article Second.
Procédés des Modernes pour construire les Plates-bandes
& les plafonds des Colonnades.

On sçait que les Architectes Goths n'exécutoient point de plate-bandes dans leurs édifices, mais qu'ils affectoient au contraire de les éviter, & de construire à leur place des arcs ogives d'une colonne à l'autre. Quand les Modernes, lors de la renaissance des Arts en Europe, travaillerent à resusciter les proportions de l'Architecture antique, soit par la difficulté de se procurer du marbre dans certains pays, soit par économie, soit enfin à cause de la facilité du travail, ils crurent devoir préférer la pierre, & changerent en conséquence les procédés des Grecs & des Romains, pour exécuter les plate-bandes des colonnades. Comme la pierre n'est pas une matiere aussi dure que le marbre, qu'elle est divisée par lits qui ont communément peu de hauteur, & que d'ailleurs elle est sujette à prendre l'humidité qui la fait quelquefois se fendre dans les gelées, ils penserent avec raison qu'il n'y avoit pas de solidité à l'employer d'une certaine longueur en architraves qui ont communément un poids à supporter, tel qu'une frise, une corniche, une balustrade & souvent même une voûte.

Ces considérations fondées sur la différence des matériaux obligent donc à construire nécessairement les plates-bandes par claveaux: mais comme ces claveaux forment des especes de coins, qui, vû leur position horisontale, ont beaucoup de poussée, ce changement de construction parut d'abord, contre l'usage antique, nécessiter d'accoupler les colonnes, principalement dans les angles & dans les retours extérieurs des édifices, afin de donner plus de force à ces endroits, & de les rendre capables de mieux résister à l'action des claveaux. Aussi pendant long-tems avons-nous vû en France qu'on n'osoit construire de plate-bandes à moins de placer des colonnes accouplées dans les angles. Souvent même on engageoit les colonnes pour leur donner plus de force, ou bien l'on faisoit ressauter les entablemens à-plomb de leur fût, dans la crainte de ne pouvoir assez efficacement contenir l'effort de la poussée des plate-bandes. De Brosse, au Palais du Luxembourg, & au portail Saint Gervais, en a usé ainsi: Le Mercier, au portail de la Sorbonne du coté de la cour, a groupé quatre colonnes à chaque extrémité, & les a accouplé à celui de la place au retour de l'avant-corps: Perrault a fait de-même au Péristile du Louvre: Le Vau, au portail des quatre-Nations, a poussé la défiance jusqu'à ne pas croire une colonne assez solide à l'extrémité de l'avant-corps, & il y a placé un pilastre quarré qu'il a de plus, par précaution, engagé dans le mur.

En effet les colonnes accouplées dans les retours extérieurs des édifices donnent la facilité de placer au-dessus de leur à-plomb de forts sommiers composés de larges quartiers de pierre, capables d'arrêter plus solidement la poussée d'une plate-bande à claveaux qu'une colonne solitaire. Il est vrai que depuis, on est devenu moins circonspect, & qu'on a placé des colonnes seules sur les angles des bâtimens, ainsi qu'on le verra par la suite. Les premiers pas en tout genre sont toujours un peu timides; ce n'est que par réflexion & succession de tems, que l'on parvient à connoître ce que l'on peut hasarder au-delà de ce qui a été fait précédemment.

Tout ce que je viens de remarquer ne regarde que les plate-bandes qui vont d'une colonne à l'autre & qui sont voisines des murs, car dès qu'il y avoit une certaine distance jusqu'aux colonnes, c'est-à-dire, lorsqu'elles formoient portiques, alors à l'exemple des Anciens on voûtoit le haut de cet intervalle, soit en pierre, soit en brique. C'étoit ainsi qu'on l'avoit pratiqué aux colonnades qui entourent le parvis de Saint Pierre de Rome, au portail de la Sorbonne du côté de la cour & ailleurs. Jamais on ne s'étoit hasardé à faire porter en l'air des plafonds horisontaux tout en pierre d'une certaine étendue au-dessus des portiques, avant la construction du péristile du Louvre. Aussi cette nouveauté, lorsqu'elle fut proposée, parut-elle alors à tous les Architectes une témérité; les plus expérimentés, ainsi qu'on le verra dans la description de cet édifice, soutinrent qu'un pareil projet étoit inexécutable, à cause de la grande profondeur du péristile; & ce ne fut, en effet, qu'après que Perrault eut produit un modèle de cette construction, pouce pour pied, avec de petites pierres de taille de même figure, & au même nombre que l'ouvrage en grand, que l'on demeura convaincu de sa solidité.[256] (266–268)

b.   Article Troisiesme.
Construction des Plate-bandes & des Plafonds du péristile du Louvre;
PLANCHE XIII (Fig. 79)

La colonnade du Louvre est décorée d'un ordre corinthien, élevé sur un soubassement dont les colonnes sont accouplées & ont trois pieds sept pouces de diamètre par le bas: leur écartement d'axe en axe au droit de l'entre-colonnement est de quinze pieds cinq pouces & demi: la distance entre chaque couple de colonnes est de cinq pieds quatre pouces six lignes; l'éloignement du mur du péristile au nud des colonnes de la façade est de douze pieds: enfin l'entablement qui couronne cet Ordre, est le quart de sa hauteur.

La difficulté de l'exécution du péristile du Louvre ne consistoit pas dans les plate-bandes qui régnent suivant la longueur de cet édifice, on avoit des procédés reconnus pour cela, & d'ailleurs toute la poussée de ces plate-bandes pouvoit être facilement contreventée, tant par les gros pavillons des extrémités, que par l'avant-corps du milieu. Ce qui méritoit la principale attention étoit, non-seulement l'action des plate-bandes des arrieres-corps formant un portique de douze pieds de profondeur, lesquelles allant du mur aboutir sur les colonnes, devoient nécessairement pousser au vuide par leur position, mais encore le poids des larges plafonds en pierre, qui devoient remplir l'intervalle des entre-colonnemens; lesquels plafonds, par la coupe de leurs claveaux, ne pouvoient manquer d'agir à leur tour dans tous les sens, contre les architraves placés au-dessus des colonnes le long de la façade du bâtiment, en les prenant soit par le flanc, soit par les angles.

Perrault comprit avec raison que tout le succès de sa construction dépendoit de solider le plus possible ses points d'appui, & de les rendre en quelque sorte immuables. A cet effet il accoupla ses colonnes pour acquérir plus de force, & les fit construire à bas appareil d'assises de pierre dure, dite de Saint-Cloud. Il n'excepta que les chapiteaux qui furent faits de deux assises de pierre de Saint-Leu, c'est-à-dire de pierre tendre, dans la vue sans doute de faciliter la sculpture de leurs ornemens, & de la rendre moins dispendieuse. Dans le milieu de chaque colonne il plaça un axe de fer d'environ trois pouces de gros, divisé en trois parties entées l'une dans l'autre, dans toute la hauteur.[257] On prétend (car on ne le sçait que par tradition) qu'entre chaque assise du fût des colonnes, il y a une croix de fer plat qui embrasse le mandrin d'axe, dont deux branches cramponnent par leurs extrémités l'assise supérieure, & les deux autres l'assise inférieure.

Quoi qu'il en soit, les assises des colonnes ainsi que celles des murs de cet édifice, furent posées sur cales, & coulées avec mortier de chaux & sable. A-plomb de chacune, il fut placé un fort sommier M [Fig. 79, upper left (fig. 6)], de toute la hauteur de l'architrave, à travers lequel passe la continuation du mandrin de la colonne A: on posa ensuite tous les claveaux des architraves taillés à crossettes par le bas, tant suivant la longueur du péristile que suivant sa profondeur; entre les joints desquels il fut placés de grands Z de fer K, d'environ quinze pouces de long, cramponnés par le haut dans l'un des claveaux, & par le bas dans l'autre: ce qui leur donne une inhérence parfaite, & les empêche de pouvoir descendre en contre-bas.

Sur la tête des claveaux de l'architrave, il fut fait dans le milieu une tranchée pour recevoir deux tirans horisontaux H, I [Fig. 79, lower middle (fig. 2)], ou B & C [Fig. 79, upper left (fig. 6)], d'environ deux pouces un quart de gros, dont l'un sert à lier ensemble les deux axes des colonnes de l'entre-colonnement, & l'autre à contenir les deux axes des colonnes accouplées.[258]

Perpendiculairement à ces tirans H, & I [Fig. 79, lower middle (fig. 2)], il en fut placé à la même hauteur, vis-à-vis chaque couple de colonnes, trois autres, K, K, L, dont les deux premiers, K, K, sont fixés chacun par une de leurs extrémités dans le mandrin d'axe G [Fig. 79, lower middle (fig. 2)], de chaque colonne, & par l'autre dans un ancre M, placé derriere le mur du péristile. Le troisieme tiran L, intermédiaire, est accroché d'une part au milieu du tiran I, & est aussi retenu de l'autre par un ancre M, placé entre les deux précédens. La fig. 8 [Fig. 79, upper middle] fait voir en S, T, S, la coupe de ces tirans & leur situation.

Après cette opération on continua d'élever la frise R [Fig. 79, upper left (fig. 7)], ou N, L [Fig. 79, upper left (fig. 6)] suivant la longueur du bâtiment: quand on eut posé les sommiers Q ou N, à-plomb des colonnes, en les faisant toujours pénétrer par le mandrin A, on plaça les claveaux, en mettant encore entre leurs joints de grands Z, L, semblables à ceux qui avoient été employés précédemment pour l'architrave; ensuite on construisit les plafonds dont les voussoirs furent disposés de la même maniere, & des dimensions représentées dans les *figures* 1, 2 & 3 [Fig. 79, lower row]: enfin l'on finit par poser le bouchon U, servant de fermeture au plafond, lequel est d'une seule pierre de six pieds de diametre par le haut, & de cinq pieds & demi par le bas: entre ses joints il fut placé, dans l'épaisseur du plafond, des T renversés C, [Fig. 79, lower right (fig. 1)] & X [Fig. 79, lower left (fig. 3)], dont on voit la représentation particuliere à part [Fig. 79, extreme lower left (fig. 4)]: l'objet de ces T renversés qui ont par le haut de grosses têtes, est de soutenir le bouchon U, plus également sur les voussoirs qui l'environnent, & de l'empêcher d'appuïer de tout son poids contre leurs arrêtes inférieures.

Sur le sommet des claveaux de la frise, on fit aussi des tranchées, comme on avoit fait sur ceux de l'architrave, pour recevoir deux autres tirans [h]orisontaux P, Q [Fig. 79, lower left (fig. 3)] & F, G [Fig. 79, upper left (fig. 6)]: celui P [Fig. 79, lower left (fig. 3)] sert à lier ensemble à cette hauteur les axes des colonnes de l'entre-colonnement, & celui Q sert à contenir les axes des colonnes accouplées. Au milieu du tiran Q est accroché par un bout un tiran S, perpendiculaire dont l'autre est fixé par un ancre V commun au tiran L [Fig. 79, lower middle (fig. 2)], qui est au-dessous.

Toute la différence qu'il y a entre l'arrangement des tirans de la frise, & de ceux qui sont à la hauteur de l'architrave, c'est qu'au lieu d'en avoir deux perpendiculaires correspondans à ceux K, K [Fig. 79, lower middle (fig. 2)], Perrault les a placés comme ils sont représentés en R, R [Fig. 79, lower left (fig. 3)], c'est-à-dire, diagonalement, & de maniere que chacun de ces tirans traversant en croix l'entre-colonnement, va se fixer dans le haut des ancres qui ont déja servi à contenir les tirans K, K; par ce moyen les colonnes sont contreventées dans toutes leurs directions.

Ces tirans R, R, ainsi que ceux S & L [Fig. 79, lower middle and lower left (figs. 2, 3)], sont divisés en deux parties unies à l'aide d'un moufle [Fig. 79, extreme lower left (fig. 5)], servant à les bander plus ou moins suivant le besoin: pour faciliter le service du moufle du tiran L [Fig. 79, lower middle (fig. 2)], & ne le point charger d'un poids inutile, on a pratiqué un vuide en cet endroit en forme d'auge, dont on voit le profil en V [Fig. 79, upper middle (fig. 8)].

Après que l'architrave, les plafonds & la frise eurent été terminés, on construisit la corniche de l'entablement qui est composée [Fig. 79, upper left and upper right (figs. 6, 9)] de trois cours d'assises posées en liaison à l'ordinaire: ces assises sont placées en encorbellement intérieurement, non-seulement à dessein de procurer plus de queue aux pierres & de les rendre plus capables de soutenir efficacement la bascule, mais aussi pour donner moins de longueur, & conséquemment plus de solidité aux dalles de la terrasse qui couvre cet édifice, dont les joints paroissent avoir été faits avec de la limaille d'acier & de l'urine.[259] Il est évident que cet arrangement laisse un vuide Z [Fig. 79, upper middle (fig. 8)] & N [Fig. 79, upper right (fig. 9)] dans l'épaisseur de la frise & de la corniche au-dessus du plafond, par où l'on peut aller travailler avec facilité, soit à bander davantage les tirans en resserrant les clavettes des moufles, soit à faire dans l'entable[ment] les réparations nécessaires.

Il est à remarquer que toutes les pierres employées pour la construction de l'entablement & des plafonds de cet édifice, sont de pierres dites de Saint Leu, & qu'il n'y a eu que l'assise supérieure de la corniche, comprenant la cymaise, qui ait été exécutée en pierres dures.

Cette description doit convaincre combien la construction du péristile du Louvre est solide & bien entendue; tout y a été prévu & obvié, tellement que, si par évenement un entre-colonnement venoit à être renversé, soit par l'effet de la foudre, soit par d'autres causes, il ne seroit pas à craindre que celui qui est voisin pût être entraîné par sa chûte. Ce qui me paroît principalement donner une force inébranlable à sa bâtisse, c'est que le fer ne porte rien & ne fait exactement que la fonction de tirer pour retenir la poussée des architraves & solider l'axe des colonnes; procédé qui doit nécessairement produire la plus grande résistance que l'on puisse espérer de la part du fer. (269–273)

c. *PLANche* XIII [Fig. 79]

La Figure premiere [lower right] représente le plan du plafond d'une entrecolonne du péristile, vu par-dessous.

A, Colonne dont l'axe est traversé par un mandrin d'environ trois pouces de gros, lequel est embrassé entre chaque assise, à ce que l'on prétend, par une croix formant un crampon de fer plat, dont deux des branches sont encastrées dans l'assise supérieure, & les deux autres dans l'assise inférieure.

B, Exprime le dessous du bouchon de pierre du plafond, qui est d'un seul morceau.

C, Position des T renversés qui soutiennent le bouchon.

D, Dessous des plate-bandes.

E, Plan de l'entablement où l'on distingue les joints des assises horisontales de la corniche, posées en liaison, tellement qu'il n'y a ni modillons ni rosettes coupés par le milieu, à dessein de donner plus de solidité à leurs sculptures.

F, F, Oeil de différens tirans.

. . . .

La Figure deuxieme [lower middle] exprime un plan au niveau du haut de l'architrave, où l'on a supposé que le plafond n'est pas encore construit.

G, Colonne avec son mandrin.

H, Grand tiran horisontal liant les axes des colonnes de l'entre-colonnement.

I, Petit tiran horisontal liant les deux axes des colonnes accouplées.

K, K, Tirans perpendiculaires fixés par une extrêmité dans le mandrin G, & de l'autre par un ancre adossé au mur du péristile.

L, Autre tiran perpendiculaire accroché d'une part au milieu du tiran horisontal I, & de l'autre par un ancre.

M, M, Ancres.

N, Vuide où doit être posé le plafond.

La figure troisieme [lower left] fait voir le plan des plafonds, pris entre la frise & la corniche.

O, Mandrin d'axe des colonnes.

P, Tiran horisontal contenant à ladite hauteur l'axe des colonnes de l'entre-colonnement.

Q, Autre tiran horisontal pareil au tiran I [in the preceding figure, lower middle], liant ensemble les colonnes accouplées.

S, Tiran perpendiculaire au précédent, embrassant par un bout le milieu du tiran Q, & fixé par l'autre dans un ancre V qui contient déjà le tiran L [in the preceding figure, lower middle].

R, R, Tirans placés diagonalement, fixés chacun d'une part au mandrin O, & de l'autre par le même ancre qui a déja servi à contenir le tiran K [in the preceding figure, lower middle] de la colonne placée de l'autre côté de l'entre-colonnement: il est à observer que ces tirans R ont chacun dans leur milieu un moufle à clavettes pour les bander plus ou moins.

T, Représente en lignes ponctuées la situation d'un tiran déjà désigné par K dans [the preceding figure, lower middle].

V, Bouchon du plafond vu par-dessus, lequel a six pieds de diametre.

X, Têtes des T renversés.

Y, Claveaux du plafond.

Z, Vuide pratiquée au-dessus des plafonds des colonnes accouplées pour élégir ces endroits.

La figure quatrieme [extreme lower left] représente à part la forme d'un des T renversés qui soutiennent le bouchon du plafond.

La figure cinquieme [extreme lower left] exprime en grand, la forme du moufle d'un des tirans L, R, S [in lower middle and left].

La figure sixieme [upper left] fait voir la coupe de la moitié d'un entre-colonnement, par le milieu de l'axe des colonnes.

A, A, Mandrins d'axe des colonnes, lequel est embrassé entre chaque assise par une croix de fer, dont deux des branches cramponnent l'assise de dessus, & les deux autres celle de dessous.

B, Tiran horisontal liant les axes de l'entre-colonnement à la hauteur de l'architrave.

C, Autre tiran horisontal liant les axes des colonnes accouplées.

D, Extrêmité d'un tiran perpendiculaire au précédent.

E, Extrêmité d'un autre tiran aussi perpendiculaire, dont l'oeil est passé dans le mandrin d'axe.

F, Tiran horisontal placé au-dessus de la frise, pour lier à cette hauteur les axes des colonnes de l'entre-colonnement.

G, Autre tiran horisontal, liant chaque couple de colonnes.

H, Oeil d'un tiran perpendiculaire au précédent.

I, Oeil d'un tiran diagonal.

K, L, Grands Z placés entre les joints des claveaux, tant de la frise que de l'architrave.

M, Sommier de l'architrave.

N, Sommier de la frise.

O, Trois assises de pierres horisontales, posées en liaison, & composant la hauteur de la corniche.

La Figure septieme [upper left] représente l'élévation extérieure de l'entablement avec l'arrangement de ses voussoirs.

P, Sommier de l'architrave.

Q, Sommier de la frise.

R, Claveaux dont ceux de l'architrave sont terminés en crossettes par le bas.

La Figure huitieme [upper middle] fait voir la coupe d'un entre-colonnement par le milieu, suivant la ligne W, W [in the lower figures] de la longueur du péristile.

S, S, Tirans perpendiculaires placés à la hauteur de l'architrave.

T, Autre tiran perpendiculaire.

U, Coupe du bouchon.

V, Tirans perpendiculaires à la hauteur de la frise.

X, Tirans diagonaux.

Z, Vuide pratiqué derriere l'entablement.

Y, Dalles de pierre formant le plancher de la terrasse qui couvre le péristile.

&, Mur du fond du péristile.

La Figure neuvieme [upper right] est un profil sur la largeur du péristile.

a, Coupe de l'architrave où l'on voit exprimé en lignes ponctuées le mandrin d'axe.

b, b, Tiran perpendiculaire placé à la hauteur de l'architrave.

c, Tiran horisontal de l'entre-colonnement.

d, Bout du petit tiran horisontal entre les colonnes accouplées.

e, Tiran horisontal placé à la hauteur de la frise.

f, f, Tiran perpendiculaire aux précédents.

g, Extrémité du petit tiran horisontal liant les axes des colonnes.

h, Ancres communs à deux tirans.

i, Coupe du bouchon.

k, T renversé.

l, Assises placées en encorbellement pour donner plus de queue aux pierres qui forment la saillie de la corniche.

m, Grande dalle de pierre de la terrasse.

n, Vuide entre le plafond & la terrasse. (274–277)

d.   CHAPITRE HUITIEME.
*Description de la construction
de la Colonnade du Louvre.*

A peine M. Colbert fut-il nommé Contrôleur-Général des Finances, place à laquelle étoit jointe alors celle de Surintendant des Bâtimens du Roi, qu'il résolut de signaler son administration par l'achevement du Louvre; ouvrage commencé par François I, & laissé toujours imparfait par ses successeurs.

Pendant le ministere du Cardinal de Mazarin, le Vau, alors premier Architecte du Roi, avoit élevé la façade du Vieux-Louvre du côté de la riviere [Fig. 17], laquelle subsiste encore, & est masquée par celle que l'on voit aujourd'hui [Fig. 95]. Il ne restoit plus que la décoration de la principale entrée, dont même les fondemens étoient déjà jetés, ainsi qu'à terminer le deuxieme & le troisieme étage de la plus grande partie de la cour.[260]

Comme M. Colbert n'étoit pas content de ce que le Vau avoit fait exécuter, non plus que de son projet de continuation, il invita les Gens de goût & les principaux Artistes à dire leurs avis à ce sujet, & même à proposer des projets en concours, promettant de faire exécuter l'idée la plus heureuse, & celle qui annonceroit avec le plus de majesté & de magnificence le frontispice du Palais de nos Rois.

La décoration de la façade de le Vau, qui étoit toute en pilastres [his final design (Figs. 33, 35) had engaged columns], fut beaucoup censurée; elle fut jugée sans noblesse, sans dignité, ayant trop peu de relief; sa porte fut unanimement trouvée petite, & de trop peu d'importance pour servir d'entrée à un pareil monument.

Parmi les projets qui furent exposés en concours avec celui de le Vau, il y en avoit un de Claude Perrault, savant Médecin, & Membre de l'Académie des Sciences, qui ne s'étoit point fait connoître; lequel projet étoit décoré d'un portique en colonnades, semblable à celui qui a été exécuté depuis. Tous les Connoisseurs furent surpris d'admiration en voyant cette magnifique pensée: comme on ne savoit à qui l'attribuer, chacun s'épuisa en conjectures pour deviner quel en pouvoit être l'Auteur, attendu qu'il n'y avoit personne de connu pour composer avec tant de noblesse, & pour dessiner l'architecture avec autant de goût & de correction.

[There follows an account of Bernini in France.]

ARTICLE QUATRIEME.
Raisons qui firent abandonner l'exécution du projet du Cavalier Bernin; & comment celui de Claude Perrault fut préféré.

Lorsque le Cavalier Bernin fut parti, les critiques se déchaînerent ouvertement contre lui. On adressa des mémoires à M. Colbert où l'on faisoit voir que son projet ne pouvoit être exécuté qu'au détriment du Louvre: on y démontroit qu'il falloit abattre pour cet effet la plus grande partie de ce que les Rois prédécesseurs avoient fait construire; que cet Artiste ne s'étoit assujéti à aucune des conditions qu'on lui avoit essentiellement imposées; que l'appartement du Roi seroit d'ailleurs, en suivant son plan, distribué sans aucune des commodités d'usage; & qu'enfin, malgré l'immensité de cette maison-royale, il n'y auroit pas de logemens pour la moitié des Officiers.

Ces raisons ayant frappé le Ministre, le déterminerent à abandonner le projet du Cavalier Bernin, pour jetter les yeux sur quelqu'autre qui n'eut point ses inconvéniens. Le choix seul l'embarrassoit, quoiqu'il n'ignorât pas l'applaudissement général qu'on avoit donné au dessein de Claude Perrault, lors du concours, il hésitoit à l'adopter: il lui paroissoit singulier de préférer le projet d'un homme qui n'étoit connu dans le monde que pour un sçavant Médecin & une personne de goût, à toutes les pensées des Maîtres de l'Art. Dès les commencemens même que le bruit se répandit de la préférence de ce Ministre, les gens à bons mots ne manquerent pas d'en plaisanter, en disant qu'il falloit que l'Architecture fût bien malade, puisqu'on étoit obligé d'avoir recours à un Médecin.

Néanmoins pour n'avoir rien à se reprocher en pareille circonstance, M. Colbert fit faire un modele en bois du projet de Perrault, ainsi que de celui de Levau, &

les présenta tous deux à Louis XIV, qui étoit alors à Saint Germain-en-Laie avec toute sa Cour. Le Roi avant que de s'expliquer sur le choix, demanda au Surintendant son sentiment sur ces deux modeles; celui-ci ayant répondu que s'il en étoit le maître, il donneroit la préférence au projet décoré en pilastres qui étoit celui de Levau; & *moi*, répliqua Louis XIV, *je choisis celui à colonnade, la pensée en est bien plus noble, plus majestueuse, & plus digne enfin d'annoncer l'entrée de mon Palais.* Il est à croire que ce Ministre avoit agi dans cette occasion en Courtisan, pour laisser tout l'honneur du choix à son maître; car personne n'ignoroit son inclination pour le projet de Perrault.

Afin de ne rien donner au hasard pour la parfaite exécution d'un semblable édifice dont la construction paroissoit extrêmement difficultueuse, M. Colbert associa à Perrault, Levau, qui avoit la plus grande expérience, & Lebrun, premier Peintre du Roi, qui entendoit très-bien l'Architecture, & qui étoit un des plus beaux génies que la France ait produit. Ces Artistes eurent ordre de s'assembler deux fois la semaine pour conférer sur les difficultés qui pourroient survenir dans la bâtisse de ce monument; & pour les engager à travailler de bonne foi, le Ministre décida qu'aucun des trois ne pourroit se dire, en particulier, l'auteur du projet. Malgré toutes ces précautions, il y eut entre ces Artistes beaucoup de discussions qui transpirerent dans le public. Levau & Lebrun disoient sans cesse que le dessein de Claude Perrault ne pouvoit être beau qu'en peinture; mais que l'exécution en étoit impossible, attendu que le péristile avoit trop de profondeur, & que les architraves qui alloient du mur correspondre sur les colonnes, ayant douze pieds de longueur, pousseroient nécessairement au vuide, sans espoir de pouvoir les retenir.

Pour lever toutes les difficultés & les inquiétudes que M. Colbert paroissoit avoir au sujet de la construction de cet édifice, Perrault fit un modèle de la grandeur de pouce pour pied, composé de petites pierres de taille de même figure, & au même nombre que l'ouvrage en grand en devoit avoir: lorsqu'il fut achevé & qu'on eut fait attention comment étoit retenue la poussée des architraves, par de petites barres de fer d'une grosseur proportionnelle à celle qu'elles devoient avoir dans l'exécution; quand on eut remarqué surtout l'arrangement des tirans disposés en diagonale, dans l'épaisseur de l'entablement, où étoit ménagé un vuide d'où il seroit aisé de remédier en tous tems aux inconvéniens qui pourroient survenir par la suite, tout le monde fut convaincu de la fermeté de cette construction, & que rien ne pouvoit être plus solide.[261]

Cet édifice qui avoit été interrompu depuis le départ du Cavalier Bernin, fut recommencé sur le nouveau plan en 1667, en faisant toutefois usage d'une partie des fondations du projet de l'Architecte Italien. On travailla sans interruption jusqu'en 1670, tant à la façade du côté de l'entrée qu'à celle du côté de la riviere, & à l'autre opposée du côté de la rue Saint Honoré.

Il seroit superflu de se répandre en éloges sur la composition & l'Ordonnance d'Architecture de la colonnade du Louvre; il y a peu de monumens qui jouissent d'une réputation aussi distinguée & dont les Etrangers fassent généralement plus de cas. C'est un de ces édifices qui fera dans tous les tems le plus grand honneur au régne sous lequel il a été élevé. Parcourez toute l'Europe, vous ne trouverez nulle-part aucun Palais, ni aucune Maison-royale qui offre un aspect plus noble, plus recommandable, & peut-être même, malgré toutes les descriptions pompeuses qu'on nous a laissé du Palais des Césars & des demeures des anciens Rois de Perse, n'a t-il point existé de frontispice d'édifice aussi magnifique & aussi-bien entendu dans son ensemble.

Ce n'est pas que cet édifice soit absolument sans défaut, nous ne pouvons dissimuler que bien des connoisseurs paroissent regretter que la galerie ne régne pas dans l'avant-corps du milieu, & qu'aussi cet avant-corps soit coupé par une grande arcade qui semble être assommée par le plein énorme qui se trouve au-dessus: d'autres ont encore désiré que les pavillons des extrémités eussent été décorés de colonnes, comme le reste, au lieu de pilastres; & qu'enfin pour donner un air moins froid, moins bas-relief, à la façade vis-à-vis la riviere, Perrault eût du moins décoré ses avants-corps de colonnes. Au surplus, s'il se trouve quelque chose à redire dans quelques-unes des parties de ce monument, son ensemble, la beauté de ses proportions, de ses profils, & de sa construction, méritent les plus grands applaudissemens: on en jugera par les développemens que nous donnerons après l'article suivant, lesquels nous avons levés & dessinés avec la plus scrupuleuse exactitude.

ARTICLE CINQUIEME.
Preuves que nul autre que Claude Perrault n'est l'Auteur de la composition de la Colonnade du Louvre.

Quoique nous ayons dit précédemment que Lebrun, Levau & Perrault avoient été chargés conjointement de veiller à la construction du Louvre, l'on ne sçauroit douter que l'honneur de l'invention ne soit dû entierement à ce dernier. Ce ne fut qu'après la mort de Perrault, c'est-à-dire, vingt ans après la construction de cet édifice, que [Boileau-]Despreaux, dans ses remarques sur Longin,[262] s'avisa de dire que Dorbay, Elève de Levau, étoit en état de démontrer, papier sur table, que la façade du Louvre étoit de son maître. Une seule remarque suffit pour détruire cette allégation. Indépendamment de ce que toute la Cour avoit été témoin des deux projets présentés à Louis XIV, & de ce que tout Paris les avoit vû exposés en concours avec les desseins des autres Architectes, pourquoi auroit-on associé à Levau, Claude Perrault? Ce n'étoit certainement pas pour lui donner des leçons de construction; car Levau passoit pour l'Architecte le plus expérimenté de son tems; ce n'étoit pas non-plus pour lui digérer ses desseins, car il étoit accoutumé à tous ces détails, vû les grands travaux qu'il avoit fait exécuter de toutes parts. Il est tout naturel de penser qu'au contraire on l'avoit associé à Perrault, tant parce que celui-ci n'étoit pas censé, quoiqu'il eut beaucoup étudié l'Architecture ancienne, avoir l'acquis nécessaire pour diriger, sans quelque conseil éclairé, la construction d'un édifice de cette importance, que parce qu'il étoit dans l'ordre que le premier Architecte du Roi eut une sorte d'inspection sur tout ce qui se construit dans les maisons-royales.

Si cette réflexion ne suffit pas, il est aisé de citer des témoins irréprochables qui déposent contre tout ce qu'on pourroit objecter dorénavant à cet égard. Ceux qui, d'après les ennemis de la réputation de Perrault, ont répété que le péristile du Louvre, l'Observatoire, l'arc de triomphe du Trône, (car dès qu'on vouloit lui ôter la gloire de l'un, il falloit nécessairement lui ôter celle des deux autres) sont du dessein de Levau, ont fait voir beaucoup de malignité, ou qu'ils se connoissoient bien peu au génie & aux talents des Artistes, puisqu'ils ne s'appercevoient pas de l'énorme différence qu'il y a entre le goût de ces deux Architectes par la comparaison de leurs ouvrages. Si quelqu'un venoit dire qu'un tableau de Raphaël est de Rubens, qu'une figure du Puget est de Girardon, qu'une simphonie de Rameau est de Lulli, il ne trouveroit assurément aucune créance, parce que chaque Auteur a une maniere caractèristique, qui est telle que les ouvrages de l'un ne sçauroient être attribués à l'autre, sans blesser le jugement de ceux qui ont du goût & des connoissances dans les Arts. De même aussi dans l'Architecture, la maniere de Desbrosses n'est point celle de Mansard, de Lemercier, ou de Bullet. Si le péristile du Louvre, l'Observatoire & l'Arc-de-triomphe du Trône sont de Levau, il faut nécessairement lui attribuer la composition des desseins de la traduction de Vitruve que l'on n'a point contesté à Perrault; il faut également que tous les ouvrages connus pour être véritablement de ce premier Architecte du Roi, tels que les Châteaux de Vaux-le-vicomte, les deux grands corps de bâtimens de Vincennes du côté du parc, les Hôtels de Lionne, & du Président Lambert à Paris, enfin le Collège des quatre Nations, soient composés dans le même esprit & dans le même caractère d'Architecture que les trois autres; mais c'est précisément tout le contraire: il seroit même difficile de trouver deux manieres de traiter l'Architecture, plus opposées. Autant Levau est lourd dans ses proportions générales, & mesquin dans ses profils; autant Perrault est élégant, noble, & pur dans les détails comme dans l'ordonnance de ses édifices: ce dernier s'étoit frayé une route dans l'Architecture, qu'il ne tenoit que de son génie, & que Levau ne connut jamais. En voilà certainement plus qu'il ne faut pour démontrer qu'on ne sçauroit contester, sans injustice, à Perrault la gloire d'avoir donné le dessein de la colonnade du Louvre; & si nous avons insisté, c'est afin qu'il ne puisse y avoir désormais le plus léger doute sur ce qu'on doit penser à cet égard.

ARTICLE SIXIEME.

Description des proportions & profils de la Colonnade du Louvre, cottés & numérotés. . . .

La Planche XVII [Patte's plates XVII–XXIV are not reproduced] représente le plan général du vieux Louvre, pour donner une idée de l'ensemble de cet édifice. Au dessus est une petite élevation de la principale entrée de ce Palais qui a environ quatre-vingt-huit toises de longueur, sur quatorze toises six pieds deux pouces de hauteur. Son ordonnace d'Architecture est corinthienne, & consiste en trois avants-corps séparés l'un de l'autre par deux colonnades ou péristiles dont les colonnes sont accouplées: elle est élevée sur un soubassement tout lice & sans ornement, qui la fait valoir; enfin elle est terminée par une terrasse bordée d'une balustrade, dont les piédestaux devoient porter des trophées & des vases.

La Planche XVIII offre dans le bas le plan d'une entre-colonne des arriere-corps du péristile du Louvre, & vers le haut le plan des plafonds de la même entre-colonne.

Il y a quatre manieres différentes d'arranger les plate-bandes d'un péristile, lorsqu'elles vont d'une colonne aboutir sur un pilastre, dont on voit des exemples dans les bâtimens antiques. Cette différence provient de ce que le pilastre n'ayant pas d'ordinaire de dimension comme la colonne, il est difficile que la largeur de l'architrave puisse répondre à plomb de l'un & de l'autre.

La premiere consiste à faire l'architrave d'une largeur égale à la diminution de la colonne, comme on l'a pratiqué au Pantheon; c'est-à-dire, de faire porter l'architrave sur le nud de la colonne, & de le faire retirer de toute sa diminution sur le pilastre.[263]

La seconde, à faire porter l'architrave à plomb sur le nud du pilastre, & à faux sur la colonne, ainsi qu'on le remarque au Temple de la Concorde à Rome.[264]

La troisieme, à diminuer le pilastre également comme

la colonne: ce qui est observé au Temple d'Antonin & de Faustine.[265]

La quatrieme enfin est de faire passer l'architrave, en sorte qu'il porte à faux sur la colonne seulement de la moitié de sa diminution & qu'il se retire sur le pilastre d'autant, comme au Marché de Nerva à Rome.[266] C'est ainsi qu'en a usé Perrault: après avoir donné aux plate-bandes qui vont d'une colonne à l'autre sur le devant du Péristile, la même largeur que la diminution de la colonne par en haut, c'est-à-dire, trois pieds un pouce, il a donné aux plate-bandes qui correspondent des colonnes aux pilastres qui n'ont pas de diminution, une largeur moyenne proportionnelle arithmétique entre le diamètre du bas de la colonne & celui du haut, c'est-à-dire, trois pieds quatre pouces.

Les plafonds des entre-colonnemens ont été tenus quarrés, & sont décorés de différens ornemens disposés avec beaucoup de goût. On remarque au milieu un soleil qui étoit l'emblême ordinaire sous lequel on se plaisoit à représenter Louis XIV.

Le plan du bas de cette entre-colonne auquel nous avons mis toutes les cottes & mesures, comparé avec celui du haut, fait voir toute leur correspondance, que les développemens suivans rendront encore plus intelligibles.

Avant d'aller plus loin, il est important d'observer, pour l'intelligence des cottes des planches, 1°. qu'à cause du peu d'espace qui n'a pas permis d'exprimer les noms des toises, pieds, pouces & lignes, au-dessus des mesures, nous avons designé les toises par *toi.* au-dessus du nombre; les pieds, par un petit trait aussi au-dessus; les pouces par deux petits traits, & les lignes sans aucune marque: ainsi 2$^{toi.}$ 3′. 4″. 5. veulent dire deux toises, trois pieds, quatre pouces, cinq lignes; 2°. que par pieds on doit entendre le pied de Roi ou le pied parisien; 3°. que je suppose le module divisé en trente parties, & chaque partie en quarante-trois autres, à cause du diamètre de la colonne qui est de quarante-trois pouces, & que, par abréviation, nous avons exprimé le mot module par *m* après le nombre, & le mot partie, par deux points placés l'un au-dessous de l'autre; par conséquent 4^m 2:4/43 signifiera quatre modules, deux parties & quatre quarante-troisiemes de partie; 4°. qu'afin d'éviter la confusion qu'auroient apporté sur chaque planche, les mesures cottées en toises, pieds, & en modules en même tems, nous avons placé à la fin de ce Chapitre une Table à l'aide de laquelle on pourra trouver à toute rigueur les rapports des toises, pieds, &c. avec le module & ses parties; 5°. que toutes les saillies des profils doivent être toujours comptées, soit du nud de la colonne, soit du nud du mur auquel ils sont adossées.

La Planche XIX représente l'élevation & le profil d'une entre-colonne.

Toutes les proportions des parties principales de cet édifice y sont cottées en toises, pieds, pouces, ainsi qu'en modules. On remarquera que le soubassement est les deux tiers moins un 14me de l'ordre corinthien qu'il supporte, y compris le socle, & qu'il est un des moins élevés de ceux qui sont exécutés dans la plûpart des meilleurs édifices; car le soubassement de la Place des Victoires, celui du Château de Saint Cloud, & celui de la Place de Louis XV [de la Concorde] à Paris, sont les deux tiers juste de l'ordre qu'ils supportent: le soubassement de la façade du Château de Versailles du côté des jardins, a les deux tiers plus un cinquieme de l'ordre; enfin celui de la Place de Vendôme [a] les deux tiers moins un quarante-neuvieme.

Une autre attention à faire, c'est que les colonnes sortent de la proportion ordinaire assignée par les plus célebres Auteurs; car elles ont vingt-un modules quatre parties de hauteur. Perrault en a usé ainsi, soit par la raison que les colonnes cannelées, & surtout accouplées, ont toujours coutume de paroître à la vue plus grosses que lorsqu'elles sont lisses & une à une, soit parce que le grand exhaussement de cet ordre, à trente-trois pieds de terre, lui a fait juger qu'il devoit être autrement proportionné pour produire son effet, que s'il étoit placé au rez-de-chaussée; quoi qu'il en soit, cette proportion générale réussit parfaitement.

De plus, les colonnes renflent au tiers inférieur de leur fût de deux pouces sur la totalité du diamètre, ce qui est contre tout exemple antique; car les Grecs & les Egyptiens diminuoient leurs colonnes depuis le bas jusqu'en haut, au lieu que les Romains ne commençoient cette diminution qu'au tiers inférieur de leur fût. On ne trouve que ces deux maniere[s] de diminuer les colonnes dans l'antique; & comme elles sont toujours constantes, il est à croire qu'elles proviennent de la différente pratique que les ouvriers employoient pour les tailler dans les carrieres de marbre, soit de Grece, soit d'Egypte, soit d'Italie, d'où on les transportoit dans chaque Ville toute taillées. . . .

Vitruve à la vérité, parle du renflement qu'on peut donner aux colonnes vers le tiers à la fin du second Chapitre de son troisieme Livre;[267] sur quoi il est à remarquer que Perrault, en commentant cette opinion particuliere à cet ancien Architecte, dit dans ses notes,[268] . . . qu'indépendamment qu'il n'y a point d'exemple de ce renflement, il est désapprouvé par la plûpart des Auteurs. Ils opposent, continue t-il, à la comparaison que l'on veut faire des colonnes avec le corps de l'homme qui est plus gros au milieu que vers la tête & les pieds, celle du tronc des arbres qui ont été le premier & le plus naturel modèle de la tige des colonnes. De plus, ils disent qu'il est nécessaire que les colonnes qui sont faites pour soutenir, ayent une figure qui les rendent plus fermes, telle qu'est celle qui, d'un empattement plus large, va toujours en se rétrécissant. Il est sans doute singulier, qu'après ces remarques, Perrault ne nous ait pas fait part des raisons qui l'ont porté à faire renfler les colonnes de l'édifice que nous décrivons.

Quant à l'accouplement des colonnes qui régnent le long de la façade du Louvre, quoique les Anciens ne fussent pas communément dans cet usage, ce sont certainement des raisons de solidité qui ont engagé cet Architecte à cet arrangement. Comme il n'avoit point été exécuté jusqu'alors, dans ce pays-ci, de péristile, & que l'on paroissoit effrayé de la hardiesse de l'exécution de ces larges plafonds en pierres, soutenus sur des colonnes éloignées de douze pieds du mur, il crut devoir multiplier les points d'appui: une preuve que ce fut cette raison qui engagea Perrault à l'accouplement, c'est qu'à la *page* 79 de la deuxieme Edition de Vitruve, en entreprenant de réfuter François Blondel, qui avoit avancé dans les dixieme, onzieme & douzieme Chapitres du premier Livre de son *Cours d'Architecture,* que l'usage d'accoupler les colonnes étoit une licence, cet Architecte n'oppose d'autre raison, si ce n'est que le bout d'un architrave qui pose sur une colonne entiere, lors de l'accouplement, est mieux affermi que quand il ne pose que sur la moitié de la colonne, & qu'il plie plus facilement, quand il est supporté par son extrémité, que lorsque cette extrémité passe au-delà de la colonne qui le soutient; car, dit-il, ce bout qui passe par-delà la colonne au droit du petit entre-colonnement a une pesanteur qui résiste au pliement de la partie opposée, qui est au droit du grand entre-colonnement.[269] Depuis l'exécution du péristile du Louvre on est devenu plus hardi, & l'expérience a fait voir par les exemples de la Chapelle de Versailles, & des bâtimens en colonnade de la Place de Louis XV, que l'on pouvoit également sans rien craindre, solider ces sortes de constructions avec des colonnes solitaires.

Quoi qu'il en soit, l'accouplement produit, à l'édifice que nous décrivons, un bon effet à l'oeil; outre que cet arrangement assure la solidité des angles d'un bâtiment, il permet aussi d'espacer davantage les colonnes pour donner de plus grandes ouvertures aux portes, aux croisées, & de pouvoir les orner de chambranles, de consoles, de fronton; au lieu qu'en plaçant les colonnes une à une suivant l'usage antique, il faut de toute nécessité tenir les entre-colonnes serrées, si l'on veut qu'elles ayent de la grace; ce qui n'est pas le plus souvent aussi commode ni aussi avantageux.

L'intérieur du portique, ainsi que l'exprime le profil, forme un plafond horisontal supporté par un simple architrave: le but de cet arrangement est, non-seulement de diminuer la grande charge des plate-bandes qui vont des colonnes aboutir au mur du péristile, mais encore d'empêcher les plafonds de paroître trop enfoncés, comme il seroit arrivé si l'on y avoit mis au-dessus une frise & une corniche. D'ailleurs, l'usage des corniches étant de défendre le haut des murs & des colonnes de la pluie, il est certain qu'elles sont inutiles dans les lieux couverts, & qu'elles ne servent qu'à derober le jour des fenêtres qui sont au-dessus. . . .

La Planche XX fait voir les détails de l'ordre Corinthien. La hauteur de l'entablement est un peu moindre que le quart de la colonne: celle de la base a plus d'un module: celle du chapiteau a deux modules dix-huit parties de haut 6/43, proportion qui a très bonne grace, & qui réussit surtout parfaitement pour les pilastres, lesquels n'ayant pas de diminution par le haut comme les colonnes, ont coutume de paroître bas & écrasés. Perrault a dû avoir d'autant plus d'égard à cette raison, que la façade en retour du côté de la riviere, est entierement décorée en pilastres.

On remarquera que, dans le chapiteau, les volutes angulaires pénétrent de quelques lignes dans le tailloir, que celles du milieu se touchent sans laisser aucun intervalle, & qu'enfin la colonne n'est diminuée par le haut que d'un septieme.

Cet Architecte n'a point fait de denticules dans la corniche de son entablement, à l'exemple de ce qui est pratiqué au Pantheon. La vraie raison, à ce qu'il paroît, est parce que les modillons étant enrichis de feuillages & d'ornemens, aussi-bien que le quart de rond & les autres moulures, au milieu desquelles se trouve le membre quarré du denticule, il a craint que, s'il l'eût taillé parmi tant de moulures ornées de suite, cela n'eût opéré de la confusion.[270]

Quoique dans le plan de l'entablement l'espace sous le plafond du larmier entre les modillons ne soit pas quarré, cet Architecte a fait ensorte de le faire paroître tel, en laissant un champ inégal autour du quarré qui renferme les rosettes, ce qui du bas de l'édifice ne s'apperçoit pas.

Ceux qui sont instruits que Perrault a fait un Traité des cinq ordonnances de colonnes,[271] doivent être portés à croire qu'il n'aura pas manqué de proposer pour modèle, son corinthien du péristile du Louvre, qui réussissoit si bien; mais tout au contraire, les proportions qu'il propose ne s'accordent nullement avec celles de cet édifice; il ne donne à sa colonne que dix-huit modules, c'est-à-dire, qu'il fait son fût beaucoup plus court qu'à l'ordinaire, après l'avoir tenu au péristile plus long qu'on ne le remarque dans aucun ouvrage antique.[272] Il n'est que trop commun de voir ainsi les Architectes en contradiction avec eux-mêmes: les Anciens, à ce qu'il paroît, n'étoient pas plus d'accord que nous; à peine trouve-t-on deux exemples où ils ayent suivi les mêmes proportions. . . .

La Planche XXI représente les proportions de la niche qui décore le bas de l'entre-colonne du péristile.

La seule remarque qu'il y ait à faire regarde la saillie singuliere du quart de rond qui couronne la console, au-delà du larmier. Les developpemens des différentes parties de cette niche ne laissent rien à desirer pour en donner une connoissance complette.

La Planche XXII exprime le détail du médaillon avec les profils de la plinthe ou de l'imposte qui régne le long de la façade de cet édifice, & du chambranle de la niche. On y trouve aussi le profil de l'archivolte de la grande arcade du milieu, & enfin celui de la balustrade qui termine ce bâtiment.

La Planche XXIII fait voir les développemens de différentes parties du soubassement.

La Planche XXIV représente le détail d'un entre-pilastre de la façade du Louvre, du côté de la riviere.

La Planche XXV [Fig. 11] exprime les proportions d'une entre-colonne du premier étage de la cour de Louvre, dont l'ordonnance qui est d'ordre composite, a été exécutée sous Henri II. Nous l'avons rapporté ici, parce qu'indépendamment de ce que cette croisée est de la plus grande beauté, ce dessein sert à faire voir que la proportion de l'ordre composite qui environne cet intérieur, a quelque rapport avec celle de l'ordre corinthien du péristile. Sa colonne a vingt-un modules & quelques parties d'élévation, & elle renfle au tiers: de plus le profil de la corniche qui couronne la croisée ressemble beaucoup, tant par la saillie de la console au-delà du larmier, que par les autres membres dont elle est composée, à celui des niches du péristile. [V]raisemblablement Perrault en a usé ainsi, afin de donner une sorte d'unité entre l'intérieur & l'extérieur de cet édifice. . . . (319–339)

e. *TABLE DE COMPARAISON de la toise, du pied, du pouce, & de la ligne, avec le module de l'ordre Corinthien du Peristile du Louvre, divisé en 30 parties.*

Comme les Planches qui expriment les détails de cet édifice ne sont cottées pour la plûpart que par toises, pieds & pouces, pour avoir ces mesures à toute rigueur, relativement au demi diamètre de la colonne, c'est-à-dire en module & parties de module, ainsi qu'il est d'usage en Architecture, nous avons fait une Table de comparaison entre les toises, pieds, pouces, & lignes, avec le module & ses subdivisions.

Afin de former cette Table, qui peut servir de modèle dans tous les cas, pour trouver toujours en modules les rapports d'une ordonnance quelconque d'Architecture, dont on ne connoît les mesures qu'en pieds, pouces & lignes, nous avons fait une régle de proportion, en disant 21 pouces 6 lignes, demi diamètre de la colonne, est à 30, nombre de parties que nous supposons le module divisé, comme 1 pouce est à X; puis réduisant en lignes les deux antécédens 21 pouces 6 lignes, & 1 pouce, puis faisant l'opération, nous avons trouvé que 258 lignes est à 30 parties, comme 12 lignes est à $X = 1^{17}/_{43}$; c'est-à-dire qu'un pouce égale $1^{17}/_{43}$ de partie de modules. En ajoutant $1^{17}/_{43}$ valeur d'un pouce à lui-même, nous avons eu la valeur de 2 pouces: à la valeur de deux pouces ajoutant un 17/43, nous avons eu celle de 3 pouces; & ainsi de suite nous avons poussé cette Table jusqu'à la hauteur de l'édifice.

Lignes.
Ligne			
1		5/43	de partie de module.
2		10/43	
3		15/43	
4		20/43	
5		25/43	
6		30/43	
7		35/43	
8		40/43	
	Partie		
9	1:	2/43	
10	1:	7/43	
11	1:	12/43	

Pieds.
Pied	Parties		
1′	16:	32/43	de partie
	Module		
2′	1	3:	21/43
3′	1	20:	10/43
4′	2	6:	42/43
5′	2	23:	31/43

Pouces.

Pouce		Partie	
1″		1:	17/43
2″		2:	34/43
3″		4:	8/43
4″		5:	25/43
5″		6:	42/43
6″		8:	16/43
7″		9:	33/43
8″		11:	7/43
9″		12:	24/43
10″		13:	41/43
11″		15:	15/43

Toises.

Toise			Modules.	
1	3		10:	20/43
2	6		20:	40/43
3	10		1:	17/43
4	13		11:	37/43
5	16		22:	14/43
6	20		2:	34/43
7	23		13:	11/43
8	26		23:	31/43
9	30		4:	8/43
10	33		14:	28/43
11	36		25:	5/43
12	40		5:	25/43
13	43		16:	2/43
14	46		26:	22/43
15	50		6:	42/43

Pour trouver, par exemple, suivant cette Table, combien la hauteur de la base de la colonne, qui est de deux pieds, a de modules, en cherchant dans la colonne des pieds, on trouvera que 2 pieds valent 1 module 3 parties 21/43. Pareillement pour trouver combien contient de modules la hauteur du chapiteau qui est de 4 pieds 8 pouces, on cherchera d'abord la valeur de 4 pieds dans la colonne des pieds, laquelle est 2^m 6:42/43 puis celle de 8 pouces qui est 11 parties 7/43; & en ajoûtant ensemble ces deux valeurs, on trouvera que 4 pieds 8 pouces valent 2 modules 18 parties 6/43, & ainsi des autres. (339–341)

95. *June 17, 1771.* Minutes of the Académie royale d'architecture (H. Lemonnier, ed., *Procès-verbaux de l'Académie royale d'architecture.* Paris, 1924, VIII, 102):

L'Académie étant assemblée, il a été fait lecture du chapitre 10 de la troisième partie du *Cours d'architecture* de feu [François] Blondel, intitulé "Des colomnes accouplées," sur lesquelles l'Académie s'est entretenue.[273] Elle est convenu que l'accouplement des colomnes a été employé avec succès notamment au péristile du Louvre, et que cette pratique, lorsqu'elle est éclairée par le jugement, peut faire un très bon effet; ce qui est confirmé par plusieurs exemples modernes.

96. *1771.* Jacques François Blondel, *Cours d'architecture . . .* , Paris, 1771, II, 224–225:

La figure A [not reproduced] donne les mesures de l'ordre Corinthien du péristyle du Louvre, du dessin de Claude Perrault, qu'il a élevé sur un soubassement auquel il a donné environ les quatre-cinquiemes de la hauteur de la colonne, y compris base & chapiteau. Le soubassement est un peu élevé sans doute; mais sa hauteur assujétie à celle de l'ordre Corinthien, placé au rez-de-chaussée de la cour, n'a pu permettre à cet Architecte de le faire d'une hauteur moins considérable. . . . cet ordre Corinthien a quarante-un pouces de diamètre, & trente-huit pieds un demi-pouce de hauteur; il est élevé sur un socle de trois pieds, servant d'appui aux galleries que forme ce péristyle: l'entablement selon Vignole, a à-peu-près de hauteur le quart de l'ordre,[274] sa base est Attique, son chapiteau de feuilles d'olivier. Perrault n'a point taillé de denticules dans le larmier inférieur de sa corniche, à dessin de procurer plus de repos aux ornements distribués avec beaucoup d'art dans toutes les moulures des cimaises.[275] N'oublions pas de rappeler à nos Lecteurs que cet ordre Corinthien est accouplé, & que de l'axe d'une colonne à l'autre, il a observé trois modules une demi-minute d'intervale.

97. *1772.* Jacques François Blondel, *Cours d'architecture . . .* , Paris, 1772, III, 64–69:

Cet avant-corps [the central pavilion of the east façade] . . . est sans contredit, ainsi que toute la façade à laquelle il appartient, l'un des chefs-d'oeuvre, & de Claude Perrault & de l'Architecture Françoise. . . . Nous rapporterons encore que l'on a disputé longtemps à Perrault d'être l'auteur de ce magnifique édifice, que plusieurs Architectes l'ont attribué à Le Veau & à d'Orbay son Eleve & son neveu.[276] Nous ne releverons point ici cette erreur. Nous avons suffisamment prouvé ailleurs la fausseté de cette assertion.[277] Les Architectes qui l'ont soutenue, ne l'auroient pas avancée, s'ils eussent voulu comparer cette production de Perrault, avec le magnifique arc de triomphe du Trône, dont il a été aussi l'Architecte, . . . absolument du même style que l'ordonnance du péristyle.

Quoi qu'il en soit, disons que cet ouvrage doit être

regardé, non-seulement comme le triomphe de l'Architecture & de la Sculpture; mais encore comme le chef-d'oeuvre de l'Art, pour la hardiesse de la construction. En effet, rien de si régulier que l'ordre d'Architecture qui y préside, rien de si intéressant que les membres qui l'accompagnent; point d'ornements mieux entendus que ceux distribués dans toute cette ordonnance; enfin rien de si magnifique que sa construction: tout y est noble, imposant. Tels sont les grands traits qui caractérisent cet édifice; tel est le sentiment qu'en doivent porter les Conoisseurs, après l'avoir examiné sous son véritable point de vue; mais considérons-le à présent comme Architecte.

D'abord la grandeur de l'Architecture de ce Frontispice, frappe, étonne sans doute; mais ce prestige cesse, quand des dehors on vient à passer dans la cour de ce Palais, où l'on ne remarque plus que de petits ordres distribués dans les trois étages qui en composent les façades. Quoique cette observation ne soit pas sans fondement, il faut convenir que Perrault s'est déterminé à cette idée sublime, excité par le zèle de Colbert, & la puissance alors sans bornes de Louis le Grand; que pour cela il a cru devoir franchir la relation des dehors avec les dedans, à raison du projet qu'il avoit conçu en élevant le module de l'arc de triomphe du Trône; c'étoit de pratiquer une grande rue qui alignât ces deux édifices célebres: idée vaste, & tout ensemble digne du beau siecle de Louis XIV, & de l'opulence de la Nation: idée qui devant un jour se réunir avec celle du Bernin, qui avoit proposé une seule grande cour, entre le Vieux-Louvre & les Tuileries, auroit produit un ensemble qui eût surpassé les plus somptueux édifices de l'Europe. Mais aujourd'hui qu'on semble avoir renoncé à ces projets, les Amateurs & les Etrangers, qui ignorent les premieres idées de Perrault, blâment en quelque sorte cette disparité frappante qui se remarque entre les dehors & les dedans de cet édifice.[278]

Les hommes instruits condamnent encore, dans l'avant-corps de cette belle façade, l'ouverture réelle de la porte à plate-bande, qui donne entrée à ce Palais [Fig. 48]; ils la trouvent trop petite, quoique de douze pieds de largeur, sur vingt-quatre de hauteur. En effet, elle paroît telle, quoique Perrault ait pris soin de la renfermer dans une arcade feinte de vingt pieds de large sur trente-neuf d'élévation; car cette ressource est peu digne du génie supérieur de cet Artiste, & ne peut jamais servir d'autorité à nos Eleves, l'archivolte de cette arcade feinte, interrompant le niveau du soubassement, & ayant pour ainsi dire forcé Perrault de supprimer toute espèce d'ouverture dans le grand entrecolonnement supérieur qui se trouve au-dessus de cette porte; de maniere que le plein qui s'y remarque, quelqu'ingénieusement orné qu'il puisse être par le ministere de la Sculpture,[279] présente toujours un corps solide, où il eût été à desirer qu'on eût remarqué un percé, préférable à tous égards dans toute espèce d'édifice, particuliérement dans celui destiné pour la représentation d'une tête couronnée. L'ouverture du petit nombre de croisées qui s'apperçoivent dans cette façade, est trouvée aussi trop peu considérable, quand on vient à la comparer avec le diametre de l'ordre, & il paroît qu'on auroit desiré que ces ouvertures eussent été continuées à la place des niches qu'on remarque dans les galeries placées de chaque côté de cet avant-corps; ce qui auroit donné, dit-on, à la façade de ce Palais, un air d'habitation qu'elle n'offre point à son premier aspect. Ces niches, loin de lui procurer le caractere qu'elle devroit avoir, font ressembler cet avant-corps à un mur de face, destiné à contenir, dans son interieur, des galleries éclairées par en haut, & consacrées à renfermer une collection de tableaux précieux, ou une Bibliotheque: il paroît qu'on pense de même sur les médaillons placés au-dessus des niches & des croisées; ce genre d'ornement n'étant guère que du ressort des arcs de triomphe, ainsi que Perrault l'a fait avec plus de convenance à celui dont il a donné les dessins pour le Trône, déja cité. Peut-être a-t-il voulu rappeler, dans cette décoration, les médaillons placés du temps de Lescot dans l'interieur de la cour [Fig. 12], comme il a imité dans son soubassement la forme & la proportion trop svelte des croisées bombées qui se remarquent dans les anciennes façades du Louvre [Figs. 9, 13, 16]. Mais arrêtons ces observations, qui n'empêchent pas que plein de vénération pour ce grand Maître, nous n'admirions, avec la plus grande satisfaction, cet édifice, dont il nous paroît impossible d'apprécier les beautés; elles surpassent de beaucoup les légers défauts que nous venons de relever d'après le jugement qu'en ont porté les plus célebres Artistes, avec qui nous avons eu souvent occasion de nous entretenir sur ce chef-d'oeuvre, & qui, comme nous, sont convaincus que cet ouvrage de l'Art est digne des plus grands éloges.[280]

98. *1773.* Jacques François Blondel, *Cours d'architecture* . . . , Paris, 1773, IV, xlvi–xlvii:

Peu d'Architectes ont excellé dans la réunion de ces deux parties [rules and taste]: François Blondel & Claude Perrault sont ceux qui ont le plus réuni les regles & le goût de l'Art dans leurs productions, l'un dans le monument de la Porte Saint-Denis, qui peut passer pour l'un des nos chefs-d'oeuvre; l'autre, dans la façade du Péristyle du Louvre, Ouvrage scavant dans la construction, admirable dans l'ordonnance, & sublime dans la distribution des ornements.

99. *1773.* Marquis de Condorcet, "Éloge de Perrault." First published in a collection of Condorcet's writings (Paris, 1773). I have used Marquis de Condorcet, *Oeuvres,* ed. A. Condorcet O'Connor and M. F. Arago, Paris, 1849, II, 46–47:

Après le départ du Bernin, on voulut comparer de nouveau son dessin avec ceux des architectes français. Perrault, qui n'était point connu comme architecte, en avait donné un avant l'arrivée du Bernin; il fut mis en concurrence avec celui de l'architecte italien, ainsi qu'un troisième, dont Dorbay, élève de le Vau, était l'auteur. Heureusement pour la gloire de notre architecture, Louis XIV, qui dans les arts avait surtout le sentiment de la grandeur, préféra le dessin de Perrault; et ce péristyle majestueux et si simple fut élevé sur ses dessins, et avec des machines de son invention.[281]

On reproche maintenant à Perrault[282] d'y avoir accouplé les colonnes, mais, de son temps, on prétendait que, malgré cette disposition, l'espace de douze pieds, qu'il laissait entre les colonnes et le mur, était incompatible avec la solidité de l'édifice. [François] Blondel même, que son savoir en géométrie et en architecture faisait regarder comme un excellent juge, et que le monument de la porte Saint-Denis devait préserver de l'envie, Blondel avait joint son suffrage à la voix du peuple des architectes. Comment Perrault aurait-il donc pu proposer de simples colonnes? c'était même beaucoup que d'avoir vu que les colonnes accouplées seraient suffisantes. Ainsi, comme tous les hommes sages que leur génie pousse à tenter des choses hardies, il resta en deçà de ce qu'il aurait pu oser.

Quelques artistes jaloux, dont Boileau n'aurait pas dû se rendre l'écho,[283] ont accusé Perrault d'avoir pris à le Vau l'idée de son péristyle; mais le Collége Mazarin, élevé par le Vau, semble être placé si près de la colonnade du Louvre pour empêcher tous ceux qui les voient à la fois, d'attribuer au même architecte deux monuments d'un goût si opposé.

Une autre preuve incontestable en faveur de Perrault est le silence qu'a gardé sur ce soupçon [François] Blondel,[284] qui, dans ses écrits, fait de l'ouvrage de Perrault une critique où la rivalité se fait trop sentir, pour qu'il ait pu y négliger un reproche bien plus terrible que toutes ses objections. Ainsi, c'est l'ennemi de Perrault qui, sans le vouloir, a mis sa gloire hors d'atteinte. Si ceux qui attaquent les grands hommes sont insensibles à la honte, que du moins ils sentent l'inutilité de leurs efforts. Un jour viendra où, de tout ce qu'ils auront écrit contre un homme de génie, il ne restera que ce qui peut servir à constater sa gloire.

100. *1777.* Jacques François Blondel, *Cours d'architecture . . . ,* Paris, 1777, VI, 164–170 (chapter V). The following was written by Pierre Patte, the continuator of the *Cours.*

DE LA CONSTRUCTION DU GRAND FRONTON QUI COURONNE L'AVANT-CORPS DE LA COLONNADE DU LOUVRE.

La construction des frontons d'une certaine étendue, & qui doivent être élevés sur des plate-bandes, a toujours passé pour très-difficile à bien exécuter. Comme les plate-bandes sont par elles-mêmes peu capables de porter des fardeaux, vu qu'elles ne tirent leur principale force que des chaînes dont elles sont armées, & qu'elles ont en outre une poussée considérable vers leurs extrêmités, lorsqu'à cette poussée se joint encore l'effort des corniches rampantes contre ces mêmes extrêmités, il est aisé de concevoir qu'il faut employer beaucoup d'industrie à faire porter, & à contenir à la fois une pareille masse dans une position aussi désavantageuse. Les modeles de construction étant toujours plus puissans pour instruire, que les spéculations les plus étendues, nous nous bornerons à exposer les développemens du grand fronton du Louvre. . . .

Sa longueur est 92 pieds, & sa hauteur 18 pieds depuis l'entablement jusqu'à son sommet. Il est porté sur huit colonnes corinthiennes accouplées, de 3 pieds 7 pouces de diametre, lesquelles sont élevées sur un soubassement. [Figure 82 and Atlas, III, pls. CV and CVII] représentent l'une son plan, l'autre son élévation, & la troisieme son profil. Nous y avons exprimé, non-seulement l'appareil des pierres, mais encore leurs différentes qualités tendre ou dure, selon leur répartition.

L'entablement de l'ordre corinthien, [Fig. 82], la corniche rampante du fronton, les chapiteaux des colonnes, le mur adossé aux colonnes & celui qui lui correspond dans le fond du fronton, sont en pierre tendre, dite *de Saint-Leu,* tandis que les tambours des colonnes & les trois arcs que l'on remarque dans le fronton sont au contraire en pierre dure, dite *de Saint-Cloud,* sans compter la cimaise de la corniche rampant, qui est également de pierre dure. . . .

L'entablement est composé de quatre cours d'assise au-dessus des deux petits entrecolonnements: le premier occupe la hauteur de l'architrave; le second, la hauteur de la frise; & les deux autres, la hauteur de la corniche, sans la cimaise; nous en avons donné particulièrement sur la droite de la planche [Fig. 82] un profil, afin de les faire mieux distinguer: mais au-dessus du grand entre-colonnement du milieu, il est à observer qu'il n'y a que trois cours d'assise, vu qu'un seul cours embrasse toute la hauteur de la corniche en cet endroit.

Nous ne traiterons pas ici de la construction de ces plate-bandes: nous en avons parlé amplement dans nos *Mémoires*,[285] c'est pourquoi on peut y avoir recours: nous nous bornerons seulement à remarquer que la plate-bande du milieu a 24 pieds de longueur, & qu'elle bombe au droit de la clef A, d'environ 1 pouce & demi; ce qui a été pratiqué, tant à cause du tassement qu'un fardeau aussi considérable que ce fronton pouvoit opérer par la suite, qu'à cause de l'étendue de cette plate-bande, qui, sans cette précaution, paroîtroit à la vue baisser dans son milieu.

Les assises de la corniche rampante ont leurs joints montans d'à plomb, & non retournés perpendiculierement au rampant, comme cela se pratique quelquefois. On a placé aux angles en retour de l'entablement, c'est-à-dire, aux extrêmités du fronton, de très-grands quartiers de pierre de 8 & 12 pieds de long, qui ont des queus considérables dans les murs; le tout afin de contenir à la fois, & la bascule de la corniche de l'entablement, & l'effort de la corniche rampante, qui pousse au vuide dans cette direction. Il est d'usage de mettre au milieu de ces pierres angulaires un fort mandrin de fer quarré, qui traverse la hauteur de l'entablement, & s'éleve jusques dans la cimaise de la corniche rampante, & de bien cramponer en outre ces pierres avec celles qui les avoisinnent, à l'effet d'opérer la plus grande résistance. En se rendant attentif à la direction des joints montans des cours d'assise de la corniche droite & rampante, on s'appercevra qu'ils ne coupent, ni modillons, ni rosettes, ni même les caissons de ces dernieres; mais qu'ils sont toujours placés au milieu d'une partie unie: ce qui a été fait à dessein de rendre leurs ornemens d'une exécution plus solide, & merite d'être toujours imité en pareil cas.

La cimaise de la corniche rampante est de pierre dure, dite *de Meudon*. Chaque côté a environ 50 pieds de long, 8 pieds de large, & 16 à 17 pouces d'épaisseur, y compris le revers d'eau. Un des côtés de cette cimaise est d'un seul morceau; l'autre devoit l'être semblablement, mais elle se cassa en trois parties en la montant. On prétend que ces deux longues pierres n'en formoient qu'une seule, qui fût sciée en deux. M. Mallet, dans *Théliamet*,[286] rapporte qu'en la sciant, on trouva un gros silex ou caillou dans le milieu qui arrêta la scie, de sorte qu'on fût obligé de retourner la pierre, pour la dégager & continuer l'opération. Chacune de ces pierres pese plus de quatre-vingt milliers. . . .

Nous avons supposé enlevé, dans [Figure 82], le parpin du tympan du fronton, destiné à recevoir sa sculpture, pour faire voir tout le mécanisme de sa construction. On y remarquera qu'il y a derriere le tympan trois arcs en décharge en pierre dure, qui n'y sont qu'appliqués, & dont la fonction est de soulager les plate-bandes, ainsi que de reporter la plus grande partie du poids de la corniche rampante, directement sur les colonnes accouplées, & sur le mur qui leur est adossé: l'arc du milieu B est ogive, & les deux autres CC sont rampans.

On voit particulièrement dans la Planche suivante [Atlas III, pl. CVII], le profil du fronton, la position respective du mur tympan, de l'arc ogive, & de la corniche rampante. Le parpin du tympan est composé de trois cours d'assise de pierre de Saint-Leu, de chacune 5 pieds de haut sur 15 pieds de long, dans sa plus grande hauteur. Ce mur a main[t]enant 2 pieds 1/2 d'épaisseur, à cause du bossage qu'on a laissé pour sa sculpture; mais cette épaisseur doit être réduite, quand elle sera finie, à 18 pouces: de sorte que le bas relief aura environ un pied de saillie, ce qui est suffisant pour faire resortir & détacher convenablement ses figures. . . .

B, est la clef de l'arc ogive, auquel est adossé le mur du fond du fronton, dont le bas répond à celui qui est derriere les colonnes, & qui forme, en s'élevant vers la clef, un espece d'encorbellement en dehors, à l'effet de soulager les voussoirs de l'arc, & de les aider à soutenir plus efficacement la corniche rampante. Comme nous avons eu l'attention de mettre les pierres au même nombre que dans l'exécution, on voit combien les voussoirs du grand arc, & les assises de la corniche rampante ont de grandes queues dans les murs, ce qui contribue beaucoup à augmenter la fermeté & la liaison du tout ensemble de cette bâtisse.

On a allégé l'épaisseur de ce fronton, en y pratiquant un vuide qui sert de réservoir, dont on voit l'étendue [Atlas, III, pls. CV, CVII], & qui est terminé par une voûte rampante.

Outre les précautions rélatives à l'appareil des pierres, & à la maniere de faire porter le poids du fronton le plus avantageusement, on a lié par surcroit toutes ses différentes parties avec des chaînes, des tirans & des crampons, que nous avons marqué des mêmes lettres de renvois dans les trois Planches [Fig. 82 and Atlas, III, pls. CV, CVII], afin d'en faire voir la correspondance suivant leurs diverses situations.

D, D, sont cours de chaînes placés derriere le tympan, & servant à contenir par des ancres fixées à leurs extrêmités, les deux côtés de la corniche rampante du fronton.

E, E, deux rangs de potences de fer quarré, destinés à soulager la portée des chaînes D, au droit du vuide de l'arc ogive, & à reporter une partie du poids du mur tympan vers le mur dossier.

F, F, tirans avec des talons aux extrêmités, servant à lier les cours d'assise du mur tympan avec le mur adossé, lesquels tirans, par leur position, peuvent également aider à soutenir les chaînes D.

G, G, crampons dont la fonction est de lier le tympan avec les arcs par le haut à leur rencontre, & avec le dessous de la corniche rampante.

H, H [Atlas, III, pl. CVII], chaînes placées entre la corniche, la frise & l'architrave, pour contenir l'entablement.

I, autre chaîne avec des moufles, placée entre la frise & l'architrave, & traversant le vuide pratiqué au droit de l'entablement, & dont le but est de lier ensemble les murs opposés.

101. *1782.* [Pierre Joseph Antoine], *Série de colonnes*, Dijon, 1782, 24–25:

Claude Perrault s'est immortalisé en élevant, vers l'an 1680, la colonnade du Louvre; ce sont les plus belles colonnes corinthiennes qu'on puisse voir, & l'entablement est d'une richesse & d'une perfection qui égalent ce que l'antique nous a laissé de mieux. Les plafonds sont aussi d'une exécution merveilleuse; cependant nous ne pouvons nous empêcher de dire que cette composition n'est pas absolument parfaite.

On pense que des fenêtres y auroient été plus convenables que des niches, car il paroît singulier qu'un tel palais n'ait point de fenêtres; il falloit disposer les colonnes une à une, & non pas les accoupler; il falloit bannir les pilastres de cet édifice; il ne falloit pas à l'avant-corps du milieu, y espacer les colonnes de deux manieres différentes, sans compter celle de l'accouplement. Il faudroit que l'espacement du milieu ne fût pas coupé par une archivolte, qui fait voir qu'on ne peut aller de plein pied d'un péristile à l'autre; le fronton ne convient nullement à cet édifice. Ces remarques n'empêchent pas que cette construction ne soit du plus grand mérite, tant elle contient d'ailleurs de beautés.

102. *1783.* Luc Vincent Thiéry, *Almanach du voyageur à Paris . . . année 1784,* Paris, [1783], 408:

Louis XIV fit construire le nouveau Louvre en 1665 [*sic*]. Louis Le Vau son premier Architecte, & François d'Orbay, son Eleve, ont fait exécuter la façade du côté de Saint-Germain-l'Auxerrois, sur les dessins de Claude Perrault, que ce chef-d'oeuvre a immortalisé. Ce magnifique Monument est composé de 3 avant-corps & de 2 péristiles; 28 colonnes cannelées & accouplées, forment galerie, & soutiennent des architraves de 12 pieds de long, avec le même nombre de pilastres placés sur le mur intérieur, dont les intervalles sont ornés de niches d'une belle proportion.

L'avant-corps du milieu est composé de 8 colonnes corinthiennes, couronnées par un fronton, dont la cymaise est formée d'une seule pierre tirée des carrieres de Meudon, sciée en deux, pour en faire les deux parties qui ont chacune 54 pieds de long sur 8 de large, & 18 pouces seulement d'épaisseur. Les 2 autres avant-corps sont décorés de 2 colonnes corinthiennes & de 6 pilastres. Sur le comble, regne une terrasse bordée d'une balustrade, appuyée sur des piédestaux.

Toute cette façade, de l'aspect le plus grand & le plus imposant, a 87 toises & demie de largeur, & forme le plus magnifique morceau d'architecture qu'il y ait en Europe. La place qui est en avant, permet qu'on en découvre les beautés.

103. *1787.* Antoine Nicolas Dezallier d'Argenville, *Vies des fameux architectes depuis la renaissance des arts, avec la description de leurs ouvrages,* Paris, 1787.

a. Il y avoit déjà du temps qu'on travailloit au Louvre; une partie de sa façade avoit huit ou dix pieds de haut. Colbert devenu surintendant des bâtimens, trouva peu propres à annoncer le palais d'un puissant monarque sur dessins de le Veau qu'on exécutoit. Tous les Architectes furent donc invités à donner l'essor à leur génie, [Claude] Perrault travailla comme les autres, son dessin fut jugé le plus beau. Néanmoins, avant que de procéder à l'exécution d'un monument de cette importance, le surintendant résolut de consulter les artistes italiens. On leur envoya des copies du projet de le Veau, mais on n'en reçut que des idées désavouées par le bon goût. Le Bernin vivoit alors, il étoit regardé comme le plus beau génie de son pays. On projeta de le faire venir en France, il y vint; les honneurs incroyables qui lui furent rendus, sont consignés dans l'histoire. Cependant cet illustre artiste fut peu gouté, & repartit sans être regretté.

Le mérite supérieur de Perrault reçut un nouveau lustre par la comparaison de ses dessins avec ceux de l'Architecte italien. Il restoit néanmoins encore une difficulté à résoudre. Les idées d'un médecin, en fait d'Architecture, devoient-elles contrebalancer celles des plus habiles maîtres en cet art? Pour la lever, on forma un conseil des bâtimens, composé du premier Architecte, de le Brun & de Perrault. Son frère Charles fut le secrétaire de ce conseil, présidé par Colbert, & qui se tenoit deux fois la semaine. Toutes les difficultés ne roulèrent que sur la possibilité de l'exécution. Il fut donc résolu de construire un petit modèle du péristile, avec autant de pierres de taille qu'il devoit en entrer dans l'ouvrage en grand, & de le retenir avec des barres de fer proportionnées à la grandeur qu'elles auroient dans l'édifice. L'exécution de ce modèle fit disparoître l'ombre même des difficultés. On convint unanimement que le fer, retenant la poussée des architraves, procuroit à un bâtiment une solidité bien plus grande, que lorsqu'il y étoit employé comme soutien.

Tels furent les préliminaires de l'érection d'un monument regardé avec raison comme le chef-d'oeuvre de Perrault & de l'Architecture françoise. Fait pour annoncer le palais d'un roi, il surpasse infiniment l'idée qu'on peut se former d'un pareil édifice. Quelle majesté dans sa colonnade, dont la grande décoration, par un heureux effort de génie, se trouve réduite à un seul ordre! quelle hardiesse dans la portée des plate-bandes des architraves, qui ont douze pieds comme les entre-colonnemens! Elle paroissoit si téméraire aux yeux des Architectes de Louis XIV, qu'ils avoient assuré la ruine de l'édifice avant son élévation jusqu'au comble. (383–385)

b. Le frontispice du Louvre, élevé avec des machines de l'invention de Perrault,[287] est un de ces efforts de génie qu'on n'a point encore égalé. L'accouplement des colonnes qui ont trois pieds & demi de diamètre, y produit un superbe effet. L'antiquité ne fournit pas d'exemple de péristile isolé à colonnes accouplées: on ne connoît guère que le temple de *Scisi* rapporté par Palladio, & celui qui se voit à *Trevi* près de Spolette, dans lesquels un pilastre corinthien, accouplé avec une colonne du même ordre, soutient l'extrémité du fronton.[288] S'il est permis, comme on n'en peut douter, d'ajouter aux inventions des anciens, la beauté de celle-ci, la grace qu'elle procure aux ordres, & le dégagement qu'elle donne aux portiques, lui méritent un accueil favorable. L'accouplement des colonnes permet de tenir les entre-colonnemens assez larges pour ne point offusquer les portes & les fenêtres qui donnent sur le portique;[289] défaut dont les ouvrages des anciens ne sont pas exempts. D'ailleurs, le diamètre de deux ou trois pieds, suffisant aux colonnes accouplées, seroit trop foible pour les colonnes solitaires qui auroient à soutenir la longueur considérable d'un entablement.

Que la belle sculpture de cette colonnade & la justesse admirable de ses proportions ne nous éblouissent pas néanmoins au point d'en méconnoître les imperfections. La porte à plate-bande est trop petite pour l'entrée d'un palais, quoique renfermée dans une arcade feinte. L'archivolte de cette arcade interrompt mal-à-propos le niveau du péristile, & le soubassement est un peu nu relativement à la richesse de l'ordre qui le surmonte. (392–393)

c. Il n'est pas étonnant que Perrault ait eu des jaloux & des ennemis de sa réputation; c'est le sort de tous les grands hommes. D'après le jugement de Boileau dans ses réflexions sur Longin,[290] ils tentèrent de lui ravir la gloire de ses productions. Ce poëte n'aimoit pas les Perrault. Charles, auteur du Parallèle des anciens & des modernes, ne l'avoit pas bien traité. Incapable d'entendre Homère & Pindare, il prétendoit qu'ils étoient inférieurs aux écrivains de son temps. En falloit-il davantage pour choquer le goût délicat de Boileau? Depuis, ce poëte radouci accorda volontiers à Perrault la qualification de bon & d'habile Architecte, & avoua que *le dépit de se voir critiqué lui avoit fait dire des choses qu'il auroit mieux fait de n'avoir pas dites*.[291] Sur ce que d'Orbay avoit offert de lui montrer papier sur table, que la façade du Louvre étoit de le Veau son maître, & non de Perrault,[292] il avoue qu'il ne veut point entrer dans cette dispute, & que s'il prenoit un parti, ce seroit en faveur de Perrault.[293] Ainsi, l'autorité du poëte satyrique qu'avoient invoquée des hommes sans génie, pour décerner à le Veau la couronne de Perrault, les écrase elle-même. D'ailleurs, une comparaison impartiale des ouvrages de ces deux Architectes leur auroit aisément fait apercevoir une différence extrême entre leur style. Il est difficile en effet d'en trouver de plus disparates. Autant les proportions générales de le Veau sont lourdes & ses profils mesquins, autant les détails, ainsi que l'ordonnance des édifices de Perrault sont purs, nobles & élégans.

Enfin, une des plus fortes preuves qu'on puisse alléguer en sa faveur, est tirée du Livre des hommes illustres que son frère publia en [1696]. Claude s'y trouve placé & comblé d'éloges, l'assertion de Boileau n'y est pas même rappelée.[294] Cet ouvrage a eu plusieurs éditions, & il est notoire que personne ne s'est élevé contre ce fait qu'un consentement universel rend décisif.[295] (394–396)

104. *1792.* Francesco Algarotti, "Pensieri diversi sopra materie filosofiche e filologiche," *Opere del conte Algarotti,* new ed., Venice, 1792, VII, 59:

Nella famosa facciata, o sia nel peristilio del Louvre si trovano non pochi difetti da contrapporre alla bellezza sua. Lasciando andare le colonne addoppiate, maniera non usata dagli antichi, il vano della porta principale sembra angusto di troppo rispetto alla vastità dello edifizio: l'arco di essa porta impostando sopra la cornice del zoccolo, il qual serve di primo piano alla fabbrica, si ficca nel piano superiore, o sia colonnato, con cui non ha niente che fare. . . . La facciata ha pochissime finestre, quasi una faccia senz'occhi; e piuttosto che della fronte di un edifizio ella rende aspetto di un loggiato, o di una prospettiva da vedersi dalla lungi in capo a un gran giardino. Non ostante tali difetti à una delle più nobili fabbriche di Europa: ed è molto ben fatto, che la si vada disgombrando da quella marmaglia di casupole, che ne toglieva in gran parte la vista.

Notes

1. The sculptor Jean Varin (1604–72), the garden designer André Le Nôtre (1613–1700), Antoine Le Ménestrel, *trésorier général des Bâtiments,* and Louis Petit, the controller of the buildings of Versailles.

2. I am unable to identify this feature.

3. Undoubtedly Roland Fréart de Chambray (1606–76); on his connection with the Louvre, see Chapter III.

4. A reference to Le Vau's south façade (1660–63; Figs. 17, 18). A plan of 1667 (Fig. 64) shows a very small stair adjacent to the central pavilion.

5. Again a reference to Le Vau's south façade.

6. That is, played sharp or flat.

7. The Galerie d'Apollon.

8. The Jardin de la Reine (or de l'Infante).

9. The summer apartment of Anne of Austria.

10. The proposed gallery and terrace appear in Figure 97, as pointed out by C. Tadgell "Claude Perrault, François Le Vau and the Louvre Colonnade," *BurlM,* CXXII, 1980, 334 n. 27.

11. The critic is probably referring to Figure 96 or to another drawing like it (see Chapter III).

12. The critic errs here. According to Vitruvius (III.3.4), it is the diastyle type of intercolumniation that is three column diameters wide; the araeostyle (the widest type) is more than three diameters (III.3.1, 5).

13. Vitruvius III.2.7.

14. Vitruvius III.2.6.

15. See Sources II, no. 1.

16. Thomas Gamard (or Jamard; d. 1671); see Hautecoeur, *HAC.*

17. Daniel Gittard (1625–86). He executed the full-scale model of Perrault's Arc de Triomphe du Trône (1669–70; Fig. 120) and was in charge of its masonry construction from 1670 on (M. Petzet, "Das Triumphbogenmonument für Ludwig XIV. auf der Place du Trône," *ZfK,* XLV, 1982, 179; see also Hautecoeur, *HAC,* I, 168–174).

18. Duval *père et fils* were active at the Val-de-Grâce, Paris. See C. Bauchal, *Nouveau dictionnaire biographique et critique des architectes français,* Paris, 1887, 209. The son (Duval-Broutet) died in 1699.

19. The buildings referred to are the Val-de-Grâce, Paris, and the Pantheon in Rome. On the artistic models for the Corinthian capitals of the Colonnade, see Chapter VII.

20. Jean Pastel (Patel); see Bauchal, *Nouveau dictionnaire,* 458.

21. Pierre Cottart (or Cottard; d. 1701); see Hautecoeur, *HAC,* I, 133–138.

22. Charles Chamois (d. after 1677); see ibid., 165–168.

23. Pierre Thévenot (d. 1702). Many payments to him are recorded in the *CBR;* he worked on Perrault's Arc de Triomphe du Trône (begun 1670; Fig. 120). See Bauchal, *Nouveau dictionnaire,* 545.

24. The citadel of Cairo, founded in the twelfth century by Saladin.

25. Olry errs here; the tomb of Muhammad is in Medina, not Mecca. It is housed within the Mosque of the Prophet.

26. I have not been able to trace the Doric Temple of Bacchus of which Olry speaks. Dorus, a king of Achaea and the Peloponnese, was said to have built the first Doric temple at Argos; see Vitruvius IV.1.3.

27. The Temple of Diana at Ephesus, one of the seven wonders of the ancient world.

28. I cannot determine the meanings of "Gôle Mandarin" and "Migra japin" or whether a specific ruby palace is meant. Lines 69 and 70 may be simply "exotic" inventions of the poet.

29. The reference is to the Mausoleum of Halicarnassus, which Queen Artemisia of Caria built for her husband and brother, King Mausolus of Caria, after his death in 353 B.C. It was one of the seven wonders of the ancient world.

30. A great Egyptian city in antiquity, second in Egypt only to Thebes.

31. The reference may be to the city of Babylon, where the ruins of the palace of Nebuchadnezzar were. According to the twelfth-century Jewish traveler Benjamin of Tudela, people feared entering these ruins "propter serpentes & scorpiones locum occupantes" (*Itinerarium* . . . , Leiden, 1633, 134). If Olry is referring instead to the Tower of Babel, its ruins could have been known to him by the descriptions of Benjamin of Tudela (ibid., 136) and Pietro della Valle (*Les fameux voyages* . . . , Paris, 1670, I, 46f. [letter 16, 1616]).

32. The Greek labyrinth was situated on the Aegean island of Lemnos. According to Pliny the Elder it was man-made, not natural, and he mentions some of its architectural features (*Natural History,* XXXVI.19.86, 90).

33. I.e., Jerusalem.

34. Probably a reference to the man-made pyramidal columns erected by the Phoenicians on the coast of Friesland or Jutland (see Tacitus, *Germania,* 34), rather than to the natural Straits of Gibralter.

35. One of the seven wonders of the ancient world.

36. One of the seven wonders of the ancient world.

37. Acts, XVII.23.

38. Bernini's colonnaded Piazza of Saint Peter's, Rome, had recently been finished in 1666, only four years before Olry's poem was published.

39. Beginning in 1594, the Escorial was sometimes called the eighth wonder of the world (G. Kubler, *Building the Escorial,* Princeton, 1982, 4).

40. Justinian is meant, not Constantine. Justinian's famous exclamation—"Solomon, I have vanquished thee!"—is possibly apocryphal; it was first reported in the *Narratio de S. Sophia* (eighth or ninth century), a legendary account of the building of Hagia Sophia.

41. The palace of the sun, described in Ovid, *Metamorphoses,* II.1f. (see Chapter I).

42. For Armida's palace, see Tasso, *Gerusalemme liberata,* canto 16.

43. The quais of the Right Bank, from the Cours-la-Reine to the Arsenal. These were improved beginning in 1669.

44. The Jhelum (Gr. Hydaspes), a river in northern India.

45. Probably a reference to Louis Le Vau's proposed Pont de la Paix, linking the Louvre to the Collège des Quatre Nations. Contrary to Olry's verse, the bridge was never built.

46. The Collège des Quatre Nations.

47. The poet errs here; the Pont Neuf is decorated with grotesque human heads, not heads of cattle.

48. Probably a reference to the Place Royale (des Vosges), rather than to the Place Dauphine, the former inhabited in the seventeenth century by a number of aristocrats. Both squares were built under Henri IV.

49. Probably a reference to Antoine Léonor Houdin's comprehensive scheme for the Louvre and Tuileries, which provided Saint-Germain-l'Auxerrois with a circular forecourt ("le cirque"). Houdin's project was known by an engraving (1661) by F. Bignon (Hautecoeur, *Louvre et Tuileries,* pl. XXIX, bottom). On Houdin, see Chapter II.

50. As far as I know, in 1670 there were no official projects afoot to remove the houses from the bridges of Paris and replace them with "riches monumens."

51. Whose mausoleum? A mausoleum for Louis XIV and members of the Bourbon dynasty had been considered during the 1660s for Saint-Denis, the traditional burial place of French kings, not for Paris (see A. Braham and P. Smith, *François Mansart,* London, 1973, I, 115–119, 253–254; II, pls. 450–460, and A. Braham, "Bernini's Design for the Bourbon Chapel," *BurlM,* CII, 1960, 443–447). Olry's reference to an "auguste Mausolée" remains cryptic.

52. The references are to Bernini's equestrian statue of Louis XIV and his *Apollo and Daphne.*

53. Here begins a description of Le Brun's Louvre monument project. See R. Josephson, "Le monument du triomphe pour le Louvre: Un projet de Charles Le Brun retrouvé," *RAAM,* LIII, 1928, 21–34; see also Figure 60 and Appendix A (A1).

54. Olry seems to be referring to the Escalier Henri II, but this can in no way be described as "à jour."

55. The Appartement du Roi, in the southwest corner of the Cour Carrée.

56. I cannot identify this individual.

57. Croesus, king of Lydia (sixth century B.C.), fabled for his riches.

58. Cochin-China, a country in Southeast Asia.

59. The Cathedral of St. Basil?

60. I am unable to identify this grotto.

61. I cannot identify the pearl "Pennamas" unless it is the name given to the pearl Cleopatra dissolved in her wine and drank at her banquet with Mark Antony to show her indifference to wealth.

62. Osman is probably used here in a generic sense to stand for the Turkish sultans.

63. Probably the Cour Carrée and the Place du Carrousel.

64. Rhodope, a high mountain range in Thrace.

65. The Pierides, the nine daughters of Pieros, King of Pella, whom he called the nine Muses. They competed with the real Muses, lost, and were changed into birds. Contrary to Olry, none of the daughters was a queen. The story is told in Ovid, *Metamorphoses,* v.294–678.

66. I cannot identify this figure.

67. Probably the Porcelain Pagoda in Nanking (begun 1413, destroyed in 1853).

68. The Grande Galerie du Bord de l'Eau.

69. Rome and Constantinople.

70. Perhaps one of several unexecuted theater projects for the Louvre discussed by G. Weber, "Theaterarchitektur am Hofe von Louis XIV," *Bollettino del Centro internazionale di studi di architettura Andrea Palladio,* XVII, 1975, 262–263.

71. Probably Henri de Gissey (1621–73), *ordonnateur des carrousels et menus plaisirs.*

72. Probably the Antichambre du Roi (Salle Henri II) in the Louvre.

73. Rooms of the King's apartment in the Louvre.

74. A room on the *rez-de-chaussée,* just off the summer apartment of Anne of Austria.

75. The Salle des Machines in the Tuileries Palace.

76. The reference is probably to the royal apartments in the Tuileries Palace.

77. Undoubtedly the sculptor Jacques Houzeau (1624–91), who is known to have worked on the staircase of the Tuileries Palace (1666–70). See F. Souchal, *French Sculptors of the 17th and 18th Centuries, I. The Reign of Louis XIV,* Oxford, 1981, II, 124f. and 129, no. 15.

78. In the Tuileries Palace.

79. The Salle des Machines in the Tuileries Palace.

80. The reference is probably to a lavish theater set.

81. Olry is apparently referring to a nonexistent gallery that would have run parallel to and north of the Grande Galerie du Bord de l'Eau. It had been proposed by Houdin in 1661 (see above, note 49).

82. Perhaps a reference to a project for a Louvre chapel.

83. Probably a reference to the Galerie d'Apollon.

84. Royal stables were located in part of the ground floor of the Grande Galerie du Bord de l'Eau, although they were called "les petites écuries."

85. Taxila is a site in modern-day Pakistan that was an important center of Buddhist art; Scorialum is, of course, the Escorial.

86. The snake was Colbert's emblem.

87. The four oxen of Myron in the Temple of Apollo, Palatine Hill, Rome; see Propertius, *Elegies,* II.30.

88. It is uncertain whether a specific statue is referred to. In Marot's engraving of 1676 (Fig. 88), an equestrian statue of Louis XIV appears above the central pediment; a seated figure of the King appears within it. These would appear to be the earliest visual indications of sculptural effigies of Louis XIV for the Louvre.

89. An intercolumniation of two column diameters (Vitruvius III.3.2).

90. Active ca. 220–190 B.C. See J. J. Coulton, "Hermogenes," *Macmillan Encyclopedia of Architects,* ed. A. K. Placzek, New York and London, 1982, II, 359–361.

91. An intercolumniation of 2¼ column diameters, with 3 diameters for the central intercolumniation (Vitruvius III.3.6).

92. An arrangement of two rows of eight columns on the front and rear of temples (Vitruvius III.2.7).

93. Vitruvius III.2.6, III.3.8.

94. An intercolumniation of more than three column diameters (Vitruvius III.3.5).

95. Changed to "onze" in the 1684 edition.

96. The south façade (Fig. 95).

97. Changed to "onze" in the 1684 edition.

98. Vitruvius v.6.7.

99. Poncelet Cliquin.

100. Philips Doublet, Huygens's brother-in-law; see Sources II, no. 21.

101. The reference is to the Petite Académie; Jean Chapelain, its director; and François Charpentier, one of its members. Charles Perrault was its secretary (and member) since its founding in 1663. See R. W. Berger, *In the Garden of the Sun King: Studies on the Park of Versailles under Louis XIV,* Washington, D.C., 1985, chap. 2.

102. The reference is apparently to an early draft of the *Ordonnance des cinq espèces de colonnes selon la méthode des anciens,* Paris, 1683 (extracts in Sources II, no. 25).

103. In his *Mémoires de ma vie* (ca. 1700; see Sources II, no. 53[b]), Charles Perrault reported that Colbert chose Le Brun's design, but only to allow the King the privilege of then selecting Claude Perrault's.

104. Philippe de Bourbon, duc d'Orléans (1640–1701).

105. Louis II de Bourbon, duc d'Enghien, prince de Condé ("Le Grand Condé") (1621–86).

106. This must be Pierre Bréau, described as a master mason and *entrepreneur des bastimens de sa Majesté* in a document of 1670 concerning Perrault's Arc de Triomphe du Trône (Fig. 120; Petzet, "Das Triumphbogenmonument," 179). Payments to him as a royal mason of 30 *livres per annum* are recorded from 1668 to 1679 (*CBR,* I, index). He worked as chief mason at Clagny for both Antoine Le Pautre and Jules Hardouin-Mansart (1674–79) and also served at Versailles in 1676 and 1680 (*CBR,* I, cols. 787, 860, 931, 998, 1079, 1213 [Clagny]; 911, 1351 [Versailles]). In 1671 he was paid 1,200 *livres* "tant pour avoir levé les plans et fait l'estimation de plusieurs maisons et héritages acquis au proffit de S.M. que par gratification, en considération du service qu'il rend dans les Bastimens" (*CBR,* I, col. 547). In 1681 and 1682 his fortunes dramatically rose when he was paid 3,000 *livres per annum* as *architecte des bâtiments du roi* (*CBR,* II, cols. 107, 246). No buildings have been attributed to him in this latter role.

107. The reference is to Philibert de l'Orme's *Nouvelles inventions pour bien bastir et à petits fraiz . . . ,* Paris, 1561, read in the Academy in 1677 (*PV,* I, 153f.). On Perrault's proposed attics for the Louvre, see Chapter IV.

108. Perrault's wooden framework was perhaps based on one in de l'Orme's *Nouvelles inventions,* fol. 10r, discussed on fols. 7r–10v. See *PV,* I, v–vii.

109. The reference is to Perrault's comprehensive Louvre-Tuileries project. See [Gottfried Wilhelm Baron von Leibniz], "Le Louvre. Plans d'achèvement. Pyramide triomphale de Perrault. Fragment inédit de Leibniz," *Journal de l'instruction publique et des cultes,* XXVI, 1857, 238 239; J. F. Blondel, *Architecture françoise,* Paris, 1756, IV, 9–15, pls. I (my Figure 142), II.

110. The Galerie d'Apollon.

111. The façade of this temple has two pairs of columns-and-piers, not pairs of columns (see A. Palladio, *Les quatre livres d'architecture . . . ,* trans. R. Fréart de Chambray, Paris, 1650, pls. on 293, 294–295; this is also true of the flanks of the building [pls. on 293 and 296]).

112. The "Temple of Bacchus" is S. Costanza, Rome, with coupled columns radially disposed in the interior (ibid., pl. on 279; A. Desgodets, *Les édifices antiques de Rome dessinés et mesurés très exactement,* Paris, 1682, 63–73).

113. The Arch of the Sergii, with coupled Corinthian columns.

114. The Palazzo Caprini (ca. 1510; destroyed).

115. Antonio Labacco (dall'Abacco) (1495–1567?) is not known to have made independent designs for Saint Peter's.

116. Cardinal Georges d'Armagnac, Bishop of Rodez (ca. 1500–1585).

117. J. Androuet Du Cerceau the Elder, *XXX exempla arcuum . . . ,* Orléans, 1549.

118. Philibert de l'Orme is not known to have made a design for the Louvre. The eastern part of the Grande Galerie du Bord de l'Eau linking the Louvre and Tuileries to which Blondel refers is by Louis Métezeau (1594–1603), not de l'Orme. Paired (colossal) pilasters were also used in the original western part of the Grande Galerie by Jacques II Androuet Du Cerceau (1603–8).

119. See, e.g., the courtyard of the Château d'Ancy-le-Franc (1541–50).

120. Pierre Lescot.

121. The Fontaine des Innocents, Paris (1547–49).

122. The Château-Neuf at Saint-Germain-en-Laye (1557–59; destroyed) was by de l'Orme; for the western half of the Grande Galerie, see above, note 118.

123. The Luxembourg Palace (begun in 1615) and the façade of Saint-Gervais (1616), both in Paris.

124. See above, note 113.

125. See above, note 111.

126. Scamozzi spread coupled pilasters across the two upper stories of his Palazzo Contarini, Venice (1609–16) and used only single pilasters at the corners (!). Other examples in his *oeuvre* that belie Blondel's statement can undoubtedly be found.

127. For the triumphal arch at Pola, see above, note 113; for the temple of Trevi, see above, note 111.

128. Palladio, *Les quatre livres,* pls. on 269 (Pantheon), 240 (Fortuna Virilis), 319 (Concord), 222 (Antoninus and Faustina); Desgodets, *Les édifices antiques,* pls. on 4–5, 12–13, 16–17, 22–23 (Pantheon), 97, 99 (Fortuna Virilis), 121 (Concord), 111, 113 (Antoninus and Faustina).

129. Vitruvius III.3.11.

130. See above, note 112.

131. Columns are paired with square piers in this temple (see above, note 111).

132. For Claude Perrault's arguments about the structural advantages of coupled columns, see Sources II, nos. 12(a) and 26(a).

133. See Sources II, no. 12(a).

134. Vitruvius III.3.9: "asperitatem intercolumniorum."

135. Vitruvius III.3.

136. A reference to Perrault's proposed attics (Figs. 88, 100, 113, 122; see Chapter IV). The complaint that the Colonnade is too low was discussed previously in the "Advis de M. le Vau le jeune sur le nouveau dessin du Louvre" of 1668 (see Sources II, no. 6 [5a,b]).

137. Vitruvius III.3.5.

138. Vitruvius IV.1.8.

139. Blondel's "second étage" = le premier étage; his "premier étage" = le rez-de-chaussée.

140. The reference is to the capitals of the pilaster order of the three buildings of the Campidoglio, Rome (begun 1538).

141. It is curious and contradictory to find Perrault recommending openings behind a colonnade; in the eastern Louvre façade he closed up the walls behind the coupled columns with niches. Apparently, a royal palace constituted a special exception in Perrault's thinking (see Chapter IV).

142. Vitruvius VI.3.1, 9.

143. Vitruvius V.6.7.

144. See Sources II, no. 24(a–c).

145. On Perrault's thinking on this topic, see Herrmann, *Perrault,* chap. II.

146. The note continues on 339/342 with a description of the machine; on 340 there is an explanation of the plate on 341; on

342n. Perrault reports about the model of the machine he had made, which was kept in the Cabinet des Machines of the Bibliothèque du Roi in the Louvre.

147. Nothing more is known of this project, which was never realized. The author of the verses is Bonaventure de Fourcroy (ca. 1619–92), jurist and poet.

148. Claude Perrault, *Essais de physique. . .* , Paris, 1680, 3 vols. A fourth volume was published in 1688.

149. A room in the Petit Hôtel de Richelieu (or Palais Brion), part of the Palais-Royal, Paris. The Académie royale d'architecture was housed here until 1692, when it was transferred to the Louvre.

150. Pliny the Elder, *Natural History*, XXXVI.95–97. Pliny does not report that the architect (Chersiphron) had prayed to Diana.

151. "Nous avons été obligés de laisser quelques lacunes dans la description de *Perrault*, & de faire quelques changemens dans le texte que nous avons trouvé obscur en certains endroits, ne se rapportant pas d'ailleurs avec la plûpart des mesures que nous avons prises exactement sur les lieux avant que d'entreprendre la description que nous en donnons" (note by Blondel, *Architecture françoise*, IV, 11 n. t). On the erroneous measurements Claude Perrault gave for the Louvre, see Herrmann, *Perrault*, 117f.

152. "Il est certain que ceux qui n'ont qu'une idée imparfaite de ce monument, ont de la peine à se persuader cette magie de l'Art. En Italie même, ceux qui ne connoissent que les estampes de ce péristile, regardent cette composition comme un beau projet, plus propre à faire le fond de la décoration d'un tableau, que le frontispice d'un Palais propre à l'habitation. C'est le langage que tinrent aussi les ennemis de *Perrault* en France, lorsqu'il présenta ses desseins à M. *Colbert* & à *Louis XIV*. Ils ont pourtant été exécutés avec un tres-grand succès, & ce monument, malgré la négligence avec laquelle il est entretenu, s'est soutenu sans aucune rupture depuis qu'il a été élevé jusqu'à présent" (note by Blondel, *Architecture françoise*, IV, 11 n. u). For the arguments that the Louvre Colonnade could only be realized in painting, see Sources II, nos. 35(b), 37(a), 53(b). On the neglect, restoration, and completion of the Louvre in the eighteenth century, see M. Roland-Michel, "The Clearance of the Colonnade of the Louvre: A Study Arising from a Painting by De Machy," *BurlM*, CXX, 1978, i–vi (Supplement); idem, "Soufflot urbaniste et le dégagement de la colonnade du Louvre," in *Soufflot et l'architecture des Lumières*, Paris, 1980, 54–67.

153. "Effectivement on a fait dans les vuides, que *Perrault* nomme puits, des escaliers à noyau, dans lesquels se dégagent les eaux du réservoir, ainsi qu'on l'a pratiqué depuis aux escaliers de la nouvelle Eglise des Invalides. . . . Les eaux qui passent par ces escaliers se déchargent dans un aqueduc qui les porte dans la riviere.

"*Charles Perrault* appuie beaucoup sur la nécessité de faire usage de ces sortes de descentes, & nous avertit que c'est à propos du bâtiment dont nous parlons qu'elles ont été mises en oeuvre pour la premiere fois, & qu'elles sont absolument de l'invention de *Claude Perrault* son frere, qui depuis s'est servi de ce moyen pour écouler les eaux de la terrasse de l'Observatoire, qu'il fit bâtir en 1667. Il est certain qu'elles sont d'un bien meilleur usage que les goutieres; l'eau de ces dernieres étant repoussée par les vents sur les façades, & incommodant considérablement sur la voie publique. A l'égard des descentes de plomb ou de cuivre, dont on fait usage à la place des goutieres, elles sont sujettes à s'engorger, & déparent d'ailleurs la décoration extérieure des bâtimens, en coupant les principaux membres saillans de son architecture, ainsi qu'on le remarque aux Tuileries, au *Château de Maisons*, &c. Il est vrai que cette descente ne peut se mettre en pratique que dans de grands bâtimens, où les épaisseurs des murs sont considérables, parce qu'il faut les enfermer dans des ouvertures en forme de puits d'environ trois pieds & demi de diametre, pour parvenir à dégorger ces descentes, lorsqu'on ne peut leur donner un assez grand diametre pour descendre dedans, ainsi qu'on peut le remarquer dans l'intérieur du portail des Minimes, dont nous avons parlé dans le second vol. [1752] p. 147, & qu'on l'a pratiqué les années dernieres dans les nouveaux bâtimens de Choisi" (note by Blondel, *Architecture françoise*, IV, 11–12 n. y).

154. On Perrault's French order for the Cour Carrée, see Chapter V and Sources II, no. 84(e).

155. "On voit dans le premier volume manuscrit de *Perrault*, page 51, une élévation où il avoit substitué aux colonnes des figures de femmes" (note by Blondel, *Architecture françoise*, IV, 64 n. q).

156. "J'ai eu occasion de voir un de ces Ordres dessiné avec assez de soin, dans un Livre manuscrit qui traite des cinq Ordres d'Architecture; cet Ordre François, quoique composé dans un genre gothique, & revêtu d'ornemens dans le goût de Berin [Jean Bérain (1640–1711)], procura, à ce qu'on m'a assuré, à son Auteur le sieur *Dolivet* [the engraver Jean Dolivar (1641–92)?], Peintre du dernier siecle, une gratification de 4000 liv. & 400 l. de pension viagere, ce qui se contredit avec ce que rapporte *Charles Perrault*, qui prétend que le prix de 3000 liv. proposé n'avoit été accordé à aucun des concurrens, ni même à son frere, qui le méritoit à si juste titre, faute apparemment, dit-il, d'avoir sollicité M. Colbert à cet effet" (note by Blondel, *Architecture françoise*, IV, 64 n. r). On the competition for the French order for the Cour Carrée, see J. M. Pérouse de Montclos, "Le sixième ordre d'architecture, ou la pratique des ordres suivant les nations," *JSAH*, XXXVI, 1977, 223–240.

157. See also Sources II, no. 41.

158. In his *L'art poétique* (written ca. 1669/70–73 and first published in 1674), Boileau satirized Claude Perrault in his verses about a Florentine physician who abandoned medicine for architecture (IV, lines 1–24). In a letter to the Duc de Vivonne (September 1676), Boileau wrote:

Vous scaurés donc, Monseigneur, qu'il y a un Medecin à Paris nommé Perrault tres grand Ennemi de la santé et du bon sens, mais en recompense fort grand ami de Mr Quinau[l]t [Philippe Quinault, poet and librettist]. Un mouvement de pitié pour son Pays ou plutot le peu de gain qu'il faisoit dans son métier lui en a fait à la fin embrasser un autre. Il a lû Vitruve, il a frequenté Mr Le Vau et Mr Ratabon [Antoine de Ratabon, *Surintendant des Bâtiments du Roi*, 1656–63], et s'est enfin jetté dans l'Architecture, ou l'on pretend qu'en peu d'années il a autant elevé de mauvais batimens qu'il avoit ruiné de bonnes santés estant Medecin. Ce nouvel Architecte qui veut se [mesler] aussi de Poesie, m'a pris en haine sur le peu d'estime que je faisois des ouvrages de son cher Quinau[l]t. Sur cela il s'est déchaîné contre moi dans le monde, je l'ai souffert quelque temps avec assés de moderation: mais enfin la bile satirique n'a pû se contenir si bien que dans le quatrieme chant de ma Poëtique a quelque temps de la, [j'ay inséré] la metamorphose d'un medecin en architecte, vous l'y avés peut être veüe, elle finit ainsi:

Notre assassin renonce a son Art inhumain,
Et desormais la Regle et l'Equierre à la main,
Laissant de Galien la science suspecte,
De mechant medecin devient bon Architecte.

Il n'avoit pas pourtant suiet de s'offenser de cela puisque ie parle d'un medecin de Florence et que d'ailleurs il n'est pas le premier medecin qui dans Paris ayt quitté sa Robe pour la Truelle [probably a reference to Louis Savot, author of *L'architecture françoise des bastimens particuliers,* Paris, 1624]. Aioutés que si en qualité de Medecin il avoit droit de se facher, vous m'avoûrés qu'en qualité d'Architecte il me devoit des remercimens. Il ne me remercia pas pourtant. Au contraire, comme il a un frere chés Mr Colbert qui est lui mésme emploié dans les batimens du Roi, il cria fort haut contre ma hardiesse, jusques la que mes amis eurent peur que cela ne me fist une affaire auprés de Mr Colbert. Je me rendis donc à leurs remonstrances et pour racommoder toutes choses, je fis une reparation sincere au medecin par l'Epigramme que vous allés voir.

> Oui j'ai dit dans mes vers qu'un celebre Assassin,
> Laissant de Galien la science infertile,
> D'ignorant medecin devint masson habile.
> Mais de parler de vous je n'eûs aucun dessein,
> Perrault, ma Muse est trop [correcte].
> Vous estes, je l'avoüe, ignorant Medecin:
> Mais non pas habile Architecte.

Mais regardés, Monseig[r], comme les esprits des gens sont faits, cette reparation bien loin d'appaiser l'Architecte l'irrita encore davantage, il pesta, il se plaignit, il me menaça de me faire oter ma Pension. A tout cela je répondis, que je craignois ses remedes et non pas ses menaces. Le denoüement de l'affaire est que j'ai touché ma Pension, que l'architecte s'est broüillé auprés de Mr Colbert par une friponnerie quil a faicte dans ses bastimens et que, si Dieu ne regarde en pitié son peuple, notre homme va se rejetter dans la Medecine. (N. Boileau, *Oeuvres complètes,* ed. A. Adam and F. Escal, Paris, 1966, 781–782, letter v.)

The "friponnerie" to which Boileau refers is a mystery. The epigram was published in 1694 in Boileau's *Oeuvres diverses,* with "Perrault, ma Muse" changed to "Lubin, ma Muse," which was again altered in the 1716 edition to "P.***, ma Muse" (*Oeuvres complètes,* 254, epigramme XXXIII and 1040). Trouble between Boileau and Claude Perrault erupted in 1668 when Claude accused Boileau of satirizing Louis XIV in satire IX, line 224: "Midas, le Roi Midas, a des oreilles d'asne" (written in 1667, published in 1668; *Oeuvres complètes,* 54). On the entire battle between the Perraults and Boileau, see H. Kortum, *Charles Perrault und Nicolas Boileau,* Berlin, 1966. See also below, note 190.

159. "Envoyé le 6. Janvier 1697. a M. Dorbay pour le travail qu'il fait actuellement sur les Memoires du Louvre pour les arrêté tous les articles marques en marge M. dorbay" (AN, O¹ 2768, fol. 109 [in margin]). This anonymous annotation accompanies a list and brief descriptions of masonry contracts. D'Orbay died on September 4, 1697.

160. See Sources II, no. 53.

161. Le Petit Conseil (see Sources II, no. 1).

162. The last sentence of the first paragraph and the entire second paragraph reappear verbatim in the anonymous "Eloge de M[r]. Claude Perrault" in Cl. Perrault, *Oeuvres diverses de physique et de mechanique,* Leiden, 1721, I(9). See Sources II, no. 61.

163. I have not located this comment in Spon's writings. The Porte Basse consisted of a corbeled arch with a keystone, without orders or moldings; it was destroyed ca. 1804. See A. Blanchet, *Les enceintes romaines de la Gaule,* Paris, 1907, 272, pl. XIX, fig. 2. Blanchet surmises that the arch may have postdated the Roman period.

164. See Sources II, no. 24(b).

165. Antoine Desgodets (1653–1728). See Sources II, no. 23.

166. "Blondel acceptait cette solution" (note by Lemonnier, *PV,* I, 13 n. 3).

167. On Cliquin's machine, see Perrault, *Vitruve,* 1684, 339/342; Herrmann, *Perrault,* app. I.

168. See Figure 87.

169. On the Vatican obelisk, see D. Fontana, *Della trasportatione dell'obelisco vaticano,* Naples, 1590 (2d ed., 1604).

170. See Figure 87.

171. A fragment of the "registre" was published in the eighteenth century: see Sources II, no. 1.

172. See Sources II, nos. 39 and 41.

173. See Sources II, no. 38.

174. See above, note 165.

175. "On a trouvé l'à propos de faire le chapiteau du pilastre dans la mesme proportion par raport à la largeur du pilastre que celle du chapiteau de la colonne, par raport au diametre de la colonne par le haut, en sorte que si l'on diminue la colonne par le haut d'un sixieme, comme on fait ordinairement, on doit donner au chapiteau pilastre un sixieme de module de plus qu'on donne au chapiteau de la colonne. Et, par consequent, si le chapiteau de la colonne a de hauteur un module et un sixieme, celuy du pilastre aura un module et un tiers" (*PV,* III, 278–279 [August 17, 1707]).

176. Amédée François Frézier had published a "Dissertation sur la maniere dont les eglises doivent être baties," critical of Cordemoy's first edition (1706).

177. Sauval's manuscript was unfinished when he died in 1676, and it underwent subsequent additions and editing. Hence I have chosen to insert this extract under the date of publication, 1724. In the extract, there is a reference to Perrault's 1684 Vitruvius edition, and the penultimate paragraph and part of the last one are lifted from the 1698 edition of Brice's guide to Paris (noted by Laprade, *d'Orbay,* 308; cf. Sources II, no. 48, last par.). On the editing of Sauval's book, see A. Blunt's introduction to the facsimile edition, Westmead, 1969, and J. P. Babelon, "Bonnes et mauvaises lectures," *RA,* no. 54, 1981, 57–58.

178. See Figure 87.

179. See above, note 169.

180. The *CBR* record payments to three Italian-born sculptors for work on the Louvre: Jean Baptiste Tuby, Philippe Caffiéri, and Francesco Temporiti. Tuby and Caffiéri, however, had been in France since at least 1660 (for Tuby, see Souchal, *French Sculptors,* III [1987], 328; for Caffiéri, see T-B, V, 350). Only Temporiti may have been specially invited; he received his earliest payment for work done from October 28, 1667, to February 19, 1668 (*CBR,* I, col. 183).

181. See Sources II, no. 44.

182. Brice first attributed the Colonnade to Le Vau and d'Orbay in his third edition (1698; see Sources II, no. 48). In his first edition (1684; ibid., no. 27), no attribution is made; in his second edition (1687; ibid., no. 32), the Colonnade is given to Perrault and d'Orbay (!).

183. Le Vau became *premier architecte* in 1654.

184. D'Orbay was never advanced to this post.

185. Claude Perrault never claimed the authorship of the Colonnade in print.

186. The Observatoire is uncontestably by Perrault.

187. See Figure 87.

188. See Sources II, no. 44.

189. See ibid., no. 39.

190. See ibid., no. 44.

191. Letter of ca. 1700; see Boileau, *Oeuvres complètes,* 574: "J'avouë franchement que le dépit de me voir critiqué dans vos Dialogues m'a fait dire des choses qu'il seroit mieux de n'avoir point dites." The "Dialogues" are Charles Perrault's *Parallèle des anciens et des modernes* . . . , Paris, 1688–97, 4 vols.

192. See Chapter I.

193. See Sources II, nos. 39 and 40.

194. Perrault was enjoined not to claim responsibility for the Colonnade by the terms that created the Petit Conseil in 1667. The "Registre" of 1667 states that "aucun [of the three members] ne pourroit s'en dire l'auteur particulierement au préjudice des autres" (ibid., no. 1).

195. The Canal du Midi (1666–80).

196. The description of this emblem is borrowed from A. Félibien, *Entretiens sur les vies et sur les ouvrages des plus excellens peintres anciens et modernes,* 2d ed., Paris, 1696, I, 26. I have not succeeded in finding the original emblem.

197. On the question of the possible connection between the ancient Roman ruins of Palmyra and Baalbek and the Louvre, see Appendix D.

198. By 1752 the ruins of Persepolis were well known to Europeans, mainly due to the publication of *Persepolis illustrata* . . . , London, 1739.

199. "Il est très-certain que la grandeur des objets est absolument nécessaire pour remplir l'idée du grand beau. Une personne d'une taille médiocre, quoique très-bien proportionnée & même belle, ne sera jamais appellée une beauté parfaite, parce qu'il lui manquera l'avantage de la taille qui fait la majesté & incline à la vénération" (133n). This idea about vastness, derived from Longinus, was included by Edmund Burke in *A Philosophical Enquiry into the Origin of our Ideas of the Sublime and Beautiful,* London, 1757, part two, sec. VII.

200. "Plusieurs personnes ont disputé inutilement à Claude Perrault la gloire d'avoir donné le dessin de la Colonade du Louvre, fondés uniquement sur ce que Boileau rapporte à ce sujet dans ses Réflexions critiques sur Longin [Sources II, no. 39]. Mais le jugement particulier de cet illustre Satyrique seroit très récusable, s'il étoit contraire au général & à celui de tout le public qui l'a toujours donné à Perrault sans varier. Tout le monde sçavoit alors la haine de Boileau contre Messieurs Perrault, qui prenoit sa source dans l'ouvrage du Paralelle des anciens & des modernes par Charles Perrault frere de l'Architecte, où il donnoit la préférence entiere à ces derniers sur les premiers, & où Boileau n'étoit pas bien traité [see above, note 191]. Il eut même quelques disputes assez vives avec l'Architecte dont il avoue qu'il avoit voulu se venger par la façon dont il en parle dans son Art poëtique, auquel cependant il ne pût refuser dans la suite la qualification de bon & d'habile Architecte dans ses écrits. Il dit dans ses Réflexions critiques, *Qu'un des plus célébres Architectes* qu'il n'ose pas nommer, ce qu'il faut bien remarquer, *s'est offert de lui faire voir papiers sur table, que le dessin de la Façade du Louvre est du sieur le Vau & non de Perrault.* Si ce célébre Architecte (Dorbay disciple de le Vau) avoit pû tenir sa parole, avec quelle joye maligne Boileau eût saisi cette occasion de se venger de son ennemi, en lui enlevant la gloire dont il avoit joui jusqu'alors sans aucune contestation, d'être l'auteur de ce chef-d'oeuvre? Mais tout au contraire, Boileau déclare en rapportant ce fait, *qu'il ne veut point entrer dans cette dispute & que s'il prenoit un parti, ce seroit en faveur de Perrault* [see Sources II, no. 39]. Je ne vois pas quel avantage les ennemis de ce dernier peuvent tirer du discours de Boileau qui me paroit décider en sa faveur. Quelque mordant que fut ce grand Poëte, son esprit seul étoit satirique, mais son coeur étoit droit & aimoit passionément la vérité. Il en a donné des preuves dans sa réconciliation sincere avec Perrault dans la lettre qu'il lui écrivit: où il lui avoue, *que le dépit de se voir critiqué lui avoit fait dire des choses qu'il auroit mieux fait de n'avoir pas dites* [see above, note 191]. Il en usa de meme avec Quinau[l]t après l'avoir si injustement décrié, & se rétracta de tout ce qu'il en avoit dit.

"Je joins à la réfutation de cette autorité, le bel éloge que fit à la mort de Claude Perrault le célébre & sçavant [Henri] Basnage dans son histoire des ouvrages des sçavans au mois de Novembre 1688. dont voici un extrait. '. . . Il sçavoit parfaitement l'Architecture, & M. Colbert ayant fait faire des dessins pour la façade du Louvre par tous les fameux Architectes de France & d'Italie, celui de M. Perrault fut préféré à tous les autres, & a été exécuté tel qu'on le voit aujourd'hui, sur les profils & les mesures qu'il en a donnés. C'est aussi sur ses dessins qu'a été élevé l'Observatoire de Paris avec toutes les commodités qui s'y trouvent pour observer. Cet édifice est d'autant plus à estimer qu'il est d'une espéce singuliere & nouvelle en France, ce qui demandoit beaucoup de génie & de science. M. Perrault fit aussi le grand modéle de l'Arc-de-triomphe du fauxbourg S. Antoine, dont une partie a déja été construite sous ses yeux' [see Sources II, no. 34].

"Un autre témoignage bien puissant, c'est celui de M. de Boffrand [Germain Boffrand (1667–1754)] qui vit encore, & dont la réputation d'excellent Architecte, & sur-tout d'homme d'honneur & de probité, n'est point équivoque. Son aveu est d'un poids accablant par l'avantage d'avoir été son contemporain. Il m'a dit il y a plus de 20 ans, qu'il avoit vû dans le tems de la construction du Louvre, le dessin de sa Façade signé par Claude Perrault. A cette preuve oculaire & invincible il ajouta, qu'il n'en auroit eû nullement besoin pour décider dans la suite par ses lumieres & son expérience, quel étoit l'auteur de cet admirable édifice. *Il n'est point de véritable Architecte,* me dit-il, *qui n'apperçoive les rapports qu'ont entr'eux ces trois excellens édifices. On y trouve les mêmes proportions, mêmes profils, même sublimité de génie, surtout dans l'Arc-de-triomphe & le Péristile.* Les sçavans en Architecture & en Peinture peuvent juger affirmativement des ouvrages d'un Artiste, comme l'on juge de ceux d'un Ecrivain par son stile & son génie, & par l'élévation ou la médiocrité de l'un & de l'autre. C'est ce que pense fort sensément M. Piganiol [de La Force] dans sa description de Paris . . . où il dit 'Que de tous les Bâtimens construits par le Vau, on n'en voit aucun où il y ait la moindre ressemblance de leur Architecture avec la magnificence & la grandeur de celle de Perrault,' & ensuite . . . 'Quoique le Vau, dit-il, fut un habile homme dans sa profession, ce n'étoit pourtant qu'un Architecte *de tradition* comme tous ses confréres, c'est-à-dire, un observateur exact des régles qu'on lui avoit apprises; mais nul génie, nulle imagination, nulle invention au-delà' [see Sources II, no. 68 (b,c)].

"Après ce que je viens de rapporter, je crois qu'on n'exigera pas de nouveaux témoignages en faveur du sieur Perrault. Il en est cependant encore un de la plus grande force, & égale à celle d'une démonstration Géométrique, au sentiment d'un des meilleurs juges & des plus grands hommes qui nous reste du siècle de Louis XIV. Charles Perrault frere de l'Architecte publia en [1696] les Hommes illustres du dix-septiéme siécle, au nombre desquels il rangea avec justice Claude Perrault. Il lui donne les éloges qui lui sont dûs, c'est-à-dire, les plus grands, pour avoir imaginé ces trois chefs-d'oeuvres d'Architecture ci-dessus nommés, sans dire un mot de l'attaque de [Boileau-]Despreaux dans ses Réflexions critiques, ni daigner le refuter par le défaut de vraiesemblance, & le peu d'impression qu'avoit fait sur les esprits, un Paradoxe tombé de lui même & mort dès sa naissance [Sources II, no. 44]. Il se fit plusieurs éditions de son ouvrage in-folio & in-douze, sans que qui que ce soit ait pensé à disputer à Claude Perrault ses belles productions. C'étoit donc un fait de notorieté publique. Or je ne sçai point d'argument plus fort & plus décisif en sa faveur, que ce silence, & ce consentement universel. Combien de voix se seroient élevées si Charles P. eut eû l'impudence de donner pour vrai, un fait non-seulement faux, mais même douteux, & de l'affirmer du vivant de Louis XIV. sous les yeux duquel il s'étoit passé, & de M. Colbert de Villacerf alors surintendant des Bâtimens? D'ailleurs, pourquoi le Vau a-t-il laissé jouir paisiblement pendant toute sa vie l'usurpateur, de sa réputation & de son bien? Pourquoi le sieur d'Orbay a-t-il attendu la mort de le Vau & de Claude Perrault pour dire qu'il avoit des papiers & des titres si décisifs en faveur de son maître? Pourquoi enfin ne les a-t-il jamais produits?

"Voilà beaucoup plus de preuves qu'il n'en falloit pour écraser les ennemis de Perrault qui ont toujours été des hommes médiocres & sans génie, & pour terminer une dispute où leur parti est si mal défendu. Je ne crains point que la postérité refuse à la mémoire de cet illustre François la gloire & l'immortalité dûe au plus grand génie en Architecture qui ait jamais existé" (142–149n).

201. On optical adjustments, see Herrmann, *Perrault*, chap. III.
202. On the completion of the Louvre in the eighteenth century, see above, note 152.
203. On the courtyard, see Chapter V.
204. On Callimachus (d. 405 B.C.), the supposed inventor of the Corinthian capital, see B. M. Boyle, "Kallimachos," *Macmillan Encyclopedia of Architects*, II, 548–549.
205. "Non sans doute, le Censeur a pu le dire en général de tout siécle où l'on n'auroit pas les lumieres nécessaires pour distinguer ce qui est digne d'admiration de ce qui est répréhensible; il n'y a nulle apparence que dans le siécle passé ce grand ouvrage ait échappé à la critique de tant d'habiles Artistes qui se distinguerent alors; mais il est arrivé ce qui arrivera toujours: quelques défauts qu'on puisse démontrer dans un bel ouvrage, ce qu'il a de beau lui attirera l'admiration, & payera avec usure pour les défauts qui peuvent s'y rencontrer: de là l'inutilité des critiques, si ce n'est pour l'instruction de ceux qui étudient, de peur qu'ils n'imitent ces défauts comme consacrés" (144–145 n. c).
206. "L'Auteur tombe ici dans le même défaut qu'il reproche à son adversaire, en faisant la critique d'un morceau qui est rempli d'assez de beautés pour mériter son respect; d'ailleurs, quand son antagoniste a dit ce qu'il lui reproche, ce n'est point à cette partie du Louvre qu'il faisoit allusion, mais à celle qui du côté de la riviere [Le Vau's south façade, Figure 17] se trouve masquée par ce que M. Perrault a bâti devant [Fig. 95], & on a en effet lieu d'en regretter la perte, cette partie etant, au sentiment de plusieurs, plus belle que ce qui la cache. il est vrai qu'elle ne pouvoit s'allier avec le péristile du Louvre; mais est-il ridicule de desirer que Perrault eût trouvé le moyen de faire une belle chose sans en sacrifier une autre déja faite?" (146 n. d).
207. A reference to Aristarchus of Samothrace (ca. 217–145 B.C.), director of the Alexandrian Library and the founder of scientific literary scholarship.
208. "L'Auteur veut ici excuser un défaut inexcusable, & qui est reconnu universellement pour tel. Je parle de cette porte ceintrée [Fig. 48] qui interrompt le péristile en dedans & en dehors, ce n'est pas là-dessus qu'il faut défendre Perrault: d'ailleurs il est inutile qu'une porte soit dans une autre, la porte quarrée suffisoit" (148 n. e).
209. Claude Desgots (d. 1732) and Germain Boffrand (1667–1754).

210. Perrault's Arc de Triomphe du Trône, Paris (Fig. 120).
211. "Toutes les raisons que l'Auteur apporte ici autorisent Perrault à faire un monument de la plus grande magnificence & d'une grandeur colossale, mais nullement à interrompre par une arcade son architecture, & à faire le milieu plein & massif comme il est. A l'égard du défaut de croisées, il est très-bien justifié, parce qu'en effet les niches présenteront toujours un plus riche spectacle que des fenêtres" (150 n. f). On the situation of the Louvre within the urban fabric of Paris, see A. Chastel and J. M. Pérouse de Montclos, "L'aménagement de l'accès oriental du Louvre," *MHF*, n.s., XII, 1966, 176–249 (entire issue).
212. "Le projet du Bernin n'étoit pas à rejetter parce qu'il y avoit des croisées, mais parce qu'il ne valoit rien d'ailleurs" (150 n. g). On Perrault's omission of windows and his specific criticism of Bernini's design on this point, see Chapter IV.
213. "Il ne s'ensuit pas de ce que les fêtes publiques pouvoient se donner dans la cour des Tuileries, qu'il fût nécessaire de remplir le milieu du péristile, de telle maniere que personne ne pût s'y placer pour voir le beau coup d'oeil de cette grande rue, projetée jusqu'à l'arc de triomphe du fauxbourg S. Antoine" [Perrault's Arc de Triomphe du Trône, Figure 120] (151 n. h).
214. This passage indicates that as late as 1755 an important part of the south façade was not yet executed. On the completion of the Louvre in the mid-eighteenth century, see above, note 152.
215. "L'Auteur défend mieux la façade du côté de la riviere, qui seroit en effet plus riche si les pilastres étoient cannelés & les ornemens finis; mais on ne peut nier que cette suite de pilastres n'ait quelque chose de [m]onotone, & que si les avant-corps étoient ornés de colonnes il en résulteroit plus d'agrément & de variété, sans qu'elles ôtassent le jour, comme il le croit, puisqu'il y en a à la façade de Versailles qui n'obscurcissent point la grande galerie" (153 n. i).
216. Still unexecuted in 1755; see above, note 214.
217. Another indication of the incomplete state of construction; see above, notes 214 and 216.
218. "Le résultat de ces deux écrits est que l'Auteur de la lettre est fondé dans le reproche qu'il fait au Censeur du Louvre d'avoir parlé avec trop peu de ménagement d'un édifice qui fait & qui fera toujours, malgré ses défauts, l'admiration de tous les gens de goût; cependant on ne peut pas dire que la censure de ce Critique manque de justesse, mais qu'elle est déplacée, dans un tems où tous les vrais citoyens voyent avec un plaisir qui tient du transport les préparatifs qu'on fait pour achever ce superbe monument. Elle paroit d'autant plus répréhensible que la multitude non instruite peut en conclure, que ce n'est pas la peine de finir un ouvrage dont on releve les défauts avec tant d'amertume, & que d'ailleurs il y a quelque ingratitude à reconnoître si mal le zéle de ceux qui s'occupent du soin de le faire porter à son entiere perfection" (155 n. k).
219. On these volumes, see Blondel, *Architecture françoise*, IV, 4–5 n. d, and Sources II, no. 38. They were destroyed in 1871.
220. Vitruvius III.3.11–13.
221. "Le module est divisé en 18 parties, & la partie en 18 minutes" (43 n. d).
222. "Les mesures que nous donnons dans cette description, sont prises sur l'édifice avec la précision la plus exacte: nous n'avons point eu d'égard aux planches gravées; d'ailleurs la petitesse de l'échelle, & l'inégalité du papier, produisent toujours des erreurs assez considérables dans les épreuves. Certainement cet édifice méritoit ce travail important" (43 n. e).
223. Blondel is slightly in error here. The ratio of the entablature height to column height in the Corinthian order

(including capital and base) is indeed 1 : 4 in Vignola, but it is 1 : 475 in Palladio and 1 : 5 in Scamozzi. See R. Fréart de Chambray, *Parallèle de l'architecture antique et de la moderne,* Paris, 1650, pls. on 75, right; 73, left and right.

224. A reference to the finishing of the Louvre.

225. Blondel, *Architecture françoise,* IV, 85.

226. Cf. Fréart de Chambray, *Parallèle,* pl. on 75, right.

227. Blondel, *Architecture françoise,* I, 90–95.

228. Pierre Patte in 1777 gave ca. 50 *pieds* (length), 8 *pieds* (width), and 16–17 *pouces* (thickness) (Sources II, no. 100).

229. On the medallion-garland motif, see Chapter VII.

230. Blondel here describes the sculptures as if they existed, but a painting by Pierre Antoine de Machy of the Colonnade (ca. 1773; Paris, Musée Carnavalet) clearly shows that the space above the entrance arch of the central pavilion was still uncarved. It remained thus until 1807, when Pierre Cartellier carved *Victory in a Quadriga Distributing Wreaths* (Fig. 48).

231. On the iron reinforcement, see Chapter VI.

232. On these niches, see Chapter IV.

233. On the sculpture of the medallions, see Appendix A (A8).

234. On Perrault's desire to close up the façade, see Chapter IV.

235. On these attics, see Chapter IV and Sources II, no. 20(a–d).

236. On the 1693 manuscript volumes, destroyed in 1871, see Sources II, no. 38.

237. See above, note 234.

238. *Architecture françoise,* IV, 42.

239. Blondel is referring to the horizontal molding that separates the upper two floors of the south façade (Fig. 95); such a molding is absent from the buildings of the Place Vendôme and Place des Victoires.

240. A description of the as-yet-unfinished façade; see above, notes 214, 216, 217.

241. A reference to a passage in the destroyed 1693 manuscript; see Sources II, no. 38.

242. "Ces ornemens ne sont point sculptés sur le lieu; sans doute *Perrault* les auroit traités autrement: au reste nous n'en avons trouvé aucun vestige dans le Recueil de cet Auteur que nous avons déja cité tant de fois" (61 n. k).

243. On the problems concerning the completion of the Cour Carrée, see Chapter V.

244. See above, note 180.

245. For the machine used for the laying of the mortarless foundations of Perrault's Arc de Triomphe du Trône (Fig. 120), see Petzet, "Das Triumphbogenmonument," 180. Contrary to La Font, this machine was not used for the foundations of the Colonnade, which were laid in the early 1660s to support Le Vau's ill-fated east wing (see Chapter II).

246. La Font (114) includes the following letter concerning the moat:

"Lettre ecrite à un particulier en province, sur les réparations du Louvre [July 15, 1755]: 'On ne doute pas que les fossés, tels qu'ils étoient anciennement, ne soient rétablis au bas de la face de la Colonnade du côté de l'Eglise de S. Germain [-l'Auxerrois], & que la partie qui en existe encore du côté de la rue Fromenteau [formerly a north-south street running through the present Place du Carrousel, to the west of the Cour Carrée; it is indicated in Figure 90], ne soit continuée à la place des remises & des vils bâtimens que l'on y a addossés. Par-là on découvrira au public la beauté de la construction de la partie de cet édifice jusqu'à présent enseveli, & qui est aussi admirable à vingt pieds de profondeur que celle qui est au niveau du rez de chaussée.'" Fragments of the moat along the western exterior façade of the Cour Carrée are shown on the Plan Turgot (1739) and in Figure 90.

247. I know of no evidence for this statement.

248. See above, note 209.

249. Perrault's drawings (destroyed) for the south façade were described by J. F. Blondel in 1756 (see Sources II, no. 84[c]).

250. Claude Guillot-Aubry (1703–71), a member of the Académie royale d'architecture from 1737 on; see T-B, II, 231, and L. Hautecoeur, *Histoire de l'architecture classique en France, III: Première moitié du XVIIIe siècle, le style Louis XV,* Paris, 1950.

251. Lemonnier (*PV,* VI, 256 n. 2) believed these drawings had been destroyed in the fire that gutted the Bibliothèque du Louvre in 1871. I believe these drawings are in the Cabinet des Dessins of the Louvre (see Appendix A [A12]). Hautecoeur (*Louvre et Tuileries,* 177 n. 2) had earlier surmised that these sheets were in the *Recueil du Louvre* there.

252. I have been unable to find such an engraving. Patte's note is a comment on Charles Perrault's text, wherein the latter reports that Le Vau's design had no colonnade (see Sources II, no. 53[b]).

253. The *directeur des bâtiments* from 1746 to 1773.

254. Laugier probably knew Claude Perrault's manuscript note on the ground floor, as summarized by J. F. Blondel in 1756 (see Sources II, no. 84[b]).

255. For these machines (not by Perrault), see above, note 167.

256. This model is reported in Charles Perrault's *Mémoires* (Sources II, no. 53[b]). Patte had published an edition of Perrault's autobiography in Avignon in 1759 (Sources II, no. 88).

257. "Quoiqu'on ne puisse appercevoir la grosseur des fers enfermés, tant dans l'intérieur de l'entablement que dans les colonnes, il est pourtant aisé de les estimer: en voyant que les tirans apparens dans le vuide de l'entablement ont deux pouces un quart, on peut conclure sans crainte d'erreur que les autres sont d'égales grosseurs, & qu'aussi le mandrin d'axe des colonnes qui les contient, doit avoir encore plus de force" (270 n. a).

258. "Pour ôter toute équivoque, j'ai affecté dans tout ce Chapitre de toujours nommer *tirans horisontaux,* ceux qui sont le long de la face d'un bâtiment, & *tirans perpendiculaires* ceux qui sont suivant sa profondeur" (271 n. a).

259. "Les eaux ayant filtré à travers les joints de cette terrasse par le défaut d'un entretien exact, & ayant endommagé plusieurs endroits des plafonds, on a pris le parti, depuis quelques années, de la couvrir par un toit bas de charpente" (273 n. a).

260. On the completion of the courtyard, see Chapter V.

261. This paragraph is based on Charles Perrault's *Mémoires* (cf. Sources II, no. 53[b]).

262. See Sources II, no. 39.

263. Desgodets, *Les édifices antiques,* 19, pl. v; 34, pl. x.

264. The Temple of Concord in the Roman Forum is now known as the Temple of Saturn, but it has no pilasters.

265. Its "pilasters" consist only of capitals and bases.

266. Desgodets, *Les édifices antiques,* 163, pl. III.

267. Vitruvius III.3.13 (in modern editions).

268. Perrault, *Vitruve,* 1684, 82/84 n. 25.

269. See Sources II, nos. 24(a–c) (Blondel), 26(a) (Perrault), and Appendix B.

270. See also Sources II, no. 81.

271. Cl. Perrault, *Ordonnance des cinq espèces de colonnes selon la méthode des anciens,* Paris, 1683.

272. On these contradictions in Perrault, see Herrmann, *Perrault,* 117f.

273. See Sources II, no. 24(a).

274. Fréart de Chambray, *Parallèle,* 74, and pl. on 75, right.
275. On the absence of dentils, see also Sources II, nos. 81 and 94(d).
276. D'Orbay was not Le Vau's nephew, nor was he related to him in any way.
277. See Sources II, no. 84(a).
278. In 1679, Louis XIV ordered a continuation of the Cours de Vincennes westward to the Abbaye de Saint-Antoine in the rue du Faubourg Saint-Antoine (Petzet, "Das Triumphbogenmonument," 182, 183 n. 150). There is no evidence that this avenue was to be extended to the Louvre.
279. See above, note 230.
280. For Blondel's project for improving the Colonnade, see his *Cours d'architecture,* III, 69–73.
281. On the machine (not by Perrault) used to hoist the pediment stones, see Figure 86 and Herrmann, *Perrault,* app. I.
282. "Ce reproche n'est pas général" (note by Condorcet).
283. For Boileau, see Sources II, no. 39.
284. François Blondel attributed the Colonnade to Perrault in his Savot edition (see Sources II, no. 13).
285. See Sources II, no. 94.
286. I cannot identify the author or the publication.
287. See above, note 281.
288. The temple at Scisi does not have coupled columns (Palladio, *Les quatre livres,* 297, figs. on 298–300); for the temple at Trevi (with pairs of columns and piers, not pilasters), see above, note 111.
289. It is curious that Dezallier does not mention the niches, which were not replaced by windows until 1807 (see Chapter IV).
290. See Sources II, no. 39.
291. See above, note 191.
292. See Sources II, nos. 39 and 41.
293. See ibid., no. 39.
294. See ibid., no. 44.
295. The argument is borrowed from La Font de Saint-Yenne (see above, note 200).

BIBLIOGRAPHY

(Books listed in Abbreviations are not repeated here.)

Aldridge, A. O. "Ancients and Moderns in the Eighteenth Century." In *Dictionary of the History of Ideas*, ed. P. P. Wiener. New York, 1968, I, 76–87.

Algarotti, F. "Pensieri diversi sopra materie filosofiche e filologiche." In *Opere del conte Algarotti*, new ed. Venice, 1792, VII, 3–253.

Amat, F. d'. "Fréart." In *Dictionnaire de biographie française*, fasc. 83. Paris, 1979, col. 1136.

[Antoine, P. J.]. *Série de colonnes*. Dijon, 1782.

Antonini, A. *Memorial de Paris, et de ses environs, à l'usage des voyageurs*, new ed. Paris, 1744.

Arvieux, L. d'. *Mémoires . . .* , 6 vols. Paris, 1735.

Aulanier, C. *La Petite Galerie (Histoire du Palais et du Musée du Louvre, V)*. Paris, 1955.

——. *Le Pavillon du Roi (Histoire du Palais et du Musée du Louvre, VII)*. Paris, 1958.

[Aviler, A. C. d']. *Les oeuvres d'architecture d'Anthoine Le Pautre*. Paris, [1681].

——. *Cours d'architecture . . .* , 2 vols. Paris, 1693–94.

Babeau, A. "Note sur les fossés du Louvre." *Mémoires de la Société nationale des antiquaires de France*, ser. 7, III, 1902, 155–164.

Babelon, J. P. *Demeures parisiennes sous Henri IV et Louis XIII*. Paris, 1965.

——. "Le château de Sucy-en-Brie, oeuvre de François Le Vau." *BSHP*, CI/CII, 1974–75, 83–102.

——. "Bonnes et mauvaises lectures." *RA*, no. 54, 1981, 56–60.

——. "La Cour Carrée du Louvre. Les tentatives des siècles pour maîtriser un espace urbain mal défini." *BMon*, CXLII, 1984, 41–81.

——. "D'un fossé à l'autre. Vingt ans de recherches sur le Louvre." *RA*, no. 78, 1987, 5–25.

Bachaumont, L. P. de. *Essai sur la peinture, la sculpture, et l'architecture*. [Paris], 1751.

Baltard, L. P., and Duval, A. P. *Paris et ses monumens . . .* , 2 vols. Paris, 1803–5.

Batiffol, L. "Le Louvre et les plans de Lescot." *GBA*, ser. 4, III, 1910, 273–298.

Bauchal, C. *Nouveau dictionnaire biographique et critique des architectes français*. Paris, 1887.

Bazin, G. "L'erreur du fossé du Louvre." *Le Monde*, 20 August 1981, 2.

Benjamin of Tudela. *Itinerarium . . .* , Leiden, 1633.

Berckenhagen, E. *Die französische Zeichnungen der Kunstbibliothek Berlin*. Berlin, 1970.

Berger, R. W. "Antoine Le Pautre and the Motif of the Drum-without-Dome." *JSAH*, XXV, 1966, 165–180.

——. *Antoine Le Pautre: A French Architect of the Era of Louis XIV*. New York, 1969.

——. "Charles Le Brun and the Louvre Colonnade." *AB*, LII, 1970, 394–403.

——. "Louis Le Vau's Château du Raincy." *Architectura*, VI, 1976, 36–46.

——. "Le Vau, François," *Macmillan Encyclopedia of Architects*, ed. A. K. Placzek. New York and London, 1982, II, 695.

——. "Louis Le Vau's Château du Raincy: An Addendum." *Architectura*, XIV, 1984, 171.

——. *In the Garden of the Sun King: Studies on the Park of Versailles under Louis XIV*. Washington, D.C., 1985.

———. *Versailles: The Château of Louis XIV.* University Park, Pa., and London, 1985.
Berty, A., and H. Legrand. *Histoire générale de Paris. Topographie historique du vieux Paris: Région du Louvre et des Tuileries,* 2 vols. Paris, 1866–68.
Blanchard, A., *Les ingénieurs du 'Roy' de Louis XIV à Louis XVI,* Montpellier, 1979.
Blanchet, A. *Les enceintes romaines de la Gaule,* Paris, 1907.
Blegny, N. de. *Le livre commode des adresses de Paris pour 1692,* ed. E. Fournier, 2 vols. Paris, 1878.
Blomfield, R. *A History of French Architecture from the Death of Mazarin till the Death of Louis XV, 1661–1774,* 2 vols. London, 1921.
Blondel, J. F. *Architecture françoise,* 4 vols. Paris, 1752–56.
[———]. "Denticule" (article). In *Encyclopédie ou dictionnaire raisonné des sciences, des arts et des métiers.* . . . Paris, 1754, IV, 847.
———. *Cours d'architecture* . . . , 6 vols. and atlas (3 vols.) (vols. 5 and 6 by P. Patte). Paris, 1771–77.
Blunt, A. *Art and Architecture in France, 1500 to 1700,* 2d rearranged impression. Harmondsworth, 1957, and later eds.
———. Review of M. Lyttleton, *Baroque Architecture in Classical Antiquity,* London, 1974. In *BurlM,* CXVIII, 1976, 320–324.
Bodart, D. "Une description de 1657 des fresques de Giovanni Francesco Romanelli au Louvre." *BSHAF,* 1974, 43–50.
Boileau, N. *L'art poétique.* Paris, 1674.
———. *Réflexions critiques sur quelques passages du rheteur Longin.* Paris, 1694.
———. *Oeuvres complètes,* ed. A. Adam and F. Escal. Paris, 1966.
Bonnefon, P. "Claude Perrault architecte et voyageur (premier article)." *GBA,* ser. 3, XXVI, 1901, 209–222.
Boyle, B. M. "Kallimachos." *Macmillan Encyclopedia of Architects,* ed. A. K. Placzek. New York and London, 1982, II, 548–549.
Braham, A. "Bernini's Design for the Bourbon Chapel." *BurlM,* CII, 1960, 443–447.
———, and Smith, P. *François Mansart,* 2 vols. London, 1973.
———, and Whiteley, M. "Louis Le Vau's Projects for the Louvre and the Colonnade—II." *GBA,* ser. 6, LXIV, 1964, 347–362. (See also Whiteley and Braham.)
Branner, R. *La cathédrale de Bourges et sa place dans l'architecture gothique.* Paris and Bourges, 1962.

Brauer, H., and Wittkower, R. *Die Zeichnungen des Gianlorenzo Bernini,* 2 vols. Berlin, 1931.
Brice, G. *Description nouvelle de ce qu'il y a de plus remarquable dans la ville de Paris,* 2 vols. Paris, 1684. (Later editions here cited [titles vary]: Paris, 1687, 2 vols.; Paris, 1698, 2 vols.; Paris, 1713, 3 vols.)
Brinckmann, A. E. *Baukunst des 17. und 18. Jahrhunderts in den romanischen Ländern,* 4th ed., 2 vols. Berlin-Neubabelsberg, 1919.
Brönner, W. D., *Blondel-Perrault: Zur Architekturtheorie des 17. Jahrhunderts in Frankreich,* publ. diss., University of Bonn, 1972.
[Brown University, Department of Art]. *The Origins of the Italian Veduta,* exhib. cat. Providence, 1978.
Bruyn, C. de. *Voyages de Corneille Le Bruyn* . . . , 5 vols. The Hague, 1725 (also Paris, 1732, 5 vols.).
Bullet, P., *Architecture pratique.* . . . Paris, 1691 (new ed., Paris, 1768).
Burke, E. *A Philosophical Enquiry into the Origin of our Ideas of the Sublime and the Beautiful.* London, 1757.
Cassan. "La nymphe de Chanceaux, ou l'arrivée de la Seine au château de Marly." *Le Mercure galant,* May 1699, 130–154.
Catherinot, N. *Distiques sur le Louvre au Roy.* Bourges, 1672.
Céleste, R., "Les piliers de Tutelle." *Revue philomathique de Bordeaux et du Sud-Ouest,* IX, 1906, 1–22.
Chardon, H. *Amateurs d'art et collectionneurs manceaux. Les frères Fréart de Chantelou.* Le Mans, 1867.
Charles Le Brun, 1619–1690, peintre et dessinateur, exhib. cat. Versailles, 1963.
Chastel, A., and Pérouse de Montclos, J. M. "L'aménagement de l'accès oriental du Louvre," *MHF,* n.s., XII, 1966, 176–249.
Chatelain, U. V., *Le surintendant Nicolas Foucquet.* Paris, 1905.
Chenesseau, G. *Sainte-Croix d'Orléans,* 2 vols. and album. Paris, 1921.
Chennevières, P. de. *Notice historique et descriptive sur la Galerie d'Apollon au Louvre,* 2d ed. Paris, 1855.
Christ, Y. *Le Louvre et les Tuileries.* Paris, 1949.
Clément, P., ed. *Lettres, instructions, et mémoires de Colbert,* 7 vols. Paris, 1861–70.
Colbert, J. B. (See Clément.)
Collections de Louis XIV, dessins, albums, manuscrits, exhib. cat. Paris, 1977.
Condorcet, marquis de. *Oeuvres,* ed. A. Condorcet O'Connor and M. F. Arago, 12 vols. Paris, 1847–49.

Coope, R. *Salomon de Brosse and the Development of the Classical Style in French Architecture from 1565 to 1630.* University Park, Pa., and London, 1972.

Cordemoy, J. L. de. *Nouveau traité de toute l'architecture. . . .* Paris, 1706 (2d ed., Paris, 1714).

Cordey, J. "Le grand salon ovale de Vaux-le-Vicomte et sa décoration." *RAAM,* XLVI, 1924, 232–248.

———. *Vaux-le-Vicomte.* Paris, 1924.

Coulton, J. J. "Hermogenes," *Macmillan Encyclopedia of Architects,* ed. A. K. Placzek. New York and London, 1982, II, 359–361.

Cronström, D. (See Weigert and Hernmarck.)

D.J. "Louvre" (article). *Encyclopédie, ou dictionnaire raisonné des sciences, des arts et des métiers. . . .* Neufchâtel, 1765, IX, 706–707.

Daufresne, J. C. *Louvre & Tuileries: Architectures de papier.* Liège, 1987.

Delamair, P. A. *La pure verité,* Paris, Bibliothèque de l'Arsenal, MS 3054.

Depping, G. B., ed. *Correspondance administrative sous le règne de Louis XIV,* 4 vols. Paris, 1850–55.

Desgodets, A. *Les édifices antiques de Rome dessinés et mesurés très exactement.* Paris, 1682.

Deshairs, L. *Le château de Bercy.* Paris, [1911].

[Dezallier d'Argenville, A. N.]. *Voyage pittoresque de Paris . . . ,* 2d ed. Paris, 1752.

———. *Vies des fameux architectes depuis la renaissance des arts, avec la description de leurs ouvrages.* Paris, 1787.

Du Cerceau, J. A. *XXX exempla arcuum. . . .* Orléans, 1549.

Dumolin, M. *Études de topographie parisienne,* 3 vols. Paris, 1929–31.

Dussieux, L. et al., eds. *Mémoires inédits sur la vie et les ouvrages des membres de l'Académie royale de peinture et de sculpture,* 2 vols. Paris, 1854.

Erlande-Brandenburg, A. "Les fouilles du Louvre et les projets de Le Vau." *VU,* n.s., XXXI, 1964, 241–263; XXXII, 1965, 12–22.

———. "Un projet d'élévation pour la façade orientale du Louvre." *BSHAF,* 1965, 115–118.

Essays à la louange du roy. Paris, 1672.

Etienne, R. "Bordeaux." *Enciclopedia dell'arte antica, classica e orientale.* Rome, 1959, II, 138–139.

Euclid. *La perspective,* trans. R. Fréart de Chambray, Le Mans, 1663.

Feldmann, D. *Maison Lambert, Maison Hesselin und andere Bauten von Louis Le Vau (1612/13–1670) auf der Île Saint-Louis in Paris,* publ. diss., University of Hamburg, 1976.

Félibien, A. *Des principes de l'architecture, de la sculpture, de la peinture, et des autres arts qui en dependent.* Paris, 1676.

———. *Rapport de l'Académie d'Architecture sur la provenance et la qualité des pierres employées dans les anciens édifices de Paris et des environs,* BN, Manuscrits, MS fr. 12341 [1678]. Published in L. de Laborde, ed., "Rapport demandé par Colbert en 1678 à l'Académie d'architecture," *Revue générale de l'architecture et des travaux publics,* X, 1852, cols. 194–242, 273–293, 321–344, and in idem, *Mémoires et dissertations,* Paris, 1852, 151–290. Also published in *PV,* I, 168–249.

———. *Mémoires pour servir à l'histoire des maisons royales et bastimens de France,* ed. A. de Montaiglon. Paris, 1874 [1681].

———. *Entretiens sur les vies et sur les ouvrages des plus excellens peintres anciens et modernes,* 2d ed., 2 vols. Paris, 1696.

Ferrier-Caverivière, N. *L'image de Louis XIV dans la littérature française de 1660 à 1715.* Paris, 1981.

Fitchen, J. *The Construction of Gothic Cathedrals.* Oxford, 1961.

Fontaine, P.F.L. *Texte explicatif joint au n°ˢ du Journal des monuments de Paris. . . .* Paris, [1891].

Fontana, D. *Della trasportatione dell'obelisco vaticano,* ed. A. Carugo. Milan, 1978. (Facsimile of Rome, 1590 and Naples, 1604 eds.)

Fontenelle, B. de. *Oeuvres de Fontenelle . . . ,* 8 vols. Paris, 1790–92.

Foville, J. de, and Le Sourd, A. *Les châteaux de France.* Paris, n.d.

Francastel, P., ed. "Relation de la visite de Nicodème Tessin à Marly, Versailles, Clagny, Rueil, et Saint-Cloud en 1687." *RHV,* XXVIII, 1926, 149–167, 274–300. (See also Weigert.)

Frankl, P. *The Gothic: Literary Sources and Interpretations through Eight Centuries.* Princeton, 1960.

Fraschetti, S. *Il Bernini.* Milan, 1900.

Fréart de Chambray, R. *Parallèle de l'architecture antique et de la moderne.* Paris, 1650.

———. *Idée de la perfection de la peinture démonstrée par les principes de l'art.* Le Mans, 1662. (See also Euclid, Leonardo da Vinci, Palladio.)

Fréart de Chantelou, P. *Journal du voyage du Cavalier Bernin en France,* ed. L. Lalanne. Paris, 1885.

Germann, G. *Einführung in die Geschichte der Architekturtheorie.* Darmstadt, 1980.

Geymüller, H. de. *Les Du Cerceau.* Paris and London, 1887.

Gould, C. *Bernini in France: An Episode in Seventeenth-Century History.* Princeton, 1982.

Guerrini, L. " 'Las Incantadas' di Salonico." *Archaeologia classica,* XIII, 1961, 40–70.

Gurlitt, C. *Geschichte des Barockstiles, des Rococo und des Klassicismus in Belgien, Holland, Frankreich, England.* Stuttgart, 1888.

Haas, W. "Hölzerne und eiserne Anker an mittelalterlichen Kirchenbauten." *Architectura,* XIII, 1983, 136–151.

Hallays, A. *Les Perrault.* Paris, 1926.

Hautecoeur, L. "L'auteur de la colonnade du Louvre." *GBA,* ser. 5, IX, 1924, 151–168.

———. *La Bourgogne: L'architecture,* 3 vols. Paris and Brussels, 1927.

———. "Le Louvre de Pierre Lescot." *GBA,* ser. 5, XV, 1927, 199–218.

———. *Histoire du Louvre. Le château—le palais—le musée à nos jours, 1200–1928.* Paris, [1928].

———. *Histoire de l'architecture classique en France, III: Première moitié du XVIIIe siècle, le style Louis XV.* Paris, 1950.

Heawood, E. *Watermarks, Mainly of the 17th and 18th Centuries.* Hilversum, 1950.

Hedin, T. *The Sculpture of Gaspard and Balthazard Marsy.* Columbia, Mo., 1983.

Henkel, M. D. "Illustrierte Ausgaben von Ovids Metamorphosen im XV., XVI., und XVII. Jahrhundert." In *Vorträge der Bibliothek Warburg, 1926–1927.* Leipzig, 1930, 58–144.

Hernandez, A. *Grundzüge einer Ideengeschichte der französischen Architekturtheorie von 1560–1800,* publ. diss., University of Basel, 1972.

Herrmann, W. *Laugier and Eighteenth-Century French Theory.* London, 1962.

Hesse, M. *Von der Nachgotik zur Neugotik.* Frankfurt-am-Main, 1984.

Hillairet, J. *Dictionnaire historique des rues de Paris,* 2d ed., 2 vols. Paris, 1963.

Hubala, E. *Die Kunst des 17. Jahrhunderts* (Propyläen Kunstgeschichte 9). Berlin, 1970.

Huygens, C. *Oeuvres complètes de Christiaan Huygens,* 22 vols. The Hague, 1888–1950.

Jal, A. *Dictionnaire critique de biographie et d'histoire,* 2d ed. Paris, 1872.

Jestaz, B. "Le Trianon de Marbre ou Louis XIV architecte." *GBA,* ser. 6, LXXIV, 1969, 259–286.

Josephson, R. "Quelques dessins de Claude Perrault pour le Louvre." *GBA,* ser. 5, XVI, 1927, 171–192.

———. "Le monument du triomphe pour le Louvre: Un projet de Charles Le Brun retrouvé." *RAAM,* LIII, 1928, 21–34.

———. *L'architecte de Charles XII, Nicodème Tessin.* Paris and Brussels, 1930.

———. *Kungarnas Paris.* Stockholm, 1943.

———. *Barocken,* 2d ed. Stockholm, 1967.

Jouin, H. *Charles Le Brun et les arts sous Louis XIV.* Paris, 1889.

Jullian, C. *Histoire de Bordeaux depuis les origines jusqu'en 1895.* Bordeaux, 1895.

Kalnein, W. Graf. Review of A. Laprade, *François d'Orbay, architecte de Louis XIV,* Paris, 1960. In *ZfK,* XXV, 1962, 184–190.

Knabe, P. E. *Schlüsselbegriffe des kunsttheoretischen Denkens in Frankreich von der Spätklassik bis zum Ende der Aufklärung.* Düsseldorf, 1972.

Konvitz, J. F. "Grandeur in French City Planning under Louis XIV: Rochefort and Marseille." *Journal of Urban History,* II, 1975, 3–42.

———. *Cities & the Sea: Port City Planning in Early Modern Europe.* Baltimore and London, 1978.

Kortum, H. *Charles Perrault und Nicolas Boileau.* Berlin, 1966.

Krause, E. *Die Mythen-Darstellungen in der venezianischen Ovidausgabe von 1497.* Würzburg, 1926.

Kubler, G. *Building the Escorial.* Princeton, 1982.

[La Font de Saint-Yenne]. *Remerciment des habitans de la ville de Paris à Sa Majesté, au sujet de l'achevement du Louvre.* Paris, 1749.

———. *L'ombre du grand Colbert, le Louvre, & la ville de Paris, dialogue. . . .* The Hague, 1749 (new ed., Paris, 1752).

[———]. *Le génie du Louvre aux Champs Élisées. Dialogue entre le Louvre, la ville de Paris, l'ombre de Colbert, & Perrault.* [Paris], 1756.

Lambeau, L. *Bercy.* Paris, 1910.

Lambert, C. F. *Histoire littéraire du règne de Louis XIV.* Paris, 1751.

Lange, L. "La grotte de Thétis et le premier Versailles de Louis XIV." *Art de France,* I, 1961, 133–148.

Langenskiöld, E. "Louvren, Tuilerierna och Versailles: Slottens byggnadshistoria i belysning av ritningar i Cronstedtsamlingen på Nationalmuseum." *Nationalmusei Årsbok,* 1942–43, 106–142.

———, and C. D. Moselius. *Arkitekturritningar, planer och teckningar ur Carl Johan Cronstedts Fullerösamling,* exhib. cat. Stockholm, 1942.

Langner, J. "Zum Entwurf der französischen Ordnung von Le Brun." In *Kunstgeschichtliche Studien für Kurt Bauch zum 70. Geburtstag von seinen Schülern.* Berlin, 1967, 233–240.

Laprade, A. "François d'Orbay (1634–1697)." *BSHAF,* 1953, 85–95.

Laugier, M. A. *Essai sur l'architecture*. Paris, 1753.

――――. *Observations sur l'architecture*. The Hague, 1765.

Le Comte, F. *Cabinet des singularitez d'architecture, peinture, sculpture et gravure*, 3 vols. Paris, 1699–1700.

Legrand, J. G., and C. P. Landon. *Description de Paris et de ses édifices . . .* , 2 vols. Paris, 1809.

[Leibniz, Gottfried Wilhelm, Baron von]. "Le Louvre. Plans d'achèvement. Pyramide triomphale de Perrault. Fragment inédit de Leibniz." *Journal de l'instruction publique et des cultes*, XXVI, 1857, 235–241. [1676].

Le Maire, C. *Paris ancien et nouveau*, 3 vols. Paris, 1685.

Leonardo da Vinci. *Traité de la peinture*, trans. R. Fréart de Chambray. Paris, 1651.

Le Rouge, G. L. *Les curiositez de Paris, de Versailles, de Marly, de Vincennes, de S. Cloud, et des environs*. Paris, 1716.

Leroy, J. D. *Histoire de la disposition et des formes différentes que les chrétiens ont données à leurs temples. . . .* Paris, 1764.

Lewis, W. H. *Levantine Adventurer: The Travels and Missions of the Chevalier d'Arvieux, 1653–1697*. London, 1962.

Lister, M. *Voyage de Lister à Paris en MDCXCVIII*. Paris, 1873.

Lossky, B. *The National Museum of the Château de Fontainebleau*. Paris, 1971.

Lothe, J. "Images et monarchie: Les thèses gravées de François de Poilly." *Nouvelles de l'estampe*, no. 29, September–October, 1976, 6–12.

Louis XIV. *Mémoires for the Instruction of the Dauphin*, trans. and ed. P. Sonnino. New York, 1970.

Le Louvre et son quartier: 800 ans d'histoire architecturale, exhib. cat. Paris, 1982.

Lyttelton, M. *Baroque Architecture in Classical Antiquity*. London, 1974.

Manesson-Mallet, A. *Description de l'univers . . .* , 5 vols. Frankfurt-am-Main, 1685–86.

Marie, A. *Naissance de Versailles: Le château. Les jardins*, 2 vols. Paris, 1968.

Marot, J. *L'architecture françoise*. Paris, n.d. ("*Le Grand Marot*").

Mazerolle, F. "Réfection des ponts de l'Isle-Adam (28 juillet 1663–8 janvier 1666)." *BSHP*, XXIII, 1896, 124–128.

Menestrier, C. F. *Histoire du roy Louis le Grand par les médailles . . .* , new ed. Paris, 1691.

――――. *Histoire du règne de Louis le Grand par les médailles . . .* , new ed. Paris, 1700.

Mérot, A. "Décors pour le Louvre de Louis XIV: La mythologie politique à la fin de la Fronde (1653–1660)." In *La monarchie absolutiste et l'histoire en France*. Paris, 1987, I, 113–137.

――――. *Eustache Le Sueur (1616–1655)*, Paris, 1987.

Michaud, C. "François Sublet de Noyers, Superintendant des bâtiments de France." *Revue historique*, CCXLI, 1969, 327–364.

Middleton, R. "The Abbé de Cordemoy and the Graeco-Gothic Ideal: A Prelude to Romantic Classicism." *JWCI*, XXV, 1962, 278–320.

――――. "The Abbé de Cordemoy and the Graeco-Gothic Ideal, Part II." *JWCI*, XXVI, 1963, 90–123.

――――. "Architects as Engineers: The Iron Reinforcement of Entablatures in Eighteenth-Century France." *AA Files*, no. 9, Summer 1985, 54–64.

[Milizia, F.]. *Le vite de' piu celebri architetti. . . .* Rome, 1768.

Monconys, B. de. *Journal des voyages . . .* , 3 vols. Lyon, 1665–66.

Monnier, G. "Dessins inédits pour la Colonnade du Louvre." *MHF*, n.s., 1972, no. 3–4, 130–137.

[――――]. *Dessins d'architecture du XVe au XIXe siècle dans les collections du Musée du Louvre*. Paris, 1972.

Montagu, J. "The Early Ceiling Decorations of Charles Le Brun." *BurlM*, CV, 1963, 395–408.

Montfaucon, B. de. *L'antiquité expliquée et représentée en figures*, 2d ed., 10 vols. Paris, 1722.

Moreri, L. *Le grand dictionnaire historique . . .* , new ed., 4 vols. Amsterdam and The Hague, 1722.

Nativelle, P. *Nouveau traité d'architecture. . . .* Paris, 1729.

Nivelon, C. *Vie de Charles Le Brun & description détaillée de ses ouvrages*, BN, Manuscrits, MS fr. 12987.

Noehles, K. "Die Louvre-Projekte von Pietro da Cortona und Carlo Rainaldi." *ZfK*, XXIV, 1961, 40–74.

Nyberg, D. "*La sainte Antiquité*: Focus of an Eighteenth-Century Debate." In D. Fraser et al., eds., *Essays in the History of Architecture Presented to Rudolf Wittkower*. London, 1967, 159–169.

Olry de Loriande, C. *Le heros tres-chrestien*. Paris, 1669.

――――. *Le superbe dessein du Louvre. Dedié a Monseigneur Colbert*. Paris, 1670.

Omont, H. *Missions archéologiques françaises en Orient aux XVIIe et XVIIIe siècles*, 2 vols. Paris, 1902.

Orme, P. de l'. *Nouvelles inventions pour bien bastir et à petits fraiz. . . .* Paris, 1561.

Ovid. *Les XV. livres de la Metamorphose d'Ovide. . . .* Paris, 1539.

――――. *Les Métamorphoses d'Ovide . . .* , trans. P. du Ryer. Paris, 1655.

———. *Metamorphoses* (Loeb Classical Library), 2d ed., 2 vols., trans. F. J. Miller. Cambridge, Mass. and London, 1921.

Palladio, A. *Les quatre livres d'architecture d'André Palladio*, trans. R. Fréart de Chambray. Paris, 1650.

[Paris, Ministère de la Culture]. *Colbert, 1619–1683*, exhib. cat. Paris, 1983.

[Paris, Musée du Louvre, Cabinet des Dessins]. *Le Brun à Versailles*. Paris, 1985.

Patte, P. *Monumens érigés en France à la gloire de Louis XV*. . . . Paris, 1765.

———. *Mémoires sur les objets les plus importans de l'architecture*. Paris, 1769. (See also Blondel, J. F.)

Perdrizet, P. "Les dossiers de P. J. Mariette sur Ba'albek et Palmyre." *Revue des études anciennes*, III, 1901, 225–264.

Pérouse de Montclos, J. M. "Le sixième ordre d'architecture, ou la pratique des ordres suivant les nations." *JSAH*, XXXVI, 1977, 223–240.

Perrault, Ch. *La peinture. Poëme*. Paris, 1668.

———. *Parallèle des anciens et des modernes* . . . , 4 vols. Paris, 1688–97.

———. *Le cabinet des beaux-arts*. . . . Paris, 1690.

———. *Les hommes illustres qui ont paru en France pendant ce siècle*, 2 vols. Paris, 1696–1700.

———. *Mémoires de Charles Perrault* . . . , ed. P. Patte. Avignon, 1759 [ca. 1700].

———. *Mémoires de ma vie*, ed. P. Bonnefon. Paris, 1909 [ca. 1700].

Perrault, Cl. *Description anatomique d'un caméléon, d'un castor, d'un dromedaire, d'un ours et d'une gazelle*. Paris, 1669.

———. *Voyage à Bordeaux (1669)*, ed. P. Bonnefon. Paris, 1909.

———. *Abrégé des dix livres d'architecture de Vitruve*. Paris, 1674.

———. *Essais de physique* . . . , 4 vols. Paris, 1680–88.

———. *Ordonnance des cinq espèces de colonnes selon la méthode des anciens*. Paris, 1683.

———. *Oeuvres diverses de physique et de mechanique*, 2 vols. Leiden, 1721.

Persepolis illustrata. . . . London, 1739.

Pesco, D. del. *Il Louvre di Bernini nella Francia di Luigi XIV*. Naples, 1984.

Petzet, M. "Un projet des Perrault pour l'Église Sainte-Geneviève à Paris." *BMon*, CXV, 1957, 81–96.

———. "Quelques projets inédits pour la chapelle de Versailles." *Art de France*, I, 1961, 315–319.

———. "Entwürfe zur Louvre-Kolonnade." *Neue Zürcher Zeitung*, October 4, 1964 (Beilage: "Literatur und Kunst," 5).

———. "Entwürfe zur Louvre-Kolonnade." In *Stil und Überlieferung in der Kunst des Abendlandes: Akten des 21. Internationalen Kongresses für Kunstgeschichte in Bonn 1964*. Berlin, 1967, III, 159–163.

———. "Claude Perrault als Architekt des Pariser Observatoriums." *ZfK*, XXX, 1967, 1–54.

———. "Das Triumphbogenmonument für Ludwig XIV. auf der Place du Trône." *ZfK*, XLV, 1982, 145–194.

———. "Der Obelisk des Sonnenkönigs: Ein Projekt Claude Perraults von 1666." *ZfK*, XLVII, 1984, 439–464.

Picon, A. *Claude Perrault, 1613–1688, ou la curiosité d'un classique*. Paris, 1988.

Piganiol de La Force, J. A. *Nouvelle description de la France*, 2d ed., 7 vols. Paris, 1722.

———. *Description de Paris* . . . , 8 vols. Paris, 1742 (also Paris, 1765, 10 vols.).

Pigler, A. *Barockthemen*, 2d ed., 3 vols. Budapest, 1974.

Portoghesi, P. "Gli architetti italiani per il Louvre." In *Saggi di storia dell'architettura in onore del professor Vincenzo Fasolo* (Quaderni dello Istituto di storia dell'architettura, ser. 6–8, fascs. 31–48). Rome, 1961, 243–268.

Pradel, A. du. (See Blegny, N. de.)

Rambaud, M. "Nouvelles recherches sur Saint-Louis-en-l'Île." *Cahiers de la rotonde*, V, 1982, 17–41.

Robert, C. *Die antiken Sarkophag-Reliefs*, 4 vols. Berlin, 1890–1952.

Roland-Michel, M. "The Clearance of the Colonnade of the Louvre: A Study Arising from a Painting by De Machy." *BurlM*, CXX, September 1978, i–vi (Supplement).

———. "Soufflot urbaniste et le dégagement de la colonnade du Louvre." In *Soufflot et l'architecture des lumières*. Paris, 1980, 54–67.

Rondelet, J. B. *Traité théorique et pratique de l'art de bâtir*, 7 vols. Paris, 1802–17 (and later eds.).

Rondorf, D. *Der Ballsaal im Schloss Fontainebleau: Zur Stilgeschichte Primaticcios in Frankreich*, publ. diss., University of Bonn, 1967.

Rose, H. *Spätbarock*. Munich, 1922.

Rosenberg, P. "Quelques dessins inédits de Romanelli préparatoires à la décoration du Louvre." *BSHAF*, 1974, 51–53.

Rosenberg Henderson, N. "Le Sueur's Allegory of Magnificence." *BurlM*, CXII, 1970, 213–217.

Rosenfeld, M. N. *Sebastiano Serlio on Domestic Architecture*. Cambridge, Mass., and London, 1978.

Rouchès, G., ed. *Inventaire des lettres et papiers manuscrits de Gaspare, Carlo et Lodovico Vigarani*. . . . Paris, 1913.

Röver, A. *Bienséance: Zur ästhetischen Situation im Ancien Régime, dargestellt an Beispielen der Pariser Privatarchitektur.* New York and Hildesheim, 1977.

Saddy, P. "A 'Construct' of Modernity: The Reinforced Lintel." *Daidalos*, no. 8, June 15, 1983, 54–65.

[Saint-Yves]. *Observations sur les arts.* . . . Leiden, 1748.

Sainte Fare Garnot, N. de. *Le décor des Tuileries sous le règne de Louis XIV.* Paris, 1988.

Saisselin, R. G. *The Rule of Reason and the Ruses of the Heart: A Philosophical Dictionary of Classical French Criticism, Critics, and Aesthetic Issues.* Cleveland and London, 1970.

Salet, F. "Le Vau et le Bernin au Louvre." *BMon*, CXXIII, 1965, 144–148.

Saugrain, C. M. *Dictionnaire universel de la France* . . . , 3 vols. Paris, 1726.

Sauval, H. *Histoire et recherches des antiquités de la ville de Paris*, 3 vols. Paris, 1724.

Sauvel, T. "Les auteurs de la colonnade du Louvre." *BMon*, CXXII, 1964, 323–347.

Savot, L. *L'architecture françoise des bastimens particuliers.* Paris, 1624.

———. *L'architecture françoise des bastimens particuliers*, ed. F. Blondel. Paris, 1673 (also 1685).

Saxl, F., and H. Meier. *Verzeichnis astrologischer und mythologischer illustrierer Handschriften des lateinischen Mittelalters, 3: Handschriften in englischen Bibliotheken,* 2 vols. London, 1953.

Schnapper, A. "Colonna et la 'quadratura' en France à l'époque de Louis XIV." *BSHAF*, 1966, 65–97.

Schubring, P. *Cassoni,* 2 vols. Leipzig, 1915.

Scudéry, M. de. *Clélie,* 10 vols. Paris, 1654–61.

Semenzato, C. *The Rotonda of Andrea Palladio.* University Park, Pa., and London, 1968.

Souchal, F. *French Sculptors of the 17th and 18th Centuries, I: The Reign of Louis XIV,* 3 vols. Oxford, 1977–87.

Soulange-Bodin, H. "Le château de Sucy-en-Brie." *BSHAF*, 1925, 32–36.

Szambien, W. "Bienséance, convenance et caractère." *Les cahiers de la recherche architecturale,* no. 18, 1985, 38–43.

———. *Symétrie, goût, caractère: Théorie et terminologie de l'architecture à l'âge classique, 1550–1800.* Paris, 1986.

Tadgell, C. *Ange-Jacques Gabriel.* London, 1978.

———. "Claude Perrault, François Le Vau and the Louvre Colonnade." *BurlM*, CXXII, 1980, 326–337.

Tempesta, A. *Metamorphoseon.* Amsterdam, [1606?].

Tessin the Younger, N. *Nicodemus Tessin D.Y.:s Studieresor* . . . , Osvald Sirén, ed. Stockholm, 1914. (See also Francastel, Weigert, and Weigert and Hernmarck.)

Teyssèdre, B. *L'art au siècle de Louis XIV.* Paris, 1967.

Thiéry L. V. *Almanach du voyageur à Paris* . . . *année 1784.* Paris, [1783].

Tooth, C. "The Private Houses of Louis Le Vau," diss., University of London, 1961.

Trouvelot, J. "Le dégagement des fossés de la Colonnade du Louvre." *MHF*, n.s., XIII, 1967, 12–54.

Vachon, M. *Le Louvre et les Tuileries.* Lyon, 1926.

Valle, P. de. *Les fameux voyages* . . . , 2 vols. Paris, 1670.

Vermaseren, M. J. *Corpus inscriptionum et monumentorum religionis mithriacae,* 2 vols. The Hague, 1956–60.

Vertron, C.C.G. de. *Le nouveau Pantheon.* . . . Paris, 1686.

Vigarani Family. (See Rouchès.)

Viollet-le-Duc, E. E. *Dictionnaire raisonné de l'architecture française du XIe au XVIe siècle,* 10 vols. Paris, 1854–68.

Vitet, L. "Le Louvre." *Revue contemporaine,* I, no. 3, 1852, 363–446.

———. *Le Louvre et le nouveau Louvre,* new ed. Paris, 1882.

Vitruvius. *Di Lucio Vitruvio Pollione de architectura libri dece* . . . , trans. C. Cesariano. Como, 1521.

———. *M. L. Vitruvio Pollione de architectura* . . . , trans. Durantino. Venice, 1524.

———. *Architettura con il suo commento et figure Vetruvio,* trans. G. B. Caporali. Perugia, 1536.

———. *Architecture ou art de bien bastir,* trans. J. Martin. Paris, 1547.

———. *Vitruvius teutsch* . . . , trans. W. Ryff. Nuremberg, 1548.

———. *I dieci libri dell'architettura di M. Vitruvio,* trans. D. Barbaro. Venice, 1556.

———. *On Architecture* (Loeb Classical Library), trans. F. Granger, 2 vols. Cambridge, Mass., and London, 1955.

———. *The Ten Books on Architecture,* trans. M. H. Morgan. New York, 1960.

Vivanti, C. "Henri IV, the Gallic Hercules." *JWCI*, XXX, 1967, 176–197.

Voltaire, F.M.A. de. *Le siècle de Louis XIV,* 2 vols. Berlin, 1751 (also London, 1752, 2 vols.).

[Walton, G., et al.]. *Versailles à Stockholm,* exhib. cat. Stockholm, 1985.

Weber, G. "Theaterarchitektur am Hofe von Louis XIV." *Bollettino del Centro internazionale di studi di architettura Andrea Palladio,* XVII, 1975, 259–281.

Weigert, R. A., ed. "Notes de Nicodème Tessin le Jeune relative à son séjour à Paris en 1687." *BSHAF,* 1932, 220–279.

———, and C. Hernmarck, eds. *Les relations artistiques entre la France et la Suède 1693–1718: Nicodème Tessin le jeune et Daniel Cronström, correspondance (extraits).* Stockholm, 1964.

Whiteley, M., and A. Braham. "Louis Le Vau's Projects for the Louvre and the Colonnade—I." *GBA,* ser. 6, LXIV, 1964, 285–296. (See also Braham and Whiteley.)

———. "Les soubassements de l'aile orientale du Louvre." *RA,* I, no. 4, 1969, 30–43.

Wiebenson, D. *Sources of Greek Revival Architecture.* London, 1969.

Wiegand, T., ed. *Baalbek,* 2 vols. Berlin and Leipzig, 1921–23.

———. *Palmyra: Ergebnisse der Expeditionen von 1902 und 1917,* 2 vols. and album. Berlin, 1932.

Wilcox, R. P. *Timber and Iron Reinforcement in Early Buildings* (Society of Antiquaries of London, Occasional Paper, n.s., II). London, 1981.

Wildenstein, D. "Les oeuvres de Charles Le Brun d'après les gravures de son temps." *GBA,* ser. 6, LXVI, 1965, 1–58.

Wolf, C. *Histoire de l'Observatoire de Paris de sa fondation à 1793.* Paris, 1902.

Wood, R. *The Ruins of Palmyra, otherwise Tedmor, in the Desert.* London, 1753.

———. *The Ruins of Balbec, otherwise Heliopolis in Coelosyria.* London, 1757.

———. *The Ruins of Palmyra and Balbec.* London, 1827.

INDEX

Abalipas, 137
Abbate, Nicolò dell', 4 n. 4
Abundance (personification), 15 n. 22, 48
Académie Française (Paris), 168
Académie Royale d'Architecture (Paris), 18, 52f., 59, 65, 70 n. 11, 76, 76 n. 1, 78 n. 7, 84, 85 n. 3, 92, 95, 96, 103 n. 15, 110 n. 9, 145, 146, 159, 163, 166f., 170, 172, 190–91, 203, 212 n. 149
Académie Royale de Peinture et de Sculpture (Paris), 9
Académie Royale des Sciences (Paris), 100, 145, 161, 164, 197
Adelcrantz, Göran Josuae, 166
Airault, Jean, 113 [43.]
Alexander the Great, 134, 139
Alexandria, Lighthouse, 134
Algarotti, Francesco, 208–9
Amboise, Château, 81 n. 11 (Chapel of Saint Hubert), 100
Ancy-le-Franc, Château, 211 n. 119
Anne of Austria, 11
Antaeus, 15 n. 22
Antoine, Pierre Joseph, 207
Antonini, Annibale, 171
Apollo, 1f., 15, 29, 40, 48 n. 3, 63, 86, 88, 92, 107, 109 n. 38, 135, 137, 139, Figs. 1–4
Argos, 105
  Temple of Bacchus, 209 n. 26
Argus, 141 [29.]
Aristarchus of Samothrace, 179
Aristotle, 139
Armagnac, Cardinal Georges d', 147
Armida, 135
Arnauld, Antoine, 83, 161
Artemisia of Caria, 134
Arvieux, Laurent d', 105f.
Athena, 92
Athens
  Hephestaion (Temple of Theseus), 108 n. 16
  Parthenon, 108 n. 16
Audran, Gérard, 86, Figs. 7, 8
Augustus, 101, 103, 162, 174

Ausonius, 100, 101
Autumn (personification), 3
Aviler, Charles Augustin d', 58 n. 2, 70 n. 11, 95

Baalbek, 104f., Figs. 127–29, 136, 137
  Propylon, 104–6, Figs. 138–41
  Temple of Bacchus, 105–7, 108 n. 10, Figs. 130–35
  Temple of Jupiter, 105
Babel, Tower, 134
Babylon, Palace of Nebuchadnezzar, 209 n. 31
Bacchus, 15 n. 22, 137
Bachaumont, Louis Petit de, 3, 173
Barbillon, 115 [72.]
Baron, Laurens, 113 [39.]
Basnage, Henri, 159, 214 n. 200
Baur, Johann Wilhelm, 4, Fig. 3
Beaumont-la-Ferrière, factory, 72
Belleville, 115 [73.]
Benedetti, Elpidio, 20
Benjamin of Tudela, 209 n. 31
Bérain, Jean, 212 n. 156
Bercy, Château, 16, 18
Berger, 116 [95.]
Bergeron, Antoine, 31, 57, 111 [3.], [4.], [8.], 112 [10.], [27.], 113 [31.], [32.], 114 [54.], 115 [78.], 116 [93.], 118 [124.], [137.], 119 [141.], [147.]
Bernini, Gianlorenzo, 6, 7, 20, 21 n. 51, 23, 25–27, 28 n. 8, 30 n. 12, 36–38, 41 n. 50, 51, 84, 125, 135, 141 [44.], 145, 159, 160–62, 167, 169, 173–76, 179, 197, 198, 204, 205, 207, Figs. 40, 41
Bignon, François, 210 n. 49, Fig. 23
Billon, Anne, 112 [12.], [13.], [28.]
Blois, Château, 100
Blondel, François, 18 n. 45, 55–56, 59 n. 4, 71, 76, 84, 85, 94f., 110, 144, 147f., 156, 163, 191, 201, 203–5
Blondel, Jacques François, 21, 26, 44, 44 n. 61, 48, 49, 54, 55 n. 17, 61 n. 12, 63 n. 24,

70 n. 11, 75, 76f., 80, 93, 104, 107, 173, 176, 180f., 203f., 205, Figs. 82, 90, 91, 103, 106
Blondel, Jean, 112 [15.]
Boffrand, Germain, 179, 190, 214 n. 200
Boileau-Despréaux, Nicolas, 83, 161, 170, 173, 198, 205, 208, 214 n. 200
Bongars, 115 [77.]
Bonneval, Comtesse de, 106
Bonnivet, Château, 100
Bordeaux
  Bourse, 100
  Cathedral of Saint-André, 100
  Château Trompette, 100
  Citadelle, 101, 103
  Hôtel de Ville, 100, 102
  Palais des Plaideurs, 100
  Piliers de Tutelle, 99f., 162, Figs. 123–25
  Porte Basse, 162
Boubert, 116 [95.]
Boudin, Simon, 113 [43.]
Bourdon, Sébastien, 191
Bourges, Cathedral, 69 n. 8
Bouverie, John, 104
Bramante, Donato, 147, 157
Branche, Jean, 113 [43.]
Bréau, Pierre, 74, 146
Briant, Jean, 113 [49.]
Briault, 115 [72.]
Brice, Germain, 15 / f., 158f., 163f., 167, 169
Brie, 116 [86.]
Brion, Simon, 112 [26.]
Brosse, Salomon de, 10, 95, 97, 148, 157, 191, 193, 199
Bullet, Pierre, 199
Burke, Edmund, 214 n. 199
Butay, Suzanne, 5 n. 10

Caffiéri, Philippe, 112 [16.], 114 [60.], 117 [120.], 118 [132.], [138], 119 [144], [150], 213 n. 180
Cairo, Citadel, 134
Caius Julius Vindex, 102
Callimachus, 178

Calliope, 137
Calvas, 114 [50.]
Campra, André, 191
Canal du Midi, 174
Candiani, 20, 23, 30 n. 12
Carcavy, Pierre de, 108 n. 17
Cartellier, Pierre, 216 n. 230
Cassan, 164–65
Catherinot, Nicolas, 140f.
Century (personification), 3, 6
Cerberus, 15 n. 22
Chambord, Château, 100
Chamois, Charles, 70–72, 132, 133
Champion, Denis, 113 [39.]
Chapelain, Jean, 14 n. 20, 145
Charité, Mathieu, 112 [15.]
Charpentier, 115 [68.]
Charpentier, François, 145
Charuel, 119 [155.], [156.]
Chaumeton, Étienne, 13 [46.]
Chauveau, François, 88
Chaveton, 113 [44.]
Chersiphron, 99 n. 29, 212 n. 150
Choisy, Château, 212 n. 153
Clagny, Château, 211 n. 106
Claudius, 101
Cleopatra, 137
Cliquin, Poncelet, 59, 115 [68.], 116 [101.], 117 [111.], 118 [127.], 120 [160.], 144, 164, 168, 169
Clymene, 3
Cochin, Noël, 23 n. 59, Fig. 39
Colbert, Jean Baptiste, 6, 9, 13, 14, 17, 19–22, 22 n. 56, 25f., 54, 55, 59 n. 6, 61, 63, 65, 72 n. 17, 73, 90, 91, 98, 105, 109 n. 45, 110, 123–25, 131–34, 142 [70.], 145–47, 159, 160, 162, 165, 166, 170, 172, 174f., 179, 182, 189, 197, 198, 204, 207, 212 n. 156, 213 n. 158, 214 n. 209
Colbert, Jean Baptiste, Marquis de Seignelay, 88, Fig. 60
Colbert, Édouard, Marquis de Villacerf, 215 n. 200
Columns of Hercules, 134, 136
Condorcet, Marquis de, 205
Constantine, 134
Constantinople, Hagia Sophia, 134
Copin, Nicolle, 118 [135.]
Coquart, Louis, 113 [44.]
Cordemoy, Jean Louis de, 81–82, 167
Corneille, Pierre, 171
Cortona, Pietro da, 20, 23, 30 n. 12
Costé, Simon du, 115 [80.], [81.], [82.]
Cottart, Pierre, 16 n. 27, 21 n. 51, 22, 30 n. 12, 70, 119 [145.], 132–33, Fig. 38
Couet, 114 [66.], 119 [142.]

Courtois, 117 [121.]
Coysevox, Antoine, 112 [20.], 191
Croesus, 137
Cronström, Daniel, 34 n. 23, 90, 161, 162
Cupid, 137–38

Dambroiseville, 115 [79.]
Dawkins, James, 104
Dawn (personification), 5, 139
Day (personification), 3, 6
De Baure, 116 [98.]
Delamair, Pierre Alexis, 169
De(s) Monceaux, 105f., Fig. 135
Demy, 113 [46.]
Desgodets, Antoine, 76, 77, 147, 163, 166, Figs. 57, 58
Desgots, Claude, 179, 190
Deslauriers, 113 [43.]
Dezallier d'Argenville, Antoine Nicolas, 173, 207
Diana, 98, 159
Dieburg, Mithraeum, 4 n. 4
Dioscurii, 29, 92
Dolivar, Jean, 212 n. 156
Dorus, 134
Doublet, Philips, 144, 146–47
Doyart, Étienne, 74, 113 [33.], [34.], 114 [57.], [58.], 116 [83.], [102.], 118 [125.]
Drusus, 101
Dubreuil, Toussaint, 10, Fig. 20
Du Cerceau, Jacques Androuet I, 101, 148, 157, Fig. 9
Du Cerceau, Jacques Androuet II, 211 n. 118
Du Cerceau, Jean Androuet, 40 n. 49
Du Corroy, 117 [122.]
Dumont, 113 [46.]
Durant, 113 [46.]
Durant, Isaac, 14 n. 21, Fig. 28
Duval, 70, 76, 132

Ephesus, Temple of Diana, 98, 134, 159
Erinys, 140 [7.]
Errard, Charles, 6 n. 15
Escorial, 134, 140 [19.]
Este, Cardinal Rinaldo d', 124
Euclid, 36

Fame (personification), 92, 184
Félibien, André, 58 n. 2, 66 n. 4, 84, 85, 85 n. 3, 110, 145, 159
Fer, Nicolas de, 54, Fig. 122
Fleury, 117 [108.], [113.]
Flora, 140
Fontaine, P.F.L., 59 n. 8, 62
Fontainebleau, Château, 4 n. 4 (Salle de Bal), 10, Fig. 20 (Galerie des Cerfs)

Fontana, Domenico, 59, 164, 168
Fontenay-le-Comte, 100
Fontenelle, Bernard de, 159
Fouquet, Nicolas, 5, 6, 86
Fourcroy, Bonaventure de, 158
Four Elements, 6
Fournier, 118 [139.]
France (personification), 48
Francoeur, Vincent, 115 [81.]
François I, King of France, 197
Fréart de Chambray, Roland, 29 n. 10, 35f., 42–45, 60 n. 10, 85, 209 n. 3
Fréart de Chantelou, Paul, 6, 36–38
Frézier, Amédée François, 167
Friolet, Étienne, 116 [94.]
Fronde, 11, 42 n. 51

Gabriel, Ange Jacques, 62, 92
Galen, 212–13 n. 158
Gallois, Julien, 113 [41.]
Gamard (Jamard), Thomas, 61, 70, 132
Ganymede, 137
Girardon, François, 61 n. 11, 199
Gissey, Henri de, 210 n. 71
Gittard, Daniel, 70, 81, 132
Gordier, Jean, 115 [73.]
Goujon, 118 [140.]
Goujon, Jean, 59 n. 8, 148, 157
Gresset, Étienne, 112 [23.]
Grimaldi, Giovanni Francesco, 11
Grou, 117 [115.], [116.]
Guillaume, Pierre, 113 [41.]
Guillemin, Simonne, 112 [22.]
Guillot-Aubry, Claude, 92, 191

Halicarnassus, Mausoleum, 209 n. 29
Halifax, William, 105
Hardouin-Mansart, Jules, 81, 162, 211 n. 106
Hayes, Jean des, 116 [92.]
Hebert, 117 [106.]
Henri II, King of France, 202
Henri IV, King of France, 135, 136, 148
Henriet, Israël, Fig. 14
Henrietta Maria, 109 n. 24
Hercules, 5, 15, 92
Hermogenes, 94, 96, 97, 143, 151, 152, 155–57
Hesselin, Louis, 17
Hippocrates, 174
Historia (personification), 11, Fig. 15
Homer, 176, 208
Houdin, Antoine Léonor, 12f., 18, 22, 30 n. 12, 85, 210 nn. 49, 81, Fig. 23
Hours (personifications), 3, 6, 136
Houzeau, Jacques, 117 [104.], 118 [131.], 139

Hurault, Jacques, 115 [74.]
Huygens, Christian, 58, 144, 146
Huygens, Lodewijk, 144
Hydra of Lerna, 15 n. 22

Isle-Adam, l', bridges, 17 n. 39

Jerusalem, Temple of Solomon, 134
Jombert, 119 [145.]
Joseph, 116 [99.]
Jourdain, Jean, 116 [89.]
Jubé, François, 116 [91.]
Julien[ne], François, 113 [45.], 116 [90.]
Jumeau, René, 115 [74.]
Jupiter, 5, 5 n. 13, 86, 139, 142 [56.], 156
Justice (personification), 15 n. 22
Justinian, 209 n. 40

Labacco, Antonio, 147, 157
La Baronnière, 116 [103.]
La Font de Saint-Yenne, 123, 171f., 173f., 189f.
La Grande, Simon, 118 [130.]
La Hyre, Laurent de, 4 n. 4
Laisné, 108 n. 17
Lambert, Claude François, 172–73
Lambert, Nicolas, 17
Langrand, 115 [72.]
La Planche, Sébastien François de, 36
La Rivière, Abbé de, 17
La Roche, 117 [109.], [119.]
La Rochelle, 100
La Taille, 115 [73.]
Laugier, Marc Antoine, 176, 192
Laury, 116 [86.]
Le Brun, Charles, 5f., 9, 10, 12, 13, 18, 24, 25f., 61, 62, 72, 73, 85–88, 92–93, 123, 124, 145, 146, 165, 166, 170, 171, 176, 180, 198, 207, Figs. 5–8, 60, 61, 93, 94
Le Clerc, Sébastien, 48, 49, 53, 59, 59 n. 6, 63, 184, 185, Figs. 86, 117, 119, 120
Le Comte, Florent, 165
Le Fouin, François, 114 [53.]
Le Gendre, Nicolas, 45, 113 [36.]
Legoux, Guillaume, 113 [48.]
Legrand, 114 [62.]
Le Grue, Jean, 112 [17.], 113 [35.], 114 [59.], [65.]
Le Hongre, Étienne, 45, 60 n. 11, 112 [21.], 114 [64.], 118 [133.]
Leibniz, Gottfried Wilhelm, Baron von, 27, 38, 73, 74, 84, 85, 109 n. 45, 145f.
Le Maire, C., 158

Le Ménestrel, Antoine, 115 [69.], [70.], [71.], [75.], [76.], 124
Lemercier, Jacques, 10, 11, 29, 34 n. 25, 43 n. 56, 44, 60, 61, 157, 191, 193, 199, Fig. 22
Lemnos, Greek Labyrinth, 134
Le Noir, 115 [79.]
Le Nôtre, André, 124
Le Pautre, Antoine, 12, 95, 211 n. 106
Le Pautre, Pierre, Fig. 124
Le Raincy, Château, 12
Leroy, Julien David, 191
Le Rouge, Georges Louis, 167
Le Roux, 118 [134.]
Lescot, Pierre, 10–12, 15 n. 23, 29, 32, 43, 51, 52, 57, 58 n. 1, 60–63, 79, 80, 148, 161, 204
Lespagnandelle, Mathieu, 112 [16.], 114 [60.], 117 [120.], 118 [132.], [138.], 119 [144.], [150.], [154.]
Le Sueur, Eustache, 4, 11, Figs. 4, 15
Le Tendre, Jean, 113 [45.]
Le Vau, François, 3, 13f., 16f., 20–22, 30 n. 12, 32, 34–35, 37, 41f., 74, 75, 77, 84, 85, 109, 125, 134, Figs. 24–32
Le Vau, Louis I, 16
Le Vau, Louis II, 3, 11f., 13, 14 n. 21, 16, 17 n. 33, 18 nn. 45, 46, 20, 22 n. 56, 24, 25f., 58 n. 1, 61, 72, 73, 78 n. 6, 83f., 87–93, 123, 124, 145, 146, 159, 161, 162, 164–71, 173, 176, 180, 189, 191, 193, 197–99, 203, 205, 207, 208, 212 n. 158, 214–15 n. 200, Figs. 17–19, 33–35, 59, 62–64, 73, 77, 92, 96–98, 107, 108
Liégeard, 114 [55.]
Lignières, Château, 16, 18
Lister, Martin, 164
Longinus, 214 n. 199
Louis II de Bourbon, Duc d'Enghien, Prince de Condé ("Le Grand Condé"), 146
Louis XIII, King of France, 10, 11
Louis XIV, King of France, passim
Louis XV, King of France, 64, 171
Louis, le Grand Dauphin, 136, 164
Lubin, 213 n. 158
Luçon, 100
Lully, Jean Baptiste, 191, 199
Lusignan, 100

Machy, Pierre Antoine de, 216 n. 230
Magnificence (personification), 11, Fig. 15

Maisons, Château, 212 n. 153
Mallet, 206
Mallet, Allain Manesson, 158
Malon, Charles Henri de, 16
Mansart, François, 22, 25, 30 n. 12, 95, 157, 191, 199, Fig. 36
Marchand, Paul, 116 [90.]
Marie-Thérèse, Queen of France, 136–38
Marigny, Marquis de, 191
Mark Antony, 210 n. 61
Marot, Jean, 17 n. 33, 22, 30 n. 12, 53–56, 63, 91, 105f., 184, 210 n. 88, Figs. 17, 18, 22, 37, 40, 88, 100, 128–34
Mars, 5, 134, 135, 138, 139, 140 [5.]
Marsyas, 137
Martin, Jean, 50
Massou, Benoît, 45, 113 [36.]
Mausolus of Caria, 209 n. 29
Mazarin, Cardinal Jules, 11, 197
Mazières, André, 31, 57, 111 [3.], [4.], [8.], 112 [10.], [27.], 113 [31.], [32.], 114 [54.], 115 [78.], 116 [93.], 118 [124.], [137.], 119 [141.], [147.]
Medina, Mosque of the Prophet, 209 n. 25
Ménestrier, Claude François, 166
Mercury, 86
Messalina, 101, 102
Métezeau, Louis, 148, 157, 211 n. 118
Meudon, Château, 12
Meusnier, Jean, 113 [42.]
Michelangelo, 147, 154, 157
Midas, 213 n. 158
Mignard, Nicolas, 29 n. 11
Milizia, Francesco, 193
Millet, Louis, 111 [5.], 112 [18.]
Minerva, 48 n. 3
Mithras, 4 n. 4
Modena, Duchess of, 124–25
Modène, Pierre, 118 [130.]
Molart, Michel, Fig. 85
Molière (Jean Baptiste Poquelin), 171
Monconys, Balthasar de, 105f., 109 n. 45, Fig. 127
Monpipaux, Château, 17
Montfaucon, Bernard de, 106, Fig. 135
Months (personifications), 3, 6
Montpensier, Duchesse de ("La Grande Mademoiselle"), 16, 17
Moreau-Desproux, Pierre Louis, 92
Morel, Louis, 118 [135.]
Moreri, Louis, 167
Morin, Pierre, 116 [86.]
Moscow, Cathedral of St. Basil, 210 n. 59

Mouton, 112 [11.], 116 [96.], [97.], 117 [118.], 118 [126.]
Muhammed, 134, 177
Muses, 15 n. 22, 210 n. 65
Myron, 142 [72.]

Nanking, Porcelain Pagoda, 137
Napoleon, 59 n. 8, 64
Nasses, 115 [79.]
Nativelle, Pierre, 169
Nemean Lion, 15 n. 22
Niobids, 29, 92
Niort, 100
Nivelon, Claude, 5
Noizet, 114 [50.]
Nouveau, Jérôme de, 16

Olry de Loriande, Claude, 1f., 14, 16 nn. 31, 32, 17 n. 35, 19, 20, 84, 133f., Figs. 29–32
Olympian gods, 5, 5 n. 13
Orbay, François d', 27, 29, 30, 33 nn. 20, 23, 34 n. 23, 35 n. 29, 39–41, 41–42 n. 51, 43, 60, 62, 83, 84, 87–93, 159, 161, 162, 164, 166–71, 173, 176, 198, 203, 205, 207, 208, 214–15 n. 200, Figs. 73, 77, 92, 96–98, 107–10
Orléans, Saint-Croix, 18
Orme, Philibert de l', 54, 70 n. 11, 146, 148, 157, 211 n. 108
Oudin, Gervais, 112 [22.]
Orpheus, 137
Oustry, 113 [46.]
Ovid, 1f., 10, 86, 135, 173

Palladio, Andrea, 13, 36, 38, 53 n. 15, 95, 96, 103 n. 15, 109 n. 40, 148, 157, 183, 208
Palmyra, 104–5, 107
  Temple of Bel (the Sun), 104, 107, Fig. 126
Paris (sculptor), 114 [61.]
Paris
  Abbaye de Saint-Antoine, 217 n. 278
  Arches
    Arc de Triomphe du Trône, 33 n. 20, 34 n. 23, 48, 55, 70, 74, 78 n. 7, 83, 84, 100, 132, 145, 147, 160, 161, 166, 170, 173, 179, 180, 184, 190, 191, 199, 203, 204, 209 nn. 17, 23, 211 n. 106, 214 n. 200, 215 n. 213, Figs. 117, 120
    Porte Saint-Denis, 204, 205
  Bridges
    Pont-Neuf, 76, 128, 135
    Pont de la Paix (project, Louis Le Vau), 210 n. 45

Churches
  Dôme des Invalides, 212 n. 153
  Minimes, 95, 212 n. 152
  Notre-Dame, 69, 161, Fig. 84
  Saint-Étienne-du-Mont, 10
  Saint-Eustache, 18 n. 45
  Saint-Germain-l'Auxerrois, 135, 210 n. 49 (Houdin)
  Saint-Gervais, 95, 97, 148, 193
  Saint-Louis-en-l'Île, 18
  Sainte-Chapelle, 135
  Sainte-Geneviève (project, Perrault), 69, 72 n. 20, 73, 78 n. 6, 81, 98, 162f.
  Sorbonne, 193, 194
  Val-de-Grâce, 76, 132, 209 n. 18
Collège des Quatre-Nations, 12, 135, 191, 193, 199, 205, 210 n. 45
Fontaine des Innocents, 148
Garde-Meuble, 187
Gobelins, 9
Hôtels
  De Monceaux, 106
  Hesselin, 17 n. 33
  Lambert, 4, 18 n. 46, 191, 199
  La Rivière (Place Royale), 17
  La Vrillière, 51
  Lionne, 191, 199
  Lully, 81
  Mazarin (Chevry-Tubeuf), 51
  Rostaing, 44
  Sully, 16, 42 n. 51
  Petit Hôtel de Sully, 40 n. 49
  Petit Hôtel de Vendôme, 114 [51.]
Île Saint-Louis, houses, 17
Louvre
  Apartment of Anne of Austria, 129
  Appartement du Roi, 137, 210 nn. 72, 73
  Cour Carrée, 10–12, 15, 19, 21, 27, 33, 41, 55, 58, 59, 60f., 66, 79, 80, 131, 132f., 136, 137, 146, 158, 160, 161, 166, 169, 176, 178, 180, 188–89, 192, 197, 202, 204, 216 n. 246, Figs. 10–12, 14, 39, 64, 65, 67, 76, 90, 91, 105–15
  Cour du Sphinx, 41
  East Façade (anonymous projects), 10, Figs. 20, 21
  East Façade (Louis Le Vau), 12, 24, 26 n. 7, 34 n. 25, 197, 216 n. 245, Figs. 33–35
  East Façade (Colonnade), passim, Figs. 42–56, 59–62, 64–67, 69–75, 77–82, 85, 86, 88, 89, 114, 115, 121, 122
  East Façade (project without col-

onnade), 28f., 123, Figs. 92–94
  East Wing, Galerie Basse, 59
  East Wing, Vestibule, 59
  Foundations, 57–58 n. 1, 124, 125
  Galerie d'Apollon, 9 n. 3, 24, 129, 140, 147
  Grande Galerie du Bord de l'Eau, 13, 35 n. 29, 138–39, 148, 161, 210 n. 84 (stables), Fig. 39
  Jardin de la Reine (de l'Infante), 129, 187
  Monument (project, Le Brun), 88, 135–36, Figs. 60, 61
  North Façade, 34, 44f., 66, 124, 161, 187–88, 198, Figs. 101–4
  North Wing, 11, 44, Fig. 14
  Pavillon de Beauvais, 44, Fig. 14
  Pavillon de l'Horloge, 10–12, 29, 34 n. 25, 43 n. 56, 62, 179, Figs. 13, 14
  Pavillon du Roi, 10–12, 15 n. 23, 29, 32, 41, 43, 55, 57, 63, Figs. 9, 16, 97
  Petite Galerie, 24, 41, 42, Figs. 96, 97
  Place du Carrousel, 137
  Salle des Antiques, 139
  Salon Carrée, 6
  South Façade (Lescot), 10, 43, 51, 79, 204, Figs. 9, 16
  South Façade (Louis Le Vau), 11–12, 23, 29, 30, 34, 37, 41–43, 56 n. 19, 93, 125f., 189, 197, 209 nn. 4, 5, 215 n. 206, Figs. 17–19, 39
  South Façade, 41f., 55, 58, 60, 66, 81, 95, 125f., 131, 143, 146, 147, 158–59, 161, 164, 168, 177, 180, 186–87, 189–91, 197, 198, 201, 202, Figs. 95, 96, 98–100
  West Façade, 10, 41, 43, 51, 79, 161, 204, Figs. 9, 13, 97
Obelisk Project (Perrault), 26 n. 1, 72, Fig. 116
Observatoire, 25, 34 n. 23, 35, 48, 48 n. 3, 70, 72, 83, 84, 88, 100, 145, 158, 160, 161, 166, 169, 170, 173, 191, 199, 212 n. 153, 214 n. 200, Figs. 68, 119
Palaces
  Louvre. *See* Louvre
  Luxembourg, 10, 51, 148, 193
  Palais-Royal, 212 n. 149
  Tuileries, 13 (Houdin), 23, 29 n. 11, 32, 72 n. 19, 84, 87,

107, 138, 139 (Salle des Machines, royal apartments chapel), 159, 174, 179, 180, 183, 204, 210 nn. 49 (Houdin), 77 (stair), 211 n. 118, 212 n. 153, 215 n. 213, Figs. 39, 142
   Squares
      Place Dauphine, 210 n. 48
      Place Louis XV (de la Concorde), 80, 200, 201
      Place Royale (des Vosges), 210 n. 48
      Place Vendôme (Louis le Grand), 81, 182, 186, 200
      Place des Victoires, 79, 81, 182, 187, 200
   Streets, Quais
      Cours de Vincennes, 217 n. 278
      Quais, 135
Pastel (Patel), Jean, 70, 132
Patte, Pierre, 18 n. 45, 66, 66 n. 5, 68, 70 n. 12, 71, 75, 76, 79f., 91, 99 n. 26, 103, 191, 193f., 205f., 216 n. 228, Figs. 11, 79, 125
Percier, Charles, 59 n. 8, 62, 71 n. 14
Perignon, 112 [25.]
Perrault, Charles, 21, 22, 22 n. 56, 25, 26, 26 n. 1, 27, 29, 30, 30 n. 12, 34 n. 23, 36, 38, 42 n. 51, 52, 55 n. 18, 59 n. 4, 60–62, 69, 72 n. 20, 73, 83, 85, 86 n. 5, 88, 90, 91, 98, 105, 110, 145, 159, 160f., 162, 165, 166, 168–70, 187, 189, 207, 208, 214–15 n. 200, 216 n. 252
Perrault, Claude, 21, 22, 25f., 47f., 58, 59, 60f., 69f., 76, 79, 80f., 83f., 88–91, 93, 94f., 99f., 104, 105, 107, 109, 110, 123, 124, 143f., 145, 151, 154f., 156f., 158–62, 164–76, 179–94, 197–205, 207, 208, Figs. 65, 67–72, 87, 113, 116–20, 124, 142
Perrault, Jean, 99, 100
Persepolis, Palace, 175
Petit, Jean, 116 [85.]
Petit, Louis, 124
Phaethon, 2f., Figs. 1–4
Philip the Arab, 107
Philippe de Bourbon, Duc d'Orléans, 146
Pierides, 137
Piganiol de La Force, Jean Aymar, 26, 123, 167, 169f., 214 n. 200
Pindar, 208
Pliny the Elder, 159
Poilly, François de, 31 n. 19, 88, Fig. 60

Poissant, Nicolas, 114 [62.], 115 [67.]
Poitiers, 100
Pola, Arch of the Sergii, 147, 148
Polyphemus, 141 [29.]
Potel, Jean, 112 [23.]
Potery, 116 [96.], [97.]
Poussin, Nicolas, 4
Primaticcio, Francesco, 4 n. 4
Puget, Pierre, 191, 199

Quinault, Philippe, 212 n. 158, 214 n. 200

Racine, Jean, 171
Rainaldi, Carlo, 20, 23, 30 n. 12
Rameau, Jean Philippe, 199
Raphael, 6, 199
Ratabon, Antoine de, 6, 20, 212 n. 158
Regnard, 124
Renault, 31, 111 [2.]
René, Claude, 116 [87.]
René, Jullien, 116 [87.]
Rhodes, Colossus, 134
Richelieu (town and château), 100
Rigaleau, Michel (La Chapelle), 114 [56.], 115 [80.], [82.], 117 [110.]
Rigault, 118 [128.]
Rinaldo, 135
Ripa, Cesare, 11
Rochefort, 18 (arsenal), 100
Rohan, Maréchal de, 16
Romanelli, Giovanni Francesco, 11
Rome
   Arch of Titus, 38
   Capitol, 140 [15.], 141 [39.], 154 (Michelangelo)
   Column of Antoninus and Faustina, 136
   Column of Trajan, 136
   Forum of Nerva, 200
   Frontispiece of Nero, 147
   Golden House of Nero, 4 n. 5
   Obelisk, St. Peter's, 59, 164, 168
   Palazzo Caprini, 147
   Pantheon, 12, 29, 76, 78, 80, 132, 149, 154, 199, 201, Figs. 57, 58
   Piazza of St. Peter's, 134, 194
   St. Peter's, 134, 147
   Sta. Costanza ("Temple of Bacchus"), 95, 96, 147, 149
   Temple of Antoninus and Faustina, 149, 200
   Temple of Apollo (Palatine Hill), 210 n. 87
   Temple of Fortuna Virilis, 38 n. 45, 53, 149
   Temple of Jupiter (Quirinal Hill), 53 n. 15

   Temple of Saturn, 109 n. 40, 149, 199
   Temple of Venus Genetrix, 109 n. 40
   Tomb of Hadrian, 136
Rossi, Mattia de', 27, 37
Rose (Roze), Arnoul, 112 [9.], [29.], [30.], 119 [148.], [152.], 120 [158.]
Rubens, Peter Paul, 191, 199

Saint-Cloud, Château, 80, 200
Saint-Denis, Basilica, 109 n. 24, 210 n. 51
Saint-Fargeau, Château, 16
Saint-Germain-en-Laye, Château-Neuf, 148
Saint-Maixent, 100
Saint-Sépulchre, Château, 17, 18 n. 46
Saint-Yves, 171
Saladin, 209 n. 24
Salonica, "Las Incantadas" (Roman building), 103 n. 9
Sangallo the Younger, Antonio da, 147, 157
Saturn, 5, 86, 156
Saugrain, Claude Marin, 168–69
Sauval, Henri, 17, 59, 167–68
Savot, Louis, 70 n. 11, 84, 95, 144, 213 n. 158
Scamozzi, Vincenzo, 38, 96, 147, 148, 157, 183
Sceaux, Château, 5 n. 8, 160 (chapel), 166 (chapel)
Scisi, Roman Temple, 95, 208
Scotin, Gérard, Fig. 117
Scudéry, Madeleine de, 5, 6
Seasons (personifications) (see also Spring, Summer, Autumn, Winter), 4 n. 5, 6
Seglas, Joachim, 116 [88.]
Seglas, Marin, 116 [88.]
Selincart, 114 [52.]
Serlio, Sebastiano, 107–8, 148, 157, Fig. 143
Simon (New Testament), 5, Fig. 6
Simon, 113 [46.], 114 [56.]
Sixtus V, 164, 168
Solomon, 134
Soufflot, Jacques Germain, 92
Spon, Jacques, 162
Spring (personification), 3
Sublet de Noyers, François, 36
Sucy-en-Brie, Château, 17, 18
Sully, Duc de, 16
Summer (personification), 3

Tallement, Paul, 144
Tempesta, Antonio, 4 n. 4

Temporiti, Francesco, 114 [63.], 120 [159.], 213 n. 180
Tessin the Younger, Nicodemus, 34 n. 23, 84–85, 90, 159, 161, 162, 166
Thevenin, Didier, 113 [49.]
Thévenot, Pierre, 70–72, 132, 133
Thiéry, Luc Vincent, 207
Tornemine, Père de, 167
Treaty of the Pyrenees, 11
Trevi (nr.), Temple of Clitumnus (S. Salvatore), 95, 147–50, 208
Troyes, Carmelite Church, 18 n. 45
Tuby, Jean Baptiste, 45, 112 [19.], [21.], 213 n. 180
Turenne, Vicomte de, 1 n. 1

Varin (Warin), Jean, 124
Vatavoualpas, 137
Vaures, Scaron de, 114 [51.]
Vaux-le-Vicomte, Château, 5f., 9, 12, 18, 85, 86, 191, 199, Fig. 5

Venice, Palazzo Contarini, 211 n. 126
Versailles, 63, 146, 174, 211 n. 106
 Chapel, 76, 81, 172, 201
 Enveloppe, 42, 182, 200, 215 n. 215
 Galerie des Glaces, 29 n. 11
 Petit Château, 40 n. 49
Vertron, Claude Charles Guyonnet de, 158
Vertumnus, 140
Vézelay, Sainte-Madeleine, 69 n. 8
Vicenza (nr.), Villa Rotonda, 13, 109 n. 40
Victory (personification), 15, 216 n. 230
Vigarani, Carlo, 124–25
Vigneron, 115 [79.]
Vigneux, Louis, 34 n. 23
Vignola, Jacopo Barozzi da, 77, 78, 182, 183, 203
Vincennes, Château, 33 n. 20, 78 n. 6, 191, 199

Vinci, Leonardo da, 36
Vinet, Elias, 100–103, Fig. 123
Viollet-le-Duc, E. E., Figs. 83, 84
Vitruvius, 49f., 52f., 77, 80, 81, 84, 94f., 101, 102, 130, 144, 149, 151, 152, 154, 156, 182, 192, 200, 209 nn. 12–14
Vivonne, Duc de, 212 n. 158
Voltaire, François Marie Arouet de, 173

War of Devolution, 26 n. 5
Wellington, Duke of, 92
Winds (personifications), 5
Winter (personification), 3
Wood, Robert, 104, 106, 107, Figs. 126, 139, 140

Xenophon, 145

Year (personification), 3, 6
Yvon, 119 [156.]

ILLUSTRATIONS

FIGURE 1. Anonymous Flemish, *Phaethon before Apollo*. Manuscript illumination, 1470–80.

FIGURE 2. Anonymous Venetian, *Phaethon before Apollo*. Painting, ca. 1500–1510.

FIGURE 3. Johann Wilhelm Baur, *Phaethon before Apollo*. Engraving, 1639.

FIGURE 4. Eustache Le Sueur, *Phaethon before Apollo*. Painting, early 1650s.

FIGURE 5. Charles Le Brun, Design for the Cupola of Vaux-le-Vicomte. Drawing, late 1650s.

FIGURE 6. Charles Le Brun, *Supper in the House of Simon*. Painting, ca. 1653.

FIGURE 7. Charles Le Brun, *The Palace of the Sun or the Course of the Year* (*Assembly of the Gods*). Engraving by Gérard Audran, 1681.

FIGURE 8. Detail of Figure 7.

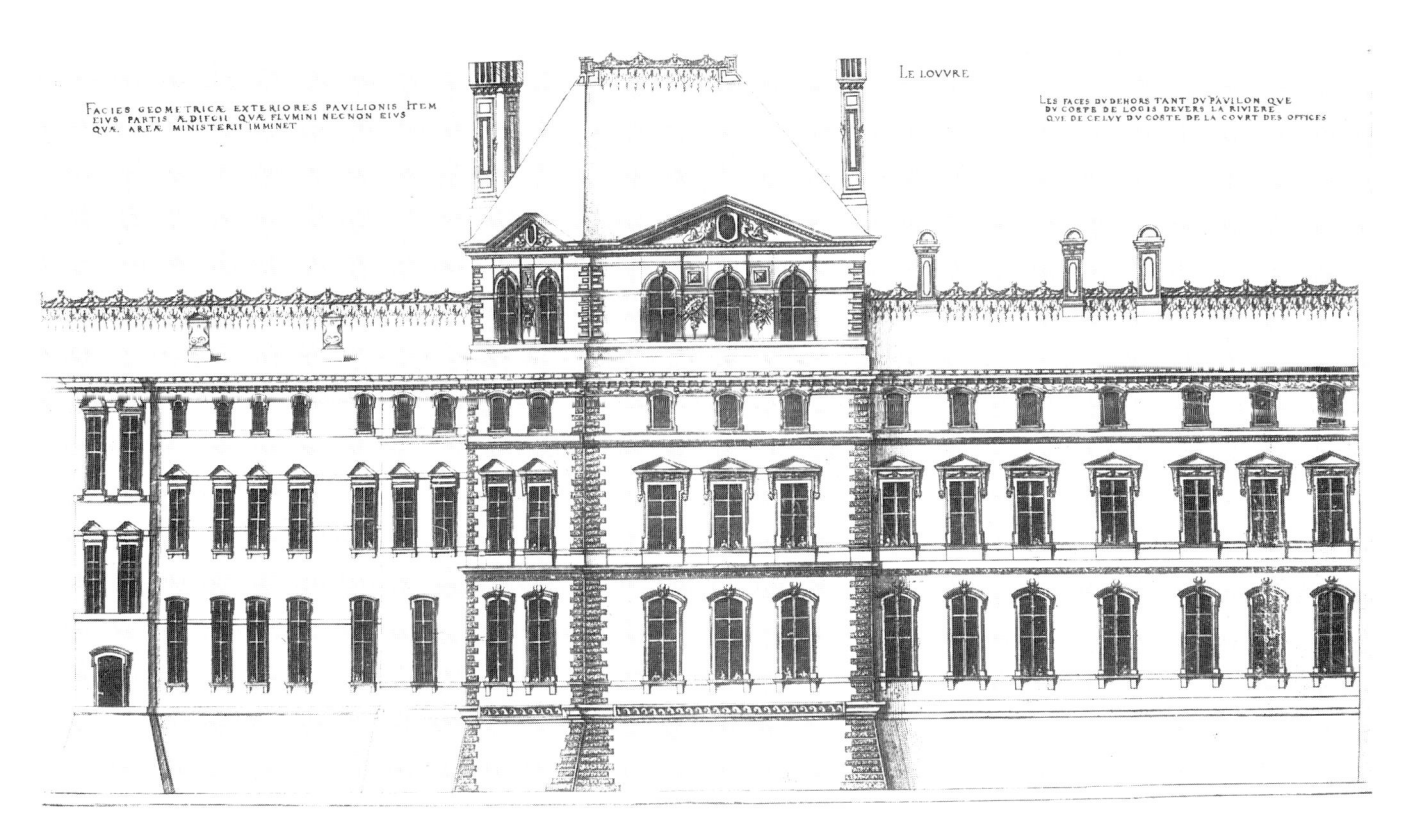

FIGURE 9. Louvre, Pavillon du Roi and west and south façades. Engraving.

FIGURE 10. Louvre, Cour Carrée, Lescot wing.

FIGURE 11. Louvre, Cour Carrée, Lescot wing. Details of *Premier Étage*. Engraving.

FIGURE 12. Detail of Figure 10.

FIGURE 13. Louvre, west façade with the Pavillon de l'Horloge. Engraving.

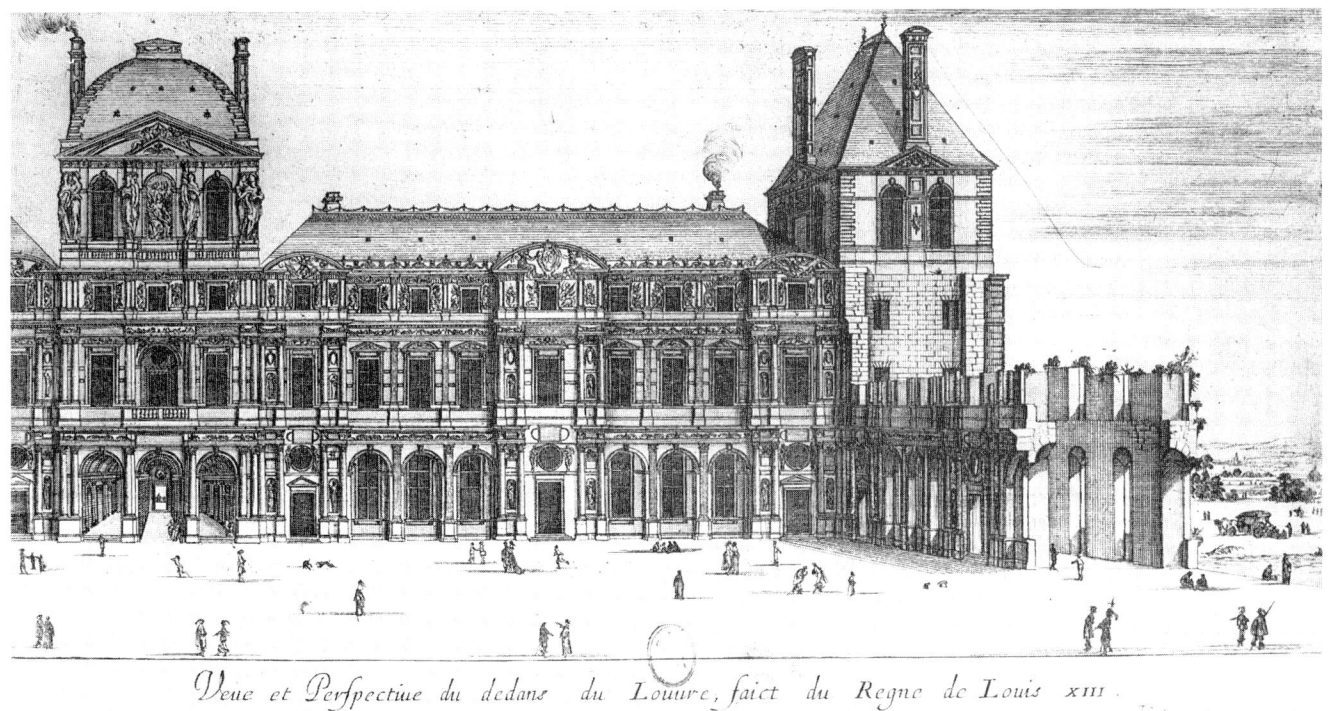

FIGURE 14. Louvre, Cour Carrée with the Pavillon de l'Horloge. Engraving by Israël Henriet.

FIGURE 15. Eustache Le Sueur, *Allegory of Magnificence*. Painting; 1654–55.

FIGURE 16. Louvre, Pavillon du Roi and south façade before 1660. Engraving.

FIGURE 17. Louvre, south façade, 1660–63, by Louis Le Vau. Engraving by Jean Marot.

FIGURE 18. Louvre, south façade, central pavilion, 1660–63, by Louis Le Vau. Engraving by Jean Marot.

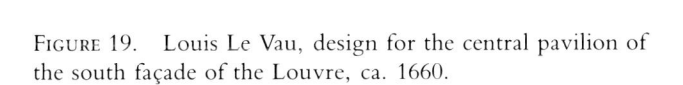

FIGURE 19. Louis Le Vau, design for the central pavilion of the south façade of the Louvre, ca. 1660.

FIGURE 20. Anonymous architect, Louvre project, shortly after 1600. Painting by Toussaint Dubreuil (restored).

FIGURE 21. Anonymous architect, design for the east façade of the Louvre, early seventeenth century. Drawing.

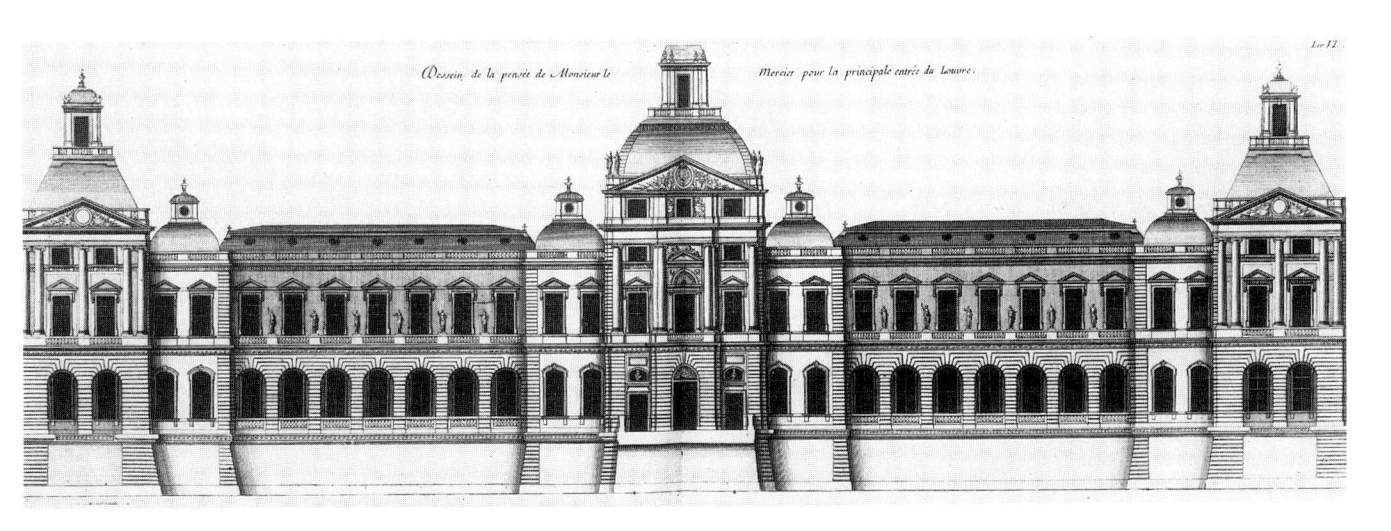

FIGURE 22. Jacques Lemercier, design for the east façade of the Louvre, before 1654. Engraving by Jean Marot.

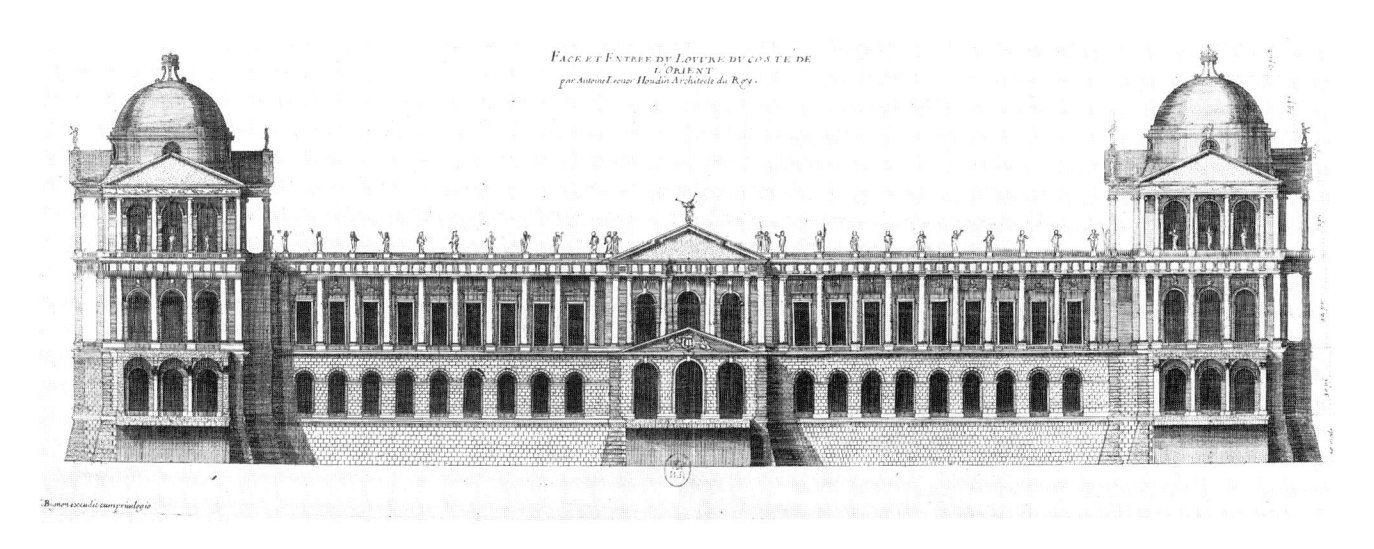

FIGURE 23. Antoine Léonor Houdin, design for the east façade of the Louvre, 1661. Engraving by François Bignon.

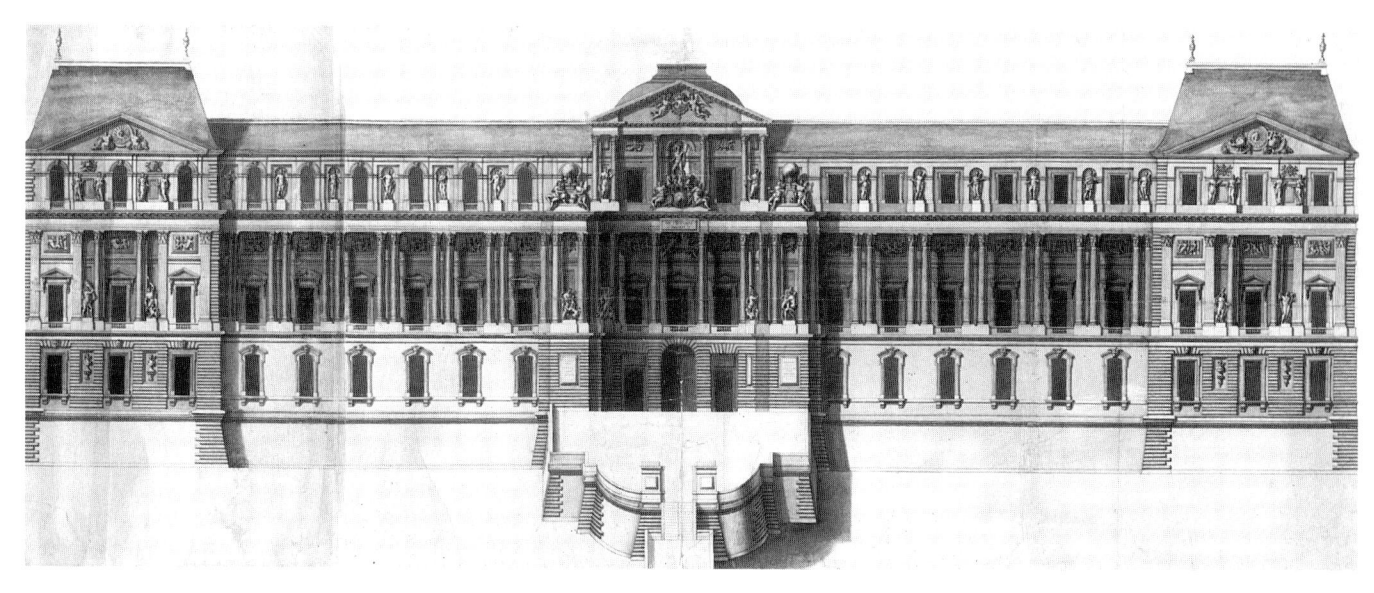

FIGURE 24. François Le Vau, design for the east façade of the Louvre, ca. 1662–64. Drawing.

FIGURE 25. Detail of Figure 24.

FIGURE 26. Detail of Figure 24.

FIGURE 27. Detail of Figure 24.

FIGURE 28. François Le Vau, design for the central pavilion, east façade of the Louvre. Engraving by Isaac Durant.

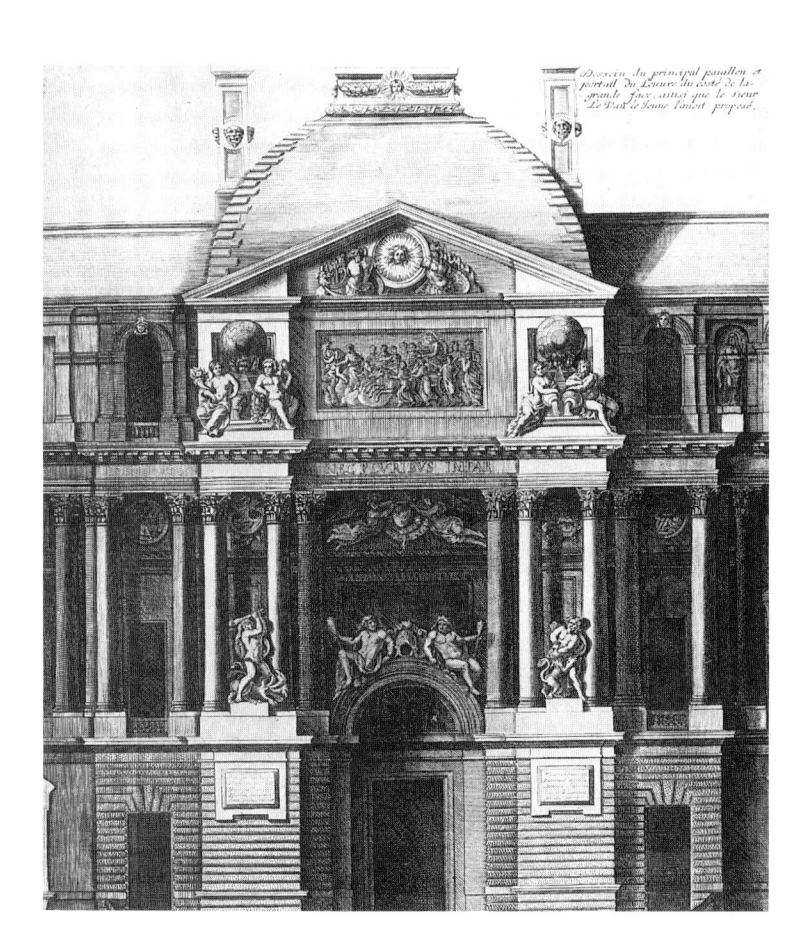

FIGURE 29. François Le Vau, design for the central pavilion, east façade of the Louvre. Engraving by Claude Olry de Loriande.

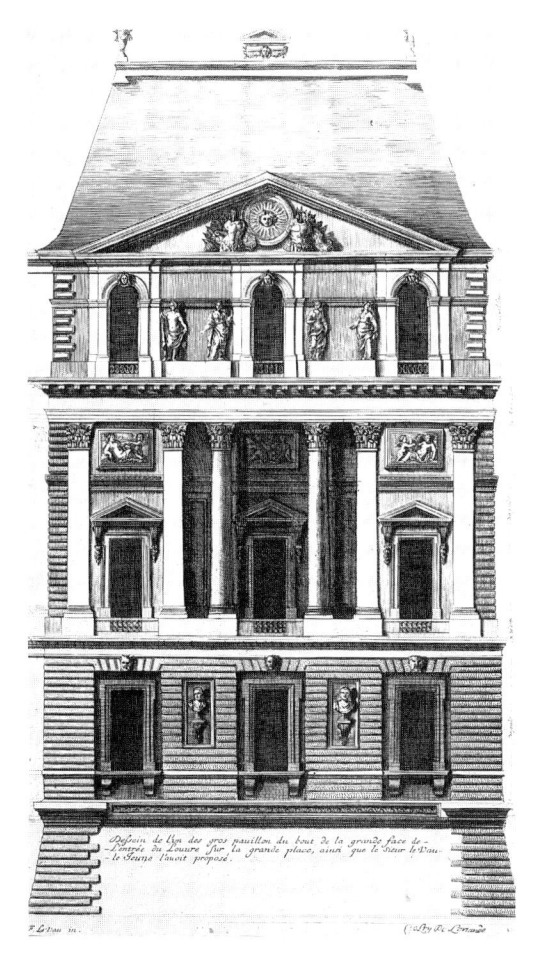

FIGURE 30. François Le Vau, design for the end pavilion, east façade of the Louvre. Engraving by Claude Olry de Loriande.

FIGURE 31. François Le Vau, design for the east wing of the Louvre, section. Engraving by Claude Olry de Loriande.

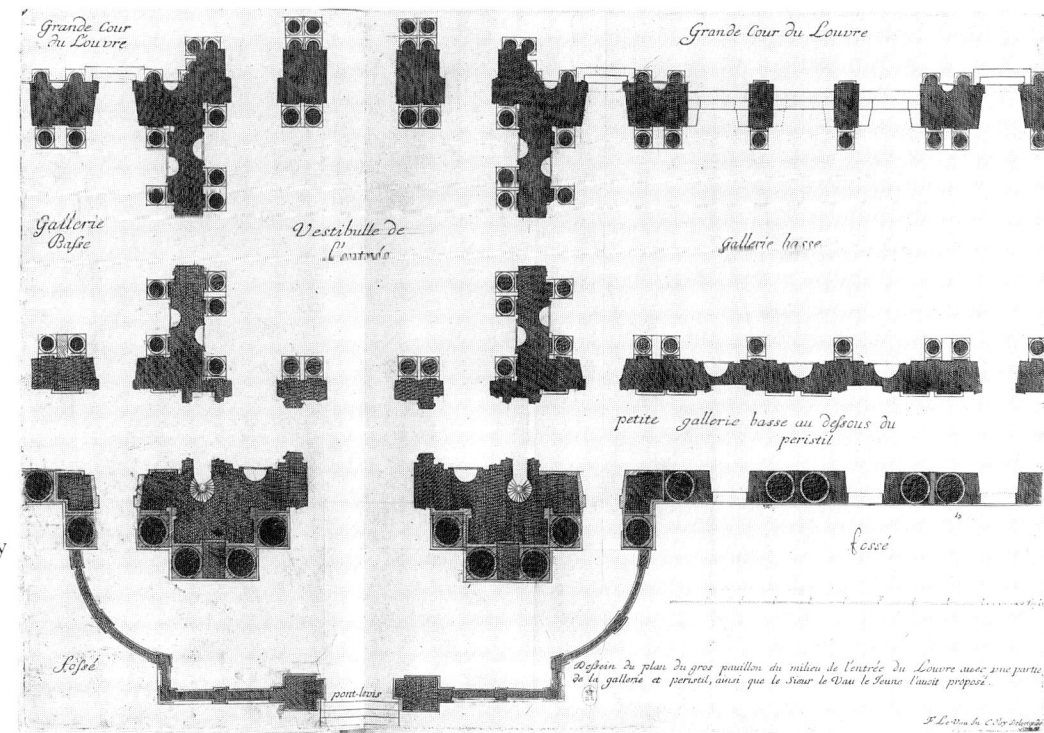

FIGURE 32. François Le Vau, design for the east wing of the Louvre, plan. Engraving by Claude Olry de Loriande.

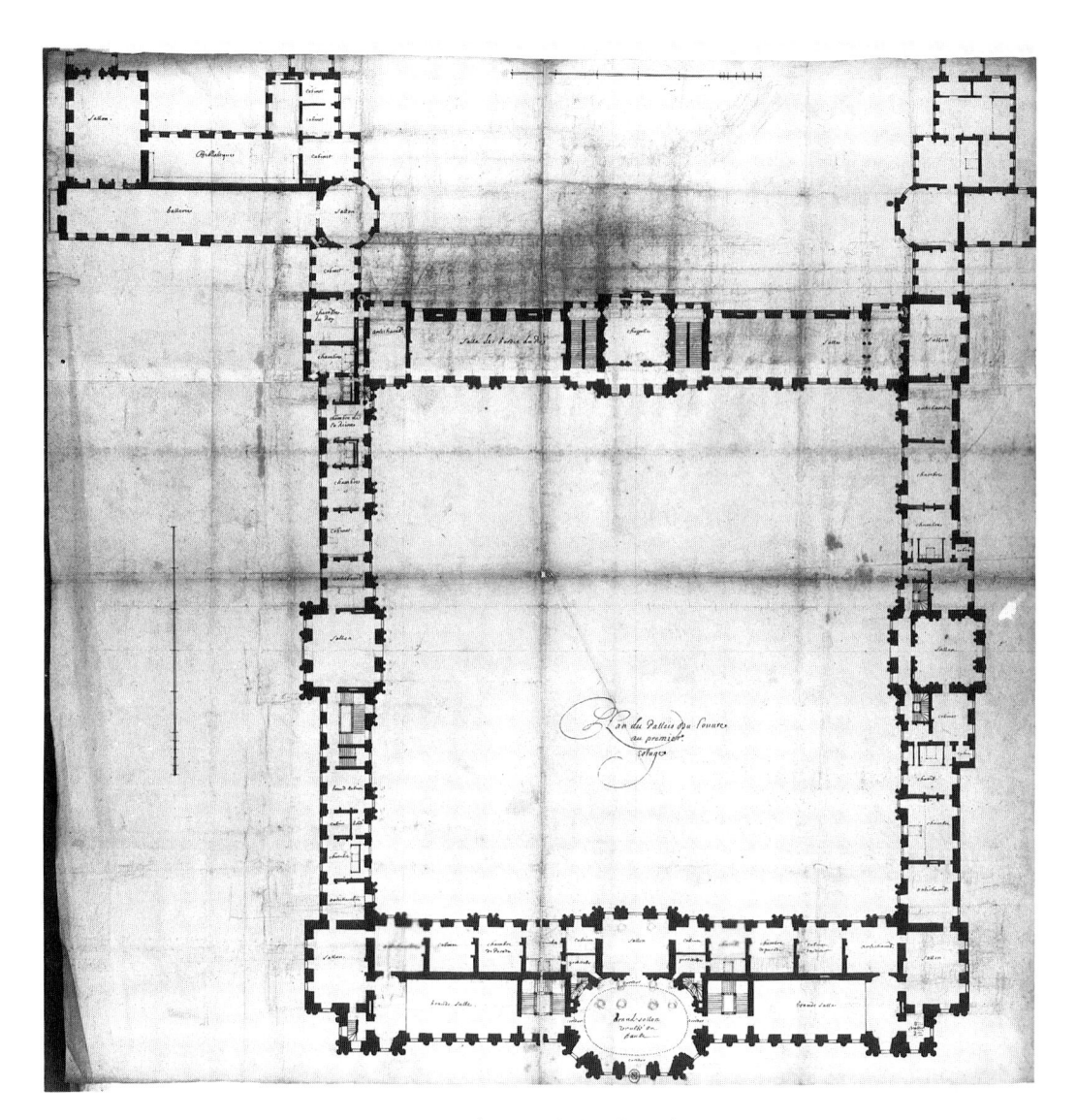

FIGURE 33. Louis Le Vau, Louvre project, plan, 1663–64. Drawing.

FIGURE 34. Louis Le Vau, Louvre project, section of the east façade, 1663–64. Drawing.

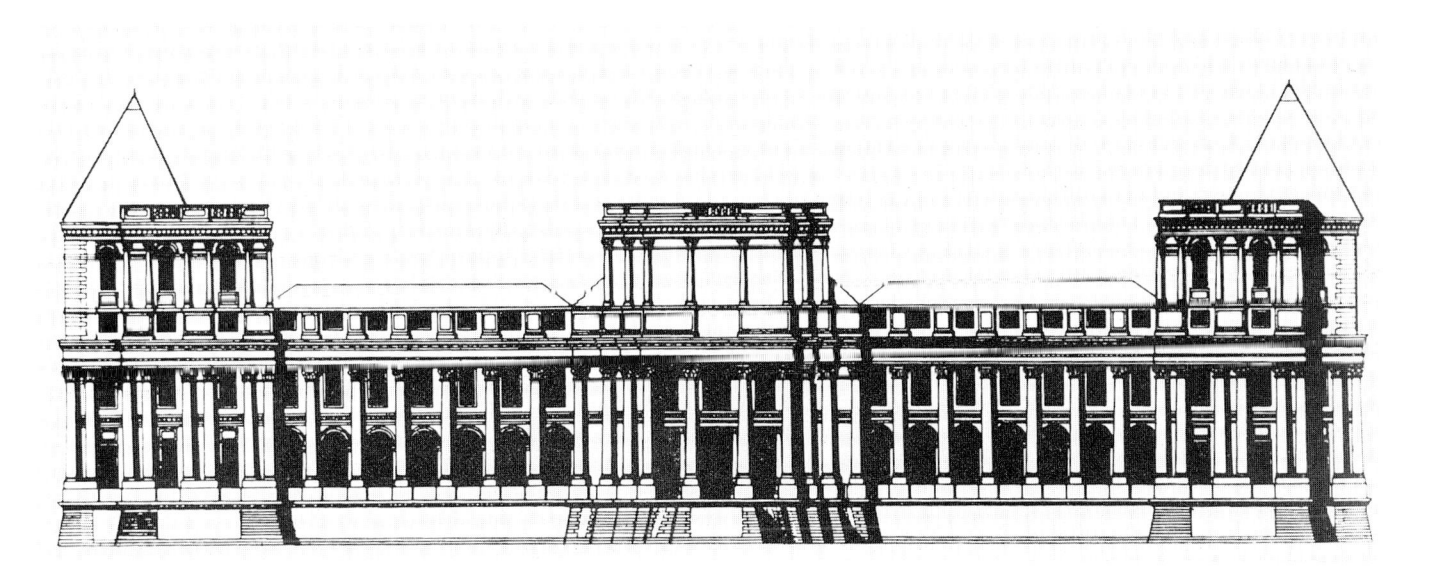

FIGURE 35. Louis Le Vau, design for the east façade of the Louvre, 1663–64. Reconstructed elevation by Trevor K. Gould.

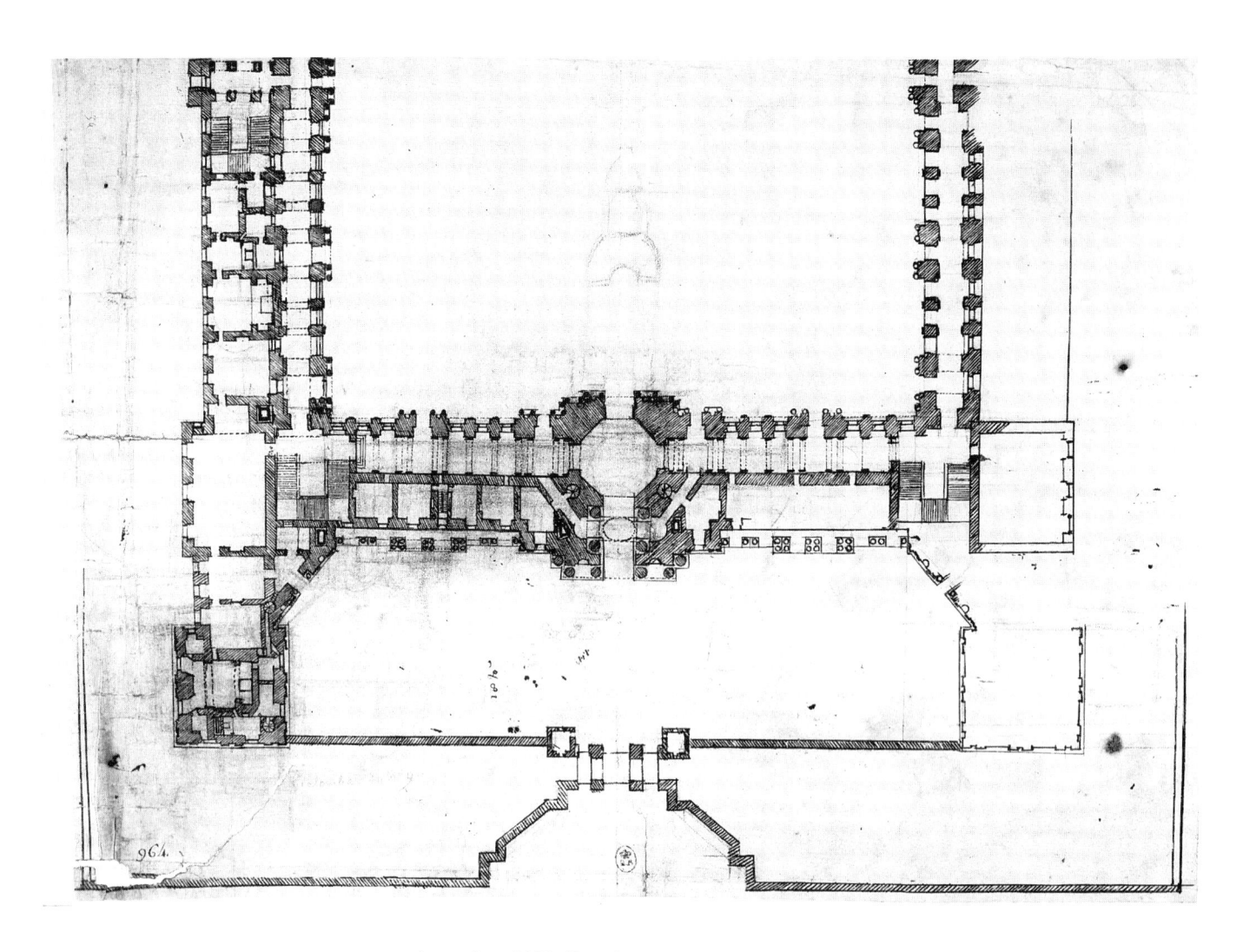

FIGURE 36. François Mansart, Louvre project, plan, 1664. Drawing.

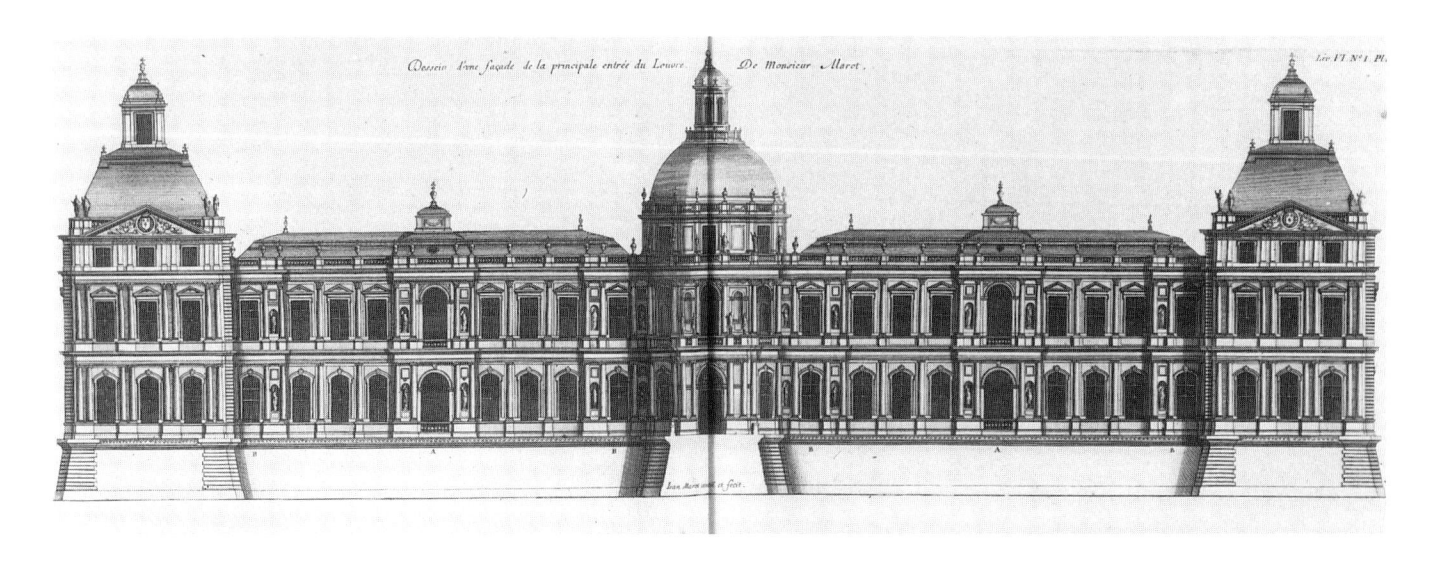

FIGURE 37. Jean Marot, design for the east façade of the Louvre, 1664(?). Engraving by Jean Marot.

FIGURE 38. Pierre Cottart, design for the east façade of the Louvre. Engraving, 1665.

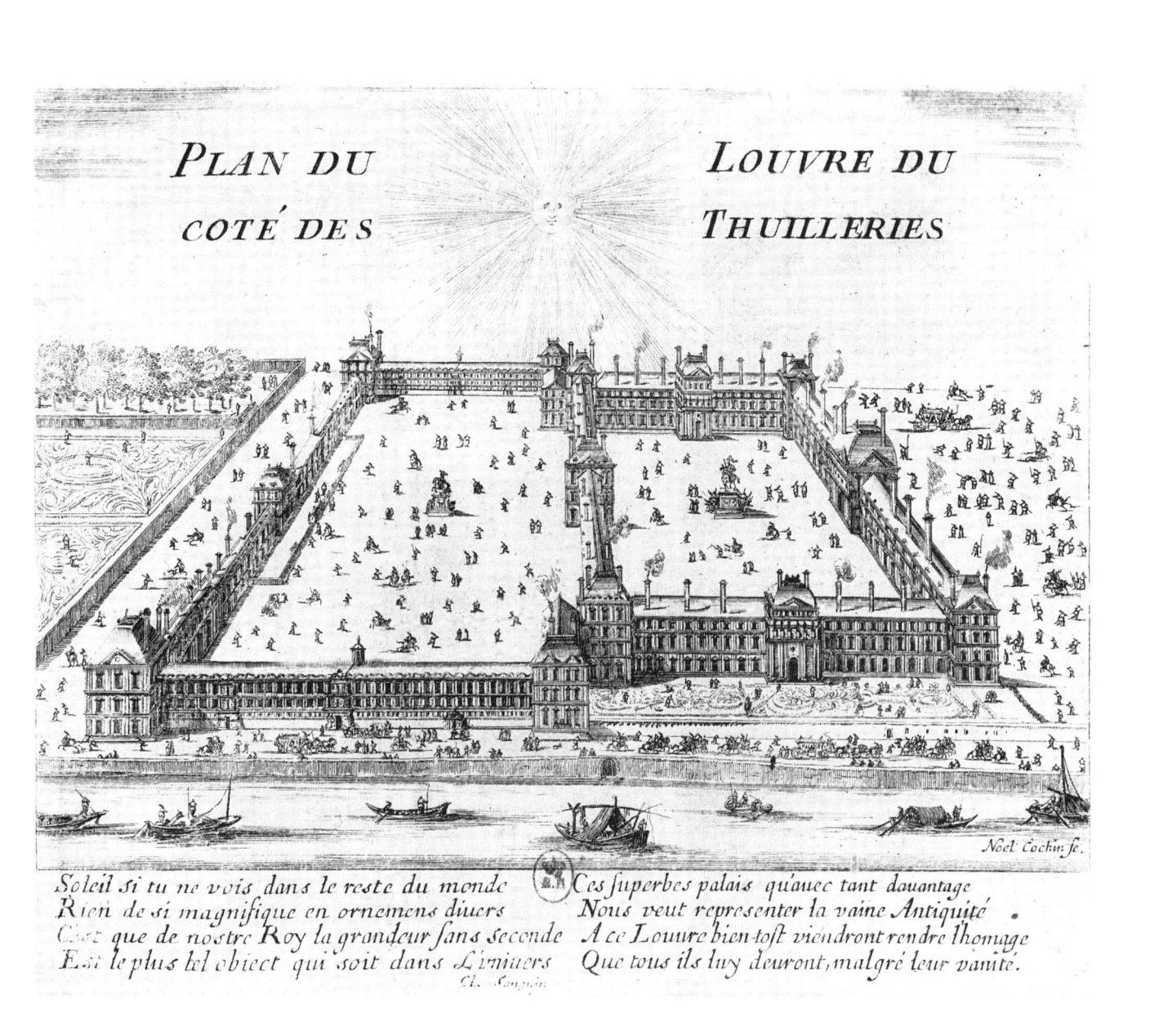

Soleil si tu ne vois dans le reste du monde
Rien de si magnifique en ornemens diuers
C'est que de nostre Roy la grandeur sans seconde
Est le plus tel obiect qui soit dans L'vniuers

Ces superbes palais qu'auec tant dauantage
Nous veut representer la vaine Antiquité
A ce Louvre bien-tost viendront rendre l'homage
Que tous ils luy deuront, malgré leur vanité.

FIGURE 39. Louvre and Tuileries. Engraving by Noël Cochin.

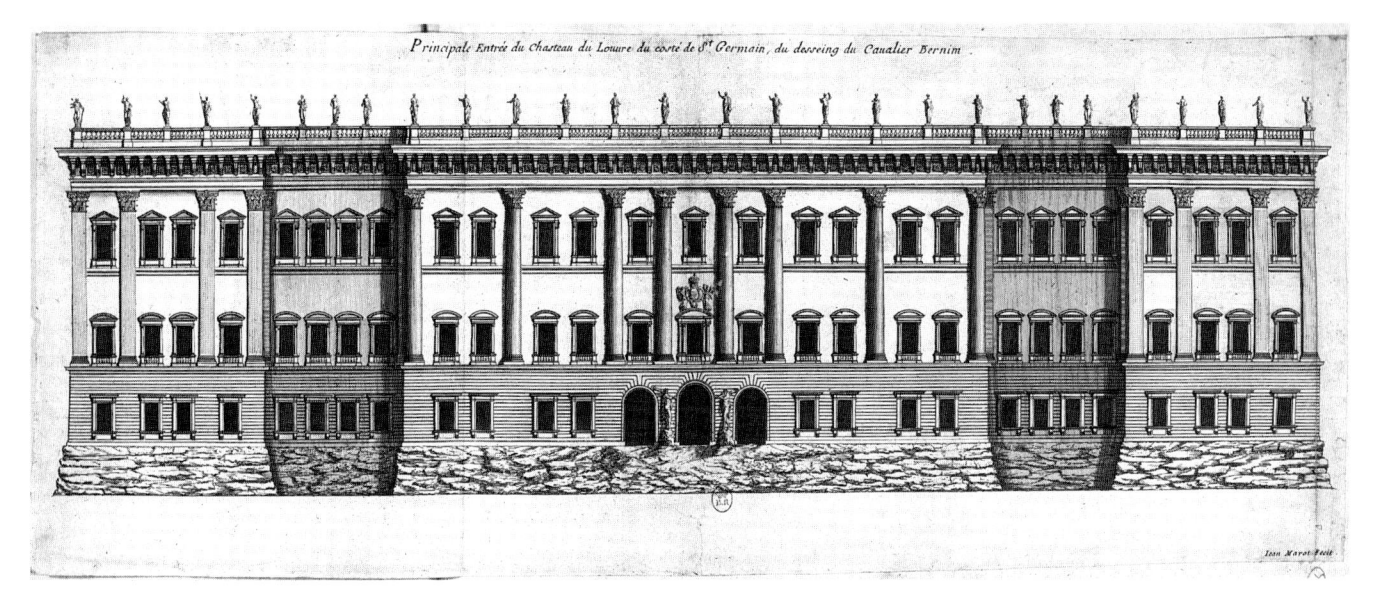

FIGURE 40. Gianlorenzo Bernini, design for the east façade of the Louvre, elevation, 1665. Engraving by Jean Marot.

FIGURE 41. Gianlorenzo Bernini, design for the east façade of the Louvre, elevation, 1665. Drawing.

FIGURE 42. Louvre, east (Colonnade) and south façades.

FIGURE 43. Louvre, Colonnade.

FIGURE 44. Louvre, Colonnade.

FIGURE 45. Louvre, Colonnade with moat.

FIGURE 46. Louvre, Colonnade. Windows of ground floor.

FIGURE 47. Louvre, Colonnade. Detail of ground-floor window.

FIGURE 48. Louvre, Colonnade. Central pavilion.

FIGURE 49. Louvre, Colonnade. Northern end pavilion.

FIGURE 50. Detail of Figure 49.

FIGURE 51. Louvre, Colonnade.

FIGURE 52. Louvre, Colonnade.

FIGURE 53. Louvre, Colonnade.

FIGURE 54. Louvre, Colonnade. Capitals.

FIGURE 55. Louvre, Colonnade. Balustrade.

FIGURE 56. Louvre, Colonnade. Details of the order. Engraving.

FIGURE 57. Pantheon, Rome. Interior columnar order. Engraving.

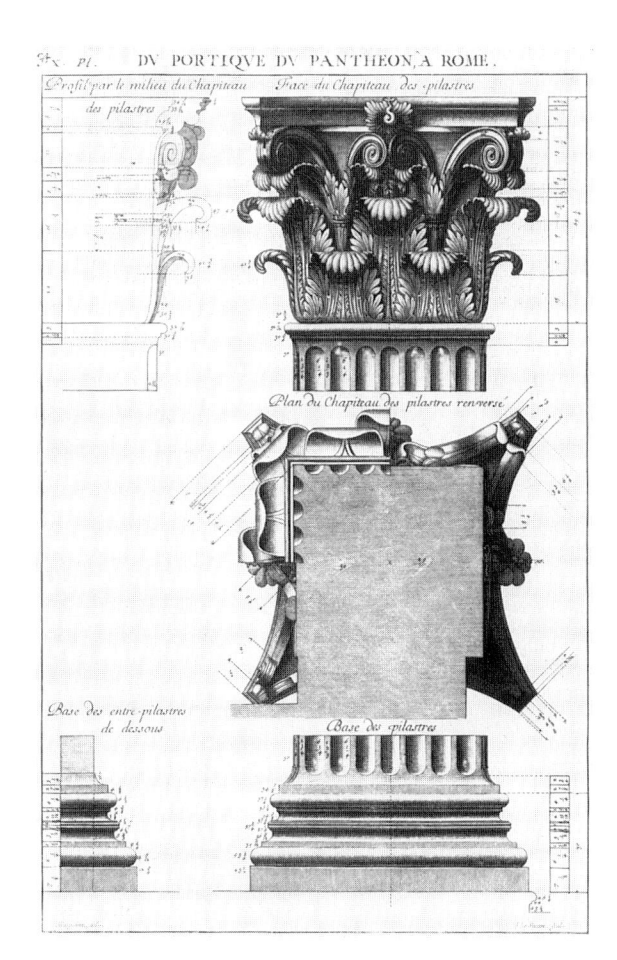

FIGURE 58. Pantheon, Rome. Pilaster order of the portico. Engraving.

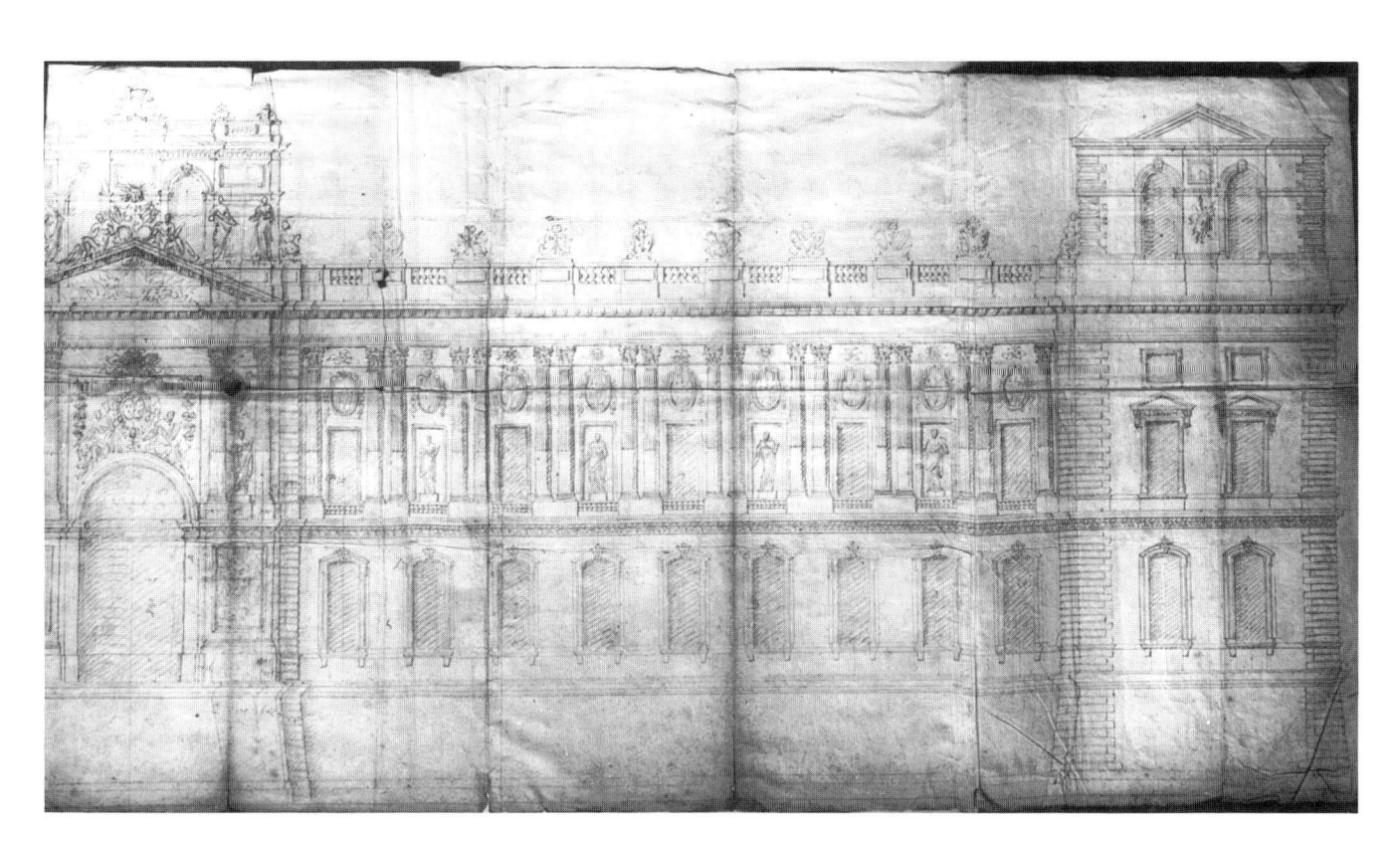

FIGURE 59. Studio of Louis Le Vau, elevation of the east façade with the Colonnade. Spring 1667. Drawing. (Appendix A, A1).

FIGURE 60. François de Poilly after Charles Le Brun. Frontispiece (1668). Engraving (detail).

FIGURE 61. Charles Le Brun, preparatory drawing for Figure 60.

FIGURE 62. Studio of Louis Le Vau, elevation of the end pavilion of the east façade. Spring 1667. Drawing. (Appendix A, A2).

FIGURE 63. Studio of Louis Le Vau, design for a triumphal arch. Drawing.

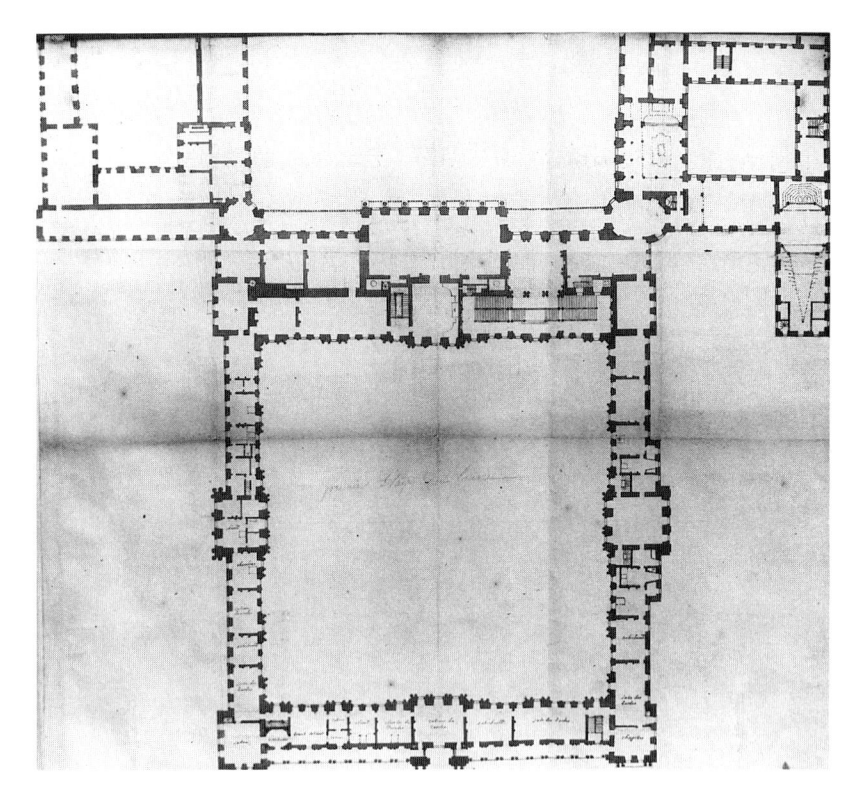

FIGURE 64. Studio of Louis Le Vau, plan of the Cour Carrée. Spring 1667. Drawing. (Appendix A, A3).

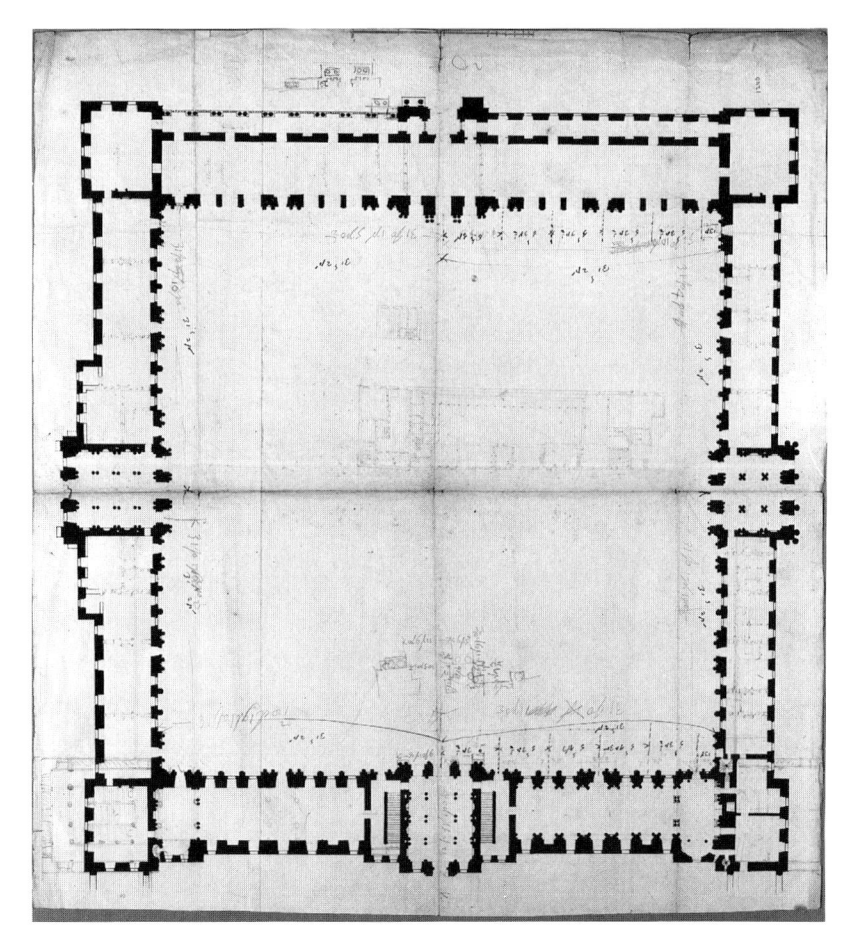

FIGURE 66. Elevation of central portion of the east façade with the Colonnade. 1667. Medal. (Appendix A, A5).

FIGURE 65. Claude Perrault (?), plan of the Cour Carrée. Spring 1667. Drawing. (Appendix A, A4).

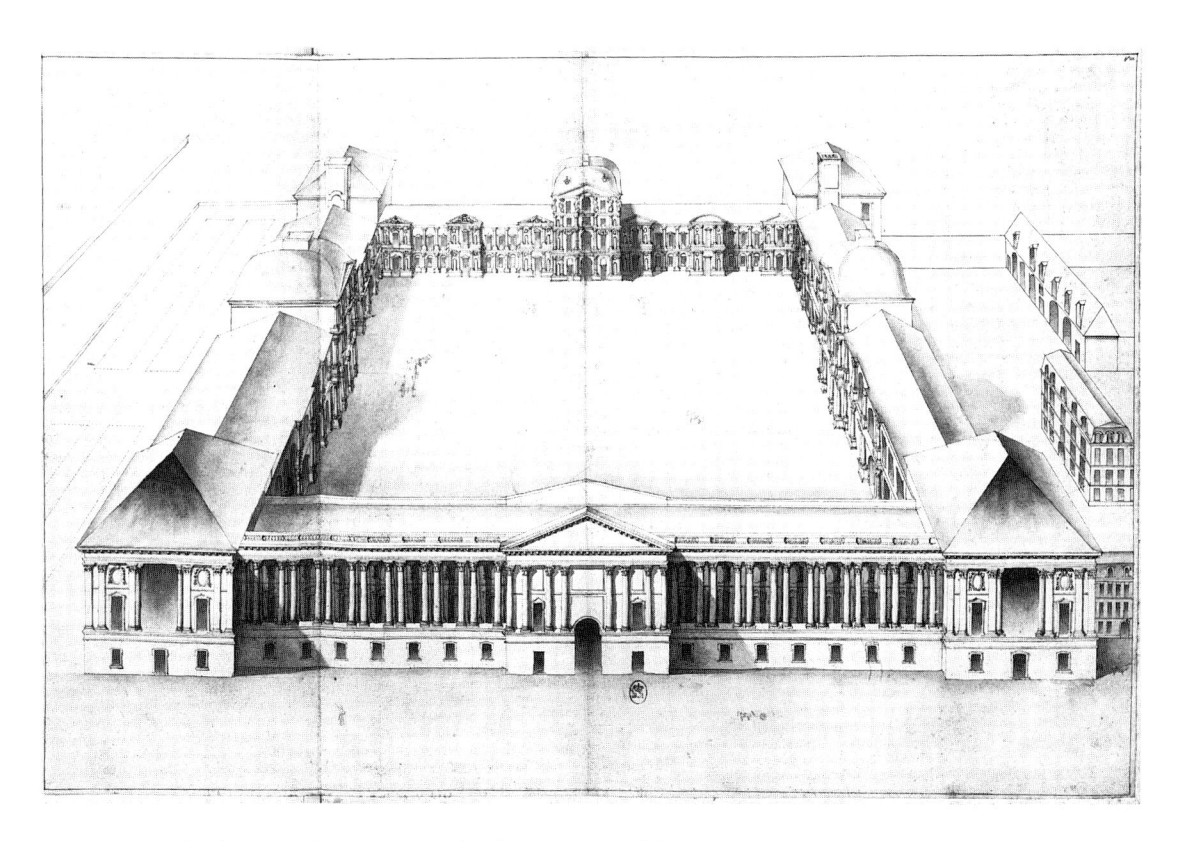

FIGURE 67. Claude Perrault, perspective bird's-eye view of the Louvre from the east. Early 1668. Drawing. (Appendix A, A6).

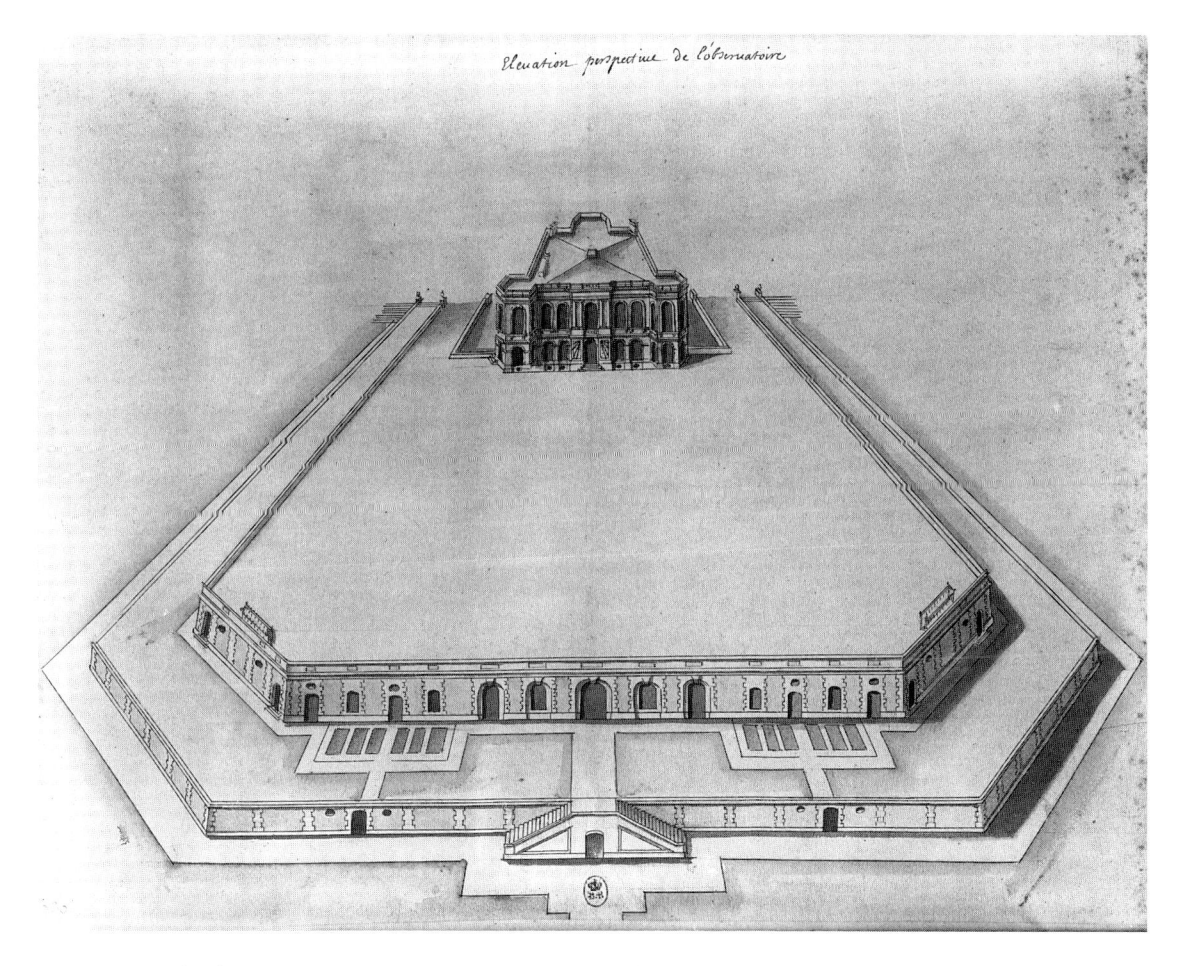

FIGURE 68. Claude Perrault, perspective bird's-eye view of the Observatoire, Paris. Early 1667. Drawing.

FIGURE 69. Claude Perrault, elevation study of end (south) pavilion of the east façade with the Colonnade. 1668. Drawing. (Appendix A, A7).

FIGURE 70. Variant of Figure 69.

FIGURE 71. Variant of Figure 69.

FIGURE 72. Variant of Figure 69.

FIGURE 73. Studio of Louis Le Vau, François d'Orbay, draftsman. Elevation of end (north) pavilion of the east façade with the Colonnade. 1668. Drawing. (Appendix A, A8).

FIGURE 74. Anonymous draftsman, east façade with the Colonnade. 1668. Drawing. (Appendix A, A9).

FIGURE 75. Detail of Figure 74.

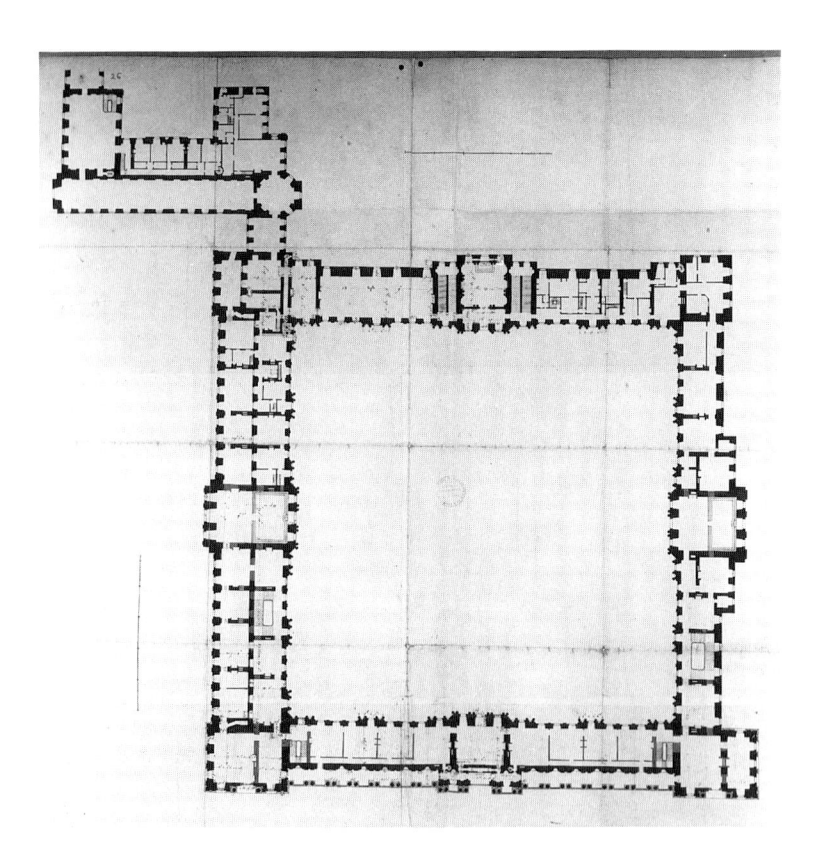

FIGURE 76. Anonymous draftsman, plan of the Cour Carrée. 1668. Drawing. (Appendix A, A10).

FIGURE 77. Studio of Louis Le Vau, François d'Orbay, draftsman. Studies of the rear wall and ceiling of the Colonnade. 1668. Drawing. (Appendix A, A11).

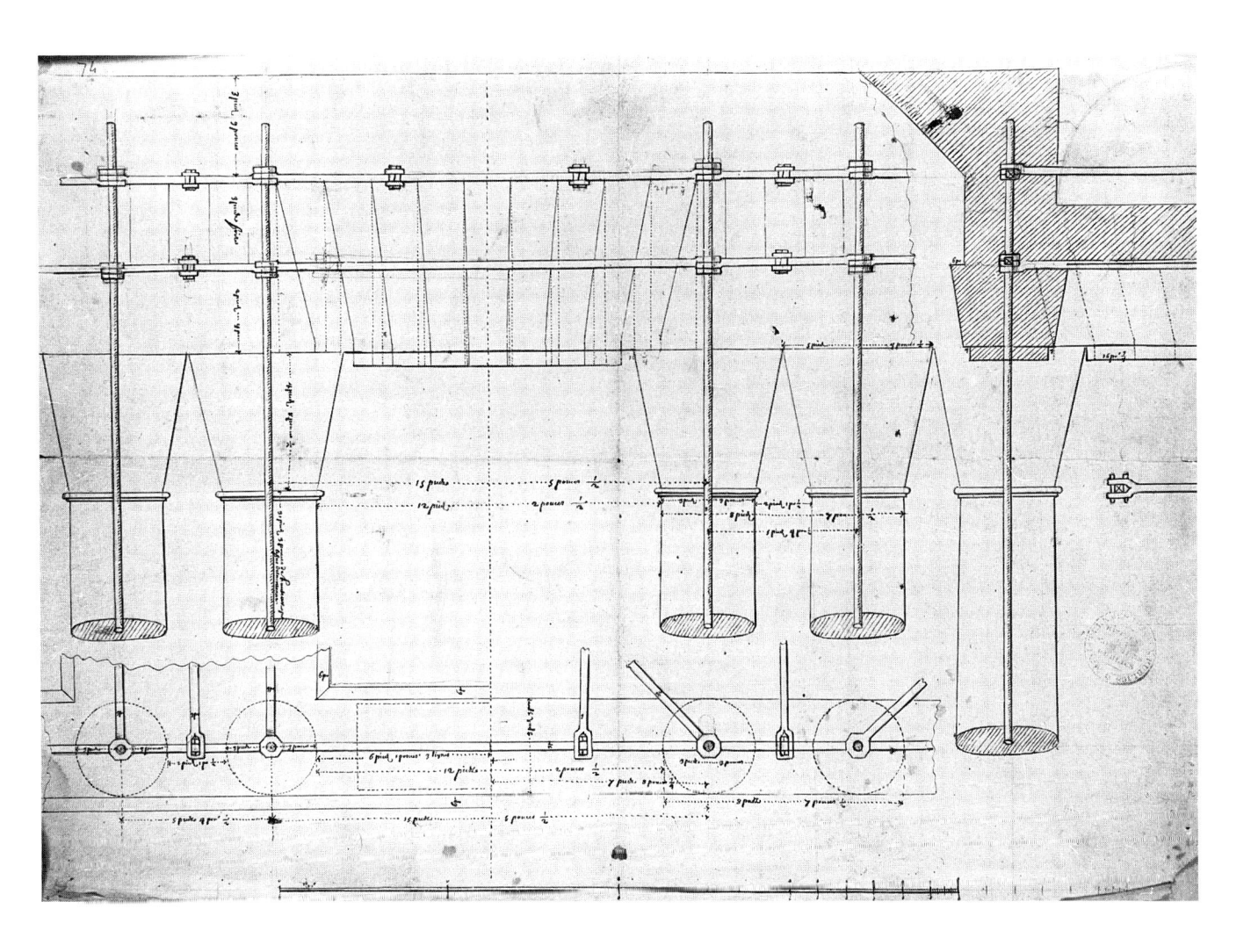

FIGURE 78. Anonymous draftsman, studies of the iron reinforcement system of the Colonnade. 1668. Drawing. (Appendix A, A12).

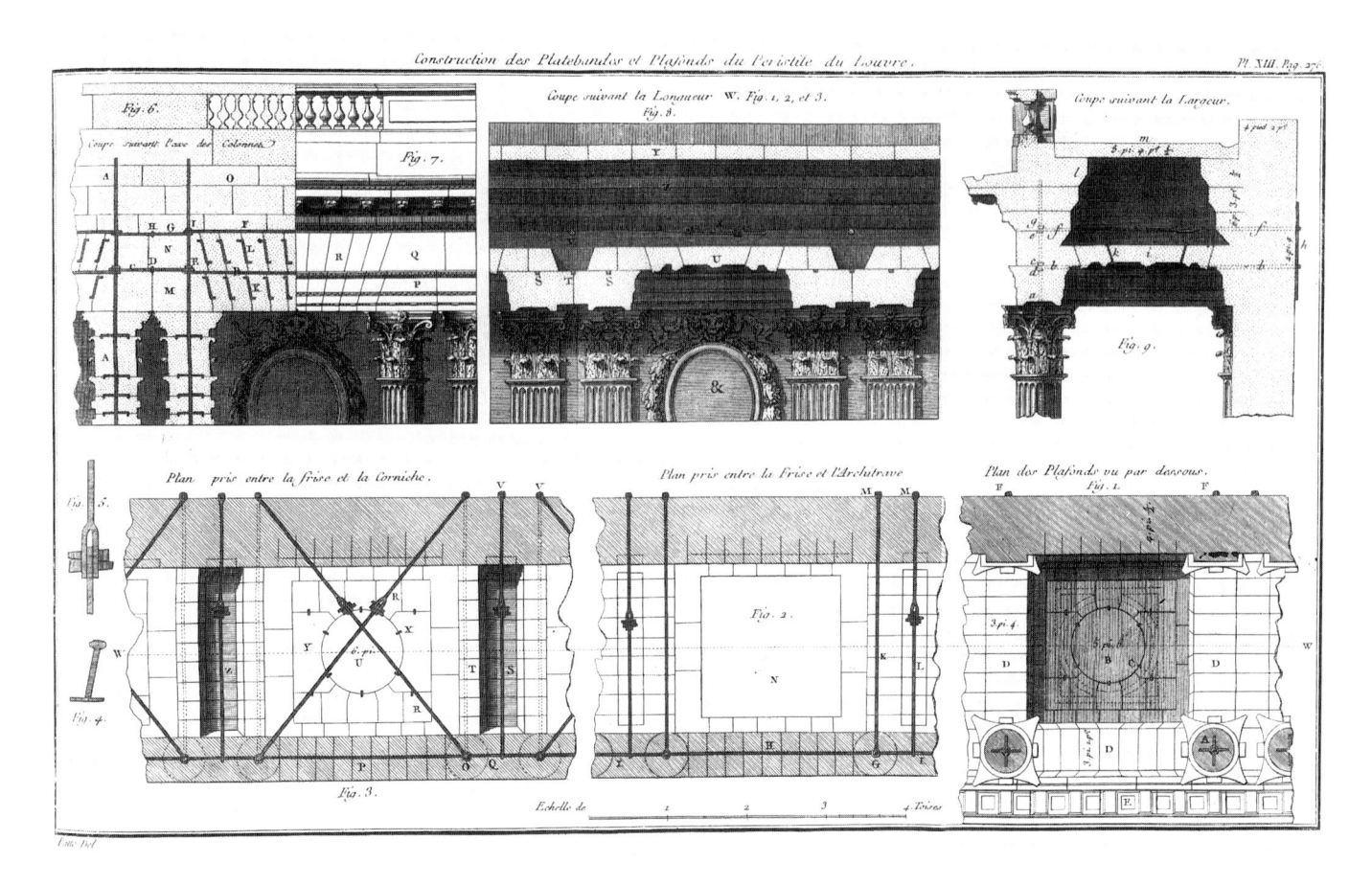

FIGURE 79. Louvre, Colonnade. Iron reinforcement system. Engraving from Pierre Patte, *Mémoires sur les objets les plus importans de l'architecture,* Paris, 1769.

FIGURE 80. Louvre, Colonnade. View of tunnel within the north entablature, with iron tie-rods.

FIGURE 81. Louvre, Colonnade. Iron tie-rods with *moufles*.

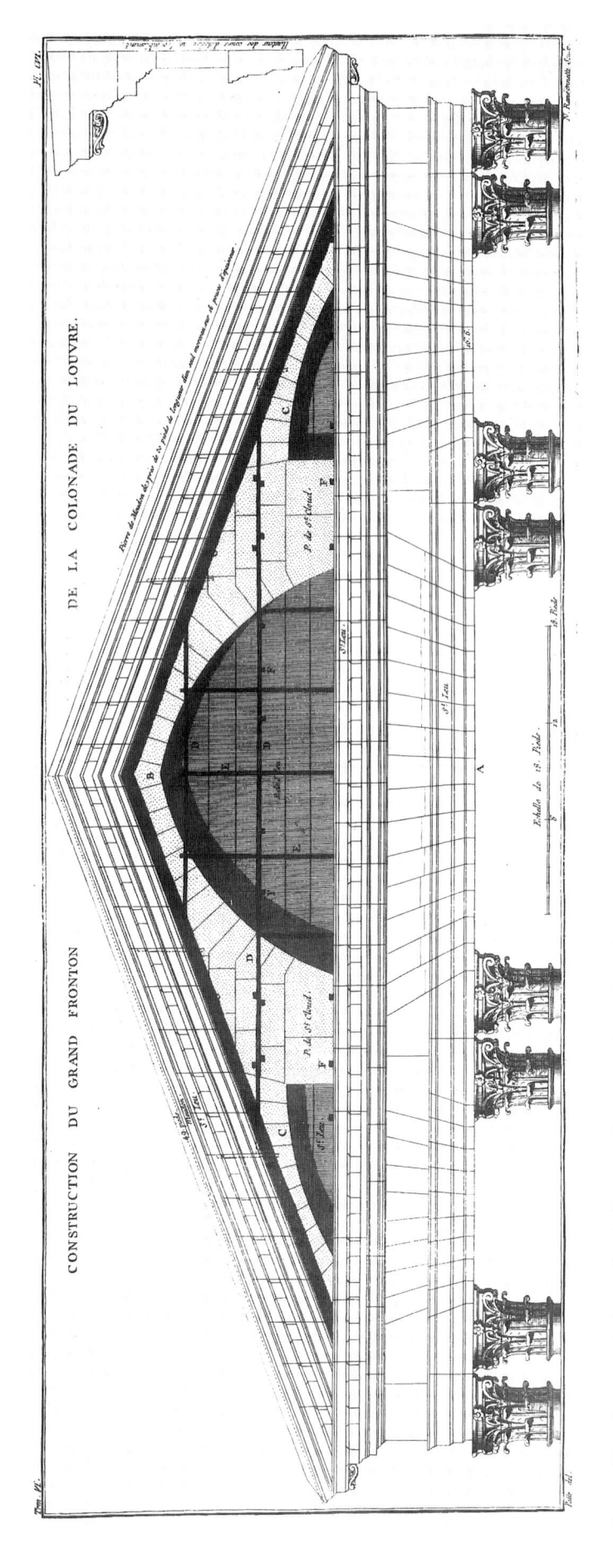

FIGURE 82. Louvre, Colonnade. Pediment of the central pavilion showing the iron reinforcement system and relieving arches. Engraving.

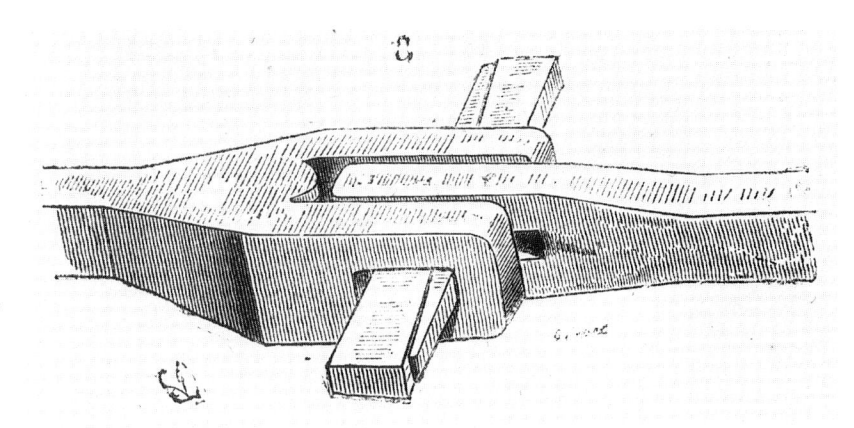

FIGURE 83. Iron "free chain," French, fifteenth century. Engraving.

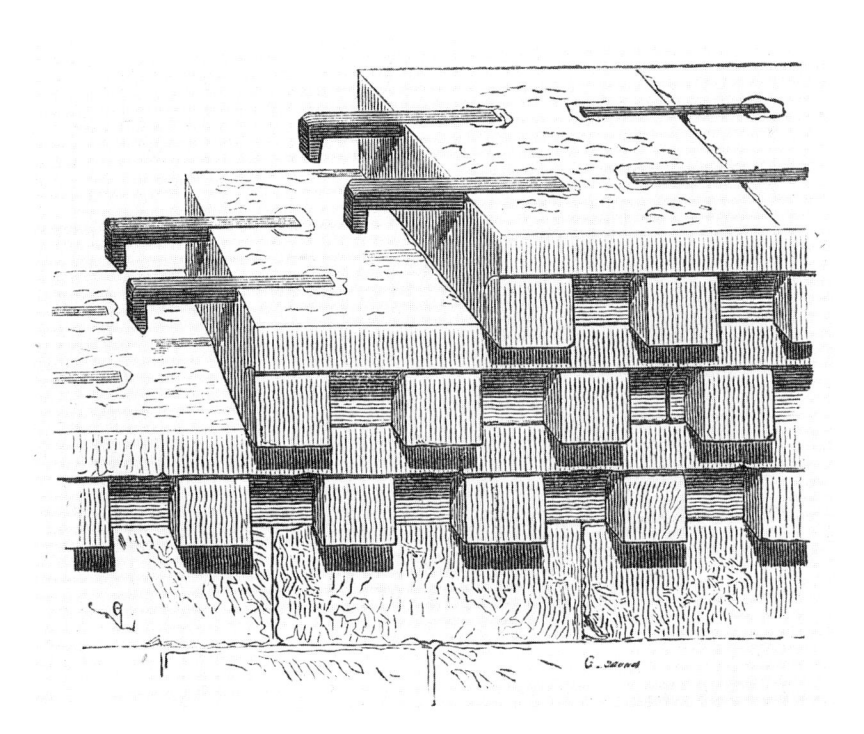

FIGURE 84. Iron cramps, Notre-Dame, Paris, late twelfth century. Engraving.

FIGURE 85. Michel Molart, medal of the Louvre Colonnade, 1673.

FIGURE 86. Sébastien Le Clerc, *Lifting of the Louvre Pediment Stones, 1674.* Engraving, 1677.

FIGURE 87. Machines for moving and lifting the Louvre pediment stones. Engraving by Pierre Le Pautre from Claude Perrault, trans. and ed., *Les dix livres d'architecture de Vitruve,* 2d ed., Paris, 1684.

FIGURE 88. Louvre, Colonnade. Elevation and plan. Engraving by Jean Marot, 1676.

FIGURE 89. Louvre, Colonnade. Elevation and section (details) of the central pavilion. Drawing, 1678.

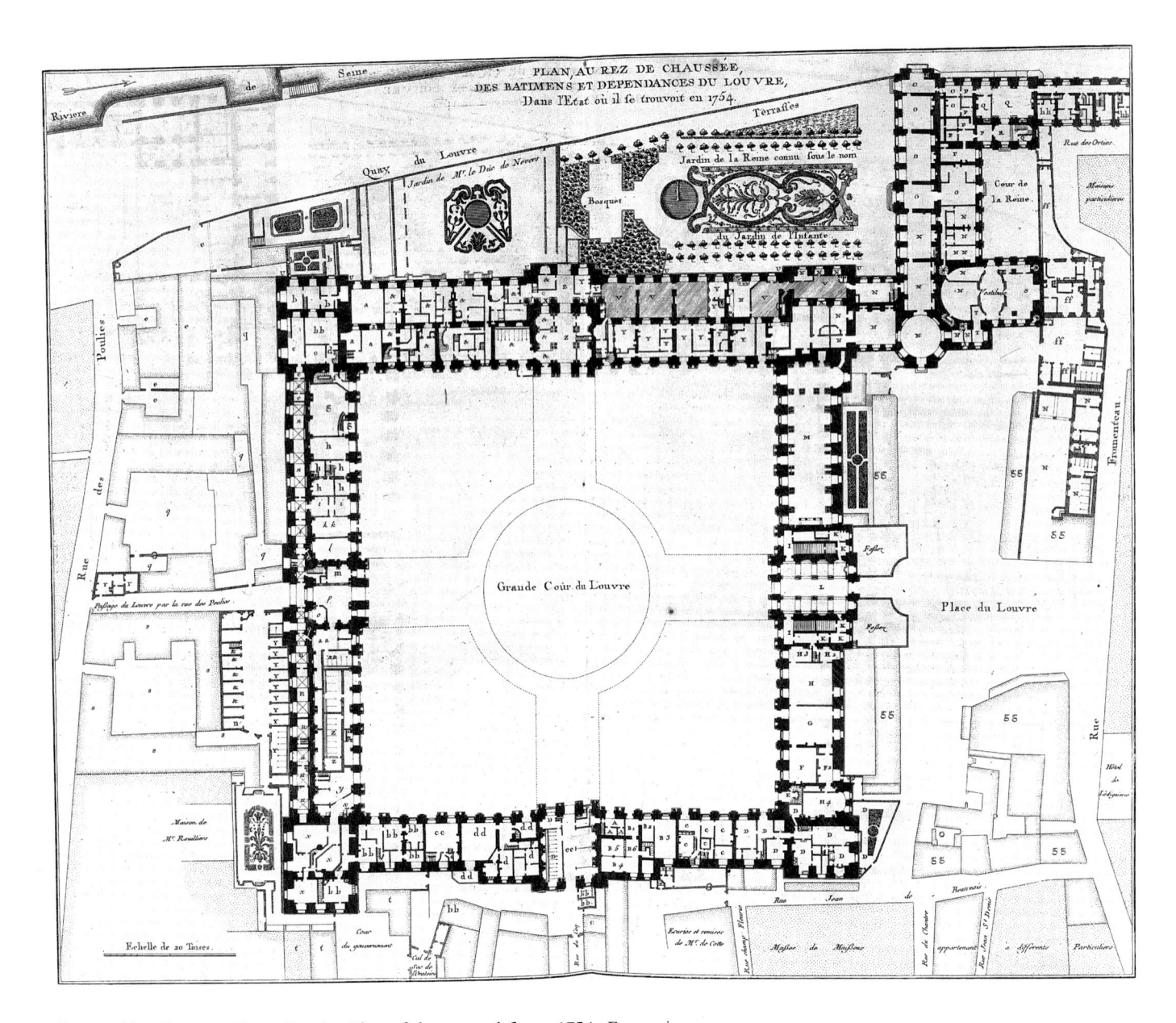

FIGURE 90. Louvre, Cour Carrée. Plan of the ground floor, 1754. Engraving.

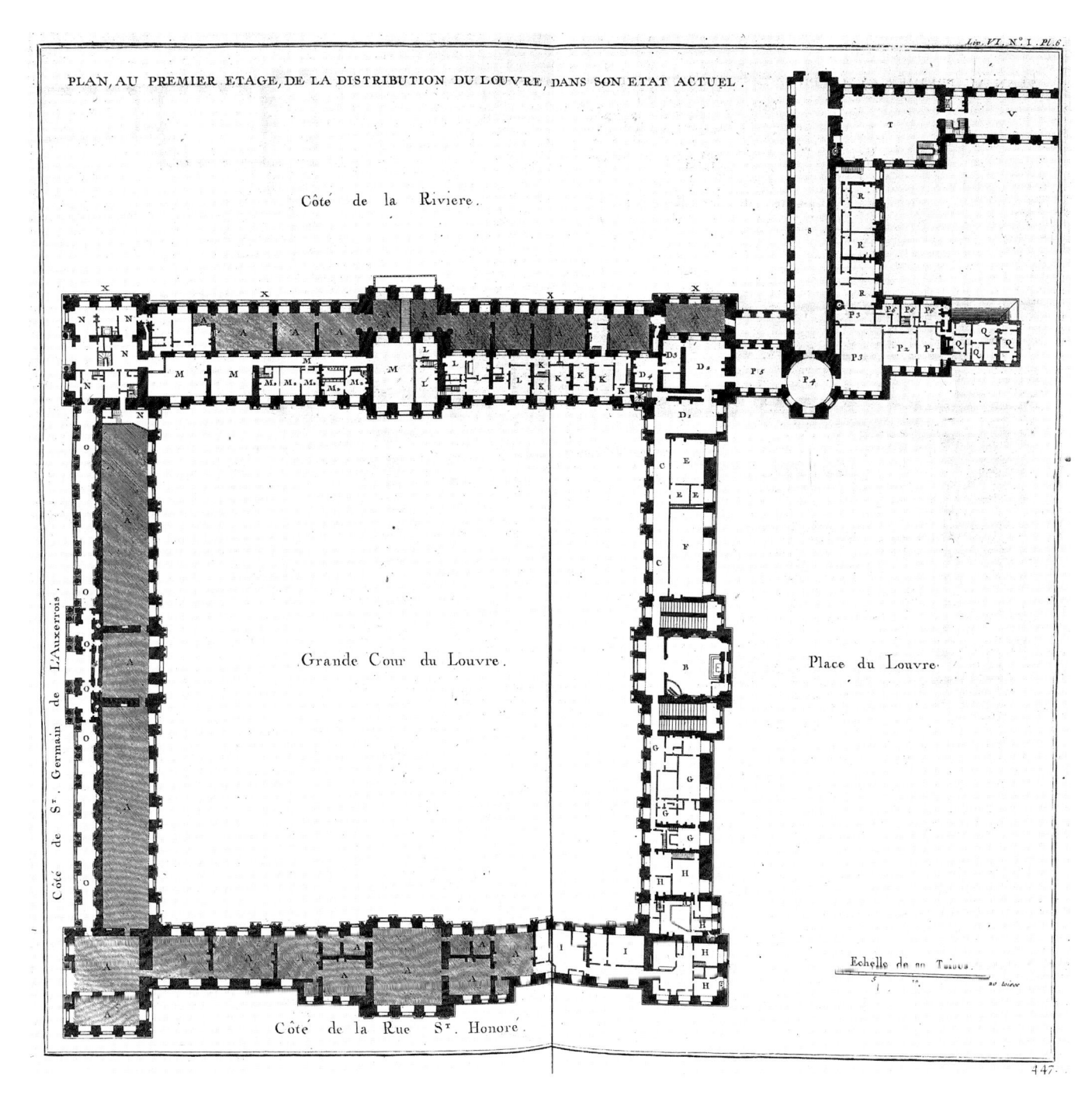

FIGURE 91. Louvre, Cour Carrée. Plan of the first floor. Engraving.

FIGURE 92. Studio of Louis Le Vau, François d'Orbay, draftsman. Elevation of the east façade without the Colonnade. Spring 1667. Drawing. (Appendix A, B1).

FIGURE 93. Studio of Charles Le Brun, elevation of the east façade without the Colonnade. Spring 1667. Drawing. (Appendix A, B2).

FIGURE 94. Studio of Charles Le Brun, elevation of the central pavilion of the east façade. Spring 1667. Drawing. (Appendix A, B3).

FIGURE 95. Louvre, south façade.

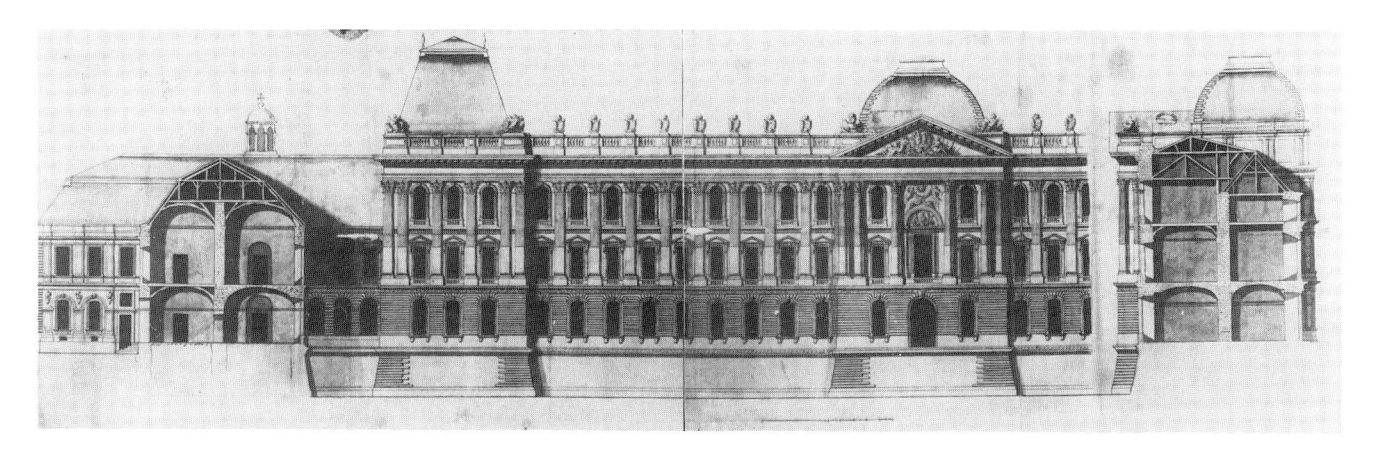

FIGURE 96. Studio of Louis Le Vau, François d'Orbay, draftsman. Elevation and section of the south façade, with a section of the Petite Galerie. 1668. Drawing. (Appendix A, C1).

FIGURE 97. Studio of Louis Le Vau, François d'Orbay, draftsman. Partial elevation of the western façade of the Cour Carrée and the Pavillon du Roi, with section of link to the Petite Galerie. Drawing, 1668. (Appendix A, C2).

FIGURE 98. Studio of Louis Le Vau, François d'Orbay, draftsman. Elevation of the south façade. 1668. Drawing. (Appendix A, C3).

FIGURE 99. Louvre, south façade. Elevation, section, and plan (details). Drawing, 1678.

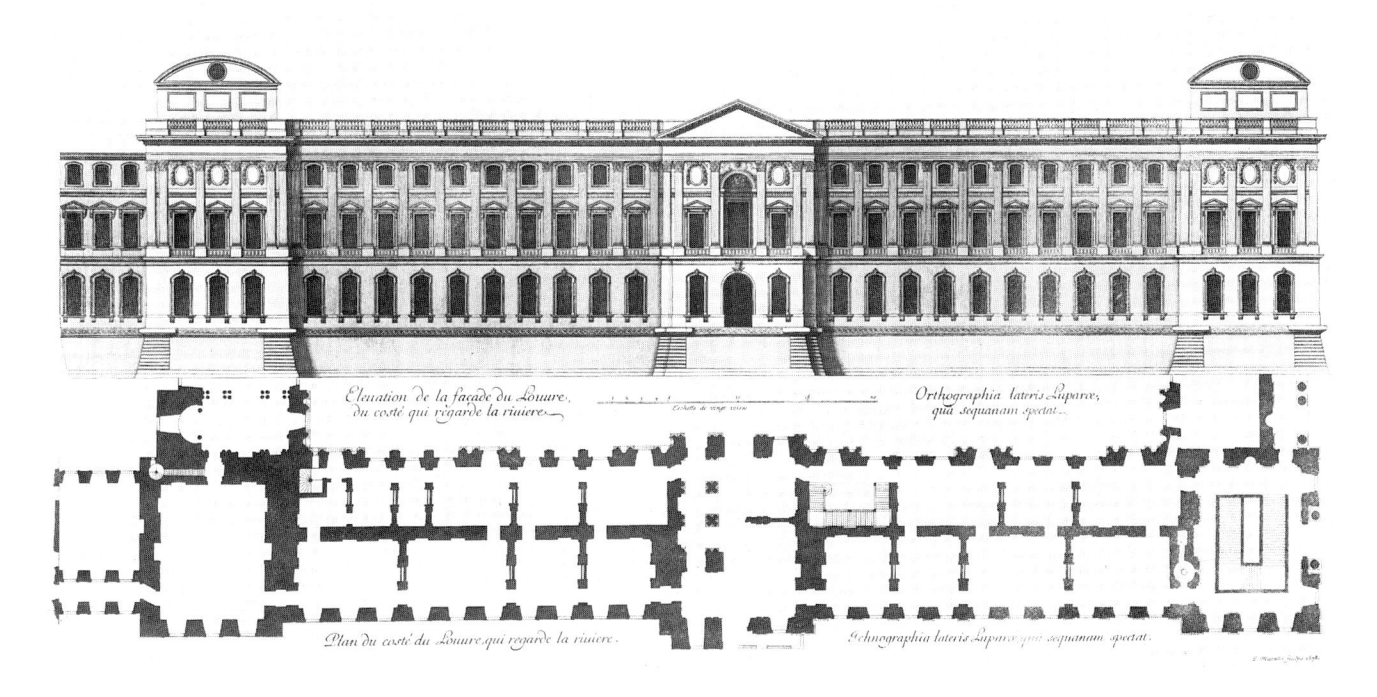

FIGURE 100. Louvre, south façade. Elevation and plan. Engraving by Jean Marot, 1678.

FIGURE 101. Louvre, north façade.

FIGURE 102. Louvre, north façade. Elevation, section, and plan of the central pavilion (details). Drawing, 1678.

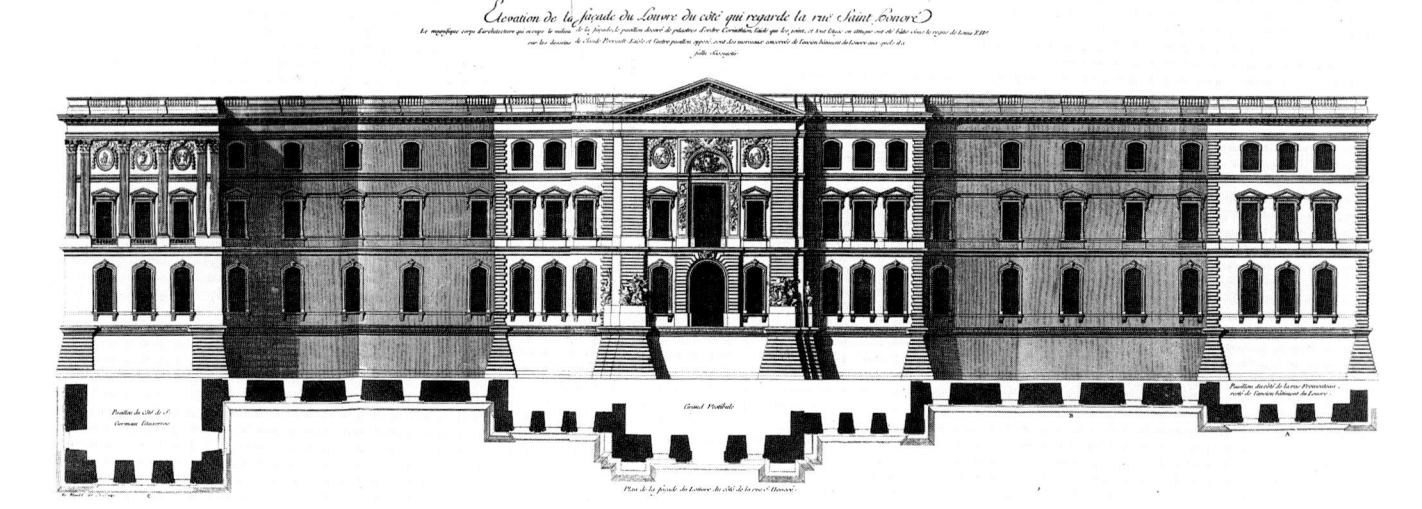

FIGURE 103. Louvre, north façade. Elevation and plan. Engraving by Jacques François Blondel.

FIGURE 104. Louvre, north façade, central pavilion. Elevation and plan. Engraving.

FIGURE 105. Louvre, Cour Carrée.

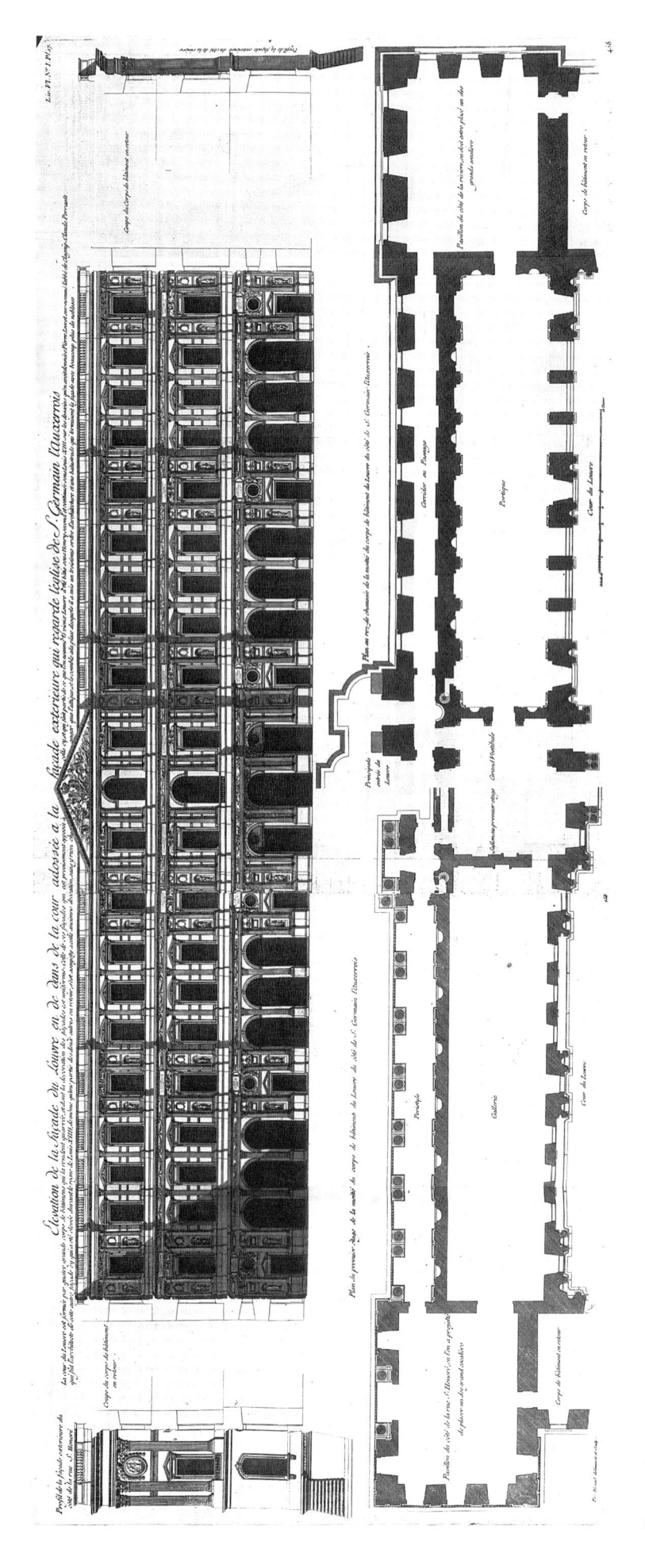

FIGURE 106. Louvre, Cour Carrée. Elevation and plan. Engraving by Jacques François Blondel.

FIGURE 107. Studio of Louis Le Vau, François d'Orbay, draftsman. Study for the top floor of the Cour Carrée, Louvre. Drawing, 1668. (Appendix A, D1).

FIGURE 108. Studio of Louis Le Vau, François d'Orbay, draftsman. Study for the top floor of the Cour Carrée, Louvre. Drawing, 1668. (Appendix A, D2).

FIGURE 109. François d'Orbay, project for Lescot wing, Cour Carrée, Louvre. Drawing, ca. 1675.

FIGURE 110. François d'Orbay, project for Lescot wing, Cour Carrée, Louvre. Drawing, ca. 1675.

FIGURE 111. Anonymous draftsman, studies for the top floor of the Cour Carrée, Louvre. Drawing, ca. 1676.

FIGURE 112. Louvre, Cour Carrée. Elevation, profile, and plan of the top floor (details). Drawing, 1678.

FIGURE 113. Claude Perrault, elevation of the Cour Carrée of the Louvre with sections of the north and south wings. Drawing, ca. 1676.

FIGURE 114. Elevation, section, and plan of the ground floor of the east wing of the Louvre (details). Drawing, 1678.

FIGURE 115. Elevation of the ground floor of the Cour Carrée (detail) and section of passageway from the vestibule of the east wing to the Cour Carrée, Louvre. Drawing, 1678.

FIGURE 116. Claude Perrault, obelisk project. Drawing, 1666.

FIGURE 117. Gérard Scotin after Sébastien Le Clerc, engraved frontispiece to Claude Perrault, trans. and ed., *Les dix livres d'architecture de Vitruve,* Paris, 1673.

FIGURE 118. Detail of Figure 117.

FIGURE 119. Sébastien Le Clerc, engraving from Claude Perrault, trans. and ed., *Les dix livres d'architecture de Vitruve,* Paris, 1673.

FIGURE 120. Claude Perrault, Arc de Triomphe du Trône, Paris. Engraving by Sébastien Le Clerc, 1679.

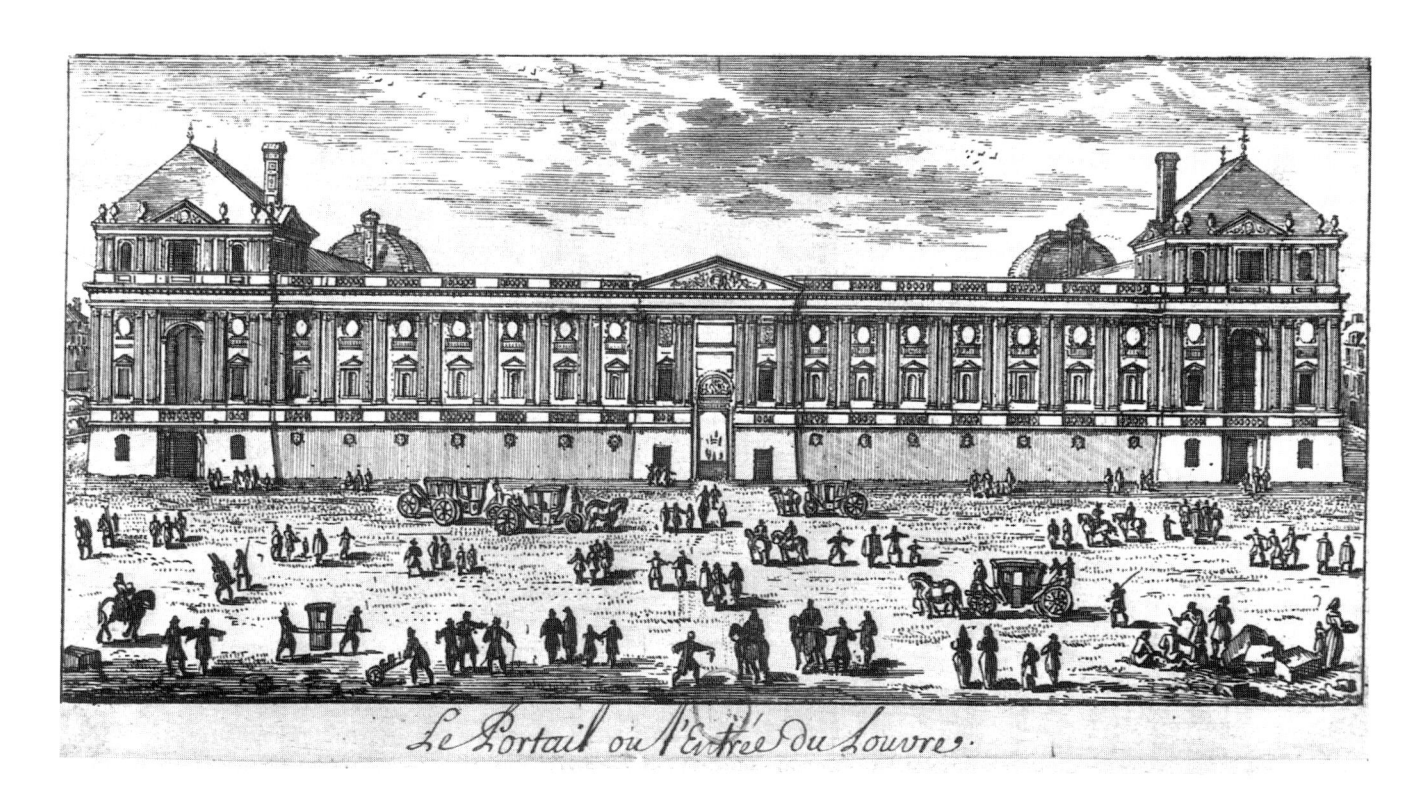

FIGURE 121. Louvre, Colonnade. Anonymous engraving.

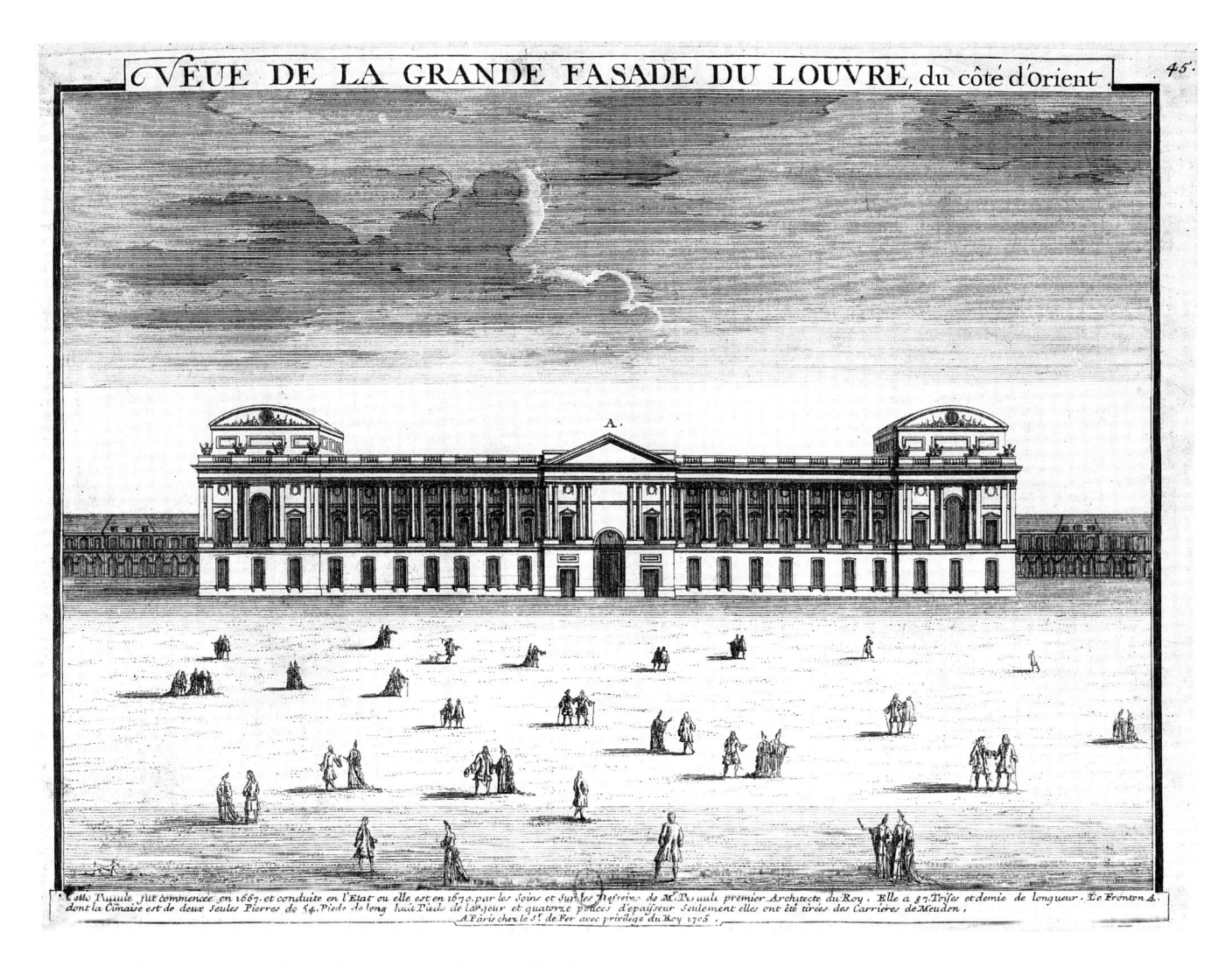

FIGURE 122. Louvre, Colonnade. Engraving by Nicolas de Fer, 1705.

FIGURE 123. Piliers de Tutelle, Bordeaux. Engraving.

FIGURE 124. Piliers de Tutelle, Bordeaux. Engraving by Pierre Le Pautre. From Claude Perrault, trans. and ed., *Les dix livres d'architecture de Vitruve,* 2d ed., Paris, 1684.

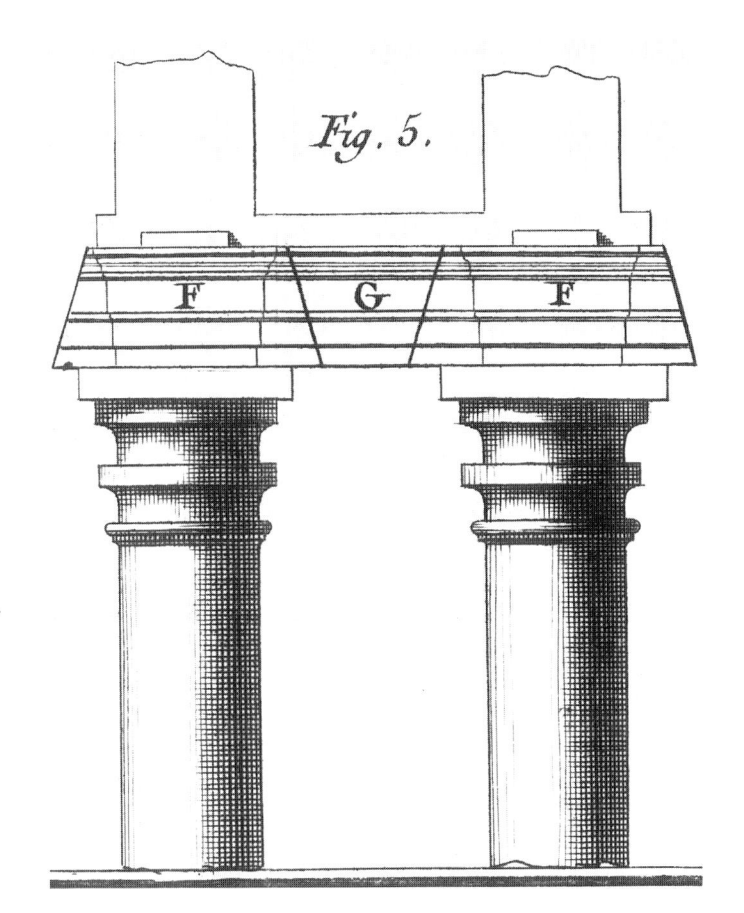

FIGURE 125. Piliers de Tutelle, Bordeaux. Diagram of entablature. Engraving.

FIGURE 126. Courtyard façade, Palmyra. Reconstruction by Robert Wood (1757). Engraving.

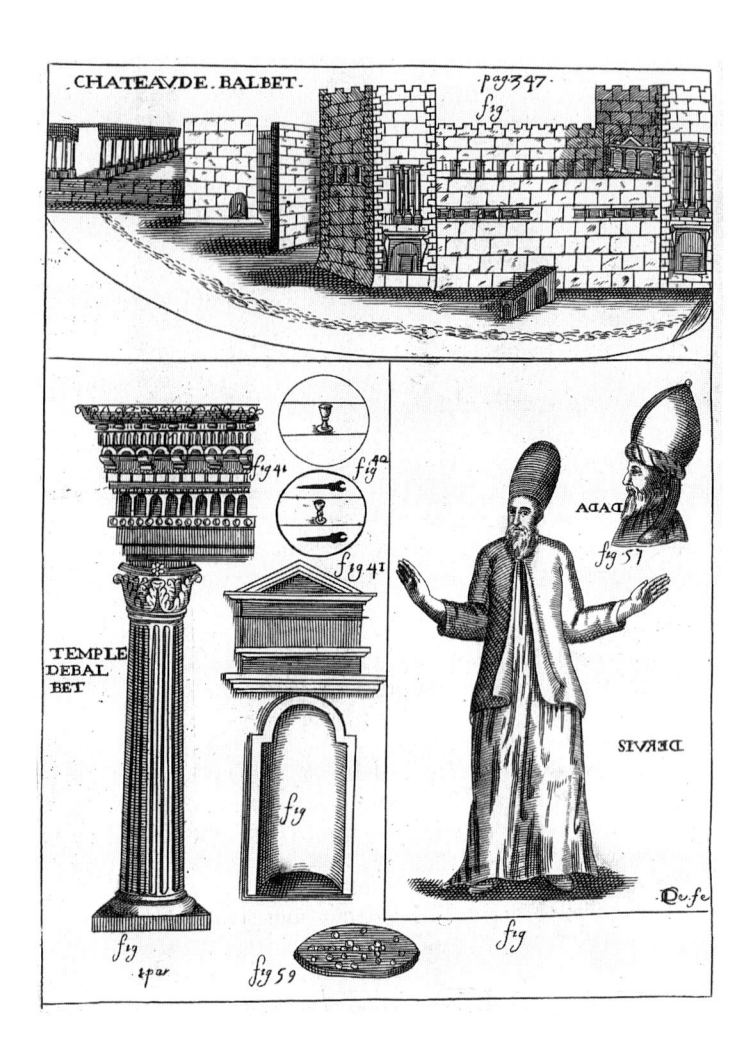

FIGURE 127. Baalbek. Engraving.

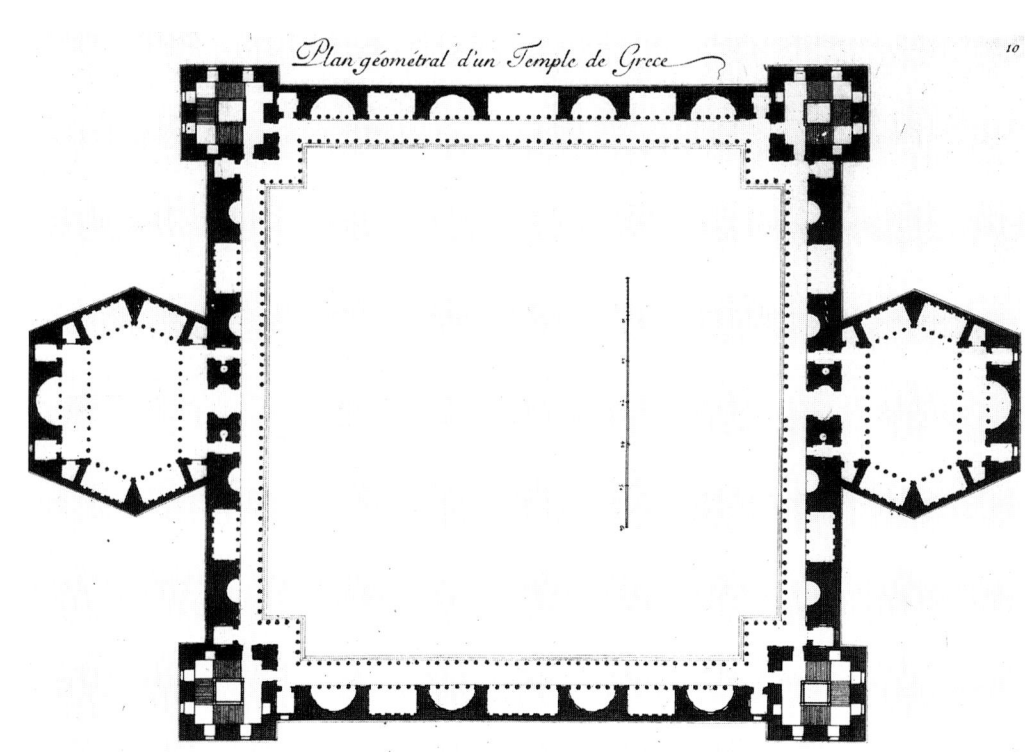

FIGURE 128. Plan of Baalbek. Engraving by Jean Marot.

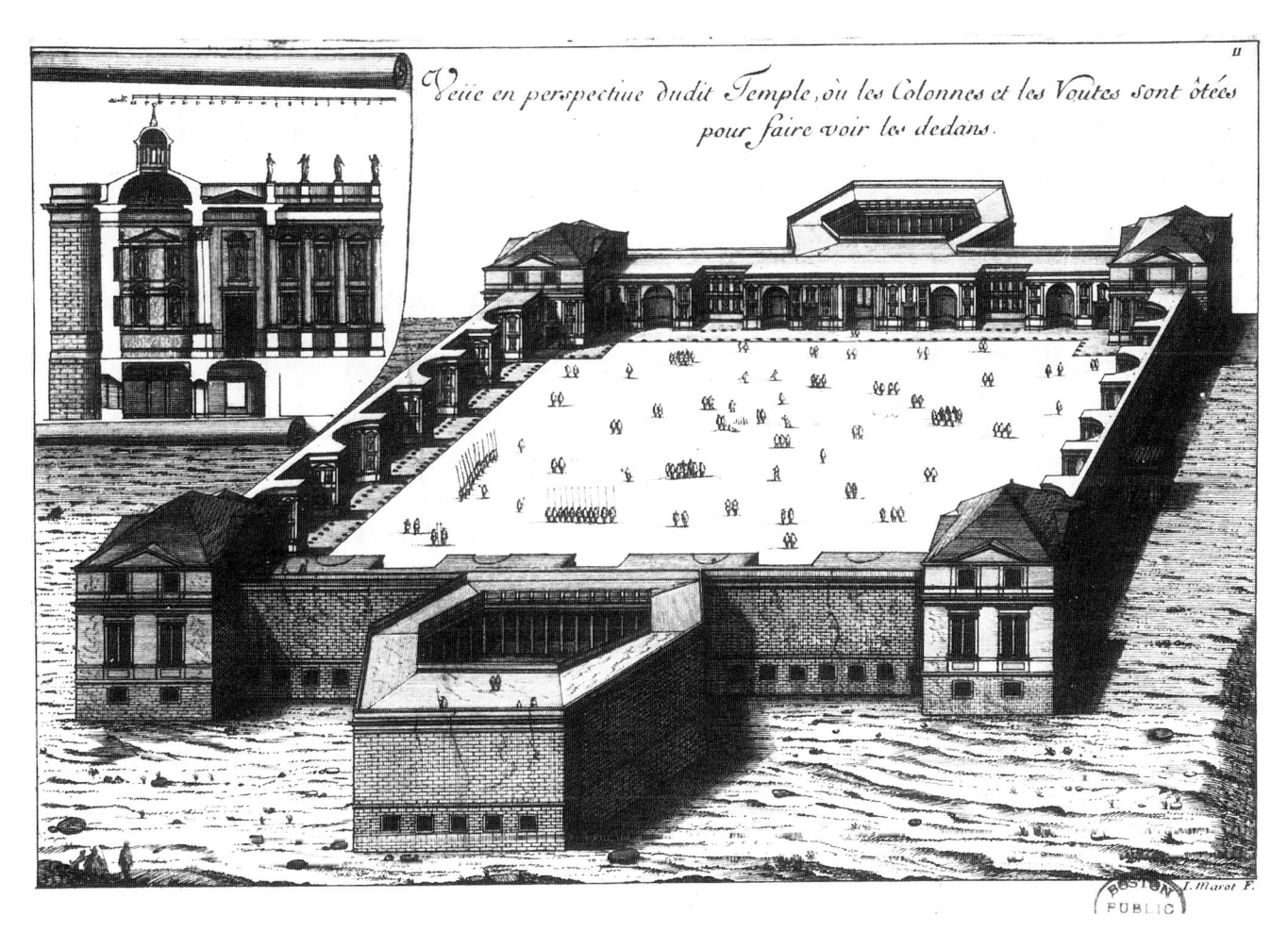

FIGURE 129. Bird's-eye view of Baalbek. Engraving by Jean Marot.

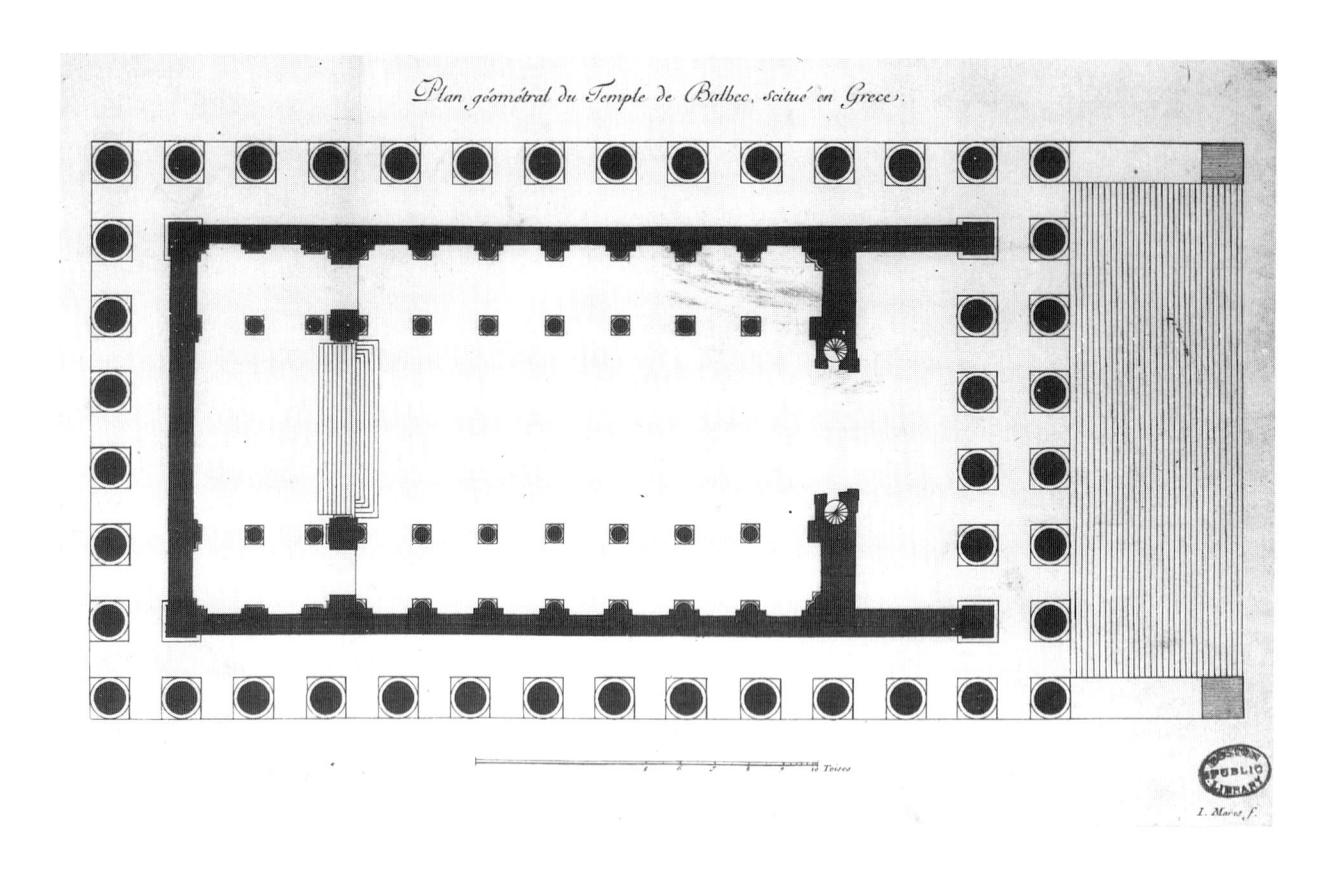

FIGURE 130. "Temple de Balbec" (Temple of Bacchus). Plan. Engraving by Jean Marot.

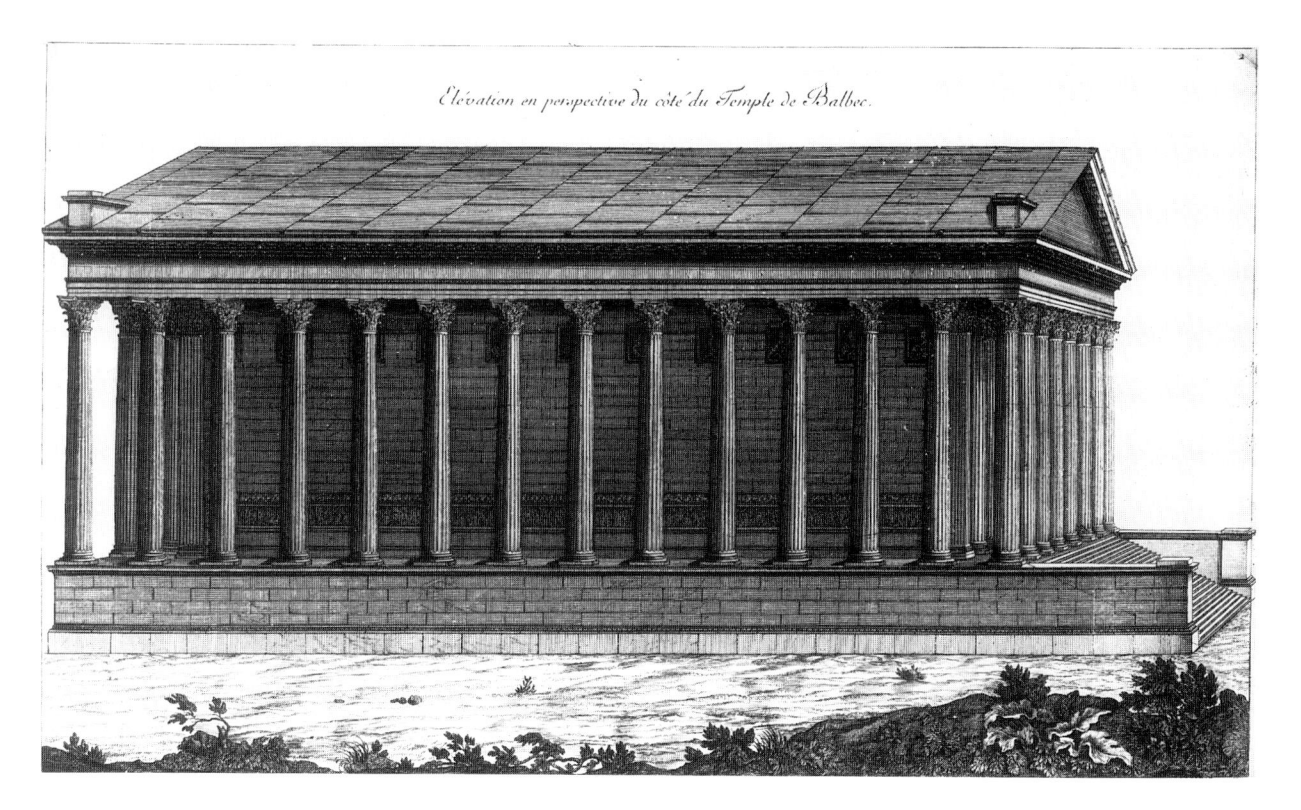

FIGURE 131. "Temple de Balbec" (Temple of Bacchus). Elevation. Engraving by Jean Marot.

FIGURE 132. "Temple de Balbec" (Temple of Bacchus). Elevation and detail of order. Engraving by Jean Marot.

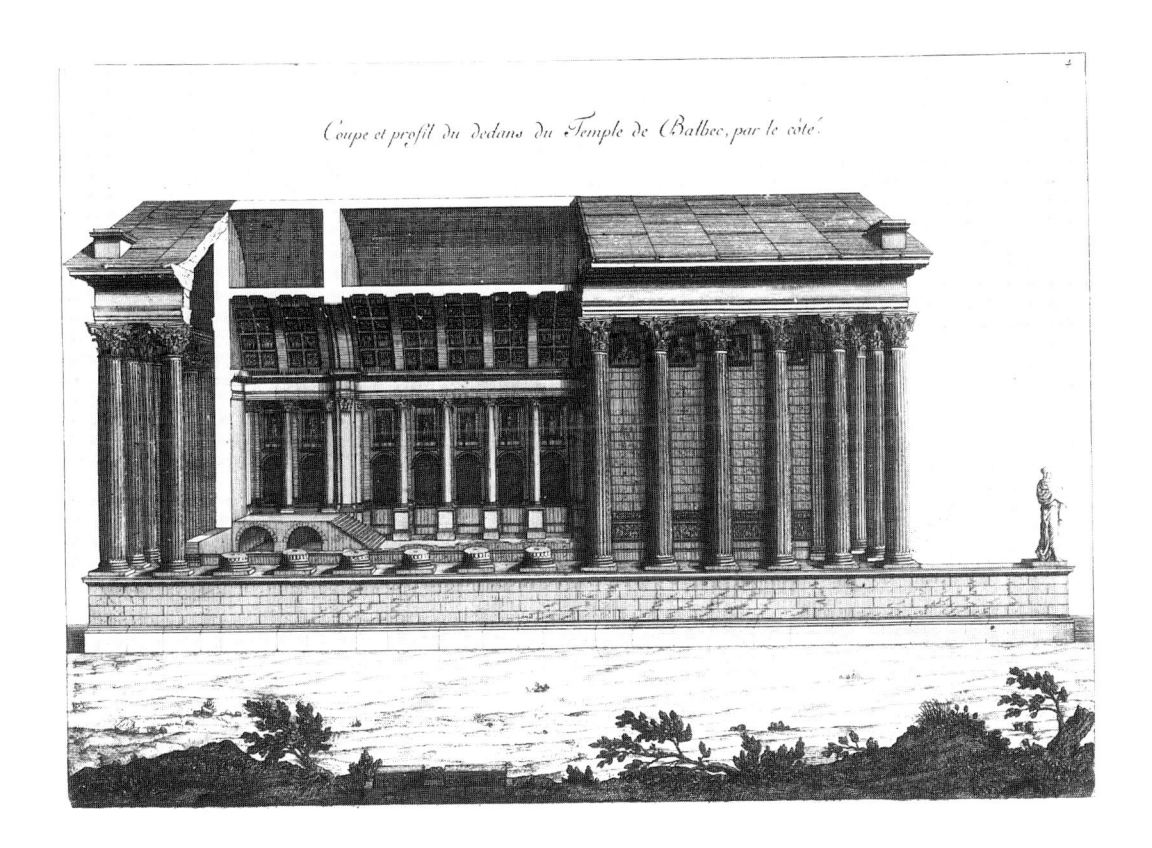

FIGURE 133. "Temple de Balbec" (Temple of Bacchus). Elevation and section. Engraving by Jean Marot.

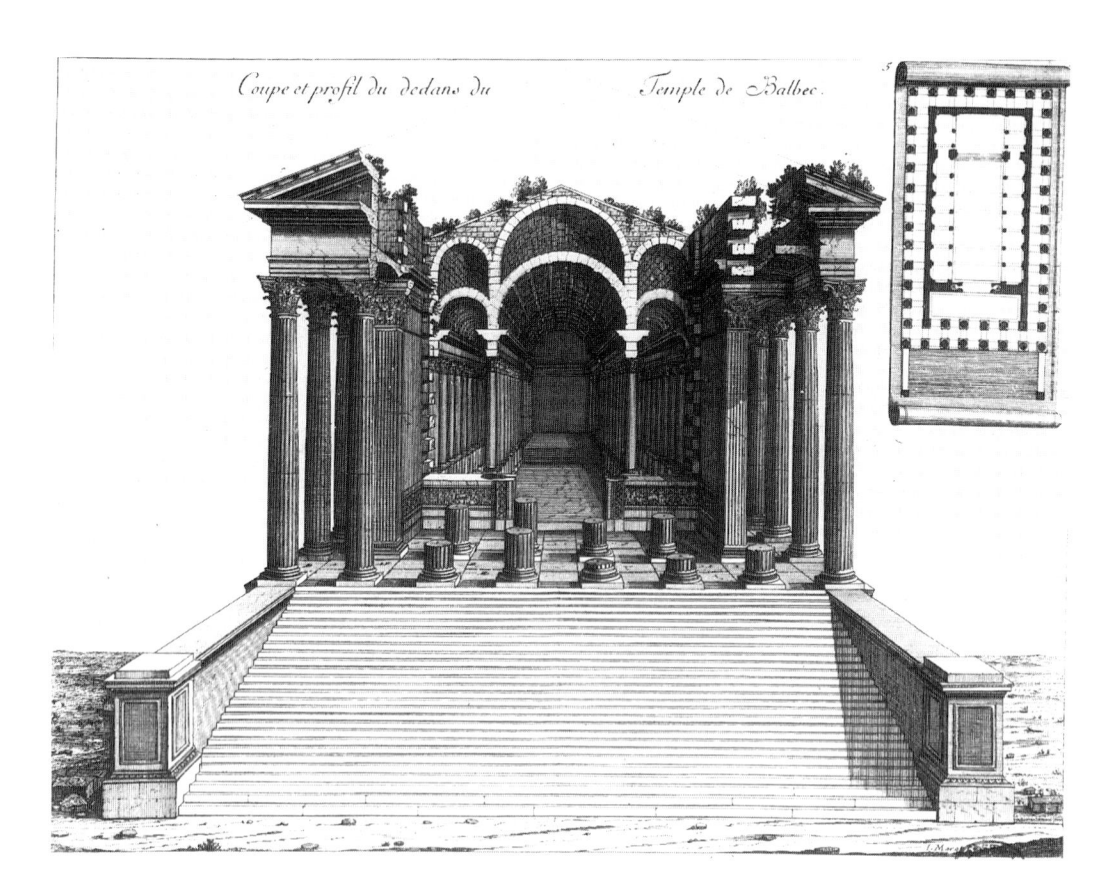

FIGURE 134. "Temple de Balbec" (Temple of Bacchus). Section and plan. Engraving by Jean Marot.

FIGURE 135. Temple of Bacchus, Baalbek, after De Monceaux. Engraving.

FIGURE 136. Baalbek. Aerial view.

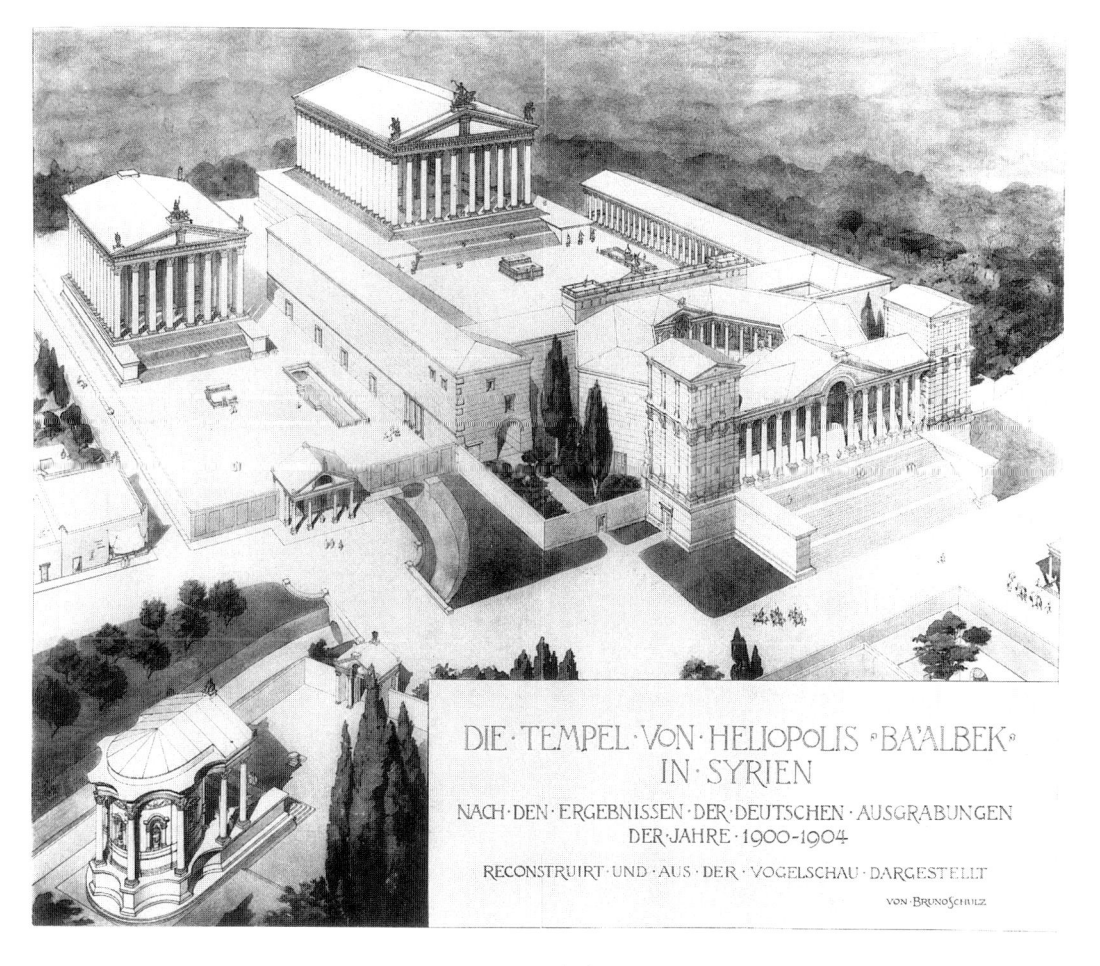

FIGURE 137. Baalbek. Reconstruction by Bruno Schulz.

FIGURE 138. Propylon, Baalbek. Reconstruction.

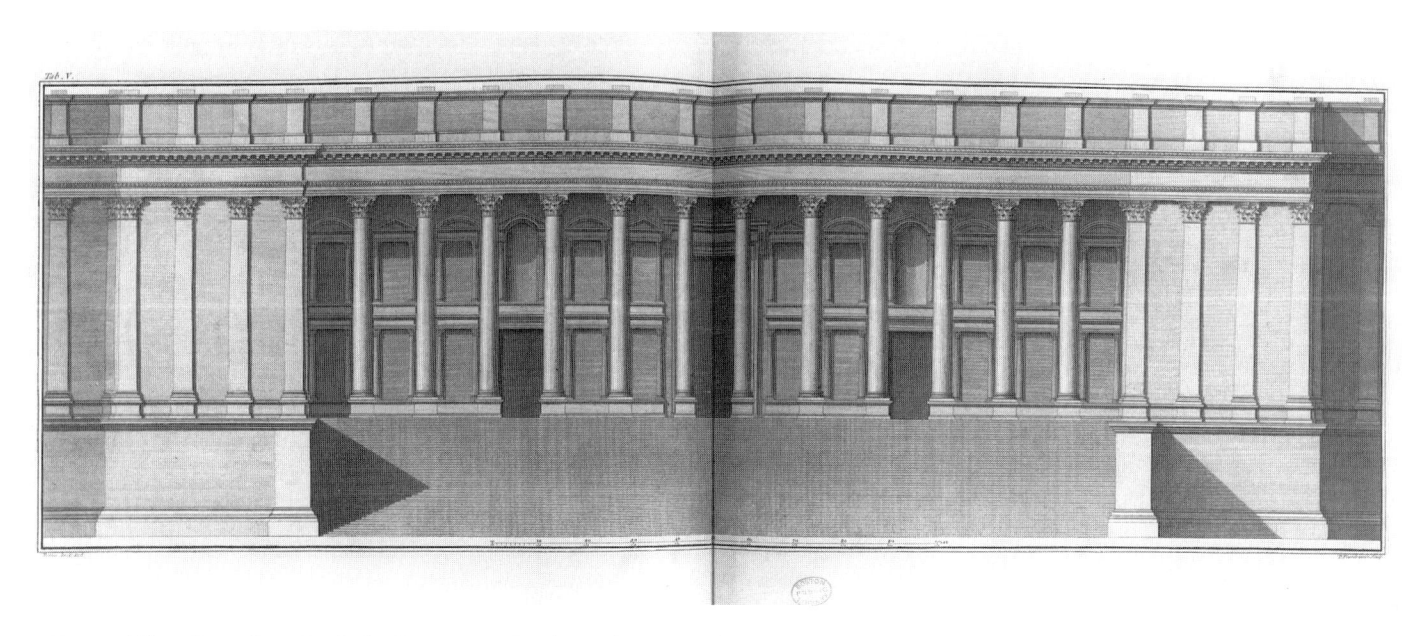

FIGURE 139. Propylon, Baalbek. Reconstruction by Robert Wood (1757). Engraving.

FIGURE 140. Propylon, Baalbek, with Arab fortifications. Engraving.

FIGURE 141. Propylon, Baalbek, with Arab fortifications.

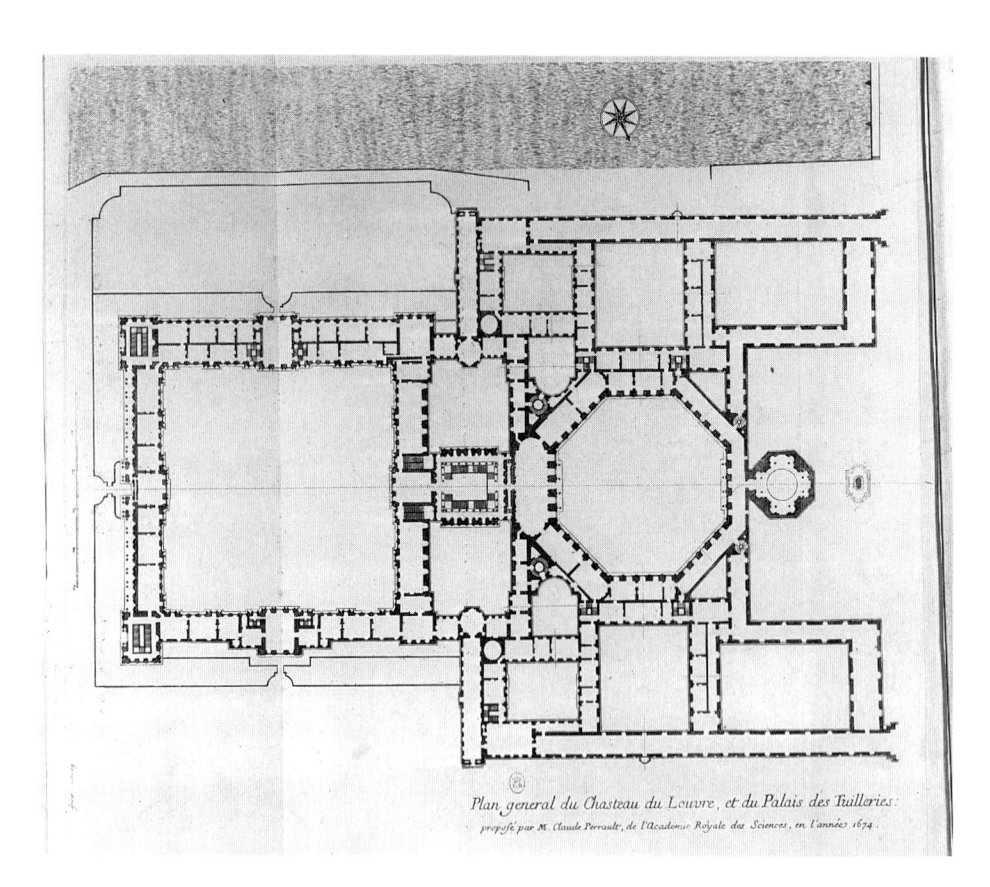

FIGURE 142. Claude Perrault, plan for the union of the Louvre and the Tuileries. Engraving, 1674.

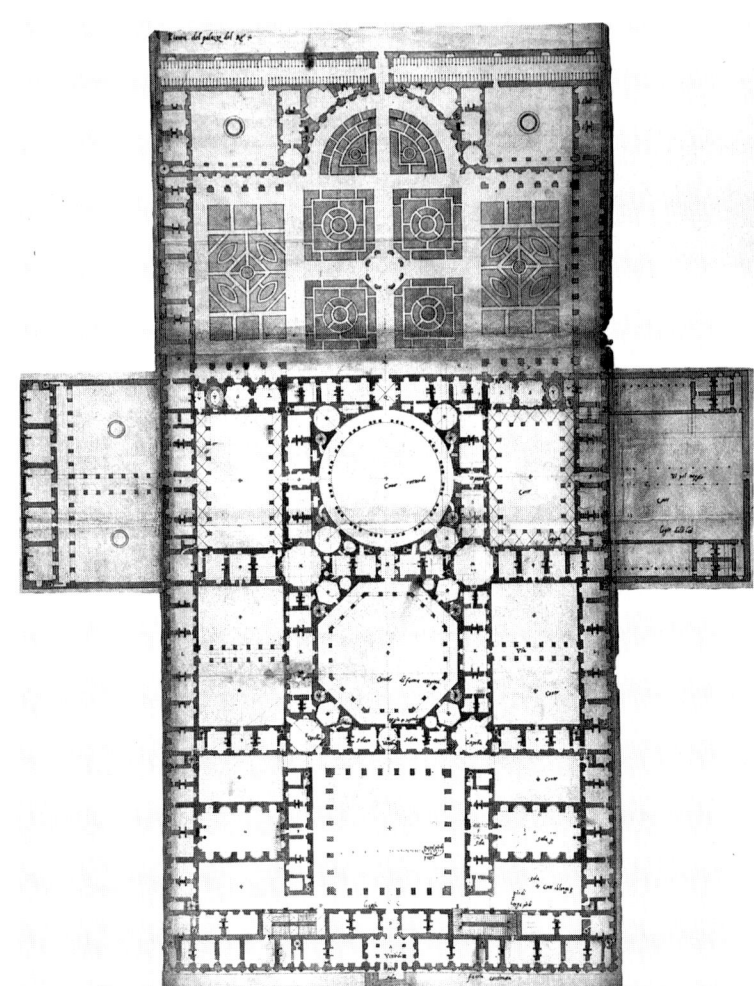

FIGURE 143. Sebastiano Serlio, plan for the Louvre, 1540s. Drawing.